# A GUIDE TO BULGARIA

**ALEXANDER TOUR**
**TANGRA TanNakRa Publishing House**
**Sofia 2002**

## WE ARE EVERYWHERE IN BULGARIA YOU WOULD LIKE TO GO!

**ALEXANDER TOUR**
Head Office:
44, Pop Bogomil Str,
1202 Sofia - BULGARIA
tel./fax: ++359/2/9833322,
9832371, 9833090, 9835568
http://www.AlexanderTour.com
e-mail: alextour@omega.bg

Alexander Tour is one of the first private tourist companies in Bulgaria, licensed tour operator (Licence No. 03392/2001) and travel agent (Licence No. 00172/2001).

The company is a member of the Bulgarian Association of Travel Agents – BATA and of the International Air Transport Association – IATA and is an authorised agent of all international airlines represented in Bulgaria.

The company is specialised in business tourism – business trips and hotel bookings, congresses, seminars, participation in international fairs. Recently active business contacts are maintained especially with the fairs in Berlin, Frankfurt/Main, Munchen, Stuttgart, Koeln, Hanover, etc. for organising the participation of Bulgarian companies and individual exhibitors and visitors. Alexander Tour enjoys good client relations with well-known state-owned and private companies.

In February 1999, Alexander Tour was selected for the "Arch of Europe for Quality" Award, held in Paris - France, the criteria for selection being: customer satisfaction, communication strategies, planning and decision-making, business results, human resources, etc.

The company makes hotel reservations and provides bus transport with its own vehicles to destinations in the country and abroad.

Since 1998 the company is handling Bulgarian tour operator together with foreign partners in the "Off the Beaten Path" and "Cultural Series – Central and Eastern Europe" routes.

The company is a member in the Internet Hotels Reservation Service for Bulgaria at http://www.HotelBulgaria.com offering up to 40% discount on room rates as compared to the prices offered at hotel reception desks. Up to now clients from more than 130 countries enjoyed the services of the company. For its appearance in Internet, the web-pages of Alexander Tour are conferred the European Award of Quality and on 01 December 1999 the site of HotelsBulgaria was nominated "site of the day" in Central Europe Online. The site was among the best 6000 Internet sites, selected by Guis Internet, Spain.

Since June 2001 Alexander Tour is a member of the International Hotel Reservations System in Internet at http://www.NewTravelAge.com.

- **Business trips – arrangements and handling**
- **Congresses, conferences, seminars**
- **Hotel reservations in Bulgaria and worldwide**
- **Airlines tickets**
- **Transport and rent-a-bus services**
- **Holiday trips to destinations worldwide**
- **By the sea and mountain tourist, balneotherapy and hobby tourism**
- **Tailor-made tours**
- **Vacations for students and graduates**

**TANGRA TanNakRa ALL BULGARIAN FOUNDATION and the CENTRE FOR RESEARCH ON BULGARIANS** actively promote the truth about the historic place of the Bulgarians in the world civilization; they help studies and the popularization of facts about the role and significance of the ancient Bulgarian culture. This is performed with the series of books "Bulgarian Eternity", published by the Foundation. A special emphasis is laid upon the latest scientific research about the origin, history and culture of the Bulgarians since ancient times until today.

**TANGRA** TanNakRa ALL BULGARIAN FOUNDATION for five consecutive years has been publishing and distributing around the world the Eternal Calendar of the Bulgarians. UNESCO recognizes this calendar as the most precise among the calendars known to world science.
"It has been proven that ancient Bulgarians had one of the most advanced calendars in the world, more acceptable than the Chinese and the Indian systems of chronology, more comprehensible and more practical", says prof. Michele Longon in "Population et Societe" Journal, France. Emphasis is laid on the historic and cultural contacts of Bulgarian civilisation with peoples, some of them non-existent any more. "The Bulgarian medieval culture is among the seven civilisations in the history of the world which played an essential mediating role because of its mission as a link between the East and the West", ascertains the Japanese historian Shigioshi Matsumae.

The Bulgarian Fireplaces of Civilization

Гербове на някои от най-старите градове в Европа
The coats of arms of some of the oldest cities in Europe

**The States of the Bulgarians – a Shield for Europe**

**TANGRA** TanNakRa ALL BULGARIAN FOUNDATION published the album "THE BULGARIANS" in close collaboration with leading historians and scientists at Sofia University St. St. Cyril and Methodius and at the Institute in History with the Bulgarian Academy of Science. It tells about our eventful thousand-year old history, about our forefathers from the valleys of Pamir and the Caucasus, from the banks of Volga, Kama and the Danube, from the Black Sea steppes to the Apennines.

"THE BULGARIANS – ATLAS" with maps and commentaries on them traces almost three thousand years of the historical route of our forefathers and is a natural continuation of "THE BULGARIANS". The role of the Bulgarians and their states in Europe – Old Great Bulgaria, Volga Bulgaria and Danubian Bulgaria as the alive shield of European civilization is outstanding. "The historic merit of Bulgaria is in the fact that it barred the Turks from Europe. It paid for that in blood, paid with its faith, its freedom and with the decline of its high culture at that time", says the Italian Prof. Sante Grachotti.

The essence of our common efforts is the Bulgarians to have their deserved place in the modern world of global integration, to live in peace with the other peoples and be proud of their name.

**TANGRA TanNakRa    ALL BULGARIAN FONDATION**
Tel.: ++359 2 / 986 44 19, Fax: ++359 2 / 986 69 45
E-mail: Tangra@bitex.com   http://members.bitex.com/tangra   P.O. Box 1832. 1000 Sofia, Bulgaria.

Издателите ще бъдат благодарни на всички читатели на Пътеводителя, които изпратят допълнителни данни и сведения за историята и културните забележителности на България, предания, легенди и пр. на адрес **1000 София, ПК 1832**, за **ПЪТЕВОДИТЕЛ-БЪЛГАРИЯ**.

**A GIUDEBOOK TO BULGARIA**
Second revised and expanded edition
© TANGRA TanNakRa Publishing House, 2002
© ALEXANDER TOUR, 2002
© Design and pre-press Aquagraphics Ltd., 2002
   ISBN 954-9942-35-X
All rights reserved. The publication of the book or parts of it in any form whatever - electronic, mechanical, photocopy, transcript or any other mode - without writtent publishers' consent is forbidden.

*DEAR READERS,*

*This is a joint publication of TANGRA TanNakRa Publishing House and ALEXANDER TOUR.*

*We hope that this GUIDEBOOK TO BULGARIA will present the Bulgarian and foreign tourists with detailed, topical and useful information, at a time when tourism is the world's number one industry and when one in every 100 persons travels for the purposes of tourism.*

*This book is intended for all Bulgarians and visitors to Bulgaria. We believe that it will reveal to you the small secrets, wonders and challenges of TRAVELLING, facilitate your encounters with the traditions, culture and modern life of our ancient and hospitable people and bring you in touch with the magic and charm of Bulgarian scenery.*

*GOOD LUCK IN BULGARIA!*

# Contents

- **GENERAL INFORMATION** ............................................................................. 16
  - HISTORY ............................................................................................................ 17
  - GEOGRAPHY ..................................................................................................... 31
  - Climate ............................................................................................................... 32
  - Population .......................................................................................................... 32
  - Economy ............................................................................................................ 33
  - LANGUAGE ....................................................................................................... 34
  - CULTURE ........................................................................................................... 36
  - OPPORTUNITIES for CULTURAL TOURISM in BULGARIA ........................... 44
  - RELIGION .......................................................................................................... 46
  - HOLIDAYS, CEREMONIES, CARNIVALS and FESTIVALS ............................ 47
  - NATIONAL PARKS and RESERVES ................................................................ 49
- **INFORMATION for VISITORS** ...................................................................... 51
  - KEY TELEPHONE NUMBERS in SOFIA ......................................................... 51
  - VISAS ................................................................................................................. 51
  - CUSTOMS REGULATIONS .............................................................................. 52
  - CURRENCY, PAYMENTS and FOREIGN EXCHANGE .................................. 53
  - FOOD, WATER and DRINKS ........................................................................... 54
  - ACCOMMODATION .......................................................................................... 55
  - POSTAL SERVICES ......................................................................................... 56
  - TRANSPORT CONNECTIONS ......................................................................... 57
  - ROAD NETWORK CONDITIONS ..................................................................... 59
  - TOURIST INFORMATION ................................................................................. 60
  - HAZARD AND SAFETY .................................................................................... 60
- **SOFIA** ............................................................................................................... 62
  - EMBASSIES and DIPLOMATIC SERVICES ................................................... 76
  - THE ENVIRONS of SOFIA ................................................................................ 79
  - PARKS in SOFIA ............................................................................................... 80
- **SOUTHWESTERN BULGARIA** ..................................................................... 82
  - PETRICH ............................................................................................................ 83
  - SANDANSKI ...................................................................................................... 85
  - GOTSE DELCHEV ............................................................................................. 87
  - BANSKO ............................................................................................................ 90
  - RAZLOG ............................................................................................................ 92
  - BLAGOEVGRAD ............................................................................................... 94
  - DOUPNITSA ...................................................................................................... 97
  - SAMOKOV ......................................................................................................... 99
  - KYUSTENDIL .................................................................................................. 101
  - PERNIK ............................................................................................................ 103
  - PIRDOP and ZLATITSA .................................................................................. 105
  - PANAGYURISHTE .......................................................................................... 107
  - KOSTENETS .................................................................................................... 109
  - VELINGRAD .................................................................................................... 111
- **CENTRAL SOUTHERN BULGARIA** ........................................................... 114
  - BATAK ............................................................................................................. 115
  - BRATSIGOVO .................................................................................................. 117
  - PEROUSHTITSA ............................................................................................. 119
  - PAZARDZHIK .................................................................................................. 120
  - KOPRIVSHTITSA ............................................................................................ 123
  - SOPOT ............................................................................................................. 126
  - KARLOVO ....................................................................................................... 128
  - KALOFER ........................................................................................................ 130
  - HISSARYA ....................................................................................................... 132
  - PLOVDIV ......................................................................................................... 135
  - ASSENOVGRAD ............................................................................................. 142

| | |
|---|---|
| CHEPELARE | 146 |
| SMOLYAN | 148 |
| DEVIN | 151 |
| PAVEL BANYA | 154 |
| KAZANLUK | 155 |
| STARA ZAGORA | 160 |
| CHIRPAN | 165 |
| DIMITROVGRAD | 166 |
| HASKOVO | 168 |
| KURDZHALI | 170 |
| **SOUTHEASTERN BULGARIA** | **172** |
| SVILENGRAD | 173 |
| ELHOVO | 174 |
| YAMBOL | 175 |
| SLIVEN | 178 |
| KOTEL | 180 |
| KARNOBAT | 184 |
| AITOS | 185 |
| MALKO TURNOVO | 186 |
| **NORTHWESTERN BULGARIA** | **188** |
| BERKOVITZA | 189 |
| CHIPROVTZI | 191 |
| BELOGRADCHIK | 194 |
| VIDIN | 196 |
| LOM | 198 |
| KOZLODUI | 199 |
| ORIAHOVO | 201 |
| MONTANA | 203 |
| VRATSA | 204 |
| MEZDRA | 207 |
| BOTEVGRAD | 208 |
| ETROPOLE | 210 |
| YABLANITZA | 212 |
| CHERVEN BRYAG | 213 |
| LOUKOVIT | 214 |
| **CENTRAL NORTHERN BULGARIA** | **216** |
| TETEVEN | 217 |
| TROYAN | 219 |
| APRILTZI | 222 |
| LOVECH | 224 |
| PLEVEN | 227 |
| NIKOPOL | 232 |
| SVISHTOV | 233 |
| PAVLIKENI | 236 |
| SEVLIEVO | 237 |
| GABROVO | 239 |
| TRYAVNA | 242 |
| DRYANOVO | 245 |
| ELENA | 247 |
| VELIKO TURNOVO | 250 |
| GORNA ORYAHOVITSA | 259 |
| BYALA | 262 |
| ROUSSE | 263 |
| **NORTHEASTERN BULGARIA** | **270** |
| PLISKA | 271 |
| SHOUMEN | 272 |
| VELIKI PRESLAV | 276 |
| TURGOVISHTE | 279 |

| | |
|---|---|
| RAZGRAD | 282 |
| TOUTRAKAN | 284 |
| SILISTRA | 285 |
| DOBRICH | 288 |
| PROVADIA | 290 |

## BULGARIAN BLACK SEA COAST — 292

| | |
|---|---|
| SHABLA | 293 |
| ROUSSALKA | 294 |
| KAVARNA | 295 |
| BALCHIK | 297 |
| ALBENA | 299 |
| ZLATNI PYASUTSI (GOLDEN SANDS) | 301 |
| St. St. KONSTANTIN AND ELENA | 302 |
| VARNA | 303 |
| KAMCHIA | 311 |
| OBZOR | 312 |
| ELENITE | 313 |
| SLUNCHEV BRYAG (SUNNY BEACH) | 313 |
| NESSEBUR | 315 |
| POMORIE | 318 |
| BOURGAS | 319 |
| SOZOPOL | 323 |
| DYUNI | 326 |
| PRIMORSKO | 326 |
| KITEN | 327 |
| TZAREVO | 328 |
| AHTOPOL | 329 |

## BULGARIAN MOUNTAINS — 330

| | |
|---|---|
| RILA | 334 |
| RILA MONASTERY | 337 |
| BOROVETZ | 339 |
| MALYOVITZA | 341 |
| MAJOR DEPARTURE POINTS FOR HIKING TOURS | 342 |
| PIRIN | 343 |
| MELNIK AND THE ROZHEN MONASTERY | 346 |
| SHILIGARNIKA | 348 |
| MAJOR DEPARTURE POINTS FOR HIKING TOURS | 349 |
| STARA PLANINA | 350 |
| THE GORGE OF THE RIVER ISKAR | 354 |
| TROYAN MONASTERY | 357 |
| MAJOR DEPARTURE POINTS FOR HIKING TOURS | 358 |
| 1. In Western Stara Planina | 358 |
| 2. In Central Stara Planina | 359 |
| 3. In Eastern Stara Planina | 362 |
| KOM - EMINE ROUTE | 362 |
| THE RHODOPE MOUNTAINS | 363 |
| PAMPOROVO | 366 |
| BACHKOVO MONASTERY | 367 |
| SHIROKA LUKA | 367 |
| MAJOR DEPARTURE POINTS FOR HIKING TOURS | 369 |
| 1. In the Western Rhodopes | 369 |
| 2. In the Eastern Rhodopes | 371 |
| VITOSHA | 372 |

## OPPORTUNITIES FOR NON-STANDARD TOURISM IN BULGARIA — 377

## INDEX OF TOWNS AND RESORTS — 380

## INDEX OF LANDMARKS — 381

# Political map of Europe

# Geographical map of Bulgaria

# Tourist sights in Bulgaria

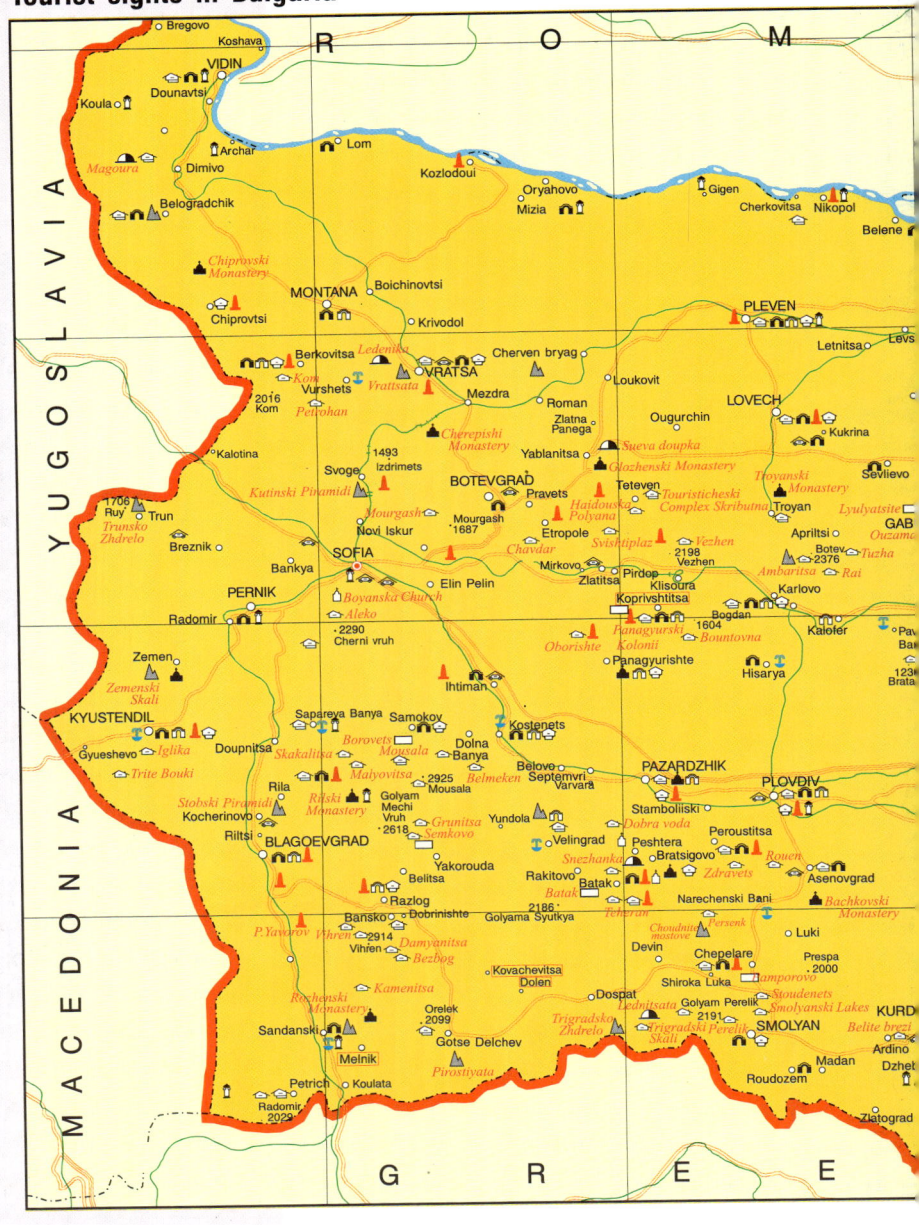

# GENERAL INFORMATION

*The amphitheatre in the Old Town of Plovdiv*

# GENERAL INFORMATION

Bulgaria is a country in Southeastern Europe and is situated on the Balkan Peninsula. To the north the country borders Rumania, to the east – the Black Sea, to the south – Turkey and Greece, and to the west – Yugoslavia and Macedonia.
Bulgaria is a parliamentary republic with a National Assembly (One House Parliament) of 240 national representatives. The President is Head of State.

Coat of Arms
Of the Republic of
Bulgaria

National Flag
Of the Republic of
Bulgaria

*Mila Rodino (Dear Motherland)*
(Anthem of the Republic of Bulgaria)
*Dear Motherland,*
*Proud Balkan Mountains,*
*The Danube next to it in blue,*
*Sunshine over Thrace,*
*Bright skies above the Pirin.*

*Dear Motherland, you are Heaven on Earth,*
*Your beauty, your charm,*
*Oh, they are infinite!*

## HISTORY

The Republic of Bulgaria is situated in the middle of the Balkan Peninsula on a busy crossroad of different cultures. According to statistics our country is among the first in the world for the number of its archaeological monuments. Today's land of the Bulgarians is one of the ancient springs of civilisation in Europe. The first traces of human activities in these territories date back to the Paleolithic Age (Old Stone Age). Human activities and culture immutably follow their course through all pre-historic epochs. The **Karanovska mound** near the town of Nova Zagora reveals exceptionally interesting findings, which allow cultural layers from the beginning of the Neolithic Age to the end of the Early Bronze Age ($6^{th}$ millenium BC - $1^{st}$ half of $3^{rd}$ millenium BC) to be distinguished. The ancient inhabitants of Bulgarian lands reached their zenith in the Eneolithic (Halkolithic) Age. It was namely in Bulgarian lands that three decades ago a civilisation was found out - dating back far before Mesopotamia and Egypt - the findings in the **Varna Halkolithic Necropolis** of $5^{th}$ millenium BC. Among them is the most ancient golden jewelry in the world and symbols of authority. The **Treasure of Hotnitsa** found in a village mound from the Late Eneolithic Age nearby the village of Hotnitsa (Lovech region) dates back to the same period. Quite impressive are the findings in the **Magoura Cave** (which was inhabited even in the Early Bronze Age) and the exceptional drawings (dating back to the Late Bronze Age) made of guano stuck to the rocks. The ancient people have depicted hunting scenes, dances, totemic and pantheistic cult figures.

During the **Bronze Age** (3100-1200 BC) the life of the local people changed. These were the **ancient Thracians** who formed themselves as a people by the end of the $1^{st}$ millenium BC. The Thracians are not only the most ancient historically proven inhabitants of our lands - modern science identifies more and more evidence that namely Ancient Thrace was one of the centres for consolidation of the **Indo-Europeans**. The most ancient Thracian monuments date back to the same historic period as was the Old Kingdom in Egypt. The Thracians exerted a profound impact on world culture due to their contacts

# GENERAL INFORMATION

with the civilisation of Ancient Greece. **Herodotus** mentioned the Thracians as the second numerous people in the Ancient World. **Homer** described them as allies of the Trojans during the 8th century BC. **Eschiles, Euripides, Aristophanes** and others also wrote about the ancient Thracians.

The Thracian culture as a culture of synthesis and illustrates the powerful Hellenistic influence in its mature expression. The cult of the Thracian god **Dionissius** played an essential role in the emerging of Greek tragedy and comedy. The myths and the cult of the Thracian singer **Orpheus** (so-called **Orphism**) nestle deeply in the spiritual life of the ancient civilisation.

Orpheus was probably a Thracian king-priest from the Mycenaean Epoch whom mythology turned into **heros** (a man who had become immortal and had turned into a god) who symbolised art, ancient wisdom, music and healing, prophetic and management abilities. Similar to Orpheus's is the image of **Zalmoxis** (a Getti priest who spent years long living as a hermit), famous prophet and healer. Some Orphic elements can be traced even in modern world religion - Christianity.

Thracian art is known mostly from the tombs and necropolises, which are great in number in some regions. Its zenith is referred to the end of the $4^{th}$ millenium and the beginning of the $3^{rd}$ millenium BC. This is the period when the notorious **Tomb of Kazanluk** was built, famous for its wonderful frescoes, as well as the Thracian mounds in the so-called Lowland of the Thracian kings in the Kazanluk Valley, which recently provoke great interest. The **treasures of Panagyurishte, Vulchitrun and Rogozen** are classic example of the Thracian art achievements. Findings dating back to Thracian times are still excavated - for example, the monumental temple near the **village of Starossel**, Plovdiv region ($5^{th}$-$4^{th}$ century BC) found in the summer of 2000; the domed tomb near the **village of Alexandrovo**, Haskovo region (the second half of $4^{th}$ century BC); the temple near **Perperikon**, etc. The exhibitions of Thracian culture in Western Europe and America during the last three decades raised its prestige far beyond Bulgarian borders.

The Thracians have expressed their beliefs in numerous monuments - the cult stone plates of the **Thracian Horseman** (Heros), golden and silver plate of various treasures. Some

*The fortress near the town of Lovech*

# GENERAL INFORMATION

Thracian gods (**Ares/Mars** (Lat.), **Artemida** - her original was that of the Thracian great mother-godess **Bendida, Dionissius, Asklepius**, etc.) were worshiped by the ancient Greeks and thence - by the Romans. These Thracian gods are well known today, their names have acquired deep symbolic meaning related to war, medicine, etc. However, few are those who know that no ancient-old Greek mythological images are meant but **borrowings** from Thracians' religion. Same is often true for such a great son of Ancient Thrace as **Spartacus** who was born on the territory of present-day town of Sandanski, at the foot of the Pirin Mountain. As an adolescent he was sold in slavery in Rome. There he became a gladiator and later a leader of the biggest slave uprising in Antiquity.

In 346 BC Thrace was conquered and remained under domination of the Macedonian Kingdom for about 50 years. **Ancient Macedonians** were a people closely related to the Thracians and according to some scientists they were even their tribal structure, similar to Thracian tribes like the **Odrissi, Bessi, Dacians**, etc. In the 5th century BC Macedonia played essential role in the Pulpiness Wars and it acquired hegemony in the Balkan Peninsula for the following hundred years. The Hellenisation of the ancient Macedonians was strongly expressed as compared to the other Thracians despite that the former and the latter remained "barbarians" for the ancient Greeks. **Philip of Macedonia** reconstructed the Thracian town of Poulpoudeva and named it after himself - Philipopol. The world hegemony established by Alexander III the Great (336-323 BC) in fact did not correspond to the interest of ancient Macedonians or the Thracian "world" as a whole but rather to the newly formed Hellenistic military-administrative oligarchy.

Thracian land became part of the **Roman Empire** by 46 AD after continuous wars and resistance. During the 2nd-3rd centuries AD our lands are among the most prospering Roman provinces with highly developed towns: **Philipopol** (Plovdiv), **Augusta Trayana** (Stara Zagora), **Serdica** (Sofia), **Naissus** (Nis), **Pautalia** (Kyustendil), **Durostorum** (Silistra), **Martsianopol** (Devnya), **Nikopolis ad Istrum** (near Veliko Turnovo), and many others. Thracian territories at-

tracted settlers from the Middle East as well as Roman veterans. Comfortable roads were built and a clear system of communication was established (it was unsurpassed till modern times - 19th-20th centuries), lifestyle raised to that in the metropolises. The establishment of Roman statehood, demographic and ethnic contacts led to the dominant role of the Latin language (especially to the north of Stara Planina Mountain) while the Hellenistic cultural features were preserved in Thrace and along the Black Sea coast.

In 330 AD Constantine I the Great moved the capital city of the Roman Empire from the "old" Rome to Byzantion (Constantinople/Istanbul) called by the Bulgarians **Tsarigrad (The Town of Tsars)**. This act was implemented after some hesitations as one of the options for a new capital city was todays' Bulgarian capital Sofia (**Serdica** in the Antiquity). After the Empire broke in two parts (395) our lands remained in the Eastern Empire (Byzantium). Among the prominent Byzantine personalities not a few were those of Thracian origin, including emperors. "Most Orthodox" of them were Emperor **Markian** (450-457, born in the region of today's Plovdiv) and **Justinian I the Great** (527-565) who was the most notorious ruler in the centuries old Empire. The Early Byzantine culture in Bulgarian lands was established in its mature forms. The population was among the early adherents to Christianity in Europe. Important ecclesiastic events, as for example the **Council in**

# GENERAL INFORMATION

Serdica (343) cut a deep imprint in the religious life of the Christian world.

The **ancient Bulgarians** were the basic ethnic component in the structure of the Mediaeval Bulgarian State. Since Antiquity they were a highly organised people of statehood. Their original homeland was in Central Asia, in the mountainous region of Pamir and Hindukush. There were founded two famous states called **Balgar** and **Balhara** according to some sources. As a highly developed civilisation, the Bulgars had culturally dominated the territories of Central Asia for a long time. They had left to the world a rich cultural heritage in the field of the philosophic understanding of the world as well as in state administration, social structure, military art, writing, linguistic culture, construction, astronomy and mathematics. Eloquent proof of this is their **eternal Bulgarian sun calendar**, which is perfect from astronomical and mathematical point of view. Its structure consists of an original 12 months calendar and an excellent 12-year cycle calendar. The constellations in this masterpiece of ancient Bulgarians' thought bear the names of animals. UNESCO has recognised it as one of the most accurate ancient calendars known so far.

The presence in Europe of the ancient Bulgarians as a statehood people can be traced about the 2$^{nd}$ century AD, which is confirmed by the "Name List of Bulgarian Khans" (the calculations refer to the 165 AD when the legendary ruler **Avitohol** from the **Doulo** Dynasty took power). These least known centuries of Bulgarian history were connected with the vortex of the Great Migration of Peoples when some Bulgarian communities were forced to migrate to Armenia (so-called Bulgarians of **Vund**), to Panonia (today's Hungary, where later Panonian Bulgarians came to be known), etc. The basic part of the people fought against powerful emenies like Avars and Turks and maintained contacts with Byzantium. The year 451 is memorable for the important battle that Bulgarians and Armenians led in the Avarair Plain in defence of Christianity. The Bulgarians who gave their lives in this battle were canonized saints of Armenian Church. In the 7$^{th}$ century the Bulgarians led by the he great **Khan Koubrat** established a powerful state unity known as **Old Great Bulgaria**, which was ally to Byzantium in its grandiose wars with Avars and Persians. As an expression of honour the Emperor Iraklius conferred on Koubrat, who had already converted to Christianity, the high Roman-Byzantine title of patrician and valuable presents. One of sensations of modern East European archaeology was the treasure of the **village of Mala Pereshchepina**, nearby today's town of Poltava (Ukraine) where the great ruler was buried. The precious findings, golden jewelry, scepter, wonderful sword, etc., are kept in the Hermitage in Saint Petersburg. Those are eloquent evidence of the great political power of Great Bulgaria and the prestige of its ruler.

After the Hazars' aggression in the middle of the 7$^{th}$ century part of the Bulgarians remained within the new Hazars' khaganat (namely the tribes of Bat-Bayan, which created in the 10$^{th}$ century the state of the so-called **black Bulgarians** by the Azov Sea) but the greater part migrated and founded new states - **Volga Bulgaria** and **Danubian Bulgaria.** They also tried to found their states in the territories of today's **Macedonia (the Bulgarians of Kouber)** and in Italy **(the Bulgarians of Altsek)**. The Bulgarians from Panonia had their autonomy within the Avars' khaganat, while part of them probably moved to today's Macedonia led by Kouber. Among those "**many Bulgarian states**" most perspective in historical point of view proved to be today's Bulgaria on the Balkan Peninsula, founded by **Khan Asparuh** and Volga Bulgaria (today's Autonomic Republic of Tatarstan within the Russian Federation) founded by **Khan Kortag**. The two big medieval Bulgarian states were far to each other - at a distance of more than one thousand kilometres. In the 9$^{th}$ century the Danubian State chose the road to Christianity

# GENERAL INFORMATION

and grew as the third state of cultural importance in Medieval Europe, while the Volga State in the 10th century chose Islam as official religion. The Bulgarians from the state by the river Volga built a great Islam civilisation, having in mind the local historical and cultural features, fighting with the peoples from the steppes and the Russian kingdoms. In the 13th century after severe resistance they were compelled to accept the status of a vassal province within the Tatarian (Mongolian) "Golden Horde" and their state was completely ruined by the Russian King Ivan Grozni in the middle of the 16th century. Today the remains of their capital city **Bolgar Veliki** (the Great) are still an imposing sight. Volga Bulgarians were subjected to strong assimilation pressure by the Russian Empire, which continued even after the revolutionary changes in 1917 when they were assigned the incorrect in ethnic point of view name of Tatars. Today in the Republic of Tatarstan there is a civil movement of intellectuals for regaining the name of Bulgarians and the ancient-old name of the country - **Bulgaristan**.

On the Balkans the powerful Bulgarian State headed by **Khan Asparuh** (680-700) united the ancient Bulgarians with the successors of the ancient Thracians and the **Slav tribes** of the so-called Bulgarian Group, which settled there in 6th - 7th centuries. This group included tribes, which inhabited Mizia, Thrace, Macedonia, part of today's territories of Greece, Albania, Serbia (Kosovo incl.) and Rumania. The ambissions of Byzantium to conquer those tribes met a powerful barrier - the state founded by Khan Asparuh. So after the crucial success in the battle with the Byzantine troops by the delta of the Danube River in 681 emerged Danubian Bulgaria (today's Bulgaria) at the crossroad between Europe, Asia and Africa. Pliska became the first capital. The territories of the state covered Mizia with today's Dobroudzha and further northward of the Danube. Due to the ethnic tolerance Danubian Bulgaria attracted the neighbouring

*The Vulchitrun golden treasure*

Slavs and they gradually accepted Bulgarian way of life and traditions. About 700 Asparuh was killed to the north-east in a war with the Hazars. Archaeologists found his burial tomb near the village of Boznessenka, today's Ukraine. Tradition turned the Khan-founder into an epic hero who built "**great towns**" and ramparts "**between the Danube and the sea**" to defend his people. His brother, **Khan Kuber** founded **Bulgaria by the Vardar River** in today's Macedonia on the Balkan Peninsula (about 680) after he rebelled against the Avars and settled in the area of the town of Bitolya in present-day Macedonia. Khan Kouber had less authority; he acknowledged the supremacy of Byzantium and established close contacts with the neighbouring Slavs.

**Khan Tervel** (700-721) was at the head of the powerful Danubian Bulgaria and stopped the Arabian invasion thus saving Byzantium and the whole of Europe from the invasion of the Arab Halifat in 718 when the Islamic troops were on their way to conquer the "world capital" of Christianity - Constantinople. Thanks to Bulgarian support to the Emperor Justinian II in 705 Khan Tervel was conferred on the highest ranking Byzantine title of **kessar**, after the name of the great Gay Julius Cesar. This act was unique in the history of Byzantium and Medieval Europe.

**Khan Krum** (802-814) introduced a new type of legislation and strengthened the image of Bulgaria as a well-organised and modern state for that time. Byzantium attacked the Bulgarian State in 811 and burned down the capital Pliska. The Bulgarians immediately counterattacked - the warriors of Khan Krum defeated the Byzantine army in a pass in the Balkan Mountain. Emperor Nikiphorus I was killed in the battle. Since the reign of Emperor Valent (378) there was no emperor to die in a battle. Byzantium, being obsessed of fear, sought union with the Frank King Carl the Great and to facilitate it, acknowledged his title of emperor.

During the rule of **Khan Omourtag** (815-831) the pre-Christian Bulgarian culture reached its zenith and in political aspect the state expanded to the Middle Danube and Tissa River (today's Hungary) and to the Dnepur River (today's Ukraine). The administrative reforms established by Krum were further developed and improved. **Khan Pressian** (836-852) expanded further the Bulgarian territories and the borders almost reached the Aegean Sea and Albania. Bulgaria became the third Great Power in Medieval Europe along with the Byzantine and the Franks' Empires.

**Khan Boris I** (852-889) converted the Bulgarians to Christianity after long diplomatic negotiations, almost two centuries after the foundation of the Bulgarian State on the Balkans. He accepted the name Mihail and was the first to built Bulgarian churches and monasteries. The Bulgarian Church canonised him and in history he remained as St. Tsar Boris-Mihail. The creation and the establishment of the Bulgarian-Slavic writing by the brothers **St. St. Cyril and Methodius** is especially important in both cultural and historical terms. The Vatican acknowledged them patrons of Christian Europe. The alphabet created by them was adopted by other nations through the Orthodox religion. Nowadays it is used in Macedonia, Russia, Ukraine, Belarus, Yugoslavia, and Mongolia. In the past this graphic system dominated in the Wallachian and Moldova Kingdoms in Romania, in Lithuania, etc.

The one who continued the policy of Boris-Mihail was his son **Tsar Simeon the Great** (893-927). Simeon received a brilliant education in Constantinople and had the talent of a writer and the exceptional qualities of a statesman. He organised the translation of a number of Christian Orthodox books from Greek into Bulgarian, patronised the Pliska-Preslav and Ohrid Literary Schools and himself was a man of letters. He moved the capital to Veliki Preslav and expanded almost twice the territory of Bulgaria. The country bordered three seas the Black Sea, the Aegean Sea and the Adriatic Sea. A connoisseur of the antique Greek and Byzantine culture, he transformed the Bulgarian State into a mighty power with a great impact on the then existing world. The period of his reign is known as **The Golden Age**.

In its greater part the Bulgarian people were adherents to their **grandparents'** Orthodox faith. However, the many-faced Bulgarian society was not at all "sterile" and was open to various spiritual phenomena and processes. The birth of the Bulgarian **Bogomil heresy** took place during the reign of **Tsar Peter** (927-969). Its rise was due to the influence of the old dualistic doctrines as well as to the possibility the Gospel to be read and interpreted by various people in their own language. Priest Bogomil is considered its founder. The Bogomil heresy possessed a number of original features - at first place, moderate dualism and open asceticism. Bogomils' doctrine regarded

*Drinking-fountain in the village of Shiroka Luka*

# GENERAL INFORMATION

the sinful world full of injustice as a Satan's deed as compared to the Lord's Kingdom of Heaven and it expanded the Bulgarian borders. The heresy exerted strong impact in the Christian world - the **Catars** and **Albigenses** in France, the **Patarens** in Italy, the **heretics from Bosnia** (their successors are todays' Bosnian Muslims), the "strigolnitsi" in Russia, everyone sharing different than the official ideas in Serbia, Croatia, Hungary, even in distant England, considered the Bogomils their spiritual fathers. The French religious rebels were proud to call themselves **Burges** ("Bulgarian in faith") thus outlining their connection with the senior Bulgarian brothers in faith. These ideas, persecuted with sword and fire by the Catholic Church, had their impact on the Reformation and the Protestant doctrines in Western Europe.

Despite the difficulties the Bulgarian Kingdom remained an important political power during the reign of Tsar Peter but the intrigues of Byzantium provoked the aggression of Svetoslav - the ruler of the Rus of Kiev. The Norman-Russian occupation led to the pretended "help" of Byzantium and as a result the Bulgarian Kingdom suffered a great stroke - pushing back Prince Svetoslav, the Emperor Joan Tsimishi in 971 conquered the eastern Bulgarian territories with the capital Veliki Preslav. The lands to the west, whose centre is today's Macedonia, preserved their freedom. It was then that the genius of **Tsar Samuil** (997-1014) showed itself. During his reign the capital was moved to Ohrid. The "Bulgarian Epic" in the wars with Byzantium was marked with great victories, including the liberation of the former capital Preslav, as well as with great defeats. In 1014 the troops of Samuil were defeated and the Byzantine Emperor Vaslilii II (called The Killer of Bulgarians) captured 15, 000 Bulgarian soldiers. He ordered that 99 out of 100 be blinded and left the $100^{th}$ one-eyed so that he could lead them. Such was the barbarism and the national catastrophe that put an end to the first period in the history of Danubean Bulgaria. Bulgaria fell under Byzantine oppression for almost 170 years.

In 1186-1188, after a number of more or less numerous uprisings, the noble brothers **Peter and Assen** managed to unite the Bulgarians in Mizia and to gain back the independence of their country from Byzantium. Veliko Turnovo became the capital of the Bulgarian Kingdom. The reign of **Tzar Kaloyan** (1197-1207) and that of **Tsar Ivan Assen II** (1218-1241), who were great army leaders and exceptionally good diplomats, was a very fruitful and favourable period for the Bulgarian nation. They made a multitude of brilliant steps, striking war actions, and tactful peace treaties, which expanded the boundaries of Bulgaria and brought stable peace and welfare to the Bulgarians. In 1204 Tsar Kaloyan became the first ruler in Eastern Europe to defeat the knights' cavalry up to then considered invincible. Tsar Ivan Assen II gained new territories for Bulgaria and the state expanded as it was during the reign of Tsar Simeon the Great. During the next decades the Bulgarian Kingdom suffered the hegemony of the Tatars (Mongolians) as well as political crises (including the great uprising of the rural **Tsar Ivailo**) but withstood the hardships. The reign of Tsar Ivan Alexander (1331-1371) was called the Golden Sunset of Medieval Bulgaria. Bulgarian arts and culture from that period developed rapidly and were akin to the pre-Renaissance in Western Europe. However, the days of the free Bulgarian Kingdom were numbered because of the advancement of the Muslim-Turkish wave from the south-east. In 1393 the Tsar's metropolis Turnovo was conquered by the Ottomans and in 1396 the last free territories fell under their domination.

The Turnovo Literary School, especially during the work of the great man of letters and clerical leader **Patriarch Euthimius** (1375-1394), exerted powerful influence on the Orthodox world, mostly to the emerging new great power - Russia of Moscow. At the end of the $14^{th}$ and

# GENERAL INFORMATION

## Bulgaria during the reign of Tsar Simeon the Great (893-927)

the beginning of the 15th centuries the clerical leaders, heads of the Churches in Russia, Lithuania, Moldova, Wallachia, Serbia were Bulgarians. St. Kiprian of Moscow (in Russia), St. Efrem of Serbia, St. Hikodim Tismanski (in Wallachia) were honoured by those peoples as national saints. The Bulgarian clergymen and writer Grigorii Tsamblak who escaped from Ottoman rule, possessed the unique quality of representing several national schools of literature from that epoch - the Bulgarian, the Serbian, the Moldovan, the Russian and the Byzantine.

The most obscurant period in Bulgarian history started to continue several centuries. During those hard times for the Bulgarian people the Ottoman Empire conducted a policy of discrimination of the Christian population, especially as regards Bulgarians, as well as made attempts for assimilation. As a result of the Ottoman invasion many mosques were built, the Arabic alphabet was introduced for official and religious documents and many Christian sanctuaries were destroyed or turned into Muslim shrines. Many Turks, mainly soldiers, settled in the territory of today's Bulgaria. The Bulgarians suffered the so-called "blood tax" most of all. Blood tax required that a boy from the family be taken to Asia Minor where he would be converted into Islam and trained for a janissar - a warrior with no knowledge of parents, kin and motherland. Those janissars as well as the Turkish army of volunteers - the bashibozouk - were the real ruthless masters of the situation in Bulgaria.

Rebellions and uprisings became the expression of the live Bulgarian strive to freedom and independence. Most numerous they were at the end of 17th century when only in the period 1686-1689 three big uprisings broke out: The **Second Turnovo Uprising** (the first was in 1598), the **Chiprovtsi Uprising** and the **Uprising of Karposh** in Northern Macedonia. The fire of the haidout (outlaw rebels) movement burned during the centuries of foreign domination - the lands between the Danube to the Aegean Sea and to the mountains of today's Albania were roved by armed Bulgarian detachments, which revenged for the abuses and oppression by the authorities. This military and political experience later grew into organised movement for liberation of Bulgaria.

Bulgarian Revival began in the middle of the 18th century. The struggle for independent church and freedom of religious belonging, the publishing of books, and later of Bulgarian periodicals, the foundation of Bulgarian secular schools as well as the official establishment of Bulgarian language and culture, were the steps towards the revival of the nation.

The writing of the History of the Slav-Bulgarian People by Father **Paisii of Hilendar** (1762) and its later spreading, at first in manuscript version, marked an important moment in our history. The traditional for Bulgaria cultural centres - **chitalishta** (pubic libraries, cultural clubs) were created to preserve and elate the national spirit. Thus they gave the chance to many young Bulgarians get in touch with the treasures of European culture, which made national self-awareness and strive to political freedom grow further. The struggle for church and national freedom, which in the middle of the 19th century grew into a large scaled civil movement, did not possess clerical but rather secular features. It turned into struggle for national emancipation, which made the Porte acknowledge the Bulgarians as an independent nation and not just as part of the amorphous mass of "rum millet" (the Christians in the Empire). Thus the Bulgarians got their way before the Oecumenical Patriarchy in Istanbul, which was a channel for the assimilation tendencies of the Greek "megali idea", aimed at spiritual melting of Bulgarian population. The zenith of this unsurpassed in scale whole-nation activities was marked by the "**Bulgarian Easter**" in 1860 when the Bulgarians bravely raised their requests in defence of the national, religious and human rights.

Bulgaria was also strongly influenced by the Russian-Turkish Wars waged in the 18th - 19th centuries. The myth about **Grandpa Ivan** was created then - it was the story about the strong Russian hero who would come from the north and would liberate his Christian brothers living on the Balkans. Russia also nurtured this faith because of its actual interests for permanent influence on the Balkan Peninsula. To our regret, these wars did not yet bring freedom to Bulgaria but made thousands Bulgarians emigrate to the north - in Danubian Kingdoms and Besarabia, which was then part of Russia. Still today hundred thousands of ethnic Bulgarians live in the southern regions of Moldova and Ukraine, preserving their origin, language and traditions.

The participation of Bulgarian volunteers in those wars, especially in the Crimean War during 1853-1866, was a good reason for Russia, depite rather late as compared to its policy towards Serbia and Greece), to plan and organise the liberation of Bulgaria from Ottoman rule. The situation on the Balkans was more than unfavourable to the Bulgarians who lived in close proximity to the big centres of the neighbouring empires, which were main source of supplies for the Ottoman military machine and bureaucracy. The neighbouring Wallachia and Moldova (united in Romania in 1859), Serbia and Greece had managed to overthrow the Ottoman domination far more easily thanks to their geopolitical features. And yet the Bulgarians did not give up as they had to fight not only against the degraded Ottoman State but with the aspirations of their neighbours.

In 1862 **Georgi Rakovski**, ideologist of the Bulgarian National Revolution, organised the **First Bulgarian Legion** in Belgrade. Young people were trained in military art with the aim of organising an uprising. A great number of Bulgarian emigrants received excellent military education abroad, while some others took prominent positions in the Ottoman Empire and were seeking for diplomatic ways to obtain independence of Bulgaria. In 1869 the **Central Bulgarian Revolutionary Committee** was set up in Bucharest (with the writer Lyuben Karavelov being its chairman), which organised the preparation for the uprising from Romanian territory.

A key figure was **Vassil Levski** (1837-1873), simply called by the Bulgarians the **Deacon** (i.e. the **Monk**) or the **Apostle**. Casting off the cassock he managed to create an intricate network of secret revolutionary committees in Bulgaria united in a Central Revolutionary Committee with the town of Lovech as Headquarters. Persecuted for years by the Ottoman police the genius conspirator was captured, sent to trial and hanged in Sofia without betraying any of his assistants. Still today Levski is worshiped and considered a saint and the dearest victim of Bulgaria throughout its millenium-old history. The **April Uprising** from 1876 was a turning point in the movement for national liberation of Bulgaria. The uprising, which enjoyed widest support in Thrace (there **Georgi Benkovski** was its leader) took numberless innocent victims. Thousands of revolutionaries gave their lives for Bulgaria and among them stands **Hristo Botev** - the genius national poet.

The sanguinary suppression of the April Uprising placed the "**Bulgarian issue**" in the schedule of the world democratic community. A wave of protests, gatherings, fund-raising about the Bulgarian victims spread through the whole of Europe, from Slav Russia to England and Ireland far away. The "**horrors in Bulgaria**" retold in touching articles by the American journalist **McGahan** occupied the headers of the press in Europe and worldwide. *"The Empires, which kill should be put to an end"*, exclaimed the great French writer **Victor Hugo**. **William Gladston** and **Otto Von Bismarck** - notorious political figures expressed support to the cause for liberation of Bulgaria. The following brightest intellects in Europe raised protests and expressed sympathy and support to the Bulgarians - **Darwin**, **Mendeleev**, **Dostoevski**, **Tolstoi**, **Tourgenev**, **Garibaldi** and many more.

# GENERAL INFORMATION

This time it was not possible for the Great Powers to ignore the Bulgarian cause - purposefully overlooked for decades. A conference was held in Tsarigrad in 1875, which aimed but did not succeed in the diplomatic effort to grant autonomy to Bulgaria within its ethnic boundaries (divided in two parts, eastern and western, with Veliko Turnovo and Sofia as capitals, respectively). The Russian Emperor Alexander II declared war on Turkey in 1877. Finns, Polish volunteers, Romanians and numerous Bulgarian volunteers took part in it together with the Russian and Ukrainian soldiers. After heavy and epical battles fought for about a year, the most memorable of which took place in Shipka Pass and around Pleven, Turkey was forced to declare capitulation and sign the San Stefano Peace Treaty in front of the walls of Istanbul. That was how Bulgaria gained back its independence on 3rd March 1878 and its territories should have expanded to the old Bulgarian lands (Mizia, Thrace and Macedonia) whose ethnic-cultural features were defined by the dominant Bulgarian element.

But in July of 1878 at the **Berlin Congress** the Great Powers revised the **San Stefano Peace Treaty** and divided the Bulgarian people. An autonomic **Principality of Bulgaria**, subjected as vassal to the Sultan was established on the territory north of the Balkan Mountains (Mizia), including Sofia region. Southern Bulgaria (Thrace) became **Eastern Roumelia** (with Plovdiv as centre) under the political and military domination of the Port even though it enjoyed administrative autonomy. Macedonia and the Odrin region of Thrace remained under Turkish rule, Northern Dobroudzha was given to Romania and the Moravian region with the big town of Nis - to Serbia. An epic struggle for liberation started in the Bulgarian lands, which remained under foreign domination, especially in Macedonia. It followed the traditions of the Apostle Levski and its peak was marked by the **Ilinden-Preobrazhenie Uprising** in 1903.

Despite the bitter disappointment with the unfair Berlin Treaty the Bulgarians took up with reviving their state. The historical capital Veliko Turnovo hosted the Constituent (Great) National Assembly, which passed the **Turnovo Constitution** - on of the most democratic in the world at that time. Bulgaria became a constitutional monarchy with a strong Parliament and modern legislation. The first Knyaz (Prince) of liberated Bulgaria was **Alexander I of Battenberg** (1879-1886). He ruled a people who managed on their own to unite the two separated territories of Bulgaria in 1885 against the will of all the Great Powers. In the Serbian-Bulgarian War to follow (1885), the Bulgarians defended their right to be united in a non-divided territory. During the term of office of the Prime Minister **Stefan Stambolov** (1887-1894) - prominent politician and statesman, called "Bismarck of Bulgaria", Bulgaria was recognised as a European country of international prestige. During the reign of Prince (later King) **Ferdinand Saxe-Coburg Gotha** (1887-1918) the role of the monarch grew due to objective and subjective reasons but the multi-party political system had al-

*Vassil Levski*

# GENERAL INFORMATION

**The territory of Bulgaria as stipulated at the Ambassadors' Conference in Tsarigrad**

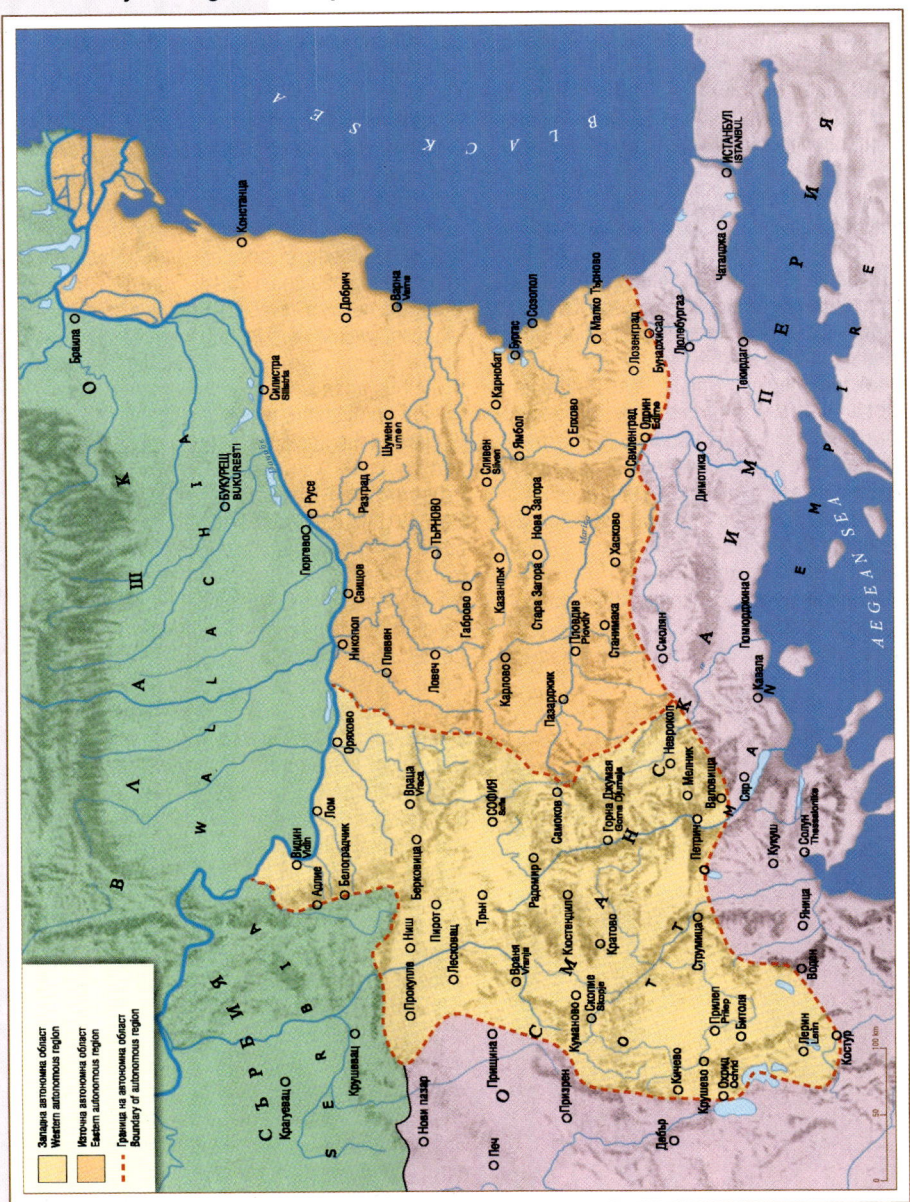

ready established solid grounds. In 1908 Bulgaria declared independence thus rejecting the last elements of unequal position as regards the Ottoman Empire. In 1912-1913 Bulgaria was the backbone in the efforts of the Balkan countries, which united against the Empire for liberation of the "**brother slaves**" in Macedonia. Bulgarian soldiers demonstrated unsurpassed bravery and heroism, the airplane was used for the first time in military actions, new methods in artillery were adopted, etc. The nation-wide exultation was nipped by the selfish policy of the allies Serbia and Greece, by the stab in the back by Romania, facilitated by inadequate diplomatic steps. During the World War I Bulgaria, with view to the not effected national liberation, had no chance and suffered a catastrophe together with Germany and the other defeated countries out of the so-called Central Powers. The heroism of the Bulgarian army remained in vain after all attempts for the liberation of Macedonia and its accession to Bulgaria failed. The national catastrophe became even worse after a Peace Treaty was signed in Neuilly, a Paris suburb in 1919.

During the reign of Tsar Boris III (1918-1943) the country was with reduced territories and hostile neighbours, and experienced deep social cataclysms and fierce interior political struggle. Despite that, all branches of economy were modernised, scientific research, education and arts enjoyed support.

One of the Prime Ministers at that time was Alexander Stamboliiski (1919-1923) - an ideologist and leader of the Bulgarian Agrarian People's Union. He implemented some successful reforms but made big mistakes in his interior policy and diplomatic efforts. The political situation in the country became more complex due to the uprising in September 1923 and the terrorist attack in St. Nedelya Church in Sofia two years later, which were followed by fierce repression on the part of the right-wing forces. Despite these extremes and hardships Bulgarian people still had faith in the Turnovo Constitution and strived to democracy and just social life.

The non-precedent salvation of the **Bulgarian Jews** from being sent to German concentration camps during World War II is associated with the name of Tsar Boris III. Thanks to the pressure of the democratic forces, the Bulgarian Orthodox Church and prominent intellectuals 50,000 Jews did not leave the country in the echelons of death. Bulgaria did not send troops to the Eastern Front to fight as an ally of Fascist Germany. Our army participated in the final stage of the war on the side of the Soviet Union and its allies. To our regret, at the Paris Peace Conference in 1947 the historic and ethnic rights of Bulgaria were once again not observed and Macedonia was included in the territories of Yugoslavia of Tito. This part of Bulgaria became a test field for an experiment a Macedonian nation and language to be created on an anti-Bulgarian basis. However, being a state of centuries-old historical experience marked of severe and unsurpassed suffering, Bulgaria was the first to acknowledge today's Republic of Macedonia (1991) and to continue rendering it assistance in the complex reality on the Balkans in the end of the 20$^{th}$ and the beginning of the 21$^{st}$ century.

After 9$^{th}$ September 1944 the democratic trends in Bulgaria were revived. However, the Soviet intervention put forward the Communist Party. In 1945 **Georgi Dimitrov** returned from Moscow. He is known as "the victor in the trial of the 20$^{th}$ century" in Leipzig when he was accused by the Nazi authorities together with three more Bulgarians of having put the Reich-stag on fire. In 1946 Dimitrov was elected Prime Minister and at the same Secretary General of the Bulgarian Communist Party. The period, when at the head of the Bulgarian state was **Vulko Chervenkov** (1950-1956), was marked by the so-called "cult of personality", which got deep roots in society. The long period of totalitarism during the term of office of Todor Zhivkov (1950-1989) was the time when state and party

# GENERAL INFORMATION

completely merged. During the 1970-s national economy achieved stabilisation and was modernised.

Democracy in Bulgaria revived in November 1989. In the new situation of real parliamentary democracy, the Bulgarian people chose their leaders - Presidents Zhelyo Zhelev, Peter Stoyanov and Georgi Purvanov, and Prime Ministers Andrei Loukanov, Dimiter Popov, Philip Dimitrov, Lyuben Berov, Zhan Videnov and Ivan Kostov. Since 2001 Prime Minister of Bulgaria is Simeon Saxe-Cobourg Gotha, the son of Tsar Boris III. The country made quick steps for integration with the big European family, creating its own model of ethnic tolerance based on traditional Bulgarian democratic values and historical experience. It is no mere chance that today's Bulgaria is a factor of stability on the Balkans nevertheless the hard and complex social and economic transition.

Ancient and strong blood runs in the veins of today's Bulgarian people - the blood of acient Bulgarians and Slavs, who settled on the Balkans in the 7$^{th}$ century winning their land in arms. This same land they turned into a cradle of Medieval European civilization by their hard work, energy and talent. The ancient Thracians and other old inhabitants of Mizia, Thrace and Macedonia joined their magnificent river of peoples thus giving birth to one of the most ancient in origin, restless in spirit and full of life people - the Bulgarians. A people, who established notorious traditions in statehood and culture, who adopted and rethought the achievements of ancient and modern cultures, who emitted strong civilisation impulses to other peoples, especially in Orthodox Europe. This people gave Europe the saint brothers Cyril and Methodius, Priest Bogomil - the religious rebel, the great musician St. Yoan Koukouzel, prominent figures like St. Kliment Ohridski, St. Yoan Ekzarh and St. Patriarch Eutimius of Turnovo, as well as a multitude of clerical leaders of other Orthodox peoples, starting from St. Mihail "the Bulgarian" - the first Metropolitan of the Rus of Kiev at the end of the 10$^{th}$ century. And in the dramatic 14$^{th}$ - 15$^{th}$ centuries there were St. Kiprian - Metropolitan of Kiev and Moscow, Grigorii Tsamblak - his successor in Kiev and Lithuania, St. Patriarch Efrem of Serbia, the leader of Romanian clergymen St. Nikodim Tismanski and many others… All of them - Bulgarians, who promoted the development of spiritually close peoples like Russians, Ukrainians, Belorusians, Serbians, Romanians, Moldovans, etc.

In the end, the creative spirit of Bulgarians - in Bulgaria and abroad - was suppressed neither by the five centuries-long Turkish yoke, nor by the dramatic turns during the last hundred years, which led to national catastrophes and hard social and political experiments, to open deprivation of ancient-old Bulgarian lands.

The creative spirit of Bulgarians survived regimes, wars, oppressions and rivers of Bulgarian blood. It gave the world even its most remarkable invention - the computer, invented by John Atanassov, whose father survived, by miracle in the April Uprising of 1876. Let us outline the names of Assen Yordanov, the constructor of Boeing, of Ivan (John) Nochev under whose skilful (and strictly confidential) guidance man first stepped on the Moon. Could we not mention the cult names of the opera singers Boris Hristov and Nikolai Gyaurov, Gena Dimitrova and Raina Kabaivanska? Or the "Mystery of Bulgarian Voices" which charmed not a one of world rock music stars! Or Bulgarian artists throughout the world including Kristo (Hristo Yavashev) - the legend of modern art.

These outlines are not an attempt of modest "self-promotion", nor provoked by romantic national understandings - nevertheless we believe or not, nevertheless we understand the essence of what was achieved, these are the truth, the truth, which we shall not forget, which obliges us before our successors and ourselves.

# GENERAL INFORMATION

## GEOGRAPHY

The Republic of Bulgaria covers a territory of 110 993 square kilometres. The average altitude of the country is 470 metres above sea level. The Stara Planina Mountain occupies central position and serves as a natural dividing line from the west to the east. It is a 750 km long mountain range stretching from the Vrushka Chuka Pass to Cape Emine and is part of the Alpine-Himalayan mountain range. It reaches the Black Sea to the east and turns to the north along the Bulgarian-Yugoslavian border.

A natural boundary with Romania is the Danube River, which is navigable all along for cargo and passenger vessels. The Black Sea is the natural eastern border of Bulgaria and its coastline is 378 km long. There are clearly cut bays, the biggest two being those of Varna and Bourgas. About 25% of the coastline are covered with sand and host our seaside resorts.

The southern part of Bulgaria is mainly mountainous. The highest mountain is Rila with Mt. Moussala being the highest peak on the Balkan Peninsula (2925 m). The second highest and the mountain of most alpine character in Bulgaria is Pirin with its highest Mt. Vihren (2914 m), followed by the Rhodope Mountains and Vitosha.

The plains and the lowlands in the country cover large areas to the north and the south of the Stara Planina Mountain. The Danube Plain is the biggest, bordering Yugoslavia to the west, the Dobroudzha region and the Black Sea to the east, the river Danube to the north and the Balkan Mountains to the south. Its relief is noted for the numerous plateaus, hills and river valleys cutting through the mountain. Dobroudzha is a hilly plain, situated in the north-eastern corner of Bulgaria. It is also referred to as "the granary of Bulgaria". The Rose Valley is located to the north between Stara Planina and the long and low mountain chain of Sredna Gora Mountain. Besides the widespread crops, the valley is typical for the oil-yielding rose grown there. It is one of the patents of the unique climate of Bulgaria. Another is the world-famous Bulgarian yogourt, made with the help of the yeast-type "bacillus Bulgaricum" (Lactobacterium Bulgaricum Grigoroff).

The Thracian Lowland is the second biggest in the country, starting from the mountains that surround Sofia to the west and reaching the Black Sea to the east. It stretches between the Sredna Gora to the north and Rila, the Rhodope Mountains and Strandzha to the south. Crops typical for the southern longitudes are grown there and sometimes two harvests are gathered.

Many European travellers claim that Bulgaria is Eden on Earth. It has everything: a sea; rivers and lakes, high mountains, virgin forests, plateaus and plains, hot and cold mineral springs.

*Sedemte Rilski Ezera*
*(The Seven Rila Lakes)*

# GENERAL INFORMATION

## CLIMATE

Bulgaria as a whole is sutiated in the moderate climatic zone. The country can be conditionally divided into two climatic zones. The Stara Planina Mountain is considered the watershed between them. Winters are colder in Northern Bulgaria and much milder in the Southern part of the country. Winter temperatures vary between 0° and 7°C below zero. Very rarely temperatures may drop below 20°C below zero. Typical continental and changeable is the climate in spring. It is exceptionally favourable for the growth of fruit-bearing trees, for whose fruit Bulgaria has been renowned in Europe for centuries. Summer is hot and sweltering in Northern Bulgaria, especially along the Danube River. The climate in Southern Bulgaria is determined by the air-currents from the Mediterranean. Summer temperatures do not reach the extremes as in Dobroudzha and along the Danube and are usually moderate: about 28°-30°C. The highest readings are usually taken in the towns of Rousse and Silistra, sometimes reaching above 35°C. Autumns are mild and pleasant in Bulgaria. The multi-coloured forests in autumn add to the picturesque landscape. Autumn showers in principle are more frequent than in spring. May, October and November are the rainiest months.

As is natural, in the high mountains the temperatures depend on the altitude. There are different climatic zones suitable for the growth of one or another rare species or crops. Typical examples are the Sub-Balkan valley, referred to as the Rose Valley, some regions in the Rhodope Mountains where one can find the unique flower of Orpheus, the region of the town of Sandanski where olives and citrus fruit are grown, etc.

There are some interesting areas from a climatic point of view, such as the Sofia Plain, the regions of Sliven and Varna, where strong winds blow almost throughout the year. In the first two cases they are due to the proximity with the Balkan Mountains and its passes, which let all winds blow constantly through them. In the case with Varna this phenomenon is due to the specific microclimate of the Bay of Varna and the sea air-currents coming from the north.

## POPULATION

The last census (in 2001) showed that 7 973 673 people live in Bulgaria. The average life expectancy for women is 74, and for men - 67. About one quarter of the population is at the age of pension. Most of Bulgarian population lives in cities. More than a million and a half people live in the capital city of Sofia, which is approximately one fifth of the total population. There are many ethnic groups living in Bulgaria (Turks, Gypsies, Armenians, Jews, Greeks, Wallachians, and Albanians) as a consequence of its historical and geographical specifics. All minorities live in harmony with the Bulgarian population without any social or ethnic pressure.

# GENERAL INFORMATION

## ECONOMY

The first steps made by Bulgarian economy in the modern sense of the word date back to the beginning of the 19th century when Bulgaria became famous for its agricultural production. In the beginning of the 20th century the country was one of the biggest exporters of early vegetables, fruit, milk, cheese, butter and meat in Europe. Up to the middle of the 20th century Bulgaria was considered a typically agrarian country.

The development of industrial production and manufacture date back to the first third of the 19th century. The factories in Sliven, Gabrovo, Veliko Turnovo and Stara Zagora, the development of crafts in these towns and in many others near the Balkan Mountains, gained good markets for Bulgaria and made it popular among the partners from the east and the west. The national industry advanced at a moderate pace till the middle of the 20th century when the government decided to turn the country into an industrial giant on the Balkans. This strategy was successful to a certain extent but it was at the expense of significant investments and a number of mistakes, connected with the lack of sufficient natural resources. The basic doctrine of the government was to increase the number of the working class, which implied opening of new enterprizes, construction of new factories and works, power plants, industrial enterprises and dams. The volunteer brigades of school children, soldiers and university students contributed as a free work resource.

At that time Bulgarian economy was bound with the economy of the USSR and the socialist countries through participation in COMECON and that gave impetus to certain branches of the national industry and revived the trade between those countries. On the other hand, Bulgaria did not have a choice and could not apply the principles of marketing and competition to the import and export of goods because of the lack of alternative trade partners.

Today Bulgaria is looking again for partners and markets. The collapse of planned economy and the introduction of the free market economy and competition caught the Bulgarian producers unprepared. A lot of companies went bankrupt. Privatisation is still in progress. There were no preferential laws until recently to give impetus to local production. There were

not enough tax and customs preferences to make Bulgarian producer assure prime quality and expand production. The foreign investments soon after November 10, 1989 clashed against walls of old decrees and regulations that deterred potential investors. The country has been in a situation of a currency board since 1997 tying the national currency to the DEM, and since

# GENERAL INFORMATION

1st January 2002 - to the Euro. This stabilised the Bulgarian Lev, put an end to the financial chaos and devaluation, and restored the hope of the people for realistic and stable savings and investments. The Parliament passed a packet of laws, which helped for modernisation of legislation and revival the production. The restitution of land and other real estate property as well as the privatisation advancing at full speed gave Bulgarians a chance to work and earn from their labour. There is a nation-wide opposition to the industrial racketeering, the disloyal competition, the production and distribution of low quality products and the piracy in the industrial and intellectual sphere. A reform in the field of banking is still to be imlplemented because of the emergence of a great number of banks and their bankruptcy at the expense of their clients. The financial, industrial and insurance companies and groups are also fought against because of the unfair deals, concealing of taxes, etc.

Today Bulgaria exports mainly agricultural products, electrics transporters, electricity and non-ferrous metals. It is especially famous for its yogourt and dairy products as well as oil-yielding roses, flowers and a variety of wines and brandies. The country imports various technical equipment, computers, audio and video equipment, electric appliances and household ware, ready-made clothes and raw materials. Tourism, which used to be an emblematic feature of the country's economy, is also successfully developing. Tourist establishments are to be totally privatised, modernised and renovated so that a better image and promotion of Bulgaria is achieved through it. Bulgaria possesses an incredible amount of natural resources which, with a little effort, better organisation and loyalty, could be turned into attractive centres for tourists and sportemen from all over the world. Many tourist companies have already met the world standards and attract their own guests to Bulgaria.

## LANGUAGE

Ancient Bulgarians belonged to the Indo-Iranian (East European) group of peoples; as a race type they are defined as Caucasus people as well (according to the West European scientific terminology). Their language was in a written form and the runic script was used. The language of the Bulgarians inhabited Danubian Bulgaria was formed in respect to the need of accession to Christianity on the basis of the Old Bulgarian language and the language of the Slav tribes from the Bulgarian group. It was the third language besides Latin, Greek and Hebrew, which was officially acknowledged by the church.

In historical aspect, the language of the Bulgarians contained few Thracian lexical elements, which had penetrated into the language through Old Greek sources.

Many words from Old Greek and Latin have become part of many European languages as terms in various branches of science, culture and politics. Bulgarian vocabulary by the end of the 19th and the beginning of the 20th century was full of Turkish words, which later gradually

# GENERAL INFORMATION

came out of use and today only add colour to the language. Some Russian words entered the Bulgarian language after the liberation of the country from the Ottoman rule.

At the beginning of the 20th century a campaign for purifying the language from foreign borrowings began but still many of them were preserved in specialised vocabularies. Science, medicine, law, political and social science traditionally use words of Latin origin. French words and terms are used in arts, German - in technical sciences, Italian - in musical terminology. The English language also provided a lot of borrowings for Bulgarian vocabulary. Alongside with the computer terminology, music, politics, business and culture, many other English words and terms are considered fashionable and are widely used by the younger generation. This is a linguistic problem that will have to be solved in the years to come for the uniqueness of the Bulgarian language to be preserved.

**Modern Bulgarian literary language** was formed during the Revival Period. Some of the characteristic features included dropping out of the case forms, post-noun position of the definite article, nine verb tenses, etc. Today there are many local dialects in Bulgaria that can be divided in two big groups - eastern and

*St. St. Cyril and Methodius*

western tongues. The difference in the vocabulary is negligible - about 20% different words, mainly in the words used in everyday life. More significant feature of the dialect and even of the literary language is pronunciation. Western tongues are specific for their harder pronunciation, few vowels and similarity to the Serbian-Croatian and Czeck languages. The eastern tongues have soft pronunciation, accent on the vowels, specific "singing" pronunciation of the words and are akin with the Russian, Ukranian and Belarus languages.

The Bulgarians use the **Cyrillic alphabet**. In the middle of the 9th century Konstantin-Cyril the Philosopher with the help of his brother Methodius created the first Bulgarian alphabet - the **Glagolitic alphabet.** They translated many

# GENERAL INFORMATION

liturgical service books and in fact created literature in the Bulgarian language. At the end of the 9th century the other Bulgarian alphabet was created - the Cyrilic alphabet, which was a prototype of the alphabet used by today by Bulgarians, Serbians, Russians, Ukranians, etc.

The first language reform was implemented as a natural process in the 19th century along with the development of Revival ideas. About ten obsolete letters and combinations were dropped out.

A second reform was carried out after the liberation from the Ottoman rule, the changes being mainly in the word order and syntax. There was a third reform after 1945, when several more letters were dropped out and the alphabet was reduced to 30 letters.

Most of the classics and modern writers are translated into Bulgarian, there are numerous scientific and specialised publications, as well as publications on science, culture, sports, religion and travel. The richest fund of books in Bulgaria is kept at the St. St. Cyril and Methodius National Library.

## CULTURE

One can get acquainted with the **pre-historic culture** of Bulgaria mainly through the exhibitions displayed at the Archaeological Museum and the National Museum of History in Sofia and through the exhibits in the local museums in Plovdiv, Stara Zagora, Nova Zagora, Varna, Rousse, Veliko Turnovo, Razgrad, Vidin, Bourgas, etc. The sights of particular interest include the famous Karanovska Mound near Nova Zagora, as well as the incredible drawings on the walls of the Magoura Cave (the Rabisha Cave). There are remains from Palaeolithic cultures in several caves in the Stara Planina Mountain and the Rhodope Mountains, while traces of Neolithic and Palaeolithic cultures by the sea are preserved in the areas of Cape Kaliakra to the north along the coast to the southern town of Ahtopol.

Most of the remains are indicative of high level masterful use of materials such as clay, kaolin, stone, wood, bronze and iron. The remains of pottery and other household ware dating back

# GENERAL INFORMATION

to the late Palaeolithic and the early Neolithic Ages found near Nova Zagora are extremely interesting and unique. This is the reason why the Karanovska Mound was called "the Noah's Ark" of European civilisation as it exhibits seven consecutive archaeological cultural layers. There are some of the first signs of the future archaic Mediterranean culture in it, which, along with the development of trade, became a model to the whole Old World. The Hotnitsa treasure, which was found among the remains of a late Eneolithic building ($2^{nd}$ half of $5^{th}$ millenium BC) and mostly the findings in the Necropolis of Varna (the late Eneolithic period) are indisputable evidence of the existence of well-developed civilisation in Southeastern Europe. Quite impressive are the settlement mounds ($8^{th}$-$6^{th}$ centuries BC) in the Eastern Rhodopes, Strandzha and Sakar Mountains, which illustrate the construction mastership of the Thracians in the early Iron Age.

The **culture of the Thracians** is represented in some of the most brilliant examples of their applied arts. The ancient Thracians were unsurpassed in processing different kinds of metals. The pots made of different metals combined in one and skillfully decorated with filigree are a challenge for researchers and antique admirers from New York to Tokyo. Most famous are the Gold Treasure Collection from Panagyurishte, the Silver Treasure Collection from Rogozen, the Vulchitrun Treasure, the flying pegasus from Sveshtari and the burial urns from the Thracian tombs. Despite being built under the strong influence of the Old Greek architecture, the thombs illustarte the passion of the Thracians for different architectural styles, their aesthetic and theological beliefs in those archaic and antique times. The racing chariots in the Kazanluk tomb and the caryatids in the tomb near Sveshtari are really very impressive. There have been discovered some new unique findings from Thracian times over the past few years thanks to the initiative and the organisational talent of a team of Bulgarian archaeologists with Professor Georgi Kitov at the head. The excavations they have made reveal some unknown aspects of the everyday life of the Thracians, as well as their burial customs and rituals. All of these have written new pages in our history books on the Thracians. About 100 mounds have been explored, more than 30 architectural constructions, and more than 5000 items of high scientific, artistic and museum value were found. Alexander Fol, Bogdan Bogdanov and Ivan Marazov with their intriguing research have contributed to our better understanding of the history of the Thracians. There already exists sufficient scientific material on the ancient Thracian and Hellenic traces on the Balkans. According to Herodotus, the Thracians were second in number and cultural achievements in the world after the Indians.

Throughout the country there are numerous remains from Thracian, Hellenic and Roman culture. Whole town sites have been preserved, restored and opened to public. Some of them are Augusta Trayana, Trimontsium, Nicopolis ad Istrum, Pautalia, Akre, Messembria, Apolonia and many others. Bulgarian museums abound in exhibits of the ancient everyday life, cult related and military items, statues, tombstones and monuments, masks, mosaics, statuettes of ancient gods, patrons of the home, and heroes. Under the capital city of Sofia have been excavated about 150, 000 square metres of ruins from the ancient city of Serdica. Almost every new building site in the centre of Sofia reveals some cultural layers from the Antiquity.

Many scientists considered that the civilisation on the Balkans was secondary and a kind of satellite to the Greek civilisation. However, there are preserved remains and cultural evi-

# GENERAL INFORMATION

dence proving that it was actually a synthesis of the Thracian culture and the cultures of the tribes who later settled here. Increasing number of archaeological finds confirm the complete autonomy of Thracian culture as regards the Greek culture till the zenith of Aegean settlements (polisi) in the 5th century BC. The famous Old Greek and Roman pantheon borrowed one third of the gods of the neighbouring Thracians - Dionisus - Ares (Mars), Zagrei become Zeus (Jupiter), Bendida became Hera (Yuniona), etc. The Thracians not only enriched Greek and Roman mythology but also the borrowings included some of their mysteries, cults and part of the holiday calendar of the Mediterranean and Black Sea regions, which is preserved, although somewhat reduced, to this day. All the town museums of history in Bulgaria have rich collections, consisting of antique cultural exhibits that reveal the town life of the people of that distant past, with their religious, cultural and daily needs. The amphitheatres and the spa in Plovdiv, Sofia and Varna are of great historical

*Drawings in the Magoura Cave*

value. A great number of scientists have written about the Antiquity and Hellenic history of the Balkans; works on these topics in Bulgarian and in the most widespread European languages date back to the middle of the 19th century till today.

The invasion of the **Slavs** and the **ancient Bulgarians**, alongside the foundation of Bulgaria, brought about some new tendencies in the cultural development of the country. The Bulgarians introduced a new symbol system of writing (tamgova). The Old Greek letters were rarely used, mainly in bilingual chronicles and texts concerning the wars between the Eastern Roman Empire (Byzantium) and Bulgaria. These texts can be deciphered only partially because of the lack of sufficient lexical sources, bilingual texts and the lack of a good systematic order in the writings. Most of them are petroglyphs, preserved on stone. Part of the symbols may also be found on the bottoms of pottery and on terracotta tiles, while others have been preserved on papyrus and parchment manuscripts from Byzantium, in Arabian scrolls, on cult plate and warriors' accoutrements. Numerous ceremonial and sanctuary accessories used by the ancient Bulgarians were found, as well as calendar devices. Many legends, songs and customs from that period are also preserved.

Some interesting finds of gold and bronze collections date back to that time, too, for example the treasure from Nagy St. Miklos, rings of Bulgarian rulers and nobility, burial sites of army leaders and khans, the sword of Khan Kubrat, the golden treasure accompanying his burial, etc. A number of scientists have devoted their lives and exerted a lot of effort to reveal this layer of our history of culture, about which very little is known. The pro-Soviet and pro-Slavic policy was a great obstacle in doing serious historic research.

The names of Ivan Venedikov, Slavi Donchev, Peter Dobrev, Yordan Vulchev, and those of the late Stanishev and D. Sussulov are well known for their contribution to the world science with a number of hypotheses and facts about the original homeland of the so-called "horseback" tribes, their culture, religion, and language. The very fact that the name "Bulgaria" was preserved in the Balkans shows that the ethos from the steppes of Central Asia had a strong cultural identity. Very little has reached our time from the Slavic culture as it served

# GENERAL INFORMATION

late kin-tribal relations. One can learn about it from Byzantine chronicles and some inscriptions in the Cyrillic alphabet.

The adoption of Christianity marked a new epoch in Bulgarian history. Besides the pre-Christian monuments in the capital Pliska and the Madara Horseman (the biggest bas-relief in Europe) quite interesting are the early churches and buildings, which can be found in Veliki Preslav as well as in many early mediaeval towns along the Black Sea coast and in the country's inland. The 9th century - called "Golden Age" of Bulgarian culture, is considered to mark the beginning of the Bulgarian literature as well. Besides the translations of Christian religious texts, apologies, prayers and church songs were created, too.

Some of the names that are emblematic to national culture include Cherorizets Hrabur, identified by some scientists as Tsar Simeon I, Joan Kukuzel the Angel Voice - a singer and composer of many marvelous religious songs, the disciples of the brothers Cyril and Methodius - Kliment Ohridski (of Ohrid), Sava, Naum, Gorazd and Angelarii, canonised by the Orthodox Church for their spiritual contribution to their people. The various ethnic groups that form the Bulgarian nation add to the richness of its culture. Many holidays, customs and songs, fairy tales, sayings and riddles have been preserved and are unique in Bulgarian and European culture as a whole.

The early Christian monasteries are very interesting in cultural and architectural respect. The most imposing of them is the Rila Monastery dating back to the 10th century - a stronghold of Bulgarian spirit and literature. The combination of Central Asian, Thracian and Early Christian elements on the domes and the columns in the churches, in the construction of the buildings, and in the layout of the early fortresses and settlements is unique of its kind. All of them show the fine taste of the Bulgarian rulers, their profound knowledge and skills to intertwine elements from different cultures without showing any uncivilised eclecticism characteristic of countries at a low level of their civilisation. Some Roman buildings, mainly Christian Orthodox churches from the period of Byzantine domination (11th and 12th centuries) are also preserved. They are being used even today, after a certain cultural assimilation and with some new icon paintings. The cultural development of the country after its liberation from Byzantine rule is overwhelmingly rich and shows the unique Bulgarian identity. The magnificent fortresses in Vidin, Cherven, Beroe, Sredets, Assenovgrad, Belogradchik and many other Mediaeval Bulgarian towns are still preserved and nowadays are being used as settings for the shooting of historical films. University students, archaeologists and architects carry extensive research work there. They are remarkable not only for the scale of their construction but mainly for the extraordinary mastership of their builders and the strategic location chosen in such a way as to completely merge with the landscape.

There are magnificent frescos in the churches and the monasteries from that period. The wall paintings in the Boyana Church near Sofia are compared to the best Renaissance models, though actually preceding them with a century and a half. The hesichastic monasteries, among which the Ivanovo, the Aladzha and the Bachkovo Monasteries, are stunning examples of the mastery of their builders, icon painters

# GENERAL INFORMATION

and wood carvers, of the brilliant combination of the surrounding landscape with the location of the religious building. The restored archaeological complex of the ancient capital Veliko Turnovo is very imposing, indeed. There is the Tsarevets Hill with the incredible town layout, the walls, churches, turrets and everyday life facilities. The churches and monasteries nearby the town, as well as the nearby village of Arbanassi are stunning for their uniqueness and bespeak the erudition and mastery of the Bulgarian rulers, their intellectual superiority and Renaissance way of thinking. Some of the frescos found in the Bulgarian churches and monasteries of that period depict diabolical, theatrical, dancing and Bogomil scenes. Considered a heresy, these frescos are material evidence of the cultural history of Bulgaria, an unwritten textbook about the unknown aspects of Orthodoxy.

The literary work of this period is remarkable. Presviter Kozma and Patriarch Evtimii are two of the most prominent men of letters and clerical leaders of Bulgarian people. A great number of religious songs written in symbols (writing notes without the note lines), which now comprise part of the church choirs repertoire, have been preserved to this day and have made Bulgaria world famous. Some ancient marginalias (notes in the margins of old-printed books) and transcripts of the Holy Book are famous exhibits in museums all over the world, the most well known of which is the Tetraevangelia of Tzar Ivan Alexander exhibited in the British Museum in London. It is a real piece of art containing superb calligraphic letters, title letters with incredibly beautiful ornaments and drawings in the margins that equal the best of their kind in the world.

After the invasion of the Ottoman Turks Bulgaria's culture went on the decline. Many mosques and buildings in Oriental style were constructed then, part of which are still preserved. During the first decades of foreign domination the building of Orthodox churches was officially banned. Later it was permitted again but only if they were built under the ground so they would not be taller than a Turkish soldier on horseback would. The art of calligraphy and marginal drawing was developed only in monasteries far from the vigilant eyes of the Ottomans. The transcripts were scarce, at least during the first two centuries. The construction of new monasteries started only in the 17th and 18th centuries after the official permission of the Porte. Various schools in icon painting, wood carving of altars, and constructions of churches and monasteries were established. Despite the official independence of the Bulgarian church, it was subordinate to the Greek Orthodox Church and had to observe the order of the Turkish Sultan, which stipulated that all the icon inscriptions were written and all the church services were conducted in Greek. The struggle for the freedom of the church lasted for more than a century and eventually finished with gaining total independence of Bulgarian church. This gave a new impetus to the development of the icon painting and woodcarving schools, the most famous of which were the ones in Tryavna, Debur and Bansko.

Zahari Zograph is a name known to every Bulgarian as one of the greatest icon painters of the time. His disciples created a new style in icon painting by introducing the portraying of ordinary people, church donors and benefactors of the spiritual life in Bulgaria. The somewhat forgotten and banned holidays in the secular and religious calendar were revived and the Bulgarian customs and rituals, as well as the folk songs and dances started to thrive. Songs were sung about heroes, haiduti, work, love, battles, nature and God. It was then that the country enjoyed its National Revival. Father Paisii of Hilendar wrote his "**History of the Slavonic Bulgarian People**" - reminding the Bulgarians of their historical origin and restoring their self-confidence, spirit of national belonging and freedom. This thin book had numerous rewritings and did what many fruitless uprisings could not have done. There were two other books on Bulgarian history written by Blazius Kleiner and Raino Popovich preceding it, but they were known only to a few Bulgarian intellectuals living in exile and were too incomplete. One of the re-writers of Paisii's history was Sofronii Vrachanski, himself a writer and spiritual leader.

The architecture during the Revival had very distinctive features. Today one can see many quarters and town centres as well as settlements perfectly accomplished by the constructors of the time. Cobbled streets, houses on sloping terrain, bow-window balconies, small windows, colour palmettes on the side walls, and especially the bright colours in which the houses, one close to another, were painted, were typical for that period. Wood, stone and limestone were the basic construction materials. The houses' interior is usually very intimate. The earthen floors, the little fireplaces, the wood-carved ceilings, the low doors and the window seats were characteristic for this new architectural style, later called "a la Franga". Some fine examples of it may be found in Koprivshtitsa, Veliko Turnovo, Plovdiv, Shiroka Luka, Tryavna, Gabrovo, Elena, Kotel, Bozhentzi, Melnic and many other places in the country. They are frequently visited by artists, poets and musicians as well as by many tourists from the five continents. Of particular interests are the crafts of that time best preserved and displayed in the Etura open-air museum of art crafts near the town of Gabrovo, in Dobrich, Plovdiv, Tryavna, etc. The original architecture of buildings and bridges created a unique atmosphere in the towns of the Revival. One of the most renowned masters of building from that period is Nikola Fichev (Usta Kolyo Ficheto) ("usta" meaning master), whose hands created masterpieces of churches and belfries, unique bridges, buildings and drinking-fountains.

The new Bulgarian literature was also gaining momentum. During that time, alongside with the teachers' poetry and didactic prose, appeared the first Bulgarian plays, the first published books and the periodicals. Dobri Chintoulov, Petko Slaveikov, Lyuben Karavelov and Georgi Rakovski are Bulgarian writers of that time and Vassil Droumev, Krustyo Pishurka and Dobri Voinikov are the first Bulgarian playwrights.

The genius of Hristo Botev is a consequence of a long process of maturing of the Bulgarian intellectuals. Even the Apostle of Freedom Vassil Levski tried his hand at writing epistolary literature and an interesting autobiographical poem, which is very revealing and sounds very colloquial.

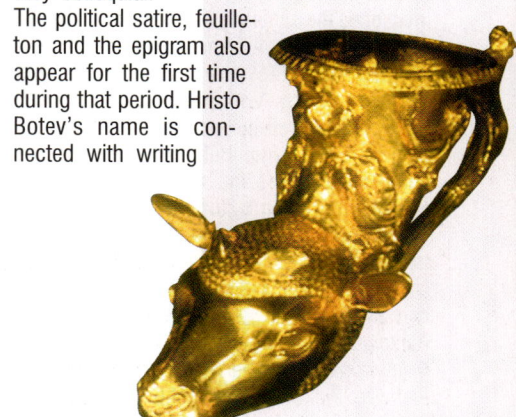

The political satire, feuilleton and the epigram also appear for the first time during that period. Hristo Botev's name is connected with writing

# GENERAL INFORMATION

the best examples of these literary genres. Petko Slaveikov collected over 150, 000 Bulgarian sayings and proverbs. The Mi-la-dinov Brothers, Grigor Purlichev and Kouzman Shapkarev also wrote down examples of the folklore of Macedonian Bulgarians and created excellent literary works.

Bulgarian culture advanced in quick pace thanks to the development of education - new schools, cultural centres and high schools were opened. Vassil Aprilov opened the famous Gabrovo High School in the middle of the 19$^{th}$ century, which bears his name today.

Dr. Peter Beron wrote the first primer, called "Riben Boukvar" (The Fish Textbook). Course books on different school subjects were also published. A great number of Bulgarians were educated abroad - in Russia, Germany, Italy and France.

After the liberation of the country from Ottoman domination the potential of the national culture sprung and many talented Bulgarians appeared in all of its spheres. In terms of literature there should be mentioned the names of Ivan Vazov, Aleko Konstantinov, Pencho Slaveikov and Zahari Stoyanov. In painting, the foreigners Vereshchagin and Mrkvichka started the realistic school in Bulgarian fine arts. Bulgaria turned to the European countries and borrowed as much as possible from their culture, trying to make up for what it had lost in the previous few centuries. Geo Milev, Yavorov, Rakitin and Liliev are representatives of symbolism, impressionism and expressionism in literature; Nickolai Rainov, Boris Georgiev, Sirak Skitnik and Ivan Milev in painting, Andrei Nikolov in sculpture; Panayot Pipkov and Pancho Vladigerov in music. All of them belonged to European cultural elite. That was the time when Bulgarian cinematography was born, represented by Vassil and Zhana Gendov. The Bulgarian theatre followed the European and Russian pattern. The National Theatre was founded in 1904, a lot of troupes performed classical plays and many great Bulgarian actors and producers worked there. Theatres went on tours and gave performances on different Bulgarian stages. Some of the most talented producers were Geo Milev and Isaac Daniel. The greatest Bulgarian dramatists of the time were Ivan Vazov, Petko U. Todorov and Peyo Yavorov. The most gifted actors were Vassil Kirkov, Adriana Boudevska and Krustyo Sarafov, who attracted wide audiences for years on end.

In the period between the two world wars Bulgarian culture sought its roots again after it had been carried away by some modern European tendencies. There appeared the themes of the country people, the life in the town, the everyday life and the feelings of the Bulgarian.

This was also a period of the development of science. The Bulgarian Academy of Sciences was founded. It attracted a myriad of scientists who specialised in Europe and the USA and with their research contributed to the development of the academic thought in Bulgaria. For a long period of time the only higher educational establishment in Bulgaria was Sofia University. The high quality of education was beyond doubt, the professors possessed exceptional erudition.

The names of the writers Yordan Yovkov and Elin Pelin, the poets Nikola Vaptsarov and

# GENERAL INFORMATION

*St. Ivan Rilski (of Rila)*

Elisaveta Bagryana, the playwrights Kostov and Stoyanov, the artists Vladimir Dimitrov Maistora and Kiril Tsonev, the sculptor Nikola Funev, the stage directors Surchadzhiev and Danovski, etc., are but a few among the names in the treasury of Bulgarian culture.

The buildings in Secession style gave way to the Bauhaus style, the city layouts became more similar to those of the West European countries, there appeared the typical cafes, cultural venues, cinemas, theatres, museums and libraries. Mihail Arnaoudov, Konstantin Zagorov and Ivan Hadzhiiski wrote some brilliant works based on their collections and analyses of our folklore.

The period after World War II was marked by the so-called "socialist realism". Some of its typical features were its heroic, ideological and demonstrative character as well as its shallowness of subject. In a positive sense it led to the accumulation of great resources in possession of the state, which used them for the development of culture. A number of significant works appeared in all its spheres. The pantomime, the puppet theatres and pop music developed and the Bulgarian circus gained world-wide recognition. Amateur culture was also on the rise and Bulgaria became a republic of amateur activities such as folk competitions and festivals, etc. Bulgarian folklore was proclaimed a national treasure. The opera school was highly appreciated and the opera singers Boris Hristov, Nikolai Guyaourov, Raina Kabaivanska and Gena Dimitrova are still one of the top singers in the world and their names may be seen on the posters of La Scalla in Milan and the New York Metropolitan Opera. Sports and tourism also developed during that period. The country had very good sports clubs in some sports. Bulgarian sportsmen won gold medals at Olympic, World and European Championships. The best represented sports were weight lifting, wrestling, track-and-field events, rhythmic gymnastics, shooting and mountaineering.

After 10th November 1989 all ideological barriers in culture were eliminated. The freedom and the lack of censorship gave a new impetus to the development of culture. Today Bulgarian creators may travel all over the world and make Bulgaria popular even in the remotest parts of the world. "The Mystery of the Bulgarian Voices", The Children's Choir of the Bulgarian Radio, the National Opera are part of our cultural identity. Cristo, Georgi Markov, Milcho Leviev and Eddy Kazassyan are no more dissidents but a few of the best representatives of our cultural identity, our face to the world. Pop music and jazz also have their new names. Simeon Shterev, Lyubomir Denev and Teodosii Spasov are well known to the world musical elite. Stefan Danailov is one of the stars of European cinematography. Dimiter Gochev, Alexander Morphov and Teddy Moskov belong to the new wave

# GENERAL INFORMATION

of top European theatre producers.

The Bulgarian press, radio and television are both state-owned and private. There are about 15 daily and more than 30 weekly newspapers published in Bulgaria, and a lot of other periodicals. The national radio broadcasts its programmes on three wavelengths - MW, SW and FW and practically all the Bulgarian towns have private radio stations. Along with the Bulgarian National Television and bTV there are private cable TV channels covering the whole country. There are also a great number of video clubs.

There are museums of history, schools, high schools, cultural centres and libraries in any Bulgarian town. Cinemas are everywhere. There are theatres in some of the bigger cities. Few of them are state-owned, greater part of them are owned by the municipalities. A number of private theatres appeared, too. There is a national circus and a lot of private circus troupes; as well as puppet theatres, opera houses, ballets, pantomime troupes, café-theatres, variety shows and night clubs, music clubs, etc.

The preservation of the **unique Bulgarian culture** is one of the problems of our times. Typical for Bulgarian folk music, for example, are the irregular rhythms, treble singing, two-part and three-part singing. The great task before the modern artists is to turn back to Bulgarian cultural roots, to study and re-create different themes from our over a thousand years old cultural treasury. This is the way to the Promised Land of the well-preserved national spirit, which to show the world the real Bulgaria - a land of an ancient, creative people of dignity.

## OPPORTUNITIES for CULTURAL TOURISM in BULGARIA

Bulgaria is a country with a very rich cultural treasury. Along with the historical monuments from the Antiquity, the Middle Ages, Revival period and from more recent times preserved in our lands, there are numerous "live" cultural monuments as well. The traditional Bulgarian customs, holidays and folk festivals may be called like that, among which the most famous are:
- The Koukeri Carnival in the region of Pernik and Doupnitsa (January);
- The Festival of Roses in Kazanluk (May);
- The festival for authentic folklore in Koprivshtitsa (May-June);

*Koukeri (Koukeri Carnival)*

# GENERAL INFORMATION

*A Koukeri mask*

- The folk festivals in Bourgas and Varna (August);
- The Festival of the Sea in Balchik and Sozopol (August);
- Festival of Dunov's followers at the Seven Rila Lakes (the second half of August);
- "Pirin Sings" Folk Festival (August) and "Rozhen Sings" Folk Festival (September);
- The festival at the Krustova Gora (Forest of the Cross) (14th September);
- The Christmas festivities in the Balkan villages and towns (December-January);
- The Days of the different monasteries after the names of their patron saints according to the religious calendar;
- Easter (in all churches and monasteries), with especially imposing ceremonies in the Alexander Nevski Cathedral in Sofia and at the Rila Monastery;
- The local folk dancing and singing festivals, etc.

Most tourist agencies have included in their packages some of the above-mentioned cultural events and the foreign visitors could get a "live" idea of the authentic culture of Bulgarians.

The national folk costumes and musical instruments are very interesting and unique. Some of the most popular nosii (costumes) are the so-called "white outfits", "black outfits", the costumes from the Thracian, Rhodope and Vidin regions, etc. The folk costumes worn on different holidays are extremely varied. Among the most picturesque are the costumes of the Koukeri, Lazarki, the fire-dancers, etc. Most of these are on display in the ethnographic museums countrywide.

Traditional Bulgarian musical instruments with original sounding are the gaida (bagpipe), kaval (shepherd's pipe), gudoulka (rebec), tupun (specific drums), gousla (a kind of mandolin), dvoyanka (double rebec), brumbuzuk (small pipe), chans and tyumbeleks (sheep's bells). One can find audio, video-cassettes and CDs with recordings of Bulgarian folk music, the phenomenal Bulgarian folk singers and ensembles, who make Bul-garia popular all over the world.

# GENERAL INFORMATION

## RELIGION

The greater part of Bulgarian population is Eastern Orthodox. Since **865 AD** when Knyaz Boris-Mikhail converted the Bulgarians to Christianity Bulgaria is considered an **Orthodox country**. Later there appeared different movements, among which the Bogomil, the Adamite and the Pavlikyan (another type of dualism) beliefs, which were considered heresy. Today all of them are history. Later the Hermeticism, Asceticism and Hesychasm were born but they lasted for even shorter periods of time before Bulgaria to fall under Ottoman domination.

After World War II and during the socialist government of the country atheism was the official doctrine, so it is considered that today one fifth of Bulgarian population are atheists. The smaller groups include Muslims, Catholics, Protestants, as well as Dunov's followers, Rosenkreuzer's followers, Mormons, etc. Some of the eastern religions are also represented in the country. Legitimate are the followers of Hinduism, Buddhism, Zoroastrianism, the various branches of Yoga - Hahta, Bhakti, Tantra, Kria, Judeans, Red Indian totems' worshipers, etc. The esoteric and occult books translated into Bulgarian are growing in number. The followers gather into groups and societies for esoteric knowledge, the books and lectures are read to large audiences, various meditation and physical techniques are demonstrated, Lamas, priests and preachers from all over the world come to Bulgaria.

Nevertheless, the majority of the Bulgarians observe the Christian traditions and more than half of them identify themselves with Orthodox Christianity. The tendency of turning back to God and the Holy Book is getting stronger, especially in the last years of democracy when the century-old beliefs and values of the Bulgarian nation were put forward. New churches, chapels and monasteries are built, old icons, altars, and churchplates are restored, dilapidated village churches are reconstructed and opened again for the believers.

The published religious literature on Christianity has also increased as well as the demand for it. The Bulgarian family celebrates the traditional Christian holidays, especially Christmas Eve and Christmas, Easter and the name days of Bulgarians, named after archangels, saints and martyrs. One can claim that it is the time of Revival of Orthodoxy in Bulgaria.

*Frescoes in the Church at Rila Monastery*

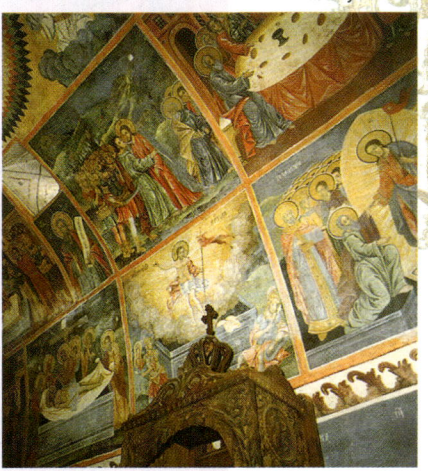

# GENERAL INFORMATION

## HOLIDAYS, CEREMONIES, CARNIVALS and FESTIVALS

The National Holiday of the Republic of Bulgaria is 3rd of March - the Day of Liberation from Ottoman rule.

### Public Holidays:
**1 January** - New Year's Day
**Easter** - according to the Religious Calendar
**1 May** - International Day of Labour
**6 May** - Day of the Bulgarian Army
**24 May** - Day of Bulgarian education, culture and Slavic script (St. St. Cyril and Methodius' Day)
**6 September** - Day of the Renion of Bulgaria in 1885
**22 September** - Independence Day
**1 November** - Day of Bulgarian Spiritual Leaders
**24-26 December** - Christmas Eve and Christmas

There are some other secular holidays and carnivals quite popular in Bulgaria:
**11 January** - Koukeri Festivals in Pernik Region (in other regions the festival is held earlier);
**1 February** - Trifon Zarezan (vines are cut)
**8 March** - International Woman's Day
**1 April** - Day of Humour and Satire
**1 June** - Children's Day
**2 June** - Day of those who gave their lives for the freedom of Bulgaria
In the **beginning of June** - Festival of Roses in Kazanluk
**15 September** - Opening School Day, Day of First-Grade Pupils
**8 December** - Students' Day.

The **traditional holiday calendar** of the Bulgarians is varied and complicated. The ancient culture on the Balkans has left its imprint on the calendar of the various holidays and ceremonies in Bulgaria. There are events and customs dating milleniums back, combining totemic, animistic, pantheist and monist elements characteristic of Mediterranean Antiquity.
In a concise version the traditional holiday calendar of the Bulgarians would look like that:

### JANUARY
| | |
|---|---|
| 1 | - Sourvaki (St. Vassil's Day) |
| 6 | - St. Yordan's Day (Epiphany) |
| 7 | - St. Ivan's Day (St. Yoan the Baptist) |
| 8 | - Grandmother's Day (Midwife's Day) |
| 17 | - St. Anton's Day |
| 18 | - St. Atanas's Day |
| 20 | - Rooster's Day (Day of Fertility) |

### FEBRUARY
| | |
|---|---|
| 1 | - St. Trifon's Day (Trifon Zarezan) |
| 2 | - Candlemas |
| 3 | - St. Simon's Day |
| 10 | - St. Haralampi's Day |
| 11 | - Vlas's Day (Shrove Day - always on Sundays, eight weeks before Easter) |
| | **Shrovetide (the first Sunday before Lent)** - always on Sundays, seven weeks before Easter |
| | **St. Todor's Day** (Horse Easter) - on Saturdays after Shrovetide |

(The last three holidays depend on Easter Day and are not fixed. For the next few years Easter will be celebrated as follows:
**2002** - May 5
**2003** - April 27
Easter is always on Sundays and is used to determine the days of the Christian holidays, which have no fixed dates.)

### MARCH
| | |
|---|---|
| 1 | - Granny Marta's Day |
| 9 | - St. St. 40 Martyrs |
| 25 | - Annunciation |

### APRIL
**St. Lazar's Day** - always on Saturdays, a week before Easter
**Palm Sunday** - on Sunday, a week before Easter
**Easter** - look at above-mentioned dates
**Low Sunday** - on Sunday after Easter

# GENERAL INFORMATION

**Sofinden** - on Monday after Low Sunday (Prayers for healthy cattle and against drought)
14 - St. Martin's Day

## MAY
1 - Prophet Yeremiah's Day
6 - St. Georgi's Day
12 - St. German's Day (Prayers against hail)
21 - St. St. Konstantin and Elena's Day
**St. Spas' Day** - always the 40$^{th}$ day after Easter
**Pentecost** (Holy Trinity) - always the 50$^{th}$ day after Easter
**Roussalya** (Holy Ghost) - the 51$^{st}$ day after Easter

## JUNE
11 - St. Bartholomew's Day
15 - Vidov Day (Prayers against hailstorms and other natural disasters)
24 - Enyo's Day
29 - Peter's Day (St. St. Apostles Peter and Pavel)
30 - Pavlyov's Day (the Day of the 12 Apostles)

## JULY
1 - St. Vrach
20 - St. Iliya's Day
22 - St. Maria Magdalena's Day
27 - St. Pantelei's Day

## AUGUST
1 - Makavei's Day
6 - Holy Transfiguration
15 - Assumption

## SEPTEMBER
1 - St. Simon's Day (Start of the ecclesiastical year)
8 - Birth of the Holy Virgin
14 - Krustovden (Day of the Cross)
17 - Faith, Hope and Love (and St. Martyr Sofia's Day)

## OCTOBER
14 - St. Petko's Day
19 - St. Yoan Rilski Thaumaturge
26 - St. Dimitur's Day
27 - Mice Day (Prayers against the evil)

## NOVEMBER
8 - Michaelmas
21 - Presentation of the Holy Virgin
23 - St. Alexander's Day
30 - St. Andrei's Day

## DECEMBER
4 - Day of Martyr Varvara
5 - St. Sava's Day
6 - St. Nikola' s Day
20 - St. Martyr Ignat's Day
24 - Christmas Eve
25 - Christmas
27 - St. Stefan's Day
31 - New Year's Eve

The Kukeri Carnival is celebrated on St. Vassil's Day and St. Trifon's Day and has been preserved since Thracian times. German is a Slavic holiday, Grandmother's Day, St. Todor's Day, Granny Marta's Day, St. Ivan's Day, Mice Day and St. Ignat's Day are ancient Bulgarian holidays, and the rest are Christian holidays from different periods.

There are church services during all of them, since they have been canonised though some are of heathen nature. Some are accompanied with public prayer processions, holy masses, hymns and prayers according to the Bulgarian Orthodox rules.

There are some **family holidays** that are of great significance for the Bulgarians. The most important of them are Christening (the Holy Christening), the First Steps (to celebrate the first steps made by the small child), the Birthday, the Nameday, Offering (the offering of an animal or some food to heathen gods and saints to make them show more grace or to

# GENERAL INFORMATION

thank them for good fortune, health and long life); the Engagement, the Wedding. Inauguration of a New House, Parting (before sending out someone on a long journey). All of these have been preserved for many ages and are a live tradition in Bulgarian families regardless of their religious beliefs.

Very popular folk festivals are held in Koprivshtitza, Shiroka Luka, Rozhen, Silistra, the Pirin and the Strandzha Mountains, etc. There are folk festivals held in Bourgas and Varna. The music festivals in Sofia, Varna, Slanchev Bryag (Sunny Beach) and Rousse are well known and very prestigious, too.

Some popular theatre festivals with international participation are "Theatre in a Suitcase" and "Apolonia" (in the latter are represented all the arts); "Love is Folly" and "Golden Rose" are film festivals. There are also wine festivals, Neptune Days along the Black Sea coast, music competitions, "Mister" and "Miss" competitions, local art competitions, sports events, and international championships.

The **most interesting and unique** Bulgarian holidays and customs are the Kukeri Carnivals of the masked koukeri; the martenitzi - white and red threads and anthropomorphic pendants exchanged between relatives and friends on Granny Marta's Day to wear for health and happiness on the occasion of the coming spring; the customs German and Russalii (Mermaids); the nestinarski dances on red coals on the Day of St. St. Konstantin and Elena; the custom of well wishing by tapping people on the back with a "sourvachka" - decorated cornel-tree twig on Christmas and New Year's Day; the Day of Humour and Satire; Krustovden (Day of the Cross) with an imposing prayer procession and pilgrimage in Krustova Gora (Forest of the Cross) area in the Rhodope Mountains., etc. Many Bulgarians and foreign tourists visit these celebrations, the former celebrate them the way their forefathers did for centuries on end and the latter take pictures and participate in them, too.

## NATIONAL PARKS and RESERVES

The following categories of protected territories are operative according to the Law of Protected Areas:
- **National Park** - Pirin, The Central Balkan, Rila;
- **Nature Reserve** - The Vratza Balkan, Sinite Kamuni (The Blue Rocks), etc.;
- **Reserve** and **Maintained Reserve** - The Siloxia, Sreburna Bioshpere Reserve;
- **Natural Sight;**
- **Protected Area**.

Rocks, waterfalls, caves, earthen pyramids, areas with various ecological systems, specific remarkable landscapes and objects of non-living character are included in the last two categories.

A Law on Protection of the Culture Monuments and Museums is also operative.

Nine national sites are included in UNESCO List of World Cultural and Nature Heritage.

**The Boyana Church**. It is admired for the unique frescoes dating back to 1259, which

*Rila landscape*

# GENERAL INFORMATION

are considered masterpieces of European Medieval art of painting. It is located in Boyana Quarter, 8 km from Sofia.

**Ivanovski Rock Monasteries.** A monastery complex in the rocks with tens of well preserved inscriptions and wonderful wall paintings - an exceptional monument of Bulgarian Medieval art. It is located in the rocks above Roussenski Lom River, about 18 km from the town of Rousse.

**Kazanluk Tomb.** A Thracian tomb dating back to the end of the $4^{th}$- the beginning of the $3^{rd}$ century BC. The frescoes in the burial chamber and in the corridor are of extreme artistic value. It is situated on the Tyulbeto Hill nearby the town of Kazanluk.

**Madara Horseman.** A bas-relief cut in Madara rocks. It is the most impressive piece of monumental art from the Early Medieval Epoch, evidencing that the Bulgarians are of Indo-European origin and culture and a highly civilised statehood people. This monument is the only of its type in European cultural history and is located nearby the village of Madara, about 16 km from the town of Shoumen.

**Pirin National Park.** Being part of the beautiful Pirin Mountain, the National Park is noted for its specific relief and unique flora and fauna species. It includes the Bayuvi Doupki-Dzhindzhiritsa Biosphere Reserve, as well. The park occupies the highest ridges of Western Pirin.

**Nessebur, the Old Town.** An architecture-historical and archaeological reserve with ancient archaeological remains of various periods, original churches from the $5^{th}$ - $17^{th}$ centuries and more than hundred authentic Revival houses.

**Sreburna Reserve.** A biosphere reserve including the Sreburna Lake and the neighbouring areas. It is created to preserve rare flora and fauna species. The reserve is situated 16 km west of the town of Silistra.

**The Rila Monastery.** The most monumental monastery complex in Bulgaria of extremely high architectural and artistic value. Founded in the $10^{th}$ century, rebuilt and expanded in $13^{th}$ - $14^{th}$ centuries, centre of literature in the $15^{th}$ century and completed in its present magnificent outlook in the $19^{th}$ century. It is situated in Northwestern Rila, about 3 km from the town of Rila and about 120 km from the city of Sofia.

**Sveshtari Tomb.** A Thracian tomb dating back to the first half of the $3^{rd}$ century BC. The central burial chamber is heavily decorated and with imposing high relief of caryatids. It is located nearby the village of Sveshtari, 7m south-west of the town of Isperih.

The first four sites were included in the list of world heritage in 1979, the next four - in 1983 and the last one - in 1985.

The diverse natural, cultural and religious features of these venues make them attractive to visitors and at the same time offer excellent opportunities for having a walk, making observations and research, for taking photos, spending one's holidays, for sports and tourism.

There are plenty of souvenirs sold in specilised shops in the parks and reserves, which in the greater part are hand-made and may be found decorating Bulgarian houses. They attract the foreign visitors with their craftsmanship and are taken abroad as a small piece of the spirit of Bulgaria.

*An old church in the town of Nessebur*

# INFORMATION for VISITORS

## KEY TELEPHONE NUMBERS in SOFIA

| Ambulance | 150 |
| --- | --- |
| Fire Brigade | 160 |
| Police | 166 |
| Road Service | 1286 |
| Mountain Rescue Service | 963 20 00 |
| Telephone Information Services | 144 |

## VISAS

The Republic of Bulgaria requires no visas for the citizens of a number of countries in the world, but every tourist is advised to obtain preliminary information in this respect because some kinds of visas require longer time for processing and issuing. Bulgarian citizens are not required visas for travelling in the European Community countries and in most of the remaining European countries, as well as in some countries in Asia, Africa and America, with which Bulgaria maintains enduring friendly, cultural and economic relations.

All data below are subject to frequent change as far as terms, costs and visa requirements with each specific country are concerned, so the prospective visitors should first check the state of the contacts between their own country and Bulgaria.

**Entry of foreign citizens in Bulgaria**. A foreign citizen may enter Bulgaria only if he possesses a valid document for travelling abroad or any substituting document instead, as well as an entry visa, visa for a stay or a transit visa, when such is required. **Visas** cover:

- Transit visa
- Short-term visa
- Group visa
- Long-term visa.

The term of stay in the country on the grounds of a visa may not exceed 90 (ninety) days. Visas are issued by the diplomatic and consular offices of the Republic of Bulgaria, long-term visas are issued upon the approval of the foreign citizens control authorities.

Since 1st January 2002 the Ministry of Foreign Affairs commenced issuing a new type of Bulgarian visa. It is in the form of a sticker and for the first time in Europe a photo on it is required.

**Transit visa.** A foreign citizen who enters Bulgaria on the grounds of a transit visa at a particular border checkpoint from one country shall leave Bulgaria within 24 (twenty-four) hours through the border checkpoint with another country. In order to obtain a transit visa the foreign citizen shall have visa for the country of his final destination. Should he travel not by airplane or no visa is required for the country of final destination, the foreign citizen shall have visa for the first country along the route, for which visas are required. **Single** - valid up to 3 (three) months and allowing only 1 (one) transit through the country. **Double transit** - 3 (three), 6 (six) or 12 (twelve) months validity, allowing 2 (two) transits through the country. **Multiple** - 3 (three), 6 (six) or 12 (twelve) months validity, allowing unlimited number of transits through the country.

**Short-term visa.** Such visa is issued to a foreign citizen when he enters the country once or multiple times for a stay of up to 90 (ninety) days within a 6 (six) months period considered from the date of his first entry. The **multiple** short-term visa is valid for up to 1 (one) year. The validity may be extended by the foreign citizens control authorities for humanitarian reasons. **Single (tourist) visa** - valid up to 3 (three) months and allowing 1 (one) entry and stay in the country. **Multiple entry visa** - 3 (three), 6 (six) or 12 (twelve)

# INFORMATION for VISITORS

months validity, allowing unlimited number of entries in the country.

**Group visa.** Group visa is issued for a transit stay or entitling to a stay up to 30 (thirty) days to foreign citizens who had formed a group before their departure to Bulgaria, are registered in a group passport and only if they enter, stay and leave the country as a group.

**Long-term visa.** It is issued to a foreign citizen who is willing to stay for a longer term or settle in the country. It entitles the foreigner to 1 (one) entry and to a stay of up to 90 (ninety) days. The validity may not exceed 6 (six) months.

**Application for visa for a private visit.** Nevertheless the term of stay, the applicant shall present: invitation to a foreign citizen on a private visit; banking statements certifying solvency or available funds amounting to USD 40 (forty US Dollars) per day for the term of stay; documents evidencing the extent of social integration (position, workplace, family); should the host be a relative, the applicant for visa shall present documents evidencing the kinship ties with the inviting person.

**Application for a single entry business visa.** The obligatory documents include: invitation to a foreign citizen on a business visit; certificate of the valid court registration of the foreign company; certifying letter from the foreign company about the position of the applicant, unless the latter is not an owner; should the applicant certify that he has registered a company according to Bulgarian legislation, a certificate from the tax authorities is required for the preceding year, evidencing the absolute figure of the declared income and the tax paid.

**Application for a multiple entry business visa for a 12 (twelve)-month period.** The obligatory documents required include: certificate from the foreign association of commercial banks or the chamber of commerce and industry; certificate of the valid court registration of the foreign company; customs, tax, banking and other documents, evidencing the existence of "enduring relations".

**Business trip.** The obligatory documents required from the Bulgarian company include: invitation to a foreign citizen on a visit and a letter evidencing the purpose of the trip; from the foreign company: a letter evidencing the purpose of the trip and the position of the applicant for visa.

The tourists are advised to take particular care of keeping possession of their documents. Any loss or damage of passport and customs documents is quite unpleasant and entails lengthy operations on their renewal, since each case is processed by the Ministry of the Interior, the Ministry of Foreign Affairs, the embassy of the respective country whose citizen the tourist is, and the customs authorities.

## CUSTOMS REGULATIONS

Every tourist visiting the Republic of Bulgaria may import a limited amount of food, cigarettes and liquor for personal use. Depending on the length of his stay, the admissible number and quantity of the imported goods is indicated at every customs checkpoint.

A special **customs declaration** is filled should the imported amounts exceed the stipulated ones, together with an explanation for the reason of this excess. Subject to obligatory declaring are golden articles, valuables in excess of personal jewellery, photographic cameras, electronic devices and apparatus of greater value. The same objects shall be declared also upon leaving Bulgaria, whereby the tourist certifies that the objects have not been made present or sold to other persons. Presents and objects carried for Bulgarian citizens or foreigners residing in Bulgaria shall

# INFORMATION for VISITORS

be declared as well.

Subject to a **special regime** of import and export are the antiquarian objects, works of art, historic and cultural treasures, rare coins of numismatic value and securities. The latter require particular permits and accompanying documents, which may be obtained in the respective country by the local authorities and the Bulgarian representations upon import, and by the Bulgarian authorities upon export of the same.

Bulgarian **business partners** enjoy special conditions for the import and export of raw and prime materials, finished products, foreign exchange, numismatic valuables and works of art.

Subject to special control are the deficient raw materials, and protected birds, animals and plants. The import and export of works of art for participation in auctions or sales, in exhibitions, fairs or art expositions, require special documents, which shall obligatorily accompany the exhibits or the works of art. The same applies to medicines, narcotics, weapons and ammunition.

The customs offices in Bulgaria most frequently used by tourists and business partners respond to the following phone numbers:

| Central Customs Office | (02) 931 15 12 |
|---|---|
| Sofia Customs Office | (02) 931 41 91 (2,3) 931 51 52 |
| Sofia Airport | (02) 71 70 51 |
| Plovdiv Customs Office | (032) 22 01 30 |
| Varna Customs Office | (052) 22 55 32 |
| Bourgas Customs Office | (056) 4 23 01 |
| Rousse Customs Office | (082) 44 99 98 |

## CURRENCY, PAYMENTS and FOREIGN EXCHANGE

The official monetary unit in the Republic of Bulgaria is called the **LEV**. As since 1997 the country has been in the conditions of a currency board, the Lev was attached to the German Mark (at a fixed exchange 1 Lev for 1 DM) and since 1st January 2002 the Lev is attached to the Euro. Through the cross rates of all other currencies, foreigners and Bulgarian citizens willing to exchange foreign currency can easily compute the respective value of their money.

The Leva in Bulgaria are of emissions not earlier than 1999. The following coins are in circulation:

**1 stotinka**
**2 stotinki**
**5 stotinki**

The above mentioned coins are of yellow metal.

**10 stotinki**
**20 stotinki**
**50 stotinki**

These coins are made of white metal. The value of one stotinka amounts to 0.01 of 1 Lev. The Bulgarian paper notes comprise the following denominations:

- **1 Lev**, with the effigy of St. Ivan Rilski;
- **2 Leva**, with the effigy of Paissii Hilendarski;
- **5 Leva**, with the effigy of Ivan Milev;
- **10 Leva**, with the effigy of Dr. Peter Beron
- **20 Leva**, with the effigy of Stefan Stambolov
- **50 Leva**, with the effigy of Pencho Slaveikov

# INFORMATION for VISITORS

Currency may be exchanged in all Bulgarian banks from Mondays through Fridays in the regular working hours without any commission charged.

A lower bank exchange rate is quoted a rule by the exchange bureaus at the major hotels, railway stations, bus stations, maritime ports, and international airports. Money can be exchanged also in the numerous private exchange bureaus, some of which are open through the week round, and others operate non-stop.

Payments in the Republic of Bulgaria are effected **only in Leva** or in Leva equivalent. In larger resorts and at places authorised to effect foreign exchange, certain payments may be effected in foreign currency. There are shops selling only for foreign currency and duty free shops at the border checkpoints and in the tax-free zones of the country.

As a rule every article in a shop (selling in Leva or foreign currency) must have a price tag. Bargaining over prices is not customary in Bulgaria. The bargaining habit known from markets in Africa, Latin America and Asia may be done only on the free private market, on flea markets, and in wholesale trade - on commodity markets, ramp-side trade or auctions.

The main international credit cards can be used in the country. In every major town there are cash dispensers (Bancomats) at the larger banks. A growing number of services can be paid for with credit cards - mainly hotel bills, tickets of large agencies, luxury shops and restaurants, vacation costs, certain more expensive souvenirs, etc. Bulgarian citizens or residents may pay with debit or credit cards for their phone, central heating, water supply bills, as well as for big purchases, cellular phone bills or Internet service, etc.

## FOOD, WATER and DRINKS

Bulgarian **food** does not particularly differ from the traditional European cuisine. The basic food products of the traditional Bulgarian cuisine are beans, sour and fresh milk, cheese, tomatoes, paprika, potatoes, onions, apples, water-melons, and grapes. Bulgarians consume all kinds of meat from industrially bred animals and fowls, freshwater and sea fish, more seldom (wild) game. Bread is invariantly present on Bulgarian dinner table. The tradition of meeting visitors with bread and salt is very much alive. The Bulgarians' cuisine is moderate, with meals seldom too salted, hot or sour. Food products can be purchased in all food stores and supermarkets, as well as on the direct producer-consumer market. Cooked food is served in catering establishments, pizza stands and restaurants, the prices depending on the category of the catering establishment.

In recent years the country has been flooded with thousands of private catering establishments, which serve traditional Bulgarian cuisine. The most frequent meat specialities are kebapcheta (minced-meat rolls) and kyufteta (meatballs), shish kebab (grilled meat) on skewers, steaks, and loukanka (salami); tarator (cold summer soup), cheese a la Shopski, breaded yellow cheese, beans soup cooked in a monastery manner, banitsa (sheeted pastry with cheese), paprika stuffed with eggs and cheese, Russian salad, aubergine puree, Shopska salad and caramel custard - of the meatless dishes. Bulgarian sour milk is worldwide famous - cow's milk, sheep's milk and buffalo-cow's milk - all of various taste and cream content. By no chance the microorganisms that are

# INFORMATION for VISITORS

of a yeast-type and make this divine product are called **Lactobacterium Bulgaricum (Grigoroff).** Along with the oil-yielding rose, which is part of every nice perfume, the milk of Bulgarian origin is among the most demanded goods at the stocks worldwide. Fruit and vegetables grown in Bulgaria are of unique taste. The fruits and vegetables purchased from the market should be abundantly washed in flowing water before consumption. In small booths one can buy edible kernels, baked seeds and popcorn, dried, caramel- or chocolate-coated kernels and fruits.

A breakfast in an ordinary restaurant costs about 3 Leva, a dinner - 8 Leva, and supper - around 10 Leva. If you order wine or 50 grams liquor, the bill is almost doubled.

**Water** in Bulgaria is usually good to drink. Irrespective of this tourists must seek information on the current state of tap water in the respective settlement. Mineral water is sold everywhere; it is of exclusively good quality, factory-bottled and duly sealed. Everywhere on sale are also **natural juices** without preservatives, manufactured by Bulgarian and foreign producers. The Bulgarian juices cost no more than 2 Leva a litre, the imported ones cost around 3 Leva. Tea and coffee is offered everywhere in the country. Boza, an Arab boiled-grain drink popular in Bulgaria is also widely sold. **Fresh milk,** obligatorily pasteurised, is sold in a wide diversity of packaging. **Beer**, locally brewed and imported is very popular, either tapped or bottled. The products of Coca-Cola, Pepsi, and Bulgarian **soft drinks** can be found in every food or specialised shop. **Alcoholic drinks** are on sale in most food shops, and in numerous specialised pubs. Bulgarian **wines** are famed for their exceptional quality; indeed, Bulgaria is one of the world's major wine exporters. The price of one bottle of 0.75 litres of good dry wine varies between 3 and 5 Leva.

Alcoholic concentrate traditional for Bulgaria is called **rakiya.** The price of a 0.5-litre bottle varies between 3 Leva and 15 Leva, depending on the quality of the product, the manufacturing technology and the region of origin. Prime quality rakiya are used as a medicine in traditional medicine. Imported brand drinks are available everywhere. Their price is close to that in the producer countries. All alcoholic drinks should mandatory bear an excise band.

## ACCOMMODATION

Being a country of a traditionally developed tourism, Bulgaria offers a wide variety of opportunities for accommodation, at a wide range of rates, and various extra services in addition.

For the **prime hotels** one shall make preliminary reservation by phone, fax or e-mail. A good number of foreign agencies and Bulgarian representative offices perform this service. The price of hotel rooms depends on the category, the season, proximity to resorts or to places of cultural interest and the size of the local settlement. As a rule the most expensive hotels are of the world chains of "Sheraton" and "Hilton". Recently across the country there have been a large number of private hotels in construction, with excellent facilities offered to tourists.

Also available in the vicinity of the towns are **motels and bungalows**, as well as **camping sites**. Prices there are relatively high for the former, and low for the latter. Particularly numerous are the spots for camping at the seaside, where prices get reduced according to the season.

An approximate idea about accommodation prices in hotels:

# INFORMATION for VISITORS

| | |
|---|---|
| **5-star Hotel** | 220 USD for a double room, 180 for a single; |
| **4-star Hotel** | 140 USD for a double room, 120 for a single; |
| **3-star Hotel** | 90 USD for a double room, 60 for a single; |
| **2-star Hotel** | 40 USD for a double room, 20 for a single; |
| **1-star Hotel** | 25 USD for a double room, 15 for a single. |

Off the active tourist season these prices usually fall twice. Most hotels offer breakfast included in the price; it is possible to make arrangements for full or half board, with reducing the price of a single night accommodation.

Spending the night in **private lodgings** is customary during the active season at the seaside and in the country's tourist centres. For foreign tourists the cost for a good room is about 15 US dollars for a two-bed room with a bath and toilet. Private lodgings can be booked in the accommodation bureaus at resort centres and tourist towns.

To less choosy tourists one could recommend the **tourist houses, chalets** and **tourist hostels.** The conditions are decent. Bringing sleeping bags or light mattresses into the chalets or public bedrooms is not necessary.

## POSTAL SERVICES

To send **a letter within the country**, one shall buy a postal card or an envelope, affix the necessary postal stamp of 0.25 Leva (25 stotinki) and write the address of the recipient and one's own (sender's) address. This can be done at any post office. As a rule, post offices are open for letters. parcels and excise bands from Monday through Friday; telephone and cable services are open through the week round.

To send a letter **abroad,** one shall obligatorily have the envelope weighed and charged according to its weight in grams. For printed matter a lower tariff is applied, and excise bands may not exceed 2 kilograms.

**Parcels and small packages** (not exceeding 2 kg) are subject to mandatory customs control. Packaging services are available at the post offices in bigger towns, and where no such service is available, the public and tourists are expected to pack up their parcels in the post office hall after examination by the customs authority.

**Registered, express and special deliveries** are charged under a higher tariff. All kinds of parcels must bear sender's and recipient's name and address clearly written.

**Telephone services** in the country comprise local urban, interurban and international calls. Local urban phone services are effected by means of automatic street telephones operated with tokens or electronic cards.

The price of one token is 0.20 Leva, and one can buy them in the post offices or newsstands. The duration of a call is limited to 3 minutes.

There are three types of card public phones for local urban, interurban and international calls and cards sold by MOBIKA and BULFON. MOBIKA cards are of 50 to 400 impulses, BULFON, cards are of 25 to 400 impulses. The price per impulse is lower for the cards of greater number of impulses. The public phones operated with cards display the remaining impulses. At post offices one pays after the call and calls are usually 1/3 cheaper than if made at card public phones.

Dialling a phone number abroad may be done with cards from public phones in the streets or at post offices. Every international dialling begins with 00 + the code of the respective country, the settlement and the

# INFORMATION for VISITORS

private phone number.
The dialling code for Bulgaria is +359.
The Republic of Bulgaria is part of the international analogous and cellular phone networks. Debit impulse cards or SIM cards could be found in specilised shops. The prices from 20 Leva to 100 Leva vary depending on the number of impulses and the validity term. Internet clubs are something natural for the first 100 bigger towns in the country. There for about 1.20 Leva - 2.00 Leva one can check his **e-mail** address, send e-mail message or open the **Web page** of interest. In these clubs one can also print out the messages either received there or from a personal diskette or CD.

## TRANSPORT CONNECTIONS

**Air, rail, road and water** transport connects Bulgaria to Europe and the world.
Railways cross all of Bulgaria's land borders. The first big European railway transport artery - **Orient Express** also cuts through the country. One may enter the country by bus or car throught the numerous checkpoints along the borders. The Danube River and the Black Sea are Bulgaria's waterways.

**Air links** are maintained through the country's local and international airports. There are three international airports in the country - in Sofia, Varna and Bourgas. Daily two-way flights link Sofia with Varna and Bourgas. During the tourist season, including late spring, the summer and early autumn, there are five to six flights daily in both directions. One-way ticket prices vary between 55 and 60 US Dollars.
Bulgarian air companies fly to most European capitals and some larger cities like Munich, Frankfurt, Milan, St. Petersburgh, etc. Some of the major European airways reciprocate with flights to Bulgaria, doubling or supplanting flights.
Bulgaria maintains air links with some of the countries of the Middle East, Central and South Africa, some countries of North Africa, Central and Southern Asia and North America. Transfers to other destinations are through foreign travel agencies and representative offices based in Bulgaria. Telephones of international airports include:

| Sofia | (02) 937 22 11 |
| --- | --- |
|  | (02) 973 22 12 |
| Varna | (052) 650 452 |
| Bourgas | (056) 684 083 |

Emergency landings may be performed in some bigger towns like Rousse, Kurdzhali, Razgard, Silistra, Plovdiv, etc. Chartered aircraft, helicopters and amateurs' gliders possessing special permits may land in the country and air corridors for them are ensured by Bulgarian air-traffic controllers.

Bulgaria's **railway border checkpoints** include: Svilengrad, Koulata, Gyueshevo, Kalotina, Vrushka Chouka (only on the Yugoslav side), Vidin (by ferryboat across the River Danube) Rousse, Silistra, and Dourankoulak. Numerous express and passenger trains reach Bulgaria or transit across the country, linking it with Europe, Asia (across Russia and the Middle East), and North Africa (across the Middle East). Travelling by train in Bulgaria is comfortable and inexpensive. The rail network connects practically all major towns and cities of North and South Bulgaria. In less accessible places and less frequented directions there are narrow-gauge railways. The price of second-class tickets for a 100 km distance amounts to about 1.5 Leva. Ticket costs generally increase in proportion to the distance travelled. Reduced-tariff tickets are granted to students against respec-

# INFORMATION for VISITORS

tive certificates, to soldiers and officers who are issued military tickets, to pensioners, war veterans, handicapped and railway employees.

Reduced tariffs are also granted to the holders of international cards for student and youth travel. The tickets are issued at railway stations, at ticket bureaus in the towns, and in tourist agencies; international travel tickets are available at special international booking offices, agencies and bureaus at the railway stations. The telephones for information are (02) 931 11 11 and (02) 932 33 33.

**The road network** in Bulgaria consists of motorways and roads of first, second and third class. Most of the network is asphalt. Motorways link Sofia with Varna ("Hemus"), and Sofia with Plovdiv and Bourgas ("Trakia").

**Local bus services** cover most directions, with express buses linking the country's major towns. Long-distance and local bus lines reach nearly 90 per cent of Bulgaria's settlements. Exceptions are made for high-mountain villages and quarters accessible only along truck roads. The price of a ticket for a 100 km distance is about 6 Leva in a luxury bus, and 4 Leva in an ordinary bus. The ticket price increases proportionally to the distance.

International bus lines are maintained with most European capitals and major cities. Via Turkey there are connections by road to the Middle East and Egypt.

Bus tickets are purchased from specialised bureaus, at bus stations and from transport and tourists agencies in the larger towns. A number of foreign travel agencies also offer these services.

The phone numbers of border checkpoints, including those with railway links, are given below:

| | |
|---|---|
| Bregovo (Vidin-Negotin) | 22 74 |
| Vrushka Chouka (Zaychar), via Vidin | 20 03 |
| Kalotina (Nis), via Sofia | 88 15 18 |
| Strezimirovtsi (Trun-Souroundoulitsa) | 2 42 89 |
| Gyueshevo (Kriva Palanka), via Kyustendil | 2 72 10 |
| Stanke Lisichkovo (Delchevo), via Blagoevgrad | 2 35 31 |
| Zlatarevo (Petrich-Stroumitsa) | 2 71 74 |
| Koulata (Sandanski-Sidirokastron) | 2 31 87 |
| Kapitan Andreevo (Svilengrad - Odrin) | 65 86 |
| Malko Turnovo (Lozengrad) | 21 98 |
| Vidin - Kalafat, (ferryboat) | 2 49 79 |
| Lom | 2 41 02 |
| Oryahovo | 23 72 |
| Rousse (Gyurgevo) | 44 01 86 |
| Silistra (Ostrov-Culuras) | 2 66 61 |
| Yovkovo | 424 |
| Kardam (General Toshevo-Constantsa) | 266 |
| Dourankoulak (Mangalia) | 244 |

**The waterway border checkpoints** are **riverside** (along the River Danube and **maritime** (on the Black Sea coast). The first riverside border checkpoint as the Danube reaches Bulgarian territory is near the village of Vruv.

Along the entire course of the River Danube

# INFORMATION for VISITORS

there are border checkpoints, which give access by water to and from Bulgaria. These are situated at the river ports of Vidin, Lom, Oryahovo, Rousse, Toutrakan and Silistra. Seaports are Varna and Bourgas.

It is possible to cross from Romania by sea by using the local small ports near Dourankoulak, and from Turkey at Rezovo. These ports can handle small vessels, which do not come from territorial waters.

Water transport for tourist passengers and cargo is available along the entire length of the River Danube and the Black Sea coast. Tourist services are effected by river and sea vessels; both the tickets for them and their timetable depend on the season, the type of vessel and its class.

Also available are numerous private boats, yachts and motorboats, which offer tours to local sites of interest and cruises on clients' wishes. As a rule, water transport costs about twice than bus ride.

List of telephones of border checkpoints and riverside (maritime) stations along the Danube:

| | |
|---|---|
| Vidin | (094) 2 49 79 |
| Lom | (0971) 2 20 57 |
| Oryahovo | (09171) 23 72 |
| Russe | (082) 44 01 86 |
| Toutrakan | (0857) 25 65 |
| Silistra | (086) 2 00 05 |
| Varna | (052) 22 23 26 |
| Bourgas | (056) 4 27 38 |

## ROAD NETWORK CONDITIONS

The international **U5** motorway links Bulgaria with Europe and with Asia Minor. It forks at Sofia, and its southern branch proceeds to Greece as **U5N**, while the second called **U5S** leads to Turkey. Most of the country's road network is first and second class. Problems may arise at roads under repair and local stretches of poor condition due to the agricultural vehicles using the same roads.

Drivers are advised to take special care of their cars and trucks in winter. Adequate tyres shall be used as well as wheel chains when driving in high mountain passes, attention and cautious proceeding at sharp turns and serpentines are required, particularly along ice-bound stretches.

The national radio and national TV broadcast daily reports on the road conditions in the country, which as a rule is listened to by most Bulgarian drivers. Visitors to the country and professional drivers could obtain information on the road conditions at the larger hotels and at the reception desks, where they would be supplied data from the daily papers.

Hitchhiking is not advisable in Bulgaria. Pedestrian movement on the first-class roads and motorways is forbidden, and bicycles are not allowed to use the high-speed lanes either. There are no toll-roads in the interior of the country so far. They would be introduced gradually up to 2004. The only road fee is paid at the point of entry into the country. Paid parking lots are available in bigger settlements and in the resorts. The prices per hour vary from 0.8 Leva to 2 Leva depending on the season and from 7 Leva to 18 Leva for 24 hours. Security is ensured. Drivers can often use roadside facilities to relax - there are sites with drinking-fountains, catering establishments, stands selling fruits, vegetables or souvenirs, roadside motels, etc. Filling stations are available at about every 30 kilometres of first-class roads, and in the larger settlements along second-class roads. The price of fuels and lubricants are close to European rates.

# INFORMATION for VISITORS

Petrol, OMV, Shell, Castrol have their filling stations, where, along with Bulgarian products, one can buy or have fixed world-class tyres.

In every bigger town one can find car-washing stands and repair services, with shops for car spares. Cars are exibited and sold in specilised shops in more than 20 towns and cities, and in more than 100 towns one can buy second-hand car. International and Bulgarian rent-a-car companies have representative offices around the country. The major hotels offer this as an extra service.

## TOURIST INFORMATION

**Tourist information centres or bureaus** can be found in most of the bigger towns and cultural centres of Bulgaria. Tourists from the country and foreign visitors can obtain there the following kinds of information:
- Accommodation;
- Booking hotel rooms and tickets;
- Excursions;
- Visits to places of interest and resorts in the region;
- Topical tourist information;
- Catering establishments.

Information can also be obtained from the **tourist councils and associations,** of which there are a total of 33 in Bulgaria. Their addresses and phones are available in the chapters for respective towns and resorts.

Another source of tourist information are **the tourist agencies, companies and local offices of the Bulgarian Tourist Society.**

Maps and leaflets, reference books and publications with tourist information can be purchased from bookshops, as well as from the above tourist information centres.

Over the past 5 years, new maps have been printed in Bulgaria for all cities, towns, resorts and mountains, which contain updated information. Guidebooks with brief and more extensive data are available in sufficient amounts; some of them have translated versions into the basic European languages.

## HAZARD AND SAFETY

One can hardly foresee all hazards and risks, which a tourist could face in a foreign country. The Republic of Bulgaria is increasingly meeting the EC criteria for ensuring security and preventive guard to its citizens and guests. Nevertheless, there are some hazards, which could be kept in mind and prevented by Bulgarians as well as by tourists travelling round the country.

Here we offer nine "golden" rules, which can help to a risk-free stay:

1. Every visitor changes money upon entering the country. Sometimes in front of the change bureau there are people offering a higher exchange rate than the official one. Avoid such gains on the cheap, if you don't want to be the victim of a street swindle.

2. When parking your car don't forget to check whether all doors and the boot are well locked. Leave no documents, bags and valuable articles exposed inside the car. Leave your car at paid parking lots, which provide security to your car and belongings.

3. Thefts happen worldwide, so you must know where the most risky places are. Above all these are the

# INFORMATION for VISITORS

markets, then the town transport, or evenings in the suburbs or the narrow streets in the centre of bigger towns, the railway stations, bus stations and airports. Do not leave your luggage unattended, nor trust any unknown persons to keep it. Carry only limited cash, and keep your documents in a safe place.

4. Leave on deposit in the hotel safes, if you don't need them for the day, any valuables like golden jewellery and ornaments, laptop computers, video-cameras and expensive photo-cameras. Don't leave them behind in your hotel rooms or lodgings, nor entrust them to new acquaintances.

5. The local guides of Asia, Africa or Latin America offering cheap services (a sight familiar to globe-trotters) are not typical of Bulgaria. If you are offered guide services without having asked for, refuse without getting involved, because the prospective guide may be up to something unpleasant.

6. Still persisting is the risk of meeting people involved in criminal business, narcotics trading, and traffic of women abroad. People of this kind can be most frequently encountered at motorways and in roadside motels, night clubs, bingo halls, fitness centres, and in the expensive resorts and restaurants. Avoid any contacts or quarrels with them.

7. Avoid buying and drinking liquor, purchased from cheap little shops. Check whether the excise bands are firmly affixed to the bottle in factory conditions.

8. When on vacation at the seaside, use mainly the beaches supervised by life-guards, and strictly observe the rules of safe bathing in the sea. Do not risk swimming in unknown and risky places, don't dive or ride a jet or motorboat near the shore. Prefer places with more people, which ensures that the sea is safe there; stay near some people for eventual assistance in case of need.

9. When hiking in the mountains, always follow the marked tracks. Carry warm clothes, comfortable footwear, a torch lights, two pairs of socks, pocket-knife, matches and rain-protecting wear. Have at hand food for at least one day, warming drink and a litre of water. Do not risk venturing out alone along unknown paths and risky venues. In winter give up hiking out in the mountain in poor visibility conditions, or without reliable equipment. If you are a mountaineer, snowboarder or ordinary skier, use only well-tried tours and frequented ski-runs. Best of all keep in group, close to people who are familiar with the tracks, ski-runs and the tours. Hire a good local guide, preferably a professional mountain guide. This would save you long inquiries, much effort and unpleasant experience, and will guarantee your health and life. Guides can be hired from licensed agencies and societies specialised in tourism, mountaineering and skiing.

# SOFIA

*Sofia, Slaveikov Square*

# SOFIA

## Sofia's motto is *"Ever Growing, Never Ageing!"*

The capital of the Republic of Bulgaria is the city of Sofia (1 096 389 inhabitants, 550 metres above sea level). The city lies in the Sofia Plain, enclosed by the Balkan Mountains to the north, the Lozen Mountain to the southeast, Mountain Vitosha to the south, the Lyulin Mountain to the southwest. The plain is open to the northwest in the direction of Yugoslavia, and to the southeast to the Thracian Lowland. Sofia is situated 55 km from the Yugoslav border at Kalotina checkpoint, 113 km from the Gyueshevo checkpoint with Macedonia, 183 km from the Greek border at Koulata, 315 km from the Turkish border at Kapitan Andreevo, 211 km from the Romanian border at Vidin, 324 km from Rousse, 392 km from our maritime border at the port of Bourgas, and 470 km from the port of Varna. In close proximity to the capital city lie Pancherevo Lake and Iskar Dam. The Iskar River flows by the city, and several smaller rivers cross the city, the most popular of these being the Vladaya and the Perlovo Rivers.

Sofia is linked by international routes with the capitals of Europe, and via Istanbul and Ankara, with the Middle East. Below is a list of the distance in kilometres to some of these cities:

|  |  |
|---|---|
| Amsterdam | 2242 |
| Ankara | 1010 |
| Athens | 863 |
| Barcelona | 2541 |
| Belgrade | 390 |
| Berlin | 1745 |
| Bern | 1773 |
| Bonn | 1973 |
| Brussels | 2196 |
| Budapest | 779 |
| Bucharest | 383 |
| Warsaw | 1691 |
| Vienna | 1044 |
| Gdansk | 2053 |
| Gibraltar | 3792 |
| Dublin | 2948 |
| Istanbul | 568 |
| Kiev | 1519 |
| Copenhagen | 2135 |
| Lisbon | 3826 |
| London | 2512 |
| Madrid | 3166 |
| Marseilles | 1908 |
| Milan | 1371 |
| Moscow | 2371 |
| Munich | 1483 |
| Oslo | 2715 |
| Paris | 2307 |
| St. Petersburg | 3079 |
| Prague | 1352 |
| Rome | 1632 |
| Rostov on the Don | 1831 |
| Stockholm | 2754 |
| Tirana | 579 |
| Hamburg | 2303 |
| Helsinki | 2920 |

**History.** Sofia is a city with a 7000-year history, which makes it a unique phenomenon in Europe, and places it among the settlements dating back to most distant antiquity. To this very day excavations in Sofia downtown bring up objects of the Neolithic man, and remnants of the Stone and Bronze Era. The reason why settlements arose so early is the abundance of thermal springs in the Sofia Plain. They

# SOFIA

cluster mainly around today's city centre - near the old mineral baths, around the Presidency building, in Lozenets Quarter, and in Gorna Banya and Knyazhevo Quarters. The water temperature varies between 21°C and 42°C, and they are curative, because of the significant amount of ions and mineral salts dissolved in them.

The first known tribes to settle in the plain were the Thracians from the triabe of *Serdi*. They gave Sofia its first name - *Serdica*.

Around 500 BC another tribe settled here, the Odrissi, known as an ethos having a kingdom of their own. For a short period during the 4$^{th}$ BC the city was in possession of Philip of Macedonia and of his son Alexander the Great. As late as in the year 29 AD Sofia was conquered by the Roman legions, and during the reign of Emperor Trayan (98-117) became the centre of an administrative region. It was given the name of *Ulpia Serdica* as a municipium, i.e. a centre of administrative region. Construction on the territory of the city expanded - turrets, protective walls, public baths, administrative and cult buildings, a civic basilica and a large amphitheatre, called bulevterion were built. In the 2$^{nd}$ century AD Sofia became the centre of the Lower Dacia province. It subsequently expanded for a century and a half, so that Constantine the Great came to call it "my Rome". The city was of moderate size, but magnificent as an urban concept of planning and architecture, abundant in amusements and of active social life. The city flourished during the reign of Emperor Justinian when it was surrounded with great fortress walls, remains of which can be seen even today.

Fully preserved and well restored now is the Roman Rotunda, transformed into the Early Christian Church of St. Georgi it now stands behind the Sheraton Hotel. Attila took the city by storm in the 5$^{th}$ century. After his death the Byzantine Empire recovered it. It remained part of the Eastern Roman till the early 9$^{th}$ century AD.

When the kingdom of Danubian Bulgaria was founded in 681 AD, many Bulgarian khans coveted Serdica. But it was only in the year of 809 that Khan Kroum succeeded in conquering and including it in the Bulgarian territory. The new name of the city was changed to *Sredets*, which in the parlance of that time meant "middle, central part, centre". Actually its location gave it all grounds to be considered the centre of the Balkan Peninsula. The city existed until the year 1018 AD when Bulgarian lands fell under Byzantine rule and it was renamed *Triyaditsa,* which meant "between mountains". After 1194 the city regained its former name.

The city was repeatedly besieged and attacked by Magyars, Serbs and Crusaders. After the liberation of Bulgaria from Byzantine rule it was re-included in the territories of the country. Its name was now Sophia. The St. Sophia Church, which stands to this day next to the St. Aleksander Nevski Memorial Cathedral, gave the city its present-day name.

Sofia quickly expanded and became a centre of crafts and trade. New buildings and numerous churches were built in the city and the neighbouring villages, the best known of these is the Boyana Church. Sofia fell under Ottoman rule in 1382. In some documents of that time the city was described as a place

*Sofia.*
*St. Petka Church*
*and the building of*
*Bulbank*

# SOFIA

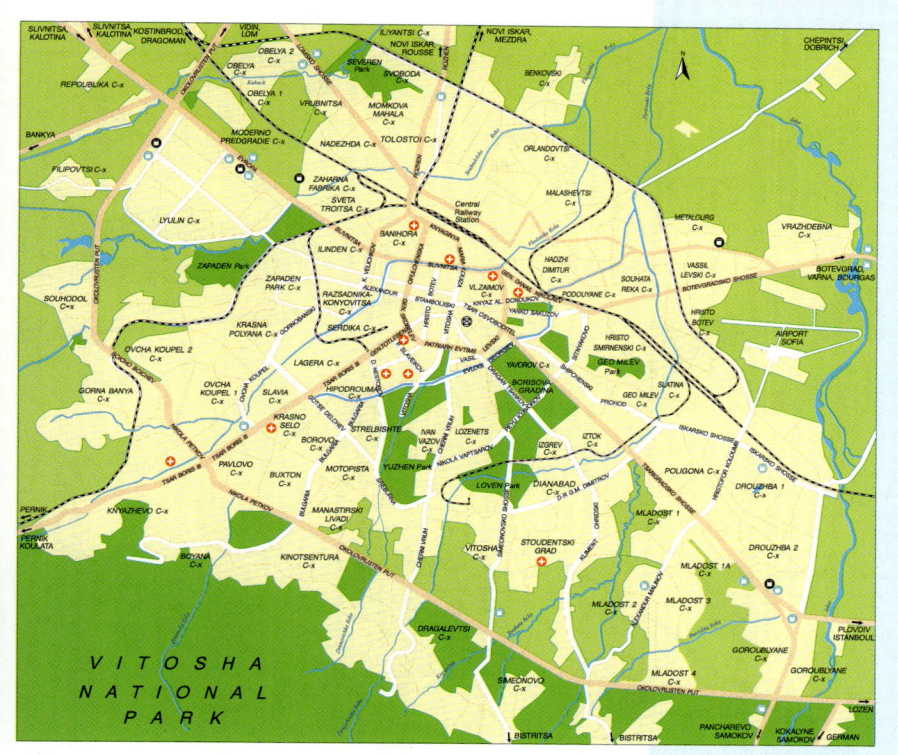

of particular charm, which evoked the admiration of the conquerors. Irrespective of that, the Turkish authorities' neglect rapidly changed the appearance of the city. Christian churches became derelict and started ruining, while Turkish administration buildings, mosques, public baths and covered markets rose in their place. The five centuries of Ottoman rule changed Sofia beyond recognition. Only recent excavations open to the world the true picture of the city such as it was during its eventful history along the centuries. Few buildings of the Ottoman period are preserved today. The Turkish administration recognised the advantageous location of Sofia as a crossroad and important centre of the Balkan Peninsula, and the city's development as crafts and market centre was promoted. During the 17th century it grew into the largest marketplace of the Balkans, and in the 18th century a stone-paved road linked it with Europe and Asia Minor. During the 19th century the first railway crossing the Balkans reached Sofia as part of the famous Orient Express. Sofia became the administrative centre of a sandzhak, large administrative unit of key importance to the Ottoman Empire. After Serbia was liberated in the 19th century, Sofia Sandzhak remained on the border. The city was repeatedly attacked and plundered by kurdzhalii (Turkish brigands), who periodically devastated its surrounding settlements.

During Bulgarian Revival and the struggle for liberation, the Apostle of Freedom Vassil Levski considered Sofia as one of the centres of a future uprising and created revolutionary com-

# SOFIA

## Sofia. Landmarks

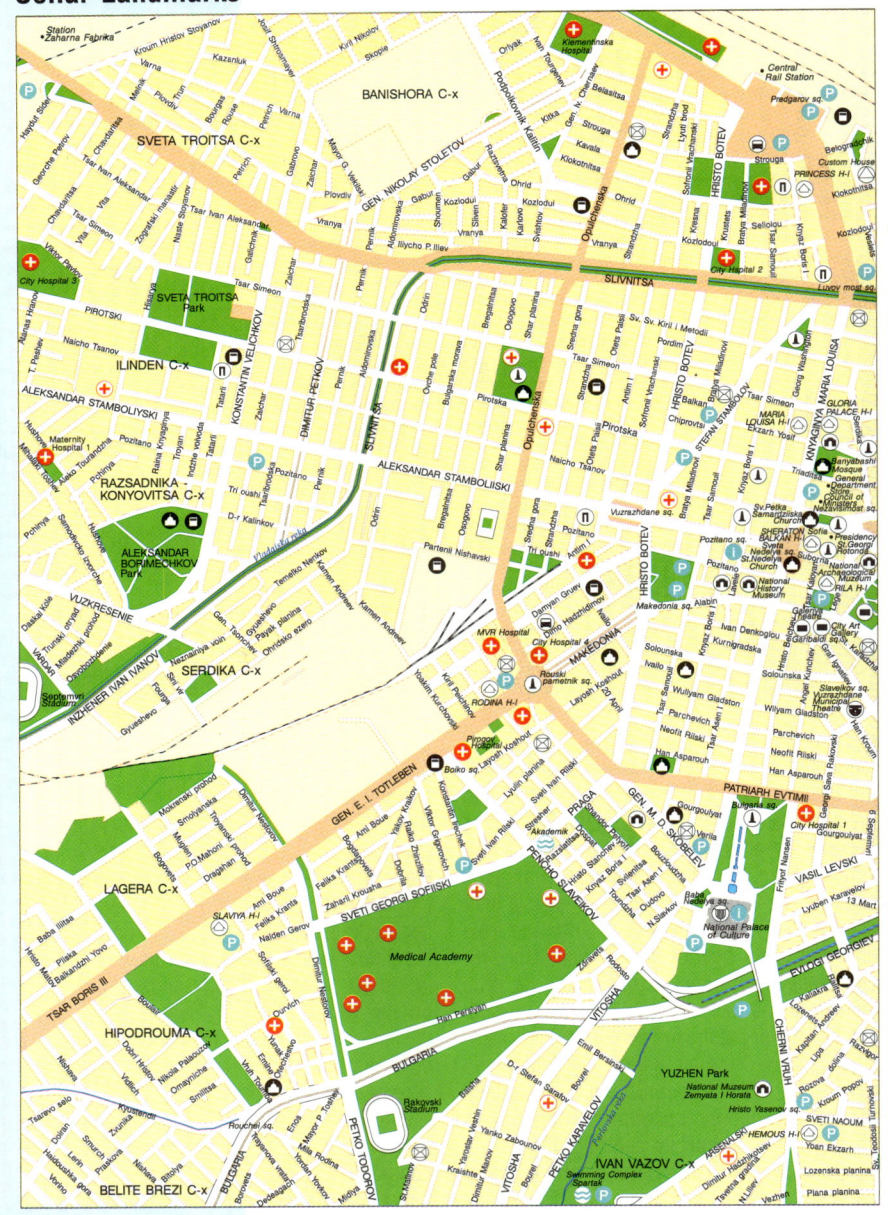

# SOFIA

# SOFIA

mittees in the city. To the irony of fate, after his arrest he was brought to Sofia, where he was sentenced and hanged in 1873.

Sofia was liberated from Ottoman rule on 4th January 1878. At that time the city had a population of only 12 000, but its favourable strategic location made it suitable for a capital and on the 4th of April 1879 Sofia was proclaimed the capital city of the Principality of Bulgaria. In a couple of years the population increased nearly tenfold, the outlook of the city radically changed; the Turkish soukatsi (narrow muddy streets) were supplanted by paved and planned streets, administrative buildings, churches, and schools were erected, public gardens laid out, a modern sewerage and water-supply system was installed, and so were telegraph and telephone lines. Sofia took on the appearance of a European city, although numerous features of the East remained. During the 20-es of the 20th century Sofia acquired a more European outlook. It developed into a truly modern city of unique charm during the reign of Tsar Boris III, when the construction of houses and buildings in Modern, Art Nouveau (Secession), Bauhaus, Neo-Classicism and European Eclecticism styles flourished. Today the centre of Sofia and the quarter between the Luvov Most (Lions' Bridge) and the Sheraton Hotel abound in buildings from the first half of the 20th century. The small streets and gas-burning street lights were preserved until nearly the World War II. US planes bombed the city during the war, causing some damage of the downtown area. At that time Bulgaria was an ally of Nazi Germany. During the 30-es and 40-es Sofia became the scene of workers' strikes, political rallies and demonstrations but also a prominent centre of culture, science and arts.

Changes in the political life in the wake of 9th of September 1944 reflected strongly on the outlook of Sofia. Buildings in urbanistic and Stalinist style were constructed, the most prominent of which is the central complex consisting of the Communist party building, Balkan Hotel and TZUM Central Department Store. Today the building of Balkan Hotel now houses one of the well-known chain of Sheraton Hotels. The Presidency of the country occupies its adjoining building. The TZUM has been radically refurbished, and the adjacent building houses the Ministerial Council. The building of the former royal palace houses the exposition of the National Art Gallery. Sofia has become the country's leading industrial centre, with one sixth of the industry of Bulgaria concentrated

*St. Alexander Nevski Cathedral Church*

# SOFIA

around it, and housing one eighth of the population, the country's political and cultural elite, and the entire state capital.

Nowadays Sofia is a very placid place to live in. Changes in its appearance are imminent. Restitution is underway, old buildings are returned to their owners, new buildings and shops emerge, private companies establish themselves on the market.

*Ivan Vazov National Theatre*

The city is in constant flux, under way is gradual restoration of its intransient cultural and architectural monuments, which make it a typically European city with ancient culture, impressive present and bright future.

**Landmarks.** Several buildings and venues vie for Sofia's emblem. The most frequent image is of the impressive edifice of **St. Alexander Nevski Cathedral and Memorial Church**. The temple is the central patriarch's cathedral of the autonomous Bulgarian Orthodox Church. It was completed in 1912 after a design of the Russian architect Pomerantsev, approved by the 1st Great National Assembly. The church rises on an area of 3170 sq. m. The altar and the patriarch's throne are cut of multi-coloured Italian marble; 13 Bulgarian and 32 Russian and Czech masters made the wood-carvings, cut the stone bas-reliefs and ornaments, painted the fresoes and the icons. The belfry rises to a height of 50.52 metres; the central dome is gold-plated with a massive gold cross on top.

The **Crypt** of the cathedral houses a collection of masterpieces of Bulgarian icon painting. Visitors can enjoy the exhibited more than 200 icons and frescos. A souvenir shop sells copies of some of the famous icons, post cards, albums and folders. A remarkable sight is the square around the cathedral, where the **Monument to the Unknown Soldier** with eternal burning flame is located. An open-air market of national costumes, embroidery and hand-knitted ware and garment and a small antiquarian and arts exposition enliven the square.

Part of the same square is occupied by the **St. Sophia Church**, dating back to the 4th-6th century AD, which gave the name of the city. In the end of 16th century it was transformed into a mosque for a short time, but soon after the Liberation it was again sanctified as an Orthodox church. Already restored, the church is open to visitors. Regrettably few of the frescoes have been preserved, but some rare icons are still in existence. A valuable exhibit kept in the church is a lock of the hair of the Apostle of Freedom Vassil Levski. Behind the church is the grave of Ivan Vazov (1850-1921), the patriarch of Bulgarian literature. A monument to the poet rises in the small garden in front of the church.

In the eastern part of the square rises the building of the St. St. Cyril and Methodius Foundation, which houses the **National Gallery of Foreign Arts**. It contains unique exhib-

# SOFIA

its of art from Africa, Asia and Europe, Spanish baroque paintings, some Rembrandts, and tableaux by the modern painter Nikolai Roerich. Opposite to the south of it rises the building of the Academy of Arts, where future artists study icon-painting, restoration of old works of art, painting, sculpture, stage design, etc. The **Ivan Vazov National Theatre** is the capital's other emblem. The theatre was founded in 1904, and its building was completed in 1907. Designed in the style of German classicism, it contains many elements of the then fashionable Secession style. The interior was twice renewed, once after the fire in the theatre in 1923, and once during the 1970-1976 period. The hall is flanked by two balconies and there are 850 seats. Two chamber stages are in operation; the one with 150 seats and the other with 100. The theatre employs some of the country's best actors and stage directors, many of whom enjoy popularity all over Europe.

The edifice of the **National Assembly** (built in 1884) is the third rightful candidate for the city's emblem. A motto inscribed on its main facade reads "Union makes Strength" - a key element of the coat of arms of the Republic of Bulgaria. Opposite its building is the monument to the King Liberator of Bulgaria (inaugurated in 1905) - the Russian Tsar Aleksander II.

To the west of the Parliament building is the Bulgarian Academy of Sciences founded in 1869, and to the east across a small garden rises the St. Kliment of Ohrid University of Sofia, founded in 1888 (and built in 1920 with personal donations by the brothers Evloghi and Hristo Georgievi, whose statues flank the parade entrance of the university) - Bulgaria's oldest higher school. The mausoleum of Battenberg is nearby the university.

**The Russian church St. Nikolai** is conspicuous from afar with its pointed golden cross. It was built in the years of 1912-1914 by Russian emigrants to Bulgaria. The interior of the church contains wonderful majolica ornaments, Russian-style icons among which stands out the icon of St. Nikolai Chudotvorets (the Wonder-worker) from the Kiev-Pechora Monastery. Next to it to the east is the **Museum of Natural Science**, with its unique collections of stuffed and live flora and fauna representatives. Visitors show particular interest in the bazaar where they can purchase small rabbits, nutria, parrots, hamsters, canaries and other household pets.

The **National Art Gallery** and the **Ethnographic Museum** are housed in the former royal palace. It was built on 1873. During the reign of Prince Aleksander Battenberg the building was entirely reconstructed on the exterior and inside in the Art Nouveau (Secession) style, with elements of Neo-Rococo and Baroque. Expensive and unique wooden pieces of furniture were arranged in the palace rooms. The National Art Gallery exhibits a collection of well over 12 000 works of art, the oldest dating back to the 18th century. The Bulgarian classical masters of painting and sculpture are represented with their most mature works. The National Ethnographic Museum exhibits a wealth of collections of national costumes, hand-made works of art from Bulgarian people's daily life, tools

*The National Art Gallery*

# SOFIA

dating from three or four centuries ago, jewellery, tissues, embroidery and other articles of typical national folk art. The exhibits include scale models of Bulgarian houses and life amenities in them, masks and costumes of the festive Bulgarian calendar rites from different ethnographic regions of the country. At the museum and the gallery there are two stands for souvenirs where one can purchase cards, albums, icons, folk music recordings, hand-made articles imitating originals of national art. Other exhibitions are often displayed in the building of the former royal palace, to fill in the vacant spaces of the impressive place. Opposite to it in diagonal rises the building of the Bulgarian National Bank. Immediately next to it, a former Turkish mosque built on top of the ruins of a Christian Church destroyed by the Ottomans, houses today's **Archaeological Museum**.

Downtown, in the interior courtyard of the Presidency and Sheraton Hotel rises the famous Roman Rotunda, transformed into the **St. Georgi Church** during the 4$^{th}$ century AD. Recently restored, it is stunning for its simple and exquisite architecture, the expressive remnants of frescoes and the entire complex of ruins behind the altar. Quite imposing as well are the ruins in the underpass opposite the Presidency, north of TZUM, in the ground-level of Sofia Shop (currently under reconstruction) in Central Hali Square, etc.

The square around the Central Hali building is also noted for its sights. The **Hali** (1911) were a covered market from the beginning of the century. Today after being reconstructed, they are a useful facility as well as an attractive place for shopping and spending some time

*Relief of guard in front of the Presidency Building*

at a cup of coffee. The mosque (1576) is in the square, the **public bath** (1913) is to the east, the ruins of the Roman fortress of Serdica with the corner turrets are to the north, the **Synagogue** (1909) is situated west of the Hali. **St. Petka Samardzhiiska Church** is located in the underpass of TZUM (south of the Hali). Vassil Levski was probably buried there, according to the hypothesis. Almost completely dug into the ground, today the whole of it is outstanding. There are attractive coffee bars and other catering establishments in the underpass, as well as many souvenir shops.

Numerous monuments adorn Sofia, and the most popular and honoured by all Bulgarians is the obelisk to the Apostle of Freedom (of 1895), which rises on the spot of his execution.

**The Russian Monument** is an obelisk rising west of the city centre; it bears a written dedication to the Russian Tsar and the Russian warriors who gave their lives in the war for Bulgaria's liberation.

**The Doctors' Monument**, dedicated to the medical staff of the Russian army who fell in the war, rises in the garden behind the National Library.

The monuments from the socialist years are

# SOFIA

more impressive and interesting as a detail of the country's past. These are the **Monument to the Soviet Army**, south of the University building and the **Monument to Freedom** in the easternmost part of the Borissova Gradina Park, crowned by a big obelisk.

The monument to **the Saint brothers Cyril and Methodius** who devised Bulgarian alphabet rises in front of the National Library. Numerous busts of leaders of Bulgarian Revival adorn the alleys of the Borissova Garden Park, as well as effigies of poets, writers and revolutionaries. Two of the most popular bridges in Sofia could well be counted among the capital's monumental spots. The **Luvov Most (Lions' Bridge)** (formerly known as Sharen Bridge - the motley crowd bridge) over the Vladaiska River lies north of the city centre in the direction of the Central Railway Station. Four lions stay on high pedestals. The **Orlov Most (Eagles' Bridge)** over the Perlovska Riover lies in the beginning of Tsarigradsko Chaussee Boulevard, which is the road to Plovdiv and Istanbul. Four bronze eagles, facing the four directions of the world, are mounted on 12-metre pylons. The Borissova Garden Park begins from that bridge, stretching to the south-east. Among the sights of Sofia one could place the streets **Graf Ignatieff, Rakovski,** and **Vitosha Boulevard.** Graf Ignatieff Street runs from east to west. It starts at the Perlovski Bridge, adorned in the sculptures of workers and peasants demonstrating the amity between the Bulgarian and the Russian peoples. Numerous shops line the street on both sides until the crossing with Patriarch Evtimii Boulevard and Vassil Levski Boulevard, where rises a **monument to Patriarch Evtimii** - a man of letters and spiriual leader of the $14^{th}$ century. Proceeding west, one comes to a small garden with the St. Sedmochislenitsi (St. St. Cyril and Methodius and their Five Disciples) Church. Further west after the crossing with Rakovski Street we come to **Slaveikov Square.** Here, in front of the City Library, is arranged the largest open-air book market of Sofia. Recently the old three-tier bronze fountain was restored. In the spring of 2000 an original monument was placed to two of the most prominent Bulgarian writers, poets and public figures - father and son Petko and Pencho Slaveikovs, in honour of whom the square was named. One can sit for a while on the bench next to them and have his photo taken for keepsake. Author of the sculpture composition is Georgi Chapkunov - prominent Bulgarian sculptor, another of whose

*Sofia by night*

# SOFIA

works is the statue of St. Sophia (opposite TZUM). There follow a couple of cinemas, company shops, photo studios and buildings of interesting architecture.

Rakovski Street lies in south-eastern direction and is considered the longest street of Sofia. It starts in the north from the railway lines of Sofia Central Railway Station, crosses the Vladaiska River, and a few streets before Dondoukov Boulevard flanks the imposing **St. Paraskeva Church**, with numerous interbuilt cupolas.

Beyond the Dondoukov Blvd. the street mounts steeply past the **National Opera** - a building, which also houses the **National Ballet** and the leadership of the Bulgarian Agrarian Party. The Opera house building is in neo-classical style, and in front of it rises a monument to Alexander Stamboliiski, one of the founders of the Bulgarian Agrarian People's Union and prime-minister of Bulgaria (1919-1923). After the steep rise the street passes by the **monument to Ivan Vazov** in the left and the square in front of the Alexander Nevski Cathedral. Further south, at the crossing of Rouski Boulevard (once called Tsarya) - or the boulevard of chestnuts and yellow brick pavement - rises the Armed Forces Club Building. To the left along Rakovski Street there is a small garden with a **monument to Stefan Stambolov**, then comes the Sulza y Smyah Theatre, the the Slavyanska Besseda Reading Club and Hotel (the oldest chitalishte - reading club and cultural centre of Sofia, with a 120 years history), Theatre 199 and the house of Ivan Vazov. To the left along Rakovski Street there is the **Theatre of the Army**, the Ministry of Finance, the **National Academy for Theatre and Film Art** (NATFIZ Krustyu Sarafov); then a crossing left leads to the **Theatre of Satire**, followed by fashion, technology and flower shops, First City Hospital, the Indian Embassy and the French Foreign-Language Secondary School. Numerous shops and restaurants adorn both sides of the street till its end at the Perlovska River.

Vitosha Boulevard starts north from the **St. Nedelya Church**. The boulevard has on both sides hundreds of shops and representative show windows and boutiques of high fashion, and numerous exchange bureaus. At the beginning of the boulevard on the right hand side rises the Palace of Justice, one of the most imposing building in Sofia with its monumental granite staircase and two bronze lion figures on each side. Lots of shops follow on both sides and a park at the crossing of Patriarch Evtimii Blvd. The park ends at the **Palace of Culture,** which features 16 halls, the largest of which seats a public of nearly 5000. Admirers of Bulgarian history could enjoy the exhibits in the **National Museum of History**, located in Boyana Quarter. Trolley-bus line No. 2 or rout-taxi line No. 21 links downtown to the museum. The **Zoo** (1, Sreburna Str.) is favourite place to youngest citizens of Sofia, as well as to the lots of visitors of the country. A list of the addresses and phone number of the most popular museums in Sofia follows:

- **Archaeological Museum** - 2, Suborna Str., tel.: 9882406;
- **Ethnographic Museum** - 6A, Moskovka Str., tel.: 9874191;
- **National Museum of History** - Boyana Quarter, 16, Vitoshko Lale Str., tel.: 9554280;
- **Boyana Church National Museum** - Boyana Quarter, 3, Boyansko Ezero Str., tel.: 685304;
- **The Earth and People National Museum** - 4, Cherni Vruh Blvd., tel.: 656639;
- **National Museum of Nature and Science** - 1, Tsar Osvoboditel Blvd., tel.: 9885115;
- **"Old Sofia" and the Sofia Museum of History** - 27, Ekzarh Yossif Str., tel.: 9831526.

# SOFIA

**Accommodation.** Sofia has a sufficient number of luxury, first class and lower category hotels, private lodgings and tourist hostels.

Sofia dialling code is 02. Telephone Information Service answers tel.: 144. One can obtain telephone information from Sofspravka - National Information System by dialling 0900 12 900 or 048 15 66.

The 5-star hotels are Sheraton, Hilton, Radisson, Hrankov, and Kempinsky-Zografski. 4-star hotels are the Sofia Princess Hotel, Rodina, Maria Louisa, TBS Ambassador, Gloria Palace, while the remaining are 3-, 2- and 1-star hotels. One can obtain latest information about the prices, reservations, transfers and accommodation at **Alexander Tour**, tel.: (02) 983 23 71, tel./fax (02) 983 33 22, e-mail: alextour@omega.bg; at the **Centre of Nationwide Information and Promotion**, tel.: (02) 987 97 78, fax (02) 989 69 39, e-mail: info@bulgariatravel.org.

**Catering.** Most of the hotels listed above have restaurants, sandwich and snack buffets, snack-bars, and some also have night clubs and discotheques. Sofia offers an exclusive variety of snack-bars, small restaurants, pizzerias, national cuisine diners, foreign cuisine restaurants, self-service restaurants, fast food places, open-air sandwich, toaster, burgers, falafel stalls, luxurious restaurants, wine cellars and clubs. Economy travel tourists will be catered for no more than 20 Leva per day - one can have lunch in a pizzeria or a small restaurant, plus a glass of wine. There are places of medium category for tourists of better means where some 60 Leva per day will be sufficient.

*Sofia. The National Palace of Culture*

Their price lists are translated into English as a rule, they have waiters and the atmosphere is very good. Food will cost about 90 Leva a-day in the restaurants of higher category. Gastronomes ordering delicacies and specialities, as well as brand drinks will need more than 100 Leva daily.

Most of the catering establishments are situated downtown. Outside its limits these restaurants and pizzerias in small streets or in the larger streets and boulevards are well visible and have the respective ad labels. As a rule restaurants are open from 11 a.m. to 11 p.m.; snack bars will open from 8 a.m. to 8 p.m.; pizzerias and fast-food restaurants may work even till 12 p.m. There are 24-hour restaurants, small stalls for local breakfasts (boza - millet-ale, yoghurt, buttermilk, cheese pasties, buns and patties, pretzels, etc.) open from 6 a.m. till 6 p.m.

The capital's visitors will have no difficulty in finding food, as there are lots of shops selling fare, fruits and vegetables, delicacies and drinks. Many 24-hour shops can be found in the city centre as well as in every quarter; tourists and visitors may thus be confident that their dinner is available at any time. Table reservation in restaurants of higher category is a guarantee of their clients' enjoyment in a calm atmosphere and good mood. Several hypermarkets are situated in the distant quarters or in the outskirts of the city, as is the European pattern. Most popular of them are Oasis, Metro and Billa.

**Cinemas and theatres.** Movie theatres in Sofia offer films with subtitles in Bulgarian, which is of significant help to foreigners. The capital's central cinemas are Moderen Teatur, Rex, Serdica, Globus, Novo Kino Slaveikov, Odeon, Dom na Kinoto, Europa Palace, Moskva, BIAD,

# SOFIA

Bezhovo Kino. There are also cinemas at the Central Railway Station and in all Sofia quarters. Cinema fans will be interested in movie theatres like Odeon - featuring return films; Dom na Kinoto - art films by famous directors; Bezhovo Kino - for late visitors after 9 p.m.

**Theatres** in Sofia in their major part were described above in the section on the landmarks in Rakovski Street. They are: Ivan Vazov National Theatre; the National Opera and Ballet; the Musical Theatre (the Operetta) and the Arabesque Ballet next to the Levski monument; the Theatre of Satire; the Theatre of the Army; the Sulza y Smyah (Tears and Laughter) Theatre; the Sofia Theatre and Beyond the Channel Theatre in Madrid and Evlogui Georgiev Boulevards; La Strada Theatre (6th of September Str. and Aksakov Str.); the Academic Theatre with the NATFIZ Kr. Sarafov; the State Puppet Theatre (Gourko Str. and Rakovski Str.); the Mladezhki (Youth) Theatre and Sfumato Theatrical Workshop at Narodno Subranie Square; and Theatre 199. A lot of private troupes also perform on other stages.

Non-verbal theatres are interesting, too. Regular performances are given by Theatredreams, tel.: 048 831 208, e-mail: theatredreams@usa.net; Alba Mimestudio, tel.: 429 886, and the pantomimic performances of the National Academy for Theatre and Film Art.

**Tourist agencies**. There are numerous tourist agencies in Sofia which offer visa services, tickets for various destinations, tourist information, trips in the country and abroad, language training courses, vacations, sports camps, accommodation in spa resorts, etc. All tourist agencies have Russian and English speaking specialists and guides. Some of the agencies employ assistants who speak several European languages.

**Transport**. Sofia is the largest transport junction of the country. The destinations of transport segments are numerous, and the routes and stopovers - most varied. The maps, which provide a general idea of the road network and railway transport, show the main overland communication lines between Sofia and the rest of the inhabited places in the country.

In general, Bulgaria's transport network divides into southern and northern routes. Thus the bus stations and the railway stations are oriented in these directions.

Here we offer the names and phone numbers for information and booking of tickets at Sofia's major stations, according to the type of transport:

| | |
|---|---|
| **Sofia Airport** | 937 22 12 |
| | 937 22 11 |
| **Central Railway Station** | 931 11 11 |
| | 843 33 33 |
| **Central Railway Station** International tickets | 987 95 35 |
| **Rila Bureau** International tickets | 65 71 86 |

(Other railway stations in Sofia are: Sofia-Sever (North), Zaharna Fabrika, Podouene and Gara Iskar).

| | |
|---|---|
| Bus Station Sever (North) | 38 31 91 |
| Bus Station Yug (South) | 72 00 63 |
| Bus Station Zapad (West) | 955 53 62 |
| Bus Station Iztok (East) (Podouene) | 45 30 14 |
| International Bus Station | 952 50 04 |
| MAT PU | 953 2481 |

In addition to these stations, well familiar to all residents of Sofia, there are dozens of private carriers starting from various places in the capital. Notably numerous are the private buses to the Balkan countries and close destinations. Information on them can be obtained at the central bus stations, especially when one is searching for alternative transport or is willing to change the date and time of the trip. Certain international destinations will be charged in hard currency.

# SOFIA

Authentically signed and duly filled-in tickets should be demanded at the counters.
**City transport** in Sofia offers wide opportunities and it is difficult to describe it without a city plan.
Every tourist should buy a detailed city map-plan of Sofia showing not only the lines but also the stops of the city transport.
As of 1998 Sofia has one subway line; dozens of bus lines connect the capital with near-by settlements, as well as covering shorter distances in the city itself; trolley buses travel in many directions; trams cut across the entire city. Fixed-route taxi minibuses serve the more outlying quarters. **Rent-a-car** companies offer their services as well. A ticket for the city transport costs 0.40 Leva, for the fixed-route taxi - 1 Lev.
The most popular **taxi cab companies** have radio taxis; their phones are: 973-21-21; 12-80; 63-99-99; 12-89; 12-63; 920-20-10; 9-733-733; 920-21-14.
A **Transport Services Centre** operates at the National Palace of Culture building, underground floor, (level 2), phones:

| | |
|---|---|
| Buses | 65 94 07 |
| Domestic trains | 843 42 80 |
| International trains | 843 42 93 |
| Sleeping cars | 843 42 94 |

Train and air tickets can be purchased from the Rila International Railways Bureau, 5, Gourko Str. and at the International Railway Bureau at the Central Railway Station.

> *SUN HOTEL* **- 100 year old, 3 star, Sofia-center**
> 16 cozy rooms, Business center, Sun pastry shop, Bellevue piano bar
> Bulgaria, 1202 Sofia,
> 89 Maria Luiza Blvd
> **Tel:** (+359 2) 9833670, 9831833, 9832338
> **Fax:** (+359 2) 9835389
> **E-mail:** sunhotel@techno-link.com

## EMBASSIES and DIPLOMATIC SERVICES

**AFGHANISTAN** - Embassy, Gorna Banya Quarter, 61, Boryana Str., block 216A, flat 15, tel.: 955 99 87; 556 196

**ALBANIA** - Embassy, 10, Krara Str., tel.: 943 38 57; Consular Office, tel.: 946 12 22

**ALGIERS** - Embassy, 16, Slavyanska Str., tel.: 980 22 50; 981 02 96

**ARGENTINA** - Embassy, 36, Dragan Tsankov Blvd., INTERPRED, block B, floor 2, tel.: 971 25 39; 971 37 91; 973 32 04

**ARMENIA** - Embassy, 11, 20$^{th}$ April Str., tel./fax: 952 60 46; 547 970

**AUSTRIA** - Embassy, 4, Shipka Str., tel.: 980 35 72; 980 35 73

**BELARUS** - Embassy, Lozenets Quarter, 20, Kokiche Str., tel.: 963 30 61; fax: 963 40 23

**BELGIUM** - Embassy, 1, Velchova Zavera Sq., tel.: 963 19 73; 988 72 85

**BRAZIL** - Embassy, 19, Frederic Joliot-Curie Str., block 156, entr.1, floor 4, flat 16, tel.: 723 527; 701 002

**CZECH REPUBLIC** - Embassy, 9, Yanko Sakuzov Blvd., tel.: 946 11 11; 946 11 10

**CHINA** - Embassy, 7, Al. Von Houmbolt Str., tel.: 973 38 73; 973 38 51; Consular Office - tel.: 971 31 06; 973 39 47

**CROATIA** - Embassy, 32, Veliko Turnovo Str., tel.: 943 32 25; 943 32 26

**CUBA** - Embassy, 1, Konstantin Shturkelov Str., tel.: 720 996; 722 014

# SOFIA

- **CYPRUS** - Embassy, Istok Quarter, 154A, Yuri Gagarin Str., floor 1, flat 2, tel.: 971 22 41; 971 92 70
- **DENMARK** - Embassy, 10, Tsar Osvoboditel Blvd., floor 4, tel.: 980 08 30; 980 22 40
- **EGYPT** - Embassy, 5, 6th September Str., tel.: 988 15 09, 987 02 15
- **FINLAND** - Embassy, 53, Simeonovsko Chaussee Blvd., Residence 3, tel.: 962 58 70; Consular Office - 16, Krakra Str., tel.: 943 11 25
- **FRANCE** - Embassy, 29, Oborishte Str., tel.: 946 03 80; 946 03 90; Consular Office - 47, Oborishte Str., tel.: 946 12 57; 962 57 85
- **GERMANY** - Embassy, 25, Frederic Joliot-Curie Str., tel.: 963 45 18; Passport & Visa Section, tel.: 963 41 01
- **GREAT BRITAIN** - Embassy, 38, Vassil Levski Blvd., tel.: 980 12 26; Consular Office, tel.: 933 92 90
- **GREECE** - Embassy, 33, San Stefano Str., tel.: 94610 27, 946 10 30; Consular Office - 19, Oborishte Str., tel.: 946 15 62; 946 15 63
- **HOLY SEE (the VATICAN)** - Embassy, 6, 11th August Str., tel.: 981 17 43; 981 21 97
- **HUNGARY** - Embassy, 57, 6th September Str., tel.: 963 11 35; 963 11 36
- **INDIA** - Embassy, 31, Patriarch Evtimii Blvd., tel.: 986 76 72; 986 77 72
- **INDONESIA** - Embassy, 53, Simeonovsko Chaussee Blvd., Residence 4, tel.: 962 52 40; 683 220
- **IRAN** - Embassy, 77, Vassil Levski Blvd., tel.: 987 85 46; 987 61 73
- **IRAQ** - Embassy, 21-23, Anton Pavlovich Chehov Str., tel.: 971 11 97; 973 33 48
- **ISRAEL** - Embassy, 1, Bulgaria Blvd., NDK Administrative Building, floor 7, tel.: 951 50 44; 951 50 46
- **ITALY** - Embassy, 2, Shipka Str., tel.: 980 77 47; 980 69 50
- **JAPAN** - Embassy, 14, Lyulyakova Gradina Str., tel.: 971 34 37; 971 27 08
- **KOREA,** - Embassy, 36, Dragan Tsankov Blvd., Interpred, Block A, Floor 8, tel.: 971 21 81; 971 25 36
- **KOREA, PEOPLE'S DEMOCRATIC REPUBLIC OF** - Embassy, Mladost-1 Quarter, Andrei Saharov Blvd., Residence 4, tel.: 975 33 40; 775 348; Consular Office - tel.: 975 33 40
- **KUWAIT** - Embassy, Simeonovsko Chaussee Blvd., Residence 15, tel.: 962 56 89; 962 51 30
- **LEBANON** - Embassy, 19, Frederic Joliot-Curie Str., Block 1, Flat 2, tel.: 971 26 67
- **LIBYA** - Embassy, Mladost-1 Quarter, Andrey Sakharov Str., Residence 1, tel.: 974 35 56; 974 31 56
- **MACEDONIA** - Embassy, 17, Frederic Joliot-Curie Str., Block 2, Flat 1, tel.: 70 50 98; 971 28 32
- **MOLDOVA** - Embassy, 17, Patriarch Evtimii Blvd., tel.: 980 42 40
- **MONGOLIA** - Embassy, 52, Frederic Joliot-Curie Str., tel.: 659 012
- **MOROCCO** - Embassy. 129, Evlogui Georgiev Blvd., tel.: 944 27 94
- **NETHERLANDS** - Embassy, 38, Galichitsa Str., tel.: 962 54 81; 962 57 85

# SOFIA

- **PALESTINE** - Embassy, 22, James Boucher Str., tel.: 963 43 24; 963 31 23
- **PERU** - Embassy, 17, Frederic Joliot-Curie Str., Block 2, tel.: 971 37 08; 971 27 16
- **POLAND** - Embassy, 46, Khan Kroum Str., tel.: 987 26 10; 987 26 60; Consular Office - te.: 981 85 45
- **PORTUGAL** - Embassy, 6, Ivats Voivoda Str., tel.: 943 36 67; 943 36 70; Consular Office - Yuri Gagarin Str., Block 154A, Flat 23, tel.: 971 34 11
- **ROMANIA** - Embassy, 4, Sitnyakovo Blvd., tel.: 971 28 58; 973 30 81; Consular Office - 1, Shipchenski Prohod Blvd., tel.: 973 35 10
- **RUSSIA** - Embassy, 28, Dragan Tsankov Blvd., tel.: 963 09 12; 963 13 14, Consular Office - 30, Nikola Mirchev Str., tel.: 963 40 21; 963 28 79
- **SLOVAKIA** - Embassy, 9, Yanko Sakuzov Str., tel.: 943 32 81/85; Consular Office - tel.: 943 32 88
- **SOUTH AFRICA, REPUBLIC OF** - Embassy, 1, Al. Zhendov Str., Block 1, tel.: 971 34 25
- **SPAIN** - Embassy, 27, Sheinovo Str., tel.: 943 30 32; 943 30 34
- **SWEDEN** - Embassy, 4, Alfred Nobel Str., tel.: 971 24 31; 973 37 74
- **SWITZERLAND** - Embassy, 33, Shipka Str., tel.: 946 01 97
- **SYRIA** - Embassy, 13A, Simeonovsko Chaussee Blvd., tel.: 962 57 42; 962 45 80
- **TURKEY** - Embassy, 80, Vassil Levski Blvd., tel.: 980 22 70; 987 29 84
- **UKRAINE** - Embassy, 24A, Boryana Str., Residence 11A, tel.: 955 40 70; 955 93 48
- **UNITED STATES OF AMERICA** - Embassy, 1, Suborna Str., tel.: 980 52 41/47
- **URUGUAY** - Embassy, 91, Tsar Ivan Assen II Str., tel.: 943 19 57; 943 40 40
- **VENEZUELA** - Embassy, 1, Toulovo Str., Floor 2, tel.: 943 30 61; 943 34 95
- **VIETNAM** - Embassy, 1, Zhetvarka Str., tel.: 658 334; Consular Office - tel.: 658 486; 963 26 09; 963 37 49
- **YEMEN -** Embassy, Mladost -1 Quarter, Andrei Sakharov Blvd., Residence 3, tel.: 704 119; 974 56 39
- **YUGOSLAVIA** - Embassy, 3, Veliko Turnovo Str., tel.: 946 16 33; 943 34 57; Consular Office - 17 Marin Drinov Str., tel.: 943 45 90

## CONSULATES

- **GREECE - General Consulate** - Plovdiv, 10, Preslav Str., tel.: (032) 232 003; (032) 238 788
- **NORWAY - General Consulate** - Sofia, 4, Alfred Nobel Str., tel.: 971 24 31; 973 37 74
- **POLAND - General Consulate** - Varna, 18, Slavyanska Str., tel.: (052) 225 586; (052) 229 542
- **RUSSIA - General Consulate** - Varna, 53, Macedonia Str., tel.: (052) 602 718; (052) 602 721; **General Consulate** - Rousse, 1, Nis Street, tel.: (082) 450 238
- **TURKEY - General Consulate** - Plovdiv, 10, Philip Makedonski Str., tel.: (032) 232 309; (032) 624 010; **General Consulate**, Bourgas, 38, Democratsiya Blvd., tel.: (056) 4 27 18

# SOFIA

## THE ENVIRONS of SOFIA

Most conspicuous to the guests of Sofia are the mountains, which encircle the Sofia Plain. Vitosha, Lyulin and Plana Mountains are interesting and full of sights worth visiting. The present tour guide has a separate chapter on Vitosha Mountain.

**Lyulin Mountain** is situated south-west of the capital city, 3 kilometres from the ring road. Now virtually a part of the city, it is a good place for outings, picnics and walks. **Bonsovy polyany** are the most frequented place in the mountain. There are interesting areas with deciduous vegetation, beautiful valleys and meadows. Tourist signs mark the routes to Lyulin chalets and shelters. **Plana Mountain** also offers interesting sights for tourists. It is situated about 10 km south of the capital and can be reached by city bus transport or by car along the road to Samokov.

Most frequently visited is the **Kokalyane Monastery**, built in the 10th century by Tzar Samuil. Beautiful frescoes and murals decorate the church, built after Russian patterns. Three of the monks in the monastery serve also in the Bulgarian monastery on Athos (Greece). There is a small scenic waterfall close to the monastery in southern direction. The monastery can be reached after a 45-minutes walk along the footpath above the asphalt road from the Devil's Bridge over the Vedena River. Another popular spot is the glade with Khan Asparoukh oak, called after him because of its age nearing 14 centuries. The oak is believed to have witnessed the days in which Bulgaria was founded. Fields and a lush hazelnut forest surround the place. About 500 metres from the oak on the footpath to the village of Zheleznitsa there is a small water spring. Tourist chalets and shelters abound in this mountain.

The **Pancharevo Lake** (12 km from the capital city) is situated next to the village of Pancharevo. The lake is about 5 km long and 1 km wide. It is suitable for recreation, sunbathing, fishing and water sports - swimming, rowing, surfing, and water skiing. Rowing and

*Kremikovtsi Monastery*

# SOFIA

*Vitosha Mountain. Aleko Chalet*

water-ski competitions are frequently organised here. Pedalos are available, fishing and bathing in the lake are only allowed in strictly limited areas. Numerous small private restaurants can be found around the lake, Lebeda (the Swan) being the most popular of these.

The **Iskar Dam** is another large water reservoir near Sofia; it lies 25 km south of the city, and is a very good recreation spot where aquatic sports can be practised. The **Shturkelovo gnezdo** (Stork's nest) **Resort** is a place worth visiting. Special attention is paid to strict observance of bathing and recreation rules, because the lake is also a drinking water reservoir for the capital. There are numerous small restaurants at the lakeside; fruits and vegetables are often offered for sale.

Within Vitosha Mountain the most interesting landmarks are the **Boyana Church** (built in three stages - 11$^{th}$, 13$^{th}$ and 19$^{th}$ centuries) and the **Dragalevtsi Monastery** (14$^{th}$ century), both considered heralds of European Renaissance. Most interesting are the frescoes (1259) in the Boyana Church, which art experts today rate them as a peak of realistic art of those times. The church is inluded in UNESCO List of World Heritage. Remarkable are the frescoes portraying the donors of the church.

**Bankya** is 22 km from the capital in the foothills of Lyulin Mountain. It is one of the villa areas of Sofia. The town is a balneological center for cardiovascular and pulmonary ailments. It can be reached by bus or by a regular railway line. Wonderful places for picnic and tourist outings surround it. The small town has several galleries, many restaurants and cafè, small clubs and a race-course.

The **Kremikovtsi Monastery** (15$^{th}$ century) is located 30 km north of Sofia in the southern slopes of the Stara Planina Mountain. Its frescoes are treasured as a revelation of a new vision in church mural painting of that time. The church itself is very small yet very well preserved. Tourists rarely visit the place.

The **Kourilo Monastery** stands at the mouth of the Iskar gorge near the village of Kourilo, 18 km from the capital. It can be reached via the road to Mezdra or by a passenger train on the line connecting Sofia with Northern Bulgaria. The church was built and painted in the 15$^{th}$ century. Along the gorge, 9 km from the Eliseina station and at a 3-hour walk from the Prolet stop lies the Sedemte Prestola (The Seven Thrones) Monastery. It dates back to the 16$^{th}$ century and its icons and murals were painted in stages. The central nave of the church is divided into 7 chapels (thrones) and is adorned with a very beautiful wooden chandelier.

## PARKS in SOFIA

The main park of Sofia is the **Vitosha Nature Park**, which covers a large part of the mountain (refer to the "The Mountains of Bulgaria" chapter for more details).

The central park of Sofia is the **Borissova Gradina** (The Garden of Boris), along the Tsarigradsko Chaussee Boulevard beyond the Orlov Most (the Eagles' Bridge). At the very beginning of the park is the Ariana Lake. Further in the park are the Vassil Levski National Stadium and Bulgarian Army Stadium, as well as courts, a cycle-racing track, etc. About a kilometre from its entrance is the Maria Louisa Swimming Complex with two open-air pools and a 10-metre jumping tower. There are numerous alleys in the park, part of which are

# SOFIA

asphalted. Also near its entrance there is an open-air stage, dozens of children playgrounds and places for recreation and training. A large monument from socialist times rises in end of the park - Bratskata Mogila (the Mound to the Brothers). For this reason it was called The Park of Freedom before. It is also a place where dozens of busts stand of Bulgarian revolutionaries, national revival leaders, writers and poets. The Borissova Gradina Park is the favourite recreation place of most citizens of Sofia.

The **Gradskata Gradina (City Garden) Park** is situated in the capital's ideal centre close to the to the Sofia City Gallery. In the middle of the park, in front of the National Theatre there are fountains with a sculpture of a female dancer; a children's playground with wooden swings and an old newspaper stall designed after the fashion of the end of the last century, selling foreign language publications and press. Although small, this park attracts lots of people seeking recreation after work in the midday and afternoon hours. It is also the favourite place of chess players. More than 100 years ago a tourist group of about 300 Sofia citizens, led by Aleko Konstantinov, a writer democrat and enthusiastic mountaineer, started from this park and climbed Mt. Cherni Vruh (Black Peak) - Vitosha's highest spot.

An original continuation of this garden is the small **park** behind the National Art Gallery. It covers a sloping terrain, and about a dozen sculptures co-exist with a number of age-old protected trees.

**Yuzhen Park** (the Southern Park) is the second largest after the Borissova Gradina Park. It extends from Ivan Vazov Quarter to the Hladilnika Quarter. Numerous children's playgrounds are included in its territory; the Spartak Swimming & Sports Center at its end is the favourite spot for open-air celebrations organised by the Sofia Municipality. Hundreds of athletes, and martial arts fans exercise in it, dozens of citizens from neighbouring quarters do their morning jogging along the park alleys.

**Zapaden Park** (the Western Park) is close to the Zaharna Fabrika Quarter and the beginning of the Lyulin Quarter. Several catering spots are available in it and there is enough space for walks and games.

Sofia is one of world's greenest cities. Dozens of small parks and gardens decorate it, thousands of trees in its streets come into leaf every spring.

Particularly famous with its chestnut trees and yellow brick pavement is **Rouski Boulevard**. Green and tended as small gardens are hundreds of small courtyards in the city centre behind old blocks of flats. The Lozenets, Mladost, Zone B-5 quarters, etc., are also green spots of Sofia.

The city breathes not only through its "lung" Vitosha but also by its numerous areas and streets planted with greenery.

*In the Borissova Gradina Park*

GUIDE BOOK

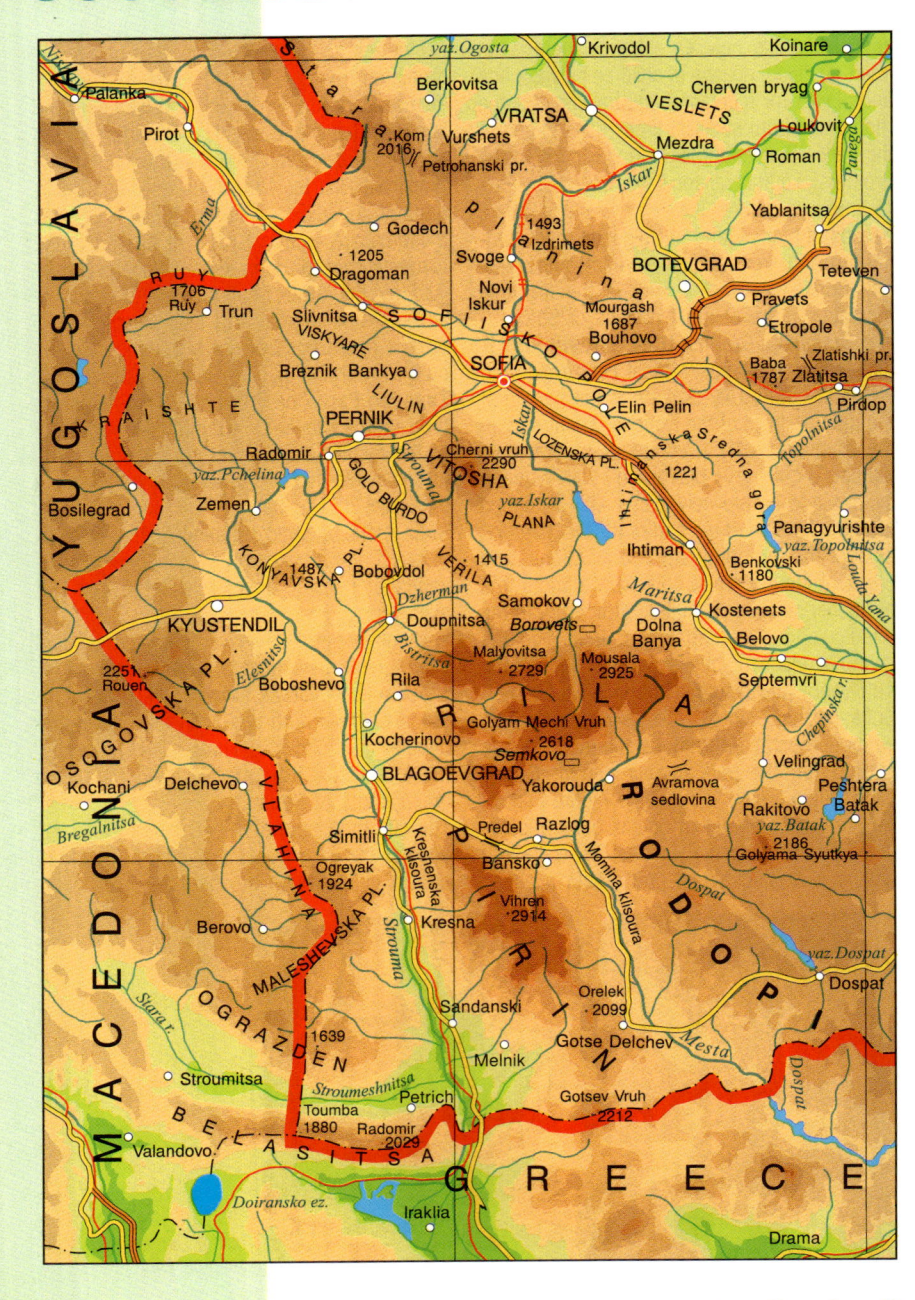

# SOUTHWESTERN BULGARIA

# SOUTHWESTERN BULGARIA

## PETRICH

The town of Petrich (population: 29 785, 200 m above sea level) is situated in the far southwestern part of Bulgaria where the Bulgarian-Greek and the Bulgarian-Macedonian borders touch. It is 13 km west of the frontier checkpoint of Koulata (at the border with Greece), 20 km east of the frontier checkpoint of Zlatarevo (at the border with Macedonia), 23 km from the town of Sandanski, 88 km from Blagoevgrad, and 189 km from the capital city Sofia. It is located at the immediate northern foothill of the Belasitsa Mountain, along the banks of the Petrich River (the right tributary of the Stroumeshnitsa River flowing into the River Strouma). The Petrich Field along the Stroumeshnitsa Valley is one of the most fertile in Bulgaria. Due to the Mediterranean influence coming through the valley of the Strouma River a number of citrus fruits grow here - lemons, kiwi, figs, etc., as well as early fruits and vegetables.

**History**. Petrich was included in the territory of the Bulgarian State during the reign of Knyaz Boris I (852-889). In the Middle Ages it was a solid Bulgarian fortress of utmost importance for Tsar Samouil's wars (997-1014) with Byzantium. Petrich preserved its Bulgarian spirit under the Ottoman rule as well. In 16th century the Christian population was 90%. In the second half of 19th century the town decayed and at the threshold of 20th century there are about 6000 inhabitants. In 1873 the first school was opened, and here in 1878 the Macedonian Bulgarians signed and sealed their appeal to the Great Powers against the resolutions of the Berlin Congress of the same year according to which the Petrich district was detached from Bulgaria. From 19th January 1892 Petrich and its district were included in Bulgarian Exarchate. The town population actively participated in the national liberation struggles of Macedonia. In 1899 a revolutionary committee of the IMRO (Internal Macedonian Revolutionary Organisation) was set up. Petrich was liberated from Turkish rule in the Balkan War (1912-1913). Part of the population emigrated but refugees from Vardar and Aegean Macedonia settled here. During the World War I the town was almost completely destroyed.

**Landmarks.** The **Town Museum of History** - situated in the centre (tel.: 0745 23092). **The Holy Virgin Church,** erected in 1857 and declared a cultural monument (tel.: 0745 24504). **The Assumption Church**, 19, 28th October Str. (tel.: 0745 22444); **St. Georgi Church**, 14, Moussala Str. (tel.: 0745 28420); **St. Nikola Church** (tel.: 0745 27139).

**Accommodation.** Bulgaria Hotel - the biggest and most luxurious hotel in the town. It is situated right opposite the bus station in the central part of the town at 21, Tsar Boris III. Agatha Hotel in the Tsar Samouil National Sports Base (near the stadium). In Petrich there are a few private family hotels.

**Transport**. There is bus and railway transport to and from Petrich connecting it with the rest of the country. The bus station is situated in the central part of the town opposite the Bulgaria Hotel (tel.: 0745 24348, 22136). There are bus lines to Sofia, Blagoevgrad, Sandanski, Koulata, Zlatarevo and all villages in the Petrich Field. Petrich is the last railway station on the General Todorov - Petrich extension of the railway line Sofia - Koulata - Athens. The railway station is located in the northern part of the town (tel.: 0745 23357, 22842); there is a public bus line to the railway station. There are several bus lines within the town itself.

**Surrounding areas**. The most significant sight near Petrich is the **Samouil Fortress** - National Museum (18 km west of the town and 6 km north of the village of Klyuch, on the right bank of the Stroumeshnitsa River). At the beginning of 11th century the Bulgarian Tsar Samouil built a defencive system against the Byzantine invasion in the Klyuch Saddle

# SOUTHWESTERN BULGARIA

(between Belasitsa and Ograzhden Mountains). In the summer of 1014 the Byzantine Emperor Vasilius II and numerous army entered the saddle. After a series of futile attacks to the Bulgarian defence he sent part of the army to march round the Belasitsa Mountain and turn up in the rear of the Bulgarians. The defenders of the fortification were taken by surprise and 15 000 of them were taken prisoners. The infuriated Byzantine Emperor ordered that all the captives were blinded, to every 100 soldiers he left one with one eye to lead them. All this broke Tsar Samouil and on 6th October 1014 he died desperate. Ever since the Byzantine Emperor has been called Vasilius the Murderer of Bulgarians. Four years after this crucial battle Bulgaria fell under Byzantine rule for nearly two centuries. The imposing bronze statue of Samouil is a remarkable sight; he is in full height with legs bent in the knees under the burden of severe anguish. On either side of the statue there are stone plates with embossed figures of the blinded soldiers. There is a museum exhibition offering significant historical information about the Bulgarian State. The biggest dwelling-place in the settlement is preserved under a glass dome. The whole of the Klyuch Saddle can be viewed from a 25 m high panoramic platform. Working hours: 08.00 a.m. - 05.00 p.m. One can use the regular bus lines from Petrich to Zlatarevo border checkpoint.

Five kilometres north-east of Petrich one can find remains dating back to the Hellenic epoch (most probably of the **ancient town of Petra**) - parts of a fortress wall, foundations of public buildings, architectural fragments. Coins dating back to 4th-3rd centuries BC were discovered. **The Roupite Nature Reserve** - 10 km north-east of the town. There is a railway station on the General Todorov - Petrich line. One can see the hot steaming mineral springs at the bottom of the dead vulcano of Kozhouh. This is an extremely beautiful and impressive place. The Bulgarian prophet Vanga lived here and helped the people in her last years. Her house and the St. Petka Church remind us of her. She herself was the initiator and donator for the construction of the church.

**The village of Marikostinovo** - a spa 13 km east of Petrich. There are a lot of hot mineral springs with water temperature of 58°-62°C. The water is good for various illnesses. An ancient necropolis of 7th-10th century is situated nearby.

**The mountain of Belassitsa** - it rises steep south above the town and in fact is its biggest natural park. The biggest area of edible chestnut trees can be found on the northern slopes. The mountain spreads in the territories of three countries - Bulgaria, Greece and Macedonia, and the crossing point of their borders is **Mt. Toumba** (1881 m), which can be climbed up for 6-7 hours starting at the village of Gabrene (only upon permission of the border authorities, there are no markings). Nine kilometres away from the town (there is an asphalt road), 720 m above sea level is the Belasitsa Chalet. One can walk the distance for 2 hours following a direct marked track. The chalet is a massive three-storied building with 80 beds in separate rooms. Tel.: 0745 22449 (Kalabak Tourist Association, Petrich). The chalet is the starting point of several marked tracks to Vodopada (the Waterfall) (0.30 min), Zaslona (the Shelter) (1 hour). Tourists can climb up the highest peak of the mountain, **Mt. Radomir** (2029 m) for about 6 hours but only upon permission of the border authorities at the piquet. There are no markings above the piquet.

# SOUTHWESTERN BULGARIA

## SANDANSKI

The town of Sandanski (population: 26 695, 240 m above sea level) is situated in South-Western Bulgaria, immediately to the west of Pirin Mountain, along the banks of the Sandanska Bistritsa River, which shortly after passing the town flows into the Strouma River. The town bears the name of the great Bulgarian revolutionary Yane Sandanski who fought for the liberation of Macedonia from the Turkish rule. It is 23 km north-east of Petrich, 22 km north of Koulata (the border checkpoint with Greece), 65 km south of Blagoevgrad and 166 km north of Sofia. The area of Sandanski has the best climate in the whole of Bulgaria and if one adds up the hot mineral springs (33°-83°C) it becomes evident why the town has turned into a resort of international significance.

**History**. On the place of the present day town there was an old Thracian settlement that had sprung up near the hot mineral springs. The first inhabitants were the tribe called *medi*. With the arrival of the Romans the small settlement was extended and improved. The curative springs were impounded and a big public bath (asklepion) was built. Most probably the settlement grew into a town during the reign of Emperor Pius (138-161) and was surrounded by fortification walls made of pebble stones from the local river. The town reached cultural and economic boom during the time of the Byzantine Emperor Justinian II (527-565). After 6th century the town was destroyed. The Slavonic tribe called *strimontsi* (*stroumentsi*) settled here; they named the settlement *Sveti Vrach*, meaning Saint Healer. According to the legend this name is connected with two folk healers - the brothers Kozma and Damyan. The settlement was included in the territory of the Bulgarian Kingdom during the reign of Khan Pressian (836-852). During the Ottoman domination Sveti Vrach fell into decay and turned into a small village. In the year of its liberation - 1912 (the Balkan War) its population was no more than 500 inhabitants (the nearby town of Melnik had a population of 12 000 inhabitants at the

*A view of the town*

# SOUTHWESTERN BULGARIA

time). A lot of refugees from the Aegean region settled in the area in 1913-1925. Nowadays the town is one of the most significant centres in Europe for treatment of diseases of the upper respiratory track and the lungs.

**Landmarks**. On entering the town along the road where the main Sofia-Koulata-Athens road forks the visitor faces **the architectural and sculptural complex** (a monument) among which the white seven-metre high stone statue of the ancient hero Spartacus rises. In the centre of the town is **the Museum of Archaeology** (2, Macedonia Str., tel.: 0746 3118, 3188, 2287, 2540) exibiting remains of the Episcopal Basilica and treasuring material evidence of more than 27 centuries. Particular attention should be paid to the **St. Georgi Church** from 1861 - it is the only building preserved from the Revival Period (10, St. St. Cyiril and Methodius Str., tel.: 0746 2428). The **Town Art Gallery,** 51, Macedonia Str., tel.: 0746 5165), **Likin Art Gallery,** 3, Melnik Str., tel.: 0746 2231.

**Accommodation.** Sandanski offers great accommodation opportunities. The biggest and most prestigious is the 4-star Sandanski Interhotel situated at the entrance of the Sveti Vrach Park. Here are 2-star hotels: Andoni, Bacheto, Kartalovets, Mramor, Sveti Vrach, in the town centre, Yug, Spartak (2, Macedonia Str.), Garant. The Sports Resort Complex (Base 1 and Base 2) near the Sveti Vrach Park offers excellent opportunities. There are several motels, rest homes with accommodation facilities and a camping site called Chetvurti Kilometre (4$^{th}$ kilometre) on the road to the village of Lilyanovo, and Popina Luka Holiday Resort. There are more than 30 private lodgings in Sandanski.

**Tourist information.** One can obtain information at Sandanski Tourist Information Bureau at 1, Bulgaria Square (Otets Paisii Communal Cultural Centre), tel.: 0746 22549, fax: 0746 2403, e-mail: bicc@omega.bg and at the Council on Tourism (2800 Sandanski, 4, General Todorov Str.).

**Transport**. Sandanski is an important point on the international road and railway lines Sofia-Koulata-Athens and this in itself determines the type of the transport links. There is bus transport to and from the town, which forms a branched net in the adjacent towns and villages. The bus station is located in the centre of the town on the right bank of the Sandanska Bistritsa River (17, Peroun Str., tel.: 0746 2130, 2134, 2137, 2140). There is railway transport connecting Sandanski to the big towns of Blagoevgrad, Doupnitsa, Pernik and the capital city Sofia as well as to the rest of the railway system of the country. The railway station is 4 km west of the town and there is a regular bus line in this direction (tel.: 0746 2213, 2235, 2413). In the town there are several regular bus lines.

**Parks**. The town of Sandanski as well as Bulgaria as a whole, are proud of the unique **Town Park** called since 1891 with the old name of the town - Sveti Vrach. Its territory is 344 decares. More than 100 tree species and more than 150 flower species grow here. One can see here old hollow plane-trees, slender cedars and sequoias, evergreen tui, branchy willows, pine-trees, pomegranates, fig trees, wild geranium, garden geranium, all sorts of roses, etc. The small stone slopes resemble the Alpine outlook of the white marble massif of Pirin rising to the east. Suspension bridges hang over the foamy and rapid Sandanska Bistritsa River. A number of alleys, wooden alcoves, playgrounds for children and other specific corners offer unique conditions for rest and entertainment. The verdure of the park surrounds the town stadium, the open-air theatre, the open-air swimming pool, an artificial lake with a bar, a lot of boats and water wheels, an original restaurant with separate niches in the shape of casks, etc. At the very gate of the park a unique ferro-concrete map of Northern Pirin was made and installed by Nikola Mironski, a well-known Bulgarian mountaineer. The Town Park has naturally merged in the bigger forest-park that sur-

# SOUTHWESTERN BULGARIA

rounds the town as in a horseshoe, which people call the green necklace of Sandanski. **Surrounding areas**. 24 km south-east is the **town-museum of Melnik**, 6 km further on is **the Rozhen Monastery** (refer to the Pirin Mountain related chapter herein). 18 km north-east within Pirin is the **Popina Luka Resort** (1230 m above sea level). A lot of private villas, bars and restaurants, and several hotels (The Vodopada (the Waterfall) Hotel, the Kotarite Hotel) are situated here. The R. Bozhinov Villa is also opened for guests. Within the holiday resort is the Yane Sandanski Chalet offering 70 beds (tel.: 0746 3198 - Edelweiss Tourist Association). The eleven-metre high **Popina Luka Waterfall** is located at the Bashliitsa River (one of the initial tributaries of Sandanska Bistritsa River) running through the Popina Luka Resort. The resort is a point of departure for several marked tourist routes in Pirin - refer to the points of departure in the section about Pirin Mountain herein. The telephone of the Mountain Rescue Service in Sandanski is 0746 4013.

## GOTSE DELCHEV

The town of Gotse Delchev (20 546 inhabitants, 540 m above sea level) is situated in the valley of the Mesta River, along the banks of its right tributary - the Nevrokop River. It is 22 km north of the Greek border, 51 km south of Bansko, 112 km away from Blagoevgrad and 212 km away from Sofia. It bears the name of legendary Gotse Delchev, ideologist and leader of the Bulgarians from Macedonia in their struggle against the Ottoman domination (till 1959 the town's name had been Nevrokop). To the west above the town is the Mid Pirin Mountain Massif, and to the east opposite to it is the south-western sub-part of the Western Rhodopes called Dubrash Mountain.

**History**. The first information about this settlement dates back to $9^{th}$-$10^{th}$ centuries and in $15^{th}$ century the name of *Nevrokoub* was mentioned. In 1625 it was registered as a town. During the Ottoman rule the town devel-

*The Mesta River*

# SOUTHWESTERN BULGARIA

oped as a crafts centre. It was famous for the production of small and large cow and sheep bells - the renowned chanove for the herds in Pirin and the Rhodopes (the tradition is been preserved only here). The crafts of skin processing and saddlery also developed. Annual trade fairs were held in the town during the second half of 14th century. In the Revival Period the inhabitants of the town showed acute national consciousness. They erected churches, a monastery school, a secular school, separate schools for young boys and young girls respectively, a communal cultural centre. As stipulated in the Berlin Treaty the

*In Kovachevista village - museum*

town remained in the territory of Turkey and was liberated in the Balkan War (October 1912). The town gave shelter to many refugees from the Serr and Drama areas.

**Landmarks. The Town Museum of History** is located in a house dating back to 1879 (Hristo Botev Str., the Central Square, tel.: 0751 23156). The **Revival Architecture Complex** of Rifat Bei (in the old central part of the town). The historical **Holy Virgin Church** dating back to 1833; the **St. Archangel Michail Church** (11, Ekzarh Antim Str., tel.: 0751 24014). The private **ethnographic collection** of Zafir Kunchev (tel.: 0751 23078).

The 500 year-old plane tree is a natural sight of the town. The tree is 24 metre high with perimetre of the trunk of 7.6 metres.

**Accommodation.** The biggest of all is the Nevrokop Hotel in the centre of the town. Smaller but cosier are Malamovata Kashta Hotel (Malamov's House) (25, Hristo Botev Str.) and Mesta Hotel. The Forest Rest House welcomes guests, too. There is a Tourist Hostel near the bus station (26, Soloun Str.).

**Tourist Information**. Tourist Information Centre, 2900 Gotse Delchev, 2, Tsaritsa Yoanna Str., tel.: 0751 22086. Council on Tourism (2900 Gotsa Delchev, 2, Tsaritsa Yoanna Str., tel.: 0751 29185). The Momini Dvori Tourist Association (in the tourist hostel).

**Transport**. The connection of Gotse Delchev to the rest of the country is only by bus transport. There are regular bus lines to Sofia, Plovdiv, Blagoevgrad, Razlog, Bansko, Dobrinishte and all the villages in the district. The town has got three bus stations - Central Bus Station (Byalo More Str., tel.: 0751 23547, 23367, 23597), Bus Station-Zapad (tel.: 0751 22417) and a private bus station (tel.: 0751 23811).

**Surrounding areas**. In honour to his victory over the Dacian tribe Emperor Trayan (98-117) built the ancient Roman town called **Nikopolis ad Nestum** whose remains are to be found 7 km east of Gotse Delchev, in the Zagrade Quarter of the village of Gurmen, on the left

# SOUTHWESTERN BULGARIA

*Remains of Nikopolis ad Nestum*

bank of the Mesta River. The fortification walls have the shape of an irregular quadrangle. Its imposing remains are an evidence of its past grandeur. It used to be an important crossing point of the roads connecting the ancient towns by the Aegean Sea with the valley of the Hebros River (Maritsa River).

Twenty-five kilometres north-east of the town, in the Dubrash Massif of the Rhodopes, high on the left bank of the Kanina River is the **village of Kovachevitsa** - a unique **architecture and historical reserve**. Time seems to have stopped forever. The Rhodope houses resembling fortresses are magnificent. The nature is magical, the atmosphere of the narrow cobble stone streets between high stone walls, the hospitality of local people are inforgettable. A number of famous people have bought houses here and spend a great part of their time in this fairy place. Kovechevitsa is a paradise not only for artists but also for anyone of poetical soul. The village is the native place of the poet Lyudmil Stoyanov. There is a regular bus line to Gotse Delchev. Some of the old houses have been turned into hotels offering specialities of the original Rhodope cuisine - these are the the Bayatev's House, the Daskalov's, the Zhechev's House, the Kapsuzov's House, the Milchev's and the Spassov's House.

Sixteen kilometres west of the **Popovi Livadi Saddle** between Middle and South Pirin is the **holiday resort** of the same name (about 1400 metres above sea level). There is no regular transport. It takes 4.30-5 hours to walk there along a marked track. The vast green fields surrounded by thick and impenetrable spruce forests create wonderful conditions for escape from the tension of the big town. There are accommodation opportunities as well - the Popovi Livadi Chalet offering 70 beds in different rooms. The Papazov Villa, the Orbel Ltd. Rest House, the Pirinplast Ltd. Rest House, the Orelyak Rest House, the Bulgartabac Hotel. One could go on hiking trails to Mt. Orelyak (2099 m above sea level, the highest peak of Middle Pirin, 2 hours), the Malina Chalet (5-6 hours), the Pirin Chalet (7 hours), and along an unmarked track to the highest peak of South Pirin called Mt. Sveshtnik (1975 m above sea level, 2 hours).

**The following sights are of great interest as well**: the ancient and medieval fortresses in the Gradishteto Area, the waterfall at the Toufcha River, the Draganov Rocks, the Momina Koula (Maiden's Tower) Fortress, the Soudin Grad Fortress dating back to late ancient times and the Middle Ages, the Holy Virgin Monastery, the St. Martyr Georgi Monastery, the meanders of the Mutenitsa River, the Mousomish mineral springs in the area of Toplika, the Pavlov's Saddle, the Manouilova Doupka Cave (Manouilov's Hole), the precipice cave called Propaduka, the Steneto rock formations in the gorge of Kochanska River, the rock formation called the Koziyat Kamuk (Goat's Stone), the rock formation called Koupena in the area of Trebichki Dol, the Pirostiyata rock formation, the Black Rock.

# SOUTHWESTERN BULGARIA

## BANSKO

The town of Bansko (9134 inhabitants; 925 m above sea level) is situated by the Glazne River (the right tributary of Mesta) at the north-eastern foothills of Pirin beneath the highest and most beautiful karst part of the mountain. Its name is related with the ancient

*Pirin in winter*

Bulgarian word *ban* (from boean, boyan) which means master. It is 160 km south of Sofia, 60 km south-east of Blagoevgrad, 6 km south of Razlog and 51 km north of Gotse Delchev. Bansko is the entrance to the most beautiful Bulgarian Mountain - Pirin and one of the biggest winter resorts in the country. If one add to this its architectural and historical value, Bansko is a pearl in the Bulgarian necklace.

**History**. The town rose up on its present location around 9th-10th centuries after the formation of the adjacent quarters of Bansko. In the middle of 18th century Bansko was a big and rich settlement developing crafts and trade. The caravans of Bansko traders travelled to the Aegean Region and to Middle Europe transporting tobacco, poppy seeds from Serr, cotton, processed skins, precious goods, gold. Bansko lived its Golden Age in the second half of 18th century and the beginning of 19th century when it reached economic and cultural boom - the Bansko School of Art was established. The representatives of this school introduced lots of secular and historical themes in art. Monastery schools and a mutual school were opened. However, Napoleon's Wars against Austria and the opening of the waterway along the Danube River put an end to its growth. In the middle of 19th century the economy of the town suffered decay. According to the resolutions of the Berlin Treaty Bansko was left within the boundaries of the Turkish Empire and its inhabitants actively participated in the consequent rebellions - Kresna-Razlog Uprising (1878-1879) and the Ilinden-Preobrazhenie Uprising (1903). The town was liberated from the Turkish rule on 5th October 1912 (the Balkan War). Bansko is the native place of the titans of Bulgarian Revival Paisii Hilendarski and Neofit Rilski.

**Landmarks**. First of all this is the **Sveta Troitsa (St. Trinity) Church** (the biggest and the richest in the region of Pirin), its construction was completed in 1835. The church strikes the viewer with beautiful frescoes and woodcarvings made by Master (Ousta) Velyan Ognev. The most outstanding representative of the Bansko School of Art - Dimitar Molerov, painted the icons. The size of the temple is impressive - too big for that time. A thirty-metre high stone tower rises up in the yard of the church (built by Master Grigor Doyuv in 1850) with a belfry and a clock made by Todor Hadzhiradonov and installed in 1869. It is located in the centre of the town behind a high stone fence. The **Holy Virgin Church** built in 14th century and restored at the end of 18th century and the beginning of 19th century has a wonderful woodcarved iconostasis. **The native house of Neofit Rilski** - preserved in its initial outer appearance and known as the Benina's House. It is located by the neighbouring St. Trinity Church at 17, Pirin Str. (tel.: 07443 4005). **The native house of the poet**

# SOUTHWESTERN BULGARIA

**Nikola Vaptsarov** - in the centre of the town, on the square of the same name. **The Velyanov's House** - a monument dating back to the Revival; one of the most beautiful houses having a rich fresco decoration and fine wood-carvings (2, Velyan Ognev Str., tel.: 07443 4181). **The Sirleshtov's House** is a small fortress. The special role of this house in Bansko is evidenced by the one-metre thick stone walls, the narrow and dark loop-holes, the iron bars on the windows and the heavy doors. **The Todev's** (Buinov's) **House** is an illustration of construction mastership and the delicate sense of beauty in everyday life. It was built in 1835. **Bansko House of Culture and Art Gallery** (tel.: 07443 2292, 5504, 5096). A **monument of Father Paisii Hilendarski** in the centre of the town at the place of his native house.

**Accommodation and catering**. As one of the biggest resorts of Bulgaria, Bansko practically offers unlimited opportunities in this respect satisfying visitors of different financial status. The tourists have at their disposal more than 40 private (predominantly family-type) hotels and more than 100 restaurants and bars. Here is a small part of them: the biggest and most luxurious hotel in the town is the 4-star Bansko Hotel (17, Glazne Str.); the Izvori Hotel (3-star), 5 km away from the town in Pirin among a beautiful coniferous wood in the area called Chalin Valog; the Strazhite Hotel Complex (2-star), one of the biggest in Bansko (Glazne Str.); the Pirin Hotel (2-star), the oldest in the town (68, Tsar Simeon Str., in the centre). The following are 2-star hotels: the Albert Hotel located in a silent street in the central part of the town; the Aneli Hotel; the Hadzhirouskovi Kashti Hotel with a big tavern; the Boyanova Kashta Hotel, the Bunderitsa Hotel (5, Bunderitsa Str.); the Dzhangal Hotel (24, Gotse Delchev Str.); the Tipik Hotel (15, Todor Aleksandrov Str.) and many others. All of them have preserved the town's typical style helping the visitor to enjoy the atmosphere of ages gone long ago. Almost every hotel offers original Bulgarian cuisine typical of the region but there are restaurants, which are worth visiting. These include the Todeva Kushta Wine Bar (7, Neofit Rilski Str.); the Dedo Pene Pub in the Pampoulov's House (1, Aleksandar Bouynov Str.); the Lovna Sreshta Tavern in the Molerov's House (29, Pirin Str.); the Poptodorov's Tavern (1, Dimitar Talev Str.); the Sharkov's House Tavern (26, $5^{th}$ October Str.,); the Alex Pizza Restaurant (14, Ohrid Str.); the Beli Noshti Restaurant in the Vakanov's House (1, Yane Sandanski Str.); the Motikata Restaurant in the western part of the town at the exit to the Mt. Vihren and Vihren, etc.

**Tourist information** regarding all issues of interest to the visitor can be obtained at: Tourist Information Centre, 2770 Bansko, 2, N. Y. Vaptsarov Sq., tel.: 07443 5048); Chamber of Tourism (Union of Private Hotel Managers), tel.: 07443 5016 and fax: 07443 5139); the Vihren Tourist Association (4, Vuzrazhdane Square, tel.: 07443 2683, 2271 and tel./fax: 07443 2641). The Mountain Rescue Service in Bansko (100, Pirin Str., in the western part of the town at the exit to the mountain, tel.: 07443 3075, 3076).

**Transport**. The basic type of transport that connects the town to the rest of the country is the bus transport. There are regular bus

*Along the narrow cobbled streets of Bansko*

# SOUTHWESTERN BULGARIA

lines to Sofia, Blagoevgrad, Gotse Delchev, Razlog, Dobrinishte and many other villages in the district. The bus station is modern and spacious. It is located in the eastern end of the town on the main road Sofia-Blagoevgrad-Gotse Delchev, by the railway station (tel.: 07443 2441, 2420). Bansko is the last but one station on the narrow-gauge line Sep-temvri-Velingrad-Dobrinishte. The railway station is behind the bus station (tel.: 07443 2215).

**Surrounding areas**. Most impressive is the legendary **Pirin Mountain**. The greater part of the tourist flow heading for the mountain goes through the town. In the immediate vicinity are the Chalin Valog Ski-Centre, the Shiligarnika Ski-Centre - one of the biggest in Bulgaria (refer to the Pirin Mountain related section herein), Damyanitsa, Bunderitsa and Vihren Chalets as well as the highest Mt. Vihren (refer to the Pirin related chapter herein). 6 km south of Bansko is **the village of Dobrinishte** (final station on the narrow-gauge line from Septemvri). It is one of the largest villages in the country with a population of over 3000 inhabitants. There are 17 mineral springs with water temperature between 30° and 43 °C, as well as a big mineral public bath. The town is a point of departure to the Gotse Delchev, Mocharata and Bezbog Chalets and to the Bezbog Ski-Centre (refer to the Pirin Mountain related section herien). There are a number of private hotels in the village as well as a Tourist House. There is a bus line to Sofia, Blagoevgrad, Razlog, Bansko, Gotse Delchev, etc. The bus station is near the railway station, about 1 kilometre east of Dobrinishte.

**Of great interest are the following sights**: the basilica and the necropolis in the Shipotsko Area; Bansko karst springs in the area of Murtva Polyana; a ceramic workshop dating back to late antiquity; the Stana Kale Fortress of late antiquity and a necropolis, a Thracian fortress and necropolis together with early Christian basilica in St. Nickola Area; Thracian mound in the area of Lisicha Mogila; the Birth of the Holy Virgin Church.

## RAZLOG

The town of Razlog (13 403 inhabitants, 825 m above the sea level) is located in the Razlozhka Valley, in the hug of 3 mountains - Rila to the north, Pirin to the south and the Rhodopes to the east. It is nestled among two hills - Golak to the north and Sarovitsa to the south. Nearby flows Mesta River. The town is 155 km to the south of Sofia, 53 km to the south-west of Blagoevgrad, 141 km south-west of Plovdiv and 6 km north of Bansko.

**History.** The past of Razlog to a great extent was predetermined by its central location. The first known settlers in these places were the Tracian tribes *satri* and *dii,* and later - the *kelts* and *slavs*. The accession of Razlog to the Bulgarian State took place in 847 during the time of Khan Pressiyan and its subjugation by the Turks - in 1382. As a name Razlog is mentioned in the Charter of the Bizantine Emperor Vassilii II from 1019. The remains of an early Christian basilica ($4^{th}$ century) near Razlog and the ruins of many churches and sacred places from the Middle Ages and from the period of the Ottoman domination testify for the heroic struggle of the Christian population in defending its faith. After the Berlin Treaty Razlog remained under Turkish domination. Its population actively participated in the struggle for Bulgarian enlightenment, independent church and national liberation. The most turbulent events during the Kressnensko-Razlozhko (1878) and Ilindensko-Preobrazhensko (1903) Uprisings in the Pirin Region developed here. The town had the name *Mehomia* until 1925.

**Landmarks.** The sightseeing tour of Razlog is a pleasant and interesting experience. 41 residential buildings of the **Razlog-Chepino house** revival architectural type have the qualities of monuments of culture. They are mostly at Macedonia Square and in Vuzrazhdane Street. Houses typical for the 1930-ies add specific

# SOUTHWESTERN BULGARIA

outlook to the main square of the town. The Parapounov's House at Macedonia Square (5 minutes from the central square, tel.: 0747 2060) functions as a **Museum of History**. **The Kiprev's House Ethnographic Museum Complex** exibits the old crafts and a wide variety of folk costumes and textiles from the region. The old **St. Georgi Church** from 1834 is not attractive in outlook, but the murals and the wooden panelled iconostasis, decorated with icons and partially with woodcarving have a high artistic value. The comparatively new **Holy Annunciation Church** from 1939 is a very imposing building whose painting still goes on.

**The water mill for processing woollen cloth** at River Yazo (10 minutes to the west of the centre) is attractive and is often used even now.

With the mediation of the museum quide, workshops and houses of masters craftsmen, weavers, knitters and creative artists can be visited - all of them being modern followers of the traditions in artistic clay., wood and textile processing.

**Accommodation and catering.** The opportunities for accommodation in the town are so far comparatively limited: N. Popov Familty-type of Hotel, G. Krainova House-Hotel, M. Kyurkchieva House-Hotel. The three of them are situated in the southern part of Razlog. Numerous catering establishments offer local Bulgarian cuisine - Zahova Maaza Tavern, Koukeri Tavern, Pirin Restaurant, Murata Restaurant and many others.

**Tourist Information.** Chamber of Tourism (tel.: 0747 6471), Pirin Tourist Association (2, Bogomil Street, tel.: 0747 2256, 5278), Mountain Rescue Service (tel.: 0747 2622).

**Transport.** Razlog is a big transport centre as regards to bus services in the region of Pirin. It has regular connections with Sofia, Blagoevgrad, Gotse Delchev, Bansko, Yakorouda, Belitsa, Velingrad and many other smaller settlements. There is a big bus station in the town (tel.: 0747 2040, 2041). Razlog has a railway station, as well, on the narrow-gauge railway line Septemvri-Velingrad-Dobrinishte (tel.: 0747 2690, 2031).

**Surrounding areas.** The central location of Razlog makes it a starting point for two mountains - Rila and Pirin. To **Rila** one can set out along a marked trail from Predela Saddle, distanced at 12 kilometres, where all buses with destination to Blagoevgrad and Sofia have a stop. One can set out from the nearby village of Bachevo (6 km to the north) to the Macedonia Chalet and Chakalitsa Chalet, but the trails are not marked. For the opportunities round **Pirin** refer to the Pirin Mountain related section herein.

In the vicinity of Razlog there are **interesting natural sights and archaeological remains**, situated in picturesque places, that are worth visiting. On the **slopes of Pirin** one can find: the Iztoka protected area (6 km south-west of the town) where the mineral water springs Iztoka and Yazo sprout out, and nearby are the Propadnaloto and Mechata Doupka Caves. The large protected area of Kroushe (7 km south-west), notorious as the only habitat of **arhangeliev lazerpizium** in Bulgaria, where the archaeological remains of a late antiquity and medieval settlement can be found, and close to it - the relics of the medieval Pisanata Church and Byalata Church, as well as the mineral water springs Babina Voda and Vurbovets. In the Kalyata Area (9 km south-west) one can visit the impressive ruins of a late antiquity fortress, the amazingly beautiful Betalovoto Area (10 km south-west) with the comfortable for accommodation and booking Hunter's Home and VANG.L Hotel-Club. On the **slopes of Rila** worthy of special attention are the Stolovatets Area (5 km north-west of Razlog) with the remains of a Thracian sanctuary and the Katarino Area (7 km to the west) with its warm mineral water spring, the remains of the late medieval St. Katerina Church and the regularly held horse races on St. Todor's day (in March).

# SOUTHWESTERN BULGARIA

## BLAGOEVGRAD

The town of Blagoevgrad (71 361 inhabitants, 430 m above sea level) is one of the largest towns in South- Western Bulgaria. It is situated at the foot of the south-western slopes of Rila mountain, on both banks of Blagoevgradska Bistritsa River, within the river-basin of the big Bulgarian River Strouma. It is situated 101 km south of the capital city Sofia, 53 km north-west of Razlog, 65 km north of Sandanski. The town is the main centre of Bulgarian Macedonia. There are 30 mineral springs in catchment with temperature up to 55ºC. This makes it a spa resort. It is a regional administrative centre as well.

**History.** The town originated at the place of the ancient Thracian settlement *Skaptopara,* evidence of which we find in the notorious Skaptoparski inscription from 238. As the town *of Gorna Dzhoumaya* it was mentioned for the first time in 1502, and with the name *Banya* - in 1576. In the past the town was an important roadside fortress. In 17th century monks from the Rila Monastery opened an monastery school. During the second half of 18th and the beginning of the 19th century the town developed as a big centre of craftsmanship and commerce. After the Berlin Treaty, *Gorna Dzhoumaya* (until 1950 the town had this name) remained within the borders of Turkey and for this reason it turned into the cradle of resistance and people's unity. The population actively took part in the uprisings that followed. The town was liberated on 5th October 1912 (the Balkan War) and then had only 7000 inhabitants.

**Landmarks**. The **Museum of History** in Varosha Quarter (tel.: 073 29020, 21170, 29173), the **house-museum of Georgi Izmirliev-Makedoncheto**, Stoyan Sotirov Art Gallery, Stanislav Art Gallery, Petit Bizhou Art Gallery, **Presentation of the Blessed Virgin Church (Vuvedenie Bogorodichno)**, as well as the Revival houses in Varosha Quarter. There are monuments to Ilyo Voivoda, Gotse Delchev, P. K. Yavorov, Cyril and Methodius and to the Macedonian-Odrin volunteers, to those who were killed in the Balkan War (1912-1913). As a cultural centre Blagoevgrad has several theatres - Theatre of Drama (tel.: 073 23475), Puppet Theatre (Varosha Quarter, phone 073 21080, 22210), Chamber Opera House (tel.: 073 20703.

The town is a university centre - American University, Neofit Rilski Southwestern University. Blagoevgrad is famous with its beautiful and functional town centre, all laid out in marble.

**Accommodation.** The accomodation facilities are not sufficient. Only several hotels are available - the 3-star Alen Mak Hotel at the central town square (1, St. St. Cyril and Methodius Street), Bor Hotel and Riltsi Motel - 2 km north of the town, by the motorway to Sofia. There are enough catering facilities, offering original Bulgarian cuisine.

**Tourist information:** Tourist Information Centre, 2770 Blagoevgrad, Varosha

# SOUTHWESTERN BULGARIA

## Blagoevgrad

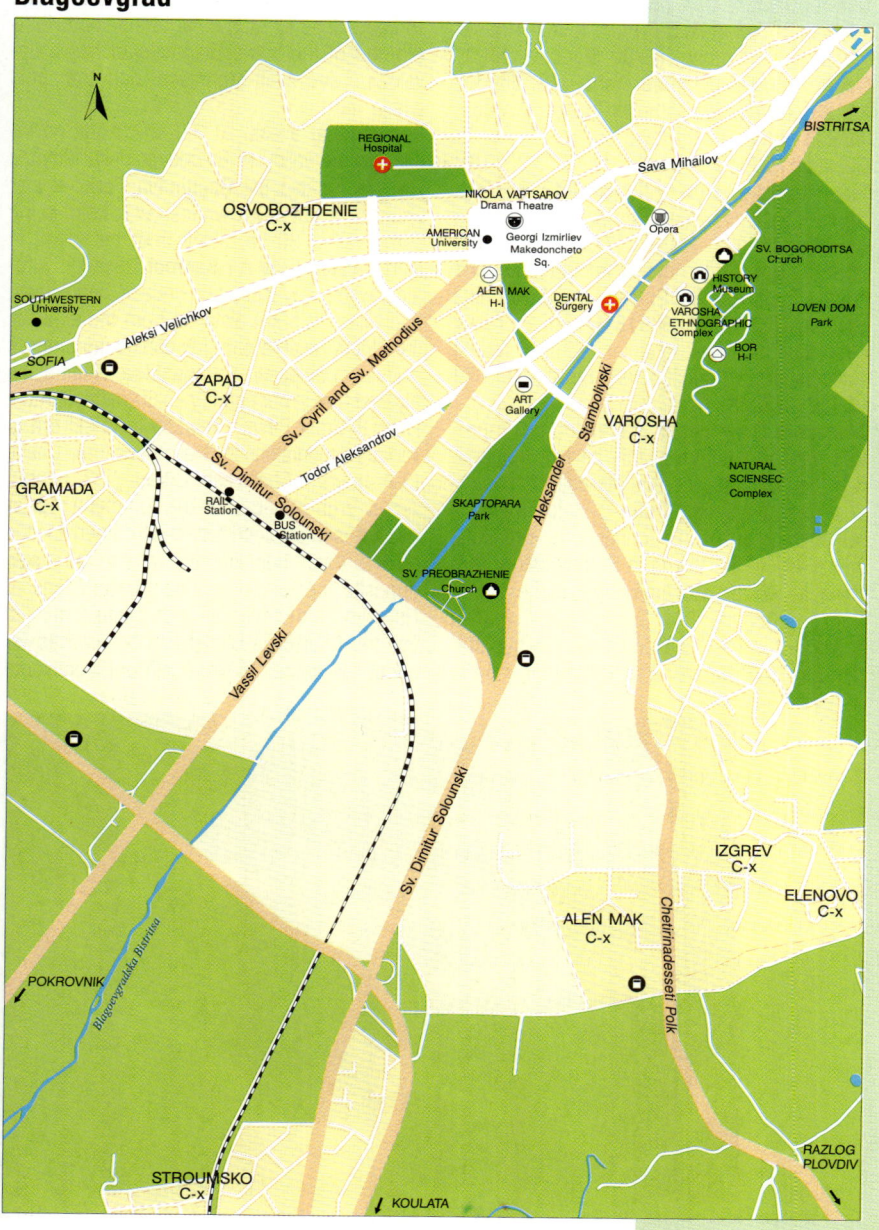

GUIDE BOOK 95

# SOUTHWESTERN BULGARIA

Quarter, tel./fax 073 65458, 36795, e-mail: scabrin@pop3.aubg.bg /Pirin Tourist House/; Council on Tourism (2700 Blagoevgrad, 1, Georgi Izmirliev Square, tel.: 073 65459, 23133); Bureau for Complex Tourist Services, located at the central town square (1, St. St. Cyril and Methodius Square, tel.: 073 23218); Pirin Tourist Forum (tel./fax: 073 65458); Orbita Chain for Youth Tourism (6, Trakiya Street, tel.: 073 23267, 22583, fax: 073 25516); Travel Bite Agency for Students' and Youth' Travel (9, St. St.Cyril and Methodius Str., tel.: 073 36917, 36918). There are many other tourist travel agencies. Aigidik Tourist Association (1, Vassil Levski Street, tel.: 073 26839, 26939).

**Transport.** Blagoevgrad is a major and important transport centre in this part of Bulgaria. It is the main stop on the international motorway and railway line Sofia-Koulata-Athens. It maintains regular bus connections with Sofia and many of the towns in Southwestern Bulgaria, as well as with the villages in the region. It has a regular bus line to the Bulgarian sanctuary - The Rila Monastery. The bus station (tel.: 073 22348, 23750) and the railway station (tel.: 073 22286, 23695, 22174) are situated close to each other at the southwestern end of the town. Blagoevgrad has a developed and well-organised bus transport within the town.

**Surrounding areas**. At 3.5 km to the northeast, in the valley of Blagoevgradska Bistritsa River is located the **Bachinovo Park**, where, annually, in June, a town festival is held. In the same valley, 30 km away from the town, in Northwestern Rila the **Bodrost Resort** is situated, with many recreation houses, bungalows, and villas. At 5 km distance from the resort is the oldest reserve park for coniferous species of trees in Bulgaria - **Parangalitsa**. There is the **highest tree** in our country - a 60-metre spruce. From Bodrost Resort, marked trails set out to various destinations in Rila - Macedonia Chalet (3-4 hours), Chakalitsa Chalet (2-3 hours), Tsarev Vruh (2 hours). In the summer a regular bus line is maintained between the town and the resort. Town bus line No. 4 can be taken opposite the railway station to the village of Hursovo, from where on foot, along a marked trail the Chakalitsa Chalet can be reached for about 5-6 hours. 16 km north of Blagoevgrad

*The Pyramids of Stob*

# SOUTHWESTERN BULGARIA

*The Dzherman River*

## DOUPNITSA

The town of Doupnitsa (38 323 inhabitants, 510 m) is situated at the north-western foot of Rila, on both banks of River German, a left tributary of Strouma, which spings from the Seven Rila Lakes. It is situated 69 km south of Sofia, 38 km south of Kyustendil, 33 km north of Blagoevgrad and 40 km west of Samokov.

**History.** The town originated after the Ottoman invasion. First accounts about it date back to 14th century. Its name is mentioned in the diary of the knight Arnold von Harf who visited the country in 1499. He described it as "a nice town".

The town is the birthplace of the activist from the Revival Period Hristaki Pavlovitch (1804 - 1848), a teacher and a scholar, who published the first Bulgarian textbooks in arithmetics and history ("Tsarstvenik ili Istoriya Bolgarskaya"), the first Bulgarian book in secular script and the first Bulgarian printed publication of Slav-Bulgarian History of Paissii Hilendarski.

**Landmarks. The Town Museum of History** (tel.: 0701 22208), the remains of the **medieval fortress Koulata,** the **clock tower** from 1782, the **St. St. Konstantin and Elena Church**, restored in 1902, the **Holly Virgin Church** from 1789, the **St. Nikola Church** from 1844. The town has its Institute of Pedagogy.

**Accommodation.** Hotel Rila (1, Svoboda Square), Moskva Hotel, in the nearby Sapareva Banya Resort and Panichishte Resort.

**Tourist Information.** Rilski Ezera Tourist Association (1, Kokiche Street, tel.: 0701 22524), Balkantourist Bureau, Mountain Rescue Service (tel.: 0701 25466).

**Transport.** The town is located on the international motorway and the railway line Sofia-Koulata-Athens. Every hour there is a bus to Sofia and Sapareva Banya. There are regular

and several km before the town of Rila is situated the village of Stob with the famous nearby **pyramids of Stob** - exceptionally beautiful and elegant earthen pyramids, finished with rounded rocky blocks. They are moulded in up to 40 metres thick reddish drifts. They are called in different ways - Samodivski Komini (Nymphs' Chimneys), Kouklite (the Dolls), Zuberite (the Pinnacles), Choukite (Rocky Peaks), Bratyata (The Brothers), Svatovete (In-laws), etc. Several regular bus lines pass through the village of Stob on their way to the town of Rila and the Rila Monastery.

**Other interesting sights** around Blagoevgrad: The antique fortress by the village of Klissoura; an ancient settlement, a necropolis and a late antique fortress - close to the Bodrost Resort; another late antique fortress - at about several kilometres from the village Selishte. There are remains of antique fortresses near the village of Gabrovo. There is a medieval fortress between the town and the village of Tserovo. The Ascension of Christ Church near the village of Pokrovnik, the St. Archangel Mihail Church and remains from a late antique fortress near the village of Leshko, the St. Ivan the Precursor Church and St. Georgi Church (built in 1861, presently a monument of culture) in the village of Bistritsa. The rock Markov Kamuk to the south of Mt. Tsarev Vruh. Chernata Skala (The Black rock) - over the right bank of Blagoevgradska Bistritsa River nearby Macedonia chalet.

# SOUTHWESTERN BULGARIA

bus connections with Kyustendil, Blagoevgrad, Razlog, Bansko, Pernik, the Rila Monastery, the town of Rila and all villages in the region. The bus station is located in the western part of the town (tel.: 0701 22368). The railway station is 10 minutes walking time to the south of the railway station (tel.: 0701 25834). There is bus transport within the town.

**Surrounding areas.** The resort town **Sapareva Banya** is 15 km south-east from Doupnitsa in the foothills of North-Western Rila. It is built on the place of an ancient Thracian settlement, which in Roman time grew into the town Germanea. The fortress of Germanea was restored by the Byzantine Emperor Justinian the Great (6$^{th}$ century). The main Roman road from Kyustendil via Samokov and Plovdiv to Tsarigrad passed through it. The fortress walls found there reveal the importance of the settlement. The **St. Nikola Church** from the 12$^{th}$ century is a sight of interest. Sapareva Banya is the birthplace of Velizarius - a renowned leader of Emperor Ustinian (527-565). The present and the past of the resort town are linked with the **curative mineral springs.** The temperature of the water varies between 57° and 100°C, and a 10 metres high gazer of 103.8°C, erupted recently in the process hydrological studies - the hottest spring in Bulgaria and extraordinary rare for Europe. Illness of the bones, joints and the locomotion system, as well as the peripheral nervous system can be treated with it.

There is a Tourist Hostel in Sapareva Banya - Verila, 400 metres to the west of the road for Doupnitsa, close to the spa. It is a complex of 13 two-room bungalows with 2-3 beds. There are several sanatorium in the town, where overnight is also possible, as well as several family hotels. Every hour there is a bus connection with Doupnitsa (at the bus station), as well as with Samokov and other settlements in the region. A private minibus to Panichishte Resort starts several times a day from the centre. There is a marked 2 hours long hiking trail. From Sapareva Banya one can set out for the St. Stefan Monastery (1.30 hours, 6 km along an asphalt road and a trail) and to the Ovcharenski (Shepherd's) Waterfall of River Goritsa (1.15 hours, 5 km along an asphalt road and trail). The resort is one of the most frequented outgoing points for North-Western Rila. Reaching from here **Panichishte Mountain Resort** (1350 m above sea level) one may set out in various directions to the numerous tourist chalets in the region - Pionerska Chalet (1 hour), Lovna Chalet (2 hours), Skakavitsa Chalet (2-2.30 hours), Rilski Ezera Chalet (2.30-3 hours), Vada Chalet (2.30-3 hours), the 7 Rila Lakes Chalet (the most beautiful lake circus in Rila, 3-3.30 hours), Ivan Vazov Chalet (6-8 hours) and others. The resort Panichishte is situated in the surrounding of beautiful old coniferous forests. There are many recreation facilities, profilactoria, big, modern information centre, ski-lift with a good ski-run and several hotels - Bor, Pondera, Doroteya, Zdravets, Lira, Temenuga, CSKA, etc. There are many catering facilities, offering delicious Bulgarian cuisine. The lowest-lying glacier-lake in Rila, the Suhoto Ezero is located in the vicinity of the resort.

From villages near Doupnitsa **interesting mountain passages across North-Western Rila** can be made to the villages of Bistritsa (at 1.30-2 hours distance along a truck road to the Samokovishteto Waterfall of River Bistritsa), Samoranovo (along a marked trail to Otovitsa Challet for 3.30 hours), Ressilovo (along unmarked tracks to Mt. Golyama Sivriya, Mt. Malka Sivriya, Mt. Kabul and others), Ovchartsi (for 30 min along Goritsa River, there is a cascade of 7 waterfalls and the penultimate, the Ovcharenski Waterfall is 39 metres high.). All villages are linked by regular town transport.

# SOUTHWESTERN BULGARIA

## SAMOKOV

The town of Samokov (27 664 inhabitants, 950 m above sea level) is situated in the northern foot of Rila Mountain in the field of the same name, which is the highest in Bulgaria. The longest Bulgarian River Iskar, springing from Rila, flows through it. It is situated 60 km south-east of Sofia, 40 km east of Doupnitsa, 36 km south-west of Ihtiman, 37 km west of Kostenets and 12 km north-west of Borovets Resort. There are 6 more resorts in the region, 2 of them being of international significance. Samokov is the biggest potato producing town in Bulgaria.

**History.** The past of the town is related to iron mining. Once there was a Roman settlement and the present town originated much later - at the beginning of 14$^{th}$ century as an ore mining settlement. At that time, Bulgarian craftsmen had direct contacts with the West-European miners - Saxons, called Sassi, and after their model Saxon furnaces (vidni) were introduced, as well as forgery workshops (madani) with blowers and big hammers (samokovi - from where originates the name of the town) set in motion by water power. When the Turks conquered the town (1372), Samokov was an economic and cultural centre.

Initially, it became municipal and later regional centre, administering today's Blagoevgrad, Doupnitsa, Razlog, Ihtiman and many other settlements. The first Bulgarian printing house of Nikola Karastoyanov was opened here (1827). It is not occasional that in the end of 18$^{th}$ and the beginning of 19$^{th}$ century the most numerous and renowned art (icon-painting, landscape and wood-carving) school of art in our country was founded here - the Samokov School of Art.

Some of the most famous Bulgarian painters were born or worked in Samokov, such as Hristo Dimitrov and his sons Dimitar and Zahari Zograf, Stanislav Dospevski, the son of Dimitar Zograf, Ivan and Nikola Obrazopisovi and others. Konstantin Fotinov, the founder of the first Bulgarian magazine, Lyuboslovie (1844) is also from Samokov. Here was initiated the struggle for independent Bulgarian church, and 50 citizens of Samokov fought as volunteers in the Russian-Turkish War of Liberation. The decline of crafts at the end of the century ruined the town and it lost its economic, cultural and administrative power.

**Landmarks.** The town is rich of cultural and historical monuments. **The Town Museum of History** keeps totems and documents, related to the most specific for the region and the town industrial branch - iron mining, which existed until 1908. The collection of typical for Samokov embroidery of folk patterns and types of textiles is interesting. The **Assumption of the Holly Virgin Church** is one of the most remarkable architectural and artistic monuments in our country. Built in 1790-1791, it is the collective labour of the talented masters of Samokov - builders, wood-carvers and painters. The most remarkable thing in it is the iconostasis created in 1793 and 1821 - a bright example of the woodcarving school of Samokov. The church of Belyo - The **Birth of the Holy Virgin Church** is a monument of culture from 15$^{th}$-16$^{th}$ century with rich mural decorations. The **big drinking-fountain** (the drinking-fountain with the ear ring) dates before 1662. The

*The old cheshma (drinking-fountain)*

# SOUTHWESTERN BULGARIA

Convent (the Metoh - maidens' monastery) was created in 1772. **St. Nikola Church, Belyo's House, Saraf's House**, **Otez Paisii Cultural Centre and memorial,** a monument to the perished in the wars 1912-1918. Many are also the **monuments** dedicated to the Russians who were killed in 1877-1878, to the first printer Nikola Karastoyanov, to Konstantin Fotinov, to Chakur Voivoda (people's defender against the Turks) and others. As a resort, Samokov is attractive with its favourable climatic conditions, the beautiful coniferous forests around, the River Iskar and mostly with its closeness to Borovets and Malyovitsa.

**Accommodation:** Hotel Iskar, the Convent (Metoh) - a romantic, serene and cheap place. There are several family hotels and private lodgings. The resorts in the vicinity offer greater choice for accommodation than Samokov itself. There is a large fruit and vegetable market in the town and many catering facilities offering tasty Bulgarian cuisine. In this respect, the old Saraf's House is recommendable.

**Tourist Information.** Council on Tourism; Rilski Tourist Tourist Society (2, Iskar Bvd., tel.: 0722 22205) - in the green area along the right bank of Iskar River.

**Transport.** Samokov is connected with the country only by bus transport. Between the town and the capital city Sofia there are state bus lines at every hour as well as private minibuses. Every 30 min there are buses to Borovets departing from the bus station. There are no direct bus lines to Malyovitsa, but one has to travel to the village of Govedartsi, from where local transport is called by phone at the Training Centre or at the Hotel. Travelling by private minibus from the town is also possible, but the cost is higher. The town is connected by regular buses with Doupnitsa, Sapareva Banya, Belchin Banya, Dolna Banya, Kostenets and other towns and resorts as well as with all villages in the region. The bus station is in the centre of the town (tel.: 0722 2640). There are bus lines within the town.

**Surrounding areas.** The town is the gate to the highest mountain in Bulgaria and the Balkans - **Rila**. Mostly through the famous **resorts Borovets and Malyovitsa** (refer to the Rila related chapter herein) any point of the mountain can be reached along marked tourist tracks. At a distance of 13 km to the southwest, near the road to Malyovitsa the big **resort village of Govedartsi** is located, also an outgoing point for hikling tours round the highest mountain (refer to the Rila related chapter herein). At 3 km distance to the south of the village there are many recreation homes, profilactoria, administrative and private villas, as well as a tourist facility of the tourist institution - Sotsialen Otdih with 100 beds (in bungalows). Among these is Mechit Chalet with one of the best ski-runs in our country, served by a ski-draw. There are several family hotels in the village, as well and many interesting catering facilities, some offering typical Bulgarian cuisine. There is an Ethnographic Museum. The famous Bulgarian writer and mountaineer Assen Hristoforov spent the greatest part of his life in Govedartsi. There is a bus connection with Samokov several times a day.

**The Belchinski Bani Spa** is siutated at a distance of 13 km to the west of Samokov by the River Palakaria. The temperature of the mineral water is 41.5°C and is curative mainly for diseases of the joints, bones and the locomotion system. There are recreation houses, and open-air pool. At a distance of 10 km from the village of Alino is situated the famous **Alino Monastery** from 16$^{th}$ century. 30 km to the east of Samokov is situated the **resort town of Dolna Banya** with mineral water temperature - 56.3°C. The recreation campus is 5 km to the south, with many recreation facilities and children camps. There is a tourist challet, called Gerginitsa (80 beds). Marked hiking tracks start from the recreation campus across Eastern Rila (refer to the Rila related chapter herein).

# SOUTHWESTERN BULGARIA

## KYUSTENDIL

The town of Kyustendil (50 243 inhabitants, 525 m above sea level) is situated in the most western parts of Bulgaria, only 27 km in the air from the three borders - Bulgarian-Macedonian, Bulgarian-Serbian and Serbian-Macedonian. The town lies in the most southern part of the fertile valley of Kyustendil, on both banks of the not large River Banshtitsa, leaning on the most northern slopes of the more than 2000 m high Ossogovo Mountain bordering with Macedonia. Quite close to the south of the town flows the big Bulgarian River Strouma. It is 90 km from Sofia to the south-west, 70 km to the north-west of Blagoevgrad, at 40 km to the west of Doupnitsa and at 22 km north-east of the border point with Macedonia - Gyueshevo. The town is a spa resort of national significance. A regional administrative centre.

**History.** Kyustendil is one of the most ancient towns in Bulgaria. Fertility and the warm mineral springs attracted the Thracian tribes of *danteleti* and *peontsi,* which founded here a settlement far back in $5^{th}$-$4^{th}$ century BC. During the $1^{st}$ century the Romans turned it into an important fortress, trade venue and renowned spa resort, calling it *Pautalia*. In $4^{th}$ century the fortress Hissarluka was built later reconstructed by the Byzantine Emperor Justinian I (572-565). After 553 the name Pautalia is not accounted any more. In 1019, in the Charter of the Byzantine Emperor Vassilii II, the town was mentioned by the name *Velbuzhd*, probably after the name of a leader. It was integrated to the Bulgarian State during the reign of King Kaloyan (1197-1207). From 1379 to 1395 feudal ruler had been Konstantin Dragash and by his name, later in the $16^{th}$ century, the town was renamed *Kyustendil* (the land of Konstantin).

From the middle of the $15^{th}$ century the Turks began to colonise massively the town and subjected the Bulgarian population to assimilation. In the end of the Ottoman domination and after the Liberation, in particular, the ethnic make up changed due to the numerous Bulgarian emigrants from the lands remaining under Ottoman rule and from the neighbouring settlements. During the Revival the town rapidly grew and developed. A church school was opened (1821), its inhabitants took active part in the ecclesiastical and national struggles. The detachments of haidouts (armed volunteers), lead by Ilyo Voivoda and Roumena Voivoda, one of the few women leaders in Bulgarian history, were very active in the surrounding mountains. Kyustendil was liberated on $29^{th}$ January 1878. After the liberation some of the crafts depending on Turkish markets declined, but tobacco production developed, as well as spa resort activity.

**Landmarks.** The Municipal **Museum of History** (tel.: 078 23534) was founded back in 1897. Each of its departments is accommodated in various cultural and historic monuments: The Department of Archaeology - in a house built in 1575 and notable for its architecture. The Revival and National Liberation Struggle Department - in the house of Ilyo Voivoda, and Ethnography Department and Post-liberation Development Department - in the **Emfiedzhiev's House,** where the commander of the Russian troops was accommodated during the Russian-Turkish War.

**The Vladimir Dimitrov - Maistora Art Gallery** is a sight of a particular interest. (tel.: 078 24469, working hours: 9.30 a.m. - 11.30 a.m. and 2.00 p.m. - 6.00 p.m., Tuesdays through Sunday). It occupies a separate building marked by an original architecture and a modern interior design. The main part of the exposition consists of over 200 masterpieces of the national painter Vladimir Dimitrov-Maistora (the Master). Works of some of the most outstanding artists like Kiril Tsonev, Assen Vassilev, Stoyan Venev, Nikola Mirchev, Boris Kolev and others, who were born or lived in the region are preserved and exhibited in the gallery. An impressive monument to the Maistora is erected in front of the gallery. The **Asclepion of Pautalia** is an impressive Roman spa and shrine, dedicated to the god of health Asclepius, built in $2^{nd}$-$3^{rd}$ century. The whole building occupied an area of 3500 square

# SOUTHWESTERN BULGARIA

metres. Large premises with a heating system, water pipes, architectural fragments and etc. have been discovered. It is located in the foundations of today's buildings of Chifte Banya and the Ahmed Bei Mosque. Other remarkable sights of the town are the following: **St. Georgi Church** (12$^{th}$-13$^{th}$ century) in Kolusha Quarter, **The Holy Virgin Church** (1816) and **St. Dimitur Church** (1866), **Pirkov's Tower** (16$^{th}$-17$^{th}$ century), the wall of the **Devehani Inn** (1606), **Lekarska House**, **Prokopiev's House**, the **old school** (from 1849). There are **monuments** dedicated to the Russian soldiers who perished for the liberation of the town from Ottoman domination, other monuments, commemorating the heroes in the wars (1912-1918), to Ilyo Voivoda, to P. K. Yavorov.

One of the most valuable treasures of the town is the mineral water which springs out of 40 springs in the foot of Hissarluka with temperature up to 73.4ºC. There are several spas, 3 open-air swimming pools, sanatorium, recreation facilities in Kyustendil. The town and its surrounding areas are well-known as the Orchard of Bulgaria - mostly cherries, plums, apples, etc. are grown there.

**Accommodation.** In addition to the resort facilities, there are several hotels in Kyustendil: Velbuzhd Hotel (opposite the railway station and the bus station, 46, Bulgaria Blvd.), Pautalia Hotel (near the central square, 1, Bulgaria Blvd), Sport Palace Hotel (15, Kalossiya Str.), Hissarluka (in park Hissarluka). As regards catering - there are no problems. The town offers a large agricultural market, shops, nice catering facilities, etc.

**Tourist information.** Ossogovo Tourist Association (in the centre, 5, Tsar Mihail Str., tel.: 078 22154, 24232, 22622). Accommodation Bureau (tel.: 078 22090).

**Transport.** Kyustendil is connected with the other parts of the country by bus and railway transport. The town maintains regular every hour bus line with the capital city, as well as with all neighbouring larger towns - Pernik, Doupnitsa, Blagoevgrad and etc. There are regular bus lines to all villages in the region. Due to its closeness to Macedonia, there are enough lines to this neighbouring country. The bus station (tel.: 078 22626) and the railway station (tel.: 078 29164) are next to each other in the northern part of the town. The town is a main station on the Sofia-Kyustendil-Gyueshevo railway line, and in near future it will be linked with the railway network of Republic of Macedonia. Town bus transport functions within Kyustendil.

**Surrounding areas.** In close proximity to the south of the town, at the lowest foothills of Ossogovo Mountain, is situated **Hissarluka Park**. The remains of a fortress, a hotel, catering facilities, walking alleys, alcoves, beautiful villas are situated amidst a splendid coniferous forest, planted in the end of 19$^{th}$ and the beginning of the 20$^{th}$ century. The Spring Festival (organised about 22 March) is annually held there. Kyustendil is the outgoing point to the beautiful **Ossogovo Mountain** with many sights of interest. A marked hiking route leads consecutively to the village of Bogoslov (1.30 hours, there is an asphalt road from Kyustendil to Trite Buki Chalet - 5 km), to Iglika Chalet (about 3 hours, it makes 11 km along the road, tel.: 078 23132), to Ossogovo Chalet (4.30 hours, 17.5 km along the road) and to Trite Buki Chalet (about 5 hours, along the road 19.5 km, the highest chalet of all abovementioned - 1550 m above sea level, tel.: 078 22332). Regular bus transport from the town can be used to the village of Bogoslov. Trite Buki Chalet is a basic outgoing point to many marked hiking tracks across Ossogovo Mountain, to many peaks around, as well as to the highest peak of the mountain - Mt. Rouen (2252 m, situated on the very border line with Macedonia - 4 hours).

More information about the mountain can be obtained by the Tourist Association in the town. 13 km to the south-east of Kyustendil in Nevestino village (a bus stop of the lines between Kyustendil and Doupnitsa) is located **Kadin (Nevestin) Bridge** over the River Strouma - one of the biggest engineering and construc-

# SOUTHWESTERN BULGARIA

tion facilities in our country from 15th century. It was built of hewn granite in 1469-1470 on the ancient and very important in the past Tsarigrad-Plovdiv-Samokov-Kyustendil-Skopie road. It has 5 impressive vaults. A commemoration inscription is preserved. The **village of Shishkovtsi** is 10 km away from the town to the north and a large collection of pictures of Vladimir Dimitrov - Maistora, who lived and worked here for 27 years are preserved in its fund. The village is a station on the railway line Sofia-Kyustendil-Gyueshevo. It has bus connections with the town. 39 km to the north of Kyustendil, on the line to Sofia, the town of Zemen is situated and in its vicinity is the historic **Zemen Monastery**, built in the 11th-12th century. Its murals are the most valuable ones from 14th century in our country. Along a 22 km distance from the town of Zemen to the village of Ruzhdavitsa, between Konyavska and Zemenska Mountains, Strouma River has created a rare, picturesque beauty, called **Zemenski Gorge**. It is a miniature copy of the Iskar Gorge. There are queer rock formations - Agapie, Saraya, Galabinski rocks, Ritlite, vigorous karst springs, unexplored caves, picturesque meanders, sideways running waterfalls, of which the most impressive is the **Polsko-Skakavishki Waterfall** (50 m) below the village of Polska Skakavitsa (there is a railway stop).

At the end of the gorge, near Ruzhdavitsa village, one can enter into the fantastic canyon of the desiccating **River Shegava** (left tributary of Strouma). The railway line Sofia-Kyustendil, from where the whole gorge can be very well observed was laid out in the Zemen Gorge in 1909. There is no road and one can only walk along the railway track.

*Kyustendil. The Mayorska (Major's) Hause*

## PERNIK

The town of Pernik (86 133 inhabitants, 710 metres above sea level) is the largest town in Southwestern Bulgaria after Sofia. It is situated in the high Pernik Plain between Vitosha, Lyulin and Golo Burdo Mountains, along the Strouma River. The town is 30 km to the southwest of Sofia, 59 km to the northeast of Kyustendil and 70 km to the north of Blagoevgrad. The largest coal mining centre in Bulgaria. Regional administrative centre.

**History.** In the 9th century the small Slav settlement of ancient history became part of Danubian Bulgaria. It was named *Pernik (Perunik, Perinik)* probably at its establishment. The town was turned into a strategic medieval centre and the 4.5 m thick fortress walls kept back the Byzantine invasions towards Sredets (Sofia) and Northwestern Bulgaria. The fortress withstood seige twice - in 1004 and in 1016. The local boyar Krakra Pernishki (from Pernik) led the defence. Already under Byzantine domination the fortress survived a devastating earthquake in the middle of 11th century. It was restored and expanded and existed till 1189 when it was destroyed and set to fire by the Serbian joupan Stefan Neman. Because of the numerous raids of kurdzhalii (Turkish brigands) during the Ottoman rule Pernik was a small,

# SOUTHWESTERN BULGARIA

scattered cattlebreeding village. It numbered barely 1000 people in 1879. After the liberation the settlement developed as a mining village. In 1891 Pernik coal mining region was declared state property (first in Bulgaria) and the village became main energy centre of developing Bulgaria. In 1929 Pernik was declared a town.

**Landmarks.** The **Town Museum of History** (in the centre of the town, 2, Phyzkoultourna Str., tel.: 076 25747) displays more than 40 000 exhibits. The **Museum of Coal Mining**. A **Thracian sanctuary** was found in Daskalovo Quarter, nearby Sofia-Koulata road, at the bank of Roudaritsa River. The sanctuary is in the form of an irregular quadrangle and existed in $2^{nd}$ - $4^{th}$ centuary. It is not the only one in Bulgaria but is the best preserved one with most complex construction. The remains of the famous **Pernik Fortress (Krakra)** are nearby the town. The Art Gallery and the Theatre of Drama are open throughout the year. Every five years Pernik hosts The Kukeri and Survakari Festival.

**Accommodation.** Krakra Hotel (near the railway station), Strouma Hotel (1, Krakra Square), Zora Hotel Complex (Iztok Quarter, 27A, Yuri Gagarin Str.).

**Transport:** Nevertheless its proximity to the capital city, Pernik is an important transport centre. The roads and the railway lines head in three main directions - Sofia, Blagoevgrad - Koulata and Kyustendil - Gueshevo. Most intensive are the transport links with Sofia where the greater part of the population of the town do their business. The buses and trains travel in short intervals. The railway station (tel.: 076 23846) and the bus station (tel.: 076 22803) are close to each other in the southwestern part of Pernik. There are railway stops within the town.

**Surrounding areas.** Pernik is a point of departure for tours in the surrounding mountains. **Roudartsi Resort Village** is 13 km to the east (in the western foothills of Vitosha Mountain) and is known for its mineral springs (28.9°C). There is a hotel, rest homes, catering establishments, 3 open-air swimming pools and it is a wonderful place for recreation during the summer. 3 km above Roudartsi in the mountain is the **village of Kladnitsa** (both villages are connected to the town by regular bus lines) which is a departure point to Selimitsa Chalet and hiking tours round Vitosha (refer to the Vitosha Mountain related chapter herein). Nearby the village is the famous **Kladnitsa Monastery.** There are three chalets and Ostritsa Biosphere Reserve in the lower **mountain of Golo Burdo**. Pernik is a strating point to these sights. One can reach Slavei (Nightingale) Chalet for 1 hour along a 4 km road (tourist marking available). Further in the mountain one can visit Kralev Dol Chalet (1.30-2 hours), Ostritsa Reserve (45 min) and Orlite (The Eagles) Chalet (1.30 hours). 10 km northwards is located the biggest village in Pernik region - **Divotino**, which can be used as a point of departure to the other low **mountain - Lyulin**. One can visit the Divotino Monastery, climb the edge of the mountain and then downwards to Bankya resort town or undertake a hiling tour to the only chalet - Bonsovi Polyani. 49 km north-west from Pernik, immediately to the boarder with Serbia is the **town of Trun**, known for its best master builders in Bulgaria. The imposing **gorge of Erma River** is 5 km to the south. The river springs in Serbia, flows in Bulgaria and again in Serbia pours into Nishava River. The high vertical rocks overgrown with lilac raise up to 150 m. A phantastic place! It was namely when he saw this beauty of nature that the famous Bulgarian writer Aleko Konstantinov exclaimed, *"What so about Switzerland!"* The Rui Hotel-Restaurant is nestled in the gorge. 4 km in the direction of the town (1 km from Trun) is Erma Chalet. The well-known St. Archangel Mihail Monastery is 30 min away from the chalet. In Trun one can find accommodation in the Virad Erma Hotel (22, Vassil Stoyanov Str.). Regular bus line links Pernik to Trun.

# SOUTHWESTERN BULGARIA

## PIRDOP and ZLATITSA

The two small towns of Pirdop (8548 inhabitants) and Zlatitsa (5648 inhabitants) of the sub-Balkan Range are located in the Zlatitsa-Pirdop Valley, between Stara Planina Mounatin (to the north) and Sredna Gora Mountain (to the south) at 680 m above sea level. The distance of 3-4 km between them is symbolic and not before long they will be integrated into one. Moreover, this area accommodates the Copper Works as well - the largest industrial enterprise in the region, providing work to the greater part of the local population. The two towns are situated 77 km east of Sofia, 27 km south of Etropole, 32 km north of Panagyurishte and 32 km north-west of Koprivshtitsa.
**History.** The territory of today's towns of Pirdop and Zlatitsa was inhabited 6000 years ago. The ancient Roman road connecting Ulpia Trayana with Ulpia Serdika passed from here. This area was often visited by Alexander the Great, by the Byzantine emperors Isaac Komnin and Isaac II Angel.
It is known that **Zlatitsa** in $4^{th}$ century BC existed under the name of *Ulpia Aurea* and it is supposed that Emperor Trayan established the settlement in its today's location in the beginning of the $2^{nd}$ century. The first written evidence is traced in the notorious Vergin Charter of King Konstantin Assen (1257-1277), where the settlement of *Zlatitsa* is mentioned. The Byzantine chronicler Dukas who visited Zlatitsa in 1445 informs about the pass (of Zlatitsa or Kashana) and the settlement. Near the town took place the notorious battle of Zlatitsa between the troops of the Hungarian King Vladislav III (Varnenchik), the Transilvanian Voivoda (leader) Yanush Huniyadi and the Serbian Prince Georgi Brankovich against the Turks.
Although the Bulgarians were a minority, in 1859 they built the Orthodox Church of St. Martyr Georgi and a school with the church. The convent with the church sheltered the Apostle Vassil Levski in 1872, who came to organise a revolutionary committee.

After the liberation of the town from Turkish rule on $3^{rd}$ of January 1878, it was almost deserted by the fleeing Turks. Many Bulgarian newcomers arrived from Macedonia. Zlatitsa gradually declined because of the absence of markets for its handicraft goods, but later cattle breeding and agriculture developed and brought it up. It is interesting to know that together with Sofia, Turnovo and Plovdiv, Zlatitsa was nominated to become the capital of Bulgaria after the liberation.
The name of **Pirdop** is among those unknown names whose origin history keeps in secret. Numerous are the legends, trying to suggest an explanation, but not a single one, so far, has become completely convincing. The Thracian mounds and the remains of medieval fortresses unequivocally indicate that various tribes interrelated their destinies here for many centuries. The first written traces of Pirdop date back to $12^{th}$ century, when the Pirdop Chronicle of Apostles' Deeds was written - a valuable monument in writing, kept in the St. St. Cyril and Methodius National Library.
During the years of the Bulgarian Revival, the entrepreneurial citizens of Pirdop managed to turn their settlement into an economic and cultural centre. In 1698, the Protopopinski (Pirdopski) collection manuscript was written by the teacher Georgi, thus initiating the literary activity in the settlement and its vicinities. The same author wrote the Tihonravov Damaskin,

# SOUTHWESTERN BULGARIA

kept in the State Library in Moscow. Originally an ecclesiastical school was founded and later, in 1820 - the first municipal school in spoken Bulgarian with the teacher Todor Pirdopski.

The local folkstyle abi (homespun coarse woollen cloth and upper men's garment made of it), shayatzi (woollen cloth), braids, woollen bed covers and blankets, candles and soap were highly valued at the markets in Vienna, Budapest, Tsarigrad, Thessaloniki, Alexandria. Only from the manufacturing of woollen braids by the 700 water-driven looms the town earned an annual income of over 9 000 000 Turkish grosh! The destiny of Pirdop after the Liberation is the same as it was of Zlatitsa - loss of markets, decline and strive for survival against a background of overall national boom.

**Landmarks.** In Pirdop these are the **Lukanov's House Museum** (17, Slavtsi Street, tel.: 07181 5073), **Nikola Poushkarov Museum** - in the native house of the scientist who put the foundations of soil studies in Bulgaria (4, Nikola Poushkarov Street). The outstanding Bulgarian writer and public figure Todor Vlaikov was born here.

The old **Revival Period houses** of Sokolov's and Boyanov's are places of interest in Zlatitsa. The **clock tower** of 1829, built of stone blocks is 16.70 metres high. The clock still strikes every hour.

**Accommodation.** In Pirdop: Borova Gora Hotel, Zdravets Tourist House (15th Street) and Sredna Gora Hotel Complex (Todor Vlaikov Square).

In Zlatitsa: Frezia Hotel (3, Al. Stamboliiski Street). There are numerous coffee-bars, confectioneries, restaurants and other recreational facilities in both towns.

**Tourist Information.** Except at the municipalities and at the hotels, information can be obtained from the Tourist Associations, as well. In Pirdop - Paskal Tourist Association (in the Zdravets Tourist House). In Zlatitsa - Svishti Plaz Tourist Association.

**Transport.** Both towns are situated on the main motorway and railway Sofia - Karlovo - Burgas. Buss connections with all villages and towns in the vicinity are regularly maintained. There is a bus station in Pirdop (Tsar Osvoboditel Blvd., tel.: 07181 5016, 5002) and separate railway stations in both towns. The Pirdop railway station (tel.: 07181 5771) is in the northern part of the town and is marked for its mamonth trees, brought from North America and planted there in 1932. The railway station of Zlatitsa is in the western part of the town (tel.: 0728 2300). Between them there is a railway stop at the Copper Works.

**Surrounding areas.** The **ruins** from the time of Justinian I are situated 6 km to the north-east of Pirdop. Near them, there are remains of an **ancient settlement,** most probably it was the ancient Thracian town *Bourdapa*. Quite close to the modern town of Pirdop there are **remnants of the Neolithic era** and in its vicinity - many **Thracian mounds.**

9 km south of Zlatitsa is located the **Old Kemer - a bridge**, spanning over the River Topolnitsa from Roman time. The **Spassovo Kladenche Church Complex** is 500 metres away from Zlatitsa. The **Kambana Park-Monument** is located in the village of Petrich, in the region of Zlatitsa. Huddled between two mountains, Pirdop and Zlatitsa are points of departure for hiking tours round them.

The Kashana Chalet is located in the Zlatitsa Pass (Kashana) in the Stara Planina Mountain, 15 km from Zlatitsa. Also from Zlatitsa, within a 3-hour walk along a marked trail (there is a 12 km long tarmac road) one can reach the Svishti Plaz Chalet. For bookings call tel.: 0728 2207. There is another chalet in the Balkan at 2-hour distance along a marked track from Pirdop - the Paskal Chalet. The three chalets are points along the Kom - Emine route. In the opposite direction, to the south, at 18 km distance, along an asphalt road in Sushtinska Sredna Gora, is located the **Panagyurski Kolonii Recreation Campus** with Raina Knyaginya Chalet. The regular buses connecting Zlatitsa and Panagyurishte stop there.

At about 10 km east of Pirdop is located the **Dushantsi Dam** - a beautiful artificial lake, a wonderful recreation place, perfect for fishing and sports.

# SOUTHWESTERN BULGARIA

## PANAGYURISHTE

The town of Panagyurishte (21 228 inhabitants, 530 m above sea level) is situated in a small valley in Sashtinska Sredna Gora, on both banks of Luda Yana River. It is 91 km east of Sofia, 43 km north of Pazardzhik and 37 km south of Zlatitsa. Its name is of Greek origin and means a fair venue but to modern Bulgarians it has become the symbol of Bulgarian strive for freedom.

**History.** Close to the present town a Thracian settlement existed even in the 4$^{th}$ century BC. In the 13$^{th}$ century the settlement at this place had the name *Kamenograd* (Litopolis). It got remarkably developed and won notoriety during the Turkish domination, when it was a privileged village for accommodating soldiers. It had a special status, which was kept until 1839. According to it no Ottoman Turk was entitled to settle or even to overnight in Panagyurishte. But the privilege did not save it from the raids of the kurdzhalii (Turkish brigands) - it was plundered and set to fire many times.

Nevertheless, in 18$^{th}$ century Panagyurishte reached its zenith. Its main way of life was cattle breeding. Woollen clothes, abi (homepsun coarse wollen cloth and upper men's garment made of it), sacks and etc. were manufactured and sold across the whole Ottoman Empire. The citizens of Panagyurishte were famous as tradesmen of cattle (dzhelepi). They were also tax collectors (beglikchii). Very early a church school was opened, which in 1839 become a mutual school. A community cultural centre was founded in 1865, which turned into a cradle of Bulgarian spirit and consciousness.

The popularity of this small town in Sredna Gora Mountain arose mostly from its particular role during the April Uprising (1876), when it became the centre of the IV Revolutionary District and in fact of all epic events. The apostles Volov and Benkovski organized a powerful and active revolutionary committee, managing to raise the whole population to an armed struggle for freedom. The first Bulgarian Republic was born with the president of the transitional government in Sredna Gora - Pavel Bobekov. Here the flag of the uprising was waved, sewn by the teacher from Panagyurishte, Raina Knyaginya, it had the words *"Freedom or Death"* embroidered on it. After exultation came defeat. In spite of the heroism and the self-sacrifice of the defendants, the much more numerous and better-armed enemy entered the town. Panagyurishte was burnt down. For their boldness to call themselves free, 650 citizens of Panagyurishte paid with their lives, *"immortalising the name of their town"* (Zahari Stoyanov). On 11$^{th}$ January the town was liberated from Turkish rule.

**Landmarks**. The **Town Museum of History** is almost wholly dedicated to the epoch of Revival and the April Uprising. The **Doudekov's House** (now an **Ethnographic Museum**) illustrates the way of life in the town at the end of the 19$^{th}$ century. Here were the headquarters of general Dandeville in 1878. The **Toutev's House** is famous for the fact that the uprising was declared in it on 20$^{th}$ April 1876. The native **house of Marin Drinov**, the famous Bulgarian historian, professor and social personality, the first minister of education in newly liberated Bulgaria. **Raina Knyaginya Museum House** with its preserved revival architecture. In its courtyard are the bones of the national heroine, who sewed the flag of the uprising. The **Lekov's, Mateev's, Landzhev's, Smol's houses, Fidzhek's shops,** etc. Interesting is the **The Holy Virgin Cathedral Church** (1818), the **St. Georgi Church** (1856) and in particular the **memorial complex**, erected at Manyovo Burdo in commemoration to the 100$^{th}$ anniversary

# SOUTHWESTERN BULGARIA

of the April Uprising. There burns an everlasting fire. Every year on 20th April, Panagyurishte is the centre of the national celebrations, commemorating April 1876. The town is the native place of Pavel Bobekov (main organiser of the uprising in the town and chairman of the transitional Bulgarian government within the short-lasting days of freedom), Nesho Bonchev - the first Bulgarian literary critic, Vasilii Cholakov - an ethnographer and dedicated supporter of Bulgarian Enlightenment, Pavel Deliradev - a notorious Bulgarian social personality and mountaineer, true follower of Aleko Konstantinov.

In 1949 near the town **the Golden Treasure of Panagyurishte** was discovered - a unique Thracian treasure from the 3rd century BC, unique in the world with its original shapes and decorations. It has been exhibited all over the world, thus making the name of its "native" town famous as well as the name of Bulgaria. At present it is kept in the Archaeological Museum of Plovdiv.

**Accommodation.** Kamengrad Hotel (House of Miners, 1, Bobekov Square. Bounai Tourist House located in the western part of the town, 15 minutes from the centre, in the boarding house of the Technical College of Optics (26, Stoyan Trendafilov Street). Some of the old houses of Panagyurishte host original taverns, offering local cuisine within the old Bulgarian folklore surroundings.

**Tourist information.** It can be obtained at the hotel, at the Tourist House and at Bounai Tourist Association (1, Doctor Long Str,).

**Transport.** The town is connected with the remaining part of Bulgaria by bus and railway transport. Regular buses run to Sofia, Plovdiv,

*The golden treasure from Panagyurishte*

Pazardzhik, Zlatitsa and Pirdop and to all smaller settlements around it. There is a bus station (tel.: 0357 3383) and a railway station - the last along the line Plovdiv - Panagyurishte (tel.: 0357 3623).

**Surrounding areas.** Ten km to the north-west is located the **historical place Oborishte**, on the small River Panova, amidst an old beech forest. Here, on 14th April 1876 convened the revolutionary committees of IV Revolutionary District (the First Great National Assembly in the history of Bulgaria), which took the decision for the declaring of the April Uprising. A modest commemorating monument was erected in 1926. 800 metres to the south of it there is a chalet with the same name with 24 beds (booking is made at Bounai Tourist Association in Panagyurishte). An asphalt road reaches it or walking takes 2.30 hours along a special trail. The chalet can be also reached by bus to the nearest village of Oborishte and from there 6 more kilometres by car or on foot.

**Panagyurski Kolonii Recreation Campus** is situated at the highest point along the road between Panagyurishte (15 km) and Zlatitsa at 1050 m above the sea level and all busses stop there. There are many recreation houses, villas, children's camps, as well as the Raina Knyaginya Chalet (Bounai Tourist Association in Panagyurishte). The **village of Banya** is located 11 km to the south-west of the town on both banks of the River Mechka. Twenty Thracian tombs were discovered round the village. Numerous are the ruins of ancient buildings and fortresses, the most famous of which is **Kaleto Fortress** (Gradishteto), erected in 11th-14th century. The **St. Nikolai Church**, dating back to 1856, is also interesting. The

# SOUTHWESTERN BULGARIA

village is the birthplace of the famous priest Gruyo Ban-ski - a colourful personality from the time of the April Uprising. There is a monument dedicated to him. The village of Banya is famous for its mineral water, which can be used for curative purposes. The spa was constructed in 1936. The village has a regular bus connection with Panagyurishte and Pazardzhik.

Panagyurishte can be a departure point for hiking tours to Sushtinska Sredna Gora. It is most convenient to go to the Panagyurski Koloni and from there to proceed along the well-marked trails to: Bratiya Chalet (2 hours), Mt. Bratiya (1 hour), Sakardzha Chalet (3 hours), Manzul Chalet (Pavel Deliradev - 2.30 hours) and also to Oborishte (4 hours). It is possible to walk through the mountain to the town of Koprivshtitsa (5-6 hours) - an easy and pleasant one day track with a respite at Manzul Chalet (Pavel Deliradev Chalet).

## KOSTENETS

The municipality of Kostenets (about 17 000 inhabitants, 500-600 m above sea level) with almost all its settlements is a spa and a resort region of national importance, situated in the valley of Dolna Banya, along the upper flow of River Maritsa. Centre of the municipality is the **town of Kostenets** (10 532 inhabitants) and the most notorious resort centres are the following: Momin Prohod (now a quarter of the town of Kostenets), **Momina Banya** (also a quarter of the town), **Kostenets** and **Pchelinski Bani recreation campuses.** The centre of the municipality is 76 km to the south-east of Sofia, 80 km west of Plovdiv, 27 km east of Borovets Resort.

**History.** The past of this region is related to many historical events. Today's village of

*A view of Panagyurishte*

# SOUTHWESTERN BULGARIA

Kostenets (7 km to the south of the town and the railway station) is proud with its longest history. It emerged in the early Middle Ages and existed from $7^{th}$ to $14^{th}$ centuries under the name of *Konstanzia*. It is mentioned in a Turkish register from 1576. According to the Turkish traveller Evliya Chelebi, Kostenets was an old Wallachian town which long resisted the Turkish oppressors. It is presumed that Kostenets is the birthplace of the man of letters Konstantin Kostenechki. The first school was opened in 1856 and the community cultural centre in 1880. At the Cherkovishte Hill, to the west of the village there are the remains of a basilica ($5^{th}$-$6^{th}$ century) and of a medieval fortress. A church from 1857 is still preserved.

**Trayanovi Vrata** is a **historical place** at the saddle between the Mt. Eledzhik and Mt. Golak of Sredna Gora. There, close to the Thracian settlement, was constructed a Roman road station, called *Sineum*. From it the Trayan Pass begins, also called Souki (narrow valley). Trayanovi Vrata (Trayan's Gates) was 15 steps wide and 24 steps high. In these area in 986 Samuil's soldiers won an important victory over the Byzantines, led by Emperor Vasilii II, delaying by this the fall of Bulgaria under Byzantine domination with 22 years. A small memorial plate commemorates this event.

During the Turkish occupation the functions of Trayanovi Vrata as a keeper of the pass declined. Unused and unkept, it started to ruin. To the south of the great gate remains of old buildings are still preserved, probably parts of a fortress with a diametre of 30 metres and thickness of the wall 2 metres. Greatest interest arises **Markova Mehana (Kaleto)** where a large building has been discovered - a garrison with a spacious inner yard, open ground floor, 6 entrances and three inner turrets made of stone and 5 layers of flat bricks. The fortress (there are preserved parts of it 2-5 metres high) had unique water equipment and an underground passage. Archaeologists definitely prove the usage of this location during the Middle Ages ($9^{th}$-$10^{th}$ century), which made it an important Bulgarian stronghold. Since antiquity, this old pass has continued to serve the people. The new Trakiya motorway passes under it. The distance between the eastern entrance of the two parallel tunnels to Trayanovi Vrata and the fortress is 500-600 metres. This historic location can be reached fastest along the motorway (from Sofia - 64 km and from Plovdiv - 72 km). The road from Kostenets or from Ihtiman to Mirovo station is convenient, and from there to the pass it takes 1.20 hours along a marked route.

**Spas.** From times immemorial the present Kostenets quarter, called **Momin Prohod** has been renowned for its spas which were used in Roman times. Now the mineral water of the 9 natural springs is collected in one catchment with a temperature of 65ºC. The output is 920 l/min, and in radioactivity it rates second in Bulgaria (after the water from Narechen), third in Europe and $25^{th}$ in the world. It cures illnesses of the bones and joints and the locomotion system, the peripheral nervous system, the respiratory system, the lungs and etc. The resort is famous abroad with its good results in healing of poliomyelitis and spasmic children's paresis. There are many sanatorium, recreational facilities, and villas.

**Kostenets Recreation Camp** is situated 9 km south of the town and the station of Kostenets and at 2 km above the village of Kostenets, right in the northern foots of the Belmeken sub-part of Eastern Rila. Three mineral springs with total capacity of 300 l/min and temperature about 47ºC have been in catchment. The water has similar curative properties with the one of Momin Prohod. There is a large spa complex, recreation homes, open-air swimming pool, villas, a pond, wonderful surrounding areas (the Kostenets Waterfall of Stara River, glorified

# SOUTHWESTERN BULGARIA

by Ivan Vazov, etc.) The combination of curative mineral water, mild mountainous climate and beautiful environment makes it attractive throughout the year.

**Pchelinski Bani** is a spa resort 8 km to the noth-west of the town of Kostenets and 2 km from the village of Pchelin. It is situated on the southern slopes of Ihtimanska Sredna Gora. The mineral water is 73ºC hot at the spring. In curative properties it is similar to the others. There is a recreational children's home, recreational facilities, numerous villas, etc.

**Accommodation.** Accommodation facilities are available in all resort centres. In the town the Konstanzia Hotel is on the central square, opposite the bus station and the railway station. Some of the rest homes accomodate guests to overnight. Private lodgings are available, as well. There is an Accommodation Bureau in the town of Kostenets.

**Tourist information** can be obtained at the municipalities, at the hotels, at the Accommodation Bureau and at Ravni Chal Tourist Associaton in the village of Kostenets (tel.: 07142 3281).

**Transport.** The town has one railway station and one railway stop (Momin Prohod) on the line Sofia-Plovdiv. The railway station is in the centre of the town of Kostenets (tel.: 07142 3126). There are regular bus lines within the whole municipality and the town has bus connections with Samokov, Dolna Banya, Ihtiman and others. The bus station is in the centre, close to the railway station (tel.: 07142 2321).

The municipality is a departure point for marked tourist routes across **Eastern Rila**, mainly through Kostenets Recreation Campus (refer to Rila related section herein). The resort of Dolna Banya, as well as Borovets Resort are in close proximity to the town. These sites can be reached by the regular bus transport and can add colour to one's stay in the municipality of Kostenets.

## VELINGRAD

The town of Velingrad (25 509 inhabitants, about 750 metres above sea level) is our largest spa resort. It is situated amidst the wonderful natural surrounding of the Western Rhodopes, in the western part of the Chepino Valley. It was formed in 1948 by 3 villages: Kamenitsa, Ludzhene and Chepino. The town of Velingrad is located 120 km south-east of Sofia, 86 km south-west of Plovdiv, 48 km south-west of Pazardzhik, 69 km north-east of Razlog, 31 km south of Septemvri and 26 km north-west of Batak.

**History.** The numerous archaeological findings, such as stone and bone tools, bronze articles and others imply existence of life since ancient times in these places. Long-lasting traces have left Thracians, Slavs, Byzantines, and Romans. The traces, however, left by the Ottomans are bloody and morbid, related with forced conversion to Islam of the local Christian population. A moving account about that time has left priest M. Draginov.

The national poet Ivan Vazov wrote at length about it in his travel notes from the Rhodopes. Later, when the spark of the Revival was kindled, the local population also made its contribution to the patriotic acts.

The St. Trinity Church was built in Kamenitsa in 1816, which by that time was just a small underground monastery, and in 1846 the first school was opened with Iliya Zhdrakov as teacher. At the liberation time the settlements, forming the modern town Velingrad were in a sorry plight. Gradually the local population become conscious of the environment granted by nature, so that the town developed into a modern resort of national and international significance.

There is a Town Museum of History (tel.: 0359 22591).

**Present.** The abundance of mineral waters, the modern spa, resort facilities, mild cli-

# SOUTHWESTERN BULGARIA

mate and wonderful natural conditions, offer recreation to over 200 000 people here every year. The valley of Chepino is famous as the sunniest part of the Rhodopes. The sunny days come up to 74% annually. Fogs are a rare phenomenon, the average January temperature is 1.8ºC and in July it does not rise above 18.7ºC. Summer is cool, winter is mild and autumn is warm and pleasant. In winter, there are wonderful conditions for skiing. Snow does not melt for a month and a half.

The greatest treasure of Velingrad are the mineral water springs (approximately 80 in number) with a temperature from 22º to 90ºC and an output capacity of 130-140 l/sec. The catchment area is about 800 km$^2$. It is formed in 3 thermal zones: Chepino, Ludzhene and Kamenitsa, whereas half of the water resources come from the Chepino basin. The mineral water of Velingrad in quality and composition combine the curative qualities of the water in Hissar, Banya (Karlovo region) and of those of Narechenski Bani. They are used for treatment of the joint and bone locomotive system, the stomach and intestinal tract, the liver, skin diseases, urological diseases and others. Tens of spas, treatment centres, recreation centres, private villas and other infrastructure are built.

The **karst spring of Kleptouza** in Chepino is a natural landmark of interest (the biggest karst spring in Bulgaria, output 570 l/sec). Near it, there is a beautiful lake and good tourist infrastructure - favourite place for rest and recreation of the local citizens and the guests of the resort as well.

**Accommodation.** As one of the biggest resort centres in Bulgaria, Velingrad offers comparatively good capacities to accommodate its numerous guests. Some of the sanatorium and the recreation facilities provide beds to tourists - Kamena Balneological Centre (Chepino Quarter, 4, Edelweiss Str.), Kolyu Ficheto Recreation House (3, Tsar Samuil Str.), Velina Hotel, Zdravets Hotel (Fontanite Square), Kleptouza Hotel (Chepino Quarter), Mariela Hotel (90, Suedinenie Blvd.), Sofia Hotel (1, Kisselets Str.), Olympic Hotel-Restaurant (300, Suedinenie Blvd.), Kislovodsk Tourist House (Ludzhene Quarter), Bulgaria Tourist House (Chepino Quarter), the family-type hotels Toto-Chance, Elbrous, Vitosha, Velingrad, Filipopol, Skaya, Markita, Topevi Elite Lodgings, Presslav, Camping Site 4th kilometre. Private lodgings are also available. There is a great choice of entertainment facilities as well as restaurants where local Bulgarian cuisine can be tasted.

**Tourist information.** Council on Tourism (4600 Velingrad, 35, Khan Asparuch Str., tel.: 0359 25659 and 02 833902), at the hotels, at Yundola Tourist Association (16, Khan Asparuch Str., tel.: 0359 28467), at the sanatorium and resort complex.

**Transport.** The resort is connected with the remaining part of the country by bus and railway transport. There are regular bus connections with Sofia, Plovdiv, Pazardzhik, Peshtera, Rakitovo, Blagoevgrad, Batak, Surnitsa and many other smaller settlements, mainly in the Rhodopes. There are two bus stations - Beev Bus Station (tel.: 0359 23073) and Tonev Bus Station (tel.: 0359 23285). Velingrad is a main stop along the narrow-gauge railway line Septemvri - Dobrinishte. There are 2 railway stations - Central Railway Station in Chepino Quarter and Yug (South) Railway station in Ludzhene Quarter (tel.: 0359 24041). Bus transport functions within the town as well.

**Surrounding areas.** At a distance of 16 km from Velingrad is situated **Yundola Recreation Campus**, spread in the saddle of the same name, dividing the Rhodopes from Rila Mountain (refer to Rhodopes related chapter herein). To the west of the town, at the narrow-gauge railway line to Dobrinishte is located the highest above sea level railway station on the Balkan Peninsula - **Avramovi Kolibi** (1455 m above sea level), also in the

# SOUTHWESTERN BULGARIA

dividing saddle between Rila and the Rhodopes, called Avramova Saddle.

**The village of Dorkovo** is 14 km north-east of the town. In its very end in 1985, the largest paleontological finding of mastodons (from 5-6 million years ago) was discovered. The village has a regular bus connection with Velingrad.

**Tsepina** - Medieval Bulgarian fortress is located 6 km (along an asphalt road) to the north-west of Dorkovo village. One can walk starting from Tsepina railway station on the narrow-gauge railway line Septemvri-Dobrinishte along a marked trail for about 2.30 hours. The fortress was erected between 11th and 13th century on the place of an old Thracian settlement. In the beginning of the 13th century it had been the stronghold of the Bulgarian boyar Aleksii Slav. The Ottoman invaders destroyed it. Remains of the fortress wall, water reservoirs, churches and other buildings are now preserved.

**The Chepino River Bed** - the valley of River Chepinska between the Rhodope subparts Alabak (to the west) and Karkaria (to the east) is about 30 km long. It is a picturesque gorge, through which pass the motorway and the narrow-gauge railway line from Septemmvri to Dobrinishte. Being carried by the low speed **romantic train,** one can admire the picturesque beauties of the surroundings. Velingrad is a point of departure for many tourist routes, mostly in the Phodopes' elevation **Alabak** (refer to the Rodopes related chapter herein).

*A view of Velingrad*

# CENTRAL SOUTHERN BULGARIA

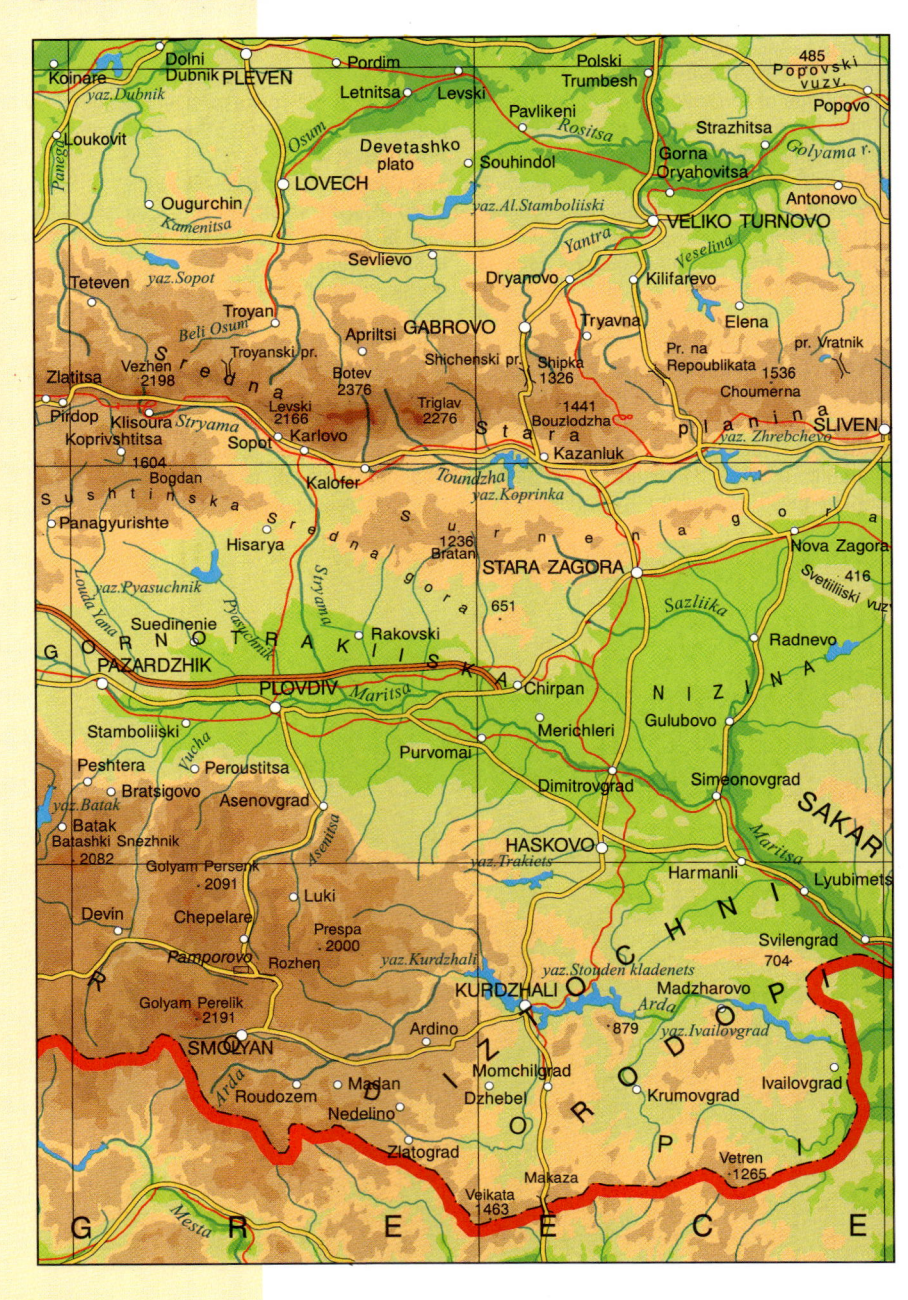

# CENTRAL SOUTHERN BULGARIA

## BATAK

The town of Batak (4488 inhabitants, 1036 metres above sea level) is situated at the northern foothill of the Batak Mountain (Western Rhodopes), along the two banks of the Stara Reka River. It is situated 36 km south of Pazardzhik, 16 km south of Peshtera, 26 km south-east of Velingrad, 51 km north of Dospat, as well as at the distance of 156 km south-east of the capital Sofia. The name of this little town is sacred for every Bulgarian. It is a symbol of martyrdom and self-sacrifice in the name of freedom!

**History.** In spite of the ruins of ancient fortresses and towns, it cannot be stated with certainty when today's Batak originated. Its name was mentioned for the first time in 1592 on the e stone embedded in the drinking-fountain (cheshma) at the Krichim Monastery. The settlement grew up substantially after the Bulgarians from the region of Chepin River and its mountain valley migrated escaping from the forceful conversion to Islam. During the pogroms by the kurdzhalii (Turkish brigands) it was repeatedly ruined and rebuilt again. In 1819 Priest Konstantin wrote that it was "a little timber village with 100 houses". According to the traveller A. Vikenel, in 1847 the village numbered 1000 houses and in 1865 Zakhary Stoyanov indicated that it had "400 houses, a lot of inns, a multitude of cuttings and 1500 inhabitants". It can be stated with certainty that as of the end of the Ottoman Rule Batak was already a big and wealthy settlement with over 9000 inhabitants. In 1813 the citizens of Batak built **St. Nedelya Church**, which was to enter the tragic history of Batak and Bulgaria 63 years later. The school was opened in 1835 and Nayden Ivanovich was the first teacher in it.

The name of the town is related most of all to the April Uprising. On 21 April 1876 its inhabitants announced the beginning of the uprising. Like everywhere else the initial enthusiasm and exultation were followed by an utter defeat but the defeat in Batak was more than terrible and reckless! Five thousand people died, the doom of the 2 thousand men, women and children who found their death in the small St. Nedelya Church, which turned out to be their last stronghold, hope and... tomb, too, being exceptionally dramatic and tragic. The stories of unparalleled heroism, self-sacrifice and inexorability told by the few people who survived this sanguinary Bacchanalia added up to dozens.

The brightest intellects of mankind raised a voice of protest and indignation in answer to this outrageous occurrence - Victor Hugo, William Gladstone, Makgahan, Dostoevski, Lev Tolstoy. Zakhary Stoyanov wrote: *"Kneel, kind readers, hats off! Batak with its ruins is in front of us. I summon everyone who is thoroughly Bulgarian, everyone who is honourable and homeland loving, to be with us here at this Bulgarian sanctuary, at this sacrificial altar to our Freedom, where, the blood of thousands of martyrs, saints, of about a hundred little children, of countless innocent lasses and lads was shed. Batak, glorious and unfortunate Batak! Should a Bulgarian heart be ever found not to palpitate at the sole pronunciation of your own name? I am standing in awe before your magnificence, History shall pay reverence to you, too."* The people's poet Ivan Vazov added: *"The Cheops Pyramid would be insufficient as a memorial to Batak."*

Those who remained alive in Batak welcomed the Russian Army of Liberation on 20th January 1878.

**Landmarks**. In the first place this is the already mentioned little stone **church of St. Nedelya**, turned into a **museum and charnel-house**. Even nowadays the bones of the heroes, chopping-log, the traces of yataghans and bullets remind of those terrible and grandiose days. It is situated in the centre of the little town. The town **Museum of History** is located in a new building and houses over 500 exhibits of the history of Batak. The several **old Batak**

# CENTRAL SOUTHERN BULGARIA

**houses** restored and proclaimed as cultural monuments are of interest, too.

**Accommodation.** Bulgaria Hotel (in the centre of the town); Kolarov's House Tourist Hostel (at the distance of 300 metres from the centre of the town, 2, Karlushka Street); private lodgings.

**Tourist information:** at the hotel, in the tourist hostel, at Batyovtsi Tourist Association (1, Osvobozhdenie Square, tel.: 03553 2285) or in the town-hall.

**Transport.** The town is connected with the remaining part of the country solely through bus transport. There are regular bus lines to Sofia, Plovdiv, Peshtera, Pazardzhik, Velingrad, Dospat and other smaller settlements within the region. Town bus station - tel.: 03553 2328.

**Surrounding areas**. **Batak Dam Lake**, which was turned into a recreation and sports zone spreads out at the distance of 3 km north-west of the town. The dam-lake offers superb opportunities for camping sites, water tourism, fishing, water sports, hiking, and recreation. The **Tsigov Chark Resort** offering greater opportunities for accommodation and entertainment than the town itself is situated on the south-west bank of the dam at the distance of about 8 km west of Batak. The complex of the Orbita Bureau of Youth Tourism is situated here with two hotels (2- and 3-star, tel.: 03542 3385, 3386, fax: 03542 3200). The Orpheus Hotel (tel.: 03542 2094, 2255, fax: 03542 2255). The regularly running buses to and from Rakitovo and Velingrad stop there.

The area of the **4 dams** is another magnificent site for recreation, sports and tourism: **Golyam Beglik Dam** (the biggest), **Shiroka Polyana Dam** (Wide Meadow) (the most beautiful), **Beglika Dam** (the smallest) and **Toshkov Chark Dam**. They are located along the road Batak - Dospat (51 km), in the middle of the distance, amongst the ravishing Rhodope countryside. There are a lot of established recreation bases, country houses, forest management, fisheries, a camping site. The conditions for hiking and water tourism, fishing, herbs and forest fruit (raspberries and strawberries) harvesting or just recreation among the magical scenery here are more than wonderful. A whole resort originated here, which is scattered upon quite a large area amongst the dam lakes. One can find accommodation in the holiday homes or in the camping site with their own bivouac facilities. There is a road to all dam lakes. All regularly running buses between Batak and Dospat stop here. Hiking tours along marked routes may be started from here in the direction to: Teheran Chalet (4 hours), the village of Surnitsa (3.30 hours), Mt. Malka Syutkya (about 3 hours), Mt. Golyama Syutkya (about 5 hours), etc. Batak itself is a good starting point for various hiking tours into the Western Rhodopes (Batak Mountain).

The route to the former **Teheran Chalet** (see the Rhodope section), passing by the first underground hydroelectric power station in our country and on the Balkan Peninsula (at the distance of 3 km south of the town) is the most popular one.

*Batak Dam*

# CENTRAL SOUTHERN BULGARIA

## BRATSIGOVO

The town of Bratsigovo (5074 inhabitants, 420 metres above sea level) is situated in the northern foothill of Ravnogor Hill (Western Rhodopes), along the two banks of the little Umishka River. It is situated at the distance of 139 km south-east of Sofia, 7 km east of Peshtera, 25 km south of Pazardzhik, 23 km north-east of Batak and at the distance of 40 km south-west of Plovdiv. It is one of those historical towns, which uphold the national spirit of Bulgarian people. A climatic and balneological mountain resort and a tourist site.

**History**. Historical records prove the existence of Bratsigovo as of the 16th century. It was the continuation of the destroyed by fire and ruined settlement of *Prevren*. Evidence was found during excavation and construction works in the town and its surrounding areas according to which these sites were inhabited by Thracians and Slavs - coins of the time of Philip of Macedonia and Justinian II, a bronze statuette of the Goddess Athena Palada, a Roman road. During the 17th century Bulgarian people from the region of Nevrokop moved to Bratsigovo to work in the mines (mulvatsite). Emigrants from the Kostur region (Macedonia) came here at the end of the 18th century, too.

A monastery school was opened in the town in 1831 and a new mutual aid school with secular training opened its gates in 1848. Gradually later on a girl's school and an intermediate secondary school were opened as well. Bratsigovo little by little turned into a big Rhodope settlement with well-developed crafts. The citizens of Bratsigovo demonstrated particularly notable skills in the field of construction creating their own Bratsigovo School of Architecture and leaving long-lasting traces in the architectural appearance of a lot of settlements in the Balkan Peninsula. It goes without saying that the masterpieces in the town of Bratsigovo itself add up to a lot more than one or two in number.

The Trendafil (Rose) People's Chitalishte (reading room or community centre) was created in 1874 under the management of Vassil Petleshkov turning into the second centre of enlightenment in the town. The first women's society Nadezhda (Hope) was founded the following year, too.

The April Uprising commenced here with enthusiasm and full of great hopes, too (21st April 1876). In spite of the exceptionally good military organisation, forces were unequal and after 18 days of desperate resistance the revolutionary committee concluded an armistice with Hasan Pasha. The hopes for survival were in vain. The Turks were not as good as their word and they started a campaign of mass terror within the little town. 141 revolutionaries were slaughtered, 252 were banished to Anadola. The leader of the Uprising in Bratsigovo - Vassil Petleshkov was captured, too. Positioned over the fire stake he responded: *"I am all alone, there are no others. I was the one who led the struggle, I was the one who commanded - do not seek for anyone else!"* He was taken more dead than alive to Tatar Pazardhik and the Ottoman bayonets stabbed the great son of the nation in the locality of Murgita. Bratsigovo welcomed the Liberation at the early January 1878.

**Landmarks**: **The Town Museum of History** (1, Kostur Str., entrance A, tel.: 03552 2035). **Vassil Petleshkov Park-Monument** is situated in the old centre of the town where during the month of April 1876 there was a revolutionary position and the Apostle of the Uprising Vas-sil Petleshkov died a heroic death. An unpretentious monument to the martyr was erected here and his bones were placed at its foundation. A humble park was formed around it.

**Sindzhirli Bounar** - a square, surrounded by Revival Period houses. It is in this square that Petleshkov announced the beginning of the April Uprising and Ana Gizdova handed the flag she made for the revolutionaries. The memorial plate is a reminder of that event and the bounar (well) itself is an interesting architectural monu-

# CENTRAL SOUTHERN BULGARIA

ment, too, erected in 1813. The **home of Petleshkov** - a fascinating architectural monument in which the great patriot was born on 14.01.1845. The house is arranged as a museum. The building of **chitalishte** (reading room or community centre) **Trendafil** - a priceless relic of the Revival Period time. During the preparation of the Uprising the building was used by the revolutionary committee for meetings and as a warehouse for arms, ammunitions and foodstuff. **The place of death of V. Petleshkov** - along the road to Pazardzhik, at the entrance to the town stadium, where a modest monument was erected. **The house of Nikola Boyanov** - an architectural and historical monument. It was in it that on 22nd February 1876 Georgi Benkovski founded the revolutionary committee of Bratsigovo. **Dzhambov's House** (1840) - with it architectural design in the style of Plovdiv's bi-symmetrical house is an attention-grabbing architectural monument in itself. **Damov's House** (1835) - an uncommon architectural monument, a complex of residential and agricultural buildings. There is a rose-distillery in the courtyard. **St. Yoan Predtecha Church** (1833) - one of the last creations of the master-builders from Bratsigovo. The belfry is 28.61 metres in height and the width of the tower adds up to 4 m. The town clock is on the third floor. Acoustics related pots were built-in in the walls of the church. A printed Gospel of 1572 was found in it. The **house of Priest Sokol** (1849) - Chairman of the Revolutionary Committee of Bratsigovo. The following sites are of interest, too: **Karamanov's House, Lukov's House, Popov's House** (1847), **Kunchev's House, the Russian Monument** and others.

**Accommodation:** Damov's House Hotel Complex (30, Bratya Popovi Str.); NEVE Hotel Complex (31, Slavi Dishlanov Str). Private lodgings are on offer, too. There are several fascinating public catering establishments offering typical Bulgarian cuisine: the Rhodopski Chanove Tavern (17, Danail Dimenov Str., working hours from 11.00 am. to 23.00 p.m.), the Markovs' Tavern (17, Bratya Gachevi Street, working hours from 11.00 a.m. to 14.00 p.m. and from 17.00 p.m. to the last customer) and others.

**Tourist information** - at the hotels, in Atolouka Tourist's Association, in the town-hall (6, Atanas Kabov Str., entrance A, tel.: 03552 2026, 2052, 2053, fax: 03552 2101, telex: 46494).

**Transport**. Bratsigovo is linked to the other settlements of the country through bus and railway transport. There are regular bus connections with Plovdiv, Pazardzhik, Peshtera, Batak and other smaller settlements within the region. The bus station is located at 79, 3rd of Mart Str. (tel.: 03552 2022). The town is also a point of the railway line Stamboliiski - Peshtera. The railway station is near the bus station - at 85, 3rd of Mart Str. (tel.: 03552 2460, 2113).

**Surrounding areas.** The town is developing as **a balneological centre**, too. There is a cold mineral water spring (18°-26°C) with the flow rate of 120 litres per minute at the distance of 500 metres west of it. There is a balneosanatorium built up here. The mineral water treats some skin diseases, the nervous system, kidney related diseases and others. There is a nice park and a country-houses zone around it. The village of Ravnogor is situated at the distance of 16 km south of Bratsigovo. Vassil Petleshkov Mountain Resort, better known as **Atolouka** is near it. One can get there by regularly running buses from the town and on foot from the village of Rozovo (2.30 - 3 hours).

**Zhaba Krepost (Frog Fortress)** - ruins of a Bulgarian military fortification with the length of the walls of 65 m and the width of 55 m, their thickness being between 1.50 and 2 m. One can get there by diverting at the 4th km along the road to Peshtera along a mountain path and for a 20 to a 30-minutes walk the visitor shall face the ruins of the fortress.

Various short and long hiking tours in this part of the Rhodopes may be started from Bratsigovo but the marked tracks are few.

# CENTRAL SOUTHERN BULGARIA

## PEROUSHTITSA

The town of Peroushtitsa (5565 inhabitants, 205 metres above sea level) is situated in the fertile Gornotrakiiska (Upper Thracian) Lowland, immediately below the most northern slopes of the Vurhovrushki hills of the Western Rhodopes. It is situated at the distance of 147 km south-east of Sofia, 24 km south-west of Plovdiv, at the distance of 12 km south of Stamboliiski and at the distance of 7 km east of Krichim. Its name is one of the symbols of the April heroic events of 1876.

**History**. The assumptions related to the origin of the name of the town are various. Most plausible seem those, which consider that it originated from *Peristitsa* - the name of a medieval Bulgarian fortress whose ruins were left over the steep rocks south of it. There was a system of 2 fortresses here - a lower one (Gradishteto) and an upper one (Momino Kale). It is assumed also that the town is the direct inheritor of the Slavonic town of *Dragovets*. Ruins of Thracian and Roman settlements were found in the surrounding areas of Peroushtitsa. This proved that the settlement is very old and its beginning dates back to ancient times.

The St. Archangels Gavrail and Mihail church (1847) and the famous Danov School in which the first teacher was the prominent Bulgarian enlightener - Hristo Danov who introduced the mutual training method in 1850 were built in Peroushtitsa during the Revival Period. It was one of the first co-educational schools in our country. In 1869 Vassil Levski set up a revolutionary committee in Peroushtitsa headed by Peter Bonev.

The citizens of Peroushtitsa took an active part in the April Uprising (1876). They courageously stood at defence against the numerous bashibozouk (Turkish armed volunteers) hordes and the regular army of Rashid Pasha for five days. They brought their resistance to an end only when the cannon grenades destroyed the roof of the revolutionary fortress - the St. Archangels Gavrail and Mihail church, in which about 600 old people, women and children were gathered. The Turks plundered the settlement and burned down 350 houses. 348 people headed by Peter Bonev - a companion and associate of Rakovski and Levski in the Belgrade Legion and leader of the Uprising in the town died there. His associate Kocho Chestimenski demonstrated an unparalleled heroism and self-sacrifice. Seeing that there was no salvation whatsoever in the church already defenceless from the attacking bashibozouks (Turkish armed volunteers), he killed his wife and children and committed suicide himself. Others followed his example, too. The remaining leaders of the Uprising died heroically as well as Spas Ginev, Father Tikev, Dr. Vassil Sokolski. The bones of those martyrs were gathered and buried in the same church so that people could remember them. The citizens of Peroushtitsa were of the first who stood for the union of the Principality of Bulgaria with Eastern Roumelia in 1885.

**Landmarks**: The **St. Archangels Gavrail and Mihail** church - museum in the centre of the town. **The Town Museum of History** is housed in a new building in the central Peter Bonev Square. **Danov's School**. The majestic **monument** on the Vlasovets Hill, south above town,

# CENTRAL SOUTHERN BULGARIA

in favour of the revolutionists who took part in the April Uprising and who found their death in it in a martyr-like manner. The unpretentious **monument to Peter Bonev** erected next to the historical church. **Chervenata Cherkva (The Red Church)** - a unique architectural monument is located at the distance of 1 km south-east of the district of Pastousha and is also known under the name Perushtenska Starina (Peroushtitsa antiquity). It was built during the early Middle Ages (5$^{th}$ to 7$^{th}$ centuries) with a skilful combination of the antique Greek with the new Byzantine style. Its imposing and eccentric architecture is amazing. It was proclaimed a monument of culture of national importance.

**Accommodation**: A big and modern tourist hostel in the centre of the town (78, Ivan Vazov Str.) offering 70 beds in 2 suites and rooms with 2, 3, 6 and more beds.

**Tourist information** - at the tourist hostel, in the Vurhovruh Tourist Association, located in the tourist hostel, at the town-hall.

**Transport**. The sole transport of the town is bus transport. The town has regular bus connections with Plovdiv (every 30 minutes), Stamboliiski, Krichim and several other smaller settlements within the region.

**Surrounding areas**. Peroushtitsa is a good point from which to set out on walks following numerous hiking tracks in the Vurhovruh Hill (Chernatitsa subpart of the Western Rhodopes), from where one can continue in various directions (see the Rodopes related section).

## PAZARDZHIK

The town of Pazardzhik (79 476 inhabitants, 205 metres above sea level) is located in the fertile Gornotrakiiska (Upper Thracian) Lowland, along the two banks of the Maritsa River. It is situated at the distance of 114 km (along the new Trakia Motorway fewer km in number) south-east of Sofia, at the distance of 36 km west of Plovdiv, 20 km north of Peshtera and 43 km south of Panagyurishte. It is located within a rich agricultural region. A regional administrative centre.

**History**. It was founded 5 centuries ago as a market settlement, which gradually turned into an important economic and administrative centre. The road Istanbul - Sofia - West-

# CENTRAL SOUTHERN BULGARIA

ern Europe on which the town was a road station contributed to it as well as the fact that it turned into a port - warehouse on the Maritsa River for cereals, rice, wine, timber from the Rhodopes and iron from Samokov, which were transported by rafts to Istanbul (through Enos). A lot of Bulgarians settled down in Pazardzhik who changed its ethnic appearance, too. A lot of European and Turkish travellers spoke enthusiastically about it. The town flourished during the 19th century and competed with Plovdiv and Sofia. In 1865 the town had 33 mahali (quarters), 3420 houses, 1200 shops and approximately 25 000 inhabitants. The Holy Virgin Church was built in 1837, a unique monument of Bulgarian architecture, wood-carving and icon-painting. Other churches were also built for the individual Bulgarian quarters. There were 5 boys' schools with 400 students and 2 girls' schools with 100 students in them in the middle of the 19th century. The famous clock tower preserved up to date was erected as early as in the 18th century, too. Chitalishte (reading room or community centre) Videlina was founded in 1862. A lot of people's enlighteners related their names with Pazardzhik - Bishop Dionisii Agatonikiiski who founded the first Bulgarian school in 1823 with his own funds, N. Popkonstantinov, Yu. Nenov, Hadzhi Tatyana - the first woman teacher in the town. The foundations of theatrical activities and of Prosveta Women's Society (Enlightenment) were laid in 1870. Levski founded the first revolutionary committee here chaired by G. Konsulov, but the detentions before trial on the part of the Turks frustrated the outburst of the Uprising. On 2 January 1878 the Army of General Gourko liberated Pazardzhik.

**Landmarks** - the **Town Museum of History**, located in one of the newest and most representative buildings of the town (15, Konstantin Velichkov Sq., tel.: 034 22505). **The Ethnographic Museum**, whose exhibition is housed in the biggest residential building in Pazardzhik of the Revival Period (the house of Nikolaki Hristovich), proclaimed as a cultural monument (8, Otets Paisii Str.). **The cathedral church of St. Bogoroditsa (the Holy Virgin)** (located at Otets Paisii Str.) - one of the most valuable artistic architectural monuments in the country erected in 1837 of pink rhyolite. The greatest piece of art in it is the wood-carved iconostasis in the traditions of the well-known School of Debur, remarkable for its exquisite open-worked wood-carving, re-creating figured compositions and plant ornaments. There are solely two similar matchless examples-work of masters of Debur and they are located in the Republic of Macedonia (in the St. Spas church in Skopje and the Bigor Monastery, not far from Debur). The monument to Stanislav Dospevski is in the courtyard of the church, work of the sculptor Ivan Blazhev. **Stanislav Dospevski House-Museum** (50, Knyaginya Maria Louisa Blvd.), in which the prominent Bulgarian painter and revolutionary from Samokov of the Revival Period lived from 1864 to 1877. The building was erected in 1864 by builders-masters from Bratsigovo in the so-called Istanbul style and was one of the most beautiful houses in the town at that time. Dospevski himself painted some of its premises. **Stanislav Dospevski Art Gallery** - a specialised state cultural educational and scientific institute of fine arts (15, Konstantin Velichkov Str.). **Konstantin**

# CENTRAL SOUTHERN BULGARIA

**Velichkov House-museum** (5, Teodor Trayanov Str.) built in 1850. The atmosphere, in which the distinguished writer lived and created, was preserved. It was in that the sister of Konstantin Velichkov - Teofana sewed the banner of the Pazardzhik Revolutionary Committee in 1876 and on 21 April Vassil Petleshkov brought the news about the beginning of the Uprising from Panagyurishte. **The Synagogue** (the Jewish Church) - erected in 1850 by the master from Bratsigovo Stavri Temelkov. Quite interesting are the arcs of the ceiling ornamented with beautiful wood-carving - an engraved sun with several round colourings and interlaced designs of geometrical figures. The internal walls are with mural paintings. It is located at 5, Assen Zlatarov Str. **Hadzhistoyanov's House** (1, Republica Str.), whose wood-carving is one of the best achievements in the Bulgarian residential architecture from the middle of the 19th century. The following are noteworthy, too: **St. Petka Church** of 1852, **St. Archangel Church** of 1860 with the icon of the same name painted by Stanislav Dospevski, **St. Sotir Church** (1862). The **monument to Aleko Konstantinov** is situated amidst a picturesque park on the island of the Maritsa River.

Pazardzhik is a town with defined cultural traditions. Three theatres function in it nowadays: the Theatre of Drama "Konstantin Velichkov" (Konstantin Velichkov Sq.) - one of the best provincial theatres in our country. The Theatre of Music "Maestro Atanasov" (Konstantin Velichkov Sq.) and the Puppet Theatre (42, Georgi Benkovski Str.).

**Accommodation**: Trakia Hotel (2, Bulgaria Blvd.). The Elbrus Hotel-Restaurant (1, Konstantin Velichkov Blvd.).

**Tourist information**: at above mentioned hotels and in the Aleko Tourist Association (19, Kliment Ohridski Str., tel.: 034 27320 and for reservations at the chalets in the Rhodopes - Milevi Skali Chalet (Milev's Rocks), Dobra Voda Chalet and Livadite Chalet - tel.: 032 274016).

**Transport**. Well developed bus and railway connections with the remaining part of the country. It is situated on the most busy road, motorway and railway line in Bulgaria - Sofia - Plovdiv that predetermined its development as a big transport centre. Further to being connected to each station of the country through the national railway network, Pazardzhik has regular bus lines to Sofia, Plovdiv, Velingrad, Panagyurishte, Blagoevgrad, etc. The bus station is situated in the central part of the town, at 6, Georgi Benkovski Blvd. (tel.: 034 26315). The railway station is in the southern part of Pazardzhik (tel.: 034 26520). There is a well organised town bus transport functioning, too.

**Surrounding areas**. The place of death of the great Bulgarian writer and democrat **Aleko Konstantinov**, founder of the organised tourist's movement in our country is situated at the distance of 14 km south, past the road to Peshtera, in the proximity of the village of Radilovo. It was in this place that on 24th May 1897 on his way back from the celebrations of the National Holiday in Peshtera he was shot by a hired assassin. An unpretentious monument was erected here and a beautiful park was formed around it. The regular buses running between Pazardzhik and Peshtera may stop there upon request.

**Bessaparskite Ridove (Bessapar Hills)** (at the distance of some 10 km east) - the archaeological research carried out indicated that the main town of the Thracians - *Besapara* was situated here. 8 burial mounds were preserved here. The pre-historic settlement **Maltepe** and the **Tri Voditsi karst spring** with the flow rate of 900 litres per second are situated near it. These sites may be reached by car in about 20 minutes or by a passenger train, stopping at the railway stations of Sinitevo and Hadzhievo and at Ognyanovo Station.

# CENTRAL SOUTHERN BULGARIA

## KOPRIVSHTITSA

The town of Koprivshtitsa (2935 inhabitants, 1050 metres above sea level) is situated along the two banks, within the upper course of the Topolnitsa River in the heart of Sushtinska Sredna Gora Mountain. It is situated at the distance of 110 km south-east of Sofia, 80 km north-west of Plovdiv, 27 km south-east of Pirdop and 24 km north of Strelcha. A town-museum and the unique settlement in Bulgaria, which preserved in compact over 250 patterns of the Revival Period architecture. A cradle of the April Uprising (1876). A tourist centre and a mountain resort.

**History**. Koprivshtitsa originated as a settlement during the 14th century. Its population dealt with cattle-breeding, manufacturing of aba (coarse homespun woollen cloth and upper men's garment made of it), furriery, dyeing and other crafts. The citizens of Koprivshtitsa proved to be good merchants, too reaching as far as Istanbul and Alexandria. The wealthy and urbanised settlement was plundered and destroyed by fire by kurdzhalii (Turkish brigands) three times and rebuilt from ashes to reach its greatest prosperity during the 19th century, when it had over 1000 houses and a population of nearly 12 000 inhabitants. Spacious houses, schools, churches, drinking-fountains, bridges were built there. In 1837 Neofit Rilski (Neophyte of Rila) opened a mutual school and 9 years later Naiden Gerov founded the first in Bulgaria independent boys' intermediate school. In 1864 a girls' intermediate school was opened here and three years later Todor Kableshkov opened the students' society Zora (Dawn). In 1869 the *chitalsihte* (reading room or community centre) was opened here. In the same year Vassil Levski established a revolutionary committee in it. During that time Lyuben Karavelov who was born in Koprivshtitsa headed the foreign Bulgarian Revolutionary Central Committee (BRCC) in Bucharest. On 20th April 1876 the first shot of the April Uprising against Ottoman Rule rang out here, which started the heroic April epic of Bulgarian people. Todor Kableshkov announced the Upris-

*Winter faity-tale in Koprivstitsa*

# CENTRAL SOUTHERN BULGARIA

ing. It was headed by another citizen of Koprivshtitsa - Gavrail Hlutev, known to the generations to come as Georgi Benkovski - the adamant and ardent leader of the people's rebellion, who died heroically in the Teteven Balkan Mountain. Unlike Batak, Bratsigovo, Peroushtitsa and other settlements-martyrs, the Osmanli Turks had mercy on Koprivshtitsa. The wealthy men of Koprivshtitsa paid for it and thanks to them Bulgaria today is in possession of its most treasured architectural wealth, untouched by the centuries.

The town is the birth place of a lot of functionaries of our Revival Period and renowned Bulgarians - Bogdan Voivoda, Doncho Vatah Voivoda, Detelin Voivoda, Dobri Voivoda ("voivoda" meaning leader of revolutionary detachment of voluneers), Dimcho Debelyanov, Nayden Gerov.

**Landmarks**. Koprivshtitsa is one of the few thoroughly preserved architectural urbanised ensembles of the Revival Period. The Revival Period houses with colourful courtyards, surrounded with high stone walls and gates, the disorderly built curved and narrow cobblestone streets and plots, the numerous stone drinking-fountains, the arch-shaped little stone bridges over the mountain brooklets and the fragrance of geranium, boxshrub, peony and pelargonium contribute to the attractiveness of the little town.

*Interior of a typical house in Koprivshtitsa*

The greatest wealth of Koprivshtitsa are its Revival Period houses, a part of which were turned into museums: **Oslekov's House** - the most famous architectural, ethnographic site in the town, ownership of a rich merchant from Koprivshtitsa in the middle of the 19$^{th}$ century. The artistically carved ceilings, the beautifully painted with geometrical figures walls, the exotic mosaics, the ancient engravings and the exquisitely elaborated applied decorative articles indicate the living standards and the spiritual wealth of the well-off citizens of Koprivshtitsa. The home of **Georgi Benkovski** - the leader of the April Uprising. The wooden gun, the banner of the Flying Detachment of armed volunteers sewed by Raina Popgeorgieva (Knyaginya) (the Princess) and the arms of the Voivoda are the most priceless relics of that tempestuous time.

**The house of Lyuben Karavelov** acquaints us with the revolutionary and journalistic activities of one of the most prominent sons of Koprivshtitsa and Bulgaria. **The house of Todor Kableshkov** exhibits the activity of the 25-years old young man who organised the rebellion in the town, the author of the famous Blood-stained letter by which it was announced to the Main Revolutionary Headquarters in Pana-gyurishte that Koprivshtitsa had risen in arms. **Lyutovs' House** Museum hosts an exposition on the subject of "Treasury of Bulgarian Construction Genius".

**The House of Dimcho Debelyanov** - the life and the literary activities of the most lyrical Bulgarian poet are reflected in it. Like in the other houses-museums, here the atmosphere, in which Dimcho Debelyanov lived and created his poems, was preserved, too.

The following houses are of interest to the visitor, too namely the houses of **Gencho Stoykov, Naiden Gerov, Desyovs', Gurkovs', Mluchkovs', Yotovs', Madzharovs', Markovs', Dogans', Pavlikyans' and the Vakarel's house** (the oldest houses in the town with over 300 years of life) and dozens of others. The **Uspenie Borgorodichno Church** (Assumption

# CENTRAL SOUTHERN BULGARIA

Church) (1817) with an iconostasis of 1821 and icons painted by Zakhari Zograph and Ioan Samokovli (1837-1838) is of a high architectural and artistic value. The **St. Nikola Church** (1842-1844) is worth seeing as well.

There are a lot of monuments in the town, too: **20th April Mausoleum-Charnel House** (in the central 20th April Sq.) of those who died during the April Uprising. **The First Gun Memorial** past the old little stone bridge where the rebel Georgi Tihanek fired the first shot of the April Uprising. The monument to **Todor Kableshkov**, the memorial complex with the key figure of **Georgi Benkovski**. One of the most moving monuments in our country - **mother waiting for her son** to return was placed on the grave of Dimcho Debelyanov. It is the work of the sculptor Prof. Ivan Lazarov.

**Accommodation**: The Koprivshtitsa Hotel (high above the right bank of the river, opposite the centre of the town). The Hadzhi Gencho Hotel (in the central part, on the left bank of the river). The Dalmatinets Hotel-Restaurant (62, Georgi Benkovski Str.). Voivodenets Tourist Hostel (in the centre of the town, at the former Pranzhev's House, 33 beds in rooms with 2, 6, 7 and more beds). Bogdan Tourist Hostel (in the restored Roussekovs' House, 33 beds in rooms with 2, 3, 4, 7, and 9 beds). Private lodgings are on offer, too, information being available at the Accommodation Bureau.

**Tourist information** - in the Tourist Information Centre, 2077 Koprivshtitsa, 1, Lyuben Karavelov Str., tel./fax: 07184 2191, e-mail: koprivshtitza@hotmail.com; at the Council on Tourism (2090 Koprivshtitsa, 15, Lyuben Karavelov Street, tel: 07184 2759 and 2104), in the above mentioned hotels, tourist's dormitories, the Accommodation Bureau as well as in Detelin Voivoda Tourist Association (tel.: 07184 2145) and in the town-hall.

**Transport**. The key transport through which the town is linked with the remaining world is the railway transport. Koprivshtitsa is at the

*Along the streets of Koprivstitsa*

principal railway line Sofia - Karlovo - Bourgas but it is situated at the distance of 10 km north of the town itself. It is connected to it through a bus line servicing each passing train. Koprivshtitsa maintains regular bus lines to Plovdiv, Panagyurishte, Strelcha and Pirdop.

**Surrounding area**. The town is a key point from which to set out on hiking tours in the highest and beautiful part of Sushtinska Sredna Gora Mountain. Marked tracks start from it in the direction of: Bogdan Chalet (3 to 4 hours), from where one can climb the highest peak of the Sredna Gora Mountain - Mt. Bogdan in less than an hour (1604 metres above sea level), Manzul Chalet (Pavel Deliradev, 3.30 - 4 hours), Krustyo Cholakov Chalet (2.30-3 hours, 11 km along a truck road), the Barikadite Chalet and Hotel (4-4.30 hours, 18 km along a road). A hiking tour to the Central Stara Planina (the Teteven Balkan Mountain) can be started from the railway station of Koprivshtitsa. It takes 6 to 8 hours to get to the Vezhen Chalet along the marked tracks (on the northern side of the ridge), passing by the peak of the same name (Mt. Vezhen, 2198 m).

# CENTRAL SOUTHERN BULGARIA

## SOPOT

The town of Sopot (12 119 inhabitants, 520 metres above sea level) is situated in the fertile sub-Balkan mountain valley of Karlovo (which is the western part of the legendary **Valley of the Roses**), immediately under the steep southern slopes of the Troyan Balkan Mountain (Central Stara Planina). It is situated at the distance of 5 km west of Karlovo, 136 km east of Sofia, 63 km north of Plovdiv and 61 km south of Troyan. It is the birth place of the Patriarch of Bulgarian Literature Ivan Vazov. A big machine-building centre.

**History**. There is information about the settlement dating back to the Ottoman Rule. During the Revival Period it was called *Altun Sopot* (Golden Sopot), because of its flourishing development, thanks to the crafts and trade. The citizens of Sopot manufactured aba (coarse homespun woollen cloth and upper men's garment made of it), braids, fur and leather of high quality and traded them predominantly round the Ottoman Empire. The town was destroyed by fire during the struggle for liberation (1877), and its population was slaughtered or expelled. The town was named *Vazovgrad* between 1950 and 1965 after which it obtained its present name again.

**Landmarks**. In the first place this is the **house, in which Ivan Vazov was born**, located at the downtown Ivan Vazov Sq. (tel.: 03134 2070). The initial house was destroyed at the end of the Ottoman Rule but at the initiative of admirers of the poet it was rebuilt in 1932 and proclaimed as house-museum. A special exhibition hall was built next to the house, which exibits key moments of the public and literary activity of the people's poet Ivan Vazov (1850-1921). A memorial to the poet was erected at the central square named after him. **Presentation of the Blessed Holly Virgin Nunnery** (located near the central square - north of it) which was founded in 1665 next to an old church from the beginning of the 15$^{th}$ century. In 1877 it was almost completely destroyed by fire. Solely the veranda with the hiding place of the Apostle Levksi (the Apostle repeatedly found a secure shelter there), the little church and the drinking-fountain in the middle of the yard survived and were preserved in their initial appearance up to date. All the remaining buildings were restored to their initial appearance. The museum corner "Rada's School", the cell of Hadzhi Rovoama and Lay Sister Rada Gospozhina - characters of Ivan Vazov's novel "Under the Yoke" are here, too.

**St. Spas Sopot Monastery** (at the distance of 2 km north-west of the centre) is located immediately at the foothill of the Stara Planina slopes, on the left bank of the Manastirska River. The date of its origin is unknown. It was repeatedly devastated and destroyed by fire. Its present appearance dates back to 1879. During the Revival Period there was a monastery school and a singing school functioning in the Monastery and it was a centre of revolutionary life, too. In 1858 Vassil Ivanov (Levski) was ordained for a Deacon here. The countryside surrounding the Monastery is extraordinary. The initial station of the open-seat lift is near it, too.

**Dyado Stoyanov's Water-Mill** (The mill of grandfather Stoyanov), described by Ivan Vazov in his novel "Under the Yoke", is located next to the road leading to the initial station of the open-seat lift, in the north-western end of the town. The following places of interest are worth seeing, too: **the Holy Apostles Peter and Paul church** of 1846, **Hadzhi Kotyov's House, Hadzhi Stoilkov's House, Hadzhi Stoynov's House, Kirkovs' House, Kopanovs' House, Konov's Bakery** and others.

**Accommodation**: Stara Planina Hotel Complex (in the central Ivan Vazov Sq.). VMZ Hotel Base. In the St. Spas Monastery (next to the initial station of the open-seat lift.

**Tourist information** - at the hotels and in the town-hall (26, Ivan Vazov Blvd., tel.: 03134 2050, 2052).

# CENTRAL SOUTHERN BULGARIA

**Transport**. Sopot is a point of the main road and railway line Sofia - Karlovo - Bourgas. There is a town bus line is functioning at short time intervals between it and Karlovo. It maintains bus connections with some of the smaller settlements within the region, too. The bus station is located at 75, Ivan Vazov Blvd. The railway station is situated at the distance of 1 km south of the town and there is a town bus going to it (tel.: 03134 2346, 2022). Not all express trains stop at it.

**Surrounding areas**. The ruins of **Anevo Kale** ("kale" meaning a fortress, stronghold") (a Bulgarian fortress of the 12th to the 14th centuries) above the Anevo Quarter, on the southern slopes of the Balkan Mountain, at about 900 metres above sea level. One can walk to it from the town for about 1.30 or 2 hours. **Sopot Kale** is located north-east of the town, too. Sopot is used as a point of departure to the **Troyan Balkan.** The open-seat lift located in the north-western part of the town (tel.: 03134 2677, 3428) takes you at the altitude of about 1600 m in a little more than 30 minutes, at a 5-minutes walk from the institutional Nezabravka Chalet. The lift has an interim station in the locality of Pochivaloto (about 1350 metres above sea level) - a favourite place for take off of delta and paragliders. One can walk to the Nezabravka Chalet from Sopot, too along a marked track starting from the lift (3-3.30 hours). Marked tracks start from Nezabravka Chalet to various directions around the Troyan Balkan Mountain: south-east towards Dobrila Chalet (1 hour), joining the Kom - Emine ridge route. Mt. Ambaritsa (1.30 hours) may be climbed from the Dobrila Chalet and one can continue in the direction of Mt. Botev (about 6 hours more) along the most beautiful and Alpine ridge of Stara Planina. It takes 4 to 4.30 hours of hiking to get to Ambaritsa Chalet and 4 to 5 hours to reach Vassil Levski Chalet. One can set out north-west from the Nezabravka Chalet to the Dermenka Chalet, too (about 3 hours) and continue westwards along the ridge.

*Ivan Vazov House-Museum*

# CENTRAL SOUTHERN BULGARIA

## KARLOVO

The town of Karlovo (25 715 inhabitants, 520 metres above sea level) is situated in the valley of the same name, which is part of the famous Rose Valley, along the two banks of Stara Reka River, left feeder of Stryama River. The town is located 141 km east of Sofia, 58 km north of Plovdiv, 55 km west of Kazanluk, 66 km south of Troyan, 5 km east of Sopot and 17 km west of Kalofer. It is the birthplace of the greatest Bulgarian - The Apostle of Freedom Vassil Levski.

**History**. Karlovo's remote past is not well explored. The village mounds, remains of Roman roads and constructions that were found in its vicinity can't be related to certain names and events. Today's town is a relatively new one. It originated on the right bank of Stara Reka River right after the Ottoman invasion in Bulgaria, as an administrative centre and a residence of the local Turkish Feudal lords, close to the old village of Sushitsa. The village was named Karlovo after the local Turkish feudal lord. The beginning of the 19th century for Karlovo was a time of rapid economic boom, cultural uplift and revolutionary ardour. Hundreds of weaving shops and watermills worked near Stara Reka River. Rich merchants bought what the skilful master coppersmiths, goldsmiths, manufacturers of woollen braids and aba (coarse homespun woollen cloth and upper men's garment made of it), leather-workers had created and traded with distant countries - Egypt, Albania, Dubrovnik, Romania, Vienna. Karlovo became a big and bustling village with a disctinct centre, town clock and nice houses. The Russian-Turkish War of Liberation put an end to the wealthy life in the town, despite the gained liberty. In 1877 the bashibozouks (Turkish armed volunteers) plundered and set Karlovo on fire. 813 people were slaughtered, most of the survivors ran away through the Balkan Mountains. Fortunately, the surviving parts of Karlovo have kept their original identity.

The town is the birthplace of the teacher Botyo Petkov, father of Hristo Botev; Dr. Ivan Bogorov, (writer from the period of Bulgarian National Revival, publisher of the first Bulgarian newspaper Bulgarski Orel (Bulgarian Eagle) in Leipzig in 1846-1847); the brothers Evlogi and Hristo Georgievi (distinguished representatives of the emerging Bulgarian bourgeoisie and patriots, who donated 6 million golden Levs for a Bulgarian institution of higher education - The University), Braiko Hadzhigenov, Hristo Popvassilev and others. Also a native of Karlovo is the famous Bulgarian mountaineer Hristo Prodanov, first to climb a peak higher than 8000 metres - Lhotse (8516 m) and the first Bulgarian to set foot on "The roof of the World" - Mt. Everest (8848 m, 20 April 1984), he remained forever in its frozen embrace. Its greatest fame, however, the town owes to the fact that it's the hometown of Mother Bulgaria's greatest son - the Apostle of Bulgarian Freedom - Vassil Ivanov Kunchev - Levski.

**Landmarks: The Town Museum of History** (Bulgarian National Revival and Ethnography, next to Levski Monument, 2, Vuzrozhdenska Str., working hours: 9.00 a.m. - 12.00 a.m. and 2.00 p.m. to 5.30 p.m., tel.: 0335 4728) in the house in the Old School - a valuable architectural and historical monument of culture since 1871. **Vassil Levski House-Museum** (57, General Kartsov Str., working hours: 9.00 a.m. - 12.00 a.m. and 2.00 p.m. - 5.30 p.m., tel.: 0335 3489). The original house was set on fire during the War of Liberation. The stairs to the cellar and the hideout are all that survived. In 1937 under the initiative of Bulgarian patriots the house was restored. In the yard there is the monument of Levski's mother - Gina Kouncheva. A spacious exhibition hall has been built, featuring materials and exhibits of the Apostle's life and revolutionary activities. From this life everyone can learn something - no

# CENTRAL SOUTHERN BULGARIA

matter if you're a Bulgarian or a foreigner, rich or poor, banker or politician. From the humble father's house to immortality on the gallows, Levski teaches us pure and simple things, shows us the path as nation and humans! **The Monument to Vassil Levski** (V. Levski Sq., in the old part of the town)- the figure of the Apostle in life-size, on a high base, with a pistol in his hand and a lion next to him. At the lower part of the base there are bas-reliefs. One can always find fresh flowers here, left by ordinary people.

The **St. Nicola Church** (next to Levski's monument). In the northern part of the yard is the grave of Levski's mother. The **Holy Virgin Church** (built in 1847) 32, Vassil Levski Str., has a nice stone drinking-fountain near the entrance. The **Chitalishte Vassil Levski** (reading room and community centre) with a permanent art gallery (20th July Sq., working hours: 9.00 a.m. - 12.00 a.m. and 2.00 p.m. - 6.00 p.m., tel.: 0335 3391). The **Alexandrovs' (Hadgivalkovs') House** (V. Levski Sq.), **Beliyat Dvor** (The White Yard) (1, Sokolova Str.), **Zoevs' House** (1, Evstati Geshov Str.), **Koprinarovs' House** (11, Rakovska Str.), **Patevs' House** (45, Vassil Levski Str., opposite Levski's monument), **Ploshtakovs' House** (8, Verkovitch Str.), **Poulevs' House** (The Union of Bulgarian Artists - 5, Dimitur Sabev Str.), **Sumnalievs' House** (1, Dragoman Str.). **The bust-monument of Hristo Prodanov** is in the town park, in the northern part of Karlovo.

**Accommodation:** Hemus Hotel (3-star, 87, V. Levski Str.). Rosova Dolina Hotel (2-star, 1, 20th July Sq.). Besh-Bounar Hotel-Restaurant. Tourist Hostel (500 metres north of the town centre, 23, Vodopad Str.). There are interesting restaurants with original Bulgarian cuisine in Karlovo, too: Vodopad Tavern (86, Vodopad Str.), Mazite Tavern (9, Verkovitch Str., working hours - 2 p.m. - 3 a.m.), etc.

**Tourist information** - available at the Tourist Information Centre - 4300 Karlovo, 35, Vodopad Str., tel.: 0335 5373, e-mail: inforcentre@mbox.digsys.bg; in the hotels, the tourist hostel, at Vassil Levski Tourist Association (1, Todor and Anna Pulevi Str., tel.: 0335 8560) and in the town-hall (1, Petko Sabev Str., tel.: 0335 3478, fax: 0335 3459).

**Transport**. Karlovo is a large transport centre. It is a main station of the main road and railroad lines Sofia-Karlovo-Bourgas. It provides regular bus lines (public and private) to Plovdiv, Kalofer, Sopot, Pazardzhik and other smaller villages in the area. The Central Bus Station is near the railway station, 77, Vassil Karaivanov Str., tel.: 0335 3155. There are also two private bus agencies: Roza-Express, whose bus station is at Subota (Saturday) Marketplace and Private Transport Agency, its bus station is opposite the railway station. The railway station (2, Teofan Rainov Blvd., tel.: 0335 4641 and 4320) is in the southern part of the town. Besides being on the main

# CENTRAL SOUTHERN BULGARIA

Sofia-Plovdiv railroad, Karlovo is also the last station of the Plovdiv-Karlovo line. Public bus transport is also functioning.

**Surrounding areas.** The 15-metre-high **Karlovski Waterfall (Suchurum)** is located 1 km north of the town, at the foot of the Balkan, above the hydroelectric power station - a favourite place of the people of Karlovo for sunbathing during the summer heats. 11 km south of Karlovo, at the village of Banya are the **Karlovo baths** - a balneotherapy resort of national importance. The mineral water temperature is 35°-54°C and its flow is 30 litres per second. It cures diseases of the muscular-skeletal system, gynecological diseases and disturbances of the peripheral nervous system. There is also a mud-cure bed and the mud is used for treatment of various diseases. Besides the resort's polyclinic there is a sanatorium, recreation facilities, an open-air beach and a lot of villas. There is regular bus transport to Karlovo. About 15 km south-east of Karlovo is the **Domlyan Dam** near the village of the same name. It is a great place for hiking and camping. There are regular buses from the town. Karlovo is a starting point of tourist routes all over the Central Balkan Range (see Stara Planina related chapter).

*Raiskoto Pruskalo (The Heaven's Sprayer) in Stara Planina Mountain*

## KALOFER

The town of Kalofer (3991 inhabitants, 600 metres above sea-level) is beautifully situated along both banks of Toundzha River, in a small valley in the eastern foot of the Strazhata Hill (The Sentry) (a natural connection between the Balkan and the Sredna Gora Mountains. Above it, spreading its mighty shoulders stands the highest peak in the Balkan Range - Mt. Botev. The town is located 17 km east of Karlovo, 158 km east of the capital city Sofia, 38 km west of Kazanluk, 75 km north of Plovdiv. It is the birthplace of the great Bulgarian poet and revolutionary Hristo Botev.

**History**. Its name can not be found in the ancient or the medieval history of our lands. On this place there were once thick, impassable and desolate woods. To the west, in the valley of Byala Reka River, was the old town *Zvanigrad*, from which there is not a trace left today. Due to the strong resistance, the Turks wiped out the town, but the proud and sturdy defenders remained unconquered. A group of 40 heroes, led by Kalifer Voivoda ("voivoda" meaning leader of a group of armed revolutionaries), roamed for long throughout the area, defending their fellow Bulgarians and arousing horror in the Ottomans. The Turks were powerless to deal with the detachment and so the Sultan gave the voivoda permission to settle in the woods along with his men, giving them privileges to establish a settlement with the statute of derventdzhii (special guards of the roads and passes in the mountains, appointed by the Turks). The haidouti (armed revolutionaries, volunteers, members of a detachment) kidnapped maids from Sopot, which was famous for its beauties, and that is how the town of Kalofer originated. It is not by chance that the his-

# CENTRAL SOUTHERN BULGARIA

tory of the town during the long Turkish yoke is full of names of famous revolutionaries, haidouts and rebels - from Kalifer Voivoda, Old Man Mlachko, Chono Chorbadzhi, Dobri Voivoda and Gulub Voivoda to the great poet and revolutionary Hristo Botev. Twice the kurdzhalii (Turkish brigands) ruined the town - in 1799 and 1804, but it quickly recovered and grew wealthy. During the first half of the 19th century Kalofer, like all our towns south of the Balkan Range, reached its zenith. Travellers notice that in it there were more than 1000 loom sites for woollen braids, a lot of mills for processing wool and dye-houses. The craftsmen and merchants of Kalofer traded with Constantinople, Vienna, Odessa, Braila. They did not call the town Altun Kalofer (Golden Kalofer) for nothing. In 1845 a big new school was built, and in 1871 a school for girls was built, too. All kinds of educational societies were formed. A lot of renowned writers and public figures are natives of Kalofer - Ekzarh Yossif I, Dimitur Mutev, Elena Muteva (the first Bulgarian poetess), Hristo Tupchileshtov, Ivan Shopov (a student of folklore and the first Bulgarian bibliographer) and others. Many people of Kalofer enrolled in the detachments of Panayot Hitov, Phillip Totyo, Hadzhi Dimitur and Stefan Karadzha, Bacho Kiro. At the end of the Turkish rule there were as much as 15 haidout detachments roaming in Kalofer's vicinity. Over 500 natives of Kalofer were members of haidout detachments and groups. During the War of Liberation (1877-1878) Kalofer shared Karlovo and Sopot's fate - it was plundered and set on fire by the bashibozouks. Almost nothing is left of the pre-liberation Kalofer.

**Landmarks**. First of all, there is the **Hristo Botev House-Museum** (downtown). It's not his native house, which burned to ashes when the town was ruined. In 1942 the house where Hristo Botev's father - the teacher Botyo Petkov had lived later, was restored. A new museum building in folk-style was added in the yard. There is a marble bust of the poet and a sculpture of his mother. Close to the centre, in its upper part, the restored building of the **school of the teacher Botyo Petkov** can be found. On its lower floor, an **Art Gallery** has been arranged, featuring pictures, dedicated to Kalofer and Hristo Botev, and the second floor hosts a **Museum of Education**. In front of the building is preserved the **stone**, on which young Botev makes his fiery speech against the Turkish rule on 24 May 1867, after which he is forced to leave Bulgaria. Next to the building a bust-monument of the **teacher Botyo Petkov** was erected. Further in this direction is the old revival **Holy Virgin Church**. In its yard was the simple church cell that gave shelter to Botyo Petkov, when he came to teach in the little town. Hristo Botev was born in it. Now there is only a memorial plate there. Monumental stairs lead from downtown to the **Memorial Complex** in the foot of the mountain, in the centre of which stands a granite statue of the Bulgarian genius, who has outspoken the prophetic words *"One, who falls fighting for Freedom, doesn't die"* and confirmed them himself.

In the north-west end, a glorious **monument of Kalifer Voivoda** stands. Other interesting sites in the town are: **the stone bridges** from the revival period over Toundzha River, some of the **old houses**, The **Maiden Monastery**, built in 1738, **St. Atanas Church**, the **rose-distillery**, the beautiful park called **Botev's meadow**, etc.

**Accommodation:** Roza Hotel (downtown), Tintyava Tourist Hostel (about 500 metres west of the centre, 58, Georgi Shopov Str.). There are many places in town, where you can have fun and taste original Bulgarian cuisine.

**Tourist information** is available in the hotel, at Haidout Tourist Association, which is housed in the tourist hostel, and in the town-hall (downtown).

**Transport**. The main road Sofia - Karlovo - Bourgas passes through the town. There are busses to Karlovo (every 30 minutes), Plovdiv and other smaller villages in the area. The bus station is downtown. The railway station (2,5 km south-east of the town, a bus line connects it to the town) is on the Sofia - Karlovo - Bourgas line and all train stop there.

**Surrounding areas.** 6 km north of Kalofer, along both banks of Toundzha River, the

# CENTRAL SOUTHERN BULGARIA

**Panitsite Resort** is situated. It has a lot of recreational facilities, mostly for children. It is a starting point for the Kalofer Mountain (see Stara Planina related chapter). During the summer, twice daily, there is a bus from the town. The **Kalofer Maiden Monastery** can be found on the right bank of Byala Reka River (White River), at about 6 km north-west of the town. Founded in 1640, it was set on fire twice (in 1799 and 1804) by kurdzhalii (Turkinsh brigands), rebuilt in 1819, with a big monastery church. During the War of Liberation it was again plundered and burnt to ashes. Today's church was built in 1880 on the foundations of the old one. The rest of the buildings are newer. One can stay for the night in the monastery against minimal payment. However, there is no regular transport to it.

The **Byala Reka Inn** is located by the bridge across the river Byala Reka (White River), with a small summer resort near it. It's a few kilometres west of Kalofer and all buses between Karlovo and Kalofer stop there. The upper part of Byala Reka has cut through the Balkan the fantastic **South Dzhendem Canyon**, declared a Nature Reserve. It is accessible only with mountaineer equipment. Near the Alpine **Rai Chalet** (Paradise) is the highest waterfall in Bulgaria - **Raiskoto Pruskalo** (The Heavens' Sprayer) (124 m), whose waters fall down the stony walls of **Mt. Botev** (2376 m) - the highest peak in the Balkan Range. One can get to this true paradise only on foot - about 4 hours from the Panitsite Resort. Besides for the Central Balkan Range (see Stara Planina related chapter), Kalofer is also a starting point for the Surnena Sredna Gora Mountain. From the railway station, along a marked tourist track, one can get to **Svezhen Chalet** in about 5 hours. The chalet is above the village of the same name, where Colonel Serafimov - a hero of the Balkan War, was born. One can also reach the village by bus from Karlovo. From Svezhen Chalet one can continue eastward along the ridge of Surnena Sredna Gora, to the Bratan Chalet and Kavakliika Chalet.

# HISSARYA

The town of Hissarya (9308 inhabitants, 364 metres above sea level) is situated in a small valley among the south-eastern outskirts of Central Sredna Gora Mountain. It is located 167 km east of Sofia, 43 km north of Plovdiv, 26 km south-west of Karlovo and 57 km east of Panagyurishte. It is a world famous balneotherapy resort and one of the biggest in Bulgaria.

**History**. The modern health resort, with its more than 20 mineral springs and mild climate, has an ancient past. During the Roman rule the town (called *Augusta* and *Sevastopolis*) was a wealthy resort centre with Emperor's palaces, wide stone streets, marble baths, a sewage system and lots of statues of Roman gods. Sick people from all over the Balkan Peninsula, Asia Minor and the Aegean Islands crowded here. The white-as-marble town could be seen from far away, like a dream among luxuriant vegetation, it was famous for its mineral springs throughout the Roman Empire. After being burnt down by the Goths in the 3$^{rd}$ century, it was rebuilt in the beginning of the 4$^{th}$ century, this time with massive and high defensive walls. During the 5$^{th}$ and 6$^{th}$ centuries the town reached its

*Hissarya Fortress*

# CENTRAL SOUTHERN BULGARIA

*Thracian temple near the village of Starossel*

zenith, being part of the Byzantine Empire. After the 6th century it slowly started to decline. Almost all the time between the 9th and the 14th century it's within the borders of Bulgaria and is known by the name of *Toplitsa*. When the Turks invaded Bulgaria, the town put up a rugged resistance, for which it was completely destroyed and the population was massacred. It was in the 17th century when the Turks finally appreciated its natural assets and re-populated the ex-resort, giving it its present name - Hissarya (fortress) because of the many fortress remains in it. While in Hissarya the population was mainly Turkish, in the nearby villages Verigovo and Momina Banya (now quarters of the town) there lived enthusiastic Bulgarians who took an active part in the struggle against the Ottoman rule. In 1868 Vassil Levski founded a revolutionary committee in Verigovo, 15 members of which took part in the Grand People's Gathering at Oborishte. The village rose in rebellion against the Turkish rule in April 1876 together with other villages in the area, but it was devastated when the April Uprising was suppressed - the village was burnt down, many people were slaughtered, others sent on exile to Cyprus Island, some were driven away.

**Present**. Today Hissarya is a flourishing town and resort of national importance. The mineral water's temperature is 24°-49°C and its output is 40 litres per second. It cures diseases of the kidneys, liver, gallbladder, gastritis, diabetes and many more. The most famous spring is the one in the Momina Banya Quarter (Maiden Bath) with its radioactive alkaline water. There is also a mud-cure establishment, which increases the quality of the therapy. There are some mineral drinking-fountains, balneotherapy establishments, a lot of sanatoriums, few dozens of recreational facilities, hundreds of private and departmental villas, a mineral water beach, many parks and gardens.

**Landmarks**: The **Archaeology Museum** with a rich archaeological (mainly) and ethnographic exposition (8, Al. Stamboliiski Str., working hours 8.00 a.m. - 12.00 a.m. and 1.30 p.m. - 5.30 p.m. all week round, tel.: 0337 2796). **The Hissarya Fortress** has the shape of an irregular tetragon with an area of 300 decares. Its 4th century walls still look impressive and are some of the best-preserved fortress defences in Bulgaria. Their total length is 2315 metres, the walls' thickness is about 2,5 to 3 metres and their height is 10 metres. The fortress were strengthened with 43 quadrangle turrets. One could enter the town through 4 gates, the main of which was the southern, called Kamilite (The Camels).

# CENTRAL SOUTHERN BULGARIA

The northern side has 2 walls, the outer of which is 10 metres away from the inner one, in front of the southern wall there was a 4-metres deep and 10-to-12-metres wide moat. Inside and outside the fortress different kinds of buildings from the ancient town were found - barracks, ancient Roman baths, a late-Roman building (with a colonnade), churches, necropolises. Out of the 5 late-ancient tombs, found in the area, the so-called **Hissarya Tomb**, also known as the 3$^{rd}$ tomb, is the biggest and most famous. It is a late-Roman (from the 4$^{th}$ century) family tomb, consisting of an overarched passage, a staircase and a burial chamber. The walls of the chamber and the passage are decorated with colour frescoes, and the chamber's floor is covered with a 4-colour-mosaic. Other interesting sites are the **banski buildings** (baths) at the springs of Havuza, Momina Banya and Indzheza, the **Old-Christian Basilicas** from the 5$^{th}$ and 6$^{th}$ century, the **Church-Tomb** from the 10$^{th}$-12$^{th}$ century, the **Holy Virgin Temple** in the Momina Banya Quarter, the **St. Dimitur Temple** in Verigovo Quarter, the **St. Pantaleimon Temple** (4, Augusta Str., tel.: 0337 2749), **St. Peter and Pavel Church** and many more.

**Accommodation**: Augusta Hotel (3-star, 3, Gen. Gourko Str.). Krepost Hotel (13, Gen. Gourko Str.). Natalis Hotel (20, Geo Milev Str.). Apriltsi Balneological Complex (66, Ivan Vazov Blvd.). Ministry of Health's Balneological Complex (12, Gladston Str.). Hissar Balneological Complex (2, Gen. Gurko Str.). These balneology complexes operate as balneo-hotels. There are a lot of private lodgings available through the Accommodation Bureau. As a resort centre Hissarya offers a wide variety of restaurants and places where one can eat and have fun.

**Tourist information** is available at the hotels, the balneo-hotels, the Accommodation Bureau, and at Orela Tourist Association (16, Augusta Str., tel.: 0337 2592).

**Transport**. Hissarya has regular bus lines to Plovdiv, Karlovo, Panagyurishte, Strelcha, the village of Krastevitch and other smaller villages in the area. The town is the last station of the local railway line Dolna Mahala - Hissarya (a deviation of Plovdiv -

*Sanatorium in Hissarya*

# CENTRAL SOUTHERN BULGARIA

Karlovo railroad). The bus station (tel.: 0337 2069, working hours: 5.40 a.m. - 7.45 p.m. all week round) and the railway station (tel.: 0337 2256, 2094) are located next to each other in the western outskirts of the town.
**Surrounding areas**. Hissarya is a starting point of tourist tracks through the Central Sredna Gora Range. From here there are marked tourist routes north-west to the Orela Chalet (from Verigovo Quarter it takes 5 hours on foot through the short cut or 22 km along a truck road, for reservations tel.: 0337 2592 in the Tourist Association). From the chalet one can proceed to the Chivira Chalet (3 hours), Bogdan Chalet (5 hours), or one can climb Mt. Alexitsa (1 hour), Mt. Fenera (20 min), Mt. Kozya Gramada (20 min). Another tourist route heads south-east to the Voden Kamak Chalet (9 km along a stony road, tel.: 0337 2534, it is 5 km away from the village of Gorna Mahala). In 2000 during archaeological excavations in the region of the village of Starossel (25 km west of the town) was discovered the grandiose **Thracian Temple** ($5^{th}$ - $4^{th}$ century BC) ever found. It is surrounded by a stone wall (up to 5 m high and 240 m long) made of huge stone blocks. The Thracian temple has one front and two side stairs, a long corridor between 5 metres high stone walls. The actual temple consists of a facade, a rectangular premise and a round premise with an unknown ceiling construction - a unique semi-cylindrical arc and dome. The entrances were closed with massive stone gates. Tens of burial mounds were found nearby, some of them containing tomb-mausoleums of Thracian rulers of the $5^{th}$ and $4^{th}$ centuries BC. The tombs contain extremely valuable articles - golden jewelry, a set of silver adorning as part of horse ammunition, full armament and other pieces of high scientific, art artistic and museum value. The cult complex is a unique evidence of the Thracian orphic belief in our lands. The complex became attractive for tourists long before its final arrangement and opening.

## PLOVDIV

The city of Plovdiv (340 638 inhabitants, 160 m above sea level) is situated in the western part of the Gornotrakiiska (Upper Thracian) Lowland, along the two banks of Maritsa, the largest river, springing out in Bulgaria, and scattered upon six unique syenite hills (called "tepeta"- hillrocks). The town is located 150 km south-east of Sofia, 270 km west of Bourgas, 140 km north-west of Svilengrad, 58 km south of Karlovo, 19 km north-west of Assenovgrad, 102 km north of Smolyan, 37 km east of the town of Pazardzhik, 90 km south-west of Stara Zagora, 75 km north-west of Haskovo. It ranks as the second Bulgarian city in population, size and significance, after the capital Sofia. The city is an important cultural, historic and tourist centre. It is a regional administrative centre, as well.
**History**. Being a crosspoint of major roads from Western and Central Europe to the Middle East, from the Baltic to the Mediterranean region and from the Black Sea to the Adriatic, Plovdiv has ancient millennial history. The most ancient inhabitants of these areas date back to the New Stone, Stone-Copper and Bronze Ages. Later, during the $1^{st}$ millennium BC, nearby the three eastern hills (Dzhambaz Tepe, Taxim Tepe and Nebet Tepe) which were practically a natural defence fortress, the Thracians founded the ancient settlement of *Eumolpias*. In 342 BC the town was conquered by Philip II, the Macedonian, renamed *Philipopole* and turned into a fortress. Later on ($3^{rd}$ - $1^{st}$ century BC, the town already being known as *Poulpoudeva*, was subject to on-going invasions of the Celts. Since $1^{th}$ century it was under Roman rule and quickly grew into a key economic, cultural and political centre of Thracia Province. The town rapidly developed and occupied the entire area around the Three-hills, as a result of which the Romans named the town *Trimontsium*.

# CENTRAL SOUTHERN BULGARIA

After the year 395, when the Roman Empire had fallen apart, the town remained in its eastern part - Byzantine. During the next two centuries the town was many times ruined and set on fire by the Huns and the Gothic tribes. The Emperor Justinian (527-565) turned it into a strategic fortress along the northern Byzantine border. At the end of 6$^{th}$ century the Slavs populated the area and named the town *Puldin* (originating from the ancient name of *Poulpoudeva*).

In 815 Khan Krum included the town within the borderlines of Bulgaria. From this moment on until it fell under Turkish rule, *Plovdiv* (already named so) was subject to numerous takeovers, frequently being under the rule of either the Bulgarians or the Byzantines. In 1364 the Ottomans conquered the town and called it *Phillibe*. Being left far in the back area of the Ottoman Empire, the town lost its strategic location and gradually declined. It was only during the Revival Period that Plovdiv regained its glorious name of a large economic and cultural centre. A new class of craftsmen and merchants was established, having a newly formed national spirit and wellbeing. A large number of residential housings and public facilities preserved as cultural monuments, date back to that Revival Period.

Prominent Revival enlighteners, cultural and political figures - Naiden Gerov (a writer, enlightener and Consul of Russia in Plovdiv), the icon-painters Zakhari Zograf, Dimitar Zograf, Stanislav Dospevski, the woodcarver Ivan Pashkula and many others worked in the town at that time. The residence and the inn of the Turpevi Brothers gave shelter to our national Apostle Levski several times, and in 1870 a local revolutionary committee was founded.

The troops of General Gurko liberated the town on January 17, 1878.

At that time this was the biggest Bulgarian town. After the Berlin Congress (1878) Plovdiv was proclaimed capital of Eastern Roumelia. It promoted an intensively diversified public and cultural life. Ivan Vazov, Konstantin Velichkov, Zakhari Stoyanov and some other reputable Bulgarians lived and worked in the town for some time. A great number of refugees came to the town from the areas of White Sea Thrace, Aegian, Pirin and Vardar Macedonia. The town hosted the proclamation of the Reunification of the Principality of Bulgaria and Eastern Roumelia on September 6, 1885 - an extraordinary in its significance revolutionary act, proving the strong and irreconcilable Bulgarian spirit in pursue of its national ideal. It is by no chance that this date - 6$^{th}$ September - is currently an official holiday of the Republic of Bulgaria.

**Present.** Today Plovdiv is a very beautiful city, coming from the past and striving forward to its future. The hills of Plovdiv are noticeable from quite a distance. This is an area of a vast flat plain and all of a sudden hills pop up! Besides the three hills already mentioned (Dzhambaz Tepe, Taxim Tepe and Nebet Tepe), around which the ancient town has been founded and which host the most interesting and precious remains of our past, stone breasts are rising Sahat Tepe, also known as the Danov's Hill (within the centre of the town, with the clock tower dating back to 16th century), Bunardzhika Tepe (west of the city centre, with the statue of a Russian soldier), and Dzhendem Tepe (The hill of Youht, further to the west). The six hills, as well as the old town of Plovdiv bring specific colour and atmosphere to the town and shape up its unique view and nature.

Maritsa River, splitting the city into two uneven parts connected by six bridges, occupies its relevant place and has its significance for the city of Plovdiv. On the area of the smaller, northern part of the city, along the riverbank, the so-called Fair City is located (37, Tsar Boris III Blvd, tel.: 032 553120). The first Bulgarian exhibition was organised back in 1892, which later on turned

# CENTRAL SOUTHERN BULGARIA

## Plovdiv

# CENTRAL SOUTHERN BULGARIA

into **International Plovdiv Fair.** Currently the fair is conducted twice annually - in the beginning of May the fair is dedicated to consumer goods and commodities, while the fair organised in September focuses on industrial goods. Plovdiv is famous as being a centre of rich agricultural area and its numerous marketplaces are exuberant with great variety of cheap fruit and vegetables.

The city plays the role of a big cultural centre. In addition to the regular opera, theatre, muppet-show and other performances, Plovdiv hosts traditional festivals, art exhibitions, biennials, some of them internationally recognised: **June** - International Chamber Music Festival, end of **May, beginning of June** - Opera days at the Amphitheatre, end of **June** - Verdi Opera days at the Amphitheatre, beginning of **August** - International Folklore Festival, **September** - International Muppet-Show Festival, **September** - "The old town of Plovdiv" National Autumn Art Exhibition. Plovdiv is also a university centre with one university and a couple of higher educational establishments.

**Landmarks**. The first ranking landmark is **the Old Town of Plovdiv Architecture Reserve**, attracting visitors from all over the world. It covers the Three-hill area, which is the original location of the town. Almost all of the most interesting history-related sights are within the old town area: cult, residential and public housings, archaeological monuments and museums, narrow cobble-paved streets. The **Holy Virgin Church** dating back to 1844 (6, Suborna Str., tel.: 032 223265, working hours: 7.30 a.m. - 7.00 p.m. all the week round). **St. Konstantin and Elena Church** dating back in 1832, **St. Marina Church** (1856) with a very interesting wood-carved iconostatis. **Ancient (Roman) Amphitheatre** is situated close to the Southern entrance of the fortress, above the road tunnel. The marble amphitheatre, built up by Emperor Mark Aurelius during the $2^{nd}$ century is the best-preserved monument of those times in our lands. It frequently hosts various performances.

**Nebet Tepe Archaeological Complex -** remains within the Northern part of the Three-

*The amphitheatre in the Old Town of Plovdiv*

# CENTRAL SOUTHERN BULGARIA

hill area. **Philipopolis fortress walls** can be seen within the central part of the Ancient town. **Hissar Kapiya** (the eastern gate of the fortress, built more than 2000 years ago). **The Yellow School** built in 1868 (Todor Samodumov Str.), the first building constructed to serve as an educational facility in Plovdiv. The **House and cellar of Hadzhi Dragan from Kalofer** - 1848-1854, 32, P.R. Slaveikov Str., currently serves as a branch of the National Cultural Monuments Institute). The house of Andrei Georgiadi (**The Hadzhikalchov's House**) dating back to 1831, 6, Mitropolit Paisii Str., currently houses the creative fund of the Union of Research Workers. The **House of Argir Koyumdzhiouglu** built in 1847 by the master Hadzhi Georgi, presently hosts the **Ethnographical museum** (2, Dr. Chomarov Str., tel.: 032 225656, working hours: 9.00 a.m. - 12.00 a.m. and 2.00 p.m. - 5.00 p.m., closed on Monday and Friday morning). **House of Artin Gidikov** from 1848, now houses the 9th regional mayor's office (15, 4th January Str.). The **House of Birdas** from 1856, now serving as official acceptance hall of the Mayor of Plovdiv (45, Suborna Str.). **House of Veren Stambolyan** (built in the second half of 19th century) now housing the creative fund of the Union of Bulgarian Artists (15, Cyril Nektariev Str.). The **House of Georgi Mavridi**, where the French poet **Lamartin** lived in 1833, now hosting the creative fund of the Union of Bulgarian Writers (19, Knyaz Tseretelev Str.). **House of Dimitur Georgiadi** (1848), now turned into a **Museum of the Bulgarian Revival** (1, Tsanko Lavrenov Str., tel.: 032 223350, working hours: 9.00 a.m.-12.00 a.m. and 2.00 p.m.-5.00 p.m., closed on Sundays). **House of Dr. St. Chomakov** (1860), now hosting the Art Gallery - **exhibition of Zlatyu Boyadzhiev** (18, Suborna Str., tel.: 032 260707. **House of Nikola Nedkovich** - 1863 (3, Tsanko Lavrenov Str., tel.: 032 626216) currently serving as **Museum of the Urban Revival Style** - a small romantic palace, located on the Three-hill area, painted in frescos and wall-paintings, exuberantly decorated with wood-carvings, columns, arches and bows. The **Balabanov's House** (the house of Hadzhi Lamisha, currently also functioning as **Museum of the Revival Traditions**). The **House of the Ritor** from the mid 19th century, now turned into a hotel-restaurant complex (8, Todor Samodumov Str.). **House of Hristo G. Danov** from the second half of 19th century, now serving as Tourist House (5, P.R. Slaveikov Str., tel.: 032 223958). These locations comprise only a small portion of the interesting sights in the Old Town of Plovdiv. **Archaeological Museum** (1, Suedinenie Sq., tel.: 032 224339) accommodating the most valuable - Panagyurishte Golden Treasure consisting of wine set masterpieces, the weight of which equals 6.169 kilos of pure gold. **History museum - "Modern History" Exhibition** (14, Angel Boukoureshtliev Str., tel.: 032 222014). **History Museum - "Reunion" Exhibition** (1, Suedinenie Sq., tel.:

# CENTRAL SOUTHERN BULGARIA

032 260252, 269959, working hours: 9.00 a.m. - 12.00 a.m. and 1.00 p.m. - 3.00 p.m., closed on Saturdays and Sundays). **Museum of Natural History** (34, Hristo G. Danov Str., tel.: 032 226663). **Art Gallery - temporary exhibition** (15, Kniaz Alexander I Str., tel.: 032 224220). **Art gallery - exhibition of icons** (22, Suborna Str., tel.: 032 226086). **Art gallery - permanent exhibition** (14A, Suborna Str., tel.: 032 267790).

**The Roman Stadium** (located in the pedestrian zone of Kniaz Alexander I Str., in the proximity of Sahat Tepe. It was constructed during the 2$^{nd}$ century reproducing the layout of the stadium in Delphi, Greece, and the marble seats accommodated 30 000 spectators of games and gladiator fights. The **Roman Forum** (located at the central city square, against the Central Post Office Building). Remains of stone-paved streets, foundations of administrative and agricultural buildings and marble columns were found out from the centre of the ancient major town of the Roman province of Thrace. **Theatres**: Theatre of Drama (36, Kniaz Alexander I Str.), Opera House (1, Gladstone Str., tel.: 032 225553), Muppet-Show Theatre (14, Hristo G. Danov Blvd, tel.: 032 223985), Plovdiv Philharmonic Orchestra (1, Central Square, tel.: 032 282750).

**Accommodation:**
**Old Plovdiv: The Lamartin House Hotel** (19, Kniaz Tseretelev Str., at the cross-section with Zora Str., avails of 2 suites, 2 singles, 2 double rooms, open from April to October, and accommodated in an old Revival house). **Hebros Hotel** (4-star, offers 4 double rooms, it is accommodated in an old Revival house). **House of the Ritor Hotel-Restaurant Complex** (8, Todor Samodumov Str., is accommodated in an old Revival house). **Tourist House** (5, P. R. Slaveikov Str., in an old Revival house).

**Downtown** (beyond the boundaries of the Old Town): **Novotel Plovdiv** (2, Zlatyu Boyadzhiev Str., 9-storied building, located at the bank of Maritsa River). **Trimontsium Hotel** (2, Captain Raicho Str., at the downtown square). **Royal Hotel** (in the downtown). **Sankt Petersburg Park-Hotel** (97, Bulgaria Blvd.). **Bulgaria Hotel** (13, Patriarch Evtimii). **Leipzig Hotel** (70, Ruski Blvd., 11-storied building). **Rhodopes Hotel** - 3-star.
**Maritsa Hotel** (42, Tsar Boris III). **Phoenix Hotel** (79, Captain Raicho Str.).

**Outside the central part of the city: Plovdiv Recreational Complex** (2-star, 3, Osvobozhdenie Blvd.). **Dounav Hotel** (100, Dounav Str.). Plovdiv has many unique and interesting restaurants and facilities, but the most pleasant ones are those, located in the old town. List of a small portion of them is provided herein: **Alafrangite** (17, Cyril Nektariev Str., working hours: 11 a.m. until midnight). **Trakiiski Stan** (5, Puldin Str., working hours: 11 a.m. - 01.00 a.m.). **Philipopolis** (56B, Konstantin Stoilov Str., working hours: 11 a.m. until midnight). **Restavratora** (The Restorer) (32, Slaveikov Str., working hours: 11 a.m. - 11 p.m. all the week round). **Puldin** (8, Kniaz Tseretelev, working hours: 11 a.m. until midnight).

*The Ethnographic Museum*

# CENTRAL SOUTHERN BULGARIA

**Tourist information** is available in every hotel and museum.

**Transport**. Plovdiv is the second significant transport centre in the country after our capital city Sofia. Two types of transport - bus and railway - connect this city to the rest of the country. There is also an existing air transport infrastructure, but currently there are no flights to and from Plovdiv. Motorway connects the city with Sofia, while major motorways connect it with Pazardzhik, Assenovgrad, Stara Zagora, Bourgas, Haskovo, Kurdzhali, Karlovo, Smolyan. The city has 3 major bus stations: **Bus Station Sever** (North) (2, Dimitur Stambolov Str., close to Philipovo railway station, tel.: 032 553011, 553705, servicing the lines to the north of the city in the direction of Rousse, Pleven, Troyan, Koprivshtitsa, etc.). **Bus Station Yug** (South) (47, Hristo Botev Blvd., close to the east of the central railway station, tel.: 032 626937, 226937, servicing the lines and routes to the southern part of the country - Blagoevgrad, Batak, Peshtera, Sliven, Svilengrad, Pazardzhik, etc.). The **Express Transport Private Association** is next to this Bus station (45, Hristo Botev Blvd., tel.: 032 265787, specialised in express bus transport services between the cities of Plovdiv and Sofia, having only a few bus stops in the capital, the last bus stop being at the railway station). There are some other private companies, servicing the routes to Hissarya and Karlovo. **Rhodopes Bus Station**, (Macedonia Str., across the central railway station - a tunnel connects the two stations, tel.: 032 779267, 777607) services the region of the Rhodope Mountains, namely: Assenovgrad, Bachkovo Monastery, Smolyan, Chepelare, Pamporovo, Devin, Kurdzhali, Haskovo, etc. Close to Trimontsium Hotel, in the foyer of the Plovdiv Philharmony (1, Central Sq, tel.: 032 224271) one can buy tickets from the City Transportation Company for **bus transport to Greece**.

**Railway transport**. There are railway lines from Plovdiv to Sofia, Bourgas, Svilengrad, Karlovo, Panagyurishte, Peshtera, Hissarya and Assenovgrad. There are two railway stations and numerous railway stops: **Central Railway Station** (44, Hristo Botev Blvd., tel.: 032 222729, 552730, 222940, info on departing trains: 032 175). **Philipovo Railway Station** (in Philipovo Quarter, tel.: 032 23433602). The **City Railway Bureau** is located in the centre of the city (29, Maria Louisa Blvd., tel.: 032 622732, working hours: 8.30 a.m. - 12.00 p.m. and 1.00 p.m. - 5.00 p.m., closed on Saturdays and Sundays). **Rila International Railway Bureau** is located opposite the Central Railway Station (31A, Hristo Botev Blvd., tel.: 032 446120, working hours: Monday through Friday, 8.00 a.m. - 6.00 p.m., Saturday - 8.00 a.m. to 12.00 p.m. and Sunday - day off). The **Airport** (no regular flights for the time being) is at a distance of 18 kilometres

# CENTRAL SOUTHERN BULGARIA

away from the city (tel.: 032 226173). **International Transport Ticket Bureau** (4, Gladstone Str., tel.: 032 633081, working hours: Monday through Friday, 8.00 a.m. - 6.30 p.m.). Gebray Company Ltd. - **Airlines Ticket Bureau** (94, Vassil Aprilov Blvd., tel./fax: 032 452166.

It is possible to rent a car from the following **rent a car** agencies: **Trakia Autotransport** (82, Hristo Botev Blvd., tel.: 032 264040), **Niko Car** (5, Maria Louisa Blvd., tel.: 032 222369). For first class cars, **Herz Company** should be contacted (located in Sankt Petersburg Hotel, tel.: 032 554409).

Plovdiv has a well organised public and private buses and trolley transport. One may also call a radio-cab, tel.: 6142, 6102, 6111, 6118, 6119, 6666.

**Foreign Countries Consular Sections**:
General Consulate of the Russian Federation (20, Ivan Vazov Str., tel.: 032 224767, fax: 032 230098). General Consulate of Greece (10, Preslav Str., tel.: 032 232003). Consular Section of the Republic of Turkey (10, Philip Makedonski Str., tel.: 032 239010).

**Surrounding areas**. The powerful shapes of the **Rhodopes** rise 10-12 km south of Plovdiv. Its vicinity and accessibility turn the mountain into a favourite site for recreation and tourism for all the citizens of Plovdiv. The existence of two resorts (Studenets and Byala Cherkva), numerous chalets (Zdravets, Ruen, Chernatitsa, Rhodopski Partizani and more distant ones) as well as hundreds of kilometres of roads into the Chernatitsa subpart of the Western Rhodopes, the dozens of kilometres of marked alleys and tracks, catering facilities and other tourist infrastructure, promote the frequent visits to the wonderful mountain sights.

Public buses start from the Rhodopes Bus Station to the villages in the foot of the mountain (Kouklen, Hrabrino, Gulabovo, and some others) which serve as starting points for various hiking tours or trips by car (see the Rhodopes related section).

# ASSENOVGRAD

The town of Assenovgrad (52 116 inhabitants, 180 m above sea level) is situated in the western part of the Gornotrakiiska (Upper Thracian) Lowland, in the northern foots of the Western Rhodopes, at a place where the Chepelarska River runs from the mountain into the valley. It is 169 km south-east of Sofia, 19 km south-east of Plovdiv, 84 km north of Smolyan, 96 km west of Haskovo and 81 km north-west of Kurdzhali. This is the most sacral Bulgarian town. A town with extremely interesting past.

**History**. This fact is explained by its favourable geographic location - the attractive combination of the mountain and the valley, its mild climate, fertile soil and the fact that here is the entrance of the most convenient passage through the Rhodope Mountains connecting Thrace with the Aegean Region. There was an ancient (Thracian) settlement on the territory of this town, and later on a medieval village was founded there. Within its surroundings more than 100 Thracian mounds with a lot of objects were found. The town played its significant role in the medieval period as a strongly fortified site, which witnessed severe battles. The town is first mentioned under the name of *Stanimahos* in the statute (1083) of the Bachkovo Monastery, whose founder, the Byzantine military commander of Georgian origin Grigorii Bakuriani, had conquered the town shortly before that. Later on the chronicles of the successive crusades within the period 1096 - 1204 gave it the names of *Stanimako, Estanimak, Skribentsion*. Under the name of *Stanimaka* (from the word of Greek origin "stenimahos" meaning fortified narrow place) the town left its deep traces in history. In 1230 Tsar Ivan Assen II fortified and expanded the strong Stanimaka's Fortress, called Petrich, which act was celebrated by putting an inscription, carved above its entrance. This is the reason for the fortress to be renamed to

# CENTRAL SOUTHERN BULGARIA

Assenova Krepost (Fortress), and the town of Stanimaka, located below it - to be renamed to Assenovgrad in 1934. Later on the town was either Bulgarian or within the Byzantine Empire. In 1364 the town was conquered by Tsar Ivan Alexander and remained within Bulgarian territories until his death when it was regained by the Turks. During the long Turkish Rule Stanimaka had lost its significance and gradually declined. The town was plundered and put on fire by the kurdzhalii (Turkish brigands) three times. Its inhabitants made their living mainly by growing vineyards (production of Mavrud type of wines) and silkworm breeding (production of silk). After the Liberation, this was a small agricultural town, which remained within the borders of Eastern Roumelia as long as 1885. At the end of 19th century the phylloxera spoiled the vineyards and mass tobbacco planting and growing commenced thereon. The glory of Assenovgrad as a sacral centre, formed during the Eneolite and existing as such until now, explains the presence of so many cult-related buildings in the town and its surroundings - 5 monasteries, 12 churches and more than 50 chapels.

**Landmarks**: The **Museum of History** (1, Trakia Square, tel.: 0331 22150) is in the centre of the town with its three sections: Archaeology, Revival Period and Ethnography. **Ethnographic Exhibition on Lifestyle in the Old Town** (31, Stanimaka Str., tel.: 0331 24030) is accommodated in a Revival style building dating back to 19th century, presenting the domestic style of living and culture of a wealthy family in the town. The working hours for the two museums are from Monday through Friday from 9.00 a.m. to 12.00 p.m. and from 2.00 p.m. to 5.00 p.m. There is also a **Paleontology Museum**, established as a branch of the Bulgarian Academy of Science in 1995. It is housed in the ex-youth house in Badelema Area. The exibits include skletons and fossils of animals, having lived 7-8 million years ago. A major sample is that of Dinoterrium Giganteum - a giant animal, quite similar to the elephant. This is the only skeleton of such an animal, found in Bulgaria, which is very well preserved. Tel.: 0331 23736, working hours: Monday through Friday, 9.00 a.m. - 12.00 p.m. and 2.00 p.m. - 5.00 p.m., Saturdays - 9.00 a.m. to 4.00 p.m., Sundays - closed. **Vine and Winery Museum** (6, Bulair Str.). Extremely valuable church in the town is **St. Joan Predtecha Church** (The Precursor) dating back to 13th-14th centuries, which has one nave, with three-wall abcide without nartex. **St. George (Ambelinski) Church** (Georgi Benkovski Str. in

*Bachkovo Monastery*

# CENTRAL SOUTHERN BULGARIA

Ambelino Quarter) looks like a natural continuation of the steep mountainous hills, with stone columns and three domes, one of which has a 12-wall shape and a high belfry. Constructed by master builders, this church is one of the most representative and imposing temples of the Revival Period. Another remarkable church is **St. Georgi (Metoshki) Church** erected in 18th century on the foundations of an old church from 12th century. The highly artistic wall paintings are drawn by Zakhari Zograf. He is also did the wall paintings in the temple and spring St. Joan Predtecha (The Precursor), next to the **St. Holy Virgin - Annunciation Church** (1836). The **Holy Virgin Church** (2, Radi Ovcharov Str.), the so called "The Deep Church", built in 1765 on the foundations of an older church, destroyed by the Turks. It has a marvellous wooden iconostasis of walnut tree, carved and painted by the masters of art from the Debur Art School. **St. Dimitur Church** was built in 1866. Special interest deserves the D. Shterev's piece of art - "Noah's Ark" because of its extremely rare iconography. The town has several **old houses of the Revival time** with original architecture and beautiful wood-carvings (for example, the houses at 30, Stamenka Str. and at 2, Bachkovska Str.).

**Accommodation**: Assenovets Hotel Complex (3, Trakia Sq., in the centre of the town, 3-star). Art Hotel (10, Kresna Str., family type of hotel, with 5 rooms). Hotel "M" (24, Slavyanska Str., 3-star, family type of hotel). Kalamandi Hotel (54, 6th January Str., on the road to Smolyan, 2-star, 5 rooms, family type of hotel). Hotel "RITZ-IV" (27, Mace donia Str., in Gorni Voden Quarter, 1-star, family type of hotel, 5 rooms). Perun Hotel (8, Gotse Delchev Str., 1-star, family type of hotel, 5 rooms). Santo Kiriko Hotel Complex (2 km away from the town). The Forty Springs Sports Complex (4 km in the direction of the town of Kurdzhali, offers a hotel, bungalows, restaurant, swimming pool). Tourist hostel (1, Kostur Str., the cheapest lodging in town).

There is even greater variety of catering and entertainment establishments.

**Tourist information** - available in the hotels, tourist agencies, Bezovo Tourist Association (6, Trakia Sq., tel.: 0331 23867).

**Transport**. Assenovgrad is connected to the rest of the country mostly by bus transport and by railway. There are regular bus lines to Plovdiv (every 30 minutes), Smolyan, Chepelare, Pamporovo, Bachkovo Monastery, Haskovo, Kurdzhali and a lot of other smaller villages and settlements within the region. The bus station (8, Vassil Levski Blvd., tel.: 0331 22862, 24853) and the railway station (10, Vassil Levski Blvd., tel.: 0331 23029, 22970, 22870) are located next to each other on the left bank of Chepelarska (Chaya) River. The town is the last station of Plovdiv - Assenovgrad railway line. Public bus transport is also available in the town.

**Surrounding areas**. 2 km south of the town, above the road to Smolyan stands the historical **Assenova Krepost** (Fortress), which had existed even during the Thracian ages, but became strategically important in medieval ages after the battle at Klokotnitsa (1230). The feudal castle of the fortress with the tower and the two water reservoirs are thoroughly studied and conserved. The relatively well-preserved building - the church "Holy Mother of God from Petrich" was restored in 1934 and 1985, and the restoration of the wall paintings was completed in 1991. The same year the church was awarded a statute of functioning temple. There is a guide, whose working hours are from 8.00 a.m. to 5.00 p.m. Wednesday through Sunday.

11 км south of Assenovgrad, along the road to Smolyan, is located the second large and significant Bulgarian monastery - **Bachkovo Monastery St. Assumption of the Holy Virgin** (refer to the Rhodope Mountains related chapter herein). This extremely interesting cultural and historical centre amazes with its architecture, wall paintings, icons and precious church plate. The guides are available from 8.00 a.m. to 4.00

# CENTRAL SOUTHERN BULGARIA

p.m. all the week round. 3 km from the town of Assenovgrad is the **St. Kirik and Yulita Monastery** (Gornovodenski Monastery). Built up in the Middle Ages its impresses with its architecture, the valuable wall paintings and icons, which made it remarkable cultural monument. 8 km east of the town, along the road to Parvomai, close to the village of Zlatovruh, is situated **St. Nedelya Arapovski Monastery** - one of the few monasteries, located and built up in the open fields. It was erected in 1856-1868 and as early as 1868 a Bulgarian school with the monastery opened its gates. The wall paintings in the church and the chapel, dating back to 1864, are very precious. In the yard of the monastery the well-known haidoutin Angel Voivoda had built a stone tower with beautiful bow-window rooms above it, which served as a watchtower and defence facility. There is a regular bus stop of all the buses to Parvomai.

One of the most interesting prehistoric sights in the neighbourhood of Assenovgrad is found in the village of Dolnoslav (13 km south-east, on the road to Kurdzhali) - the Lopkite area. There is the only **cult centre**, well studied and described, which had satisfied the religious and other spiritual needs of the prehistoric inhabitants of present South Bulgaria and North Greece. To visit this sight one may take the buses running in the direction of Kurdzhali. The **Thracian rock sanctuaries** are extremely interesting, the most mysterious of them is that of **Belantash** (in the Rhodope Massif of Dobrostan, close to Sini Vruh quarter). There was found a silver votive tablet of Hercules, presented as Dionisius. Four sanctuaries dedicated to the Thracian mounted warrior were found nearby Assenovgrad.

9 km away from the town, east of Bachkovo Monastery, is located the world famous **Chervenata Stena Biosphere Reserve** (The Red Wall) of a total area of 3029 hectares. More than 600 spices of plants grow there, large part of them being endemites and relicts, included in the "Red Book of Endangered Species" of Bulgaria.

45 км south of Assenovgrad, in the proximity of the town of Luki and above the village of Belitsa, in Gradishte Mountain (western part of the Rhodope Mountains), is located one of the most honoured Christian holy places - **Krustova Gora (Forest of the Cross)**. Close to Mt. Krustov Vruh (1413 м) there was a Christian monastery, which was burned by the Turks and the monks were killed. The place is considered a holly place - if someone overnights there, there is a chance for him to be cured, if ill. Of course, this is valid for truly religious persons. Now there is a church and always lots of people crowd there, especially on September 14th - the day of the Holly Cross. There is a regular bus transport to the village of Borovo. From there one may set out by car or on foot (1-1.30 hours). Assenovgrad is a key starting point for tourist hikes across the **Dobrostan Massif** of Western Rhodope Mountains (refer to the Rhodope Mountains related chapter herein).

# CENTRAL SOUTHERN BULGARIA

## CHEPELARE

The town of Chepelare (6067 inhabitants, 1100 m above sea level) is situated in the heart of the Rhodope Mountains, in a small valley, along the two banks of Chepelarska (Chaya) River. It is 222 km south-east of Sofia, 72 km and 53 km south of Plovdiv and Assenovgrad respectively, some 30 km north of Smolyan and about 10 km north-east of Pamporovo Resort. This is the town in Bulgaria situated at the highest altitude. It is a typical resort centre, mostly winter resort.

**History**. The valley has been populated since ancient times, which was proved by the urns with burnt bones, heads of arrow and spear, different ornaments and other objects, considered to be of Thracian origin and found in the locality of Batalski Kamuk. Some Bulgarian Christian tombs dating back to $12^{th}$-$14^{th}$ century were found on the neighbouring land of the town, yet there is no absolute proof as to the existence of an ancient and medieval settlement on the territory of the present town. An ancient Roman road from Plovdiv to the Aegean region passed through the Chepelarska river valley.

The first inhabitant of this place was Belyo-Kehaya, who built his house in 1705. Inhabitants from the neighbouring villages followed his example. In 1726 the newcomers bought the land and became owners of the valley and the surrounding hills. So the settlement of Chepelare was founded. Its name comes from the Gyumyurdzhi village of *Chepeli*, which translates into Bulgaria as stormy, cold. The basic occupation of the inhabitants was animal breeding and some craftsmanship, while some of the men, living there used to travel in the Aegean region working as fishermen or brick-laying masters. The kurdzhalii (Turkish brigands) often invaded the settlement, but they faced organised and severe defence.

In 1836 Chepelare inhabitants built St. Atanas Church and 3 stone turrets within 40 days, supported by a troop of soldiers, sent by the Sultan to guard against the Bulgarian-Mohammedans (pomaks), who opposed the construction. Later on a school was built up, while in 1867 a second temple - Holy Virgin - was inaugurated.

The Caucasus Cossacks brigade of General Cherevin liberated Chepelare on the $18^{th}$ of January 1878. The same year Captain Petko Voivoda with his detachment settled there to defend the Bulgarian Christian population against the rebels of Sinclair.

The Berlin Treaty made Chepelare a borderline village and it frequently gave shelter to the members of the detachment of Peyo Shishmanov Voivoda, who fought for the liberation of the enslaved parts of our Motherland. After the union of Eastern Roumelia with the Bulgarian Principality in 1885 the south border with Turkey was closed and the path of thou-

*Chepelare in Winter*

# CENTRAL SOUTHERN BULGARIA

sands of sheep herds to their winter pastures were barred. Then Cheperale people butchered a large number of sheep and started cutting the surrounding woods in order to provide pastures for the reduced number of sheep herds. Within the period 1879-1886 about 30 000 decares of wonderful coniferous forests surrounding Chepelare were cleared. This brought in the new occupation for the town wood-cutting and - wood-processing. The timber was transported along the river to Stanimaka (Assenovgrad). In 1922 one of the first water power stations in the country was constructed in the region. Gradually, with the beginning of the 20th century and especially during the 30-ies and the 40-ies, Chepelare was turned into a resort town.

**Landmarks**: **St. Atanas Church** (5A, General Cherevin Str.), the **Holy Virgin Church** (Chaya Str., tel.: 03051 3420). More information about these two churches is provided in the history section on Chepelare, provided above. **Museum of Speleology and Bulgarian Karsts** (9A, Shina Andreeva Str., in Peshternyak Tourist House, tel.: 03051 2289, 2041, 3041, working hours: 9.00 a.m. to 12.00 p.m. and 1.30 p.m. to 5.30 p.m. except Mondays) - it is an unique museum not only for Bulgaria, but also for the Balkan Peninsula and Europe. **Rhodopska Iskra Chitalishte** (Rhodope Sparkle Community Centre) (21, Vassil Dechev Str., tel.: 03051 2029).

**Accommodation:** Plenty of accommodation facilities exist in Chepelare, yet throughout the winter months of January, February and March it is necessary to book in advance. The family type 2- or 3-star hotels prevail in this small town (their number exceeds 20), and they are associated in Chepelare Tourist Association.

**Tourist Information** - Tourist Information Centre - 4850 Chepelare, 2A, Mourdzhovska Str., tel.: 03051 3273; Chepelare Tourism Association (tel.: 03051 2246, 3545, fax: 03051 3475). Studenets Tourist Company (9A, Shina Andreeva Str., housed in Peshternyak Tourist House, tel.: 03051 2289, 3251, 3261); at the hotels.

**Transport**. The only available transport to Chepelare is by bus. There are regular bus lines to Plovdiv, Assenovgrad, Sofia, Smolyan, Pamporovo, Devin, Shiroka Luka and other smaller villages within the region. The bus station is located on the left bank of the river (Chaya Str., tel.: 03051 2023).

**Surrounding areas**. 1.5 km south of the town, near the road to Smolyan and Pamporovo is the first station of the **two-chair lift**. It is 2471m long, its transportation capacity is 600 persons per hour and it takes the skiers and tourists for 17 minutes to Mt. Chala (1873 м) in the Chernatitsa sub-part of the Rhodopes, where the starting points of the ski-runs are located. Their total length is equal to 8 400 metres. The first ski-run is 3150 m long and 50 m wide, with a variance of 720 m, while the second ski-run is 5250 m long and 25 m wide. The long distance ski-run is 30 km. 10 km south-west of the town is one of the largest and most famous winter resorts in the country - **Pamporovo** (refer to the Rhodope Mountains related chapter herein).

Being situated in the heart of the Rhodopes, Chepelare serves as a starting point for numerous tourist routes in the mountain of Orpheus (refer to the Rhodope Mountains related chapter herein). At a road distance of 15 km (6 km deep in the Rozhen Saddle), south-east of the town, high on top of Mt. Mechi Chal (Karamanitsa). **Rozhen Observatory** is located, which is open for tourist visits against a modest entrance fee. There is no regular transport to this place, but one can climb up from Chepelare to the observatory for about 2-2.30 hours. The white building, which can be seen from the entire Western Rhodope Mountain, seems as if it has perched on the mountain ridge.

Chelepare is a beautiful mountainous small town, but even more beautiful and appealing is **the nature surrounding it** - a mixture of century old coniferous forests, luxuriant green meadows, exuberant in flowers, vigorous mountain springs, and the endless "sea" of the mild Rhodope peaks!

# CENTRAL SOUTHERN BULGARIA

## SMOLYAN

The town of Smolyan (33 153 inhabitants, 850 to 1050 m above sea level) is picturesquely scattered in the narrow gorge of Cherna River (Black River), in the most beautiful part of the Rhodope Mountains. It is about 260 km southeast of Sofia, 103 km south of Plovdiv, 87 km west of Kurdzhali, 46 km south-east of Devin and 16 km south of Pamporovo Resort. This is one of the most beautiful Bulgarian towns. A regional administrative centre.

**History**. On the 18th of June, 1960 the three neighbouring villages of Smolyan, Raikovo and Ustovo merged in a town, which was named Smolyan, and presently each one of the villages is its quarter. **Smolyan Quarter** (at the highest altitude) is the successor of the vanished village of *Ezerovo*, which was situated 3 km above the town, amidst the Smolyan Lakes. During the period of the attempts to convert the native population to Islam (17th century), its inhabitants strongly opposed this act and the Turks completely destroyed the village. Some of the inhabitants were killed, others ran to the mountains and those who adopted the Muslim religion populated the areas along Cherna River, where the modern quarter lies. The Turks named this new settlement *Pashmaklu*. This is the name mentioned by the French traveller Dr. Paul Luka (1706) and it is recorded in the inscription of the **Overarched Bridge** (Beiska Kupriya), built in 1716. The name of Smolyan was given to this neighbourhood after the Liberation and it came out of the name of the Slav tribe of *Smoleni*. **Raikovo Quarter** (the quarter in the middle) was divided in the early ages into *Gorno* (Upper) and *Dolno* (Lower) Raikovo. A legend tells us that the fellow of Momchil the Hero, Raiko founded this settlement. During the attempt to convert the population to Islam, its inhabitants strongly resisted, paying for that with more than 200 victims, but they preserved their religion and village. The first written document about this settlement dates back to the inscription on a stone of the Mazolska drinking-fountain (1572). It developed as a craftsmanship village. Its aba (coarse homespun woollen cloth and upper men's garment made of it), woollen cloths and rugs were famous throughout the Ottoman Empire. Its economic power during the Revival Period revealed in the building of nice houses of typical Rhodope architecture, churches and schools. **Ustovo Quarter** (the lowest) is an old settlement. Its name is linked to "ustie" (estuary) or "ushtelie" - i.e. it originated from the geographical location of the settlement. It is situated on an important crossroad - this was the crossing point of the old roads from Plovdiv to Xanti and Gyumyur-dzhina and from Drama through Nevrokop (modern Gotse Delchev) to Kurdzhali and Odrin. This predetermined to a greater extent its economic and historic development. Ustovo became an important market centre and significant craftsmanship settlement. Crafts like coppersmith, tinkering, shoe-making, goldsmith, and furriery, homespun wollen cloths and tailoring and others were well developed since early ages. Their products had good market, most of all in Istanbul and Smirna (Izmir). At the beginning of 19th century the village achieved great economic and cultural boom. Almost all of

*An old Roman bridge*

# CENTRAL SOUTHERN BULGARIA

the interesting sites and buildings date back to that period. In 1830 the first monastery school was founded. Priest Gligorko, one of the prominent defenders of Bulgarian population, lived and worked in Ustovo. This is the birthplace of some prominent Bulgarians, such as Sava Stratiev, fighter against Phanariotism and Stoyu Shishkov, a teacher, ethnographer and a man of letters. After the Liberation the entire Smolyan region remained under Turkish Rule until 1912.

**Landmarks.**

In Smolyan Quarter: **The Revival Period houses - Meramovs', Sarievs', Prissadovs'**, etc. The **overarched bridge** (Beiska Kupriya) across Cherna River, built in the beginning of 18$^{th}$ century. **Chinar Nature Reserve** (sycamore-tree) - a 250-years old tree. The **Planetarium** (20, Bulgaria Blvd., tel.: 0301 23074) is the biggest in Bulgaria. The **Museum of the History of Mid-Rhodope Mountains** (New Centre Complex, tel.: 0301 24603), houses more than 150 000 exhibits. The **Town Art Gallery** (New Centre Complex, tel.: 0301 23268) accommodates thousands of masterpieces of artists and sculptors.

In Raikovo Quarter: **Pangalov's House** - valuable architectural monument of culture dating back to 1860, **Alibeev Konak** - an old residential and agricultural complex in the upper part of the quarter. The **Cheshitev's House** in the **Cheshitska area** - housing interesting typical Rhodope houses from the Revival Period in Dolno Raikovo. **Memorial and Charnel-House** in honour of the inhabitants of Raikovo, who died for freedom. **St. Nedelya Church** (1836 г.) has a rich collections of icons. **Mazolev's Drinking-Fountain** bears the inscription, evidencing the first mention of the village.

In Ustovo Quarter: **Mednikarska Charshiya** (the old coppersmith marketplace), **Hadzhiivanov's House,** which provided shelter for the headquarters of the Russian troops in the region during the War of Liberation (1877-1878). The **Sheremetev's, Takov's, Hadzhichonov's Houses** are also within this area. The **Kelyav's House** bears the inscription of sergeant Parhomenko, which informs that some Cossacks from the First Squad of the II Regiment stayed there. **St. Nikola Church** is remarkable with its plentiful, rich wall paintings and original architecture.

The new, modern **centre of the town** is a skilful combination of local traditions and existing environment. Its construction was completed in 1983.

The **Rhodope Theatre of Drama** (Bulgaria Blvd., tel.: 0301 25178) is successfully functioning in this nice town. The town is also a university centre - it houses the Pedagogical Faculty of Plovdiv University "Paisii Hilendarski".

**Accommodation**: Smolyan Hotel (3-star, in the centre of the town, 3, Bulgaria Blvd.) is the biggest in the town. Cypress Private Hotel (31, Sokolitsa Str.). Markelov Private Hotel (14, Nikola Philipov Str.). Mechta Hotel (within the region of Smolyan Lakes). Ezerata Hotel (within the region of Smolyan Lakes, transport provided by bus line No. 4). Sokolitsa Hotel (47, 1$^{st}$ May Str., next to the bus station). Boarding house of the Pedagogical Faculty (32, D. Petrov Str.). Esperanto Tourist Complex. Smolyanski Ezera Chalet (Smolyan Lakes) is situated in the area of Smolyan Lakes. It has 43 beds. The public bus line No. 4 stops close to the chalet. Smolyan offers a wide variety of catering and entertainment facilities, yet one of the most authentic is Beni Tavern in Raikovo Quarter.

**Tourist Information**: Tourist Information Centre, 4700 Smolyan, 80, Bulgaria Blvd., tel./fax: 0301 38055, e-mail: Rhra@mbox.digsys.bg (Union of Rhodope Hoteliers and Restaurateurs); Regional Tourist Information Centre (4700 Smolyan, House of the Youth, TIC, tel./fax: 0301 25040); Council on Tourism (4700 Smolyan, 12, Bulgaria Blvd, tel.: 0301 28758, 24751, 22023/235). Tourist Information Centre (in Smolyan Hotel, 3, Bulgaria Blvd., tel.: 0301 24643, fax: 0301 24631, email: ticsmo@mbox.digsys.bg). Tourist Information & Reservation Centre (80, Bulgaria Blvd., tel./fax: 0301 38085, email: rhra@mbox.digsys.bg).

# CENTRAL SOUTHERN BULGARIA

Karluk Tourist Association (57, Rhodope Str., tel.: 0301 21292, 21056) as well at the hotels.
**Transport**. Bus transport is the most popular for Smolyan. There are regular bus lines to Sofia, Plovdiv (every hour), Kurdzhali, Devin, Assenovgrad, Chepelare, Pamporovo (every hour) and to other smaller villages within the region. Public bus stations: Smolyan Bus Station (located in Smolyan Quarter, at the western end of Bulgaria Blvd., tel.: 0301 34251). Bus Station Iztok (East) (in Ustovo Quarter, tel.: 0301 45161). Bus Station Yug (South) (tel.: 0301 45826). Private buses servicing long-distance lines start 7:00 a.m. from the parking lot opposite the Planetarium. 6 public bus lines are regularly functioning within the boundaries of the town. Radio-cab is also available (tel.: 0301 35059).
**Surrounding areas**. 16 km to the north, up above the town is one of the biggest Bulgarian winter resorts - **Pamporovo** (refer to Rhodope Mountains related chapter herein).
10 km west of the centre of the town is the region of **Smolyan Lakes**, known as the "emerald eyes of the Rhodope Mountain". They totalled 20 in number, but presently there are only 7 lakes. The largest one of them - Bistroto Ezero, the so-called "clear lake" - is also the deepest and the most beautiful. The whole region forms a natural park of forests, meadows, hotels, a chalet, chapels, lanes, open-chair lift to Mt. Snezhanka (Pamporovo), picturesque vertical rocks. Bus line No. 4 travels to this region.

**Smolyan Waterfall** - on Kriva (Curved) River, which is the left tributary of Cherna River. The waterfall is 20 meters high and is in the immediate surroundings south-west of the town.
27 km south of Smolyan, in the valley of Arda River is the village of **Mogilitsa**. It has beautiful Revival Period houses, but the most interesting building is that of the **Agoushev's Konak**, built in 1843. It was intended for all the year round living (in opposition to the summer **Agoushev's Konak** in the Chereshovo Area). It has 221 windows, 86 doors and 24 chimneys. It is artistically decorated inside and outside, with wood-carvings on the ceiling, cupboards, railings and shelters. The Konak tower is flower-painted, and the internal and external architectural design, all in pine, walnut and cherry-wood is splendid piece of art of an unknown Rhodope master. According to the legend, his right hand was cut by Agoush, the owner of the Konak, to make sure that the master will not build another similar masterpiece of art. This is the only preserved medieval feudal castle on the Balkan Peninsula. There are some 20 caves in the vicinity of the village, the most interesting of them being the Ultsata (Uhlovitsa) Cave (3km east of the village) noted for its miraculous cascade lakes. The cave is easily accessible. There is regular bus line from the town of Smolyan to the village.
10 km north of the town is located the extremely interesting village of **Momchilovtsi**. Its authentic Rhodope architecture, the local historic-ethnographic museum, the interesting habits and traditions, its mild and pleasant climate in all seasons, the delicious local culinary gourmets, its fantastic nature, the availability of a number of family type of hotels and other appealing features turn the village into a special site of domestic and international tourism. There is a regular bus line to

# CENTRAL SOUTHERN BULGARIA

Smolyan and Chepelare. For further information and hotel reservation one should contact the Momchilovtsi Tourist Information Centre (tel.: 03023 2212, fax: 03023 2833).

At the middle of the road connecting Smolyan and Roudozem (28 km) is located **Mt. Srednogorets** (1262 m), called the Rhodope Mt. Shipka. In 1934 a 16-metre high magnificent memorial charnel-vault was erected in honour of the soldiers of the 21st Sredna Gora Infantry Regiment commanded by the legendary Colonel Vladimir Serafimov. During the Balkan War, the above-mentioned military unit, jointly with the population from the neighbouring villages led a heroic battle against the numerous regular Turkish troops, which were times more than the Bulgarians. Colonel Serafimov disobeyed the order of the Chief Command Unit to withdraw, declaring: *"I will never betray to the enemies the villages, which have welcomed me as a Liberator just one day ago!"*

**St. Atanas Monstery** and the legendary peak of **Kralyov Kamuk** are located to the south in the Rhodope Ridge of Kainadina.

Smolyan serves as a starting point for a number of tourist routes in the neighbouring hills and ridges of Western Rhodope Mountains (refer to the Rhodope Mountains related chapter herein). The town is also a centre of the emerging national recreation and tourist complex Orpheus, enclosing in its boundaries a significant part of the most beautiful Western Rhodope landscapes.

*A chapel nestled in the Rhodopes*

## DEVIN

The town of Devin (6018 inhabitants, 710 m above sea level) is situated on the two banks of Devinska River, in a small hilly valley in the very heart of the Rhodope mountain. It is 196 km south-east of the capital city, 46 km north-west of Smolyan, 57 km and 82 km south of Krichim and Pazardzhik respectively, and 40 km north-east of Dospat. The town is a well-known balneology resort.

**History**. As early as the Thracian period an ancient settlement and a sanctuary existed at that place. The ancient settlement was situated in the present boundaries of Selishte Area, on the left bank of Vucha River and was then called *Diove*. When the Slavs came, they gave it the name of *Dyovlen*, meaning most probably a small valley, narrow lowland. The village was desolated during the attempts to convert the Bulgarian population to Islam in 1666-1671. Some of the inhabitants of the old village moved to the Vlas' huts, where they laid

# CENTRAL SOUTHERN BULGARIA

the foundations of the present town. A Medieval necropolis dating back to 13$^{th}$-14$^{th}$ century was found in the centre of the town. The names of the surrounding localities and peaks prove that this land was populated by Bulgarians ever since. The most ancient document, which mentions the name of Devin, is of Turkish origin and represents a list of dzhelepkeshani (cattle breeders) in 1576. There are no other documents on the remote past of the settlement - most probably they were destroyed during the two devastating fires, which burnt almost everything to ashes in 1904 and 1912. The town was under Turkish Rule until the year 1912. After 1912 many newcomers moved from the surrounding villages to Devin and thus they helped its economic growth. The town was named *Dyovlen* up to 1934.

**Present**. There is no other town in Bulgaria and on the Balkan Peninsula with so many healing mineral springs. At the same time its microclimate is one of the most healthy climates at all - the rocky and green hills prevent the town from the strong and cold north-west winds, there is a great number of sunny days within the year, the winter is extremely mild, the summer is cool and there is not a single industrial polluter. The proximity of the beautiful coniferous forests, the rivers, exuberant in trout, the wild goats (a scene, quite seldom for the Rhodope Mountains) and last but not least the hospitality of the local mountain dwellers give a final touch to this favourable picture. All these predetermine the development of the town as an extremely promising balneology and mountainous resort of national and international significance. This resort is strongly popular in the Scandinavian coun-

*A view of Devin*

# CENTRAL SOUTHERN BULGARIA

tries. It has its balneology sanatorium and open-air mineral beach.

**Landmarks**: **The Town Museum of History** (40, Osvobozhdenie Str., in the central part of the town). **St. Georgi Chapel** dates back to 18$^{th}$ century (in the western part of the town, close to the stadium). **St. Joan Rilski Church** (10, Drouzhba Str., in the central part of the town).

**Accommodation**: Grebenets Hotel (2A, Drouzhba Str., in the central part of the town) is the largest hotel in Devin. Manolov Hotel (50, Osvobozhdenie Str., in the central part of the town). There are family type hotels in the town as well as private lodgings, available for tourists and visitors. There are also sufficient catering and entertainment facilities.

**Tourist Information:** Tourist Information Centre, 4800 Devin (5, Osvobozhdenie Str., tel.: 03041 4161, fax: 03041 3902). Orpheus Tourist Association ( 46, Osvobozhdenie Str., tel.: 03041 2751), as well as at the hotels.

**Transport**. The only public transport available in Devin is the bus transport. It has regular bus lines to Pazardzhik, Plovdiv, Krichim, Smolyan, Dospat, Gotse Delchev, Shiroka Luka, Pamporovo and other smaller villages within the region. The bus station is at the very entrance of the town, on the right bank of the river (24, Osvobozhdenie Str., tel.: 03041 2077).

**Surrounding areas**. 22 km to the south-east is the **Village of Shiroka Luka Architecture and Ethnographic Reserve** (refer to the Rhodope Mountains related chapter herein). Only 8 km away from the town, in this same direction, are the **Bedenski Mineral Baths** - all the buses to Shiroka Luka, Smolyan and Pamporovo have stops there.

30 km south of Devin one can see a cluster of miracles of the Rhodope Mountain. Against the flow of the Vucha River one can reach the place where its two springs merge - Trigradska and Bouinovska Rivers. For million of years the two rivers had cut out some fantastic canyons, each of them "garnished" by a magnificent cave. The right tributary (viewed along the flow of the river) is the Trigradska River, which had deeply cut in the marble rocks the famous **Trigrad Gorge**, several kilometres long. Before entering it, the river falls into the **Dyavolskoto Gurlo** (Devil's Throat) - a fantastic cave, where, along the following 7000 metres, the water forms some 18 waterfalls and passing through the enormous Roaring Hall exits into the canyon. This miracle of nature is electrified and can be visited against a symbolic fee.

1.5 km south of the town is the Trigradski Skali Chalet and one can make a reservation at the Tourist Association in Devin. Visitors can use the regular bus line from Devin to the village of Trigrad, which has a bus stop close to the chalet.

The other river, the Bouinovska, had created not the less beautiful **Bouynovsko Gorge**, and a little far above it, close to the cross-section to the village of Yagodina is the **Yagodinska Cave**, famous for its unique shapes - cave pearls and stony roses. The cave is electrified. For this tour one can use the regular buses from Devin to the village of Yagodina. Within a 2-hour walk from the town of Devin against the flow of Devin River one can reach the ruins of the **Kaoursko Kale** - an old, inaccessible Bulgarian fortress (built in 8$^{th}$-10$^{th}$ century), which remained unconquered for entire 40 days in the battles with the Ottoman invaders. From the kale the path goes along the entire gorge (15 km) passing close to the **Minaretash** - a vertical rock on the left bank of the river, with a diameter at its basement of 30 meters and some 150 meters height, and reaches the famous **Kemerov Bridge**. There are some fisheries and premises, and along the road passing there one can reach the village of Borino or climb up the marked track to the Orpheus Chalet (about 2 hours).

Devin serves as a **starting point to** other marked hiking tracks in the Velish-Videnish sub-part of the Western Rhodopes (refer to the Rhodope Mountains related chapter herein).

# CENTRAL SOUTHERN BULGARIA

## PAVEL BANYA

Pavel Banya (about 4000 inhabitants, 350 m above sea level) is a town located in the Kazanluk valley to the east of the illustrious Valley of the Roses and on the banks of the Tundzha River. The northern slopes of the Surnena Sredna Gora start to the south of it. The town is 185 km from Sofia, 22 km to the west of Kazanluk, 24 km from Kalofer, 54 km south from Gabrovo, 86 km to the north of the city of Plovdiv and only 4 km from the main Sofia-Karlovo-Bourgas motorway. It is a balneological, mineral water centre of national and international importance.

**History.** Historical data on the settlement is scarce but excavations (during the construction of the new sanatorium - 1939-1940) brought to light remains of a Roman bath and an ancient Christian church, which seem to indicate that local mineral waters were in active use as early as the days of the Roman Empire. The settlement, as it is today, was founded during the Russian-Turkish War of Liberation.

**Present.** Pavel Banya owes its popularity to the healing mineral waters it is endowed with. They spring from 7 natural and drilled-in sources, all having similar chemical composition. Their total output rate is 16 litres per second at the temperature of up to 63°C. Such water is excellent for healing degenerative disorders and inflammations of the joints, chronic rheumatism, infectious arthritis, deforming oste-arthrosis, the Behterev syndrome, inflammation of the tendon, of the joint "pockets", post-traumatic and orthopaedic conditions, post bone-fracture conditions, post dislocation and post sprain conditions, anchylosis of the joints, inborn problems of the pelvis joints. Treatment results have been particularly effective in cases of deformations resulting from spine problems and the peripheral nervous system, blocked movements of the spine joints with painful and limited ability to move, disc pathic states of all kinds - plexus, radiculitis, etc. Diseases of the central nervous system, gynaecological problems are successfully treated. One characteristic feature of the Pavel Banya Sanatorium is that it treats - with particular success - disc hernia.

The resort hosts a big recuperation centre with more than 500 beds and modern medical equipment. There are many other balneological and supporting facilities. It also has 200 decares of park of various broad-leaved and coniferous trees, close to which there is an open-air sport and beach complex (an Olympic size swimming-pool).

**Accommodation:** The recuperation complex has a 2-star hotel (22 double rooms, 2 single rooms and 2 suites). The Knyaz Pavel Hotel (120 beds in double rooms). Varna Hotel (1, Goze Delchev Str., 16 beds, a snack bar). Zdravets Hotel (10 beds). Motel (40 beds, 4 suites, coffee-bar and canteen with a kitchen). The resort has a sufficient number of catering and entertainment facilities.

**Tourist information.** At the hotels and at the town-hall (tel.: 04361 2260, 3260, 2264, 2148, fax: 04361 2094 and telex: 88496).

**Transport.** Bus and railway lines connect Pavel Banya with the remaining part of the country. Hourly buses to and from Kazanluk. Bus routes to following destinations have a stop at the town: Sofia, Plovdiv, Rousse, Sevlievo and Stara Zagora. The bus station is in the very centre of the town. Pavel Banya railway station (4.5 km north of the town, connected with it by regular bus and private van transport) is a stop along the sub-Balkan Sofia-Karlovo-Burgas railway line.

**Surrounding areas.** Two kilometres west is the **Dubravata Area**, covered with mixed foliage and beautiful meadows. Extremely soothing to the heart and the coronary system as well as the lungs with a healing effect long proved. Two kilometres south is the **Izvora** (the Spring), the waters of which have a most healing effect on the excretory system. In the

# CENTRAL SOUTHERN BULGARIA

**village of Touria** (another 4 kilometres south) is the **birthplace** - and **house** - of the Bulgarian writer **Choudomir** and the Nashentsi Ethnographic Hall (Our Folks).

6-7 km to the south is located the **village of Gabarevo** with **Dzhananov's House** where Vassil Levski established a revolutionary committee in 1869. At present the house is hosting exhibition of paintings dedicated to the Apostle of Freedom, as well as an exposition of private belongings of Petrana Klissourova - a graphic painter and poetess.

In the neighbouring **village of Turnichane** there is a branch of the **Kazanluk Art Gallery** exhibiting works of the famous painters Dechko Stoev, Stefan Yankoulov, Hristo Forev, the sculptures of Ivan Topalov, as well as the permanent exhibition of the natural wood-plastics of the artist Hristo Yotov.

In the **village of Gorno Sahrane** (7 km to the north) is the "Bate Mitko" entertainment establishment (bar, discotheque, an open-air pool and an exotic zoo, giving home to crocodiles, a jaguar, turtles, roes, deer, mountain goats, parrots etc. Some 10 kilometres to the south on the way to the town of Rakovski and the city of Plovdiv one can see a rare tree (an interesting natural phenomemon ) - the Kichest Gabur Tree (the branchy hornbeam tree), now 160 year old.

Pavel Banya is the starting point of numerous tourist tracks, which lead throughout the Stara Planina and Sredna Gora Mountains. From the village of Touria one may follow the track to the Sredna Gora chalets - **Bratan Chalet** (4 hours) and **Kavakliika Chalet** (3-hour walk, 17 km by car). Stara Planina can be challenged from the village of Skobelevo (about 10 km north of Pavel Banya) for reaching the **Mazalat Chalet** (4.30 hours), the **Sokolna Chalet** can be climbed from the village of Gabarevo (2.30 hours), from the village of Tuzha (15 km north-west of Pavel Banya) one can reach the **Roussalka Chalet** (2.30 hours, 13 km truck road) and **Tuzha Chalet** (6 hours walk, 25 km of truck road).

## KAZANLUK

**Kazanluk** (54 021 inhabitants, 350 m above sea level) is a town located in the centre of the valley bearing the same name, whose eastern part is known beyond the boundaries of Bulgaria as the Valley of the Roses. It is about 200 km east of Sofia, 55 km east of Karlovo, 48 km south of Gabrovo, 75 km west of Sliven, 35 km north-west from Stara Zagora and 108 km north-east of Plovdiv. Kazanluk is an important industrial, historical and cultural centre. The town is the Capital of the Roses (rose growing) in our country.

**History.** The first settlement on the territory of today's Kazanluk was founded in Neolithic times. During the Eneolith and the Bronze Age life in the settlement went on. It was during the $5^{th}$-$4^{th}$ centuries BC that the Thracian town *Sevtopolis,* bearing the name of the Thracian King Sevt III (now the ancient settlement is

*The Memorial Church near the town of Shipka*

# CENTRAL SOUTHERN BULGARIA

under the waters of the Koprinka Dam, 7 km to the west of the town) was announced capital of the Thracian state of the Odrissi (a rich civilisation of the Tonzos valley - today's Toundzha River). From those days are more than 12 burial tombs already found, the most important of which is, by no doubt, the Kazanluk tomb offering a unique insight into the life of the ancient Thracians.

*Kazanluk Thracian Tomb. Frescoes*

Today's town of Kazanluk was established at the beginning of the 15$^{th}$ century. By the end of the 19$^{th}$ century Kazanluk had become well-known for its production of rose oil, copper plates and household articles, abi (coarse homespun wollen cloth and upper men's garment made of it), gaitani (braids). Due to the loss of markets throughout the Ottoman Empire after the Liberation the crafts declined to give way to contemporary economic activities.
**Landmarks.** The **Kazanluk Thracian Tomb** (dated back to the end of 4$^{th}$ and first half of the 3$^{rd}$ century BC) was excavated in 1944. It is one of the 9 cultural, historic and natural sites in Bulgaria included in the UNESCO list of monuments of global importance. Indeed, it is a masterpiece of the Thracian architecture and painting. It is considered to belong to the "dome-shaped" type of tombs. The tomb is located in the north-eastern part of the town, in the Tyulbeto Park. It consists of a lobby, a corridor and a round-shaped dome-roofed burial tomb. The system of ornaments in the corridor is complex and extremely interesting. The walls are covered with shining, fine plaster and a beautiful fresco - characteristic of the times - of interwoven leaves encircle its upper part. Scenes of war are depicted and in the centre of each one can see two warriors and two more coming from both sides, all of them in their battle attire and weapons. Warriors on horseback are also shown with the particulars of their battle gear and armament. This theme relates to the military and political activities of the deceased. The focal point is the main composition, which describes a burial feast. It is there that one can see a married couple of obvious eminence, painted with great skill and care. They are placed sit but next to them stands a tall woman, presumed to represent the Goddess of land and fertility - Demetra. Numerous figures of wildly galloping horses and battle carts add to the width and depth of the scene.

The tomb is embedded into a special protective building, equipped with all the necessary air-conditioning systems for preserving the frescos. Near to the original a one-to-one copy has been built for mass visitation with working hours 8.00 a.m. - 6.00 p.m. Monday through Friday. Telephone for information: 0431 24700. Another notable tomb is the **Muglizh Tomb** - 3 kilometres west of the small town of Muglizh (regular busses from Kazanluk). It dates back to the 3$^{rd}$ century BC and has an overall length of 23 meters.

**Iskra Town Museum** (Iskra Str.15) was founded in 1901, exhibits more than 70 000

# CENTRAL SOUTHERN BULGARIA

objects and is one of the oldest in the country. In 1930 director of the museum became the well-known Bulgarian writer Dimitur Hristov Chorbadzhiiski - Choudomir. At present it is divided into 5 thematic sections. The **Town Art Gallery** (located in the same building with the museum) is one of the oldest and richest in the country especially when one takes into account that Kazanluk is the birthplace of such painters as Dechko Uzunov, Nenko Balkanski, Ivan Milev, Choudomir and a number of others. Apart from great pieces of art, the gallery possesses a collection of icons and engravings form the Revival Period as well as a small collection of works from the sphere of the ornamental and applied arts. Branches to the gallery are the **houses of Prof. Nenko Balkanski,** and of the national painter **Dechko Uzunov** both exhibiting unique pieces of art. **Choudomir Museum of Literature and Art** has a year-round art exhibition called "The life and works of Choudomir" and a picture gallery - appreciation to many talents and nationally important works of Choudomir. The Choudomir Festivities are held in Kazanluk each year from 25th March (the birthday of the author) until the 1st April (Humour and Jokes Day).

**The Museum of the Rose.** The oil-yielding rose was imported in Bulgaria during the 18th century from the Middle East and found the most favourable conditions for growing in the valley of the Toundzha River - between the Stara Planina and the Sredna gora mountain ranges - the valley was later called "Valley of Roses". Founded in 1969, this museum is unique of its kind not only in Bulgaria. It working hours: 8.30 a.m. - 5.00 p.m. all the week round. Each year during the first weekend of June it becomes the focus of attention during the traditional annual Festival of the Rose - the most colourful event in the Town of the Roses.

**Koulata Ethnographic Complex** (the Tower) is located in the oldest quarter of Kazanluk at Knyaz Svetopoli-Mirski Str. Two restored houses were turned into permanent ethnographic expositions - a traditional village house of the sub-Balkan region as from the 19th century and a typical town house (the Hadzhienov's house) of mid 19th century illustrate with their interior the way old Bulgarians lived in this part of the country.

**St. Joan the Precursor Church** was built in 1844. In 1877 the greater part of the frescoes were destroyed. Stefan Ivanov, Nikola Marinov and Dechko Uzunov restored the wall paintings in 1936. Now it exibits two medallions, painted by Choudomir and Mara Chorbadzhiiska as well. **The Holy Trinity Church** - 1834. **St. Iliya the Prophet Church** of 1866. In 1877 the bashibozouk (armed volunteers) of the army of Sulleiman Pasha slaughtered more than 200 citizens of Kazanluk, seeking refuge in the church. Their bones are exhibited in the church-yard.

The **Nunnery Convent** (1828) was a hospital for Russian soldiers and Bulgarian volunteers during the Russian-Turkish War of Liberation of 1877 - 1978, many of which were buried in its backyard.

**Accommodation:** The

*The Memorial to Freedom on Mt. Stoletov*

# CENTRAL SOUTHERN BULGARIA

*A typical Kazanluk house*

Kazanluk Hotel (2, Rozova Dolina Blvd.) - 3-star hotel and the biggest in town with its 350 beds. Arsenal Hotel (52, P. D. Petkov Str.) - 3-star hotel, offers 2 suites and 21 rooms. Both hotels have their own restaurants. The MOSHI Tourist Complex - Krunsko Hanche Motel (3 km north of the town) has 12 double rooms and 4 suits, a restaurant and a bar.

Apart from these, the town has many other establishments offering traditional local cuisine: Starata Kushta Restaurant (The Old House) (4, D-r Baev Str.), Kestenite Restaurant (The Wall-nut tree) (10, 19$^{th}$ February Str.) and many others.

**Tourist information.** Tourist Information Centre - 6100 Kazanluk (4, Knyaz Alexander Batenberg Blvd. - tel.: 0431 24917). Orlovo Gnezdo Tourist Association (10, Acad. P. Stainov Str.), at the hotels.

**Transport.** Kazanluk is an important transport centre. It is cut across by major motorway Sofia-Karlovo-Burgas and the respective railway line but also by main motorway from Rousse through Veliko Turnovo and Gabrovo in the direction of Stara Zagora, Plovdiv, and Haskovo. There are regular bus routes connecting the town with Gabrovo, Stara Zagora, Karlovo, Plovdiv, Lovech, etc. The bus station (tel.: 0431 22383) and the railway station (tel.: 0431 22012) are close to one another and are located in the southern part of the town.

**Surroundings areas. Shipka-Bouzloudzha National Park-Museum** was founded in 1956. It includes the **Birth of Christ Memorial Church** (the Sipka Monastery) nearby the town of Shipka (12 km north of Kazanluk, regular bus line), **The Memorial to Freedom on Mt. Shipka** (above the Shipka Pass through the Balkan Mountain, 26 km. northwest of Kazanluk, all Kazanluk-Gabrovo busses stop there), and **the historical sites** nearby - the **Monument to Victory** and the adjacent **park close to the village of Sheinovo** (11 km north-west of the town and 3 km south of the town of Shipka, regular bus lines) and the **historical places** at Mt. Bouzloudzha (17 km north of the town and 12 km to the east of Shipka Pass, no regular bus lines) in the Balkan Mountain.

In the surroundings of the **town of Shipka**, on the southern slopes of the Balkan, Bulgarians have built the **Birth of Christ Memorial Church** in honour to the heroes of the Russian-Turkish War of Liberation of 1877-1878 - Russian soldiers and Bulgarian volunteers. Its gold plated domes and beautifully ornamented facade stand out against the mountain and attract the attention of all heading for the Shipka Pass. Sanctified on 27 September 1902, the memorial church is built in the Russian clerical architectural style of the 17$^{th}$ century with an entrance under 3 arcs, over which there is a high and impressive belfry. The names of the Russian regiments and the soldiers who gave

# CENTRAL SOUTHERN BULGARIA

their lives for the liberation of the country are engraved on 34 marble plates. In the church one can enjoy Slavic spiritual music and see the permanent exhibit of icons and church plate. Working hours: every day from 8.30 a.m. to 5.30 p.m. Professional guides available on demand.

**The Memorial to Freedom** stands proud on Mt. Stoletov (1326 metres) to the south of the Shipka Pass in the Balkan Mountain. A stairway of 894 steps gets visitors from the pass to the memorial, built in 1934 with the voluntary support of the whole nation. It is 31.5 meters high and over its main entrance one can see the proud figure of a bronze lion. The other three sides of this entrance bear inscribed the names of Shipka, Sheinovo and Stara Zagora - the battle fields reminding us of the heroes of war and the feats of Bulgarian volunteers. Working hours: every day from 9.00 a.m. to 5.00 p.m. Professional guides available on demand. The Memorial of Freedom is amidst **Shipka National Park-Museum**. Indeed, few are the museums situated in the very real theatre of battles and Shipka is one of them. It includes all the places and points of interest related to the defence of Shipka Pass and is a complex of memorials, remaks of strategic positions once held, trenches and batteries. The historical, and most noted, rocky cliff - Mt. Orlovo Gnezdo - is nearby. It became the arena of the decisive and dramatic battle for the pass from $21^{st}$ to $23^{rd}$ August 1877, which later inspired the national poet Ivan Vazov to write the immortal poem "Opalchenzite na Shipka" (The Defenders of Shipka) Each year on $3^{rd}$ March (Bulgarian National Holiday) and on $23^{rd}$ August (the most dramatic day of the battles and of the whole Russian-Turkish War) national festivities are held. As a result, a whole tourist settlement has emerged through the years.

The feat of Russian and Bulgarians during the Russian-Turkish War of Liberation has been honoured by yet another monument - the memorial at the **village of Sheinovo**. It is built exactly on the spot, where the spontaneous parade of victory was held on $28^{th}$ December 1877 to mark raising of the white flag by Veissel Pasha and the surrender of his army of 30 000. It is in the form of a sword 15.6 meters high - blade up. The memorial bears engraved the names of all Russian and Bulgarian participants in the battles and texts of gratitude as well.

Under the historic **Mt. Bouzloudzha** in the Balkan, stands the **memorial to Hadzhi Dimitur** and his volunteers, erected on a small meadow on the northern slope of the peak, where all found their death on $2^{nd}$ August 1868. It is a sculpture of the leader in front of a wall of 28 stone blocks, bearing the names of the dead warriors. There is a whole tourist settlement, including two cha-

*Picking roses*

# CENTRAL SOUTHERN BULGARIA

*Rose oil-yielding facility*

## STARA ZAGORA

Stara Zagora (143 989 inhabitants, 190 meters above sea level) is situated in the northern part of the Gornotrakiiska (Upper Thracian) Lowland, immediately under the southern slopes of Surnena Sredna Gora. Along with Kazanluk and Gabrovo it stands nearly at the ideal centre of the country. The town is located at the distance of 231 km east of Sofia, 90 km north-east of Plovdiv, 70 km south-west of Sliven, 48 km north of Dimitrovgrad and 35 km to the south-east of Kazanluk. Apart from being one of the most ancient towns in Bulgaria it is a big and important regional industrial and cultural centre.

**History.** Mostly due to its central position this town has a rich and most interesting history. In the 6$^{th}$ century BC it was a major Thracian settlement called *Beroe*. In the 2$^{nd}$ century the Romans built the town and call it *Augusta Trayana* (to the name of the emperor Trayan), which is soon to become one of the greatest and most famous towns in Roman Thrace. At the beginning of the 6$^{th}$ century the town was destroyed, later on to be populated by incoming Slavic tribes, who named it *Vereya*. For some time in the mid of 8$^{th}$ century is was conquered by the Byzantine Empire and renamed again, this time in honour of the Empress - *Irinopolis.* In th 9$^{th}$ century the town became an administrative centre of a vast district under the name of *Borui*. It was as late as the 12$^{th}$ - 14$^{th}$ century that the district was named *Zagore* wherefrom much later its contemporary name derived. Under the Turkish Rule it was known as *Eski Hisar* (old fortress) and after 1488 - as *Eski Zaara* ("zaara" meaning a fertile area).

During the Revial Stara Zagora is an important economic centre populated by Bulgarians mainly, extremely active in the sphere of Bulgarian educational revival and national liberation movement. Among the teacher in the five-class primary school of 1859 are the

lets with the same name - Bouzloudzha.
Other points of interest around the town of Kazanluk include **St. Paraskeva Church** in the village of Enina (4 km north of the town, regular buss line) built during the reign Tsar Assen II - about 1237-1238 and considered the oldest in the district. Several times partially burnt and recovered it owes its notoriety to the manuscripts found therein. **St. Nicolai Monastery** is close to the town of Muglizh (15 km east of Kazanluk and 2.5 km north of its centre, regular bus lines). It is beautifully situated on the bank of Muglizh River and represents an immortal bastion of Bulgarian spirit.

The **Koprinka Dam** is only 6-7 km to the west of the town. There are recreational and tourist facilities built around it - a wonderful place for leisure and sports out in the open air. It is easily accessible by regular bus lines from the town.

**Kazanluk Mineral Baths** (Ovoshtnik) are located 5 km to the east of the town and 2 km south of Ovoshtnik in the immediate vicinity of the Toundzha River. There one will find an open-air mineral beach. Some of the villages adjacent to the town of Kazanluk are **departure points** of several marked tourist tracks crossing the Shipka Balkan (refer to the Stara Planina related chapter herein).

# CENTRAL SOUTHERN BULGARIA

esteemed enlighteners Neofit Rilski, Ivan Bogorov, P. R. Slaveikov and among the pupils one reads the names of Vassil Levski and Raina Popgeorgieva. A revolutionary committee was established in town and it was headed by Kolyo Ganchev, Georgi Apostolov and the Zhekov Brothers under the leadership of Stefan Stambolov and Georgi Ikonomov but due to treason, the planned uprising failed before it was to start. For the third time in its history Stara Zagora was put to the torch and turned to ashes during the Russian-Turkish War of Liberation.

After the Liberation the town was built yet once again in the fashion of straight geometrical system - straight streets crossing in perpendicular. The town plan was worked out by the Czheck urbaniser Loubor Bayer. The principles laid therein are further observed in the construction works, which makes the town unique in Bulgaria.

Stara Zagora is the birthplace of the poets Kiril Hristov, Nikolai Liliev, Vesselin Hanchev of the singer Hristina Morphova; of the painters Anton and Georgi Mitovi, Atanas Mihov, Mario Zhekov. It is commonly known as the "town of lime-trees and poets".

**Landmarks.**
**The Town Museum of History** (11, Graf Ignatief Str., tel.: 042 44081, 23931).
The **Bereketska Mogila** (Hill) (west of Kolyo Ganchev Quarter) is the biggest prehistoric settlement excavated in Bulgaria. It is 17 meters high, its diametrical dimensions at the base are over 250 metres. Close to the District Hospital (16, Armeiska Str. or Bareiro Str.) scientists have found the **biggest dwelling mounds in Bulgaria.** Therein were the remains of two ancient dwellings dated back to the neolith - the middle of the $6^{th}$ millennium BC and they are the best preserved such finds in Europe to date. Working hours: 9 a.m. - 12 a.m. and 2 p.m.- 5 p.m. Tuesday through Friday. The antique **forum Augusta Trayana** (The Bishop Methodi Kousev Blvd., on the back of the Law Court) is one of the most monumental facilities built in the Roman city of Augusta Trayana. Working hours: 9 a.m. - 12 a.m. and 2 p.m. - 5 p.m. Tuesday through Friday.

**Late antiquity floorage mosaic** - $4^{th}$ century (Gen. Stoletov Str., behind the Opera House). Preserved is only the guest hall of a rich house, situated in the centre of Augusta

*Autumn in gold*

# CENTRAL SOUTHERN BULGARIA

Trayana. Only the floor has stood up to the decay of time and it is in an impressive and lavishly ornamented square hall of about 10 x 10 metres. The composition, the colours chosen and the craftsmanship employed make it one of the most impressive examples of provincial Roman art of the 6$^{th}$ century. Working hours: 9 a.m. - 12 a.m. and 2 p.m. - 5 p.m. Tuesday through Friday.

**Late antiquity municipal building with mosaics** (4$^{th}$ - 6$^{th}$ century) can be seen in the cash hall of the Central Post Office, where archaeologists have excavated a big building of the south-eastern end of Augusta Trayana in the immediate vicinity of the city walls. The floor of this official building is covered with a colourful mosaic, which employs allegorical and zoological symbols to represent and illustrate the seasons of the year and the endless spiral of life. Working hours: 9 a.m. - a.m. and 2 p.m. - 5 p.m. Tuesday through Friday.

**The Defenders of Stara Zagora 1877 Memorial Complex** is a 50 meter high monument erected in 1977 on the historical Chadar Hill to commemorate 100 years from fierce battle for the liberation of the country during the Russian-Turkish War of 1877-1878 when the Bulgarian volunteers, waving the national colour - the sacred Samara Flag - went to their maiden battle. It stands proud in the Bulgarsko Opulchenie Park on the outskirts of the town.

**Youri Gagarin Astronomic Observatory and Planetarium** (located on the top floor of the High School of Foreign Languages "R. Rolane").

**The Art Gallery** (110, Tsar Simeon the Great Blvd., tel 042 22843, 21380) hosts more than 4000 works of art from all genres. The golden fund of the gallery keeps a rich collection of medieval Bulgarian icons and prints as well as works from Georgi Danchov, Stansilav Dospevski, the Mitov Brothers, Ivan Penkov, Tseno Todorov, Vladimir Dimitrov - the Master, David Perez, Dechko Uzunov, etc. (Working hours: 9 a.m. - 12 a.m. and 2 p.m. - 6 p.m. Tuesday through Saturday).

The **Hilendar Convent** (in the yard of the St. Dimitur Church, tel.: 042 32086) is a reconstruction of the original convent with the Hilendar Monastery at Sveta Gora, which actually functioned in the town before being finally burned down when the town was put on fire for the last time. In those days Levski lived there for three years. A central place has the exhibition "Levski in Stara Zagora". (Working hours: 9 a.m. -12 a.m. and 2 p.m. - 5 p.m. Tuesday through Friday).

The **House-Museum "Town Life in the 19$^{th}$ century"** (68, Dimitur Naumov Str., close to the centre of the town) is located in Hadzhiangelov's House, which was built in 1883 by a master-builder from Debur and is a typical representative of the later type of symmetrical architecture with no portico. (Working hours: 9 a.m. - 12 a.m. and 2 p.m. - 5 p.m. Tuesday through Friday).

**Geo Milev House Museum** (37, Geo Milev Str., tel.: 042 23450) is a rich, modern and well arranged museum to visit. (Working hours: 8.30 a.m. - 4.30 p.m. Monday through Saturday).

**Metodii Koussev Park** (**Ayazmoto** - the Spring) is a big, artificial green park arranged over the slopes of the Sredna Gora in the northern part of the town. Its creator was the notable restoration activist Bishop Metodii Koussev and planting began in 1895. Today the park spreads over an area of 2600 decares and is a true botanical garden with various kinds of trees and flowers from all over the world. In the park there are the St. Theodor Tiron Church, the memorial to Aleko Konstantinov, a zoo, jogging alleys, sport facilities and is an excellent place for outdoor recreation among exotic nature. **Metodii Koussev Memorial** (1838-1922) is the work of the sculptor Valentin Starchev and the architect Tanko Serafimov. The opening ceremony was held on 1 November 1996.

Stara Zagora is a big cultural centre. The **Geo Milev Theatre of Drama** (Bishop Metodii Koussev Blvd.) stages its plays in the beautiful

# CENTRAL SOUTHERN BULGARIA

## Stara Zagora

# CENTRAL SOUTHERN BULGARIA

building of the Old Theatre House in the centre of the town (tel: 042 26978, 22267, 22273).
The **State Opera House** (111, Gen. Stoletov Str., tel: 042 24416, 29584, tel./fax: 042 41015). The **State Puppet Theatre** (46, Gen. Gourko Str., tel.: 042 25508, 25408, 48095). Stara Zagora is a university centre, as well.

**Accommodation:** Ezeroto Complex (60, Bratya Zhekovi Str.). Vereya Hotel (100, Tsar Simeon the Great Str., in the centre, the biggest hotel in town). Zheleznik Hotel (1, Peter Parchevich Str.)
Char Hotel (12, Kamenev Str.). All hotels have restaurants offering national cuisine.

**Tourist information.** At the Council on Tourism (6000 Stara Zagora, 107, Tsar Simeon Blvd., tel.: 042 39603, 26864), at Surnena Gora Tourist Association (62, Tsar Simeon Blvd., tel.: 042 38435).

**Transport.** Being an important transport junction the town maintains contacts with the other parts of the country by road and rail. Regular bus lines to the towns (Plovdiv, Kazanluk, Sliven, Chirpan, Nova Zagora, Dimitrovgrad, and Haskovo) and the villages in the region. The major motorway Sofia - Plovdiv - Bourgas and the road from Rousse to Kurdzhali cross the town. The bus station (64, Slavyanski Blvd., tel.: 042 22145, 22149) and the railway station (20, Gerasim Papazchev Str., tel.: 042 50145, 26752) are near-by each other in the southern part of the town. Railway routes to Plovdiv and Sofia, to Bourgas and Toulovo start from the town, from where one can join Sofia - Karlovo - Bourgas railway line. Stara Zagora Airport (no regular flights at present, Kolyo Ganchev Quarter, tel.: 042 20966, fax: 042 21188, telex 88530) is located at the very outskirts of the town. Stara Zagora has a very well organised inter-city transport.

**Surrounding areas. Stara Zagora Mineral Baths** is a balneological resort, 15 km northwest of the town with an open mineral pool and numerous opportunities for recuperation and rest, boarding and entertainment. In the immediate vicinity a Roman bath from the $2^{nd}$ century (161 163) was found, which the citizens of ancient Augusta Trayana used. In the area of Mechi Kladenets (Bear's Well) archaeologists have discovered old copper mines (from the Copper-Bronze Age - the $4^{th}$ millennium BC), which are one of the oldest and biggest of their kind in Europe.

The resort is a departure point for a whole-day hiking tour along a marked track to Kavakliika Chalet in the Surnena Sredna Gora Mountain. The baths are reached by regular town bus line. The **resort village of Yagoda** is located 20 kilometres north of Stara Zagora - it has an open-air mineral pool. One can get to it by passing through the 14-kilometre long historical **Zmeevski Pass**, by the famous village of Zmeevo known for its excellent zmeevski white pelin wine. All buses between Stara Zagora and Kazanluk can be taken, as well as the train for Toulovo.

# CENTRAL SOUTHERN BULGARIA

## CHIRPAN

Chirpan (20 468 citizens, 180 meters above sea level) is located in the central part of the Gornotrakiiska (Upper Thracian) Lowland mostly along the left bank of Tekirska River. It is located 201 km south-east of Sofia, 51 km east of Plovdiv and 39 km south-west of Stara Zagora. It is the birthplace of the great Bulgarian poet Peyo Yavorov.

**History.** Chirpan is considered the heir to the Roman settlement **Sherampol,** which was established close to the Roman town of Pizus (the Hissarluka Area close to the village of Rupkite, 7 kilometres to the north of today's Chirpan). It has been accepted that Sherampol (translated "the city of nice friends") was established by fleeing refugees. The present name of the town is supposed to derive from the Roman Sheramnol although todays town emerged at a much later stage - most probably in the 17$^{th}$ century around Tekira Springs under the name of *Dzherpan*. During the Bulgarian Revival (18$^{th}$ - 19$^{th}$ century) the settlement grew as a town with well-developed agriculture and crafts. During the struggle for independence of the Bulgarian Church it was the people of Chirpan who gave the first sacrifices - Velko Boyadziyata and Kaba Ivan. After the Liberation crafts were in decay due to the loss of markets in the Ottoman Empire but in their place vine-growing and wine-making underwent a rapid development. The town was severely hit by the earthquake of 1928.

It is the birthplace of the great Bulgarian lyric and revolutionary Peyo Kracholov Yavorov, of the painter Georgi Danchov - Zografina, one of Levski's comrades, of the painter Nikola Manev known far beyond Bulgarian borders and of the poet Dimitur Danailov.

**Landmarks. The Museum of History and Archaeology. P. K. Yavorov House-Museum** (22, Kracholovi Str., in the centre of the town). Among the personal belongings are the inkpot and the watch of the poet as well as a part of his library. The house of **G. Danchov** (the centre of the town, now an entertainment establishment offering Bulgarian cuisine) is a supreme example of Bulgarian Revival Art. **Tyankov's House** and **Manchev's House** stand out with their exceptional architectural design of the past century. One of the few remaining horse-driven mills in the country is preserved in the yard of the latter. Both houses are now modern restaurants with authentic 19$^{th}$ century interior, which make them unique attractions to all visitors. One of the **most interesting and best-preserved houses** from the beginning of the 20$^{th}$ century now hosts Bulbank Office. The **Holy Mother Church**, built in 1846 is one of the 4 oldest churches of its kind in the town.

Every year Chirpan celebrates **January Days of Yavorov** - a festival of literature and art in honour of the great poet. Every odd year the town hosts the **Atanaska Todorova National Contest for Country Music Performers** in memory of the great Chirpan-born singer.

**Accommodation:** Chirpan Hotel (3-star, 9, Yavorov Str.). The town has good restaurants and entertainment facilities among which one may note the 3-star Park Tavern, located in the town's central park.

**Tourist information -** at the hotels, at the Town-Hall (1, Suedinenie Blvd. at the very centre of Chirpan) as well as at Srednogorets Tourist Association (in the centre, tel.: 0416 2425).

**Transport.** Chirpan is located on the major motor- and railway line Sofia - Plovdiv - Bourgas and maintains regular bus connections with Plovdiv, Stara Zagora, Dimitrovgrad, Haskovo, Purvomai and other towns in the region. The bus station (Industrialen Quarter, P. K. Yavorov Str., tel.: 0416 3214, 2295) and the railway station are near in the eastern part of the town. All express and passenger trains stop at Chirpan railway station.

**Surrounding areas. Merichleri Balneologi-**

# CENTRAL SOUTHERN BULGARIA

cal Resort is located 17 kilometres to the east of the town. Its mineral waters have a temperature of 34°C and an output rate of 12-15 litres/min. The water is excellent for curing intestinal diseases, liver and gall disorders. One can reach the resort by the regular bus or by the train to Dimitrovgrad. 8 km north-east of Chirpan one can visit the remains of the **Roman fortress** (Sherampol - see the text above).

The **Granitski oak-tree** is the oldest tree in Bulgaria (over 1600 years of age) and stands in the village of Granit (20 kilometres north-west of the town, easily accessible by regular bus).

The **Kamenna Svatba** (the "stone wedding") is a natural phenomenon of stone 25 km north-west of Chirpan and 2 km from the village of Medovo with regular bus lines.

**Yagach Hunting Park** (5 km west of the town) is an excellent place for recreation, sports and hunting. There is a municipality owned villa where - against modest prices - one may check-in for the night.

The **Ethnographic Museum** in the village of Spassovo (8 km to the north with regular bus lines) is another point of interest; the key is hold at the mayor's office).

## DIMITROVGRAD

Dimitrovgrad (45 918 inhabitants, 100 metres above sea level) is a town in the very heart of the Gornotrakiiska (Upper Thracian) Lowland on both sides of the Maritsa River. It is located at the distance of 48 km to the south of Stara Zagora, 78 km east of Plovdiv, 13 km north of Haskovo, 215 km west of Bourgas and 220 km to the south-east of the city of Sofia. It is an important industrial centre and one of the youngest towns in Bulgaria. It is also a regional administrative centre.

**History.** The birth date of this town is well known - 3 April 1947, when the villages of Rakovski, Mariino and Chernokonyovo (earlier called the "Small Batak" due to its suffering from the Ottoman invaders) were united to place the foundations of what Dimitrovgrad is today. It was named after Georgi Dimitrov.

The vast deposits of lignite and lime as well as the proximity of the waters of the Maritsa River were the base for the construction of a cement and a chemical plants. Thousands of young people, called "brigadiri" came to participate in the construction works and populated the town. Apart from being a centre of industry, Dimitrovgrad developed as a powerful vegetable-producing region - the second in the country after Plovdiv.

In 1957 the town elected a representative and participated in the Constituent Congress of the World Federation for the Fraternity of Towns and became one of its founders. The town is also associated with the esteemed poet - Penyo Penev, called the poet with the "vatenka" (a coarse thick upper garment usually worn by builders).

**Landmarks.** The **Museum of History** (7, St. Climent Ohridski Str., tel.: 0391 23264, working hours: 9 a.m. - 12 a.m. and 2 p.m. - 5 p.m. Monday through Friday, no entrance fee). The **Penyo Penev House-Museum** is

# CENTRAL SOUTHERN BULGARIA

situated on the floor of the building, where the poet lived and the exhibit shows his life and works (9, D. Blagoev Blvd., tel.: 0391 24304, working hours: 9 a.m. - 12 a.m. and 2 p.m. - 5 p.m., Monday through Friday, no entrance fee). The **Art Gallery** exhibits paintings and hosts personal and group exhibitions (7, D. Blagoev Blvd., tel.: 0391 25846, working hours: 9 a.m. - 12 a.m. and 2 p.m. - 5 p.m., Monday through Friday, no entrance fee). The **Apostol Karamitev Theatre of Drama** (13, D. Blagoev Blvd., opposite the railway station, tel.: 0391 23312, P. O. Box 88). **Jordano Bruno Planetarium** is the first such facility in the country, opened in 1962 (Vaptsarov Park, tel.: 0391 26180, no entrance fee). **St. Dimitur Church** was built in 1880-1884. It is a three-nave basilica, which can be visited every day from 7 a.m. to 7 p.m. It is located at Rakovski Blvd., in the very centre of the town. Interesting because of its architecture is the **Rotunda** - a modern building touching the town-hall. It is located at the downtown square.

Dimitrovgrad is one of the greenest towns in Bulgaria. There are more than 4 500 decares of parks and gardens. The Maritsa Park is on the right bank of the river, the oldest is the Vaptsarov Park, while the most interesting and picturesque one is the well-known Penyo Penev Park.

Every two years since 1970 the town hosts the so-called Days of Poetry, during which poets contest for the prize "Penyo Penev". It is interesting to note that the first winner of this prize was the poet Damyan Damyanov. Since 1980 Dimitrovgrad also hosts the Bulgarian Theatrical Poster Exhibition and Contest.

**Accommodation:** The town has two 3-star hotels - Moskva Hotel (11, D. Blagoev Blvd. in the centre, opposite the railway station) and Aphrodite Hotel (in Vaptsarov Park). The least expensive and unpretentious is the Trakons-FZS Hotel (2, S. Stambolov Blvd., opposite the central bus station and close to the well-known Sunday Marketplace). All three hotels have their restaurants and coffee-bars. Penyo Penev Tourist House offers 64 beds in 2 suites and double rooms (15-minute walk from the railway station into the park).

**Tourist information.** Compact Tour Tourist Association (tel.: 0391 54010, 54009, 27460), Hebros Tourist Association (8A, Tsar Boris I Str., tel.: 0391 24093, 27586, 23981), as well as at the hotels.

**Transport.** Dimitrovgrad maintains regular bus lines to Sofia, Plovdiv, Varna, Bourgas, Stara Zagora and Haskovo as well as to the smaller towns and villages in the region. The Group Transport Company maintains bus routes to many countries in Europe, as well. The central bus station (D. Blagoev Blvd., tel.: 0391 23687, 23861, 23187, the bus station to Haskovo (D. Blagoev Blvd., next to the police office) and the railways station (D. Blagoev Bvld., tel.: 0391 23622) are close to each other on the centre of the town. Dimitrovgrad can be reached through the Sofia - Plovdiv - Svilengrad and Rousse - Toulovo - Podkova railway lines, as well as their international extensions. It has well-organised bus transport.

**Surrounding areas.** The **Sanctuary of the Nymphs** is located 15 km south-east of the town (nearby the village of Kasnakovo). It is a Thracian monument of culture of great national importance and consists of cult-related buildings ($2^{nd}$ century), an inn ($3^{rd}$ century), amphitheatre ($4^{th}$ century) and an interesting architectural decision uniting the three natural springs. Regular bus line. 16 km to the north-west of the town one can visit the **Merichleri Mineral Spring** (refer to Chirpan section herein), regular bus line from the town. The Izvora na Belonogata Tourist Complex (Spring of the White-legged Maiden) is located 35 kilometres south-east of Dimitrovgrad (near the town of Harmanli). Regular bus and railway transport available. 20 km to the south-west one can visit **Haskovo Mineral Baths** (refer to Haskovo section herein), accessible by regular bus lines.

# CENTRAL SOUTHERN BULGARIA

## HASKOVO

Haskovo (population: 80 870, 200 metres above sea level) is located at the banks of Haskovska River, among Haskovo Hills at the foothills of the Eastern Rhodopes. The town is 225 km and 75 km to the south-east of Sofia and Plovdiv, respectively; 64 km and 16 km south of Stara Zagora and Dimitrovgrad, respectively; 50 km north-east of Kurdzhali and 70 km north-west of Svilengrad. It is one of the oldest settlements is Bulgaria (in 1985 Haskovo celebrated it 1000$^{th}$ anniversary). It is a regional administrative centre.

**History.** The first settlement on this territory dates back to around 7 000 years BC in the neolith period. Throughout its existence, the town experienced innumerable periods of revival and decay. During the first half of 13$^{th}$ century near Haskovo history witnessed one of the most successful battles in Bulgarian history - the Battle of Klokotnitsa (nearby the village bearing the same name). On 9$^{th}$ March 1230 Tsar Ivan Assen II (1218-1241) inflicted a smashing defeat of the Byzantine Empire, which had violated the peace treaty. The battle at Klokotnitsa later proved to have been an event of immense importance for the entire future of Bulgaria.

The town developed into a settlement of craftsmen although much smaller than the near village of Uzundzhovo, which hosted a big fair. In fact, during some time Haskovo was called "Haskyoi by Uzundzovo".

The town was liberated on 19 January 1878 by General Gourko's army. After the Balkan Wars the population of the town grew rapidly as a result of the incoming refugees from Aegean Thrace. Gradually, it developed as the tobacco-producing centre in Bulgaria. The town is the birthplace of the noted Bulgarian scientist and social activist - Prof. Assen Zlatarov and the famous violin player Nedyalka Simeonova.

**Landmarks.** The **Museum of History** (Svoboda Sq., tel.: 038 32067) exhibiting sections in: "Archaeology", "Ethnography", "The Revival and the National Liberation Movement", "19$^{th}$ Century Town Life (in the Paskalev's House, 9, Bratya Minchevi Str., tel,: 038 32276), "Home Crafts - up to the end of 19th century" (in the Shishmanov's House), and "Prof. Doctor Assen Zlatarov". Working hours: 9 a.m. - 12 a.m. and 2 p.m. - 5 p.m. The **Gourkov's House**, now the Composers' Club (59, Benkovski Str., tel.: 038 32224). The **Museum of Literature** (32, Dobroudzha Str., tel.: 038 24241, 29877). **St. Archangel Mihail Church** (Tsar Osvoboditel Str.) with precious frescoes and wood-carvings. **St. Holy Mother Church**, built in 1837 (Bratya Minchevi Str. , working hours: 7 a.m. - 7 p.m.). **The Art Gallery** (43, Tsar Osvoboditel Str. , tel.: 038 33901, 22126). Haskovo has two theatre houses - Ivan Dimov Theatre of Drama (40, Otets Paisii Str., tel.: 038 24233) and the Puppet Theatre "Kutsoto Petle" ("the lame cockerel") (tel.: 038 20726). The town is a university centre and hosts the Territorial Systems and Administration Faculty with the University of National and World Economy, Sofia.

**Accommodation:** Aida Hotel Complex (3-star, 1, Svoboda Blvd.). Romantika Hotel (3-star, in Kenana Park). Klokotnitsa Motel (3-star, north-west of the town, on E80 motorway). Drouzhba Hotel Complex (in Kenana Park). The Rhodopes Hotel Complex (39, Bulgaria Blvd.). Andy Motel (210, Osvobozhdenie Blvd.). Oscar Hotel (20A, Tsar Osvoboditel Str.). Tony-M Hotel (32, Suedinenie Blvd., Entr. A, Apt. 15). Hadzhi Passeva Hotel (1, Aleko Konstantinov Str.) Kenana Tourist House (in the Kenana Park, offering 100 beds in rooms of 2, 3, 4 and 5 beds).

Haskovo has many establishments, offering traditional Bulgarian cuisine. Some of the best known are: Aida Restaurant (4-star, 1, Svoboda Sq.). Gourkova Kushta Restaurant (3-star, 6, Gen. Gourko Str.). Divo Kozle Restaurant (3-star, in the Kenana Park).

# CENTRAL SOUTHERN BULGARIA

Bolyarka Tavern (2-star, 18, Elbrus Str.).
**Tourist information.** Aida Tourist Association (2, Sredna Gora Str., tel.: 038 32120, 24858) and at the hotels, as well.
**Transport.** Haskovo has bus and railway transport facilities. This is a stop along the Trans-European motorway to the Middle East. Over 54 bus lines ensure the transport connections with Dimitrovgrad, Harmanli, Lyubimets, Svilengrad, Stambolov and many other towns and villages in and outside of the region. The bus station is located at 11, Suedinenie Blvd. (tel.: 038 22393, 42452) and not far from there is the railway station (27, Suedinenie Blvd., in the eastern part of the town, tel.: 038 24125, 29787). The town is a station along the Rousse - Toulovo - Podkova railway line. Apart from the central railway station there are several other stops on the territory of the town. 11 regular bus and trolley inter-town lines line operate within Haskovo.
**Surrounding areas. Kenana Park** is a beautiful natural park adjacent to the town offering excellent opportunities for recreation, sports and tourism, located 2 kilometres south-west of the town. **The Haskovo Mineral Baths** is a balneological resort of national importance, located 15 kilometres west of the town (regular, hourly bus line to Haskovo). The 12 mineral water springs have a temperature of 48.5°C and an output rate of 35 liters per second. The water is excellent for joint and other bone-structure (spinal) disorders and some gynaecological deceases are cured, as well. There is an open-air mineral pool. The resort is a starting point for hiking tours along marked tracks through the Eastern Rhodopes (refer to the Rhodope Mountains related chapter herein).
From the Baths one can reach the **Sharapanite** in about an hour walk. The Sharapani are **unique Thracian wineries** - enormous grape vessels carved out in plain rock and connected with channels for transporting the fluid (1st millennium BC). 7 kilometres to the north-west of the town and 2 kilometres from the village of Klokotnitsa one can find the remains of the A**ssenova Krepost (Hissarya)** (The fortress of Tsar Ivan Assen II) as well as the memorial in honour of the battle of 1230, when Tsar Ivan Asen II captured the Despot of Epir - Theodor Komnin. Close by is a big tourist complex. Regular bus lines to Haskovo.

20 kilometres away from Haskovo, nearby the village of Alexandrovo, immediately by Maritsa Motorway connecting Europe with Asia, the scientists have excavated a **domed Thracian tomb** dating back to the second half of the 4th century BC. The wall is covered with paintings displaying hunting scenes with 7 riders, 4 people on foot, 2 deer, 2 wild boars and 9 hunt dogs. The scenes are of unique artistic value, true, expressive, and unparalleled in the Thracian art up to now.

The **Sanctuary of the Nymphs** is located 10 kilometres to the north-west of the town, near the village of Kasnakovo (refer to Dimitrovgrad section herein). **Izvora na Belonogata Tourist Complex** is 37 km east of Haskovo (4 km east of Harmanli). Remarkable is the old drinking fountain built in 1585 the legend of which inspired the great Bulgarian poet P. R. Slaveikov to write the poem of the same name, translated as "The spring of the white-legged maiden" which gave the name of the tourist complex. Accessible by regular bus lines.

*Frescoes in the domed Thracian tomb near the village of Alexandrovo*

# CENTRAL SOUTHERN BULGARIA

## KURDZHALI

Kurdzhali (45 729 inhabitants, 240 metres above sea level) is located in the very heart of the Eastern Rhodopes, along the two banks of the Arda River, on both sides of which are the two big dams - Studen Kladenez Dam to the east and Kurdzhali Dam to the south. The town on the Arda River is situated at the distance of 250 km, 100 km and 81 km southeast of Sofia, Plovdiv and Assenovgrad, respectively, 66 km and 50 km south-west of Dimitrovgrad and Haskovo, respectively, and only 15 km north of Momchilgrad. Kurdzhali is a regional administrative centre.

**History.** This place had been a settlement as early as 6 000 years ago. Prehistoric remains of human life as well as ample examples of the presence of Thracian, Roman and Byzantine culture have been found plus medieval Bulgarian and late-Ottoman remains. The first historical finds are associated with the Thracian tribe *koelaleti*, subdued by the Romans during 1st century. Then came the Slavic tribe of *Smoleni*. During the Middle Ages the settlement frequently shifted under Bulgarian or Byzanitine rule.

Bulgarian presence is proved by the unique 3-navel Bulgarian basilica found in Vesselchane Quarter of the town dated to the 11$^{th}$ - 12$^{th}$ century. This town quarter is heir of medieval Bulgarian town *Munyak* demonstrating an architectural style, similar to that of Preslav, Messemvria and Turnovo. In the 14$^{th}$ century the settlement was conquered by the Turks, and in 1379 it was populated by colonists from Asia Minor. In the middle of the 17$^{th}$ century the town was ruled by Kurdzhi Ali - a noted army leader. It is supposed that accepted the town was named after him. During the 18$^{th}$ century bloodthirsty kurdzhalii gangs (Turkish brigands), which ruined not one and two prospering Bulgarian villages, used to gather in the town. In January 1878 the Don Cossacks of General Chernobouzov liberated the town, which was to remain within the Eastern Rumelia part of the country, as agreed under the Berlin Treaty. In 1886 it is given to Turkey again as a compensation for the Union (1885). On 8$^{th}$ October 1912 the soldiers of colonel Delov's regiment liberated the town for the second and last time. Gradually, Kurdzhali became the "tobacco warehouse of the Eastern Rhodopes" and later a centre for the development of Bulgarian non-ferrous metallurgy.

**Landmarks. The Bulgarian Basilica St. Joan the Precursor** (11$^{th}$ - 12$^{th}$ century) is located in the Vesselchane Quarter of the town. At the end of 1998 during continuing excavations a unique find was brought to the surface in it - the burial tomb of a senior Christian bishop (dated back to end of the 12$^{th}$ or the beginning of the 13$^{th}$ century) wearing his gold-knitted clerical attire. There are only three more dresses of this kind in the world but this has proved to be the first find of its kind in a burial tomb. A fantastic archaeological find!

In the former konak (the Turkish town-hall built around 1870) with its interesting exterior architecture one can visit the **Museum of History** (4, Republikanska Str., tel.: 0361 24200, 24300, 26851). The **Picture Gallery**

# CENTRAL SOUTHERN BULGARIA

(Republikanska Str., tel.: 0361 23619, working hours: 9 a.m. - 12 a.m. and 2 p.m. - 5.30 p.m.) hosts the works of such painters as Vladimir Dimitrov - the Master, Kiril Tsonev, Dechko Uzunov, Svetlin Roussev, V. Decheva, D. Kirov and others, as well as icons, prints and church plates.

Kurdzhali has two theatres - the Dimitur Dimov Theatre of Drama (1, Bulair Str., tel.: 0361 26481) and the Puppet Theatre (17, Trakia Blvd., tel.: 0361 22013). There are several senior schools in the town for teachers, nurses and midwives.

**Accommodation:** Arpezos Hotel Complex (on the left bank of the river, 46, Republikanska Str.). Oustra Hotel (1, Gen Delov Str., not far from the stadium).

**Tourist information** can be obtained at the hotels and at Mircho Spassov Tourist Association (Otez Paisii Str., Block 2, tel.: 0361 26719, 24859, 25629).

**Transport.** Bus and railway lines connect Kurdzhali to closer and far-off towns, cities and villages in Bulgaria. There are regular bus lines to Plovdiv, Haskovo, Smolyan, Ardino, Momchilgrad, Kroumovgrad, Ivailovgrad and other smaller towns in the region. Through the Makaza Pass the town is connected to the Greek Mediterranean. The bus station (94, Bulgaria Blvd., tel.: 0361 24536, 24636) and the railway station (98, Bulgaria Blvd., tel.: 0361 24095) are close by in the south-eastern part of the town. Kurdzhali is a stop along the Rousse - Tulovo - Podkova railway line.

**Surrounding areas.** The two big dams on both sides of the town are excellent places for recreation, sports, tourism and entertainment. Numerous rest homes, country houses, catering establishments, roads, and a tourist chalet (Borovitsa Chalet on the **Kurdzhali Dam**, 18 km out of town, tel.: 0361 26719, 24859, 25629 in the tourist association). Several tourist entertainment ships cross both dams..

After the wall of the **Studen Kladenets Dam** (Cold Well) one can see the incredibly narrow canyon of the Arda River, called Devil's Bridge (one can get there by bus or enjoy the sight from a ship).

Close to the village of Zimzelen, 5 km north-east of the town, visitors can see another of natures wildest whims - the natural earthen **Kurdzhali Pyramids**.

They are scattered on a steep slope over a wide area and are of most different size and shape (Gubite - The mushrooms, Vkame-nenata Svatba - The stoned wedding), etc.), coloured in white, pink and green. Tuff based they have acquired these shapes due to weather conditions in the course of millions of years. The village can be reached by regular bus lines.

The **medieval fortress of Perperek** is located in the valley of a small river, only 7 kilometres to the south-east of town (in the direction of Haskovo). This was the most powerful fortress in the Ahridos region, and during $13^{th} - 14^{th}$ century was an bishop's and fortified Bulgarian town. The Turks met fierce resistance during their invasion of the country in the $14^{th}$ century and this is why after conquering it, they slaughtered the greater part of the population, others took in slavery and the destroyed the fortress. It now stands in ruins. Only the hexagonal tower of carved stone is partially preserved. Remnans of the settlement are also preserved - they were owned by the bolyar Momchil.

A unique Thracian rock sanctuary was discovered nearby – an expression of the ancient dwellers' mystic belief in the Sun.

The picturesque valley of the **Borovitsa River** (together with Arda, one of the two main rivers flowing into the Kurdzhali Dam) can be seen to the north-west of the town and while being there, one has the feeling of being somewhere in the American wild West. The feeling one experiences while crossing the canyon cannot be explained. It is accessible by the regular bus line to the nearby villages in the direction of the Bezvodno village.

# SOUTHEASTERN BULGARIA

# SOUTHEASTERN BULGARIA

## SVILENGRAD

The town of Svilengrad (population: 19 416; 55 m above sea level) is situated on the banks of the Maritsa River, in the immediate proximity to the touching point of three state boundaries, namely Bulgarian-Greek, Bulgarian-Turkish and Greek-Turkish. It is about 70 km, 150 km, and 300 km south-east of Haskovo, Plovdiv and Sofia respectively, 2 km north of the boundary with Greece, and 14 km north-west to the boundary with Turkey, 30 km and 265 km north-west of Odrin (Edirne) and Istanbul, respectively. One of the gates to Bulgaria.

**History**. There is information about an initial Thracian settlement, and consequently a Roman one, which was later transformed into an important Roman fortress called *Bourdenis* guarding the military road to Tzarigrad. In 1205 on the same territory Tzar Kaloyan inflicted the first serious defeat on the Crusaders lead by emperor Baldwin; that was one of the greatest battles in medieval Bulgarian history. At the time of imposing the Ottoman Rule the settlement of *Kinekli* was situated there. The present town was formed in 15$^{th}$ century beside a ford on the Maritsa River. Actually the town expanded around the famous Moustafa Pasha Bridge built in 1529. It is 300 m long, 6 m wide and has 20 arches. There is a slabstone with an inscription stating the years of construction, which the generations assessed as "an eternal useful deed". The bridge is considered to be one of the best representatives of this epoch in Southeastern Europe. In the middle of 17$^{th}$ century the town had more than 700 houses and a kervan-sarai (stable for the horses of travelling tradesmen) for 700 horses. Apart from its strategic location (on the way to Tsarigrad and the bridge over Maritsa) the town was famous as a big silk-worm breeding centre. The follicles called "Odrin type" were particularly evaluated in Europe, however the main market was Turkey. The town was famous for its renowned charshiya (market street) - workshops and inns. A secular school was built in 1847, where Ivan Vazov was later a teacher (1872-1873). In 1870 the Zvezda (Star) Communal Cultural centre was opened. In 1874 Peter Stanchev, a teacher from Turnovo, proposed the name of *Svilengrad* for the town ("svila" – silk, "grad" - town), and the Bulgarians accepted this idea, however it was implemented during the Balkan War (1912).

G. S. Rakovski, Petko. R. Slaveikov, Hr. G. Da-nov would often travel through the town on their way to or back from Tzarigrad. In 1871 Levski set up a secret revolutionary committee. On 7$^{th}$ January, 1878 the Russian armies entered, however after the signing of the Berlin Treaty the town was left in the territory of Turkey. During the Balkan War a military airport was equipped near Svilengrad. For the first time in world history an army (the Bulgarian army) used aeroplanes for military purposes. The town was finally liberated during the Inter-Allies War (1913). At the time of liberation the town's ethnic composition was entirely changed, the inhabitants were predominantly Bulgarians, refugees from the areas still under yoke.

**Landmarks**. The Moustafa Pasha Bridge (See above).

**Accommodation**: Svilena Hotel (Svilena Sq., in the town centre). Ekaterina Sevova Hotel (20, Hristo Shishmanov Str.). Milena Hotel (8, Preobrazhenska Str.). Chekichev Hotel (9, V. Levski Str.). The catering and entertainment opportunities continuously expand.

**Tourist Information** - at the hotels and the Sakar Tourist Association (5, Septemvriiska Str., tel.: 0379 6275).

**Transport**. The international roads and the railway line from Europe to the Middle East and Asia cross the town. There are bus lines to Plovdiv, Haskovo, Harmanli, Elhovo, etc. All buses heading for Turkey go through the town, so the latter is practically connected to all points of the country by bus. The bus station is located at 19, Tsar Simeon Veliki Str. in the eastern part of the town (tel.: 0379 3466, 2883, working hours: 6.30 a.m. - 7.00 p.m.). The railway station is in the Novo Selo Quarter, 3 km away from the centre (tel.: 0379 7003, 4169). The town is connected with the national railway system as well as with that of Turkey by means of the international railway line.

**Surrounding areas**. There are numerous Thracian mounds 7 km south-west, in the lands of the **village of Mezek. The Maltepe Mound** (treasure mound) is a Mikena type ($4^{th}$ century BC) and it is situated 1 km south-west of the village. It recovered a **Thracian domed tomb** – Mezekska a la beehive Tomb of remarkable architecture as well as other archaeological finds. Just above the village are the remains of the Mezek **Neutzikon Fortress** ($11^{th}$-$12^{th}$ century) having the shape of an irregular polygon. It is one of the best preserved fortresses in the country. There is a regular bus line to the village of Mezek.

Some 30 km north-east, near the villages of **Matochina** and **Mihalich** is the famous **tower** ($12^{th}$ -$13^{th}$ centuries) and the **rock churches** ($10^{th}$ century). There is a regular bus line available. The border **Kapitan Andreevo** Checkpoint (on Bulgarian territory, tel.: 0379 7448, 7346) and Kapukoule (on Turkish territory) are situated 14 km south-east on the international road to Istanbul. There is a regular bus line.

# ELHOVO

The town of Elhovo (population: 13 629, 130 m above sea level) is situated on the left bank of the Toundzha River in the fertile field. It is 339 km south-east of Sofia, 60 km and 37 km south of Sliven and Yambol, respectively, 30 km north-east of Topolovgrad, 94 km and 66 km south-west of Bourgas and Sredets, respectively.

**History**. A Thracian settlement called *Orouditsa* existed at the place of the present town. The Roman conquered it, fortified it and gave it the name of *Orouditsa ao Bougoum*. Later the Byzantine called it *Malso Kastra* (fortified settlement) until the arrival of the Slavs who gave it the melodious name of *Yanitsa* which consequently changed into *Enina*.

In the years of Ottoman Rule the town was an agricultural, crafts, and administrative centre. In $17^{th}$ century it had a market street with more than 40 workshops. However, the town became depopulated after several epidemics, the devastating kurdzhalii (Turkish brigands) raids, and the Russian-Turkish War of Liberation (1877-1878). A great part of the population moved to Dobroudzha, Bessarabia and Russia. At the time of the Liberation one could count 100 houses and 900 inhabitants. In 1934 the town was renamed to Elhovo.

**Landmarks.** The **Town Museum** (4, Shipka Str., tel.: 0478 3772) possesses one of the richest ethnographic expositions in the country. Of special interest are the collections of folk crafts samples and costumes of Bulgarians immigrants from Aegean Thrace, Lozengrad region and Odrin region.

**Accommodation**: The Puldin Hotel (in the town centre, 9A, Kroum Str.).

**Tourist Information** - at the hotel or at Rodni Prostori Tourist Association (5, Turgovska Str., tel.: 0478 2040).

**Transport**. Buses and trains. There are regu-

# SOUTHEASTERN BULGARIA

lar bus lines to Sliven, Yambol, Bourgas, Sredets, Topolovgrad, Svilengrad, and other smaller villages and towns in the district. Elhovo is the last railway station (tel.: 0478 2494) on the railway line Yambol-Elhovo connecting the town with the national railway system.

**Surrounding areas.** Colchis pheasants are breeded in the area of **Papazova Koria**, 5 km north of the town. Visitors can see the birds. There is a regular bus.

## YAMBOL

The town of Yambol (population: 82 924, 135 m above sea level) is situated in the eastern part of the Gornotrakiiska (Upper Thracian) Lowland, on the banks of the Tounczha River, shortly after the river curved to the south. It is 37 km north of Elhovo, 106 km west of Bourgas, 28 km south-east of Sliven, 304 km east of Sofia. One of the oldest Bulgarian towns. A regional administrative centre.

**History.** The earliest traces of communal life were discovered in the dozens of prehistoric dwelling mounds. The so-called **Rasheva** and **Marcheva Mounds** are located on the territory of the present day town. These two date back to the Neolith, Eneolith and Bronze Epoch. Some of the finds recovered there are kept in the Parisian Louvre, the Archaeological Museum in Sofia, and mostly in the Museum of History in Yambol. The ancient town sprang up as a Thracian settlement called *Kabile* (some 10 km north-west of the town, near a village of the same name) at an important crossroad; later it became a significant fortress in the state of Philip of Macedonia. During the Roman domination the town reached its prime when people started minting coins. On his way through the town in 293 emperor Diokletian gave it the name of *Diospolis* (God's town). It existed till 378 when the Goths destroyed it. The

# SOUTHEASTERN BULGARIA

first written information dates back to 6th century. Since 11th-14th centuries it was mentioned as a Bulgarian town having different names - *Diospolis, Dianopolis, Diampolis, Yampolis, Dublin, Dublino, Douboulino*, and the Byzantine authors mentioned it *as Dimpolis, Diampolis, Hiampolis*. The town was mentioned with the name of *Dubilin* in an inscription of 1357 (the reign of Tzar Ivan Alexander). At the time it was situated on the border between Bulgaria and Byzantium, and nearby was the famous entrenchment Erkesiata. Some of the impressive fortress walls and turrets of medieval Yambol are still preserved.

The town was among the first in the Balkans to resist the Ottomans. It was conquered in 1373 after a long siege. During the Ottoman Rule many Turks settled to live around Hissarluka, and after the Russian-Turkish War of 1829 many Bulgarians from the town and the vicinity emigrated to Russia. The haidouts (armed volunteers, leaders or members of detachments) Georgi Garabdchi, Boudak Stoyan, Kara Dobri, Dyado Zhelyo and others based in countryside of the town, took part in the battles for liberation. The town is a native place of the revolutionaries Georgi Drazhev, Radi Kolessov, Zakhari Velichkov, etc. The Oriental town carried out active with agricultural products, silkworms, homespun material, predominantly with Odrin and Tsarigrad. The so-called Salty Road from Anhialo to Plovdiv passed through the town. The Russian armies liberated it in January 1878. In memory of this act people built and inaugurated the St. Alexander Nevski Temple - the first monument of the Bulgarian-Russian friendship in Bulgaria. It was erected in the Bakadzhitsite area south-east of the town. In the first half of 20th century Yambol was known for its curative mineral water, unique rail tram tugged by horses, pheasant breeders, huge hangar for zeppelins of 1917. John Atanassov, the inventor of computers, had kinship in Yambol, and it was a native place of Peter Noikov - the first professor in pedagogic, Atanas Radev - elite mathematician, Georgi Papazov and Ivan Popov - world famous painters, Kiril Krustev - Bulgarian of encyclopedic knowledge, Stiliana Paraskevova who embroidered the prototype of Bulgarian national flag.

**Landmarks. St. Georgi Church** (45, St. Georgi Str.) dates back to 1737 and it was the centre of cultural and religious life, as well as of the national struggle for liberation of the church in Yambol. A monastery school was opened in 1805 and in 1857 a class school where Dobri Chintoulov was a teacher in the period between 1857 and 1862. From 1866 onward the liturgies were carried in Bulgarian only. During the Russian-Turkish War of Liberation the church was entirely burnt down, and in 1882 restored again. There is a beautiful iconostasis there.

**The Bezisten of Yambol** (Osvobozhdenie Sq.) is one of the most interesting and well preserved architectural monuments in Bulgaria from the second half of 15th century. It is a covered market. In 1970-1973 it was restored and reorganised as a souvenir palace. **The Town Museum of History** (2, Byalo More Str., working hours: 8.00 a.m. - 12.00 a.m. and 1.00 p.m. - 5.00 p.m., Saturdays and Sundays - days off with the exception for visitors with reservations). There are more than 100 000 exhibits there. **The Georgi Papazov Art Gallery** (2, Tzar Samuil Str., working hours: 9.00 a.m. - 12.00 a.m. and 2.00 p.m. - 6.00 p.m., Saturdays and Sundays - days off with the exception for visitors with reservations). Housed in an interesting antique building it is one of the richest galleries in the country. It possesses more than 3 000 works of dozens of outstanding Bulgarian and foreign painters. Its most valuable treasure is the collection of decorative works that make the gallery rank first in Bulgaria and well known abroad. **The Astronomic Observatory and**

# SOUTHEASTERN BULGARIA

**Planetarium** (12, Tzar Ivan Alexandar Str.). There are two theatre halls in Yambol - Theatre of Drama (18, G.S. Rakovski Str.) and Muppet Theatre (1, Georgi Papazov Str.).
**The town park** (an island in the Toundzha River) and the **hill of Borovets** are nice places for recreation within the territory of the town.
**Accommodation**: The Toundzha Hotel Complex (2-star, 13, Bouzloudzha Str., 1- and 2-bed rooms and suites, restaurant and a lobby bar). The Borovets Hotel Complex (3-star, 100, Borovets Str., 2-bed rooms and suites, restaurant, night bar). There are plenty of catering establishments in the town offering nice Bulgarian cuisine and entertainment.
**Tourist Information** - at the hotels and at the Kabile Tourist Association (31, S. Karadzha Str., tel.: 034 22670).
**Transport**. Yambol is connected with the country and the world by bus and railway transport. There are bus lines to Sliven, Nova Zagora, Elhovo, Sredets, etc. The bus station is situated near the market place (Turgovska Str., tel.: 046 23654, 24417, 23885). The town is a point on the railway line Sofia - Plovdiv - Bourgas, and there the extension to Elhovo forks. The railway station is in the western part (1, Zheleznicharska Str., tel.: 046 22626, 22254). There is a railway bureau for reservations in the town (tel.: 046 22121). The town has developed a well-arranged public bus transport.
**Surrounding areas**. **The Kabile National Archaeology Reserve** - situated 6 km north of the town. It preserves the ruins of the most significant antique Thracian town of Kabile. This economic, political and cultural centre of Ancient Thrace has been investigated for more than 25 years. The remains are really impressive. There is an archaeological museum as well. Working hours: summer time - 8.00 a.m. - 8.00 p.m., winter time - 10.00 a.m. - 4.00 p.m. A bus runs from Yambol to the museum 9 times a day.
**The St. Spas Monastery with the Alexander Nevski Temple-Monument** - 14 km southeast of Yambol. The idea of its construction was suggested by General Skobelev and implemented with the help of the voluntary donations from Bulgaria and Russia. Skobelev granted a huge cross and a Testament, which are preserved to these days. The list with the names of about 900 Russians and Bulgarians who died in the struggle for the Liberation of Bulgaria is preserved, too. It was most solemnly inaugurated in September 1884. The church hosts of a big collection of icons, old printed books, and church plate most of them made in Kiev-Pechor Monastery. The iconostasis was made there, too, and was installed in the temple in parts. There is a bus running from Yambol to the temple three times a day - at 7.00 a.m., at 1.00 p.m., at 4.00 p.m. The interesting historical sight called **Erkesiata** (trench) is situated in the area called Bakudzhitsite, at the foot of the most eastern peak. It is a part of the biggest fortification on the Bulgarian territory from $7^{th}$-$11^{th}$ centuries (131 km long); it guarded the Bulgarian State from the raids of Byzantium from the south. The lowlands of **Bakadzhitsite** are a wonderful sight for tourism because of the deciduous woods, historical sights, the closeness of the town and the available accommodation facilities, including the Drouzhba Chalet offering 74 beds (tel.: 046 24151). It is the point of departure for a number of marked tracks to various sights. It is 16 km away from Yambol along an asphalt road.

# SOUTHEASTERN BULGARIA

## SLIVEN

The town of Sliven (population: 100 695, 270 m above sea level) is situated in the eastern part of the Gornotrakiyska (Upper Thracian) Lowland at the foothills of the Sliven Balkan (Eastern Balkan Mountains). It is 279 km east of Sofia, 28 km north-west of Yambol, 70 km north-east of Stara Zagora, 75 km east of Kazanlak, 114 km west of Bourgas. "The town of the 100 Voivodi" ("voivoda" - leader of a detachment of armed revolutionaries). A regional administrative centre.

**History.** Most probably the name derives from the location of the town, i.e. fusion of the field, the mountain and the three rivers of Assenovska, Selishka and Novosselska ("slivam" - to fuse). The town sprang up in the period 7th - 11th centuries by a the old military road from the Danube through the Vratnik Pass (Zhelezni Vrata - Iron Gates) in the Balkan mountains to Tsarigrad.

Idrissi, Arabian geographer, was the first to give information about the town in 1153 calling it *Istilifounos*. Later it became known with as *Silimno, Slivno*. In 1388 the town was conquered by the Turks and entirely destroyed. Father Paisii mentioned it in his "Istoria Slavyano-bulgarska" (Slavonic and Bulgarian History) (18th century) already as *Sliven*.

During the first decades of the Ottoman Rule Sliven enjoyed privileges as a settlement of people breeding falcons and people guarding mountain passes. Gradually the town became an important craft centre, growing further in size and wellbeing. It gained popularity for the weaving of the woollen cloth called 'kebe'. In 1828 there were about 20 000 inhabitants. Sliven was liberated in 1828 in the Russian-Turkish War. When the Russian soldiers withdrew more than 15 000 Bulgarians left with them and settled to live in Romania, Bessarabia and South Russia. In 1872 the population of the town numbered 25 000 inhabitants.

Sliven grew as town of crafts and trade, making use of the water power of the rivers. The craft of manufacturing aba (homespun coarse wollen cloth and upper men's garment made of it) was best developed. Up to 400 traders would annually visit the town to buy thousands of metres of woollen cloth. The craft of rifle making came second in importance. In 1836 the first woollen textile factory in Bulgaria was built in Sliven, that of Dobri Zhelyazkov the Factory Owner. It was three-storied, with 20 spinning machines, 6 mechanical looms and 500 workers. Its big stone buildings are still preserved. Traders from Turkey, Poland and Hungary would come to the annual fair in Sliven. It rivalled the fair in Uzoundzhovo.

In the Revival Period Sliven became famous as "the town of the 100 voivodi": Indzhe, Zlati, Kara Subi, Radoi, Hristo, Konda - a woman leader, Hadzhi Dimitur, Panayot Hitov, Tenyu Voivoda and many other. Georgi Ikonomov, one of the apostles of the April Uprising was born in the town. Sliven is the birthplace of Sava Dobroplodni, Dr. Ivan Seliminski, Dobri Chintoulov. After the Liberation the crafts suffered a decay, while the textile industry continued to develop and shape the economic face of the town.

**Landmarks. The Town Museum of History** (18, Tsar Osvoboditel Str., tel.: 044 22494); **the Museum of Revival Arts** (13, Tsar Osvoboditel Str., tel.: 044 22083) - a permanent exposition of works of Revival Period painters as Dimitur Dobrevich, D. Danchov, N. Pavlovich, as well as painters from the first decades after Liberation - Ivan Mrkvichka, Anton Mitov, Ivan Angelov, Yordan Kyuvliev, etc. **Hadzhi Dimitur House-Museum** (Assenova Str.) is situated in the south-western part of the town (the former Kloutsohor Quarter) and comprises a complex of several buildings restored in different periods - the native home with its interior, the inn and some of the farm houses. **The 19th Century Sliven Lifestyle House-Museum** (5, Simeon Tabakov Str., tel.: 044 23149) is located in a building of 1813 having a very interesting architecture. **Dimitur**

# SOUTHEASTERN BULGARIA

**Dobrevich Art Gallery and Exposition** (10, Mirkovich Str., tel.: 044 22796, 23395, 26643) in Mirkovich's house. **Dobri Chintoulov House-Museum** (5, Vuzrozhdenska Str., tel.: 044 22494, 25198). Modern Bulgarian art is displayed in the permanent **exposition of the painter Sirak Skitnik** (2, Tsar Simeon Str., tel.: 044 25342). **The monument to Hadzhi Dimitur** was built in 1935 in the centre of the town. The figure of the legendary leader stands on a rectangular column. At the foot of the monument, in special niches one can see the busts of outstanding people from Sliven from the period of Revival. The **Stariyat bryast (The old elm-tree)** (600 years old) can be seen in the centre of Sliven. One can also visit about ten Christian temples.

There are two theatre halls in the town - Stefan Kirov Theatre of Drama in the town centre, and a State Muppet Theatre (10, Tsar Osvoboditel Str., tel.: 044 25186, 22718).

**Accommodation**: The Dinamo Hotel Complex (3-star, 1, Sofiisko Shosse Str.). The Sliven Hotel (2, Hadzhi Dimitur Str.). Oasis Hotel Complex (in the Mollova Koria area). The Shapo Alpia Hotel (in the Sinite Kamani (Blue Stones) Park, near the initial lift station to Karandila). The Vector & Cie. Hotel (7, Hadzhi Dimitur Str.). The Spectur Hotel (119, Panayot Hitov Str.). The Start Hotel (area of Mollova Koria, the last stop of bus line No. 12, tel.: 044 88461). The Shaklian Hotel (39, G. S. Rakovski Str.). Most of the hotels have restaurants and other entertainment establishments.

**Tourist Information** - at the hotels and at the Sinite Kamuni Tourist Association (13A, Velikoknyazheska Str., tel.: 044 29361, 22431, 22432).

**Transport**. Buss and railway transport. There are regular bus lines to Yambol, Nova Zagora, Karnobat, Aitos, Bourgas, Elena, Veliko Turnovo and many other smaller villages and towns in the district. The bus station (2, Hadzhi Dimitur Str., tel.: 044 26629, 24793, 25120) and the railway station (Dame Grouev Quarter, tel.: 044 83656, 82292) are situated in the southern part of the town not far from each other. The town is a major railway station on the main railway line Sofia - Karlovo - Bourgas. There is well-arranged bus and trolley transport in Sliven.

Near the road to Kotel and Karandila, in the north-eastern end of Sliven is the initial open-seat lift station (tel.: 044 83834) in the direction to the area of Karandila. The lift brings all volunteers to roam Sliven Balkan Mountain up to more than 600 m variation in altitude for about 20 min. There is a town bus line from the town centre to the initial lift station.

**Surrounding areas**. The **area of Karandila** situated north-east of the town, among the century old forests of the Sliven Balkan Mountain. Here one can visit the **Sinite Kamuni Nature Park** (with extremely interesting rock formations like Halkata - the Ring, etc.), the Karandila Tourist House (950 m above sea level, offering 180 beds, restaurant, coffee-

# SOUTHEASTERN BULGARIA

bar, bar, etc., there is a 32-km long asphalt road to the town), the Karandila Chalet (970 m above sea level, 24 beds, 500 m away from the Tourist House). The area offers excellent opportunities for rest, sports and tourism; there is a ski-run with two ski-taglines, a football playground of Olympic size, a lake with boats, classified rock sites for mountaineering and sports climbing. This is the point of departure for a number of marked tourist tracks round the Sliven Balkan Mountain (See the Stara Planina Mountain related chapter herein). There is no regular transport with the exception of the above-mentioned open-seat lift.

**The Mineral Baths of Sliven** (also called Dzhinkovski) - situated 12 km south-west of Sliven at the village of Zlati Voivoda (former Dzhinovo), near the road to Nova Zagora. A whole balneological resort has sprung up near the mineral springs (44°-45°C and output rate of 16 litres per second). People use the water to cure diseases of the spine and bone-system, the peripheral nerve system, stomach, intestines, liver and gall-bladder, etc. Apart from the sanatorium and the other medical establishments, there are two hotels, the Central Hotel and Zhiva Voda (Water bringing back to life) Hotel. There are regular bus lines to Sliven and Nova Zagora.

**Aglikina Polyana** (the Meadow of Aglika) - 38 km north-west of Sliven, in the Elena Balkan Mountain, situated immediately next to the Vratnik Pass. A historical area that entered the Bulgarian national history as the most popular gathering place of the haidouts (armed revolutionaries). It is a large meadow (80 m wide, and 200 m long) surrounded by venerable oak-trees and beach trees. A memorable inscription was carved in a big natural stone slab. It is a point on the route from Mt. Kom to the cape of Emine along the ridge of the Balkan Mountain. There is no regular transport. An asphalt path leads from the marking booth at the Vratnik Pass to the meadow itself.

## KOTEL

The town of Kotel (population: 7433, 527 m above sea level) is situated in a picturesque small valley (kotlovina - that is where its name derives from) in the Kotel Balkan (Eastern Stara Planina Mountain. It is 328 km east of Sofia, 49 km north-east of Sliven, 38 km and 62 km south of Omourtag and Turgovishte, respectively. An old town from the Revival Period.

**History.** At the beginning of the Ottoman Rule Kotel was inhabited by Bulgarians from the adjacent towns and villages in search of rescue. A Turkish register of 1486 contains the earliest information about the town. During the first centuries of the foreign domination it was inhabited by the so-called derventdgii (special Bulgarian guards of the mountain passes and roads) and dzhelepi (traders of cattle, sheep in particular). The already mentioned obligations of Kotel towards the central authority compensated for a relative independence - municipal self-government, independently elected local governor, exemption of some taxation, prohibition of Turkish settling there. All these, as well as the economic growth in $18^{th}$ - $19^{th}$ centuries, the commercial contracts, the passionate Orthodox belief of the inhabitants of Kotel (many used to travel to Jerusalem and Sveta Gora) contributed to the transformation of the town into a lively centre of Bulgarian culture and education, of the struggle for church independence and national freedom. Kotel is the native place of Captain Georgi Mamarchev (officer in the Russian Army), Georgi Sava Rakovski (one of the main ideologists of the movement for national liberation), the Revival men of letters Neophyte Bozvelli, Dr. Peter Beron (the author of the famous "Riben Boukvar" textbook), Sofronii Vrachanski (the most outstanding representative of the literary school of Kotel who copied "Istoria Slavyano-bolgarska"

# SOUTHEASTERN BULGARIA

*The old Kotel*

(Slavonic and Bulgarian History) brought by Paissii Hilendarski himself in 1764), Stefan Izvorski, Ivan Kishelski, Vassil Beron, the socially active men Gavril Krustevich, Aleko Bogoridi, Stefan Bogoridi, etc.

In 1812 the first Bulgarian elite secular school was opened here. The town is a native place of a number of voivodi (leaders of revolutionaries - haidouts), haidouts, revolutionaries, volunteers, members of in Hadzhi Dimitur's, Panayot Volov's, Hristo Botev's detachments. Vassil Levski set up a revolutionary committee in Kotel. The town suffered hard times during the kurdzhalii (Turkish brigands) raids. Indzhe attempted to attack and rob the town but its inhabitants erected a three-metre high wall and drove back the brigands. Nevertheless, in 1848 and 1863 Kotel was put on fire. During the Russian-Turkish War of Liberation battles were held in the immediate vicinity of the town. The town itself accommodated the volunteer detachments, the volunteers' headquarters with general Stoletov, as well as the Hussar regiment from Narvsk with A. Poushkin at the head, who was son of A. S. Poushkin, the genius Russian poet. After the liberation in 1894 Kotel suffered the most devastating fire in its history when the greater part of the town was ruined down. Only the quarter called Galata survived and today it renders an approximate idea of what the old town looked like.

The craft of carpet weaving is very typical for the town and the region, which makes Kotel the oldest centre of artistic fabrics in the country and abroad, having a unique weaving school. The town has preserved precious relics of the past - sarcophagus with Georgi Sava Rakovski's skeleton in it, Dr. Peter Beron's heart, manuscripts of Levski and Sofronii Vrachanski. Its rich history, Revival architecture and marvellous vicinity make this picturesque Balkan town a desired place for national and international tourism.

**Landmarks**. The town of Kotel has been declared **an architecture and historical reserve**. There have been preserved about 110 **houses from the Revival Period** in the quarter of Galata that survived the fire in 1894, as well as in those at Durlyanka street. They are Kamchiya-style houses - one- or two-storied, made of stone and wood, with brilliant wood carvings, huge eves, curved roofs and fantastic yards.

**The Galatan School** (17, Izvorska Str., tel.: 0453 2316, working hours: 8.00 a.m. - 12.00 a.m. and 1.30 p.m. - 6.00 p.m.) - an architectural monument from 1869. There is a museum exposition of brilliant fabrics - symbol of the ancient craft of carpet weaving -

# SOUTHEASTERN BULGARIA

so typical of Kotel. **The Kyopeev's House - Ethnographic Museum** (4, Altunlu Stoyan Str,, working hours: 8.00 a.m. - 12.00 a.m. and 1.30 p.m. - 6.00 p.m.). The visitor finds himself in the romantic atmosphere of the old Kotel home, feeling its whole beauty, utility and cosiness. **The Pantheon of Kotel"s Revival men and women** (Vuzrazhdane Sq., working hours: 8.00 a.m. - 12.00 a.m. and 1.00 p.m. - 5.00 p.m.). It is an imposing building made of stone, iron, copper and wood, giving the impression of contact with the glory of the past epoch. Georgi Sava Rakovski's sarcophagus lies here.

**The Museum of Nature and Science** (situated in the park called Izvorite (the Springs), tel.: 0453 2355, working hours: 8.00 a.m. - 12.00 a.m. and 1.30 p.m. - 6.00 p.m.). It preserves approximately 30 000 exhibits which show the natural variety of the area. The museum exposition has been arranged in accordance with ecological principles and occupies 1 000 square metres. It is the only one of its kind in Southeastern Europe. Vassil Georgiev, a local teacher at the time, established it.

**The Izvorite Park** (the Springs), situated in the northern part of the town, is unique with the three springs (output flow of 2 000 litres per second). **The Sveta Troitsa (St. Trinity) Church and St. St. Apostles Peter and Pavel Church** preserve beautiful wood-carvings representing the Tryavna School of Art.

There is **Philip Koutev High School of Music** in Kotel, it is the first high school for folk singing and instrumental music in Europe (the other school of this type is located in the village of Shiroka Luka in the Rhodope Mountains).

**Accommodation**: The Mel Invest Hotel (59, Izvorska Str.) offers 50 beds. There is a restaurant and a discotheque. The Minyor House for Prophylactics offers 30 beds and a restaurant. The Vetrila Hotel (1, Vetrila Str.) offers 10 beds and a bar. There are numerous catering establishments that offer local cuisine in the town. One such restaurant is Diavena Restaurant, also Elenite Restaurant, Starata Vodenitsa (Old Water-mill) Tavern situated in the Izvorite Park, etc.

**Tourist Information**: in Kotel Tourist Association (housed in the town-hall, tel.: 0453 2030, working hours: 8.00 a.m. - 5.00 p.m., Monday through Friday) and at the hotels.

**Transport**. Buses. There are regular lines to Shoumen, Veliki Preslav, Turgovishte, Omourtag, Sliven, Yambol and other smaller villages and towns in the district. The bus station is situated in the southern part of the town near the river (Louda Kamchia Str., tel.: 0453 2612, 2052, 2460).

**Surrounding areas**. Apart from the town itself, there are four more architecture and historical reserves: the villages of Zheravna, Medven, Katounishte and Gradets. **The village of Zheravna** is 14 km south of Kotel and a regular bus runs to and from. It is one of the pearls of Bulgaria. Every building in the village is in itself a unique cultural monument. It has been preserved almost in its authentic appearance and atmosphere. The most interesting sights are: **the House-Mouseum of Roussi Chorbadzhi, the House-Mudeum of Sava Filaretov, the House-Museum of Yordan Yovkov** (that is the native home of the great Bulgarian writer), **the houses of Dimo Kehaya and Todor Ikonomov,** respectively. The village preserves remarkable ensembles of Revival town lay-out and architecture like the church complex with **St. Nikolai Church** built in 1932. It is worth mentioning the remarkable **Hilendar Convent** where "Slavonic and Bulgarian History" was copied (this particular copy is the so called Zheravna manuscript). **The class school** from 1867 houses an art gallery. The village is the native place of many outstanding Bulgarians as Yordan Yovkov, Raiko Popovich, Sava Filaretov, Todor Ikonomov, V. Stoyanov, Dr. V. Sokolski, D. Stoyanov Bradata (the Beard), etc. Accommodation facilities in Zheravna are to be found in the Zlatna Oresha Hotel Complex offering 50 beds and a restaurant. There are

# SOUTHEASTERN BULGARIA

*Museum of carpet weaving in Kotel*

private lodgings as well.

**The village of Medven** is 12 km south-east of Kotel and there is a regular bus line to it. There are more than **120 cultural monuments** dating back to the Revival Epoch. The most famous one is the **House-Museum of Zahari Stoyanov** - the native home of the remarkable Bulgarian revolutionary and writer. Of special interest are the **Yurta** and **Cherni Dol Architecture Ensembles**, as well as **St. Marina Church** built in 1882. There are remains of a big medieval fortress.

**The village of Katounishte** is 15 km southeast of Kotel. About 80 buildings in the village have been declared **cultural monuments**. There is a regular bus line from Kotel.

**The town of Gradets** is situated 17 km southeast of Kotel, regular buses run to the latter and Sliven. It is rich in **architecture Revival monuments** - houses, a church, a school. There are remains of the **medieval fortress of Grameni** near the village.

There are more than **30 caves** that have already been **investigated** (non-electrified) in the region of Kotel. Most interesting are **Ledenika Cave** (1111 m long and 242 m deep), **Dryanovska Cave** (in the area of Pizdra, one of the most easily accessible and much visited by tourists, with numerous beautiful mineral formations), **Kurvavata Lokva Cave** (The Bloody Puddle) (134 m deep, the legend tells of the murder of many soldiers of Emperor Nikifor's), **Rakovski Cave** (in 1854 Georgi Sava Rakovski started writing his poem "Gorski Putnik" ("Traveller in the Forest") nearby), etc.

Very interesting are **the Skokovete (Jumps) Waterfall** (situated on a left tributary of the Medven River; there is a marked tourist route from the town to the waterfalls), **Sini Vir Waterfall** (at the Medven River just above the village of Medven), and **Medven Springs**.

Some 7 km south of Kotel is the antique dividing wall at **Zhelezni Vrata Pass** (Vrantik, Demir Kapiya - Iron Gates) that had once been connected with the Vida Fortress on the peak of the same name. At the foot of the peak is the area called **Grutski Dol** where the Byzantine were defeated by Khan Kroum's armies in 811, and by Ivailo on 17 July, 1280. The remains of **the medieval fortresses of Kozyak, Haidout Vurban, Ticha, Acheras** and other are to be found in the environs of the town. Kotel is the only town in the country that is a point of the longest mountain tourist route in the country, that of Kom - Emine, starting at Mt. Kom (near the border with Serbia) and running along the ridge of the Balkan Mountain to Cape Emine at the Black Sea coast.

# SOUTHEASTERN BULGARIA

## KARNOBAT

The town of Karnobat (population: 22 000, 220 m above sea level) is situated in the Karnobat Plain, in the north-eastern part of Gornotrakiyska (Upper Thracian) Lowland. From the town northwards starts the Stara Planina Mountain. It is 336 km and 58 km to the east of Sofia and Sliven, respectively, 22 km west of Aitos, 54 km north-west of Bourgas, 100 km south of Shoumen and 50 km north-east of Yambol. Agricultural centre.

**History**. The territory of the present day town was inhabited in ancient times. A real evidence supporting this fact is the Karnobat mound and the Roman fortress called Markela (or Kroumovo Kale, Hissarluka), where in 8$^{th}$ century Khan Kardam won a brilliant victory over the Byzantine. Ever since the settlement has been Bulgarian.

The town fell under Turkish domination in 1372. In a document in Doubrovnik from 1595 it was registered as *Karanovo*, that is how the Bulgarians called it. In 1762 Bozhkovich from Doubrovnik first mentioned it using its present name *Karnobat*. At that time the town was an important centre of sheep breeding famous for the local breed called Karnobat sheep. Huge quantities of meat, wool, pasturma (dried thin meat), lukanka (homemade piquant sausage), candles, soap were produced. The two-week cattle fair was famous all over. After the Russian-Turkish wars in the first half of 19$^{th}$ century many inhabitants of the town moved to Besarabia. The first class school known as Karanovsko School was opened in 1862. During the Russian-Turkish War of Liberation (1877-1878) Karnobat was severely destroyed but consequently due to the rich agricultural resource of the region, the traditions in cattle breeding and wine manufacturing, as well as to the railway line Sofia-Bourgas it continued to develop and grow. From 1953 till 1962 the town was called *Polyanovgrad*, but after that it regained its present day name. It is the native place of Slav Merdzhanov who was a Macedonian and Odrin revolutionary.

**Landmarks**. **The Clock Tower** is situated in the old southern part of the town. It was built by Tryavna masters in 1841 as a Revival symbol of a prospering trade and crafts settlement. **The St. Archangel Yoan Bogoslov Church** (in the town centre, tel.: 0559 4271, working hours: 7.00 a.m. - 12.00 a.m. and 2.00 p.m. - 5.00 p.m.) with an iconostasis made by Debur masters, was built in 1880 in a Revival architectural style.

**The Town Museum** hosts a precious archaeological and ethnographic collection. **The houses of Nikifor Minkov and Saroolou Bey** are interesting with the wood-carvings in them. **The Bencho Obreshkov Gallery** (in the house of the communal cultural centre, downtown, working hours: 10.00 a.m. - 12.00 a.m. and 4.00 p.m. - 6.00 p.m.).

**Accommodation**: Karnobat Hotel (in the town centre, near Sofia-Bourgas road, 5, Asparouh Str.) offers about 100 beds. The Orlovets Motel (7 km eastward) offers 30 beds and a restaurant. The Orlovets Chalet (two buildings, 5 bungalows, 10 km east of Karnobat, and 3 km away from the village of Sokolovo, if one cuts through the town the distance is 7 km) offers 28 beds in 2 suites and two-, three- and five-bed rooms, a restaurant and a coffee-bar. There are interesting places offering traditional cuisine like the Starata Kashta Tavern (The Old House) (21, Aleksi Denev Str.), etc.

# SOUTHEASTERN BULGARIA

**Tourist Information** - at the hotels and at Orlovets Tourist Association (1, Todor Kableshkov Str., tel.: 0559 2192).

**Transport**. The town is an important transport centre with regular bus lines to Bourgas, Sliven, Yambol, Aitos, Sredets, Kotel, Shoumen, etc. Karnobat Bus Station (tel.: 0559 2043). The railway station of Karnobat (tel.: 0559 2150, 2151) is the fourth important in the country. It is a station on the line Sofia - Karlovo - Bourgas, and a point of departure in the direction of the railway station of Komounari where it forks to Northern Bulgaria.

**Surrounding areas**. The medieval **fortress of Markela** is situated 7.5 km south-west of the town. The archaeological excavations started in 1986 and so far there have been recovered a medieval basilica of $6^{th}$ century, an Old Bulgarian church of $10^{th}$ century, a Byzantine church of $11^{th}$ century. The fortress has most imposing ancient Bulgarian earth fortifications called valove (ramparts). **The town of Soungourlare** is 25 km north-west of Karnobat. It is well-known in Bulgaria and abroad for its marvellous wines. The most famous brand called Soungourlarski misket is made from the grapes grown in the adjacent vine-growing villages and towns - Grozden, Slavyantsi, Choubra, Lozitsa and Chernitsa. There is a regular bus line to Karnobat.

## AITOS

The town of Aitos (population: 25 057, 100 m above sea level) is situated on both banks of the Aitos river, in the Aitos field, in the southern foot of the Eastern Balkan Mountain (Aitos Mountain). It is 358 km east of Sofia, 30 km north-west of Bourgas and 22 km east of Karnobat. An agricultural centre.

**History**. Aitos is an old settlement founded by the Thracian tribes. Northwest of the town there are the remains of three turrets belonging to the medieval fortress called *Aetos* (in Greek - an eagle) erected between 650 and 750. And that is where its present day name comes from. It was registered with this name by the Byzantine chronicler Nikita Honiat, and in the chronicles of the French knight Geoffrois de Lavarduen. In 1206 *Aetos* was destroyed by the Crusaders. In 1488 it grew again as a fortified town. Later in $17^{th}$ century the traveller Evlia Chelebi registered it as *Chengis*, while in the Revival Period it was known as *Orlovo* or *Orlovets*. At that time it was a considerably big town with a famous fair. After the signing of the peace treaty in Odrin in 1829 many inhabitants of the towns and its vicinity moved to Bessarabia, and yet during the liberation period (1878) the town numbered 3000 inhabitants. The annual four-day long agricultural

# SOUTHEASTERN BULGARIA

and crafts fair continued to be held. The first agricultural school for young girls in the country was opened here.

**Landmarks**. Museum **Ethnographic Collection** (in the area of the Genger Hotel, tel.: 0558 6157, 6158); **Chengelievs' House-Museum** (13, Chengelievi Str., tel.: 0558 5990); **Peter Stanev House-Museum** (26 Peter Stanev Str., tel.: 0558 5643); **St. Dimitur Church** with precious frescoes (22 Tsar Osvoboditel Str., tel.: 0558 2004).

**The mineral baths of Aitos** are situated in the eastern part of the town. The water temperature is 16°-17°C, output rate - 30 litres per second. The mineral water is good for drinking and curing stomach, gastric and liver diseases.

**Accommodation**: The Aetos Hotel (1, Garova Str.) in the south-western part of the town, not far from the railway station. The Genger Hotel (60, Parkova Str.) offers a restaurant-tavern and a coffee-bar.

**Tourist Information** - at the hotels and at the Choudnite Skali Tourist Association (35A, Stancionna Str., tel.: 0558 2650).

**Transport**. Buses and trains. There are regular bus lines to Bourgas, Karnobat, etc. The railway station is in the north-western part of the town (1, Georgi Kondolov Str., tel.: 0558 2030, 2137). The railway station (in the south-western industrial zone, tel.: 0558 2111, 2113) is on the main line Sofia-Bourgas (via Plovdiv and Karlovo).

**Surrounding areas**. The remains of the **Aetos Fortress** are located north-west of the town on a small hill. The Byala Reka Resort Area (White River) is 16 km north-west of Aitos and 4 km north of the village of Topolitsa. The Zdravets Chalet is situated in its southern end (40 beds), an still further north is the zone for rest and sports, with rest homes and villas. There is a regular bus line from Aitos to the village of Topolitsa.

In the vicinity of the town the famous **Aitos green stone** (andezit) is mined, used for cladding.

## MALKO TURNOVO

The town of Malko Turnovo (population: 3 527, about 340 m above sea level) is the only town in the Bulgarian part of Strandzha Mountain. It is some 470 km south-east of Sofia, 83 km south of Bourgas, 58 km south-west of Tsarevo, and 9 km north-east of the checkpoint of the same name at the border with Turkey. Guard of the Bulgarian spirit in the region of Strandzha Mountain.

**History**. A Thracian settlement existed on the spot of the present day town; only mounds and necropolis have remained. According to the Shkorpil brothers that is where a Roman roadside station called *Outsourgas* was located. The present town of Malko Turnovo was founded by the end of 16$^{th}$ century and the beginning of 17$^{th}$ century, most probably by settlers that had moved from the adjacent huts and smaller villages to settle by the Golemiya Vris Spring where people still drink its nice water. The name of the settlement derives from the profusion of prickly thistles all over the place. Initially *Trunovo* changed into Turnovo and later the word "Malko" (small) was added to distinguish it from the name of the Old Bulgarian capital Turnovo. G. Ensholm was the first to give information about the town. He participated in Dibich Zabalkanski's march at the time of the Russian-Turkish War of 1828-1829. In his book "Notes on the Towns beyond the Balkan Mountain" he claimed that the town had 3 500 inhabitants who earned their living primarily with sheep-breeding, and all the crafts related to it - aba manufacturing (coarse homespun woollen cloth and upper men's garment made of it), tailoring, leather-processing and manufacturing, wool spinning and weaving, cattle trade, as well as masonry and pottery. There were excellent goldsmiths and money-changers. People mined marble, part of which was used for the construction and decoration of the Dolma

# SOUTHEASTERN BULGARIA

Bahche Palace in Istanbul. Trade was well developed in many workshops. In the second half of 19th century Malko Turnovo was a nice and rich town with a population of nearly 8 000 inhabitants - Bulgarians. They passionately preserved the Bulgarian spirit, customs and traditions. The first monastery school was opened at the beginning of last century. A secular school was set up in the 40s of 19th century, and about 1875 - a school for young girls. In 1902 the town had a performance hall. According to the Berlin Treaty signed after the Russian-Turkish War of Liberation (1877-1878) Malko Turnovo was left within the boundaries of the Ottoman Empire. At the time of the Ilinden-Preobrazhenie Uprising (1903) the district revolutionary committee was lodged in the town; the outstanding leaders were Stefan Dobrev, Raiko Petrov, Lefter Mechev, Diko Dzhelepov, etc. After the severe defeat of the uprising around 5 000 inhabitants of Malko Turnovo had to leave their native place. The town was liberated from foreign rule in 1912.

**Landmarks**. Some twenty or so old buildings in the typical Strandzha style have been declared monuments of culture. Some of them are **Popikonomov's House** where is the ethnographic collection, and **Velko Georgiev's workshop** with 18-metre long facade. There is a museum collection called **"Preobrazhenie Uprising of 1903"** arranged at the Prosveta Cultural Centre.

There are interesting icons (made by Sokrat Georgiev, an icon-painter from Sozopol) and frescoes in the Uspenie Bogorodichno (Assumption) Church (1830). The **Golyam Vris Spring** where the town sprang up is in the centre.

**Accommodation**. The Malko Turnovo Hotel.
**Tourist Information** - at the hotel and in the town-hall.
**Transport**. Only buses. The international road from Bourgas to Lozengrad (Kurklareli) and Istanbul passes through Malko Turnovo. There are regular bus lines to Bourgas and Tsarevo, as well as to all smaller villages and towns in the region.

**Surrounding areas**. Several kilometres north of the village of Stoilovo (the village is some 10 km away from the town) near one of the curves of the Veleka River, is **Petrova Niva** - a sacred place for every Bulgarian; it is also known as Strandzha Oborishte. This is the place where the delegates of the Odrin Revolutionary District with leaders Georgi Kondolov, Mihail Gerdzhikov, Penyo Shivarov, etc. gathered and from 28th to 30th June, 1903 worked out the plan for the uprising. It broke on the Christian holiday of Preobrazhenie (Transfiguration) (19th August in the old calendar); so people know it as the Preobrazhenie Uprising. At Petrova Niva there is a big **monument-charnel house of Georgi Kondolov** and **a museum collection**. Each year on 19th August national celebrations are held in memory of all that participated in the Preobrazhenie Uprising. There is a regular bus line to the village of Stoilovo only.

**Dolmenite** - pre-historic tombs near the village of Gramatikovo, which is situated 25 km north-east of the town. There is a regular bus transport.

**Mt. Gradishteto** (710 m) - the highest peak in Strandzha Mountain, which is on the territory of Bulgaria. It is situated on the very border with Turkey. There are remains of a Thracian fortress and a settlement.

Some twenty kilometres north of Malko Turnovo runs one of the most picturesque Bulgarian rivers - **Veleka**, a wonderful place for having a rest, fishing and practising water tourism with canoes. **The Kachoula Resort** is near the village of Gramatikovo. **The village of Bulgari** known for **nestinari dances** - dancers step on embers barefooted, is 41 km north-east on the way to Tsarevo.

In this part of Bulgaria one can find the Strandzha periwinkle - evergreen endemic bush included in the Bulgarian Red Book of Floral Species under Protection.

# NORTHWESTERN BULGARIA

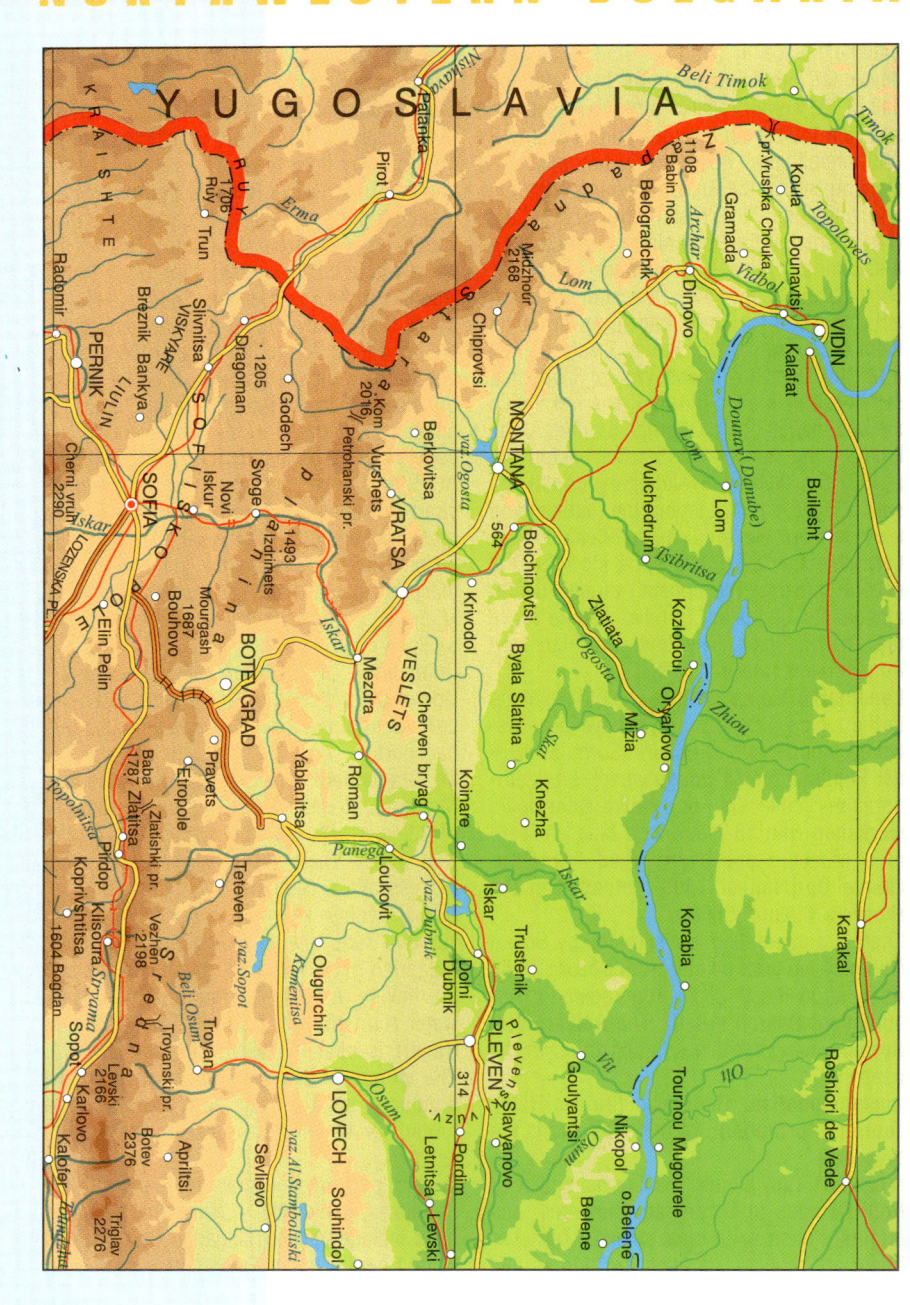

# NORTHWESTERN BULGARIA

## BERKOVITZA

The town of Berkovitsa (16 818 inhabitants, 400 m above sea level) is situated in the northern foot of Berkovski Balkan (Western Stara Planina). It is at a distance of 89 km to the north of Sofia, 24 km to the south of Montana, 53 km to the west of Vratsa and 25 km to the north of the Petrohan Pass.

**History.** Berkovitsa is an old settlement. This is confirmed by the remains of a fortress and a church from 4th century on the Kaleto Hill, situated to the north-west of the town. The settlement is known from the reign of Tsar Kaloyan (the beginning of 13th century) as well and in the time of the Vidin Kingdom (the second half of 14th century) it was a border fortress. Berkovitsa is mentioned in written form for the first time in a Turkish document of 1491. During the Turkish rule it developed as a crafts settlement - mainly in wood-processing and pottery. A great number of refugees from other parts of the country settled here. The inhabitants of Berkovitsa many times have raised their heads against the Ottomans. In 1403 they took part in the uprising of Konstantin and Fruzhin, in 1688 - in the Chiprovtsi Uprising, in 1836 - in the uprising under the leadership of Mancho Punin as well as in the uprising in 1837. After the Liberation in 1878 the town declined, because it remained away from the railway line passing through the Iskar Gorge, thus losing markets in the Ottoman Empire for its crafts goods. The national poet Ivan Vazov worked for a certain time in Berkovitsa as a chairman of the court.

**Landmarks. The Ivan Vazov House-Museum** (2, Ivan Vazov Str., tel. 0953 2235) which is in the central part of the town is arranged in the building where the poet lived in the period 1879-1880. The house itself is a precious architectural monument with an interesting exterior and interior architecture with wood-carved ceilings and original fireplace, cupboards, shelves. The atmosphere in which Vazov lived is preserved. There is a documentary exhibition showing the period of his work in Berkovitsa - the creation of the narrative poem "Gramada" ("Cairn"), the short novel "Mitrofan and Dormidolski", etc. **Permanent ethnographic exhibition -** organized also in an architectural monument of culture, in a close proximity to Ivan Vazov House-Museum. **The clock tower** is remarkable for its solid construction and beautiful upper part in which the clock mechanism still works. It was constructed in 1762 and is one of the oldest towers in our country. **The Town Picture Gallery. The Krustev's House** built in Revival style. **The Holy Virgin Church** (1843) has an original belfry, wood-carved iconostasis and the "Golden Gospel" - an exceptional work of art from 1892 is kept there. **The St. Nikola Church** (19th century).

**Accommodation.** TOBO Inn-hotel (a folk-style hotel-restaurant, 23, Nikolaevska Str.). Educational-qualification complex of the Ministry of Trade and Tourism (with 2-star hotel, 16, Ashiklar Str.). Mramor Hotel-Restaurant.

**Tourist information.** Tourist Information Bureau (4, Hristo Botev Str., at Berkovski Balkan Tourist Association, tel.: 0953 4106) and at the hotels.

**Transport.** Road and railway transport connect Berkovitsa with the rest of the world. There are regular bus routes to Sofia, Montana, Lom, Vurshets and many other smaller villages in the region of the bus station (tel.: 0953 3574) and the railway station (tel.: 0953 3014, 3015) that are in the eastern part of the town (the first is close to the centre). Berkovitsa is the last railway station of the local railway line Boichinovtsi-Montana-Berkovitsa. It is connected through the railway station Boichinovtsi with the settlements along the main railway line Sofia-Mezdra-Vratsa-Broussartsi-Vidin (Lom), as well as the whole national railway system.

**Surrounding areas.** The northern slopes of the Berkovski Balkan at the foot of which Berkovitsa is situated are famous for their

# NORTHWESTERN BULGARIA

**chestnut woods** - one of the two natural finds of tame (mordant) chestnut in Bulgaria (the other one is in Belassitsa Mountain, above the town of Petrich). Berkovitsa is a main point of departure along marked tourist tracks through the Berkovski Balkan (refer to the Stara Planina Mountain related chapter herein). **Kaleto** - a woody hill (515 m) to the northwest near the town. It is a natural forest-park and a protector of Berkovitsa from wind. Here are the remains of Roman and medieval Bulgarian fortresses built in three belts in terraces. Of interest are the two late antique Christian churches that date back to $4^{th}$-$5^{th}$ century. **The Ashiklar Area** (the valley of the singers in love) is a romantic neighborhood to the south of the town, spreading out to the chestnut woods. A favorite place for recreation in natural environment.

**Vurshets Resort** (18 km to the southeast) is a balneological centre of national importance and is the biggest in Northeastern Bulgaria. It is nestled in a small valley, surrounded to the south by the main ridge of Stara Planina and to the east by the Vratsa Balkan. Since 1860 its thermal waters (temperature from 32.6° to 36.4°C) are used for healing rheumatic, cardiovascular, gastric-intestinal, nerve and other diseases. There is a great number of sanatoriums, holiday houses, villas. Marius Hotel (126, Republika Blvd.) works, too. One could rent private lodgings. The resort is a point of departure of marked tourist tracks in the Vratsa Balkan - to the Byalata Voda Chalet (1.30 hours along a marked track and 7 km asphalt road), to Parshevitsa Chalet (about 8 hours), and to Proboinitsa Chalet (4.30-5 hours on foot). There is a regular bus transport between Vurshets and Berkovitsa.

**The Klissoura Monastery St. St. Cyril and Metodius** (about 10 km to the south east of Berkovitsa and 12 km to the west of Vurshets) was founded in 1240. It was many times burned and restored in the time of the Ottoman Rule. It remained a real fortress of Bulgarian national spirit in this region. It has a striking outlook. The walls are not painted. One is attracted by the beautiful wood-carvings of the

*Autumn in Berkovitsa*

iconostasis, made by Stoicho Fandakov from Samokov and the marvellous icons of the famous icon-painter Nikola Obrazopisov. One can spend the night there against minimal fee. Behind the monastery starts a marked tourist track up to Mt. Todorini Kukli (2.30-3 hours Vurshets) on the main ridge of Stara Planina where one may join the Kom-Emine route. There is no regular transport to the monastery but buses between Berkovitsa and Vurshets stop at the road fork from where one can walk 3 km along an asphalt road. One can also go on foot from Vurshets (through the village of Spanchevtsi) for 1-1.30 h.

**The village of Burzia** - 6 km to the south of Berkovitsa. Mountain and balneological resort of local importance. All buses going through the Petrohan Pass stop there.

**Petrohan Pass** (1444 m above sea level, 25 km to the south of Berkovitsa) is on the Stara Planina ridge and is a boundary between the Berkovski Balkan (to the west) and Koznitsa and Ponor (to the east). This is the road from Sofia to Berkovitsa, Vurshets, Montana, Lom, Vidin. It received its name after the Petrov's Inn, which had many years served those who passed by it (it is not preserved). There is a motel-restaurant, gas-station and a chalet (Petrohanski Prohod Chalet) and another big Chalet (Petrohan Chalet) to the east 30 min on foot. A point of departure for tourist routes along the ridge of the Balkan - to the west: Mt. Kom (2016 m, about 3 hours), the new Kom Chalet (3.30 hours), the old Kom Chalet (3.00 hours), the town of Berkovitsa (about 6 hours) and to the east (except to the Petrohan Chalet): to Mt. Todorini Kukli (about 2.30 hours), Proboinitsa Chalet (5-6 hours), Lakatnik railway station (7-8 hours), etc. All buses going through the Petrohan Pass stop there. The Haidoushki Waterfall is situated 9 km to the southwest from Berkovitsa in the lovely valley of Goliama Reka where the water goes down with roar on the two falls. The neighborhood district is very beautiful. One can walk to the waterfall in 1.30-2 hours.

## CHIPROVTZI

The town of Chiprovtsi (2915 inhabitants, about 500 m above sea level) is picturesquely situated in the folds between Chiprovska and Iazova Mountain (Western Stara Planina) on the banks of Stara Reka and Martinovska Ogosta rivers. It is 120 km to the northwest from Sofia and 35 km to the west from Montana. Centuries-old stronghold of Bulgarian spirit.

**History**. Chiprovtsi is a very old settlement, originating in Thracian time, when ore mining in these lands is dated back. There were ledges of copper, lead, gold, silver and iron. In Roman age the region around the village had been among the gold mining centres of greatest importance on the Balkans. The village is named after the Roman name of copper - cupprum. It was named *Kiprovets* first, then *Chiporovtsi* and finally the today's Chiprovtsi (renamed in 1956). In late antiquity ore minimg had been of great importance for the development of military production in the Rome Ritsaria (today Archar). Slav people had come here after 6$^{th}$ century and borrowed production experience in ore mining from the local inhabitants.

In 13$^{th}$-16$^{th}$ century Chiprovtsi had been a busy mining village that enjoyed great favours. Here settled Saxon miners, who gave a further impetus to this activity. It is not accidental that right here in the flourishing feudal domains of the Bulgarian boyars Soimirovi a great part of the Bulgarian aristocracy settled after the Ottoman invasion. Chiprovtsi reached its economic, political and cultural boom in the first three centuries under foreign rule. Goldsmith's trade developed most in comparison to all other handcrafts. High artistic production had outlined the town as the biggest goldsmith centre on the Balkan Peninsula in 16$^{th}$ and 17$^{th}$ century along with Tsarigrad, Thessaloniki and Belgrade. Trade with the famous cups made in Chiprovtsi flourished not only on the

# NORTHWESTERN BULGARIA

*A Chiprovtsi-style carpet*

Balkans and the Ottoman Empire but extended to Central Europe, too. Churches, monasteries, schools, rich and beautiful houses were built in this environment of considerable improvement and culture.

In 16$^{th}$ century the Literary School of Chiprovtsi emerged. Its "heights" are: "Abagar" by Fillip Stanislavov, the theological, philosophical and historical works of Petar Bogdan, Yakov Peyachevich and Krustyu Peikich. Petar Bogdan and Petar Parchevich headed the struggle for national independence in the middle of 17$^{th}$ century. In the beginning they relied on help from our western neighbours and the Pope, but were disappointed and began an independent preparation of a people's revolt. In September 1688 broke the Uprising of Chiprovtsi that was headed by Georgi Peyachevich, Bogdan Marinov, the brothers Ivan and Mihail Stanislavovi and Peter Parchevich. The decisive battle took place in the area called Zheravitsa, where the troops of the Turkish vassal - the Magyar count Emerik Tekeli - defeated the Bulgarians. Those surviving fortified themselves in Chiprovtsi and in the Chiprovtsi (Gushovski) Monastery, but their defence was overcome, too. Outrageous slaughter and brutality followed. More than half of the inhabitants were slaughtered. A great part of the survivors looked for refuge in Vlashko (Romania), Magyar and Croatia. The town was burnt down, devastated and ruined, after which it never reached its past glory. Chiprovtsi rebelled in 1836 (Manchov's buna) and in 1837 (headed by Vurban Penev). Its inhabitants took part also in the uprising in Vidin in 1850.

In 19$^{th}$ century carpet manufacturing developed very much. The famous Chiprovtsi carpets are handmade from pure wool on a vertical loom. Even today they find markets all over the world, and now in thousands Bulgarian homes the colours of nature in Chiprovtsi beam, collected and immortalized by the tender hands of the carpet masters in Chiprovtsi.

**Landmarks.** The remains of the **Santa Maria Catholic Cathedral** constructed in 1371 and burnt during the uprising in Chiprovtsi in 1688. **The Ascension Church** built probably in 14$^{th}$ century. Burnt after the uprising in Chiprovtsi and later it was restored. In 1865 master Danail from Shtip painted the iconostasis. The remains of **St. Nikolai Church** - it was constructed in 17$^{th}$ century and burnt after the uprising. **The Museum of History** is arranged in a house built in 1896 as a school. Working hours: 8 a.m. - 17.00 p.m. all the week round. The museum and the above-mentioned churches are on the **Historical Hill**. **Sharenata cheshma** (the colourful drinking-fountain) - the only monument survived after 1688. Its foundations are about 1.5 m in the ground. In the past it was covered with frescos. **Punko's House** is near the Historical museum. Now restored it bears the charm of the Revival architecture.

**Accommodation.** Punkova Kashta Hotel (the second floor of the Revival Punko's House is arranged as a folk-style hotel). The private lodgings are of 1- and 2-star category. Accommodation is made through the Tourist Council (see below).

**Tourist information.** Tourist Council (2, Vitosha Str., tel. 09554 2168). Tri Chuki Tourist

# NORTHWESTERN BULGARIA

Association.

**Transport.** There is a regular bus connection with Montana and bus transport to some of the smaller settlements in the region.

**Surrounding areas. The Monastery of Chiprovtsi St. Yoan Rilski** (6 km to the northeast, near the village of Zhelezna) was raised according to the legend about $10^{th}$ century along with the first steps of Christianity and the work of the students of Ciril and Methodius in our lands. It is a century-old centre of Bulgarian education and it has been burnt and devastated 6 times during the Turkish rule. It was the last refuge of the revolted Bulgarians in the dramatic 1688.

The monastery complex includes **St. Yoan Rilski Church,** built in 1829 (this is the oldest entire building). It is remarkable with the tracery wood-carving of its iconostasis. Hristo Enchev, an icon-painter from Koprivshtitsa, painted the icons. There is also a small chapel built after the Liberation. The inscription above the wall paintings shows that the chapel is devoted to the Russian Tsar-Liberator. The tower-charnel house was built after the Liberation (I and II floor) and the belfry - at the beginning of $20^{th}$ century. The charnel house is situated in the ground floor where are collected the mortal remains of people who died in the national-liberation struggles, including the martyrs in the uprising of Chiprovtsi. **The remains of the Gushovski Monastery** - built in $17^{th}$ century and soon after that burnt in the memorable 1688. It was the predecessor of the modern Chiprovtsi Monastery. One can get lodging in the **Chiprovtsi Monastery** at minimal fee. Annually on $6^{th}$ of September nationwide celebrations are organized here. There is a regular bus transport from Chiprovtsi. There are 34 beds in one 2-beds room and in two shared rooms in the **Kopren Chalet** (975 m above sea level, 20 km away). There is no regular transport. Chiprovtsi is a **point of departure** for hiking tours in Chiprovska Maountain - to Mt. Midzhur (the highest peak in the Western Stara Planina, 2168 m), to Mt. Martinova Chuka (2026 m), to Mt. Golema Chuka, Mt. Obov, Mt. Trite Chuki, Mt. Kopren etc., but there is no tourist marking. But one can hire a guide. **St. Yoan Predtecha (The Precursor) Lopoushanski Monastery** is about 20 km to the northeast. The people's poet Ivan Vazov had often visited it. The icons in it are done by the icon-painters from Samokov Stanislav and Nikola Dospevski. There is a regular bus transport from Montana. There are remains of an ancient Roman fortress in the area called Kaleto, situated to the southeast of Chiprovtsi. **Chiprovski Waterfall, the rock formation Kuklite** and many others.

*The Chiprovtsi Monastery*

# BELOGRADCHIK

The town of Belogradchik (6685 inhabitants, 520 m above sea level) is situated between both mountain massifs Venetsa and Vedernik (small sub-parts of Western Stara Planina), among the fantastic world of Belogradchik rocks. It is 182 km northwest from Sofia, 68 km to the northwest to Montana, 52 km southwest from Vidin and 12 km southwest from the Oreshets railway station. It is a town amidst a fantastic natural environment.

**History.** This is an old settlement, originated as early as 1st century when the Romans built a fortress among the rocks. After that the fortress and the settlement were ruined many times and built again by Byzantines, Bulgarians, Turks. A register from 1454 testifies about the Bulgarian town here. In 1837 during the reign of Sultan Mahmud II the fortress was finished in its present-day outlook and with the non-paid work of the Bulgarian population. In the period of Ottoman Rule Belogradchik was a small agrarian-craftsman town. A peasant uprising began here in 1850, but it was cruelly crushed and the last defenders of the fortress slaughtered. The name of the town comes from "beliya gradezh" (the white building) of the fortress - a natural combination of human and nature work. After the Liberation (1878) Belogradchik gradually becomes a tourist centre above all, which attracts thousands of visitors from the country and abroad.

**Landmarks. The Town Museum of History** is arranged in the Revival house of the Panovs' (1810), which in itself is an architectural monument. It is in the centre of the town (tel. 0936 3469). The **Astronomical Observatory** has one of the most powerful telescopes in Bulgaria. **St. Georgi the Victorious Church** was built in 1868.

**Accommodation.** Belogradchishki Skali Hotel. Rabisha Tourist Complex (in the park above the stadium, 99 beds in 2 suites and in 2-bed and 4-bed rooms).

**Tourist information.** At the hotel, at the Tourist Complex and at the Belogradchishki Skali Tourist Association (1, Vassil Levski Str., tel. 0936 3285, 4933).

**Transport.** There is regular bus transport to Sofia, Montana, Vidin and other smaller settlements in the region. The bus station has a tel.: 0936 3427. There is a bus connection with the Oreshets railway station (12 km to the northeast) of the Mezdra - Vidin railway line which connects Belogradchik to the national railway system.

**Surrounding areas. Belogradchik Rocks** formed from red sandstone and conglomerate - one of the natural wonders of Bulgaria! A fairy-tale stone world surrounds Belogradchik from west, south and southeast. If you come from Sofia by car you will see at first the **Falkov-Borovets group of rocks** with Momina Skala (Maiden's Rock), Pchelin Kamuk, Torlaka, Borovishki Kamuk etc. **Lipenitsa group** is to the east of the town among which biggest interest evoke the Dinosaur and the Latin Kale (a strategic fortress surrounded by a fortified wall). It is worth seeing the Lepenishka Cave in which charred wheat and vessels dating 2000 years ago were found, and the Izvozki oak - more than 1200 years old. Among the **Zbegovska group of rocks** to the west of the town a great impression make the Twins, the rocks in the area called Magaza Small and Big Zbeg, which were used as fortresses, the lonely obelisk Borich and the Belogradchik stone bridge. **The central group** rises immediately above the town. One can see about 100 m high lonely rocks named Adam and Eve, the delicate Madonna, Konika (The Rider), Uchenichkata (The Female Student), Mechkata (The Bear), the Dervish (Muslim clergyman), the impressive Borov Kamak, Monasite (The Monks), the fantastic kale with ancient fortress walls, above which the most magic rock wonders rise.

The French traveler Germon Blanky wrote the following about the Belogradchishki Skali in the distant 1841: *"Neither the famous narrow*

# NORTHWESTERN BULGARIA

passes of Aulihul in Provance, neither the Pancarbo Gorge in Spain, neither the Alps, neither the Pyrenees, nor the most eminent Tyrol mountains in Switzerland have anything, which can be compared with what I saw in Bulgaria in the town of Belogradchik". The famous Felix Kanits adds: *"It's hardly probable that a more romantic fortress than the Belogradchik one has ever been built".*

The most characteristic peculiarity of the **Belogradchik Fortress** is the perfect inclusion of the unapproachable rocks in the whole fortress system. Three construction periods can be seen in the buildings - Roman and Byzantine ($1^{st}$-$6^{th}$ centuries), Byzantine and Bulgarian ($8^{th}$-$14^{th}$ centuries) and Turkish (1805-1837). The constructions of the last period prevail in its present-day outlook. The fortress is situated at 10200 sq. m and has 5 gates, 4 of which are main. **Magourata** or the **Rabishkata Peshtera** (Rabisha Cave) is found near the village of Rabisha, 16 km west of the town of Dimovo, 50 km southwest from Vidin and 34 km northwest of Belogradchik. It was formed about 3-4 million years ago in the Magoura Hill, 463 m high. Inside one can see unique halls and formations as Triumphalnata Zala (The hall of tryumphs), Harmana (The wheat thrashing site), the Hall of the Stalactone, Glinenite Piramidi (The mud pyramids), Povaleniyat Bor (The fallen pine-tree), Vkamenenata Reka (The Stoned River), The Fiords, etc. The exit of the cave is through Vratach on the bank of the Rabisha Lake. Primitive men lived there. The wall drawings made with bat excrements are the only ones in the caves at the Balkan Peninsula. These masterpieces of late prehistoric art date back from the beginning of the Bronze Age. The cave was used by Manush Voivoda as a shelter. Magourata Cave is electrified, the length of its galleries are 2500 m. A minimal entry fee is paid. There is a hotel, a restaurant, pavilions and other buildings round it. There is a regular bus transport from Belogradchik and the town of Dimovo.

*Belogradchik Rocks with the fortress*

# NORTHWESTERN BULGARIA

## VIDIN

Town of Vidin (57 614 inhabitants, 20-25 m above sea level) is situated on the bank of the Danube River, on its big curve in the most northwestern corner of Bulgaria. It is 199 km the northwest from Sofia, 102 km northwest from Montana, 52 km north from Belogradchik, 56 km northwest from Lom and 30 km southeast from the border town of Bregovo. It is one of the oldest Bulgarian towns. It is a regional administrative centre.

**History.** The past of this town dates 23 centuries ago. As early as $3^{rd}$ century BC the Celts built a settlement here with the name *Dounonia* (a high and fortified place). The Romans put into final shape the fortress with the purpose to guard the border road along the Danube and named it *Bononia*. Bulgarians named the town *Bdin,* and Byzantines - *Vidini*. In the meantime it was ruined and built again many times. In 1003 Gavril Radomir, the son of the Bulgarian Tsar Samouil, stood the 8-months siege of the Byzantine Emperor Vassilii II. The town reached the greatest flourishing at the end of $14^{th}$ century, when it became a capital of the Bdin Kingdom of Ivan Sratsimir (1360). It has been a port on the river and an important trade centre of goods not only for domestic needs, but also for transit trade with Vlashko (Romania), Madzharsko, Dubrovnik, etc. A gospel from 1360 says that it was written in "the great and crowded town of Bdin". The rise of the town ceased in 1396 when the Turks invades it. Since then Bulgaria started counting the 482 dark years of Ottoman rule, the 127195 endless days of persecution, terror, human misery, assimilation and overt genocide.

In those centuries Vidin had been a great fortress and an important administrative centre. In $17^{th}$ century it was even called " the main town of Bulgaria". In 1794-1807 the town became a centre of the absolute Turkish military leader Osman Pazvantooglu, who declared himself an independent ruler of a considerable part of Bulgarian northwestern territories. During his rule construction on a large scale developed in the town - new streets were made, big administrative buildings rose, mosques and medreses (Islamic religious schools) were built, etc. Some of them are preserved even till now. Vidin gradually turned into an oriental town, especially after the settlement of some Turks after the defeat of the Turkish army near Vienna and the liberation of Serbia. Expression of desperate fight for national liberation was the famous Vidin Uprising of 1850 headed by Boiadzh Stanko Voivoda. Gradually with development of shipping along the Danube and with the strengthening of the trade ties with Central Europe the standard of living of its inhabitants rose. Through Vidin Port Austrian Shipping Co. bought the production of the whole Western Bulgaria, incl. Macedonia. That went on till 1866 when neighbouring Lom was connected through a road with Sofia and replaced Vidin.

After the Liberation (1877) the town changed basically its ethnical population in favour of the Bulgarians. During the Serbian-Bulgarian War after the Union of Eastern Roumelia with the Bulgarian Principality (1885) Vidin was successfully defended by captain Atanas Uzunov. The town is a birthplace of the eminent Bulgarian social activist Naicho Tsanov and of world famous post-impressionist artist Ju Pasken (Iulius Pinkas, 1885-1930), a brilliant representative of the Paris School of Art.

*Baba Vida Fortress*

# NORTHWESTERN BULGARIA

**Landmarks. Baba Vida Fortress-Museum** (tel.: 094 22884) - it is named after an old legend - it is the biggest historical sight of Vidin and is the best-preserved medieval Bulgarian fortress in the country. It has been built in different historical periods from 3rd century till the end of 19th century. Most active were the construction works under the reign of Ivan Srazimir. The main body of the fortress of that time is preserved even today - the main turrets and bastions, as well as the inner surrounding wall that connects them. A museum exhibition is arranged in the fortress. There is a theatrical scene and dramatic performances with historical plots are played among the unique scenery.

**The Vidin fortified system,** known also as the Turkish Kale, was built in 17th-18th century. Today in a comparatively good outlook are preserved the fortified wall facing the Danube, the northern sector of the fortress facing the town with its 4 gates - Stambolkapia, Pazarkapia, Nechirekapia and Florentinkapia. The system has the form of a semi-circle seesaw line of 1800 m diametre, touching the Danube River. Seen from the land the fortification consists of a moat and a ground rampart, whose corners are formed by 8 stone 5-angle bastions. With the construction of the Kale and including the Baba Vida Fortress as a main citadel in the common defencive system, in the second half of 18th century Vidin became a first-class key military point along the Danube.

**The Town Historical Museum** (tel.: 094 25609) is one of the richest and best-arranged museums in the country. It is housed in two buildings - in the former **Turkish Konak** (police office) from 18th century are arranged the Archaeology, Revival Period and National Liberation Movement sections, and the Ethnographic section is placed in the **Krustatata Kazarma** (barracks building like a crest) - an original architectural monument from the end of 18th century.

There is also the **Mausoleum of the first Bulgarian Ekzarh Antim I. The library of Osman Pazvantooglu** (from about 1800, a monumental construction with original oriental architecture and woodcarving).

**The St. Pantaleimon Church** from 1634 is the most precious monument of Bulgarian architecture and art in the town from the age of Turkish rule. The **St. Petka Church** from 1633. The **St. Dimitur Cathedral.** The building of the **military club,** in which **the Town Art Gallery** is housed, the **Teketo** (Islamic monastery) **Saldahin Baba, Hadzhi Angel's House**, the **Synagogue** and many other interesting cultural and historic monuments.

There is a Theatre of Drama in Vidin, too.

**Accommodation.** Military Club Hotel (15, Baba Vida Str.). Rovno Hotel. Bononia Hotel. Tourist House (3, Iskra Str., 300 m from the railway station and 200 m from the port). There are 90 beds in 6 suites and in 2-bed, 3-bed and 4-bed rooms. The Danube Camping (7 km to the northeast of the town and 3 km from the village of Zlaten Rog) with fourteen 2-bed and two 6-bed pile bungalows along the banks of the Danube River. There is a regular bus transport from Vidin. Reservations can be done at Bononia Tourist Association (see below). Boats for sports and water tourism are offered against payment. There are a lot of interesting restaurants and entertainment sites in Vidin, but the most original one is in the former warehouse of the traders from Dubrovnic in the centre of the town.

**Tourist information.** At the hotels, at the Tourist House and at Bononia Tourist Association (3, Edelvais Str., tel.: 094 23828, 23206).

**Transport.** Two kinds of transport connect the town to the rest of the world - road and railway. There is regular bus transport to Sofia, Montana, Lom, Vratsa, Belogradchik and many other smaller settlements in the region. Telephone of the bus station - 094 23179. The railway station (tel.: 094 23184) is the final one on the railway line Mezdra - Vratsa - Vidin (Lom) and through the railway station Mezdra it is connected with the rail-

# NORTHWESTERN BULGARIA

way system of the country. There is also a new river station (since 1992 there are is regular passengers transport from Bulgaria) and in the northern part of the town operates a ferry port (tel.: 094 24979), through which an extremely important ferry connection with Kalafat (Romania) is established. It serves a considerable part of the tourists stream to and from Bulgaria. There is a town bus transport in Vidin as well.

**Surrounding areas. The Danube**, a large European river (a border between Bulgaria and Romania) runs past the town, which is situated on its right bank. It offers wonderful opportunities for rest, sports, fishing, water tourism and many other activities. There is a big water tourist base in the northern suburbs of the town. Excursions along the river can be done with small entertainment ships, hired at the river station. The Danube is an exceptional natural wealth, which shall be used by the future generations of the ancient town.

**Ratsiaria** is the name of the ancient Roman town near the village of Archar, 27 km to the southeast of Vidin near the Danube River. Its remains are 2 km to the west of the village. During the reign of Emperor Aurelian the town became a capital of the province Dakia Ripenzis and took the name *Ulpia Ratsiaria*. It was a rich and crowded town. The masterpieces of its goldsmiths made it famous in the whole empire. In 447 the Huns devastated the town, but it rose again to be ruined in 586, this time forever. There is a regular bus transport from Vidin, as well as from Lom.

**The Bozhouritsa Park** is situated between the rivers Milchina and Vidbol, 18 km to the southwest of the town. There is a dam lake with opportunities for water sports, fishing, sun bathing and other activities. There is a chalet in the park with the same name, which has 24 beds in 2-bed, 3-bed and 5-bed rooms and 10 beds in 2-bed bungalows. Telephone 266 through the post office in the village of Sinagovtsi or through Bononia Tourist Association.

## LOM

The town of Lom (27 897 inhabitants, 50 metres above sea level) is situated on the right bank (the Bulgarian one) of the Danube River, at its estuary with the Lom river. It is 162 km north of Sofia, 56 km southeast of Vidin, 49 km north of Montana and 42 km west of Kozlodoui. It is the second most important port on the Danube after Rousse.

**History.** It was founded by the Thracians under the name of *Artanes*. After them the Romans called the fortress and the town *Almus*, from where the name of today's town and of the Lom River comes. There are no reports proving that there existed a big settlement in the Middle Ages. It was not until Turkish rule when it enlarged but for a long time it was under the shadow of the dominant towns of Vidin, Nikopol and Silistra. It is assumed that the Turkish village was founded in 1695 by Kara Mustafa and Murad Bei who were defeated at Vienna in 1683 and who came here sailing rafts along the Danube River.

The name *Lom Palanka* was mentioned for a first time in 1704. The settlement then called "palanka" was something between a village and a town in size and importance. In 1798 Lom was suffered by the kurdzhalii (Turkish brigands). With the development of shipping along the Danube after 1830 the importance of the town grew. The road to Sofia contributed to its progress and turned it into a main export port to Vienna (Austria). By 1869 there were 120 shops, 148 trade offices, 175 food shops, 34 coffee bars, 6 hotels, 2 mills. The town was centred around the old Kale (fortress), which was entered through three kapii (gates) - Vidinska, Belogradchishka, Sofiiska. The tradesmen from Lom offered goods at the biggest fairs in the region and beyond. In 1880 there were 7500 inhabitants in the town.

Lom is proud of its traditions from the period

of the national Revival. In 1856 the first community centre in Bulgaria was founded there, the first women's society in this country was founded here (1858) and one of the first theatre performances took place in the town. Krustyu Pishurka, an educator worked here.
**Landmarks. The Town Museum of History** (tel.: 0971 2466 is housed in the interesting building of the old town-hall. The foundations of the **antique fortress Almus** are preserved. **The oldest community centre in this country - Postoianstvo.** The building of the former School of Pedagogy. **The Borunska Church**. The monument to Tseko Voivoda (1807 -1881) - a participant in the battles for liberation from Serbia and pronounced by its government to be a voivoda (revolutionary leader).
**Accommodation.** The Dounav Hotel.
**Tourist information** - at the hotel and at the Asparuchov Hulm Tourist Association (5, Nikola Chukov Str., 3600 Lom, tel.: 0971 24194, 24586).
**Transport.** Two types of transport connect it to the rest of the world - bus and railway transport. There are bus lines to Vidin, Kozlodoui, Montana as well as to other smaller settlements in the region. The bus station telephone is 0971 22093. The town is a last stop on the railway line Broussartsi-Lom, through which it is connected with the national railway system. The railway station telephone is 0971 22485. There is a river port, too (tel.: 0971 22057), but so far there is no regular transport provided from Bulgaria.
**Surrounding areas.** The remains of the **Asparoukhov Rov** (The dyke of Asparoukh) (4 km southeast). **The Danube River**, along the banks there are holiday homes, establishments, places for recreation and sport. The big river offers wonderful opportunities for fishing, motor sports, water tourism and many other activities. 28 km westward there are the remains of the Roman **Ratsiaria** (refer to Vidin related chapter herein).

# KOZLODUI

The town of Kozlodoui (14 286 inhabitants, 40 metres above the sea level) is situated by the river Danube, opposite the second biggest island with the same name. It is 196 km north of Sofia, 42 east of Lom, 29 km west of Oryahovo, 15 km northwest of Mizia and 80 km north of Vratsa. It is a sacred historical town to all Bulgarians and the country's heart of energy production.
**History.** At first the settlement was spread over 3 km west of the river Ogosta in the area of Chetate (in Romanian - fortress). There are two versions of the origin of its name: the first comes from the Turkish *Kozludere* (a low gully), and the second - from the Latin meaning of *Kozlodoui* - "a corner of the ice blocks" - as sometimes in winter ice blocks pile up at this part of the river. It is not known for sure when the settlement has moved to its present place. Most probably it happened at the time of the huge flood of Danube and Ogosta in 1840. Near the town, east of the area Magoura Petra, the remains of the Roman fortification Reganium can be seen and between Kozlodoui and Hairedin are preserved parts of the Hairedin defence trench ($7^{th}$-$8^{th}$ century). In documents from $17^{th}$ century the settlement is mentioned under the name of *Kotosluk*. Kaikchii (boatsmen) from the village drew boats and vessels with ropes upstream. The traveller Domenico Sestini (1780) recorded the well-developed silkworm breeding and leather processing with the herb sumac.
In terms of history Kozlodoui is mostly connected with the name of the immortal poet and revolutionary Hristo Botev. On the $17^{th}$ ($29^{th}$ old calendar style) May 1876, 200 Bulgarian men disembarked the Austro-Hungarian steamer Radetski at the shore of Kozlodoui led by their voivoda Hristo Botev. They embarked on the steamer at different Romanian ports as civil travellers. Then they

# NORTHWESTERN BULGARIA

got off the ship (forcing the captain to stop it at the isolated area of the Bulgarian river bank) as a well-organized revolutionary detachment of volunteers, dressed in their rebel uniforms, going to help the Bulgaria which was already burning. Stepping onto their native land the rebels fell on knees and kissed it. From here started their heroic epic whose summit was later in the week on the ridge of the Vratsa Balkan. Passing through the whole of Northern Bulgaria in ceaseless fighting, under the pursuit of the Turks, the detachment entered into a decisive battle against the dozen times outnumbered enemy around Mt. Okolchitsa. There on 2 June (old calendar style) 1876 the Voivoda was shot, the detachment was defeated and scattered into small groups around the Balkan. 130 men died, 68 were captured and sent on penal servitude and only 8 escaped. The prophetic words of Botev came true: *"He, who perishes in a battle for freedom, does not die!"* After the liberation of Kozlodoui in 1877, many settlers came into the town from other parts of the country and the Bulgarians became dominant within the ethnic profile of the town. In 1974 the first nuclear power station in Bulgaria and on the Balkan Peninsula was built here (it is only one so far).

**Landmarks.** 5 km northwest of the centre of the town, by the Danube River, is the well-arranged **Botev Park**. It was created in the place where in May 1876. Hristo Botev and his detachment disembarked onto the native land. There is a **stone obelisk**, erected in 1936 with the inscription "He does not die". The old **stone cross** put there after the Liberation is preserved. The initial letters H.B. are inscribed with evergreen cypresses on the opposite Krushovski Bair (Hill). This is the beginning of a **120-kilometre Botev alley** following the path of Botev's detachment to Mt. Okolchitsa in the Vratsa Balkan. It is marked with 68 stone signs. Every year on 27th May on the shore of Kozlodoui thousands of people walk the trail (5-6 days) and reach Mt. Okolchitsa to take part in the national celebrations on 2nd June. Near the port, also in the same region, there is the Radetski Restaurant housing a **museum** in its west wing. Here is the Kozlodouiski Briag Chalet consisting of 2 buildings offering 40 beds in rooms with 2, 3, 5 and more beds. There is a bus line connecting the town and Botev Park.

To the west of the port is the area of Kiler Bair, which is the beginning of the historic Kozlodoui Val (dyke) dated back to time of Khan Asparouh's state. It was built in the end of 7th century and is 32 km long. The dyke ends southwest of the Hairedin village. The highest preserved part of it is 2.60 m. A marked path along the river bank (in the Botev Park) leads there.

**Surrounding areas.** The **Danube River** with opportunities for rest, sports, tourism and fishing. **Kozlodoui Island** - located just opposite the town and separated from it by a tributary about 200 m wide. The island is 7.5 km long and between 0.5 and 1.6 km wide. Its surface is 6.1 sq. km and is the second biggest Danube island after Belene. It raises 3-4 m above the river. It is covered with river poplars and is a favourite hatching place of many birds - wild geese, wild ducks and others. It can be reached by boats against a low fee.

**Accommodation.** Refer to the section about the Botev Park.

**Tourist information.** At Radetski Tourist Association (13, Sofia Str., tel.: 0973 3505), at Radetski Hotel and at the chalet.

**Transport.** At present there is only bus transport connecting Kozlodoui with the rest of the country. There are regular bus lines to Lom, Vratsa, Oryahovo, Miziya and other smaller settlements in the region. There is a port, but so far there is no regular passenger transport along Danube from Bulgaria. The closest railway station is the town of Miziya on the narrow-gauge railway road on the line Cherven Bryag - Oryahovo.

# NORTHWESTERN BULGARIA

## ORIAHOVO

The town of Oryahovo (7006 inhabitants, from 30 to 226 metre above sea level) is situated on the hills by the river Danube, not far away from the Ogosta and Skat estuaries. It is 190 km north-east of Sofia, 29 km and 71 km east of Kozlodoui and Lom, respectively, 74 km north of Vratsa, 14 km north-east of Miziya and 95 km west of Nikopol. One of the most picturesque Danube towns.

**History.** At the highest point on the Bulgarian shore of the Danube (226 m) existed as a settlement as far back as the Bronze Age. The Thracians have also left significant traces here. The ruins tell us about the town of *Vateria* and the *Variana* Fortress from the Roman time when the old Roman road to Constantinople passed through these lands. In the Middle Ages, in $9^{th}$-$10^{th}$ century a Bulgarian town with a fortress emerged, which was a border post to stop the advance of the Avars, Franks and Magyars. For first time the name of the town was mentioned in 1226 when the Magyar army passed through the Bulgarian settlement *Orechov*. It was many times destroyed to the grounds and rebuilt. In 1388 the settlement was conquered by the Turks, and in 1396 it suffered because of the battles between the Turks and the crusaders of the Hungarian Knyaz Sigizmund of Luxembourg during the advance of the Christian army in the direction of Nikopol. In 1444 the Polish-Hungarian Knyaz Vladisslav Yagelo (Varnenchik) succeeded in liberating it for a short time. Later, when the first Turnovo Uprising took place (1598) the Wallachian voivoda Michai Vityazul with his army fought here.

In the Middle Ages the town was also called *Vrhov*, *Orezov*, *Oreev*, and in a Hungarian document it is reported as *Oreshik*. From the beginning of $18^{th}$ century until 1888 its name was *Rahovo*, then *Orehovo* and finally today's *Oryahovo*. With the development of shipping along the Danube River in the end of $18^{th}$ and $19^{th}$ century, Oryahovo became rich. Despite the large number of Turks in the town, it kept alive the Bulgarian spirit. The Bulgarian population took an active part in the struggle for church and national independence.

In 1857 a class school was opened, later a girls' school and a community centre. The local revolutionary committee founded in 1872 served the secret channel between Oryahovo and Becket for transporting weapons and revolutionary activists. Vassil Levski visited the town twice. In the winter of 1876 Oryahovo gave shelter to the apostles Panaiot Volov and Georgi Benkovski on their way to Panagyurishte revolutionary district. Stoian Zaimov, Ivanitsa Danchev, Nikola Obretenov, Nikola Slavkov had stayed in the town, as well. The people from Oryahovo took part in the struggle of Bulgarian volunteers during the Russian-Turkish War (1877-1878). The

*On cruise along the Danube*

# NORTHWESTERN BULGARIA

town was liberated on 20 November 1877 after three days of heavy fighting.
**Landmarks.** The **Town Museum of History** in the centre (Levski Str.). **The park of Bulgarian-Romanian Friendship** is located in the eastern part of the town, above the Danube River. It was founded in 1959-1960 and there is the famous **Statue of Liberty** made by the sculptor Arnoldo Tsoki in 1882 in memoriam of the Romanian soldiers who died for the liberation of Bulgaria from Ottoman rule.

**The Loven Dom Park** is the highest point in the centre of Oryahovo, from where there is an open view to the Danube shore and the opposite Romanian settlement Becket. **Diko Iliev House-Museum** (9th November Str., in the eastern part of the town, tel.: 09171 2467), displays the environment in which one of the greatest musicians, conductors and composers, lived (1895-1985). He composed lots of popular Bulgarian hora ("horo" - folk dance) and marches for a brass orchestra. Emblematic are the Dounavsko Horo, Severnyashko Horo, Pravo Horo, etc. In the **St. Georgi Church** dating back to 1837 church plate from $17^{th}$ century and old print church books brought from Russia are preserved. It is situated in the centre near the bus station.

**Accommodation.** Asparouh Hotel (9, Asparouh Street) with 4 double rooms. Dounav Hotel (6, Alleya na Mira Str.). Seikov Hotel (34, Ivan Vazov Str.). Sladki Mechti Hotel-Tavern. Kamuka Hotel.

**Tourist information.** At the hotels and at the Tourist Association.

**Transport.** Bus and railway transport. There are regular bus lines to Vratsa, Pleven, Kozlodoui, Knezha, Byala Slatina and other smaller settlements in the region. The bus station (tel.: 09171 2307, 3147) is located in the centre of the town, next to St. Georgi Church. Oryahovo is the last station of the railroad line Cherven Bryag-Oryahovo, through which it is connected with the railway system of the country. The railway station (3, Dragomanska Str., tel.: 09171 2315, 2383) is in the northern end of the town, on the shore of the Danube.

Through the port (near the railway station, tel.: 09171 3168) the town is connected with other Bulgarian ports on the Danube River.

**Surrounding areas.** The remains of **Kamuka Fortress** are around 1.5 km west of Oryahovo (the local people call it Kaleto). The fortress, built in $12^{th}$ century is a part of the defence system along the north border of the Bulgarian State. It had an irregular form and small size. It was forever demolished in $16^{th}$ century. The 9-metre corner guard turret that was a 2-storied one is comparatively well-preserved. The building is typical Old Bulgarian and is very stable - crushed stones, white mortar and timber beams levelling the brickwork. The name Kamuka comes from its solidity ("kamuk" - stone). An asphalt road leads here. It would take 30 minutes walk from the centre of the town.

5 km east of the town (along the road to Nikopol) there is the **Esperanto Island** covered with thick foliage. On the shore opposite it is the resort zone of the town - a place for rest with a beach, park and a restaurant. The area is called **Esperanto** because here in 1937 the Esperanto World Congress took place. There is a regular bus transport from the town.

22 km southeast is the village of Ostrov (on the bank of the Danube). South of the village starts the **Ostrovski Val** (dyke) from the period of the Asparouch State. It presents a deep terraced defence system spreading to the west. Its length is 64 km and it ends between the villages Gabare and Tlachene.

**The Danube River** in the area of Oryahovo offers wonderful opportunities for rest, sun bathing, sports, water tourism, fishing and many other activities. The river here is especially beautiful because of the high and steep Bulgarian shore.

# NORTHWESTERN BULGARIA

## MONTANA

The town of Montana (49 368 inhabitants, 160 metres above the sea level) is situated on the river Ogosta immediately next to the dam with the same name. It is 113 km north of Sofia, 24 km north-east of Berkovitsa, 102 km south-east of Vidin, 41 km north-west of Vratsa and 49 km south of Lom. It is the biggest transport crossroad of Northwestern Bulgaria. A regional administrative centre.

**History.** It is a successor of the Roman fortress settlement *Castra ad Montanenzium* (fortress in the mountain) or known also as *Montana*. After archeological excavations it was proved that the long history of the settlement began on the Kalebair ridge, on the left bank of Ogosta River. The strategic position of a crossroad of important roads and the carst spring (now captured) determined the position of the Roman town.

In 3rd century it was the most significant town in the province of Dakia under the name of *Ripenziz*. It was destroyed by the Barbarians. In the Middle Ages it was small insignificant settlement. During Turkish rule it was mentioned for first time under the name of *Koutlovitsa* (a name of Slavic origin) in a document of 1575. The Liberation (1878) found it with the name of *Golyama Koutlovitsa* (Ogosta River separated it from Malka Kutlovitsa) and with less than 1000 inhabitants. Until 1891 when it was officially declared a town, it bore this name. Then the town was given the name of *Ferdinand*, after the name of the then Prince (later on Tsar). At the time it was a craft centre and a major cattle market. Tradesmen from all over the country as well as from abroad - from Turkey, Romania, Serbia participated in the annual fair. The building of the railway line Boichinovtsi-Berkovitsa (1916) which then passed through Ferdinand contributed much to the rapid flourishing of the town. After World War I many refugees from Tsaribrod and Bossilegrad areas settled here. In 1945 the town was renamed to *Mihailovgrad*, and in 1993 again, after about 20 centuries, it took the name of Montana.

**Landmarks: The Town Museum** (tel.: 096 22489). There is a Theatre of Drama as well.

**Accommodation.** Zhitomir Hotel Complex (3-star, 1, Zheravitsa Square). Montana Tourist Hostel (in the park zone, near Slaveikov Square. It offers 34 beds in rooms with 3, 4, 5 and more beds). The bus and railway stations are 1 km away.

**Tourist information** - at the Montana Tourist Association (41, Treti Mart Str., tel.: 096 25251, 20214 as well as at the Tourist Hostel.

**Transport.** Bus and railway transport are the two types of transport connecting the town with the rest of the country. The bus transport is the most important having in mind the town's position and the many roads meeting or starting from here. There are regular buses to Sofia, Lom, Vidin, Belogradchik, Chiprovtsi, Berkovitsa, Vratsa, Pleven, as well as regular connections with almost all smaller settlements in the region. The bus station (tel.: 096 23454) and the railway station (tel.: 096 23846) are near to each other. Montana is a transitional railway station on the line Boichinovtsi-Berkovitsa through which it connects with the national railway system. Regular bus transport functions in the town.

**Surrounding areas.** Immediately south of the town there is the historic **Kale Bair** with archaeological excavations of the Roman fortress Castra ad Montanezium (Montana). **Montana Dam** (immediately south of the town) has been turned into a wonderful place for rest, sports, water tourism and fishing. Many villas, rest homes, catering establishments are built here and there is a regular bus transport.

# NORTHWESTERN BULGARIA

## VRATSA

The town of Vratsa (69 423 inhabitants, 380 m above sea level) is situated along the two banks of Leva River, in the northern foots of the majestic Vrachanski Balkan. It is 116 km north of Sofia, 41 km south-east of Montana, 80 km and 74 km south of Kozlodoui and Oryahovo, respectively, 57 km and 17 km north-west of Botevgrad and Mezdra, respectively. Vratsa is the largest town in Northwestern Bulgaria. Its nature, history and culture form a unique combination. It is a regional administrative centre.

**History.** South of the town is the fantastic gorge of Leva River, coming out of the Vrachanska Mountain, which is known since a lot of time ago as *Vratsata*. In the 6$^{th}$ century there was a fortress here according to the Byzantine chronicler Prokopii. Later the medieval Bulgarian settlement *Vratitsa* emerged in this area. In the beginning of the Ottoman invasion Radan Voivoda successfully defended the area for quite a long time, taking advantage of the natural fortifications and the strong walls of the existing fortress. During the Turkish rule Vratsa was turned into a garrison settlement and was many times ruined and recovered. At first, the Wallachian ruler Mihai Vityaz ruined the town is 1596, while later on (in the beginning of 19$^{th}$ century), during the rule of Osman Pazvantooglu the town served as a battlefield for the troops of the Vidin feudal and the Sultan. At the end of the 18$^{th}$ and particularly during the 19$^{th}$ century Vratsa grew into a big craftsmanship, trade and administrative centre. Its products - aba manufacturing (a coarse homespun woollen cloth and upper men's garment made of it), leather products and goldsmith - reached Lyon, Vienna, Bucharest and Tsarigrad. At mid-19$^{th}$ century the town already had 2500 houses.

All these influenced the spirit of the town. Cathedrals, schools and beautiful houses were built at that time. Sofronii Vrachanski worked and lived in the town. Other natives of Vratsa are the prominent Bulgarians Ivan Zambin, the first Bulgarian diplomat in Russia, Dimitur Hadzhitoshev, famous political leader killed by the Turks in 1827, etc. The town was liberated from the Turkish Rule on 9$^{th}$ November 1877.

With the decline of the crafts after the Liberation Vratsa lost its significance. After the construction of Sofia - Mezdra - Varna railway line, the towns of Mezdra and Roman took off some of the town's trade and market functions. Later on, when the railway line Mezdra - Vratsa - Lom was completed (1913) and a continuation of the railway from Broussartsi to Vidin was finished (1923) Vratsa partially regained its position.

**Landmarks**: **The Town Museum of History** (at the central Hristo Botev Square, tel.: 092 20373) is famous for its extremely valuable golden Thracian treasuries, its original samples of the well-known Vratsa goldsmith school

*Vratsata Gorge*

and numerous exhibits and a lot of information about the life and last days of the **poet and revolutionary Hristo Botev**. There is an impressive monument of the poet in the central town square named after him. Immediately behind is the restored **residential and defence turret** of the **Kurtpashovs'**. 150 metres northwest is located the other turret, constructed at the same time and to serve the same purpose, namely the **turret of the Mezhchiis'**.

**The Revival-Ethnographic Complex** (General Leonov Str., tel.: 092 20209) includes the **Hadzhitoshevs' House** (the most valuable and interesting), the **house of Grigoriya Naidenov** - a member of the local revolutionary committee and a volunteer, the **house of Ivan Zambin**, **The Ascension Church** dating back to 18$^{th}$ century, which gave shelter to Levski, P. R. Slaveikov and other revolutionaries and enlighteners. Also here is the **oldest school in the town - The Ascension School** (1822). There is a **bust-monument of Vassil Levski** in front of the complex. The **Nikola Voivodov Complex** (also in the centre of the town) includes **the native house of Voivodov** and the **house-museum of the typical Vratsa urban traditions and style** from the very beginning of the 20$^{th}$ century. Also here is the **house of Gen. Kiril Botev**, (Ivanka Boteva Str.), where the brother of Hristo Botev together with their mother lived from 1900 to 1903. The **native house of Prof. Andrei Nikolov** (Andrei Nikolov Str, below the Tourist House) - the patriarch of the Bulgarian sculpture, houses a permanent exhibition of his masterpieces. The beautiful **Hristo Botev Tourist House,** situated on the **Kaleto Hill** was built in the period 1926-1931 with donations from the tourists of Vratsa. Steep stone stairs lead to the house and there is a round-routing asphalt road. In the proximity with the Tourist House is the **Monument of The Herald of Liberty.** At this place that one can hear each Sunday the sounds of a battle horn reproducing the signal of the Russian soldier, Petlak the Cossack, who had thus announced the liberation of the town on 9$^{th}$ November 1877. At about 100 metres behind the monument there is a high **white-stone obelisk** bearing the names of the volunteers from the region of Vratsa who took part in the war. The southern part of the town, where the Leva River leaves the Vratsata Gorge, houses the old craftsmanship area - the **Kemera Quarter**. All the old shops and stores are currently under restoration. Some of them are already refurbished and may be visited.

**The Town Art Gallery** has a rich collection of the works of famous artists and sculptors, among which one can spot the names of Andrei Nikolov, St. Ivanov, Tseno Todorov, Ivan Funev, Pencho Georgiev, etc.

**Accommodation**: Hemus Hotel (1, Hristo Botev Sq.). Tourist Hotel, also known as the Tourist House (1, Leva River Str., in the southern part of the town, on the way to the Vratsata Gorge), offering 150 beds in 3 suites and in single and double rooms. DNA Hotel (Mito Rozov Str). Alpine House in the Vratsata Gorge, 1 km south of the Tourist House.

**Tourist information** is available at the hotels and mostly at the Tourist House.

**Transport**. Vratsa connects to the villages and towns within the region and throughout the country by bus and railway transport. There are regular bus lines to Sofia, Montana, Kozlodoui, Oryahovo, Mezdra (at short intervals), as well as to the smaller villages, scattered around the town. The bus station (tel. 092 22558) is located on the way between the railway station and the centre of the town. Vratsa is an important railway station along the railway route Mezdra - Boichinovtsi - Broussartsi - Vidin (Lom). The town connects to the national railway network through the railway station of Mezdra. The railway station (tel.: 092 24415) is located in the northeastern part of the town. There is regular bus transport within the town.

**Surrounding areas. Hristo Botev National Park** in the **area of Okolchitsa** (located about 20 kilometres south-east of the town, in the very heart of Vrachanski Balkan). In the beginning of June 1876 this place witnessed the last drama that put an end to the heroic epic of the detachment of Hristo Botev. The detachments's voivoda (leader), as well as the majority of his men, were killed and the rest of them were either caught or scattered in the Balkan. The heart of one of the greatest and most ingenious Bulgarians, who left to the generations the example of his heroic life, his unsurpassed political journalism and some 20 poems, which are a majestic peak in Bulgarian poetry, ceased beating. And he was just 28 years old... In 1937-1938 a **35-metre monument with a volunteer's crest** was erected at Mt. Okolchitsa (it can be seen from a long distance far away in the plain and the mountain) to honour the heroism of Botev and his detachment forever. In the valley of Yolkovitsa, on a natural crag the **place of death of the poet and revolutionary** is marked. At a distance of 300 metres away from this natural monument is located the Okolchitsa Chalet (a complex of 5 panel bungalows with a restaurant, 84 beds in rooms of 2, 3, 4, 5, and 6 beds, one can make a reservation in the Tourist House in Vratsa). Each year on 2$^{nd}$ June the area hosts national celebrations in honour of Botev and all those who fought and gave their lives for Bulgarian freedom. All participants in the national tourist march along the Botev's trail from the Kozlodoui bank on the Danube River arrive on the day before the celebrations and a large campus town is erected. Besides the Botev's trail, this is the final destination of many other marked hiking tracks. During the summer there is a regular bus transport from Vratsa, and for the rest of the year - regular bus transport is provided to the village of Chelopek, and there are 8 kilometres more to the area. For about 3-4 hours one can reach the place along a marked hiking track starting from the town and passing close to the interesting waterfall of Skaklya.

**The Ledenika Cave** is also situated in the Vrachanski Balkan, south-west of the town (16 km asphalt road and approximately 2.30 hours on foot along a marked tourist track). This is one of the most interesting Bulgarian caves, which is electrified. There are several halls with wonderful formations, the most impressive being the Concert hall (60 m long, 46 m wide and 22.7 m high) which has a fantastic acoustics. It has hosted a lot of concerts. The entry fee is just a symbolic one. Next to the cave there is a tourist settlement. Ledenika Chalet (850 m above sea level, tel.: 092

Ledenika Cave

# NORTHWESTERN BULGARIA

24411, 86 beds in 2 suites and rooms of 2, 4, 5, and 6 beds) is nearby, too. In the direction to the settlement there is also an open-chair lift, its initial station being between the town of Vratsa and the village of Zgorigrad, which is located immediately to the south end of Vratsata Gorge. There is regular bus transport to the lift.

**Vratsata** - the fantastic gorge of the Leva River, immediately to the south of the town. Its western rocky massif, full of miraculous cliffs, some of them reaching 350 metres height is extremely impressive. The whole region is karst (as well as the entire Vrachanska Mountain) and is a paradise for the rock climbers. There are dozens of different categories of climbing routes. The area hosts a large and nice Alpine House and there are a lot of nice meadows scattered along the river, suitable for camping. Vratsata attracts thousands of admirers of nature both from Bulgaria and abroad. From the centre of the town the place can be reached within half an hour on foot. Another possibility to go there is to use the bus transport to the village of Zgorigrad, located on the other side of the gorge. **The Botev Alley**, 120 km long, from Kozlodoui to Okolchitsa, reproduces exactly the route of Botev's detachment with all the historic sights along the trail. The closest of these historic landmarks are the **Botev meadow** on the Veslets Hill, where the detachment had to overnight, and **Milin Kamuk**, where the detachment fought a severe all day long battle on 30$^{th}$ May and gave 15 victims, among which the colour-bearer - Nikola Simov (Kourouto). There are monuments erected on both places. One can reach these spots on foot or using the regular bus transport to the village of Kostelevo (for Botev meadow) and to the villages of Mramoren and Banitsa (for Milin Kamuk). Vratsa is an important and frequently used **departure point** for hiking tracks round the beautiful and glorious Vrachanski Balkan, which is part of Western Stara Planina Mountain (refer to the Stara Planina Mountain related chapter herein).

## MEZDRA

The town of Mezdra (13 502 inhabitants, 230 m above sea level) is spread out amphitheatrically along the left bank of Iskar River where it exits the Balkan Iskar Gorge. It is located 100 km north-east of Sofia, 58 km and 17 km south-east of Montana and Vratsa, respectively, 40 km north-west of Botevgrad. This is the biggest railway cross-section in Northwestern Bulgaria and one of the most important for the whole country.

**History.** Mezdra is a successor of ancient culture. Remains from the Stone-Copper Age and the Thracian period were found there. During Roman domination there was a big town with a castle on the rocks up above the river Iskar (remains of it can be seen south of the railway station, in the Kaleto area). It protected the roads to Sofia, Vratsa and Montana. The town declined with the collapse of the Roman Empire. During the Bulgarian Middle Ages the settlement recovered, but only to be burnt to ashes in 1393, when the Ottoman hordes devastated the area. A document dating back to the 15$_{th}$ century marked the place as "Mezra Torbaritsa", meaning an empty bag". The life in the settlement revived during the 18$^{th}$ century, yet it remained small and insignificant. Immediately after the Liberation (1878) there were only about twenty houses in Mezdra totalling 86 inhabitants. When the railway line from Sofia to Varna was constructed in 1897, the village started its rapid development, while with the construction of the railway Mezdra - Vratsa Lom (Vidin) during the period 1913-1923, it turned into an important distribution point for this part of the country. The village was proclaimed a town in 1950.

**Landmarks**. **The Kaleto Fortress** - south of the railway station, next to the new reinforced concrete bridge. A flat terrace high on the rocks houses the remains of a fortress with a well-preserved 5-6 metre wall. Archaeologists found out that the foundations of the fortress are of Roman origin, while the wall on the foundation dates back to the Old Bulgarian period. This are the best-preserved remains in the area. The fortress is within 15 minutes walk from the centre of Mezdra. **The Art Gallery** in the town houses a rich collection of masterpieces of art, among which one can see some original sculptures of Prof. Ivan Funev.

**Accommodation.** Rodina Hotel (26, Hristo Botev Str.). **Tourist information** is available at the hotel.

**Transport.** The town has well-developed bus and especially railway connections. There are bus lines to Vratsa (most frequent and regular), Botevgrad, Montana, Vurshets and many smaller villages within the area. The telephone number of the bus station is 0910 2501. Being a very big railway section, dozens of trains pass each day through Mezdra to and from Sofia, Varna, Rousse, Gorna Oryahovitsa, Vratsa, Vidin, Lom, etc. The railway station is big and modern (tel.: 0910 2551).

**Surrounding areas. The Iskar Gorge** with all its natural, historic and cultural landmarks (refer to the Iskar Gorge related chapter herein).

**Hristo Botev National Park** in the area of Mt. Okolchitsa, approximately 20 km south-west of Mezdra in the Vrachanski Balkan. There is no direct transport link from the town to park (refer to the Vratsa related chapter herein).

**The Prophet Iliya Stroupesh Monastery** is a cultural monument of national significance. It dates back to the 14th century, when there was a small church at the same place, the mural paintings of which are well preserved and it has survived in the monastery yard. In the period of 1851-1857 the presently existing three-storied monastery building was erected. The monastery provided shelter to Vassil Levski, Nikola Obretenov, Mito Ankov and many others. In the old times the monastery was a gathering place for a big cattle auction marketplace on the religious holiday of Saint Iliya, that is why the monastery is also known under the name of Turzhishki (Auction place Monastery). One can reach it from Strupets railway station, where all passenger trains have a stop and there is 1 km further walk. There is a road to the monastery as well.

# BOTEVGRAD

The town of Botevgrad (23 516 inhabitants, 350 m above sea level) is situated in the valley of the same name, in north foothills of the eastern parts of the Western Stara Planina, along the two banks of Stara Reka River. It is 62 km north-east of Sofia, 57 km and 40 km south-east of Vratsa and Mezdra, respectively, 25 km north-west of Etropole, and 39 km south-west of Yablanitsa.

**History**. Botevgrad is a successor of the medieval Bulgarian town of *Zelin*, which was located 3 km away from today's town. During the Turkish rule the village was known by the name of *Samoundzhievo,* famous with its sweet smelling loaves (samouns) of bread. In 1826 in a private house in this village the first school was opened and 20 years later a school building was constructed. Later on a church and a clock tower were erected. In 1866, after the road from Rouschuk (Rousse) to Sofia was moved from the Etropole Gorge to Arabakonak Gorge, the Rouschuk ruler Midhat Pasha issued an order, proclaiming the small village a town. It was given the name of *Orhanie* after the name of Sultan Orhan. The town served the purpose of guarding and facilitating the travellers passing along the new road. The town was built up following a civil engineering plan, characterised by chessboard-like crossing streets and houses with spacious yards.

The town rapidly grew up and the Hungarian traveller, Felix Kanits who visited it in 1871, wrote that it was the centre of a region, incorporating 25 villages, while its square was it architectural centre and glory. The same year Vassil Levski founded a revolutionary committee, while in the next year the town became a district centre of the Domestic Revolutionary Organisation. During the Russian-Turkish War of Liberation (1877-1878) severe battles were held close to it and the town was badly destroyed. It was liber-

# NORTHWESTERN BULGARIA

ated on 29th November 1877. At that time it had only 2297 inhabitants.

Its present name (after the name of the poet and revolutionary Hristo Botev) was suggested by the prominent Bulgarian scientist - Prof. Assen Zlatarov. It is the native town of the poet Stamen Panchev and of our well-known linguist, expert in Slavonic languages and ethnographer, Prof. St. Romanski.

**Landmarks**: The **Town Museum of History**. Well-preserved are the house, hosting the **Old School**, the **Ascension Church** dating back to 1864, the **Community Cultural Centre** from 1883, the **Clock Tower** - a symbol of the town, built up at the central square by master Vouno Markov from the village of Vrachesh in 1866. The town has a number of **monuments** - to Hristo Botev, to the Russian soldiers, killed in the Russian-Turkish War of Liberation, to the Unknown Soldier, to Granny Koina (heroic mother), to the poet Stamen Panchev.

**Accommodation**: Botevgrad Hotel (79, 3rd March Blvd.). Sinyo Nebe Hotel.

**Tourist information** is available at the hotels, at the Council on Tourism (2140 Botevgrad, tel.: 0723 6128), and at Venets Tourist Association (tel.: 0723 3301).

**Transport**. Only bus transport is available in the town. It is used to link it to the villages and towns in the region and countrywide. Southeast of the town passes the Hemus motorway from Sofia to Varna, which facilitates and speeds up large portion of its bus communications. There are regular bus lines to Sofia (every hour), Etropole, Yablanitsa, Mezdra, Loukovit, etc. The bus station can be reached at tel.: 0723 3346.

**Surrounding areas. Zelin Resort** - 4 km southeast of the town, scattered amidst nice deciduous forests. The monastery "Birth of the Son of God the Holy Virgin" is situated in its vicinity. The resort is a starting point of the route to the Roudinata Chalet (2-3 hours hike along a marked track) within the Bilo Massif of the Western Stara Planina Mountain. There is regular bus transport from the town to the resort. 23 km north of Botevgrad and 3 km away from the village of Bozhenitsa is situated the **Bozhenishki Urvich** - this is a nationally significant monument of culture. Remains of an early Byzantine fortress and ruins of a rock church and dwelling, where the famous Bozheniski Inscription of Sevast Ognyan was found are well preserved in this area.

**The village of Skravena** is 6 km north-west of the town and the most interesting monument there is the **church-monument**, which until recently kept the bones of the 10 Botev's rebels, killed at Rashov Dol (now the bones are kept in a charnel-house in the centre of the village, opposite the town-hall), and the **house** of the rebel Miko Stoyanov. The village is a starting point to the K & N Mukanski Chalet up at the Lakavitsa Hill (6 km - 1.30 hours walk along a marked truck road). There is regular bus transport.

**The village of Vrachesh** lies at the northern foots of Mt. Mourgash, 3 km south-west of the town. It has ancient history. The settlement has existed there since the 13th-14th century, known as *Cheshkovitsa*. Today's name of the village dates back to 1430. There are some remains of an ancient and medieval fortress. The house of T. Kamitlyarski - giving shelter to the headquarters of General Gurko - is also preserved. 4 km south-west of the village is situated the **St. St. Forty Martyrs Monastery** and to the south, on the Bebresh River is situated the Bebresh Dam - the new artificial lake and the area is turned into a recreational zone. There is a regular bus transport from the town to the village.

11 km east of Botevgrad is the small town of **Pravets**, birthplace of Todor Zhivkov - head of state for quite a long time. Close to the town there is a large artificial lake, turned into a wonderful place for recreation, sports and entertainment. There is the Pravets Hotel as well as the famous attraction restaurant Shatrata (The Marquee). The original marquee-cover was a present by the ex-shah of Iran Reza Pahlavi.

## ETROPOLE

The town of Etropole (12 386 inhabitants, 580 m above sea level) is situated at the northern foothills of Etropolska Mountain (the most eastern part of Western Stara Planina), along the two banks of Malki Iskar River. It is 87 km north-east of Sofia, 25 km south-east of Botevgrad, 28 km south of Yablanitsa, 43 km south-west of Teteven and 27 km north-west of Zlatitsa.

**History**. There was a Thracian and later on a Roman settlement in the area of the nowadays town, the main occupation of its inhabitants being ore mining. In the beginning of $9^{th}$ century the settlement was within the territory of the Bulgarian State. Thanks to the ore mining it turned into a flourishing settlement in $16^{th}$ and $17^{th}$ century (iron, silver and gold were mined). The crafts related thereto such as blacksmith, goldsmith, manufacture of knives, weapons, agricultural tools, etc., were also well developed. Some ore-miners came to this place from the Saxon area, Serbia and Bosna (the family names of the Alemans, Avramovs and Bohorovs date back to that period). Coins were minted in Etropole during $17^{th}$ century. The village was destroyed by a devastating earthquake in 1749, but the bright highlanders quickly restored it. Then the year of 1791 came, when the town was ruined 6 times by the kurdzhalii (Turkish brigands). It was once again recovered and took its deserved place in the countrywide cultural and national uplift during the Revival. A manuscript dating back to 1820 named it "the glorious town of Etropolia". Today's name of the town probably has a Thracian origin - "etr" meaning "water", i.e. a water field ("pole" - field).

Together with the old church in 1710 a town tower (turned into a clock tower in 1821) was erected, while in 1871 a community cultural centre was built. There the famous Etropole's literary school was established and the proximity of the Etropole Monastery, only 5 km away from the town, contributed to its sustained development. In 1870 Levski founded a secret revolutionary committee, headed by Todor Peev, one of the brightest leaders of the Revival. The natives of Etropole took part in Rakovski's Legiya (legion), in the detachments of Hadzhi Dimitur and Stefan Karadzha, of Panayot Hitov, Hristo Makedonski, Hristo Botev. Etropole was liberated on $24^{th}$ November 1877 by the troops of Gen. Gourko. After the Liberation the town declined. It gradually developed as a tourist centre, taking advantage of the favourable natural resources facilitating this development.

*The Etropole Monastery*

**Landmarks**: **The Town Museum of History** (107, Rouski Blvd., tel.: 0720 2124, working hours: - 8.30 a.m. - 12.00 p.m. and 1.30 p.m. - 5.00 p.m.). **St. Archangel Mihail Church** (in the centre of the town, located at Malki Pazar Square) was first mentioned in 1600, but the present building dates back to 1837, famous with its iconostasis of fine walnut woodcarving. Interesting as well are the **Jewish Tower** dating back to $14^{th}$ century and the 20 metres high **Defence Turret** (Rouski Blvd.). **St. Georgi**

# NORTHWESTERN BULGARIA

**Church** (10, Hristo Botev Str.) was erected in the middle of 17th century on the foundations of an old medieval church, completely ruined during the attacks of the kurdzhalii. It was completely built of river stones and pebbles. Twenty-five **Revival houses** attract the visitors' attention. Beautifully scattered along the river of Malki Iskar, they are distinguished for their exuberant and rich wood-carved ceilings, doors, cupboards, hearth places, columns, etc. The walls are whitewashed and colourfully wood-framed. The most typical houses are the **Pavelponchov's**, the **Hadzhigrigorov's**, the **Vulchev's**, and the **Arnaoudov's houses**. **Memorial monument to the soldiers and volunteers killed during the wars**, as well as many other monuments.

Etropole is famous with its unique annually held **festivities of the men, living in the houses of their parents-in-law**.

**Accommodation**: Etropol Hotel (Central Square). Etropole Hotel (at the street above the bus station, offering 120 beds, restaurant, bar, discotheque). Staroplaninets Tourist House (in the Lozeto area, 15 minutes away from the bus station) offers 50 beds in rooms of 2, 4, 5 and 9 beds. The Bash Samokov Tourist Hostel (7 km to the right along the road to Zlatitsa) has 40 beds in rooms of 2, 3, 4 and more beds.

**Tourist information** is available at the hotels, the Tourist House and at Staroplaninski Tourist Association (located in the building of the public forestry, P.O.Box 53, tel.: 0720 3506).

**Transport**. Bus transport is the only available. There are regular bus lines to Sofia, Botevgrad, Pravets, Yablanitsa, Loukovit, etc. The bus station (tel.: 0720 2300) is situated at the southeastern end of the town.

**Surrounding areas**. **St. Trinity Etropole Monastery (Varovitets)** is 5 km east of the town on the road to the village of Ribaritsa and the summer resort of Yamna. It was built back in 1158. During the Turkish rule it was the most significant scholar centre in the lands lying north of the Balkan. At the end of 16th and during 17th century the Etropole Literary School was established in Etropole and the nearby monastery. Its major representatives are the monk Danail Etropolski, the priest Rafail, Daskal Koyo (Kolyo the Teacher), Gramatik Boicho, Deacon Yoan, Vasilii Sofianin. The unique "Fourfold Gospel" was created here far back in the 1585 and is still well-preserved nowadays. Other remarkable manuscripts are the "Fourfold Gospel" from 15th century, the "Apostle" (16th century), "Oktoih and Tipik" (16th-17th century), the "Prologue of Danail" (1620). Varovitets monks drafted the manuscript on the life of Yoan Rilski, telling the story of the solemn transfer of the holy bones of the saint from Turnovo to the Rila Monastery in 1469. The treasury of the monastery holds two ancient silver crests with inscriptions, on one of which the year 1492 is marked. Also the silver ark is very interesting. The monastery gave shelter to our national apostle Vassil Levski. One can reach the monastery taking the bus in the direction of Yamna summer resort.

**The Thracian settlement** (5th-4th century BC) - its ruins were found on the isolated hill of Bogotvor, close to the town. It has about a dozen of sepulchral mounds. **Chertigrad** is the place of the remains from a famous Thracian fortress (this name of the area was given later). The ruins are situated east of the town on the hill between the villages of Lopyan, Broussen, Cherni Vit and Yamna. One can reach the sight by taking the bus to Yamna village and after that continuing on foot. **Ruins of a medieval fortress** are found on the St. Atanas Hill, very close to the town. The **summer resort** and the **village of Yamna** (approximately 15 km north-east of the town) are situated among the northern hills of the Zlatishko-Tetevenski Balkan. It serves as on of the departure points to the Svishti Plaz Chalet (approximately 5 hours walk). There is a regular bus transport to the village. Etropole is a **departure point** of many hiking routes in the Etropolski Balkan and Zlatishko-Tetevenska Mountain (refer to the Stara Planina related chapter herein).

# YABLANITZA

The town of Yablanitza (3312 inhabitants, 420 m above sea level) is picturesquely scattered in between the average size massifs of Dragoitsa and Lissets, offshoots of Stara Planina Mountain, along the banks of Kalenovik River. It is respectively 101 km and 39 km north-east of Sofia and Botevgrad, 28 km north of Etropole, 24 km south of Loukovit, 23 km north-west of Teteven and 65 km south-west of Lovech. The town is famous with its Yablanitsa halva.

**History.** This area was populated even during the Old Stone, Stone-Copper and Bronze Ages. There are numerous Thracian mounds scattered around the town, part of them being thoroughly explored. The name of the town - Yablanitsa has centuries old history. It was first mentioned in 15$^{th}$ century as *Ablanitsa*, but the root of the word has Old Bulgarian origin ("ablan" meaning apple tree). During the Turkish rule the village was scattered and divided into quarters, and following the construction of the road from Rouschuk (Rousse) to Sofia, these quarters grouped around it. Its inhabitants were known as the so-called "voinutsi" (partially tax exempted against certain duties to the central authorities), who kept their freedom-loving spirit alive. They took part in the detachments of Philip Totyu, Hadzhi Dimitur, and Stefan Karadzha. In 1873 the Apostle Levski and Dimitur Obshti established a revolutionary committee there. During the Russian-Turkish War of Liberation (1877-1878) its inhabitants actively supported the troops of the Russian Gen. Gurko.

The beginning of 18$^{th}$ century gave strong impetus to the development of various crafts, out of which the pottery and halva producing are still very popular for the region. The first church school was opened in 1870. In 1879 the first independent school building was built. Yablanitsa was proclaimed a town in 1969.

**Landmarks. The central street** attracts the attention of the visitors with its old houses dating back to the end of 19$^{th}$ and the beginning of 20$^{th}$ century, with its nice chestnut trees. A rich **museum collection** is exhibited in Nauka Community Cultural Centre, a Revival style building (working hours: 8.00 a.m. - 5.00 p.m.).

**Accommodation**: Balkanskal Departmental Resort House.

**Tourist information** is available at the Community Cultural Centre and at the town-hall (in the centre of the town, 5750 Yablanitsa).

**Transport**. Located along the Hemus motorway (running from Sofia to Varna and Rousse), the town takes advantage of all bus lines, passing through it. Besides a transit stop on some major bus lines, the town has regular bus lines to Teteven, Loukovit, Lovech and other smaller villages. The bus station is at the central square, where also passes the major road connecting the town with the motorway.

The closest railway station is that of Zlatna Panega on the railway line Cherven Bryag - Zlatna Panega (9 km to the north). Bus transport to the railway station is available).

**Surrounding areas. The Glozhene Monastery St. Georgi the Victor** (approximately 10 km south-west of Yablanitsa). There is no such other monastery in Bulgaria, "nestled" on the top of a rocky edge, which looks like a Medieval Castle. It is situated in the Massif of Lisets, immediately to the south high above the village of Glozhene. It was erected in 13$^{th}$ century by the Kiev Prince Glozh, after his escape from South Russia. The prince enjoyed the hospitality of the Assen Brothers and as a gesture of gratitude he built a monastery above the place where he lived, the present village of Glozhene, naming the monastery "St. George the Victorious Kievski". Out of the numerous manuscripts, drafted there only two were preserved - "The Tale" dedicated to the foundation of the monastery and the "Apostle" dating back to 1689. Vassil Levski was heartily welcomed in this monastery as well - his hiding place is kept for the generations nowadays. The devastating earthquake in 1913 seriously damaged the building (destroying completely the old church with precious woodcarvings). Extremely valuable is the ancient icon of St. Georgi the Victor, brought by Prince Glozh from the Kiev-Pechorsk Monastery. It was silver laid in 1826 by the Gabrovo native Ivan Popovich. The monastery can be reached by car if passing through the village of Malak Izvor (about 10 km away), by bus to the same village and then another hour walk or by bus to the village of Glozhene (12 km) and then having an hour and a half steep hiking.

**The Sueva Dupka Cave** (14 km north of Yablanitsa and 3 km south of the village of Brestnitsa) is electrified and has numerous very interesting formations in several naturally shaped halls. The entrance fee is just a symbolic one. There is no regular transport, though there is a good asphalt road up to the cave. One can use the regular bus lines to the village of Brestnitsa.

**Bezdunniyat Pchelin Precipice Cave (The Bottomless Bee-garden)** (5 km north-east of the town) - 105 metres deep and having a hole opening of 25-40 metres. 9 km to the north of Yablanitsa is situated the village of Zlatna Panega, close to which is the famous **karst spring Glava Panega,** the second large in Bulgaria, after the Devnya karst springs. There are also two small lakes, one above the other, out of which runs the river Panega. The flow is 2000 l/sec and the temperature is constant - 10°-12°C, due to which the lakes never freeze. There are proofs that the waters come through an underground passage from the river Vit. In the village of Batultsi (13 km north-west of the town) there is a **House-Museum of Vassil Levski,** working hours: 8.00 a.m. - 5.00 p.m.

# CHERVEN BRYAG

The town of Cherven Bryag (18 642 inhabitants, 110 m above sea level) is situated at the inflow of river Zlatna Panega in river Iskar. It is 137 km north-east of Sofia, 53 km south-west of Pleven, 12 km north-west of Loukovit, 56 km east of Vratsa, and 55 km south of Oryahovo. It is an important railway cross-section.

**History**. It first appeared as a railway station settlement in 1899 on the newly built Sofia-Varna railway line. It was proclaimed a town in 1929.

**Landmarks. St. Sofronii Vrachanski Chathedral** is located in the central part of the town (tel.: 0659 5860).

**Accommodation**: Cherven Bryag Hotel (4, Turgovska Str., in the centre of the town, opposite the railway station).

**Tourist information** is available at the hotel and Leskovets Tourist Association (14, Turgovska Str., in the centre of the town).

**Transport**. It is a large railway cross-section on the line Sofia - Gorna Oryahovitsa - Varna (Rousse). Cherven Bryag is a starting point of a narrow-gauge railway line from Cherven Bryag to Byala Slatina and Oryahovo, as well as of a normal railway line to Loukovit and Zlatna Panega. The railway station is in the southwestern end of the town, opposite the central area. The town has regular bus lines to Pleven, Vratsa, Loukovit, Byala Slatina, as well as to many smaller villages within the region. The bus station (tel. 0659 2117) is located at Hristo Botev Square, very close to the railway station (tel.: 0659 2007, 2730).

**Surrounding areas**. 6 km south-west of the town is the **village of Resselets**. Only one kilometre away from the village is the unique **natural phenomenon Propadaloto**. It is an area of approximately 250 metres long and 30-40 metres wide, which has fallen through with some 30 metres. Steep cliffs surround the place and the descent to the bottom is

# NORTHWESTERN BULGARIA

along a romantic narrow path meandering between the cliffs. This is one of the rare places in Bulgaria where one can come across a scorpion. In its vicinity is the cosy Reselets Chalet with 70 beds (in rooms of 2, 3, 4, 5 and more beds). The extension number for the chalet is 430, and it can be reached by calling the switchboard operator of the village of Reselets. There is a possibility to make a reservation at the Tourist Association in Cherven Bryag. There is a regular bus line between the town and the village, and yet another transport possibility is provided by the railway route Sofia - Gorna Oryahovitsa - Varna - Rousse, but only passenger's trains stop at the railway station of Reselets village. The picturesque chalet is some 3 km away from the railway stop. There is an asphalt road leading up to the chalet. The region provides plenty of interesting hiking tracks along impressive river canyons. The most pleasant time for visiting the area of the Reselets Chalet is in spring, when the lilac is in full blossom.

**The river Iskar** also provides wonderful opportunities for water tourism, fishing, sun bathing on the shore, having fun and recreation in the open. South of Cherven Bryag the river still runs in a canyon, and though not so impressive as the Iskar Gorge it is an attractive sight for tourists.

*Rock precipice near Lakatnik*

## LOUKOVIT

The town of Loukovit (approximately 10 000 inhabitants, 135 m above sea level) is situated on the two banks at the mouth of the valley of Zlatna Panega River. It is 125 km north-east of Sofia, 24 km north of Yablanitsa, 12 km south-east of Cherven Bryag and 49 km south-west of Pleven. It is a centre of a large and interesting karst region.

**History**. There are traces of Thracian, Roman, Byzantine and Old Bulgarian periods. Many rings, fibulas, earrings, ceramic articles and objects and the famous Loukovit silver treasure dating back to the $4^{th}$ century BC (exhibited in the museum collection of the Community Cultural Centre) were found in the numerous Thracian mounds scattered in the area. A treasure of Roman coins was also found. Byzantine coins dating back to the $12^{th}$ century as well as coins from the reign of Tsar Ivan Alexander (1330-1371) were found at the Gradishte Hill. The settlement was first mentioned in a document dating back to 1479 under the name of *Gorni Loukovit*. At the end of $17^{th}$ century the Turkish troops, defeated near Vienna and Belgrade ruined it in their retreat and forced a lot of the inhabitants to convert to Islam.

The nearby Kar-

# NORTHWESTERN BULGARIA

lukovski Monastery, where Sofronii Vrachanski found shelter and worked for the benefit of his people, promoted Bulgarian spirit. The national defenders Angel Voivoda and Vulchan Voivoda were active in the region. The Apostle Vassil Levski founded a revolutionary committee in Gorni Loukovit. The Revival upsurge found its reflection in the construction of the first school in 1849.

After 18th century Loukovit was the largest village in the Pre-Balkan region and was famous with its 14 water mills on the river Panega. The Orthodox Bulgarians mainly bred cattle, while the Bulgarian Mohammedan grew vegetables. After the Liberation in 1878 the village was proclaimed a town under the name of Loukovit. The crafts declined as elsewhere in Bulgaria after the markets in the Ottoman Empire were lost. The town made some progress in its development after the railway line Cherven Bryag - Zlatna Panega was constructed.

**Landmarks**: There is a **Historical museum collection,** housed in the **Suznanie Popular Library house** (3rd March Square, tel.: 0697 2144), established in 1895. **St. Georgi Church** is situated in the centre of Loukovit, on the left bank of the river.

**Accommodation.** Putno Upravlenie Hotel (3rd March Square).

**Tourist information** is available at the hotel, at Zlatna Panega Tourist Association and at the town-hall (74, Vuzrazhdane Str., tel.: 0697 2559, 4058).

**Transport.** Bus and railway transport is available. Loukovit is located on the major road Sofia - Pleven - Rousse and all the buses servicing this direction have a transit stop there. In addition there are regular bus lines to Cherven Bryag, Roman, Lovech, Teteven and other smaller villages within the region. The bus station is located in the central part of the town, on the right bank of the river (2, Zlatna Panega, tel.: 0697 2503, 2527). The railway station is at the northeastern end of the town (tel.: 0697 2264, 4194) servicing the railway line Cherven Bryag - Zlatna Panega, through which the town of Loukovit is connected to the national railway network.

**Surrounding areas**. The most important archaeological excavations are situated on the **Gradishteto Hill**.

**The karst gorge of Zlatna Panega River** is south of Loukovit. **The Iskara Resort** covers a large area and is about 10 km south-west of the town. The karst earth depths host numerous precipices and caves, some 150 of them already explored. Most famous among them are Prohodna Cave, Temnata Doupka Cave (the dark hole), Kucheshkata Dupka Cave (the dog's hole), etc. Here is also the village of **Karloukovo** (12 km away from the town, regular bus transport to the village is available), where the **The Assumption Karloukovo Monastery** is situated (see the historical information herein). Nearby are the **rock churches** St. Marina and St. Grigorii.

Within this region is the **Karloukovo gorge** of Iskar river, some 30 km long, beginning from the village of Roman and going down almost to Cherven Bryag. The gorge has very interesting rock formations, the most spectacular of them being The Dolls, situated east of the station of Resselets.

On the way between the railway station and the village of Karloukovo (2.5 km away from each of the locations) is situated **Peter Tranteev National Speleologists' House** offering 60 beds in rooms of 2 and 3 beds. Nearby is the Provurtenik Chalet (1.5 km away from the station of Karloukovo, 3.5 km from the village of Karloukovo and 3 km away from the Speleologists' House). It avails of 20 beds in rooms of 2, 4 and 6 beds. The chalet bears the name of the neighbouring rocky sculpture, resembling a guard turret. (Reservation can be made through the Tourist Association in Loukovit.) This incredible karst paradise can be reached either by bus from the town of Loukovit or by a passenger's train in the direction Sofia - Gorna Oryahovitsa - Varna (Rousse) to Karloukovo station.

# CENTRAL NORTHERN BULGARIA

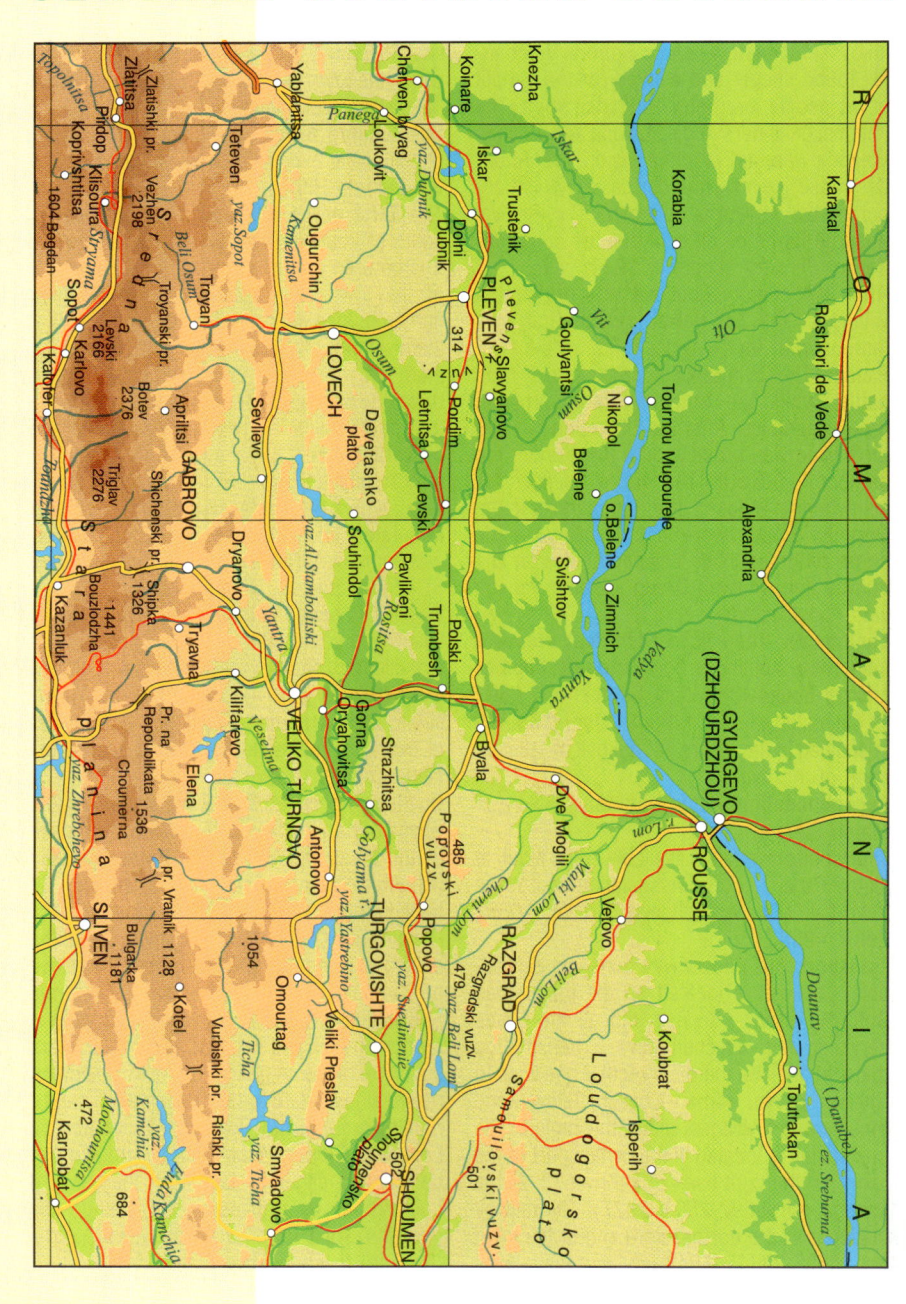

# CENTRAL NORTHERN BULGARIA

## TETEVEN

The town of Teteven (12 581 inhabitants, 410 metres above sea level) is picturesquely nestled along the two banks of the Beli Vit River between Teteven Balkan Mountain and Vassiliov's Mountain (sub-part of the Troyan Balkan Mountain). It is 116 km north-east from Sofia, 74 km south-west from Lovech, 60 km west of Troyan, 23 km south-east from Yablanitsa and 54 km east of Botevgrad. The people's poet Ivan Vazov said about it: *"Unless I had come to Teteven, I would have been a foreigner for Mother Bulgaria, too..."*

**History**. The region has been inhabited since the remote past. The tribe of the Serds lived in these places at Thracian times due to which the Romans later on included the region in the Serdica strategy. Saint Iliya Monastery dates back to Medieval Bulgaria. The oldest information about the settlement in writing is contained in a document of 1421. The name mentioned there was *Tetevyan*. An artistically elaborated cross, a gift from Tsar Ivan Shishman, was preserved in Saint Iliya Monastery up to the year 1930 (at the moment it is in London Museum). Evidently the Monastery existed during the 13th - 14th centuries and probably the settlement developed around it. During the Ottoman Rule, the inhabitants of Teteven were "voinutsi", i. e. they were assigned some military and guard duties against which they obtained certain rights and independence. Teteven developed as a prospering handicraft settlement. During the 16th and the 17th centuries the Turks carried out forcible conversion to Islam within the region but they did not dare touch the town. The popular haidouts (armed revolutionaries grouped in detachments) were Kostin, Deli Palo, Dancho, Angel, and Niagol. In 1800 there were about 3000 houses in the town of Teteven. The town merchants traded with Sofia, Bucharest, Brashov, Vienna, Thessaloniki, and Anadola. Over 60 of its inhabitants were Hadzhii (they had gone to the Holy Sepulchre in Jerusalem). In 1801 the town was completely devastated by kurdzhalii (Turkish brigands). Half of the inhabitants was slaughtered, the survivals left Teteven. Of the 3 thousand buildings only four survived... Although the settlement rehabilitated with the elapse of years, it never reached its previous heyday and welfare. The inhabitants of Teteven kept abreast with the cultural and political upsurge during the Bulgarian Revival. Churches and schools were built and Bulgarian spirit was kept and strengthened. In 1872 Vassil Levski organised the most numerous revolutionary committees in the Bulgarian lands (51 people) with a chairman and a cashier - both of them outstanding and influential wealthy men Stanio Vrabevski and Petko Miliov - Strashniya (the Terrible). Dimitur Obshti (a close associate of Levski) worked in the town, too under whose guidance the robbery of the Turkish postal service in the Arabakonak Pass was carried out on 22nd September 1872. This act, kept in secret from Levski, unfortunately led to tragic consequences for the whole revolutionary organisation and for V. Levski in person - all revolutionary committees founded by Levski during the years were now broken and the Apostle was caught and hung on 18th February 1873 in Sofia.

The final drama of the April Uprising took place at the distance of 15 km to the south-east of the town. Georgi Benkovski (the factual leader of the people's riot), Zakhari Stoyanov (who left for Bulgarian people the priceless "Notes on Bulgarian Uprisings"), Father Kiril (the cashier of the 4th Revolutionary District) and Stefo the Dalmatian fell victims to a repulsive betrayal. They were caught in a Turkish ambush in the locality of Kostina in which Benkovski and Father Kiril were murdered and Z. Stoyanov and S. the Dalmatian survived by a miracle after incredible narrow escapes. Teteven inhabitants slaughtered the traitor on the day when he was to receive his recompense.

11 members of Botev's detachment of armed volunteers, 4 members of Panaiot Hitov's detachment as of 1876 and 48 volunteers in the Russian-Turkish War were born in Teteven. The liberation of the town is related to the name of the inhabitant of Teteven Banio Marinov, who guided the squadron of Colonel Orlov through the Vassiliovska Mountain. The Turks were taken by surprise and rendered harmless. Later on the

# CENTRAL NORTHERN BULGARIA

same inhabitant of Teteven participated in the liberation of the town of Orhanie (Botevgrad), too and became its first town governor. Banio Marinov organised a detachment of volunteers and took part in the Kresna Uprising in Macedonia where he was wounded. He died of his wound in Sofia Hospital. Sava Mladenov (one of the close assistants of Hr. Botev in the last tragic days of the poet and revolutionary and his detachment of armed volunteers) was born in Teteven, too. He found his death at the distance of 8 km to the south of the town.

After the Liberation Teteven developed as a centre of tourism.

**Landmarks.** The **Town Museum of History** (3, Sava Mladenov Sq., tel.: 0678 2005). Working hours: 9.00 a.m. - 12.00 a.m. and 2.00 p.m. - 5.00 p.m. (all the week round in summertime). **St. Iliya Monastery** built up during the 14$^{th}$ century is one of the 4 buildings, which survived in the sinister year of 1801.

**All Saints Church** (situated in the central part of the town). It was built from 1834 to 1846 and is an exception among the churches built up during the years of the Ottoman Rule due to its large dimensions - it is 31.1 m long, 14 m wide with thickness of the walls of 1.5 m. Its two large bells were cast in Moscow. The pulpit is decorated with woodcarving from Debur and the iconostasis is with woodcarvings from Teteven. The ancient **house-museums** from those, which survived in 1801 are remarkable: **Bobev's house** (tel.: 0678 3205), **Tuikov's** (tel.: 0678 3097), **Hadzhi Ivan's** (with Levski's hiding-place in it) and **Iorgo's house**. Teteven has a **Picture Gallery,** too. **The monuments to Petko Strashniya** (the Terrible) (at the beginning of the town), of **Banio Marinov** and others are erected here, too. Teteven is famous for its rakiya (plum brandy). Every year at the beginning of the May the biggest mountain cycling race on the Balkan Peninsula is held here organized by the Bulgarian Extreme Sports Club "Boundless".

**Accommodation**: The Zdravets Hotel. Koznitsa Tourist Hostel (in the southern part of the town, along the banks of the Koznitsa River, a left tributary of the Beli Vit River). It has 50 beds in double rooms and in 3- and 4-bed rooms. The town offers private lodgings as well. There are good public catering establishments in Teteven with an original local cuisine and pleasant entertainment. Two of the most preferred ones are the Sinchets Restaurant and Manuel Restaurant.

**Tourist information** - at the Regional Tourist Information Bureau, 5700 Teteven (Sava Mladenov Sq, tel./fax: 0678 4217). One can obtain information here about the tourist sites in and around Gabrovo, Tryavna, Troyan and Apriltsi (participating along with Teteven in the Stara Planina Tourist Association). At Vezhen Tourist Association (7, Hr. Botev Street, tel.: 0678 3110, 2372). At the Holiday House and at the Tourist Hostel.

**Transport**. Teteven has regular bus connections with Sofia, Vratsa, Roman, Loukovit, Cherven Bryag, Oryahovo, Pleven, Lovech, and Veliko Turnovo as well as with almost all the settlements within the region. The bus station (54, 3$^{rd}$ March Str., tel.: 0678 2557) is located on the left bank of the Beli Vit River next to the stadium. There are two town bus lines, too.

**Surrounding areas**. Teteven is one of the most picturesque Bulgarian towns. It is surrounded by crown of mountain peaks Mt. Treskavets, Mt. Ostrich, Mt. Cherven, Mt. Kon, Mt. Haidoushka Polyana, Mt. Petrahilia and others. The panorama of the town is quite impressive and characteristic and it remains in the visitor's mind to the end of his life. The rocky vertical precipices of **Petrahilya** (an Alpine mountaineering site) are particularly spectacular. There is a marked tourist track up to its peak.

**The village of Ribaritsa** (at 12 km to the east) is one of the longest villages in Bulgaria and it is a famous mountainous resort. There are a lot

*Teteven in winter*

# CENTRAL NORTHERN BULGARIA

of holiday homes, country-houses, private hotels, and public catering establishments. It is among the key points of departure for hiking tours in the Teteven Balkan (refer to the Stara Planina Mountain related chapter herein). The **place of death** and **the monument to Georgi Benkovski** killed by the Turks on 25th May 1876 are located on the right bank of the Kostina River. Every year on this date celebrations are held where actors reproduce the events, which took place immediately before the death of the Voivoda. There is a regular bus line between the village and Teteven.

The area of **Prossechenik** (beside the Beli Vit River, on the road to the village of Ribaritsa, at the distance of 6 km from the town) offers perfect conditions for recreation during the summer months. The buses for the village of Ribaritsa have a stop there. The **waterfall** of the Koznitsa River (a left tributary of the Beli Vit River) is located at the distance of 3 km to the south of Teteven. The asphalt road does not go to the waterfall itself and one is to walk along a path along the river. The monument erected at the **place of death of Sava Mladenov** is also located beside the Koznitsa River (on its left bank), at 8 km to the south of Teteven. A marked track strays from the asphalt road, crosses the river and it takes 5 minutes to get to the historical site. There is no regular bus transport to it.

**Momina Poliana Chalet**, with the exceptionally beautiful countryside around it is located on the northern slopes of the Teteven Balkan Mountain. A point of departure to it is the village of Cherni Vit (13 km south-west from the town), to which there is a regular bus transport. It takes about 4 hours to get to the chalet on foot.

The Teteven Balkan is included in the territory of the **Central Balkan Mountain National Park**. The two **nature reserves** - **Boatin** (within the territory of the village of Cherni Vit) and **Tsarichina** (within the territory of the village of Ribaritsa) are located within its framework in the proximity of Teteven. The big village of Glozhene is situated at the distance of 12 km to the north west of Teteven. The historical **Glozhen Monastery** is located above it (refer to the Yablanitsa related section herein).

## TROYAN

The town of Troyan (26 541 inhabitants, 400 metres above sea level) spreads out along the two banks of the Beli Osum River (the Chernmi Osum River empties into its northern end) at the northern foothill of the Troyan Balkan Mountain. It is situated at the distance of 60 km to the east of Teteven, 180 km to the north east of Sofia, 70 km and 35 km to the south of Pleven and Lovetch, respectively, 47 km to the south-west of Sevlievo and at the distance of 25 km to the north-east from the historical Troyan Pass in the Balkan Mountains. It is a town with opulent traditions.

**History**. The name of the town comes from the ancient Roman road crossing the Balkan Mountain through today's Troyan Pass - *Via Trayana*, which linked Misia with Thrace and the Aegean Sea. The origin of the today's settlement is thought to go back somewhere at the beginning of the 15th century, when, after Bulgaria fell under Ottoman Rule, a lot of Bulgarian refugees settled down in this hard-to-reach and forested region running away from the arbitrary rule of the Turks. Later on the migrations continued and Troyan grew up but about the year 1800 the town suffered three invasions of the kurdzhalii (Turkish brigands) who devastated it. In spite of this during the 19th century the town reached a high material and cultural prosperity. The crafts were those, which reached their greatest development, pottery and woodcarving in particular. More than half of the population of the town made their living on the basis of these crafts till World War II. The bright and intelligent mountain dwellers realised that their future lays in faith and enlightenment. Talented master builders created magnificent patterns of the Bulgarian Revival church architecture in the town and within the region - in 1835 St. Paraskeva Church in Troyan and The Assumption Church in the Troyan Monastery were built (refer to the

# CENTRAL NORTHERN BULGARIA

Stara Planina related chapter herein). In 1839 the St. Nikolai Letni Church was erected in the area of Goumoshtnik whose wood-carved iconostasis is a unique of its kind work of the Bulgarian Revival Art. In 1870 a Community Cultural Centre was set up in Troyan, in which 2 years later the commencement of the theatrical activities in the town was set up with the performance of "Genoveva the Martyr". In 1872 the Yellow School was built up in the town, in which the modern secular program of teaching was introduced involving studies of the French language as well. The inhabitants of the town of Troyan did not let the revolutionary processes go past them either. In 1869 they enthusiastically met the Apostle Vassil Levski and Matei Preobrazhenski - Mitkaloto. Two years later a secret revolutionary committee was set up there at Levski's initiative. During the Russian-Turkish War of Liberation in August 1877 Troyan was devastated by the bashibozouks (Turkish army of volunteers), but its population rendered invaluable assistance to General Kartsov when his army passed the Balkan Mountain through the Troyan Pass. After the liberation the town was rebuilt out of the ashes. In 1911 the first electric bulb was lit and soon after that Troyan became the third electrified town in Bulgaria (after Sofia and Plovdiv). The building of the railway line Lovech - Troyan gave an impetus to the development of the town - it commenced in 1929 and was completed in 1948. Troyan is the birthplace of Ivan Hadzhiiski (our greatest sociologist and nations psychologist), Prof. Dr. Nikola Shipkovenski (psychiatrist) and a lot of other outstanding names. In the autumn of 1998, 130 years of the proclamation of Troyan as a town were solemnly celebrated.

**Landmarks**. **Crafts and Applied Arts Museum** (Zentralen Square, in the building of the old Municipality, tel.: 0670 22062). Working hours: 8.00 a.m. - 12.00 a.m. and 1.00 p.m. - 5.00 p.m. Day off - Monday (from April to October) and Saturday and Sunday (in winter). **Serekov's House Town Art Gallery** (6, Angel Kunchev Street, 50 m from the central square, tel.: 0670 22877). Working hours: 9.00 a.m. - 12.00 a.m. and 2.00 p.m. - 6.00 p.m., Monday through Saturday. **The St. Paraskeva Church** dating back to 1835. **An architectural ensemble** around the house of Vlassi Vlaskovski (Vassil Levski Street). **The homes** of **Ivan Hadzhiiski** and **Minko Nikolov.** An architectural ensemble (houses over the river) next to **Marko's Bridge**. The architectural complex **Nounki** (in the central town part, next to the river - restored houses of the traditional Balkan mountain architectural type). It is a hotel at the moment. **Architectural complex** at 129-137A, V. Levski Street. **The house** of **Dona Milina** (next to the church). **Architectural and ethnographic ensemble** along Tsar Kaloyan Street. **Balev's houses** at Gen. Kartsov Street. **Old houses** in Popishka Quarter. **Old houses** in Drianska Quarter. There are some annual festivities of national importance, as well, namely: A day of the Plum Tree and Plum Brandy - the last Saturday of September, Festival of Films for the Mountain - the last Saturday and Sunday of September, The Day of Troyan - 14th October (Petkovden - Name day of those named Petko).

**Accommodation**: Nounki Hotel Complex (3-star, located in the central part of the town, near the bridge over Elma River). It has 18 beds in 2 suites and 6 rooms and a restaurant. Residence Complex (owned by Troyan municipality, at a 20-minute walk from the centre of the town; there is an asphalt road, too) on the hill in the town park of Kupincho. Nikola Gaburski Tourist House in the town park of Kupincho, 2 km from the centre of Troyan (there is a lane leading directly to it). It offers 60 beds in rooms with 2 and 3 beds, a restaurant, a day bar and central heating. Troyan Resort Complex Co. manages the two Holiday Houses - Kupina 1 and Kupina 2 (200 m from each other) on the hill in Kupincho town park, offering 170 beds in total.

**Tourist information** - at the Municipal Tourist Information Bureau (with the Tourist Associa-

# CENTRAL NORTHERN BULGARIA

tion) - 5600 Troyan, 133, Vassil Levski Street, tel./fax: 0670 35064. Ambaritsa Tourist Association (tel.: 0670 26017). At the hotel, at the Holiday Houses and at the Tourist House.

**Transport**. Bus and railway transport. There are regular bus links with Sofia, Pleven, Lovech, Cherven Bryag, Veliko Turnovo, Gabrovo, Sevlievo, Plovdiv and Karlovo as well as with almost all smaller settlements within the region. There is a private Neshev Bus Line to Sofia (point of departure in Troyan - in front of the hotel, in Sofia - near the Princess Hotel, the former Novotel Europa Hotel). The bus station (21, Dimitur Ikonomov-Dimitrikata Str., tel.: 0670 22172, 24207) is located in the eastern part of the town, on the right bank of the Beli Vit River, not far from the railway station (tel.: 0670 22851, 22753, 24091), which is the last along the Levski-Lovech-Troyan railway line. Troyan is connected to the national railway network through Levski railway station. There is a town bus transport as well.

**Surrounding areas**. The historical **Troyan Monastery** is located at the distance of 10 km to the south-east from the town of Troyan (refer to the Stara Planina related chapter herein).

A local teacher in biology created the **Museum of Natural Science** in the village of Cherni Osum (12 km southeast from the town of Troyan and 2 km to the south of the Troyan Monastery). Working hours: 8.00 a.m. - 12.00 a.m. and 1.00 p.m. - 4.00 p.m. all the week round. There is a regular bus line between the village and the town. There are accommodation facilities in Cherni Osum (refer to the Stara Planina related chapter herein, Troyan Monastery section). The village is a point of departure for hiking tours around the Troyan Balkan Mountain (refer to the Stara Planina related chapter herein).

**National Fair - Crafts and Applied Arts** in the **village of Oreshak** (7 km to the east of the town). Articles of the modern masters of art crafts and the applied arts not only from Troyan and the region but from all over the country, often of foreign guests, are is exhibited in the numerous halls there. A part of the exposition is a bazaar, too. Demonstrations of masters and tasting of the famous Troyan plum brandy (rakiya) are organized upon a preliminary request. Working hours: 9.00 a.m. - 5.30 p.m., all the week round, tel.: 0670 2318, 2317. There are accommodation facilities in the village as well (refer to the Stara Planina related chapter herein, Troyan Monastery section). All the buses from Troyan to Cherni Osum, the Troyan Monastery, Apriltsi, etc. have a stop in the village of Oreshak.

**Beklemeto - a resort tourist complex** in the area of the same name, 22 km to the south-west from the town and 3 km under the Troyan Pass in the Troyan Balkan Mountain (about 1300 metres above sea level). There are a lot of private country-houses, public catering establishments, a hotel complex named "Bulgaria" with 50 beds, a restaurant.

Battles for control of the Troyan Pass by Russian units and Bulgarian volunteers were held there during the Russian-Turkish War of Liberation (January 1878). The historical **Kartsov Buk** (Beech-tree) bearing a mark of the sword of a Cossack is located at about 1 km south of the central part of the complex. Beklemeto is a point of departure for tourist hiking tours round the Troyan Balkan Mountain - for the Dermenka Chalet (about 3 hours), for the Kozya Stena Chalet (2.30-3 hours) and others. All the regular buses passing

*The Troyan Monastery. Frescoes*

# CENTRAL NORTHERN BULGARIA

through the Troyan Pass stop at Beklemeto.
**The village of Shipkovo** - 18 km to the west, on the road for Teteven, among the northern elevations of Vassiliov's Mountain. A balneotherapy resort with holiday houses, private country-houses, an open-air mineral beach with a swimming pool. Private lodgings are offered as well. The mineral spring is with the output rate of 55 l/sec at the temperature of 52°C. The mineral waters there cures hypertension, gastric, liver, kidney and nervous diseases. It is the point of departure for the Vassiliov Chalet (a 2-hour walk) under the higher peak in the Vassiliov's Mountain. 5 buses run daily between Shipkovo and Troyan. A great part of the Troyan Balkan Mountain is within the boundaries of the **Central Balkan National Park** within the framework of which the **Steneto** and **Kozya Stena** Biosphere Reserves are located. The first is included in the list of **UNESCO** and comprises an area of 3602.4 hectares around the upper course of the Cherni Osum River. It is characterised by lots of rocky formations, karst shapes and caves. A regular bus running to the village of Cherni Osum may be used and one can walk from there on. The second is the smallest reserve in the park and it was created mainly for the preservation of the endemic kind of **old mountainous edelweiss.** One of the most beautiful peaks of the Balkan Mountain is situated here - Mt. Kozya Stena. It may be reached most easily from Beklemeto (about a 2-hour walk). Troyan is one of the most important **points of departure** for tourist hiking tours around the Central Part of the Stara Planina Mountain and, in particular, around the Troyan Balkan Mountain.
**Sopot Dam** - at about 30 km to the north-west, by the village of Golyama Zhelyazna, it is a wonderful place for recreation, sunbathing, water motor sports, water tourism, fishing. There are good conditions for camping as well as holiday houses, private country-houses, public catering establishments. All the busses passing by have a stop there.

# APRILTSI

The town of Apriltsi (about 5000 inhabitants, between 500 and 600 metres above sea level) is spread out along the northern corrugations of the Kalofer Mountain, by the Ostreshka River (the Novoselska River), the Vidima River and the Zla Reka River. Its quarters (former villages) are scattered at a great distance one from the other. It is situated at the distance of 205 km to the south of Sofia, 57 km to the west of Gabrovo, 41 km to the south-west of Sevlievo, 25 km to the south-east of Troyan and 49 km to the south-east of Lovetch. It is a colourful mountain resort.

**History**. It was in 1812 when a church and a school with it were opened here and in 1850 a secular school was founded, as well. In 1872 Vassil Levski organized a secret revolutionary committee. Freedom-loving Balkan mountain dwellers took part in the April Uprising (1876), known here as Novoselo Uprising. The Republic of Novoselo was proclaimed and the rebels heroically defended the whole 9 days against the numerously outnumbering them enemy. It was drowned in blood and fire - over 150 people killed, lots of people exiled, 772 buildings were destroyed and set on fire, the convent and the church of 1812 inclusively. Voivoda Tsanko Dustabanov who came with his detachment

# CENTRAL NORTHERN BULGARIA

from Gabrovo in support of the insurgent villages was killed there, too. A great part of the survived population emigrated.

In 1976 in honour of the 100-annual jubilee from the April (Novoselo) Uprising the four villages - Novo Selo, Vidima, Zla Reka and Ostrets were proclaimed as today's town of Apriltsi. The first village is considered as central area of the new town. Apriltsi increasingly becomes an attractive winter resort.

**Landmarks.** The historical **Novo Selo Monastery** (in the eastern part of the Novo Selo Quarter). It was plundered and destroyed by fire during the Uprising. It was rebuilt after the Liberation. The following places of interest are located in Novo Selo, too: **House-monument to Novoselo Uprising, The Architectural and Ethnographical Museum**, **St. Georgi Temple Monument,** the **houses** of **P. Popnikolov** and **M. Popski.**

**Accommodation.** The Loven Dom Hotel (Vidima Quarter, 10 beds, everything needed for hunting on offer). The Tihiyat Kut Hotel (10 beds in 5 double rooms). Matev Hotel, family type of hotel (10 beds). Zora Chalet (in the Zora Quarter, past the road fork to the quarter of Vidima, 57 beds in 1 suite and rooms with 3, 4, 5, 8 and more beds). Vidima Chalet (in the southern end of the quarter of Vidima, 54 beds in 1 suite and rooms with 3, 4 and 5 beds).

There are private homes, which offer accommodation as well: Tsonevski (6 beds in 3 double rooms), Turnovski (2 beds), Perkovi (4 beds in 2 double rooms), Nikolova (4 beds). Catering is offered at all hotels, chalets and private lodgings.

**Tourist information** - in the Regional Tourist Bureau - 5641 Apriltsi (102, V. Levski Street, Stara Planina block, tel./fax: 06958 3249). At the Balkan Tourist Association. At the hotels, at the tourist chalets.

**Transport**. There are regular bus lines to Troyan, Sevlievo, Gabrovo, Pleven, Lovech and other smaller settlements within the region. The bus station is in the Novo Selo Quarter. A town bus runs between the quarters of the town.

**Surrounding areas**. **Batoshevo Monastery** (20 km to the north-east of Apriltsi and 4 km to the south of the village of Batoshevo). It was founded during the 13$^{th}$ century under the reign of the Bulgarian Tsar Mihail Assen (1248-1258). It was destroyed during the

GUIDE BOOK 223

# CENTRAL NORTHERN BULGARIA

Ottoman invasion in the 14th century and rebuilt in 1838. It was wall-painted in 1869. Father Matei Preobrazhenski Mitkaloto (the Wanderer) and Bacho Kiro studied in the monastery school. The church built up in the style of the Bulgarian Revival, the icons painted in the style of Tryavna icon-painting school and the great wood-carved iconostasis are remarkable. All the buses going in the direction of Sevlievo stop here.

**The village of Batoshevo** (at the distance of about 25 km to the north-east of Apriltsi). This is one of the villages whose population took most active part in the April (Novo selo) Uprising. There is a monument to those glorious and tragic days. All the buses passing between Apriltsi and Sevlievo stop here.

**The monument in the Ravni Bunar area** (along the northern slopes of Mt. Roussalka, known also as Mt. Mara Gidik, above Ostrets Quarter). Here on 11th May 1876 one of the last battles between the Novoselo rebels with Tsanko Dyustabanov at the head and the Turkish hordes pursuing them took place here. It can be reached on foot solely along the marked track from the quarter of Ostrets leading to Mt. Roussalka and the Tuzha Chalet. The town of Apriltsi is one of the most important **points of departure** for hiking trails around the highest and beautiful part of the Central Stara Planina Mountain - the Kalofer Balkan Mountain, at the head with the leader of the whole mountain - Mt. Botev (refer to the Stara Planina Mountain related chapter herein).

## LOVECH

The town of Lovech (44 262 inhabitants, about 200 metres above sea level) is picturesquely situated along the two banks of the Osum River, where the last elevations of the Pre-Balkan Mountain end. It is situated at the distance of about 170 km to the north-east of Sofia, 90 km and 35 km to the south, of Nikopol and Pleven, respectively, at the distance of 35 km to the north of Troyan, 86 km to the west of Veliko Turnovo and 65 km to the north-west of Gabrovo. One of the oldest and most interesting Bulgarian towns. A regional administrative centre.

*The Batoshevo Monastery*

**History.** The town is a descendant of the Thracian by-the-road town of *Melta* (in today's area of Hissarluka) which had a strategic location along the Danube-Aegean Sea main road. During the Medieval times the town remained an important military strategic centre and it was called *Lovuts* (a town of hunters) by the 11th century. During the 12th century it was moved to the right bank of the Osum River where the quarter of Varosha is situated now. After the Turnovo Uprising the Lovech Fortress firmly defended the approaches to Turnovo and after a 3-month siege the Byzantine Empire was forced to conclude the well-known Lovech Peace Treaty (1187), stipulating a new beginning for the Bulgarian state. Since the end of the Byzantine domination the town has been known by its today's name - Lovech.

# CENTRAL NORTHERN BULGARIA

During the 13th and particularly during the 14th century it was one of the biggest towns and fortresses in Northern Bulgaria and it reached an enviable economic prosperity. The town fell under Ottoman Rule in 1393. The last semi-independent ruler of the Lovech Fortress - Stanko Kussam, became a haidoutin (rebel) after its downfall. In the first centuries of Ottoman Rule the town declined and it was not until the 18th and particularly during the 19th century that it became well off, thanks to crafts and trade. It was called Altun Lovech (Golden Lovech). In 1870 the town had 11 thousand inhabitants. As early as in 1839 the struggle for an independent Bulgarian church began here. The first schools were opened in 1846-1847 and one of the first teachers here was the people's poet and writer Petko R. Slaveikov. In 1870 a chitalishte (community cultural centre and reading-room) was established here and two years later the first theatrical performance was held under the guidance of Angel Kunchev.

There was an old covered wooden bridge over the Osum River but the river carried it away in 1872. Only 2 years after that the self-studied master of genius craftsman master usta Kolyu Ficheto built up his famous covered bridge with 24 small workshops in it. Unfortunately it was burned to ashes by a fire in 1925. The present (unique in the country) covered bridge was built up on the analogy of it. During the years of the national liberation movement (the second half of the 19th century) Lovech turned into the revolutionary capital of Bulgaria. In 1869 Vassil Levski laid the foundations of the local revolutionary committee and in the following year he pointed Lovech as a centre of the Internal Revolutionary Organisation. It was from here on that the fibres entwining all the country started and they rose the Bulgarian people in battle for national independence. On 17th July 1877 Lovech was liberated by the squadron of Col. Zherebkov and Col. Parensov but 10 days later the Turks conquered it again and slaughtered over 2500 Bulgarians in the town and in its surroundings. The town was finally liberated on 3rd September 1877 by the units of Gen. Imeretinski, Gen. Skobelev and Gen. Dobrovolski. Its freedom was won at the price of 1683 Russian victims.

After the Liberation Lovech last the markets in the Ottoman Empire. The construction of the railway line Levski - Lovech (1932) and its extension to Troyan (1948) gave an impetus in the development of the town. For the last few years the town has established itself as a big cultural and tourist centre.

**Landmarks. Varosha Architecture-Historical Reserve** - the old quarter of the town, amphitheatrically situated along the right bank of the Osum River. Over 160 houses of the characteristic Revival architecture were restored in it. The houses along the street leading to the Stratesh Park are particularly outlined. The following places of interest are located in the Varosha quartert: **The Revival and the National Liberation Movement Museum** also known as **Vassil Levski Museum** (14, Marin Pop Loukanov), which is located in a special building constructed on the place where the house of Levski's follower Marin Pop Lukanov was. The **old square with the monument to Todor Kirkov** (an outstanding national revolutionary from Lovech hanged by the Turks in 1876) is situated along the river. **The house-museum of Ivan Drassov** - a follower and councellor of Levski (Marin Pop Lukanov Street). **Cheshneto House. Rasho's House. The Hristo Tsonev-Latinetsa House-Museum,** owner of Kukrinsko Hanche (Kukrina's Inn). His house gave shelter to Vassil Levski. **The Art Gallery** (9, Vassil Levski Street).

The famous **Pokritiyat Most (covered bridge)** (built by Usta Kolyu Ficheto) links Varosha with the remaining part of the town. It is a pedestrian area with shops on both sides. **The ancient Holy Virgin Church. The monument to Vassil Levski** (above the southern

# CENTRAL NORTHERN BULGARIA

end of the town). **The white and the black monuments** are dedicated to the Russian liberators of Lovech (in the Stratesh Park). It is a real pleasure to walk along the little, steep and narrow streets of old Varosh.

**The Stratesh Park** - in the eastern part, on the right bank of the Ossum River, is a wonderful place for recreation, located in a picturesque countryside with a well-developed tourist infrastructure and a zoo. There are a lot of monuments and ruins of a Medieval Bulgarian fortress. The park is also known as the Lilac Park due to the great number of this vegetative species attracting thousands of admirers of its tender blossoms and irresistible fragrance. Lilac Days of Music are held in Lovech during May every year.

**Accommodation**. The Lovech Hotel (12, Turgovska Street). The Orbita-2 Hotel (2-star, in the Varosha Quarter). The Hissarya Hotel (51, Turgovska Street). Stratesh Tourist House (in the Stratesh Park, 66 beds in two suites and rooms with 2 and 3 beds). Bash Bounar Tourist Hostel (a 30-minute walk from the centre into the direction of Troyan, in the Presechena Skala area, it may be reached with the town transport, too and a 10-minute walk, 74 beds in rooms with 3, 4 and more beds).

**Tourist information** - In the Council on Tourism (5500 Lovech, 51, Turgovska Street, at Hissarya Hotel, room No. 105, tel.: 068 23821, 23364). In the Stratesh Tourist Association (10, Prof. Ishirkov Street, tel.: 068 24663). At the hotels, at the tourist house and at the tourist hostel.

**Transport**. There are regular bus lines to Sofia, Pleven, Troyan, Teteven, Sevlievo, Gabrovo, Veliko Turnovo, Levski and other smaller settlements within the region. The bus station (tel.: 068 24425, 24475) and the railway station (tel.: 068 24935) are located not far from each other in the western part of the town. Lovech is a transitional station of the railway line Levski - Troyan, linking it to the national railway network. There is a town bus transport functioning in Lovech.

**Surrounding areas. The Bash Bounar Park** is located in the immediate proximity of the town, on the way out to Troyan. There are a lot of small and big caves in the rocky banks of the Ossum River. Bones and tools from the Paleolithic period and the Bronze Era were found in two of them - **Vassil Levski Cave and The Tabashka Cave**. One can get to the park on foot from the centre of the town in less than an hour. There is a town bus, too.

In the village of Stefanovo, 20 km southeast from Lovech and 27 km north-east from Troyan is the village of Staro Stefanovo Architecture Reserve (the only one on the territory of the region) with over 100 monuments of culture from the beginning and the middle of the 19th century. The first written information dates back to 1515 from the registers of Nikopol sandzhak (district) when the village was called Isvote. Other sources are the taxation records (1624) and

*The village of Stefanovo*

# CENTRAL NORTHERN BULGARIA

Voinugan lists from the beginning of the 18th century. Preserved as an entire ethnographical complex, the village of Stefanovo (until 1949 - Vratsa) during the Ottoman Rule enjoyed the status of a soldiers' and dervishko (Turkish monks) village. One of the oldest settlements in the Lovech district with a proven ancient Bulgarian origin. Sites of interest are also the Birth of the Holy Virgin Church built in 1864 by Usta (Master) Gencho Kunchev from Tryavna; Selskata Cheshma (the village drinking-fountain) (1830); Popovoto Bridge (1824) built by Master Marin Hristov from Lovech; the old Tser (Oak tree) - over 1300 years old - around which were the grounds for spiritual services. The first school was set up in 1854 in the house of Priest David - Father Superior in the Troyan Monastery up to 1906, follower and a courier of the Apostle Vassil Levski. In 1870 a secret revolutionary committee was founded and often the Apostle and Priest Matei Preobrazhenski - Mitkaloto (the Wanderer) visited the village. A native rebel is Ivanaki Yonkov Kyurkchiyata - Vrachancheto, who was among the leaders of the Velchova Zavera (Velcho's Conspiracy against the Ottoman Rule), hung by the Turks in 1836. In the village there is a tourist hostel offering 20 beds. Private lodgings are available at the Dzhurov's, Georgiev's and Hadzhi Minkov's houses, the last one hosting a rich private ethnographic exhibition. In the area there is an ancient Roman fortress - Kaleto and some Thracian mounds. The village is a favourite place for shooting film productions for its preserved distinctive spirit and architecture. There is a regular bus from Lovech.

**The Kukrinsko Hanche (Kukrina's Inn) Museum** is located in the village of Kukrina, at the distance of 17 km to the east of Lovech. After the treachery of Pop Krustyo (Krustyo Priest), on 26th December 1872 the Apostle of Bulgarian Freedom Vassil Levski was captured here.

## PLEVEN

The town of Pleven (122 149 inhabitants, about 150 metres above sea level) is located in the central part of the Danubian Plain, past the Vit River. It is situated at the distance of 174 km to the north-east of Sofia, 35 km to the north of Lovech, 53 km and 49 km to the north-east of Cherven Bryag and Lukovit, respectively, 146 km to the south-west of Rousse, 55 km to the south-west of Nikopol, 49 km to the west of Levski and at the distance of 76 km to the south-east of Oryahovo. It is a town-pantheon. A regional administrative centre.

**History.** Pleven has a centuries old and rich in events history. It originated in Thracian times on the place of today's park of Kailuka and it was named *Storgoziya*, which name was preserved in Roman times as well. After its destruction by the barbarians, the Slavs rebuilt it under the name of *Kamenets*. A second settlement was set up to the north of it which was named *Pleven* (from "plevel" which means weed). Later on the two settlements united and they were first mentioned under the name of Pleven in 1266 when the Magyars occupied it. After the 12th century the town developed as a craftsman's and trade centre. The town put up a ferocious resistance to the Turkish invaders and that is the reason for its being destroyed and for its population being slaughtered, expelled and converted to Islam after its downfall. In 1596 Pleven was conquered and set on fire by the Wallachian Voivoda Mihail Vityaz (Hrabri) (the Courageous).

During the 17th and the 18th centuries the Bulgarian population in the town grew in number and took the trade and crafts in their own hands and started to develop its cultural life as well. The town became famous on the Balkan Peninsula and in Anatolia for its market of cattle and sheep (as of 1842). In 1825 a Bulgarian secular school was opened there, in 1840 - the first Bulgarian girls' school was opened by Anastassia Dimitrova and a year

# CENTRAL NORTHERN BULGARIA

later a new boys' school was opened. In 1834 the St. Nikolai Church was built and in 1845 its iconostasis was made. Dimitur Dospevski and Nikola Obrazopissetsa (the Image Painter) painted the icons. In 1869 a chitalishte (cultural centre and reading-club) was founded in the town, too. In 1871 Pleven had 3101 houses with the population of 17 000 people. On $6^{th}$ May 1869 Levski set up the first secret revolutionary committee here. The citizens of Pleven took part in the detachments of armed volunteers of Philip Totyu and Hristo Botev.

Pleven became famous most of all with the events, which took place during the Russian-Turkish War of Liberation (1877-1878). After the forcing of the Danube River by the Russian troops, their Western squadron headed to that town of strategic importance. The Turkish commandment on its part dislocated the whole garrison of the Vidin Fortress here headed by Osman Pasha, in command of a 40-thousand people army. A system of defencive facilities was built up around Pleven. The Russian forces under the command of Gen. Shouldner, consisting of 7000 people, carried out the first assault of Pleven on $18^{th}$ June 1877. It was not a success. There were more than 2400 people killed and wounded (against 2000 on the part of the enemy). The second assault was held on $30^{th}$ July and despite the numerous victims (over 7000 people killed and wounded) was not a success, either. On $11^{th}$ and $12^{th}$ September a 100-thousand Russian-Romanian army carried out the third assault orientated at the town. This battle cannot be equalled to any other during the whole war in relation to its large scale and bloodshed. The units of Gen. Skobelev managed to perform a break-through at the Green Hills but the Chief Russian Headquarters did not appreciate the situation well enough and ordered a retreat... 16 000 people killed and wounded on the part of the Russians and the Romanians during the two-day not abating battles.

The outstanding military engineer Gen. Totleben arrived promptly from Russia to organize the blockade of the town. In execution of the blockade related plan, Gen. Gourko conquered the villages located by the road to Sofia - Dolni Dubnik, Gorni Dubnik and Telish, and the knot around the town got tight. Staring from the end of October Russians and Romanians gradually built up a fortifying blockade line. At the beginning of December it reached 50 km. At the same time the situation of the Turkish Army was deteriorated due to hunger, diseases and cold. It was completely isolated, the essential merit for this belonging to the epic battles for defence of the Shipka Pass. There Bulgarians and Russians at the expense of incredible sacrifices and with unseen courage and selflessness stopped the 45-thousand army of Suleiman Pasha heading towards Pleven and did not allow them pass through the Balkan Mountain. On $10^{th}$ December 1877 Osman Pasha made a desperate attempt to break through the blockade in the region of the Vit River, but suffered a complete defeat and Pleven fell after 5 months of defence at the expense of incredible efforts.

The town quickly grew up after the Liberation. The newly built railway lines Sofia - Varna (Rousse) and Pleven (Yassen) - Somovit - Cherkovitsa greatly contributed to it. Today

*The Kailuka Park*

# CENTRAL NORTHERN BULGARIA

## Pleven

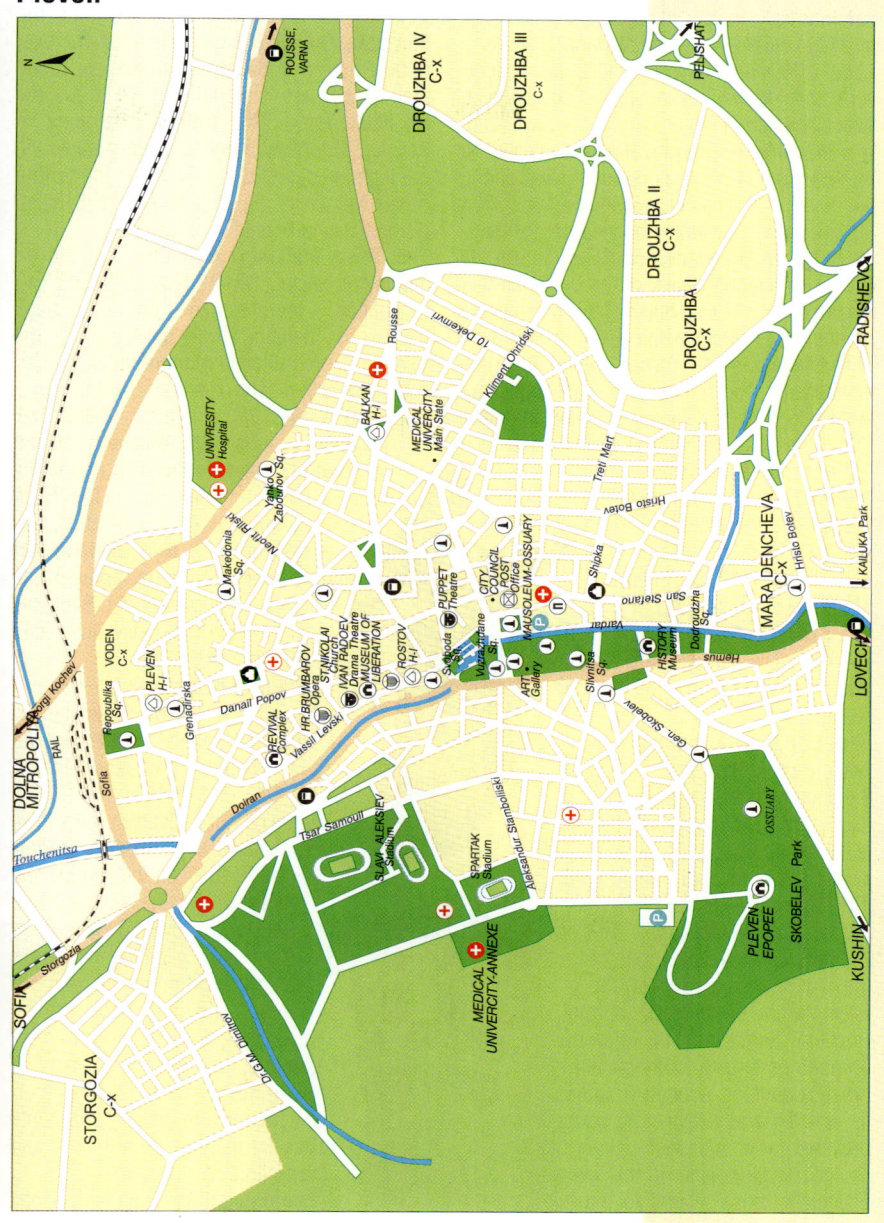

# CENTRAL NORTHERN BULGARIA

Pleven is the 7th biggest town in Bulgaria.

**Landmarks.** Almost all landmarks there are related to the Russian-Turkish War of Liberation. About 200 monuments remind to the generations about the most sanguinary battles, which took place here. In the centre of the town there is a **Mausoleum-Charnel House** dedicated to the Russian and Romanian soldiers killed during the war (5, Vuzrazhdane Square, tel.: 064 30033). It was solemnly opened on 16th September 1907 in the presence of General Stoletov (the Commanding Officer of the Bulgarian volunteer forces). The architect of this outstanding monument is Pencho Koichev, and Prof. Ivan Truvnishki made the wood-carved lime-tree iconostasis. The iconostasis was highly acknowledged at the Paris exposition in 1906. Prof. Mrkvichka and Prof. A. Mitov painted the icons. The Mausoleum is 24 m high. The **Museum to the Liberation of Pleven** is not far from there (157, V. Levski Street, tel.: 064 22435).

**The Skobelev Park** was built up in the southwestern part of the town, on a low hill (in the place of the old-time redoubts Isa aga and Kovanluka). **Bratskata Mogila** (common grave) (which preserves the bones of thousands Russian soldiers) as well as a lot of militant relics of that time is situated among its greenery and lanes. The renowned **Pleven Epic 1877 Panorama** is situated at the top of the hill, too (tel.: 064 37306), created in honour of the 100th anniversary of the Pleven Epic on analogy of the Borodin Panorama in Moscow. Through its original combination of artistic paintings, sculpture, authentic articles and explanatory texts, it provides for a sufficiently clear idea of the development of the events, especially those related to the third assault of the town.

**The Kovanluk second redoubt** and the **Murtvata Dolina** (Death Valley) where over 6000 Russian and Romanian soldiers found their death are situated not far from the Skobelev Park. **The Totleben rampart** in Kailuka. **The Monument to Victory** raises on the high hill past the Vit River, and the **bridge** of the river where the white flag of the defeated Osman Pasha waved is under it.

**The Town Museum of History** (3, Stoyan Zaimov Street, tel.: 064 22623, 22691, 23569) is situated in the green zone on the left bank of the Touchenitsa River, not far from the centre. The remarkable **monument** to the citizens of Pleven who died in the Serbian - Bulgarian War of 1885 is situated in the small garden opposite it. **Museum of the Hunters' and Fishermen's Society** (15-17, D. Popov Blvd.). **The Town Art Gallery** (75, Doiran Blvd, tel.: 064 38342). **Iliya Beshkov Art Gallery** (at the beginning of the steps leading to the Skobelev Park, 1, Gen. Skobelev Blvd., tel.: 064 30030, 30090).

There are two theatres in Pleven - Theatre of Drama (155, Vassil Levski Str., tel.: 064 34376, 22087) and the Puppet Theatre (14, Tsar Simeon Street, tel.: 064 24121, 28807).

The unique of its kind **Kailuka Park** is situated in the immediate proximity of the town on the south in the valley of the Tuchenitsa River. Sheer rocks, over 20 metres high (here rock climbing races are held), exuberant vegetation, lakes, swimming pools, lanes, recreation corners, sports playgrounds, the eccentric Peshtera (Cave) Restaurant and another tourist infrastructure make it a favourite place for the citizens of Pleven and the visitors of the town.

**Accommodation:** The Pleven Hotel

# CENTRAL NORTHERN BULGARIA

(2, Republica Square). The Rostov Hotel (2, Osvobozhdenie Street). The Balkan Hotel (68, Rousse Blvd.). Garrison Military Club (77, Doiran Street). Kailuka Tourist House (at the beginning of Kailuka Park). It offers 70 beds in 5 suites and in 2-, 3- and 4-bed rooms.

**Tourist information** - at the Council on Tourism (5800 Pleven, 2, Vuzrazhdane Square, Municipality of Pleven, tel.: 064 24119, 26229). At Kailushka Dolina Tourist Association (23A, D. Konstantinov Street, tel.: 064 29014). At the hotels.

**Transport**. Pleven is a big transport centre. There are regular bus lines to Sofia, Veliko Turnovo, Lovech, Troyan, Cherven Bryag, Levski, Knezha and a lot of other big and small settlements. The Central Bus Station (Republica Square, tel.: 064 22961) and the Central Railway Station (6, Republica Square, tel.: 064 23455, 24127, 23843, 31133, 23446, fax: 064 24006) are situated next to each other and are located in the northern end of the town. Pleven is situated on the main railway line Sofia - Gorna Oryahovitsa - Varna (Rousse), and the local railway line for Somovit and Cherkovitsa starts from it, too. There is a town bus and trolley-bus transport functioning in Pleven.

**Surrounding areas**. **The village of Grivitsa**, a railway station on the railway line Sofia - Varna (Rousse) is situated at the distance of 6 km to the east of the town. During the War of Liberation sanguinary battles between Russians and Romanians on the one hand and the Turks, in defence of Pleven took place within the region of the village. A mausoleum in memory of the Romanian soldiers killed here was built in the village after the liberation. It is located amongst a spacious park with a lot of monuments and a common grave. One can go there from the town by a passenger train or by bus.

**The town of Pordim** is situated at the distance of 21 km to the east of Pleven. The General Headquarters of the Russian Army and of Emperor Alexander II was located here during the War of Liberation. The General Headquarters of the Russian Army Museum was set up here. There is another museum - Romanian Soldier 1877-1878, set up in the immediate proximity of a little house (preserved in its original appearance up to date) which accommodated the Headquarters of the Romanian units during the siege of Pleven. Pordim is also a station on the Sofia - Varna (Rousse) railway line. There is regular bus transport.

A **green zone** was arranged around Pleven of about 25 thousand decares, including the parks of Kailuka, General Lavrov, General Genetski, Grivitsa and others, which, serve as a filter against air pollution as well. The village of Vulchitrun is situated at the distance of 22 km south-east of Pleven, in which the **Vulchitrun gold treasure** was found in 1924 - a priceless monument of the late Bronze Era in our country. It is preserved in the National Museum of History in Sofia. There is a regular bus transport to the village both from the town and from Pordim.

**The town of Dolni Dubnik** - a town at the distance of 15 km to the west of Pleven with a lot of monuments from Pleven Epic. It is the greatest oil filed deposit in Bulgaria, natural gas is yielded here, too. The three dams in its surroundings are a favourite place for recreation, water motor sports, water tourism, and fishing. It is a station at the railway line of Sofia - Varna (Rousse). There are bus connections with Pleven.

**The village of Gorni Dubnik** (at the distance of 23 km to the west of Pleven), also a station at the railway line of Sofia - Varna (Rousse). Great battles during the War of Liberation took place here, too. The General V. N. Lavrov Park-Museum is located in the proximity of the village in the area connected with one of the most important moments related to the siege of Pleven. A lot of Russian soldiers headed by the regimental commander Lavrov found their death here. Today there are lots of monuments and common graves reminding of those dramatic days when Bulgarian freedom was born. In addition to railway transport it can be reached by bus, too.

# CENTRAL NORTHERN BULGARIA

## NIKOPOL

The town of Nikopol (5108 inhabitants, at about 100 metres above sea level) is amphitheatrically situated along the slopes of several hills, on the high right bank of the Danube River, at the distance of 3 km to the east of the mouth of the Ossum River. It is situated 229 km to the north-east of Sofia, 95 km to the east of Oriahovo, 55 km to the north-east of Pleven, 51 km to the north-west of Svishtov, 25 km to the north-east of Gulyantsi and 6 km to the east of the railway station of Cherkovitsa. It is the smallest Bulgarian town situated along the Danube River.

**History**. Independently of its small size today, Nikopol has a long and interesting past. It is the successor of the antique settlements of *Sekouristka* (the remains are by the road between Nikopol and Cherkovitsa) and *Nikopolis* (town of victories). It is thought that the town got its today's name from the Byzantine Emperor Iraklii in honour of the victory over the Persians in 639. The Roman - Byzantine fortress of Tourissa on the opposite Danubian bank, together with Nikopol, were expanded after the 7th century by the Bulgarians, Tourissa being called Little Nikopol and

*Sunrise by the Danube*

Holuvnik. Today it is the Romanian town of Turnu Mugurele. Nikopol was the last stronghold of the Turnovo Kingdom, defended by Tsar Ivan Shishman. He died here in an unequal battle with the Turkish invaders. The Turks called it *Kyuchuk Stamboul* (Little Tsarigrad) and preserved it as a port and an important military, administrative and trade centre on the Danube River. The town was a powerful fortress for centuries and the battle of the Polish King Vladislav Varnenchik and the Magyar King Sigismund with the Turks was held here. During the 18th century Nikopol was the biggest town and fortress along the lower Danube River. The Turkish traveller Evliya Chelebi wrote that there were 16 drinking-fountains and two kaleta (fortresses) in the town - Tuna Kale and Pech Kale. There were barracks for 20 000 nizami (regular soldiers). The town had a completely Oriental appearance. As of 1860 Nikopol was a river station of Austrian ships as well.

After the Liberation, thanks to its natural and historical endowments, the town turned more and more into a tourist site.

**Landmarks. The drinking-fountain of Elia (Syutliika)**, built up during the 2nd century by the ordinary citizen of Rome Frontona in memory of his early deceased wife Elia, who gave vent to his grief in verse over the stone. During the 19th century archaeologist Dijardin, moved by all that, placed another inscription. A nice lane takes us to the fountain nowadays.

**Shishman's fortress** - remains from the fortress, defended by the last Bulgarian Tsar before the Turkish invasion - Ivan Shishman. One of the gates to the fortress, called Shishman's Gate, is very well preserved.

**The old St. St. Peter and Pavel Church** dates back to the 13th century. The **house** in which **Vassil Levski** was hiding during his visit to the town on the way to Romania is preserved, too. In the house of Tsvyatko Smolyanov one can see the epitaph of the author of "Abagar" (the first printed book in the Cyrillic alphabet published in Rome in 1651) - the Catholic Bishop

# CENTRAL NORTHERN BULGARIA

Philip Stanislavovitch who died in 1654. The **Monument to the Russian soldiers** who died during the Russian-Turkish War of Liberation, led by General Studler-Krinder rises on one of the town hills. There are several **houses** of the **Bulgarian Revival** period, which were declared as cultural monuments in the town as well.

**Accommodation**: The Town Hotel. Nikopol Camping (in Shishman Park, at the distance of 4 km from the town). It has 52 beds available in 9 bungalows with 4 beds each and 2 vans with two rooms, 4 beds in each room.

**Tourist information** - at the town hotel and in the Danube Tourist Association (tel.: 0651 2616). Such information may be obtained in the Town-hall as well (situated in the centre of Nikopol).

**Transport**. There are regular bus lines to Pleven, Svishtov, Guliantsi and other smaller settlements within the region. The telephone number of the bus station is: 0651 2436. The station of Cherkovitsa is situated at the distance of about 6 km to the west of Nikopol and it is the last station on the line of Pleven (Yassen) - Somovit - Cherkovitsa. There is a regular bus transport from the town to it. Nikopol has a river port on the Danube River as well but for the time being there are no regular passenger's transportations along the Danube River on the Bulgarian part.

**Surrounding areas**. At the distance of 0.5 km east of the town (past the Fishermen's Base), on the bank of the Danube River there are remains of an **old rock monastery**. The ruins of the **ancient settlement of Sekuristka** are situated past the road to the village of Cherkovitsa. The regular buses in this direction may be used. **The Danube River** within the region of Nikopol provides great opportunities for recreation, sunbathing, sports activities, water tourism, fishing, etc. **Shishman Park** is situated at the distance of 4 km from the town, on the bank of the river in a well-preserved countryside. There is camping site as well.

## SVISHTOV

The town of Svishtov (30 591 inhabitants, about 100 metres above sea level) is situated at a high terrace on the right bank of the Danube River, in the place where the river reaches its most southern point. It is situated at the distance of 250 km north-east from Sofia, 51 km south-east from Nikopol, 97 km south-west from Rousse, 76 km north-east from Pleven, 45 km north-west from Byala, 47 km north-east from Levski and 31 km east from Belene.

**History**. The town is a successor of the Roman (and later on of the Early Byzantine) town of *Nove* (1$^{st}$ century) - an important strategic centre with naval functions. During the Middle Ages it was called *Stuklen*, and in the map of Fra Mauro of 1459 it was marked under the name of *Sistovo*, which is the transcription of today's name of the town. Svishtov comes from "svesht" (candle). During the first centuries of the Ottoman Rule there were several huts here, which lit up with fires along the river

*The Clock Tower*

# CENTRAL NORTHERN BULGARIA

banks to light the way of boats and sailing-vessels during night-time. Gradually the future town of Svishtov was formed around them. The town reached an enviable development during the 19th century in spite of its complete destruction during the Russian-Turkish War of 1810. In 1865 Dr. Ivan Bogorov described Svishtov as "the most commercial place" of our towns. In 1869 there were 957 stores and 720 warehouses there. The first high school of commerce in Bulgaria was established in Svishtov (1873). The well-known traveller of 19th century Felix Kanits wrote: *"Svishtov has been enjoying the reputation of an European town with an European market for a long time."* Within the time period from 1850 to 1860 in the port of Svishtov there were about 150 vessels sailing along the Danube with water displacement of 120 000 tons, a part of which belonged to Svishtov merchants. In 1867 the Danubian Steam Society was established with the merchant from Svishtov Nikola Stanchov as the chief shareholder. The Society purchased the Austrian-Hungarian ship "Commencement" and three tank barges for transportation of cereals. The tangible welfare of the town was reflected in its cultural life as well. In 1841 Hristaki Pavlovich established a new Bulgarian school and a secular school for girls. One of the first in Bulgaria chitalishta (reading-clubs) with a museum with it was set up here in 1856. In 1884 the first in Bulgaria Commercial High School opened its gates (today's High School of Economy). The outstanding Revival public figures Nikolai Pavlovich, Emanuil Vaskidovich, Hristaki Pavlovich and a lot of other eminent functionaries worked here as well. Schools, churches, beautiful houses were built in thse years.

On 26th and 27th June 1877 the key forces of the Russian Army disembarked on the bank of the Danube River in the locality of Tekirdere (at the distance of 4 km east of Svishtov) and the Russian-Turkish War of Liberation began. Although the Turks did not anticipate the crossing of the Danube River by the main Russian units to take place namely here, they put up ferocious resistance and it was in the first battle for Bulgarian freedom that 814 Russian soldiers and officers found their death.

The town lost its initial first-grade significance after the Liberation, but it remained an important economic, cultural centre and grew as a tourist centre as well. Since 1936 Svishtov has been an academic town, too in relation to the opening of the Higher Institute of Finance and Economics "Dimitur Tsenov" (in the name of an outstanding Bulgarian patron).

Svishtov is the birthplace of Dragan Tsankov, Grigor Nachevich, Nikolai Pavlovich, Dimitur Tsenov, Alexander Bozhinov, Tsvetan Radoslavov (author of the song, on the basis of which "Mila Rodino" ("Dear Motherland") - Bulgarian national anthem was composed) and of the great Bulgarian writer - humorist, democrat and creator of the organized hiking movement in our country - Aleko Konstantinov.

**Landmarks**: In Svishtov there are more than 120 archaeological, art and architectural monuments of culture of local and national significance. **The Town Museum of History** (tel.: 0631 22888), considered one of the oldest museums in Bulgaria (1856).

**The Ethnographic Museum** (tel.: 0631 22448). **The Aleko Konstantinov House-Museum** (not far from the centre, tel.: 0631 25452), in which the heart of the great Bulgarian is preserved in a glass vessel.

**The Holy Trinity Church** (1867, in the centre of the town, tel.: 0631 25492) is the most interesting architectural monument. It was the work of the great Bulgarian builder of the Revival period usta Koliu Ficheto ("usta" - master). The citizen of Svishtov Nikolai Pavlovich painted the icons. The temple suffered a lot during the earthquake in 1977 but in 1992 its restoration was completed. **The ancient St. Dimitur Church** (1640) and **St. St. Peter and Pavel Church** (1644). Bulgarian masters erected the **clock tower** (1760, in the centre of the town). **The School of Hristaki Pavlovich** (1815). **The House of Peace**, in which in 1791

# CENTRAL NORTHERN BULGARIA

an Austrian-Turkish Separation Peace Treaty was signed. **The old Revival houses - Sladkarov's, Danailov's, Hrulev's, Bruchkov's, Cherkezov's, Radoslavov's,** the **house of the Subevs Brothers,** etc.

**Accommodation**: The Academia Hotel (1, Tsanko Tserkovski Street). The Dunav Hotel (2, Tsar Osvoboditel Street). Kaleto Tourist Hostel (in Kaleto Park, 2, T. Panteleev Street). It offers 26 beds in double rooms, a restaurant, a bar and a coffee-bar. Yug Complex. Kirilov Hotel. Sviloza Hotel. Emili Hotel.

**Tourist information** - can be obtained at the hotels, at the Tourist Hostel and at Aleko Konstantinov Tourist Association (21, D. Shishmanov Street, tel.: 0631 22131).

**Transport**. Bus and railway transport. There are regular bus lines to Rousse, Pleven, Veliko Turnovo, Lovech, Byala, Levski and other smaller settlements within the region. The telephone of the bus station is 0631 23205. Svishtov is the last station of the railway line Levski - Svishtov (Belene), through which it is connected to the national railway network. The telephone of the town railway bureau is 0631 22461. There is a river station, as well but since 1992 there is no regular passenger transport along the Danube River on the Bulgarian part. There is a town bus transport functioning in Svishtov, too.

**Surrounding areas**. **The Pametnitsite Park** (the Monuments) is situated at the distance of 4 km east of the town in the locality of Tekirdere. The Russian-Turkish War of Liberation began here and in the place where the Russian troops disembarked a big commemorative park with white marble and granite monuments, military attributes of that time, was created. Now there are public catering establishments, a beach among a lot of greenery and regular town transport.

The remains of the **ancient town of Nove** (1st century) and the **Medieval town of Stuklen** are located in the immediate proximity, at the distance of 1 km east in the Kaleto area, to the right above the road to the Pametnitsite Park.

Several buildings with interesting architecture, town gates and others were found and investigated. A museum was set up and functions here as well. The town bus to the Pametnitsite Park may be used.

**Pisanite Kamuni** (Inscribed Stones) - an area 2 km east of Svishtov, where articles and tools of the early Paleolithic period were found.

The Danubian **island of Vardim** is situated at about some 10 km east of the town, which is the third biggest Bulgarian island (after Belene and Kozlodui). It was declared a natural reserve due to the birds' colonies of great cormorants, herons and others. The well-known Vardim oak tree grows here, too.

There is a white stone **monument** marking the place where on 18th June 1868 the detachment of armed volunteers of Hadzhi Dimitur and Stefan Karadzha disembarked from the gemiya (the sailing-vessel) on the native bank to write down another heroic page in Bulgarian history. It is situated at the distance of about 20 km east of Svishtov in the **Yankovo Gurlo** area (near the mouth of the Yantra River in the Danube River). It was also near the mouth of the Yantra River, in the proximity of the village of Krivina that Bulgarian and German archaeologists found the ruins of the **Limmes Kastel** (fortress) of **Yatrus.** There is a regular bus transport to the village.

GUIDE BOOK 235

# CENTRAL NORTHERN BULGARIA

## PAVLIKENI

The town of Pavlikeni (about 14 000 inhabitants, 115 metres above sea level) is situated in the central part of the Danubian Plain, at a distance of about 4 km north of the Rositsa River. It 230 km north-east of Sofia, 43 km north-west of Veliko Turnovo, 22 km south-east of Levski, about 40 km north-east of Sevlievo and about 50 km south-west of Byala.

**History**. Emigrant Paulicians who had come from Southern Bulgaria during the Middle Ages founded the town. They were followers of a religious heresy, which originated in Western Armenia during the 7$^{th}$ century. The settlement figured under the name of *Bavlikian* or *Pavlikian* in documents of 1430. During the Liberation (1878) it was a small village. After the building up of the railway line Sofia-Varna (1899) it developed as a handicraft and trade settlement. In 1943 it was proclaimed a town. Part of the population of the town professes the Catholic religion.

**Landmarks: The Art Gallery** (in the central part of the town, 1, Bacho Kiro Street, tel.: 0610 7149). **The Zoo** (in the southern end of the town, 75, 3$^{rd}$ March Blvd., tel.: 0610 2415). **The monument to those who perished in the wars.**

**Accommodation**: The Poltava Hotel (in the centre of the town, 2, Svoboda Square). There are nice public catering establishments, too, which offer typical Bulgarian cuisine. One of them is the Strandzhata Restaurant (1, Al. Stamboliiski Street, working hours: 6.00 a.m. - 11.00 p.m.).

**Tourist information** - at the hotel or in the town-hall (4, Ruski Blvd., tel.: 0610 3580, 6195, 3526).

**Transport**. Bus and railway transport links the town. There are regular bus lines to Veliko Turnovo, Lovech, Pleven, Sevlievo, Levski, Polski Trumbezh, Suhindol, Byala Cherkva and other smaller settlements within the region. The bus station (32, 3$^{rd}$ March Blvd, tel.: 0610 4064, 4041) and the railway station (tel.: 0610 3433, 3033, 3071) are next to each other and they are situated in the southwestern part of Pavlikeni. The town is a station at the main railway line Sofia - Gorna Oryahovitsa - Varna (Rousse).

**Surrounding areas**. **A ceramic centre** (of 2$^{nd}$ - 3$^{rd}$ centuries) is found to the north-west of the town in the Vurbovski Livadi area (Willow Meadows) with a great number of pottery workshops and furnaces for the production of artistic, construction and every-day ceramics, and near it there is a country-house of a Thracian landowner with a lot of agricultural tools.

**The village of Gorna Stoudena** is situated at the distance of 24 km to the north of the town, past the road Pleven - Rousse. There is a military-historical museum arranged in the building where the General Headquarters of the Russian Emperor Alexander II was located for some time during the Russian-Turkish War of Liberation. An old Russian cemetery is preserved in the northern part of the village.

The small **town of Byala Cherkva** is situated at the distance of 4 km to the south of Pavlikeni. The town is birthplace of the hero of the April Uprising, the teacher Bacho Kiro, who set up the first chitalishte (community cultural centre) in a village in Bulgaria Selska Lyubov (Rural love) in 1869 and who led out 101 rebels from Byala Cherkva only during May 1876. The whole detachment of armed volunteers (over 200 people) under the leadership of Pop (Priest) Hariton, Peter Parmakov, Hristo Karaminkov and Bacho Kiro was defeated at the Dryanovo Monastery after a siege which lasted for about 10 days. The people's teacher, enlightener, poet and traveller Bacho Kiro was hung in Turnovo on 28$^{th}$ May 1876.

In the town there is a monument to those who were killed in the Uprising as well as monuments to Bacho Kiro and Tsanko Tserkovski who was also born here. The famous Bulgarian Prof. Alexander Burmov was born in Byala Cherkva, too.

# CENTRAL NORTHERN BULGARIA

A **monument-belfry** was built in 1929 next to the old white church St. Dimitur, in which there are built-in columns of the antique Nikopolis ad Istrum in honour of the Russian liberators. There is a **town museum and a house museum of Tsanko Tserkovski.**

St. Yoan Monastery was situated at the distance of 4 km south-west of Byala Cherkva which was destroyed by the Turks during the Turnovo Uprising (1598) in which the local population also actively participated. There is a regular bus transport from Pavlikeni to the town as well as from Veliko Turnovo and Sevlievo.

The **town of Souhindol** is situated at the distance of 14 km south-west of Pavlikeni - a big vine-growing and wine-producing centre. The prominent Hungarian traveller, scientist and artist Felix Kanits visited the old settlement in 1872.

It was as early as in 1897 when its population used vine sprinklers and grapevines imported from France. In the eve of the Liberation as well as after it Suhindol was a big cultural centre for its time. The community centre dates back to 1870 and the clock tower dates back to 1895. Newspapers were published here, too. In 1908 the first independent vine-growing and wine-producing co-operative company in Bulgaria was established here - Gumza. Nowadays there is a great demand for the red Suhindol Gumsa on the international market, too and it is one of the best-sold Bulgarian wines. There is a museum and an art gallery in the town. The picture "Suhindol Maiden" painted by Felix Kanits in 1872 is preserved and exhibited in the art gallery.

There is a regular bus connection between Pavlikeni and Suhindol.

The **Emenski Canyon** and the **Momin Skok (Maiden Jump) Waterfall** declared as natural sights are situated at the distance of 16-17 km south-west of Pavlikeni, on the Negovanka River. There is a regular bus to the village of Emen.

## SEVLIEVO

The town of Sevlievo (about 25 000 inhabitants, 200 metres above sea level) is situated in the mountain valley of the same name, along the left bank of the Rossitsa River, a little after its spillway with the Vidima River. It is situated at the distance of 190 km north-east of the capital city, 28 km north-west of Gabrovo, 50 km west of Veliko Turnovo, 37 km south-east of Lovech, 47 km north-east of Troyan, 40 km south-west of Pavlikeni and 41 km north-east of Apriltsi.

**History**. The settlement emerged in the $15^{th}$ century as a village producing timber boards but it is likely that it had existed before that, too ($10^{th}$-$12^{th}$ centuries).

It was mentioned under the name of *Selvi* for the first time in 1618 where its present name comes from (it is related to the surrounding vegetation). It was completely devastated and put to fire by the kurdzhalii (Turkish brigands) in 1798. The settlement recovered comparatively quickly as an administrative centre with a well-developed craftsmanship - woodworking, leather processing and tailoring, weaving. There was a well-known cattle market here, too but it was the silkworm breeding and the silk-trade which brought the greatest glory to the town and made it famous. There was a great demand for silkworm seed and silk from Sevlievo in Austria, France, Romania. The population of the town was affected by the great plague in 1838.

The town did not neglect its cultural develop-

# CENTRAL NORTHERN BULGARIA

ment, either. A community centre was founded there (1870) by Dr. Stoicho Zografski, schools, churches, a clock tower (1777), beautiful houses and bridges were built as well. Petko R. Slaveikov and Martin Sofroniev were teachers here. Hadzhi Angel Ivanov translated the text of church hymns into the language of Slavs and Bulgarians and the Priest Pencho Nestorov translated the Gospel into the Bulgarian language. After the Liberation the town at first declined as a craftsmanship centre but quickly developed after that.

**Landmarks**: **The Town Museum of History** located in the building of the first secular (Hadzhi Stoyanov's) **school** (in the centre of the town, 6, Petko R. Slaveikov Street, tel.: 0675 4463, 4852), built in 1844, where P. R. Slaveikov was a teacher for a short time. **The clock tower** (in the centre of the town) built by Bulgarian builder masters (1877-1879) of stone, bricks, mortar and wood. It has an original architectural appearance and is 18 m high.

**St. Prophet Iliya Church** (in the centre of the town, 12, Skobelev Street, tel.: 0675 3296), built up in 1834 and having a valuable wood-carved iconostasis. The **Holy Trinity Church** (in the centre of the town, 12, Sv. Troitsa Street, tel.: 0675 4495) of 1870. **The stone bridge** over the Rossitsa River built by Master Kolyu Ficheto during 1857-1858 and restored after the flood in 1939.

**The Monument to Freedom** (in the centre of the town) was erected in 1894 and was designed by Otto Horeishi and Arnoldo Zocci (Italian sculptor, author of monuments in Sofia, Rousse, Oriahovo). The pillar of the monument is an original stone column from the Roman town of Nikopolis ad Istrum (beside the village of Nikyup, Turnovo region), and the figure was made in Vienna. The gallows on which the revolutionaries from Sevlievo were hanged in 1876 was in the place of today's monument. **Tabahanata** (tannery) - restored and open to visitors.

**Accommodation**: The Rossitsa Hotel (1, Svoboda Square, in the centre of the town). There are several public catering establishments, which serve delicious traditional cuisine. Here are two of them: the Royal Restaurant (in the centre of the town, 10, Slavianska Street, working hours: 9.00 a.m. - 12.00 p.m.) and the Loven Dom Restaurant (on the right bank of Rossitsa River, to the south of the stadium).

**Tourist information** - at the hotel and at the Rositsa-Mazalat Tourist Association (34, Iv. Presnakov Street, tel.: 0675 3005, 3004).

**Transport**. Bus transport provides regular connections with Sofia, Gabrovo, Veliko Turnovo, Lovech, Pleven, Troyan, Apriltsi, Pavlikeni and other smaller settlements within the region. The bus station (Stoyan Buchvarov Street, tel.: 0675 3628, 3627, 3625) is situated in the western part of the town.

**Surrounding areas**. **The Monument to Father Matei Preobrazhenski** (1926) is situated about 30 km on the east by the Sofia - Varna road, between the villages of Novo Selo and Balvan, which was built in memory of the outstanding Revival enlightener and revolutionary, follower and friend of Levski, also called Mitkaloto (the Wanderer), who was born in Novo Selo. There is a monument to Father Matei in front of the museum (author Nenko Nenkov). All the buses running between Sevlievo and Veliko Turnovo can be used to get there.

**Baagdalata Park** (10 km south-east of the town, the detour is at the 7th km along the old road to Gabrovo). The Momina Sulza Chalet is located here, too (tel.: 0675 6336), providing 60 beds in rooms with 2, 4, 6 and 8 beds. There is no regular bus transport.

**Al. Stamboliiski Dam** spreads its waters at about 6 km north from Sevlievo offering wonderful conditions for recreation, water motor sports, water tourism, fishing, sunbathing on the beach. There are holiday homes, public catering establishments and country houses. The regular buses running to the villages of Gradishte, Gorsko Kosovo and Mladen can be used.

**The Batoshevo Monastery** is situated at the distance of 20 km south of the town, past the village of the same name (refer to the town of Apriltsi related section herein).

# CENTRAL NORTHERN BULGARIA

## GABROVO

The town of Gabrovo (67 350 inhabitants, 390 metres above sea level) is situated along the two banks of the Yantra River, at the northern foot of the Shipka Balkan Mountain (Central Stara Planina). It is situated 220 km north-east of Sofia, 274 km south-west of Varna, 150 km north-east of Plovdiv, 46 km south-west of Veliko Turnovo, 48 km north of Kazanluk and 28 km south-east of Sevlievo. It is situated in the immediate proximity of the geographical centre of Bulgaria and in itself is a centre of humour and jokes. A regional administrative centre.

**History.** Gabrovo originated during the Middle Ages as a strategic settlement in the proximity of the Balkan Mountain passes. According to the legend Racho Kovacha (Racho the Blacksmith) established the settlement, but there is no explicit evidence in support of this statement.

At the end of the $12^{th}$ century due to the proximity of the town to the capital of the Bulgarian state Turnovo, the handcrafts and trade developed here as well as crafts related to the maintenance and guard of the passes through the Balkan mountain - blacksmiths, armour and weapon smiths, etc.

The first known name of the settlement dates back to 1430 (already under the Ottoman Rule) - *Gabruva*, and today's name - Gabrovo appeared as late as the $17^{th}$ century. The name comes from the horn-beam tree (Carpinus betulus, in Bulgarian "gaber"). During the years of Ottoman Rule Gabrovo was a big craftsmanship and trade centre. During the $19^{th}$ century 26 crafts were practiced here - blacksmiths (horseshoes), knives and cutlery, pottery, manufacture of braids, leather processing and tailoring, silk-worm breeding and a lot of others. The first manufacturing enterprise Ivan K. Kalpazanov opened in 1860 - a textile factory. In the same year Gabrovo was proclaimed a town. Felix Kanits said about it that during the 70-es of the $19^{th}$ century *"Gabrovo is a big workshop"* and that it is *"a town living on water"*, having in mind the widely used waterpower. The good quality of the Gabrovo made articles was known all over the Ottoman Empire and even beyond it. There is a street in Bucharest now still named "Gabroveni".

The quick economic growth and the national revival were the reason for the opening of the first Bulgarian secular school called after the name of its founder - Vassil Aprilov as early as in 1835. In 1872 it grew into a secondary school and in 1889 it was called Aprilov's High School, functioning up to date. Beautiful Revival houses, churches, bridges, drinking-fountains, a clock tower (1835) were built then. The inhabitants of the town took an active part in the Uprising of Captain Dyado (Grandfather) Nikola in 1856, in the Turnovo Uprising of 1862, in the detachments of armed volunteers of Hadzhi Dimitur and Stefan Karadzha (1868), of Hristo Botev (1876), of Tsanko Dyustabanov (1876 - completely formed in Gabrovo). In 1868 Levski set up a revolutionary committee here. The town is the birthplace of Vassil Aprilov, Tsanko Dyustabanov, Pop (Priest) Hariton, the composer Emanuil Manolov and a lot of others.

Gabrovo continued to develop as the biggest textile centre of Bulgaria after the Liberation and it was not by accident that it was nicknamed "the Bulgarian Manchester". The town has been famous for the stinginess and sharp-wittedness of its inhabitants from time immemorial due to which the unique in the world House of Humour and Satire is located here.

**Landmarks:** The unique **House of Humour and Satire** (64, Bryanska Street, tel.: 066 27228, 29300). Works of authors from 153 countries are exhibited in 10 halls with an area of 8000 square metres. This House not only collects but also investigates and popularises humour and satire in all the genres. Every odd year the House and the whole town become the centre of the International Biennale of

# CENTRAL NORTHERN BULGARIA

Humour and Satire in the Arts, which is a part of the big May Cultural Festivals of Gabrovo. The **unique** in Southeastern Europe **open-air museum - the architectural ethnographic complex of Etura** is situated at the distance of 8 km south of the centre of the town in the immediate proximity of the Etara quarter and past the Sivek River (at the distance of 3 km from the road-fork to Shipka). It is the most interesting place of interest in the town and one of the most visited sites all over Bulgaria. Located over an area of 60 decares the complex lives the authentic life of a typical craftsmanship settlement from the period of Bulgarian Revival. The way Bulgarian people lived 150 years ago can be perceived and felt here. One can hear the rattle of wheels and mills moved by water, the whiz of the mills for woollen cloths and for flour. Metal ornaments, pottery articles, copper utensils, braids, hot buns and whatever else come out from the skillful hands of the masters there. The little cobblestone streets, the stone cheshmi (drinking-fountains), the gas lanterns, Sakov's house, the house with the tavern, the clock tower and a lot of other authentic details complete the whole picture. All of these is predominantly the work of the great patriot Lazar Donkov who dedicated his life to this noble cause - to create this authentic ethnographic complex. There is a town bus running to Etura.

**The Town Museum of History** (19, Opulchenska Street, tel.: 066 25218). **The National Museum of Education** (tel.: 066 24071) and **the Aprilov's High School** (in the centre of the town), in which a lot of well-known Bulgarians studied (Aleko Konstantinov, Emanuil Manolov and others). Master Gencho Kunev built it at the initiative and with the funds of the rich merchant, enlightener and scholar Vassil Aprilov.

**The Hristo Tsokev Art Gallery** (10, Cyril and Methodius Street, tel.: 066 23381) exhibits Bulgarian and foreign works of art. **Bayov Bridge,** built in 1855. **The Assumption Church** (1865), whose icons and wood-carved iconostasis (work of masters from Tryavna) are among the masterpieces of Bulgarian art. **The clock tower** (1835, in the centre of the town), whose clockwork was made by local blachsmiths, and its bell was made in Vienna. The cobblestone **Opulchenska Street** and the old commercial **Radetski Street** are of interest to the visitors, too.

**The monument to Racho Kovacha** (Racho the Blacksmith) - the legendary founder of the town. It is located on a small rocky island in the Yantra River (the central part of the town). **The Aprilov drinking-fountain** built up in 1762 by Krustio Aprilov, a relative of V. Aprilov. It has 2 drinking-founatin heads and an interesting decoration. **The Planetarium** and the **Zoo** are located in the direction of the Gradishte area.

*Aprilov's High School and the monument to V. Aprilov*

# CENTRAL NORTHERN BULGARIA

Being a big cultural centre, Gabrovo nowadays has 3 professional theatres - the Racho Stoyanov Theatre of Drama (2, Timok Street, tel.: 066 26722), The Puppet Theatre (11, Cyril and Methodius Street, tel.: 066 29051) and the Experimental Theatre of Satire and Variety (64, Brianska Street, tel.: 066 26594).

Every year during August a Balkan youth festival is held in Gabrovo called Youth on the Balkans, and at the end of September - the beginning of October the town hosts the Days of Chamber Music.

Gabrovo is a university centre, too - the Higher Institute of Mechanical and Electrical Engineering (1963).

**Accommodation**: The Balkan Hotel (in the centre of the town, 14, Emil Manolov Street). The Panorama Hotel (also in the centre, 18, Benkovska Street). The Corona Hotel (in the Etura Quarter, 27, Grigorovska Street). The Stranopriemnitsa (The Inn) Hotel (in the architectural ethnographic complex of Etura). Private house White River (in the quarter of Aprilovo).

### HIGH SCHOOL of RESTAURATEURSHIP and HOTELIERSHIP
Gabrovo, 18, Benkovski Str.
**Tel./fax:** 066 44023
Trhgabrovo@mbox.stemo.bg
*Educational and Training Complex:*
Restaurant (education and training)
**60 places**
Hotel (education and training)
**120 beds**

**Tourist information** - in the Gabrovo Municipal Tourist Information Bureau (5300 Gabrovo, 2, Vuzrazhdane Square, tel./fax: 066 28483). The Regional Tourist Bureau is located at the same address (tel./fax: 066 29161), which can provide information not only about Gabrovo but about the towns of Teteven, Troyan, Apriltsi and Tryavna, included in Stara Planina Association. Uzana Tourist Society. Char-dafon Hunters"Society (65A, Svishtovska Street, tel.: 066 23459), and at the hotels, too.

**Transport**. Railway and bus transport. There are regular bus lines to Sofia, Veliko Turnovo, Gorna Oryahovitsa, Kazanluk, Troyan, Tryavna, Sevlievo, Apriltsi, the Shipka Pass and a lot of other smaller settlements and recreation zones. The bus station is in the central part of the town (tel.: 066 23277, 25577). Gabrovo is the last station on the railway line of Vurbanovo - Gabrovo, a branch of the main line Russe - Gorna Oryahovitsa - Stara Zagora - Podkova. All trains stop at Vurbanovo Station and through it Gabrovo is connected to the national railway network. The telephone number of the railway station is 066 25301. There is a town bus transport, too.

**Surrounding areas**. One can admire the panoramic view to the town and have a look at the ruins of the old fortress wall in the **Gradishte area** - at the distance of 3 km from Gabrovo. **The Assumption Sokolski Monastery** (4 km from Etura and 12 km south-east from the centre of Gabrovo) was built in 1833 with donations by the citizens of Gabrovo and Bulgarians in immigration. Its foundation and activity further on are closely connected to the name of Yossif Sokolski. The Monastery turned into an educational centre and Neofit Bozveli was a teacher there. In 1856 the detachment of armed volunteers of Dyado Nikola found shelter here. After the defeat 8 of the revolutionaries were hanged in the cave by the monastery. The place of these gallows is a charnel-house now and the hooks for the ropes are hammered into the wall. Later on (1868) Master Koliu Ficheto erected a stone drinking-fountain with eight fountain heads which slakes the thirst of the exhausted traveller. During the rebellious spring of 1876 the detachment of 220 rebels of Tsanko Dyustabanov was blessed in the monastery before it set off on the way to immortality. Before that the Apostle Vassil Levski found shelter here, too. During the Russian-Turkish War of Liberation the monastery was turned into a military

# CENTRAL NORTHERN BULGARIA

hospital. A modest museum collection preserves relics from the struggles for enlightenment and freedom. Old icons painted by the hand of Zakhari Zograf complete the precious exhibits of the museum. There is bus transport available or one can walk to the museum from Etura along a marked track for 1-1.30 hours.

**The Liuliatsite Resort** is situated at the distance of 15 km west of Gabrovo whose name is related to the abundance of lilac within the region. The climate is favourable for treatment of pulmonary diseases. There is a rest house, private and institutional country-houses, catering establishments. A marked hiking track starts from here in the direction of the central ridge of Stara Planina which joins the Kom-Emine route along the ridge of Stara Planina Mountain. There is a regular bus transport.

**Uzana Mountain Resort** is situated at the distance of 22 km south-west of the town on the ridge of Stara Planina (Shipka Balkan Mountain) - there are institutional holiday houses, several hotels, 3 chalets, a ski-lift, a base of the Mountain Rescue Service, catering establishments. **The geographic centre of Bulgaria** is located within the region, too and is marked with a memorial sign. There are regular buses during the holidays.

The historical **Shipka Pass** is situated at the distance of 21 km south of Gabrovo and the Monument to Freedom is located above it (refer to the Kazanluk related section herein). **The historical Mt. Bouzloudzha** is at the distance of 12 km east of the pass (refer to the Kazanlak related section herein). All buses running between Gabrovo and Kazanluk stop at the Shipka Pass and there is no regular transport to Bouzloudzha. The **village of Bozhentsi - an architecture and ethnographic reserve** is situated 15 km east of Gabrovo (refer to the Tryavna related section herein). Gabrovo is a key **point of departure** for hiking routes around the Shipka Balkan Mountain (refer to the Stara Planina related chapter herein).

## TRYAVNA

The town of Tryavna (12 226 inhabitants, 440 metres above sea level) is situated in a small valley expansion of the Tryavna Balkan mountain (Central Stara Planina), along the two banks of the Dryanovska River. It is situated at the distance of 242 km north-east of Sofia, 22 km east of Gabrovo, 17 km south of Dryanovo, at 42 km south-west of Veliko Turnovo and 7 km north of Plachkovtsi. Cradle of the unique in its kind Revival Art School - the Tryavna School.

**History**. According to the legend the settlement originated during the 12$^{th}$ century during the reign of the Assen Dynasty. The youngest brother Kaloyan erected the St. Archangel Michail Church in the area of *Truvna* (named after the resilient grass around), around which a whole village gradually grew up. During the Ottoman Rule Tryavna was a privileged settlement, whose inhabitants guarded the pass through the Balkan to Odrin and Istanbul. The settlement reached prosperity at the end of the 18$^{th}$ and at the beginning of the 19$^{th}$ century when the crafts, the applied arts and the trade established themselves on the market. The influence of the representatives of Tryavna Art School is strongly felt. Masons built beautiful houses, schools and churches. Icon-painters ornamented them with icons and mural paintings and joiners (woodcarvers) completed their work with unparalleled altars, ceilings and windows. Felix Kanits who visited the town in 1872 called in the "Bulgarian Nuernberg". A lot of Tryavna citizens took an active part in the struggles for an independent Bulgarian church, for national awareness and liberation. The town is the birthplace of Levski's associate Ange Kunchev. Petko R. Slaveikov lived there, too and his eminent son, the poet Pencho P Slaveikov was born in Tryavna.

The exceptionally healthy climate and the divine countryside of Tryavna made it a para-

# CENTRAL NORTHERN BULGARIA

mount resort as early as in 1896. Later on the first in our country children's sanatorium for chest diseases was built up here with a donation from Tsaritsa Ioana (wife of Tsar Boris III).

**Landmarks**. Tryavna has preserved its Revival appearance even today. The old part was proclaimed an **architecture reserve** with about 140 monuments of Revival architecture. The brightest evidence of it are the ensembles at **Dyado Nikola Square, P. R. Slaveikov Street, Peter Bogdanov Street, Kachaunska Mahala (quarter)**. The **Daskalov's House** (1804) is incomparable (27A, P. R. Slaveikov Street, tel.: 0677 2166), in which the **Museum of Woodcarving and Icon-Painting** is located. The two magnificent woodcarved ceilings created by Dimitur Oshanina and Ivan Bochukovetsa in 1808 after a bet made between them. **The Tryavna School of Icon-Painting Museum** (1, Breza Street, tel.: 0677 3753) contains over 160 icons. **The Slaveikov's House Museum** (1830, 50, P. R. Slaveikov, tel.: 0677 2206). **Angel Kunchev House-museum and monument** (39, Angel Kunchev Street, tel.: 0677 2398). **The House of Dyado (Grandfather) Dobri** (1834). **Popangelov's House** (from the end of the 18th century) - the oldest in the town. **Raikov's House** (1846, 1, Prof. Pencho Raikov Street). **St. Archangel Mihail Church** dating back to 1819 (tel.: 0677 3442) with its magnificent richly carved iconostasis (work of Vitan Koyuv-Junior), the unusually beautiful bishop's throne made by Priest Koyu Vitanov about 1821. The church possesses a relic - over-throne cross of palisander wood carved with 12 scenes from the Bible.

**St. Georgi Church** (1848-1852) has a remarkable iconostasis, work of the masters Dimitur Deikov and Nikola Dragoshinov (1852). In **Shkoloto (The School) Museum** (7, Captain Dyado Nikola Square, tel.: 0677 2278) there are permanent exhibitions, among which the donation of the world famous Bulgarian painter Dimitur Kazakov stands out. The exhibits in the collection "Time-measuring devices and technology of Medieval times up to the end of the 19th century" are quite original. **The Clock Tower** (1814, in the central Captain Dyado Nikola Square). **The upper bridge** (1844). **The Totyo Gubenski Art Gallery** in the ancient Kalinchev's house (45, P. R. Slaveikov) dates back to 1830. It is in possession of 500 pictures donated by the collector Gubenski. **The Ivan Popdimitrov House-Museum** (P. R.

*The Tryavna School of Icon Painting Museum*

**GUIDE BOOK**

# CENTRAL NORTHERN BULGARIA

Slaveikov Street) with pictures, donated by his grandson. There is a permanent exhibition, too - a donation by the sculptor Ivan Kolev.

Every odd year on 26th and 27th May **Slaveikov's Days** are held here including various cultural events. The town is host of the unique in the country **International Plain-Air Painting on Wood Plastics "Bet in Tryavna"**, which is held each year.

**Accommodation.** Brushlyan Hotel-Restaurant, known also as the Tourist House (above the town, 6, Panorama Street, offers 10 beds in 5 double rooms). Ralitsa Hotel-Restaurant. The Tiger Hotel (7A, Dimitur Gorov Street, offers 4 double rooms). Tryavna Hotel-Restaurant (46, Angel Kanchev Street, offers 100 beds in 4 suites and in 1-, 2- and 3-bed rooms). There are other private hotels as well.

**Tourist information** - at the Municipal Tourist Information Bureau (5350 Tryavna, 22, Angel Kunchev Street, tel./fax: 0677 2247). Planinets Tourist Association. At the hotels.

**Transport.** Bus and railway transport. There are regular bus lines of Gabrovo, Dryanovo, Plachkovtsi, Veliko Turnovo and other smaller settlements within the region. The bus station (2A, Stara Planina Street, tel.: 0677 4378) and the railway station (tel.: 0677 2510) are next to each other and they are located in the northern part of the town. Tryavna is a station on the main railway line Rousse - Gorna Oryahovitsa - Stara Zagora - Podkova.

*Wood-carved ceiling in the Daskalov's House*

**Surrounding areas.** The recreation town of **Plachkovtsi** (at the distance of 7 km to the south of Tryavna) is an important point of departure for the Tryavna Balkan Mountain (refer to the Stara Planina related chapter herein). The natural phenomena **Vikanata Skala** (The Called Rock), **Muhnatite Skali** (the Mossy Rocks) and **Stolishta** are located here. There is a tourist house, too. There is a bus and railway transport functioning between the two towns.

**The village of Bozhentsi - Architecture and Ethnographic Reserve** (at the distance of 28 km west along the road to Dryanovo; on foot it mat be reached for about 1-1.30 hours from the Sechen Kamuk Hill on the road to Gabrovo) - almost all the buildings here were built during the 18th and mainly during the 19th century in the typical of this region of Bulgaria Revival style. In Bozhentsi one is carried away into the past and finds out an unsuspected idyll and calmness among the spirituality of the old houses. There is a museum, too. Every year in the beginning of September the village hosts a plain-air "Autumn in Bozhentsi", and from June to September - an exhibition-bazaar of works of art is held there, too. It is possible to find accommodation in some of the houses - Ivan Karadimitrov's House (19th century), Maria Savekova's House (18th-19th century), Tsana Mihova's House (19th century), Ivan-tsa Boncheva's House (20th century), Parlapanov's House. Tel.: 363 through telephone orders for Bozhentsi. There is a regular bus transport from Gabrovo and Dryanovo. Patterns of ancient architecture are preserved in the near small **villages** of **Skortsi, Dobrevtsi, Kereni, Kissiitsi, Genchevtsi**. There are regular buses from Tryavna.

# CENTRAL NORTHERN BULGARIA

## DRYANOVO

The town of Dryanovo (9707 inhabitants, 270 metres above sea level) is amphitheatrically situated along the two banks of the Dryanovska River, a right tributary to the Yantra River. It 241 km and 21 km north-east from Sofia and Gabrovo, respectively, 17 km north of Tryavna, 25 km south-west of Veliko Turnovo, 32 km east of Sevlievo and 15 km west of Kilifarevo. A cradle of Bulgarian construction genius.

**History**. The settlement is mentioned as a fortress on the Strinava Plateau by Byzantine chroniclers in 1186 for the first time in relation to the Uprising led by the members of Assen dynasty (1185-1187). It is mentioned under the name of *Diranav (Diranava)* in a Turkish register of 1430, and today's name of Dryanovo is found in a book of the Zograf Monastery of 1500. The name originated from the cornel-tree commonly found here.

The settlement reached its greatest prosperity (since 1883 it has already been proclaimed as a town) during the Revival Period. Dryanovo became famous for its masters - builders and wood-carvers. The most outstanding representative of Bulgarian construction genius during the Revival period - the self-educated architect and masterbuilder Nikola Ivanov Fichev (Master Kolyu Ficheto, 1800-1880) was born here.

The inhabitants of Dryanovo took an active part in the national liberation movement. There were citizens of Dryanovo in Velcho's Conspiracy, in Georgi Rakovski's legion in Belgrade, in the detachments of armed volunteers of Stefan Karadzha and Hadzhi Dimitar, of Hristo Botev. In 1875 Georgi Izmirliev established a revolutionary committee here. During the fateful spring of 1876, in spite of the readiness of the citizens of Dryanovo for struggle, due to the lack of an eminent leader, no uprising burst out here. The settlement, however, gave revolutionaries for the detachment of armed volunteers of Pop Hariton and Bacho Kiro, which heroically fought for more than a week in the Dryanovo Monastery under siege. During the Russian-Turkish War of Liberation 88 citizens of Dryanovo fought in the Bulgarian volunteer forces.

Nowadays the town and its surrounding areas develop more and more as a center of internal and foreign tourism. Dryanovo is the birthplace of the writers Racho Stoyanov, Atanas Smirnov and of the composer Todor Popov. In relation to its healthy climate and high average life expectancy the town is often referred to as the "town of centenarians".

**Landmarks**: The **Kolyu Ficheto Museum** (in the eastern part of the town, Kolyu Ficheto Square, tel.: 0676 2079, also known as a museum of the Bulgarian Revival Architecture), in front of which the impressive bronze figure of the self-educated genius rises, work of the sculptor Boris Gondov. The home of the Master was not preserved. **Lafchiev's House** (the eastern part of the town, Kolyu Ficheto Square) of 1840, is a genuine masterpiece of the Revival Architecture. Even a nail was not used in its construction. **The Holy Trinity Church** is remarkable for its magnificent wood-carved ceilings. **The St. Nikola Church,** built up by Kolyu Ficheto, is located in the central part of the town. Elevated on the Bryasta ridge (the Elm-tree), at its time it dominated over the whole town. Interesting buildings of the old-time **Dryanovska charshiya (marketplace)**, as well as the restored **houses - Ikonomov's, Afazov's, Romounov's, Taninov's** in the **Boiuv Yaz** area are preserved. **The Clock Tower** (the old one was destroyed in 1944) and **the Art Gallery** (Shipka Street) are located in the centre of Dryanovo, near to each other.

**Accommodation.** Momini Skali Hotel Complex (in the south-eastern end of the town, Apriltsi Residential Area, Block No. 12). Milkana Hotel Complex (in the central part, near the river). **Tourist information** - at the hotels or at the Bacho Kiro Tourist Association (9, Stefan Stambolov, tel.: 0676 2332).

**Transport**. Bus and railway transport connect

# CENTRAL NORTHERN BULGARIA

the town with the country. There are regular bus lines to Gabrovo, Veliko Turnovo, Tryavna and other smaller settlements within the region. The bus station (1, Pop Hariton Street, tel.: 0676 2045) and the railway station (8, Zheleznicharska Street, tel.: 0676 3209) are located one opposite the other, on the two banks of the river (the bus station is on the left bank and the railway station is on the right bank of the river), in the southern part of the town. Dryanovo is a station of the main railway line Rousse - Gorna Oryahovitsa - Stara Zagora - Podkova.

**Surrounding areas**. **St. Archangel Mihail Dryanovo Monastery** (at the distance of 4 km south-west of Dryanovo, tel.: 0676 2389, 4058), huddled in the gorge of the river of the same name, is one of the symbols of the insubordinate Bulgarian spirit, a glorious and martyr's page, inscribed in blood into Bulgarian history. It was this monastery which 220 revolutionaries led by Pop Hariton, Daskal (teacher) Bacho Kiro and Lieutenant Peter Parmakov turned into an unassailable fortress for the whole of 9 days and nights during the spring of 1876. Thousands of bashibozouks (Turkish army of volunteers) and regular troops swooped down over the handful of defenders. An unfortunate hazard exploded the gunpowder arsenal and made Voivoda (Leader) Pop Hariton blind, but the resistance became even more fierce and more desperate... The rebels answered the proposal of Fazlu Pasha to surrender with the letter written by Bacho Kiro: *"Pasha, we want the government to acknowledge our rights as a people and until this is done, we shall not surrender to your tormentor's hands as long as we are alive - we have made our decision to die and we shall keep our oath! And you shall bear responsibility for your tyrannies before Europe ..."* After the Turkish artillery destroyed the monastery walls, it was solely the night which helped the survived rebels but it did not succeed in saving them from martyr's death. Only the captured Bacho Kiro was brought to trial but he behaved with dignity and was hanged on the gallows, paying for the love for the Motherland with his life.

Dryanovo Monastery dates back to the time of reign of the Assen dynasty, the 12th century. It was built in relation to the celebration of the victory of Bulgaria over Byzantium in 1187. It

*The church at the Dryanovo Monastery*

# CENTRAL NORTHERN BULGARIA

was twice destroyed and then rebuilt. After the dramatic events in May 1876 solely the charred stonewalls of the church and a part of the stone walls protruded from it. It was rebuilt but the holes from the shells of Fazlu Pasha were left in the stonewalls and the museum collection tells us about the epic battles. Several old icons painted by Gabrovo masters are preserved, too. There is a regular bus transport from Dryanovo to the monastery.

**The Bacho Kiro Cave** is located near the monastery, known also as the Dryanovo Cave. It was opened in 1890 and since 1964 it has been electrified. For as long as 1200 m a fairytale underground world reveals itself to the eyes of the visitor. The formations follow one after another - "Bacho Kiro's Throne", "the Dwarfs", "The Sleeping Princess". The "Throne Hall", the "Reception Hall", the "Haidouti Meeting-Ground", the "Fountain", the "Sacrificial Altar" evoke the admiration of the visitors. Remnants of people who lived during the Paleolithic Age were found in the cave.

The Bacho Kiro Chalet is situated on the other side of the river, opposite the monastery (tel.: 0676 2106, offering 85 beds in rooms with 2, 3, 5 and more beds, a restaurant, a coffee bar). The Strinava Camping is situated at a 10-minute walk from the chalet (it has 20 two-bed bungalows and a restaurant). The camping site is a seasonal one. The Dryanovo Monstery Hotel is located in this area as well.

Extremely interesting **remains of an ancient customs house** and a market-place of the Roman town of the 2nd century **Discodura-terra** - located on the ancient road from Nove and Nikopolis ad Istrum to Vereya were found at the distance of about some 10 km north-east of the town, near the village of Gostilitsa. There is a regular bus transport to this place of interest.

The architectural atmosphere of the Revival period is preserved in the nearby-situated **villages of Kalomen** and **Kerenite**, which in combination with the beautiful surrounding countryside is appealing to tourists.

## ELENA

The town of Elena (7471 inhabitants, 300 metres above sea level) is situated in the mountain valley of the same name, in the northern approaches of the Elena-Tvurditsa Balkan Mountain (Central Stara Planina). It is situated at the distance of 280 km north-east of Sofia, 40 km, 36 km and 33 km south-east of Veliko Turnovo, Gorna Oryahovitsa and Lyaskovets, respectively, 18 km south of Zlataritsa, 28 km south-east of Kilifarevo, 40 km north of Tvurditsa and 79 km north-west of Sliven. A Revival town.

**History.** The region of the today's town was inhabited even during the late Neolite. There was a settlement there before the Ottoman Rule, but it was mentioned as a deserted village with the names of *Mezra Istromena* (Sturmena) and *Iliyana* (Elyana) in a document of 1430. It was known under the name of *Gelendzhik,* too. At the end of the century it was already registered as a settlement guarding the passes of Stara Planina.

By the 16th century Elena has already grown as a village. It reached prosperity during the 18th and the 19th centuries as a craftsmanship, trade, Revival and revolutionary centre (in 1860 it was proclaimed a town). Crafts were developed - manufacturing of aba (coarse homespun woolleen cloth and upper men's garment made of it), ironmongers, production of ropes, silkworm breeding and others. In 1854 there were 1000 houses in Elena, a result of an active construction of public and civil buildings.

In 1843 the citizen of Elena Ivan N. Momchilov (Russian graduate) established the first Teacher Training School (called "Daskalolivnitsa" - moulding of teachers, by Petko R. Slaveikov), preserved up to date. In 1874 Doino Gramatik made the Elena transcript of Paisii's History. The citizens of Elena took part in Velcho's Conspiracy (1835), in Captain Dyado Nikola's Uprising (1856), in the Turnovo

# CENTRAL NORTHERN BULGARIA

Uprising (1862). Georgi Sava Rakovski stayed in the town several times, and the Apostle Vassil Levski came twice (1868 and 1871), and during his second stay he organised the Elena secret revolutionary committee. During the Russian-Turkish War of Liberation the town and its surrounding areas were an arena of fierce battles. Elena was destroyed by fire, but fortunately not completely.

The town developed as an architecture and historical town-museum whose future was in the development of tourism most of all. It is the birthplace of the plotter Hadzhi Y. Bradata (the Beard), of the great church activist Ilarion Makariopolski, of the writers Stoyan Mihailovski and Petko Yu. Todorov, of Sava Katrafilov, of the Kurshevski Brothers.

**Landmarks.** The town has preserved its ancient Revival appearance up to date. **130 buildings** of that time are preserved, grouped in several ensembles. Most renowned are the **Daskalolivnitsata** (first teachers' training school in the country) of 1844 in which **the Museum of the Town of Elena** is located. **Museum of Revival and the Struggles for National Liberation. The clock tower** of 1812, which counts every hour still today. **The Ilarion Makariopolski Museum** in his home (the house itself being a valuable architecture monument of 1710-1715). **Popnikolov's house** of 1830 is perhaps the most beautiful building of the Revival Period in the town almost completely made of wood. The five **Razsukanov's houses** date back to the end of the 18th century and the beginning of the 19th century. The two old **churches** - **St. Nikola Church** (1804) and **Assumption Church** (1837) are the work of builders from the village of Bolertsi and are distinguished by the rich wood-carvings in style of the Tryavna School, the second evoking respect by its big dimensions. They are located next to each other. **The Art Gallery** is located in the home of the writer **Petko Yu. Todorov and** exhibits a priceless collection of icons and modern works of art. The **five Hadzhi Dimitrov's houses**, the **Poryazov's**

*The monument to Stoyan Mihailovski*

house. There is special charm and romance in the **ensemble of houses along S. Petkov Street, S. Yovchev Street and Hadzhi Sergii Street.**

**Accommodation**: The Elena Hotel Complex (1, Hristo Stanev). Dr. Momchilov Tourist Hostel (in the centre of the town, 3, Stoyan Mihailovski Street). It has 40 beds in rooms with 4, 5 and more beds.

**Tourist information** - at the Tourist Information Centre, 5070 Elena (located in the building of the Elena Hotel Complex, 1, Hristo Stanchev Str., tel.: 06151 3732, 3632, e-mail: elena_hotel@abv.bg). Choumerna Tourist Association (located next to the tourist hostel, tel.: 06151 4191, 4091).

**Transport**. Bus and railway transport connect the town of Elena with the country. There are regular bus lines to Veliko Turnovo, Gorna Oryahovitsa, Lyaskovets, Zlataritsa, Tvurditsa, Sliven, Stara Zagora and other smaller settle-

# CENTRAL NORTHERN BULGARIA

ments within the region. The town is the last station of the railway line Gorna Oryahovitsa - Elena, through which it is connected to the national railway network. At present there are trains functioning only during the summer season on holidays.

**Surrounding areas**. **The St. Nikola Kapinovo Monastery** (at the distance of about 25 km to the north-west of Elena) was founded in 1272 during the reign of Tsar Konstantin Assen-Tih. It is one of the most impressive monasteries in Bulgaria. It was a religious, cultural and revolutionary centre during the Ottoman Rule. In 1630 it was devastated by fire and in 1793 by kurdzhalii (Turkish brigands) after which it was rebuilt as a fortress and the monks themselves took the defence of the Monastery in their own hands. At the end of the 18th century Father Superior of the Monastery was Sofronii Vrachhanski who brought here the copy of "Slavonic-Bulgarian History" of Paisii Hilendarski made by himself. "The History" was read and copied behind the thick monastery walls, aimed at being spread throughout Bulgarian land and enlightening souls and hearts. In 1835 the plotters of Velcho's Conspiracy found shelter in the monastery. The rebellious Captain Mamarchev repeatedly visited the monastery. The monks planned an uprising with Hadzhi Stavri from the Lyaskovski Monastery but they did not succeed. The restored in 1835 monastery church, work of masters from Dryanovo is of special interest to visitors. The Composition "Doomsday" covering the whole external wall of the church is distinguished for its high artistic value. Yoan Popovich from Razgrad painted it in 1840.

There is a bus line from Veliko Turnovo to the Monastery and the nearest railway station is Debelets (at the distance of 15 km north-west). There is an entire tourist settlement located amongst picturesque surroundings nearby the Monastery.

**St. Iliya Plachkovo Monastery** (near the village of the same name, at the distance of 2-3 km north-west of the Kapinovski Monastery) was founded during the reign of Tsar Ivan Assen II, but it was destroyed when the country succumbed to Ottoman Rule (only ruins called "Balaklii" remained from it, located not far from the today's monastery). It was ruined five times and it was rebuilt for the last time in 1845, after the pogrom, which followed Velcho's Conspiracy with the active participation of Kolyu Ficheto. It is namely in relation to the Conspiracy that the greatest glory of this ecclesiastical cloister was achieved. In 1835 the serious merchant from Turnovo Velcho Atanasov - Dzhamdzhiyata (the Glazier), Captain Georgi Mamarchev, Hadzhi Y. Bradata (the Beard) and several other plotters planned an uprising against the Ottomans in the region of Turnovo. A traitor brought the Turks to the monastery (the fundamental base of the plotters). The greater part of the plotters were slaughtered, the uprising was crushed, and the monastery became subject to plunder, destruction and fire. The holy place was often visited by Sofronii Vrachanski and Neofit Bozveli. In 1856 Master Kolyu Ficheto built up the high monastery belfry, the church and probably - the residential part of the building. There are several extraordinary icons in the monastery, the most valuable of them "Christ Great Prelate" (work of Zakhari Zograf (the Icon-painter) is a masterpiece of art. The transport connections are the same in relation to the Kapinovski Monastery.

**Yovkovtsi Dam** spreads its waters at the distance of 4-5 km west of Elena - a perfect site for recreation, water motor sports, sunbathing, water tourism and fishing. There is tourist infrastructure, too. The regular buses running into the direction of the above-mentioned monasteries, Kilifarevo and Debelets can be used. Elena is a **point of departure** for hiking tours around the Elena - Tvurditsa Balkan Mountain (refer to the Stara Planina related section herein).

# CENTRAL NORTHERN BULGARIA

## VELIKO TURNOVO

The town of Veliko Turnovo (66 998 inhabitants, 210 metres above sea level) is regally situated along the historical hills of Sveta Gora, Tsarevets and Trapezitsa, on the two banks of the Yantra River, cutting a peculiar gorge through Turnovo Hills. It is situated 240 km north-east of Sofia, 86 km east of Lovech, 46 km north-east of Gabrovo, 50 km east of Sevlievo, 43 km south-east of Pavlikeni, 42 km north-east of Tryavna, 106 km south-west of Rousse, 7 km south-west of Gorna Oryahovitsa and 100 km south-west of Targovishte. The old metropolis of Bulgaria. A regional administrative centre.

**History**. Veliko Turnovo is the town with the most glorious historical past in Bulgaria. It is a symbol of Bulgarian statehood and a source of national pride for every Bulgarian. Each little place in it is history.

The earliest traces were found on the Trapezitsa Hill (dating back to first half of the 3$^{rd}$ millennium BC). Remnants on Tsarevets Hill date back to the end of the Bronze Era (13$^{th}$ century BC). This oldest settlement was inhabited by Thracians (the tribes of Uzdicenses and Crobises) and existed by the end of the Iron Era. Its prosperity is related to 6$^{th}$ century BC - till 1$^{st}$ century AC. Its traces in the first centuries of the Roman Rule are lost on our lands (at the beginning of the new era).

The next layer of Tsarevets is early Byzantine, from the 5$^{th}$ to the first half of the 7$^{th}$ century when there was a fortified town on the hill (one of the supporting points of Byzantium in the northern part of the Balkan Peninsula), which withstood for 3 centuries. A big Slavonic-Bulgarian settlement of the 8$^{th}$ to 10$^{th}$ century was founded on the ruins of this town. At the end of the 10$^{th}$ century the hill was already densely populated and in the 12$^{th}$ century it was a fortified town and a significant economic centre.

The origin of the name is related to the Slavonic word "tern" or "trun" (thorn) and during the years it developed into *Ternov, Trunov, Turnov, Turnovgrad, Turnovo* and *Veliko Turnovo*, being called "Veliko" (Great) in relation to its size, beauty and grandeur. In 1187 the Uprising of Assen and Peter was successfully completed, the Byzantine Rule was thrown off and Turnovgrad became the capital (the third capital in the history of Bulgaria) of the restored Bulgarian Kingdom. The following two centuries are "golden" in the history of the town.

The Tsar's Palace and the Bulgarian Patriarchy were situated on the Tsarevets Hill and the houses of the boyars and the senior priesthood as well as a lot of churches were situated on Trapezitsa Hill. Assenova Mahala (quarter), located between the above mentioned hills, by the Yantra River, was inhabited by craftsmen. The district of foreign merchants (Franks) was to the south-east of the Baldwin Tower. Thick fortified walls of the "internal town" protected Tsarevets and Trapezitsa. The other two quarter also had fortified protection and formed the "external town". Solely the dwellings of the destitute among the non-privileged people remained outside the fortifications at the foothill of the Momina Krepost (Maiden's Fortress) Hill, in the immediate proximity of the Yantra River. During the 13$^{th}$ and 14$^{th}$ centuries the capital of Bulgaria was a big political, economic, trade and cultural centre in Europe. The Bulgarian State reached the heights of its development during this period. Along with Byzantium it was the first power on the Old Continent. Magnificent palaces, monasteries, churches, fortifications, bridges, big houses were built here. The Turnovo School of Painting and the Turnovo Literary School, whose founders, organisers and most prominent representatives are Patriarch Evtimii and Teodosi Turnovski (of Turnovo), developed and carried out their versatile activities here. All the prosperity and spiritual upsurge was discontinued on 17$^{th}$ July 1393, when after a 3-month siege Veliko Turnovo, and gradually the whole of Bulgaria succumbed under Ottoman Rule.

# CENTRAL NORTHERN BULGARIA

## Veliko Turnovo

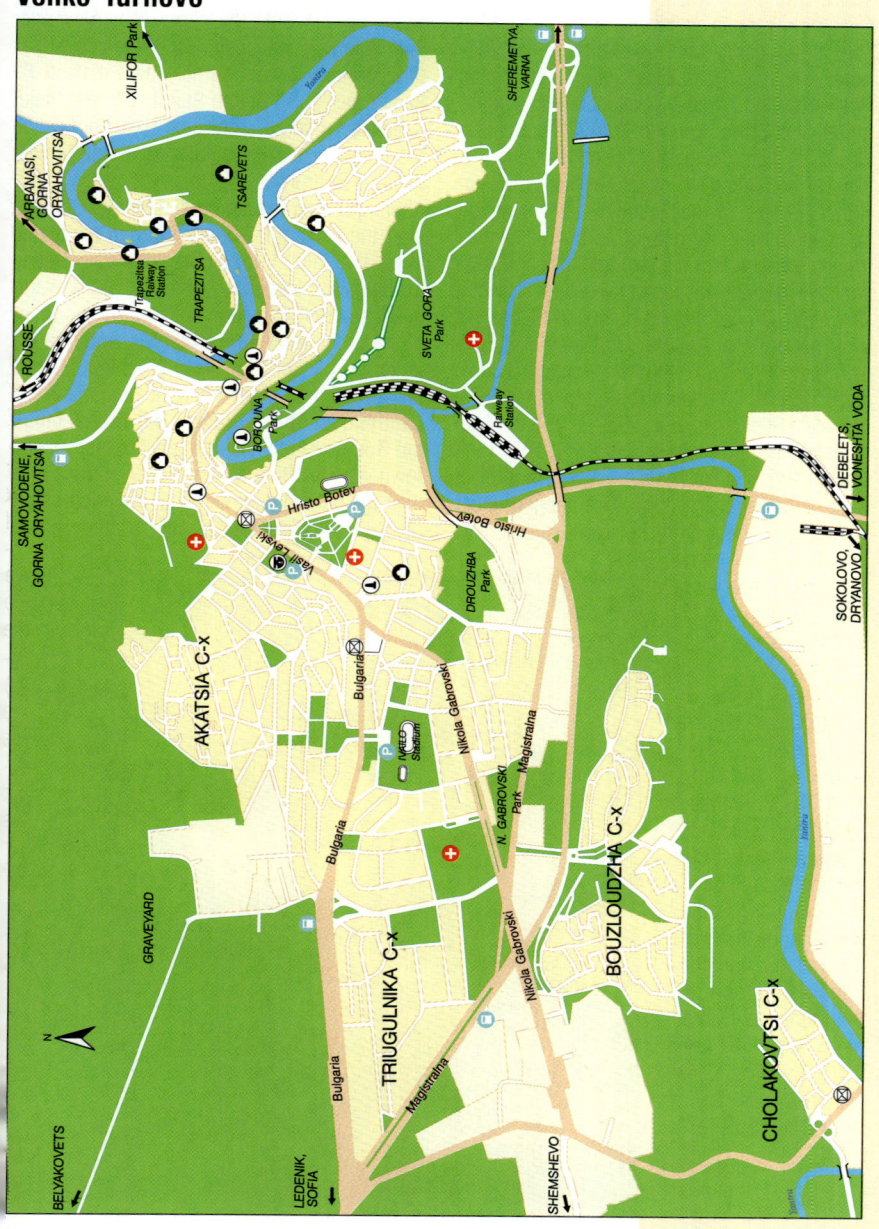

# CENTRAL NORTHERN BULGARIA

The Metropolitan town was in ashes. Centuries were to pass before the town was able to recuperate and experience a new economic, cultural and political upsurge during the Revival period. Crafts developed, trade flourished, beautiful houses, public buildings, churches (with the greatest contribution in that respect belonging to the unsurpassed Master Kolyu Ficheto), the aspiration for enlightenment and national self-awareness started to find their implementation and the struggle for ecclesiastical and national independence gained strength. The population of the old Bulgarian Metropolis took part in the Turnovo Uprisings of 1598, 1686 and 1700, in Velcho Conspiracy (1835), in the Uprising of Captain Dyado Nikola (1856), in Hadzhi Stavrev' Revolt (1862) and in the April Uprising of the rebellious year of 1876. Then Bacho Kiro, Tsanko Dyustabanov and a lot of other fighters for freedom were hanged under the gallows erected in the town square. The Apostle Levski came here more than once (the last time in 1872, unfortunately enchained).

On 7th July 1877 Veliko Turnovo was free again. From 10th February to 16th April 1879 the Constituent Assembly, which developed the First Bulgarian Constitution - the Turnovo Constitution, one of the most democratic constitutions in Europe for that time, convened here. On 17th April 1879 the first Great National Assembly of liberated Bulgaria convened in Veliko Turnovo to elect a head of state. On 27th July the same year Alexander Battenberg was elected as Bulgaria's knyaz (first prince). It was namely here that on 6th September 1885 Stefan Stambolov and Petko Karavelov made the decision to acknowledge the union of the Principality of Bulgaria with Eastern Roumelia.

Although Sofia became the capital of Bulgaria after the Liberation, Veliko Turnovo continued to be a sanctuary for all Bulgarians, a bastion of Bulgarian national spirit and self-awareness. It is the birthplace of Petko R. Slaveikov, of the great actor Konstantin Kissimov, of the writers Emiliyan Stanev and Dimitur Mantov and of a lot of other eminent Bulgarians.

**Landmarks**. **The Tsarevets Hill Archaeological Reserve** in the eastern part of the modern town - **the fortified wall,** which in combination with the natural endowments, provided safety of the institutions which were of the greatest

*The Metropolitan town of Veliko Turnovo*

# CENTRAL NORTHERN BULGARIA

importance for the Bulgarian state, is restored. The so-called **Baldwin Tower** in which Tsar Kaloyan confined the Latin Emperor Baldwin after his capture during the defeat of the Crusaders in 1205 near Odrin rises in its most southern part. One of the most interesting sites is **the Palace of Bulgarian Tsars** representing an independent fortress situated on the area of 4872 square metres. The most impressive premises in the Palace were **the Throne Hall** and **St. Petka Palace Church.** The Palace whose building was expanded several times during the 13th and the 14th century, was completely destroyed after the town fell under Ottoman Rule.

The second largest architectural complex of Tsarevets is **Bulgarian Patriarchy.** The Patriarchal complex rose at the highest place, above the Tsar's Palace. It occupied an area of about 3000 square metres, as an individual fortress in the shape of an irregular polygon. The **Lord's Ascension Patriarchal Church** with a belfry tower - a phenomenon scarcely met in the ecclesiastical architecture on the Balkans rose in the centre of the yard. The excavated foundations of residential buildings and churches along the steep slope of Tsarevets, east and south of the Patriarchy, forming a little quarter of the Medieval town are of a special interest. A big boyar settlement north of Tsarevets was studied, too which with its architectural pattern is the prototype of Bulgarian Revival house. One of the most valuable Medieval Bulgarian monuments - **Forty Holy Martyrs Church** is situated at the western foothill of Tsarevets Hill, near the river. It was erected by order of Tsar Ivan Assen II in honour of his great victory over the Byzantines at Klokotnitsa on 22nd March 1230. During the 18th century the Turks turned it into a mosque but a part of the valuables contained in it are still preserved. Thus, for instance, the three preserved stone columns - Assen's, Omourtag's and the one from the Rodosto Fortress are of an exceptional importance to historical science and prove the succession in the Bulgarian statehood.

Tsar Kaloyan's grave and his golden 61-gram ring-seal were found during excavation works in the 1970-ies. **The St. St. Peter and Pavel Church** rises at the foothill of the northern slope of Tsarevets - the only better preserved church from Medieval Turnovgrad. After the town succumbed to Ottoman Rule the Bulgarian Patriarchy and the whole Patriarchal library was moved to it. The last Bulgarian Patriarch - Evtimii served in this church for about two years before being sent in exile.

Tsarevets Hill finishes in its north-eastern end with a strongly protruding over the Yantra River Lobna Skala (Rock at the place of death) from which traitors were thrown down.

**The Trapezitsa Hill** is related to the earliest manifestations of the Bulgarian rulers in the 12th century. In 1185 the **St. Dimitur Solunski Church** was built in the outskirts of the hill and during its consecration the brothers Assen and Peter proclaimed the Uprising against the Byzantine invaders. It was a royal church up to the year 1230 and Assen, Peter and Kaloyan were crowned in it. Here on 7th November 1204 Archbishop Vassilii was promoted to the rank of Patriarch of Bulgarian church. The church was shown mercy after Turnovo fell under Ottoman Rule. A lot of fighters for spiritual and national liberation were buried in its courtyard during the 19th century. The church was almost completely destroyed during the second half of the 19th century. The **St. Georgi Church** is also situated in the eastern outskirts of the hill. It was erected in 1612 in the place of a destroyed Medieval Bulgarian church. The most interesting things in it are the mural paintings whose unknown author had shown himself as a follower of the best traditions of Turnovo School of Painting. A lot of dwellings of boyars were found during excavation works and there was a little family church in nearly each of them.

In 1195 by an order of Tsar Ivan Assen I, the relics of St. Ivan Rilski were rested in a monastery located on the hill. The relics of the

# CENTRAL NORTHERN BULGARIA

St. Gavrail Lesnovski were moved by Tsar Kaloyan to the **Holy Apostles Church** located on the same hill.

The quarter on the two sides of the river between Tsarevets and Trapezitsa Hills where the 4 valuable historical churches are located (St. Dimitur Solunski, St. Georgi, Forty Holy Martyrs and St. St. Peter and Pavel) is called **Assenova Mahala** (Assen's quarter) and constituted the fundamental part of the so-called "external town". It originated during the reign of Tsar Ivan Assen II (1218-1241).

**Sveta Gora** is the third hill of the Metropolis Turnovgrad. It rises south of Tsarevets and was a cultural and spiritual centre of the Bulgarian State in Medieval times. There were a lot of churches and monasteries here. The Turnovo Literary School and the Turnovo School of Painting developed a versatile and vivacious activity in the biggest of the monasteries - **Holy Virgin Odigitriya**. The Titans of the Medieval Bulgarian spirit - Patriarch Evtimii and Teodosii Turnovski did creative works here. Today the buildings of St. St. Cyril and Methodius Veliko Turnovo University rise on the place of the monastery.

After Veliko Turnovo fell under Ottoman Rule the town started to expand to the west little by little. Predominantly Turks settled down along the hills of Tsarevets and Trapezitsa and predominantly Bulgarians settled down in the new quarters. Construction of a lot of new private and public buildings commenced with the growing economic prosperity of the Bulgarians during the Revival period, a great part of which still adorn the Old town (between the hills of Trapezitsa and Sveta Gora, separated from them through the meanders of the Yantra River).

The self-educated Bulgarian architect and builder Master Kolyu Ficheto greatly contributed in this respect. He created several of them - **the Konak** (police station) (1872), related to a lot of historical events (to the interrogation of the captured Levski in 1872, to the Turkish court trial of the revolutionaries Bacho Kiro, Tsanko Dyustabanov, Georgi Izmirliev, Ivan Semerdzhiev, Ekim Tsankov and others in 1876, to the welcoming of the Russian liberators in 1877, to the Constituent Assembly in 1879 and the First Great National Assembly convened during the same year, to the decision for the acknowledgement of the Union in 1885). **The Inn of Hadzhi Nikola** (1858), one of the most interesting architectural monuments of the Revival period. The **St. St. Cyril and Methodius Church** (1861), **St. Spas (Ascension) Church** (1862-1863) and **St. Konstantin and St. Elena Church** (1872), as well as the **House with the Monkey** (1849, in the centre of the town), taking its name form the sitting monkey placed above the ground floor with an inscribed sign plate under it. **The Museum of the Second Bulgarian State** is located near the Konak. **The home of Petko R. Slaveikov**. The **St. Nikola Church** (1836) during whose construction Kolyu Ficheto worked as an apprentice. **The prison-museum** (1862) where a lot of freedom-loving Bulgarians were sent, among them Levski, Philip Totyu, Stefan Karadzha, Bacho Kiro. **The house of Kokona (Grand Lady) Anastassia** (of the end of the 18th century). **Stambolov's Inn** (was owned by Stefan Stambolov's family, the rebellious Captain Dyado Nikola worked here, too). **The monument to Velcho Conspiracy** in the square of the same name. **Gourko Street** with a lot of Revival Period houses in it adds romantic atmosphere to the Old Town. Built steeply above the river, it seems as if they have perched one over the other. One of the most beautiful buildings in this street is **Sarafkin's House** (Money-changer's) (1861).

**The Art Gallery** (tel.: 062 38951) and **the monuments to the Assens' Dynasty** in front of it are located on a picturesque peninsula (Borouna), rising above the Yantra River. There are a lot of other interesting old houses, public buildings, squares, dozens of monuments, too. It is difficult to describe Veliko Turnovo, it is worth seeing with one's own eyes!

**Accommodation.** The Veliko Turnovo Interhotel (2, Alexander Penchev Street). The Yantra Hotel

# CENTRAL NORTHERN BULGARIA

(3-star, 2, Opulchenska Street). The Sveta Gora Motel (in the south-eastern end of the Sveta Gora Park). Orbita Hotel (downtown, offers 50 beds, 'tourist' category). Trapezitsa Tourist House (in the centre of the town, 79, Stambolov Street, it has 73 beds in 2 suites and in 2-, 3- and 4-bed rooms). Momina Krepost Tourist House (Maiden's Fortress) (in the Ksilofor Area, east of town, near the last stop of town bus lines No. 7 and No. 11 and 2-km further walk, it offers 178 beds in 3 suites and in 2-, 4- and 5-bed rooms). There are cosy and typical Bulgarain public catering and entertainment establishments offering traditional Bulgarian cuisine in Veliko Turnovo. One of them is the tavern in the House with the Monkey, working hours: 11.00 a.m. - 12.00 p.m., 14, Vustannicheska Street).

**Tourist information** - at the Tourist Information Centre - 5000 Veliko Turnovo (13A, Hristo Botev Str., P. O. Box 5000, at the Veliko Turnovo Hotel, tel.: 062 22148, e-mail: dtour@vali.bg), at the Council on Tourism, 5000 Veliko Turnovo (at Veliko Turnovo Hotel, tel.: 062 30571, 30353, 528057); at Trapezitsa Tourist Association (79, Stefan Stambolov Street, tel.: 062 21593, 35185); at the hotels and in the tourist houses.

**Transport**. The town of the old Metropolis is connected with bus and a railway transport. There are regular bus lines to Sofia, Gabrovo, Rousse, Lovech, Kazanlak, Tryavna, Dryanovo, Sevlievo, Gorna Oryahovitsa (a town bus line), Lyaskovets (a town bus line), Pavlikeni, Turgovishte, Popovo, Byala and other smaller settlements within the region. The bus station (86, Nikola Gabrovski Street, tel.: 062 40908) and the central railway station (tel.: 062 620065) are far from each other, the first being located in the western end of the town, and the second - in the southern end of the town immediately under the Sveta Gora Hill. There is another railway station - Trapezitsa, north-west under the hill of the same name. Both stations are at the main railway line Rousse - Gorna Oryahovitsa - Stara Zagora - Podkova. Moreover, the railway station of Gorna Oryahovitsa (the biggest railway junction of Northern Bulgaria) is located at the distance of only several kilometres northeast of Veliko Turnovo. At the railway station there is a taxi service for Veliko Turnovo passing through the village of Arbanassi. The following travel agencies are located there, too: Group (for bus tickets in the country and abroad, 1, Al. Stamboliiski Street, tel.: 062 628292), Rila Railway Bureau (13A, Hr. Botev Street, tel.:

*On the Tsarevets Hill*

GUIDE BOOK 255

# CENTRAL NORTHERN BULGARIA

062 22130), Rila International Travel Bureau (13A, Hr. Botev Street, tel.: 062 22042), Inter-tour (an agent of Balkan Airlines, 13A, Hr. Botev Street, tel.: 062 21545) and Sema Express (airlines ticket bureau, 25, Nikola Gabrovski Blvd., tel.: 062 621586). The town has a regular town bus and trolley-bus transport.

**Surrounding areas. The village of Arbanassi - Architecture and Historical Reserve** located at the distance of 4 km north-east of Veliko Turnovo. Its flourishing as a trade and craftsmen's centre was during the 16$^{th}$ to the 18$^{th}$ century when the monumental houses and churches with a rich interior decoration, woodcarvings and mural paintings were built. These are unique monuments of our architectural and artistic heritage. The Arbanassi type of houses may be defined as dwellings - fortresses. The most interesting are **Konstantsaliev's House** (housing a museum collection), **Hadzhiiliev's House, Kandilarov's House, Nikolchokostov's House** and others. The following churches deserve special attention, too - Birth of the Holly Son Church, Archangel Michail and Gavrail Church, St. Atanas Church, St. Georgi Church. Arbanassi is the birthplace of Ilarion Dragostinov, chief apostle of the Sliven Revolutionary District in the April Uprising. One can find accommodation here at: the Arbanassi Palace Hotel, the Arbus Hotel & Tavern, the Raiski Kut (Paradise Corner) Hotel & Tavern, Konstantin and Elena Hotel Complex, Bolyarska Kushta (Boyar's House) Hotel & Tavern and others. There is a taxi service running every 30 to 40 minutes between Gorna Oryahovitsa and Veliko Turnovo passing by the road fork for the village (1 km).

**The Preobrazhenski Monastery** is situated at the distance of 6 to 7 km north of Veliko Turnovo, under the inaccessible sheer rocks of the left bank of the Yantra River. It flourished during the 14$^{th}$ century. It was repeatedly ruined and destroyed by fire during the years of Ottoman Rule and rebuilt in the first half of the 19$^{th}$ century. One of the most remarkable

*The House with the Monkey*

monuments of Bulgarian Revival Period architecture and iconography. It includes 4 churches. The Central **Transfiguration Church** was started to be built by Master Dimitur Sofialiyata (of Sofia) who was hanged because of his participation in Velcho's Conspiracy (1835). Master Kolyu Ficheto completed it. It was painted by Zakhari Zograph (the Icon-painter), two of his compositions being of a particularly high artistic value - "Doomsday" (on the whole eastern wall of the nartnex) and the "Wheel of Life" (on the southern outside wall). The wood-carved iconostasis and the iconostasis icons, work of masters form Tryavna are remarkable, too. The masterpiece of the painter of the Revival Period Stanislav Dospevski - "St. Apostle Andrei" is exhibited here as well.

The next **Annunciation Church** was built by the Master Kolyu Ficheto and Stanislav Dospevski painted the icons. Dimitar Sofialiyata built the little underground St. Andrei Church, and the

# CENTRAL NORTHERN BULGARIA

icons were painted by the unique icon-painter and wood-carver Papa Vitan, one of the most eminent representatives of the Tryavna School of Art. The last of the monastery churches is **Lazar's Ascension Church** (of 1891), whose icons were painted by the citizen of Tryavna Ivancho Kunchev. A bell tower with a clock built by Kolyu Ficheto (1860) rises in the courtyard of the monastery. The largest bell was a gift by the Russian Emperor Alexander II for the services of the monastery as a Russian military hospital during the Russian-Turkish War of Liberation. Matei Preobrazhnski - Mitkaloto (the Wanderer), Pop (Priest) Hariton, Father Zotik lived and worked in the monastery. Vassil Levski, Angel Kunchev, Philip Totyu, Stefan Stambolov, Georgi Izmirliev found a safe shelter here. There is a regular bus to the motorway and it is about a 30 to 40-minute walk from there.

**One of the oldest monasteries around Veliko Turnovo - Sveta Troitsa Monastery (The Holy Trinity)** is located on the right bank of Yantra River opposite the Preobrazhenski Monastery. It originated about the year 1070. It was called Assen's, Shishman's (after Bulgarian tsars), Patriarch's Monastery. It is related to the literary activities of Monk Evtimii up to his election as a Patriarch in 1375. Having returned back to Bulgaria from the Sveta Gora Monasteries on Athos in 1371, he settled down here and created the renowned literary school known as the Turnovo School. This School developed the great spelling reform and established the language standards. Master Kolyu Ficheto erected the present Monastery Church in 1847.

It can be reached by bus and on foot from Veliko Turnovo and from the village of Samovodene or along a picturesque track under the rocks of the Yantra River in about a 2-hours' walk from the town.

Teodosii Turnovski founded **The Birth of the Blessed Virgin Kilifarevo Monastery** (at the distance of 17 km south of Veliko Turnovo and 4 km south-east from the town of Kilifarevo) in 1348-1350 with the generous help of Tsar Ivan Alexander. Solid stone walls surrounded it. It was a centre of Hesychasm (Medieval religious doctrine teaching that unity with God could be achieved through quietness and solitude) and a centre of education and literature. Over 400 disciples of the first teacher Teodosii Turnovski were taught there. It was repeatedly ruined and destroyed by fire during the years of Ottoman Rule. Its last restoration commenced about the year 1830, Master Kolyu Ficheto taking an active participation. Under his hands were erected the residential part of the building and **St. Dimitur Church** (1844). The wood-carved iconostasis of the church is a genuine piece of art, joint work of Kolyu Ficheto and S. Marangozina.

There is regular bus transport from Veliko Turnovo and the nearest railway station is Debelets (at the distance of 10 km north).

**The Lyaskovets Monastery** is at the distance of 6 km north-west of the Old Metropolis town

*The resideitial part of Kilifarevo Monastery*

# CENTRAL NORTHERN BULGARIA

and at the distance of 3 km south-west of the town of Lyaskovets. It is situated on a high inaccessible rock on the Arbanassi Hill. Its remote history is based on legends and traditions. It is related most of all to the struggles for national liberation - uprisings, detachments of armed volunteers, conspiracies. Vassil Levski, Matei Preobrazhenski, Hristo Ivanov - Golemiya (the Big), Bacho Kiro and others often came here from 1869 to 1871. The monastery provided shelter to the revolutionaries during the preparation of the April Uprising. Ilarion Makariopolski opened the first ecclesiastic school (St. St. Peter and Pavel School of Theology) here in 1874, the first lecturer in it being Nedyu Zhekov. Archbishop Kliment Branitski (Vassil Droumev), Sofronii Vrachanski, Georgi S. Rakovski and a lot of other people's enlighteners are connected with this School. In 1877-1878 the Slavonic Charity Committee set up an orphanage with the monastery for all those who had suffered from the Ottoman ferocities during the Russian-Turkish War of Liberation, Dobri Voinikov being appointed as its Manager.

There is an asphalt road to the monastery from Lyaskovets, Veliko Turnovo and Arbanassi. It takes not more than an hour walk from

*Kapinovo Monastery*

Lyaskovets and 45 minutes from Arbanassi. Accommodation against minimal fees can be found in all above mentioned monasteries.

**Nikopolis Ad Istrum** (at the distance of 18 km north of Veliko Turnovo and at the distance of 3 km south-east of the village of Nikyup) - ruins of the majestic Roman town founded by Emperor Trayan at the beginning of the 2nd century AD in honour of his victory over the Dacians. Deep moats and high stone walls surrounded it. A forum (square), straight and wide streets, temples of Roman, Greek and Eastern Gods, white-stone private and public buildings were found there during archaeological excavation works. The town was provided with sewerage and water-supply systems. An enormous water pipeline, 26 km in length, supplied abundant mountain spring water from the cave near the village of Moussina. Veterans, big land-owners, merchants and craftsmen who had come from different parts of the Roman Empire - Asia Minor, Syria, Egypt, inhabited the town. Nikopolis Ad Adstrum was one of the biggest trade centres of Lower Moesia. Over 900 kinds of colonial coins were minted here. A network of stone roads connected it with the other Roman centres in Moesia and Thrace. A Roman marble statue of the God of Love - Eros, a bronze head of Emperor Gordian III (238-244), architectural details, statuettes, inscriptions and others were found here, too. Most imposing is the sculpture of the God of Medicine - Ascleteus - 1.83 m man-high statue, weighing about 800 kg, which is now kept at the Museum of Archaeology in Veliko Turnovo.

The ancient town reached its zenith during the 2nd-4th centuries. It existed up to the beginning of the 7th century when the Avars destroyed it. A Bulgarian settlement was set up here during the 10th century, which survived through the Middle Ages but was of secondary significance. It was not mentioned during the years of Ottoman Rule.

There is regular bus transport to the village of Nikyup.

# CENTRAL NORTHERN BULGARIA

## GORNA ORYAHOVITSA

The town of Gorna Oryahovitsa (35 621 inhabitants, 160 metres above sea level) is situated at the northern outskirts of the Turnovo Hills, at the distance of 7 km north-east from Veliko Turnovo, 3 km north-west of Lyaskovets and 247 km north-east of Sofia. The biggest railway junction of Northern Bulgaria.

**History.** The first information about life in a settlement dates back to the second half of the 5th millennium BC (Middle Neolithic Age) and is related to the ruins in the area called Blatoto (the Swamp) (located in the town within the region of the high school). The rectangular houses were made of hedge and clay. There are traces of the earliest Thracian settlement in the area of Pchelno Myasto (Bees' Place) at the distance of about 2 or 3 km east of the town, between the Kamuka Hill (the Stone) and the Arbanassi Hill. Its inhabitants were from the tribe of Krobizi. The settlement was of significant dimensions (with an area of over 100 decares). The Kamuka Fortress was erected to provide security for the people. It existed from the 5th century BC to the 1st century BC, when the Romans built up their own fortified settlement over its ruins. It gradually acquired economic power mainly through cultivating grapes and producing wine. During the 2nd and the 3rd centuries the Roman Province Lower Moesia was the only province enjoying protection on the part of the central authority for cultivating grapes and for the production of premium quality wine. The life of that settlement continued up to the coming of the Slavs (6th - 7th centuries). There is no substantiated evidence of a settlement life during the period 7th-12th centuries.

After the restoration of Bulgarian State at the end of the 12th century a need arose of protection of the new Metropolis Turnovgrad. Several sentry fortresses were built up, among which Rahovets, too (at the distance of 4 km north-west of today's town). This happened between 1187 and 1190, when the task of the new fortress was to protect the road from Cherven (the region of Rousse) to Turnovgrad. The name originated from the Persian "rah" - road, motorway. Today's name of the town originated from there in the course of time. During the Ottoman invasion the fortress was conquered by the Turks after the water pipeline to it was discontinued (without destroying the fortress). Rahovets existed up to the year 1444 when Vladislav III Varnenchik destroyed it. Three individual small villages existed during the first centuries of the Ottoman Rule there - Mala (Little), Sredna (Middle) and Golyama (Greater) Rahovitsa.

Gorna Oryahovitsa gradually (with certain rights granted by the Sultan in 1538) turned into an economically powerful settlement, particularly during the Revival Period. Crafts prospered and trade was among the most active in Northern Bulgaria. Every Friday there was a big market of cattle, agricultural production, timber, and charcoal. As early as in 1822 a monastery school was opened here and in 1827 - the private school of Father Gerassim Stoikov (it became public school in 1835), in 1850 - the first girl's school opened its gates and in 1859 the first intermediate high school was founded by Ivan Momchilov. The chitalishte (the reading room and community centre) was opened in 1869. In 1870 Gorna Oryahovitsa was proclaimed a town. It numbered 4700 inhabitants at that time, there were 1200 houses and 5 churches.

The population of the town took part in almost all actions in the region being part of the struggle for national liberation. Vassil Levski organised a revolutionary committe here during the first half of 1869 and after that visited the town twice more. During the preparation of the April Uprising Gorna Oryahovitsa was designated as centre of the First Revolutionary District with Stefan Stambolov as Chief Apostle but Ivan Semerdzhiev, Georgi Izmirliev and the Gruncharov Brothers worked most actively in the town. After a series of treacheries the

# CENTRAL NORTHERN BULGARIA

large-scale uprising failed. There was only one battle between a handful of rebels and the Turkish hordes with tragic consequences. On 28th May 1876 Ivan Semerdzhiev (together with Bacho Kiro and others) was hanged in Turnovo, Georgi Izmirliev was hanged on the gallows on the same day in the centre of Gorna Oryahovitsa with the words: *"It's a good thing to give your life for the freedom of your Mother country!"*. Sider Gruncharov (Sider Voivoda) died at the head of a detachment of armed volunteers under Mt. Mourgash. Mortal danger threatened Gorna Oryahovitsa, but the courageous chairwoman of the women's society Elena Gruncharova gathered women, children and old people and set off for Turnovo where by entreaties they obtained patronage by Reuf Pasha who sent regular army and protected the town from Circassians and brigands. Three citizens of Gorna Oryahovitsa fought in Botev's detachment of armed volunteers and 132 people joined the Bulgarian volunteer forces during the Russian-Turkish War of Liberation. The Russian Army liberated Gorna Oryahovitsa from the Ottoman Rule on 26th June 1877. Major Emiliyan Senkevich (brother of the Polish writer Henrich Senkevich) was amongst the liberators who married a woman from Gorna Oryahovitsa.

After the Liberation the town developed as a big transport (predominantly railway) centre as it is nowadays. Its proximity with the Old Metropolis town of Veliko Turnovo, with Arbanassi, with the magnificent monasteries around and with a great number of other sites of interest makes it a tourist centre as well.

**Landmarks. The Town Museum of History** (6, Antim I Street, tel.: 0618 41464, 43738). **The house of Sider Voivoda. The Joint School. St. Georgi Church** (25, St. Knyaz Boris I, tel.: 0618 45687). The **monument to Georgi Izmirliev** in the centre of the town as well as the monuments to **Vassil Levski, Hristo Botev** and **Sider Voivoda**. The **Neolithic settlement** near the high school.

**Accommodation**: The Rahovets Hotel (1, Georgi Izmirliev Street). Etoal Private Hotel is located at the distance of 150 m from the railway station.

**Tourist information** - at the hotel and at the Kamuka Tourist Association (2, M. Todorov Street, tel.: 0618 41421).

**Transport**. The biggest railway centre of Northern Bulgaria. The two main railway lines - Sofia - Gorna Oryahovitsa - Varna and Rousse - Gorna Oryahovitsa - Stara Zagora - Podkova cross here. The local railway line Gorna Oryahovitsa - Zlataritsa - Elena branches off from here. The railway station is located in the northern end of the town (106, Tsar Osvoboditel Street, tel.: 0618 56050, 56007). There is a railway bureau in the centre of the town as well (1, Tsar Osvoboditel Street, tel.: 0618 42134).

Gorna Oryahovitsa has regular bus connections with Veliko Turnovo (a town bus line), Lyaskovets (a town bus line) and a lot of other towns and villages in this part of the country. The bus station is located in the central part of the town, on the left bank of the small Dereto River (10, Yanko Boyanov Street, tel.: 0618 42123, 42096). There is a taxi service between Gorna Oryahovitsa and Veliko Turnovo every 30-40 minutes departing from the railway station and passing through the village of Arbanassi. There is a town bus transport, too.

**Surrounding areas.** The already mentioned ruins of Medieval **Rahovets** are located at the distance of 4 km north-west of the town. The fortress (about 250 m in length) was amongst inaccessible rocks in the area. Nowadays only parts of its foundations can be seen. It takes about an hour walk from the centre of the town. Within 1 km from there are the following interesting sites: the **locality of Bahadur** with the late Medieval necropolis, the **St. Petka Cheshma** (drinking- fountain) and the locality of the same name where was the settlement of Temnigrad (Dark Town) of the Late Medieval Period, the **Ovchar's Cheshma** (shepherd's drinking-fountain) which supplied water to the Rahovets Fortress by means of a pipeline.

# CENTRAL NORTHERN BULGARIA

The ruins of the **Thracian Fortress** on the **Kamuka** (Stone) Hill are located immediately south of Rahovets. The wall of the fortress adds up to 350 m in length, and there are ruins of a Thracian sanctuary in the middle - a square indented into the rock with the side being 2 m long and the depth of 0.5 m. A little cave goes on from there downward. The site of the Thracian sanctuary has its following interesting explanation - the high temperature of the limestone during the summer causes a powerful ascending stream which splits the storm- and hail-bearing clouds and throws them aside. That is why hail falls on the northern slopes of the Kamuka and not on its south-eastern slopes where the vineyards and the settlement itself were located.

**Bozhoura Forest Park** (at the distance of 7 km west of the town, behind the Rahovets Fortress). The Bozhur (Peony) Chalet offering 40 beds in 5- or 6-bed rooms is located here. There is no regular transport running to it but there is an asphalt road as well as a marked hiking track from Gorna Oryahovitsa (1.30 hours) as well as from Veliko Turnovo (2.30 hours).

**The town of Lyaskovets** - an old horticultural, vine-growing and wine-producing centre which has preserved its foremost role in this respect up to these days is located at the distance of 3 km south-east of Gorna Oryahovitsa. Lyaskovets is a picturesque town of the Revival Period with about 80 old houses grouped mainly in 5 little romantic streets. There are several churches with valuable icons and wood-carvings on their altars, too - St. Atanas Church, restored in 1835 after a fire, St. Dimitur Church of 1724, St. Nikola Church, St. Georgi Church and St. Vassilii Church with a clock on its belfry. There is a Museum of History and a Museum of Gardening (unique of its kind in Bulgaria). A town bus line is functioning between the two towns and it is possible to get here by train on the Gorna Oryahovitsa - Elena railway line.

The village-museum of Arbanassi is situated not far from Gorna Oryahovitsa (at the distance of 4 km south-west, refer to the Veliko Turnovo related section herein), as well as the ancient monasteries - **Preobrazhenski Monastery**, The **Holy Trinity Monastery**, the **Kilifarevo Monastery**, the **St. St. Peter and Pavel Monastery** (refer to the Veliko Turnovo related section herein) and the **Kapinovo** and **Plachkovo Monasteries** (refer to the Elena related section herein).

# CENTRAL NORTHERN BULGARIA

## BYALA

The town of Byala (approximately 11 000 inhabitants, 60 metres above sea level) is situated along the Yantra River in the central part of the Danube Plain. It is 294 km north-east of Sofia, 52 km south-west of Rousse, 54 km north of Veliko Turnovo, 45 km south-east of Svishtov, 93 km east of Pleven and 50 km north-west of Popovo.

**History.** The name Byala (White) comes from the colour of the surrounding limestone rocks. The settlement emerged around 1596 and was mentioned for the first time in 1618. In 1831-1837 there was an outbreak of an epidemic of plague. Felix Kanits described the settlement in 1871 as a craftsman's centre with a bazaar and many workshops. In 1845 Petko R. Slaveikov was a teacher in this town. After the April Uprising was put to rout, one of its last tragedies took place in the town of Byala. Pursued by a Turkish horde and trying to cross the river and escape Panaiot Volov, Georgi Ikonomov and Stoyan Angelov drowned in Yantra. At the time of the Russian-Turkish War of Liberation, the Headquarters of the Russian Commander - Emperor Alexander II was located in the town of Byala. After the Liberation Byala had about 4000 inhabitants. In 1891 it obtained the status of a town.

**Landmarks: The Military-Historical Museum War of Liberation** (2, Julia Vrevskaya Street, tel. 0817 2466) is in the old house in which the Headquarters of the Russian Army was accommodated. A beautiful park is situated in the surrounding area where old guns and a part of the pontoon bridge, which was used by the Russian troops to cross the Danube River near Svishtov on 27$^{th}$ June 1877, are exhibited. Here is the tomb of **Baroness Julia Vrevskaya,** who was a volunteer medical nurse during the war.

The famous **Belenski Bridge** is situated between the town and the railway station (near the bridge on the Rousse - Veliko Turnovo route) on the Yantra River - an outstanding monument of Bulgarian architecture, designed and built by Master Kolyu Ficheto in 1865-1867 by the order of Mithad Pasha. It is 276 m long and 9 m wide. Its vault arches are decorated with sculptures of animal heads. A part of the bridge was carried away in a flood and then restored, but in disharmony with the old part. The bridge is closed to vehicles. There is a monument to the Great Master on the left bank in front of the bridge.

The **white monument to the three revolutionaries** who tried to swim across the river on

# CENTRAL NORTHERN BULGARIA

25th May 1876 is situated near the bridge on the left bank of the river.

**The Clock Tower**, built in 1872 by the local craftsmen's organisation is located in the centre of the town. Its height is 15.20 m. Other historical sites of interest are **Alexander II House-Museum, the monuments** to the Russian officers and to Julia Vrevskaya.

**Accommodation.** The Yantra Hotel.

**Tourist information** - at the hotel and at Yantra Tourist Association (3, Ekzarh Iosiff Square, tel. 0817 2474).

**Transport** Byala has a bus and railway connection with the other parts of the country. There are regular bus lines to Rousse, Veliko Turnovo, Svishtov, Popovo and other smaller villages in the region. The railway station is located at the distance of 5 km from the town (there is a regular bus line with the town) on the main railway line Rousse-Gorna Oryahovitsa-Stara Zagora-Podkova.

**Surrounding areas.** The **Belenskata Forest** is located at the distance of 6 to 7 km from the town. Here the Yantra Chalet can accommodate up to 40 people in 4 suites and in rooms with 2, 3, 5 and more beds. There is no regular transport, but there is an asphalt road leading to it. It would take about 1.30 hours walk to reach the chalet.

Near the village of Pepelina, 31km to the north-east of Byala the beautiful **Orlova Chouka Cave** is located (in the Cherni Lom River valley). The total length of the galleries is about 12km thus being the second longest cave in Bulgaria. It is electrified. The cave can be reached for about 45 minutes walk starting from the railway station of Tabachka. It is at a distance of 6 km from the town of Dve Mogili. There is a regular bus line from Rousse to Pepelina and from there - 3 km along a truck road (30 minutes walk). Near the cave there is a mountain chalet of the same name (it offers 21 beds in two rooms with 3 beds each and a room with 15 beds, for reservations: tel. 082 224705, 225454 - Prista Tourist Association, Rousse.)

## ROUSSE

The town of Rousse (162 128 inhabitants, 50 metres above sea level) is located on the high right bank of the Danube River, 496 m from the outflow of the big river. It is 320 km north-east of Sofia, 203 km north-west of Varna, 106 km north-east of Veliko Turnovo, 146 km north-east of Pleven, 97 km north-east of Svishtov, 122 km south-west of Silistra, 66 km north-west of Razgrad. The greatest and the most important Bulgarian town on the Danube River, known also as "Little Vienna" because of its ancient architecture. It is a regional administrative centre.

**History.** The famous Rousse mound - a prehistoric settlement existed more than 5000 years ago is located within the boundaries of the modern town. At the beginning of the new era on a part of the territory of the modern town of Rousse an ancient settlement of *Sexaginta Prista* (The sixty ships) emerged, where "prista" means a particular type of a Greek river guard vessel. Probably it was founded by the Roman Emperor Vespasian (69-79). Later on it was known under the names of *Pristis* and *Pristapolis*. It existed up to the 6th century, when the Avars brought it to ruins. In Medieval times a new settlement emerged near the ruins of the ancient settlement, and information about it was found for the first time in the Broush Guidebook of the 16th century under the name of *Rossi*. In the Sultan Register of 1431 and in a Peace Treaty concluded between the Ottoman Empire and the Magyar state dated 20th of August 1503 the settlement was mentioned under the name of *Roussi*. In Ahmed Neshri chronicles as well as in many other old maps the town was shown as a wholesome town together with the settlement of Giurgiu on the opposite side of the Danube River named Yorgogi, Yorgovo, Yuroukova, Roussi on both sides of the Danube River, Giurgiu on both sides of the Danube River.

# CENTRAL NORTHERN BULGARIA

In 1595 the Wallachian ruler Mihai Vityazoul (the Courageous) made an attempt to liberate Bulgaria with an Wallah-Bulgarian army and the town was brought to ruins. After its reconstruction at the beginning of the 17th century it was given the name of *Rouschuk* (little Roussi). The town turned into an important port and a strong border fortress. In 1811 the Russian General Koutouzov carried out the famous Rouschuk battle and became known as a talented military commander. In 1864 the town became the centre of the Danube District of the Ottoman Empire. In 1866 the building of the first railway road in Bulgarian lands - Rouschouk-Varna was completed. The first modern agricultural farm was founded under the name of Noumine (Exemplary farm). The River Management was founded as well and in a short period of time 7 steam ships and 15 barges were purchased. A printing house was opened with printing machines from Vienna where newspapers, books and textbooks were printed. The bookshop of Hristo G. Danov was opened at that time. To meet the needs of the secular education in Rouschouk in 1843 Alexander Rousset published in Strasbourg the first geographical map in Bulgarain.

European influence penetrated into the town through the active river transport along the Danube River (predominantly Austro-Hungarian ships) and this had positive impact on the development of the town. Architecture developed, too and the construction of private and public buildings resembling the style of the capital of the Austro-Hungarian Empire - Vienna commenced. The European fashion in clothing also penetrated first in this Bulgarian town.

On the 1st January 1866 the first in Bulgaria meteorological observations began here with modern Austrian equipment.

Rouschouk was not left aside from the struggle for spiritual and national liberation either, moreover that in its capacity of being a gate to Europe it was here that the modern freedom-loving ideas of the Old Continent made their way into the country. Zora (Dawn) Chitalishte (reading room and community centre) and the home of the extraordinary Bulgarian woman patriot baba (grandmother) Tonka Obretenova became centres of the national struggle. A lot of revolutionaries were assisted to leave the Empire or to return to their Motherland. It was here that Angel Kunchev - one of the most faithful and ardent followers of Vassil Levski died during an exchange of fire with the Turkish police. Baba Tonka, her sons and daughters, revolutionaries who gave their lives for the freedom of Bulgaria - Stefan Karadzha, Angel Kunchev, Zahari Stoyanov, Lyuben Karavelov, Panayot Hitov, Hristo Makedonski, Dimitur Tsenovich and a lot of other great Bulgarians were buried in this town.

A Pantheon-Charnel House of the national Revival heroes with an everlasting fire was opened in Rousse in 1979. The bones of many of the 453 dignified Bulgarians, who were born in or who linked their lives with this town and whose names are inscribed in the Pantheon were collected in it. On 20th February 1878 the Russian Army led by General Totleben entered Rouschouk and was enthusiastically welcomed by the population led by Archbishop Kliment Branitski (Vassil Droumev).

The town was the biggest in the liberated Bulgarian lands - over 20 000 inhabitants. On 31st July 1879 the Bulgarian flag of the ships donated by Russia was risen which marked the beginning of the organised Bulgarian river navigation. The first marine technical school, later on moved to Varna, was opened here in 1881. The same year was found the first Bulgarian bank - Girdap. In 1889 the first Bulgarian Chamber of Commerce, and two years later the first joint-stock insurance company - Bulgaria - were established in Rousse. As of the end of the 19th century a lot of celebrated architects did their creative work in the liberated of Rousse (Edward Winter, Udo Ribau, Georg Lang, Edwin Petritski, Ne-

# CENTRAL NORTHERN BULGARIA

## Rousse

# CENTRAL NORTHERN BULGARIA

gos Bedrossyan, Todor Tonev, Nikola Lazarov and others), painter-decorators (Karlo Francescani, Giovanni Pitor and others), landscapers (Ferdinand Halober, Rihard Noyvirt and others). It is not due to randomness that Rousse is being considered the most European Bulgarian town even nowadays. The writers Elias Kaneti, awarded the Nobel Prize for literature for 1981, Dobri Nemirov, Michael Arlan were born here, Lyuben Karavelov, Ivan Vazov, Stoyan Mihailovski, the poet Tsvetan Radoslavov, author of the text of the Bulgarian national anthem, the painter Joul Pasken (Pinkas), the pianist Otto Liebih, the opera singer Mimi Balkanska, Academician Mihail Arnaoudov lived here.

The role of the town grew up even more with the construction of the so-called Bridge of Friendship between the Bulgarian and the Rumanian banks in 1954. It was here that at the end of the 1980-ies the civil movement for protection of the town from the pollution of the Giurgiu Chemical Works (Rumania) originated and it marked the beginning of the democratic changes in Bulgaria. Nowadays Rousse is a big economic, transport, cultural and tourist centre.

**Landmarks**. About 200 building in Rousse are considered part of architectural historical heritage of Bulgaria, 12 of which are especially valuable. In the first place this is the **Dohodnoto Zdanie** (The Profitable Building) with the winged Mercury on its roof (the Old Theatre), built in 1902 by the architects Raul Brank, Georg Lang and Frank Scholts, which together with the **Monument to Freedom** (1908), a remarkable work of the architect and sculptor from Florence Arnoldo Zocci, are the symbols of Rousse. The following are also among the most outstanding cultural and historical monuments: **The High School of Music; the Catholic Church** (Episkop Bossilkov Street, tel.: 082 228188) with coloured stained-glass; the buildings of the **Savings Bank, the Chamber of Commerce and Industry** (Lyuben Karavelov Library), **the boys' high school Knyaz Boris** (now a secondary vocational school Hristo Botev); **The house of the sailor; the Regional Administration** (granted for a museum); **The Club of the Culture Functionaries; The Duty-Free Zone Administration; the Simeonov Brothers' House. The native home of Elias Kaneti** is located at 13, Gurko Street.

Rousse is a town of the museums: **The Pantheon to the National Revival Heroes** (tel.: 082 28913); **The Town Museum of History; the Baba Tonka Museum** (phone: 082 32364); **the Zakhari Stoyanov House-Museum**; **Toma Kurdzhiev House-Museum**; **The Museum of the Town Lifestyle** arranged in Kaliopa's House (tel.: 082 27742). **The National Museum of Transport and Communications** is housed in the building of the oldest railway station of Bulgaria. Carriages of Sultan Abdul Aziz, of Tsar Ferdinand and Tsar Boris III are preserved in it. **The Town Art Gallery.**

The ancient sites of interest of the town also include **Leventabia Fortress** (a restaurant complex now), **the Kyuntukapiya Gate from Mitiriza, the Mahmoud Column, the Holy Trinity Church** (8, Holy Trinity Square) dating back to the beginning of the 17th century, **the Fleet Tower,** built in 1884 by architect Franz Gruenanger for meteorological observations. There are **monuments to those killed in the Serbian-Bulgarian War of 1885,** to **Russophilles,** to **Baba Tonka,** to **Lyuben Karavelov, Stefan Karadzha, Raycho Nikolov**, etc.

There is an Opera House in Rousse (Sveta Troitsa Square, tel.: 082 234303, 225358), a Philharmonic Orchestra (12, Rayko Daskalov Street, tel.: 082 225680), Theatre of Drama and a Puppet Theatre. **The International Festival "March Days of Music"** is annually held in the town.

There is a higher educational institution, too the University of Rousse.

**Accommodation.** The Riga Hotel Square (Svoboda Square). The Danube Hotel (Svoboda Square). The Splendid Hotel. The Yordan Petrov

# CENTRAL NORTHERN BULGARIA

Hotel (Prista Western Park, on the bank of the Danube River opposite the island of Lyulyaka (Lilac), working hours: 8:00 a.m. - 11:00 p.m., there is a restaurant). The Dom na Armiyata (House of the Army) Hotel (2, Odrin Street). The Rai (Paradise) Motel. The Prista Chalet (in the western park of the same name, offering 132 beds in 3 suites and in 2-, 4-, 5- and 7-bed rooms, there is a town bus line to it). Lyulyaka Camping (in the Prista Western Park, on the bank of the Danube River opposite the island of the same name, it has 24 beds in double rooms - two rooms in a bungalow.

**Tourist information** - at the hotels and at the tourist chalets. At Prista Tourist Association (1, Knyazheska Street, tel.: 082 224705, 225454) and at Akademik Tourist Association (8, Studentska Street, tel.: 082 450887).

**Transport**. Bus, railway and river transport services the inter-town and international connections of the town. There are regular bus lines to Sofia, Varna, Pleven, Veliko Turnovo, Shoumen, Razgrad, Turgovishte and a lot of other towns and villages of the country. There

*Dohodnoto Zdanie (The Profitable Building) in Rousse*

# CENTRAL NORTHERN BULGARIA

are two bus stations functioning in the town – Iztok (East) Bus Station (10, Ivan Vedar Street, tel.: 082 443836, 228151, 444810) and Yug (South) Bus Station (156, Alexander Stamboliiski Square, tel.: 082 222974, 228151, 228100). Rousse is the initial (or the final) station of two railway lines Rousse - Gorna Oryahovitsa Stara Zagora Podkova and Rousse - Kaspichan - Varna. It is connected through them to the national railway network. There are two railway stations in the town - one in the eastern part and the Central Railway Station (in the western part, tel.: 082 222213, 224320). There is a town railway ticket bureau (082 222845) and an office for sleeping car reservations (082 224202).

The river station of Rousse is a big one. Since 1992 the river passenger transport along the Bulgarian Danubian riverside has been discontinued but its continuance is solely a matter of time. There are cruises only along the international route Rousse - Belgrade - Novi Sad - Budapest - Bratislava - Vienna - Linz - Pasau with Bulgarian and mainly foreign tourists. Tourist cruises on little ships are organised during the summer. Since 1993 the ferryboat line Rousse - Giurgiu has been in operation, too. There is town bus and trolley bus transport in Rousse.

**Surrounding areas**. Prista Western Park is located at the distance of 6 km from Rousse along the road to the town of Byala. There are beautiful deciduous forests, well shaped lanes, tourist can visit the the Danubian island of Lyulyaka, Prista Chalet, Lyulyaka Camping, the Danube Motel, Ribarska Koliba (Fisherman's hut) - interesting restaurant. There are town bus lines - No. 6 and No. 16 running to the park. Another big site for recreation, sports, tourism, sunbathing and all other kinds of entertainment is situated at the distance of 12 km east of Rousse - the **Lipnik Forest Park**. There are country houses, restaurants, artificial lakes, a hotel, a zoo corner, a sports base and a camping site. There is a town bus line functioning in this direction.

**Obraztsov Chiflik (Exemplary Farm)** is situated at the distance of 3 to 4 km from the Lipnik Forest Park and possesses beautiful deciduous forests, fertile land and vineyards (an example of the economic development in the past) and two little sprightly tourist chalets - Zdravets Chalet (40 beds in 1 suite and in 2-, 4-, 5-, 6- and 9-bed rooms, tel.: 082 233609) and Minzuhar Chalet (45 beds in 2-, 3-, 5- and 14-bed rooms, tel. for reservations - in the Prista Tourist Association, Rousse). There is a regular bus line (Rousse - Obrzatsov Chiflik) and one can walk to the Minzuhar Chalet in 30 minutes from the last stop and another 30 minutes to the Zdravets Chalet along a marked track.

**The Roussenski Lom River Valley**, along with its tributaries Beli (White), Malki (Little) and Cherni (Black) Lom represents a unique world in itself in which the amazing nature is entwined into our remote past history. Part of the valley with the territory of 3260 hectares was proclaimed a **Nature Park** (at the distance of 20 km south of Rousse). The rivers have created incredibly beautiful gorges into the limestone rock foundation. It is genuine joy for the eyes and real paradise for rock climbers.

One of the most significant military, economic and cultural centres of Bulgaria during the 13$^{th}$ and the 14$^{th}$ centuries was located there the **Medieval Town of Cherven** (on the right bank of the Cherni Lom River, by the name of the same village, at the distance of 31 km south of Rousse). Out of the preserved ruins most interesting are the parts of the fortified walls, the defensive tower (used as a model for the restoration of the Baldwin Tower on Tsarevets Hill in Veliko Turnovo), the two gates, the castle, the foundations of a great number of churches, the foundations of the boyar palaces, the two unique in their kind water pumping facilities with vaulted staircases, etc. There is a regularly functioning bus transport to the village.

Many monks-hermits settled down in the valley

# CENTRAL NORTHERN BULGARIA

during the late Middle Ages. Whole monastery complexes were created there - Ivanovski, Maluk Rai (Little Paradise), Golyam Rai (Great Paradise), Koshouta (Doe) and churches with exquisite mural paintings, a part of which was preserved. The mural paintings of the **Ivanovski Rock Churches** (on the Roussenski Lom River) are one of the summits of Medieval Bulgarian art (work of masters from the Turnovo School of Painting). In 1983 they were entered into the cultural list of UNESCO protected sites. There is a regularly functioning bus transport to the village of Ivanovo.

The Alpinist Chalet is situated on the bank of the Roussenski Lom River, at the distance of 6 km south of the Prista Chalet (14 beds on plank-beds and 6 bungalows with 36 beds in 2-, 3- and 4-bed rooms, reservations at Prista Tourist Association, Rousse) with perfect possibilities for rock climbing along routes with different categories of complexity. It is located at the distance of 1 km south-east along an asphalt road from the village of Bassarbovo. There is regular bus transport to the village.

**The Bassarbovo Monastery** is situated at the distance of 2 km from the chalet. **The village of Pissanets** with the **Mamoulya rock phenomenon** and the strongly fortified **Pissansko gradishte** (ruins of an ancient town) are situated at the distance of about 25 km south of Rousse, on the banks of the Beli Lom River. There is regular bus transport to that site.

**The Danube River** provides great opportunities for recreation, water sports, water tourism, fishing and lots of entertainment. There are wonderful little places, like the islands of Lyulyaka and Mateya, the riverside at Stulpishte, Marten and so on. The shelters for accommodation are not few in number, there are attractive public catering establishments, sports bases, tourist chalets, beaches and all of them are accessible either by car or by public transport.

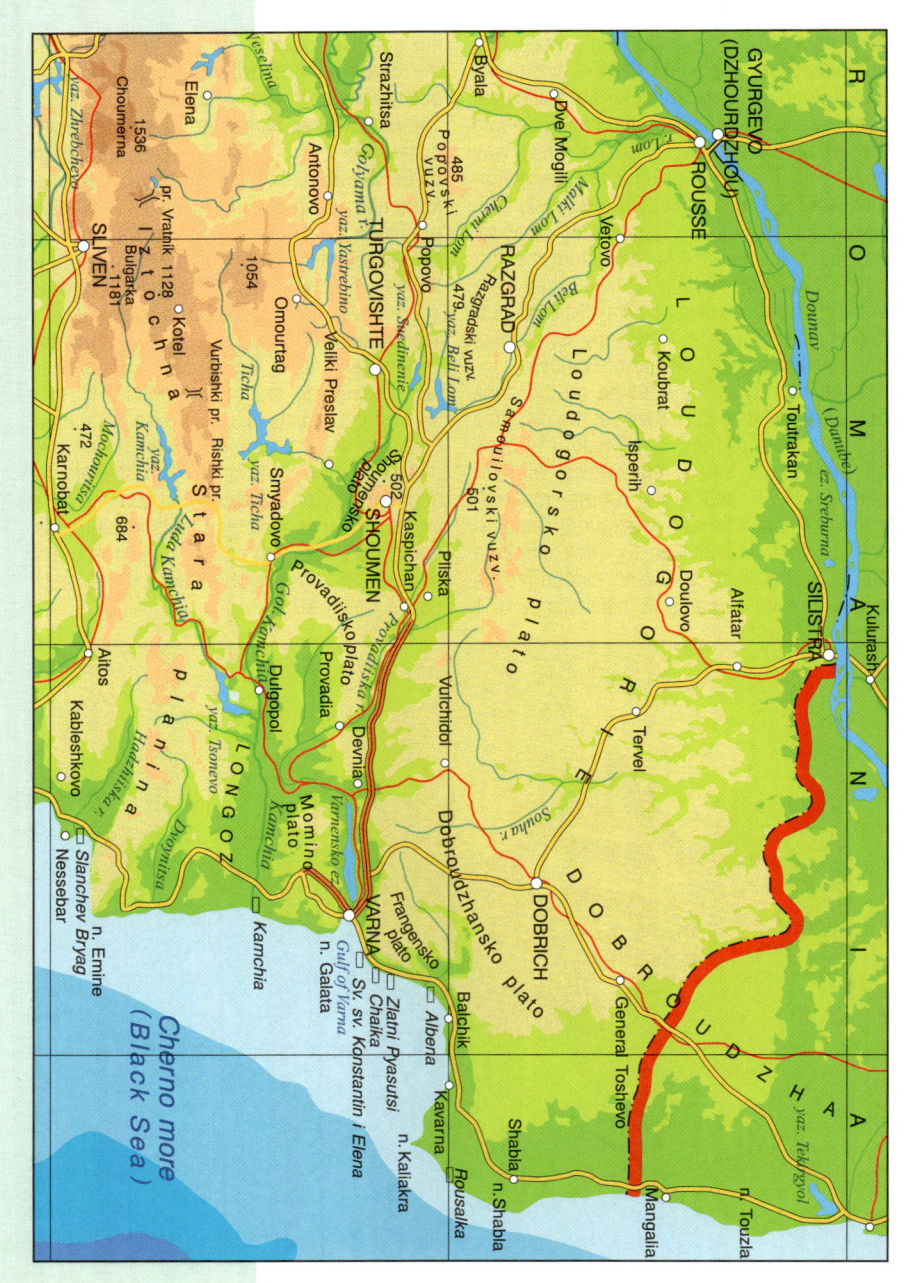

# NORTHEASTERN BULGARIA

# NORTHEASTERN BULGARIA

## PLISKA

The town of Pliska (population: 1243; 140 m above sea level) is situated in the south end of the Loudogorie Plateau. It is 404 km north-east of Sofia, 24 km north-east of Shoumen, 6 km north-west of Kaspichan, 6 km west of Novi Pazar, and 2 km south of the remains of the first Bulgarian capital of the same name. **The first capital of Danubian Bulgaria**. Two kilometres away from the present day town are the remains of the imposing construction of Pliska - the first capital of Danubian Bulgaria in 681, the year of its foundation by Khan Asparouh until 893-894 when the capital was moved to Preslav by Tsar Simeon I the Great. The town consisted of three concentric fortifications. The **Exterior City** is marked by a moat in the ground with a rampart enclosing a rectangular territory of 23 square kilometres. Almost in the middle of the Exterior City is **the interior fortress** surrounding the Interior City. The fortress has a solid stone wall (2.5 m wide), made of huge ashlar slabs. At each corner there was a trapezium-shaped tower, and on each of the four walls there were two five-angled towers and a gate. The main entrance is the east gate. The third inner defensive zone is a solid-built brick wall surrounding the citadel situated in the centre of the **Interior City**.

The most characteristic and interesting architectural monuments whose remains have been preserved until these days are:

**The Grand Palace** (the best preserved building in the Interior City) - the throne-room of the Bulgarian rulers was a formal representative building for the Khan's Council, the official receptions of foreign envoys, and for rich parties. His throne was there, as well. The size of the palace is as follows: 52 m long and 26.5 m wide.

It was built by Khan Omourtag (814-831) whose merit is the turning of

# NORTHEASTERN BULGARIA

Pliska into one of the biggest East-European centres in early Middle Ages.
**The Small Palace** (the most imposing building in the citadel), occupying an area of 568 square metres was the Khan's residence. Unlike the Grand Palace the Small Palace is more exquisite and richer. Besides the Small Palace the citadel houses the temples, the catchment basin, the swimming pools, the farm houses. Pliska underwent not only great constructions but also a high degree of improvements, i.e. floor heating installation, drainage system of clay and lead pipes for the clean and dirty water, glass windows!

Prince Boris erected the **Grand Basilica** (situated in the Exterior City, 1.5 km north-east of the Interior City. It has three naves (the biggest on the Balkan Peninsula) and is imposing in size (100 m long, 30 m wide) - one of the most stately Bulgarian architectural works dating back to the second half of 9th century.

It is in Pliska that one can trace back the development of Bulgarian architecture from the ancient Bulgarian epoch to the period of adoption of European features. There is a rich archaeological museum near the excavations (tel.: 05323 2271). The oldest source of information about Pliska is the inscription on the stone column of 821 (Khan Omourtag's) in the vicinity of the village of Chatalar (at present Tsar Kroum railway station)

Under the Turkish rule the name of the settlement was changed to *Aboba*, which was preserved till 1925. After that it was called *Pliskov*, and in 1947 - *Pliska*.

**Accommodation**: A motel situated in the immediate neighbourhood of the excavations. A hotel in the modern town.

**Tourist Information** - at the hotel, the motel and the town-hall of Pliska.

**Transport**. There are regular bus lines to Shoumen, Novi Pazar and Kaspichan as well as to other smaller towns and villages in the district. It is only 6 km away from Kaspichan railway station where there are connections to Sofia, Varna, Bourgas, Rousse and Silistra.

## SHOUMEN

The town of Shoumen (population: 89 054; 220 m above sea-level) is situated at the eastern mouth of the Shoumen Plateau, on either bank of the Bokloudga river (Poroina - which means torrential). It is 380 km northeast of Sofia, 115 km south-east of Rousse, 90 km west of Varna, 140 km north-east of Veliko Tarnovo, 41 km east of Turgovishte, 49 km south-east of Razgrad, 113 km south of Silistra, and 56 km north-east of Vurbitsa. An old Bulgarian fortification. A regional administrative centre.

**History**. Shoumen is an old town of fortresses. Its foundation and development were connected with the fortresses at the eastern end of the Shoumen Plateau (in the area of Hisarluka). The famous fortress of Shoumen was built in four basic periods: early and late Antiquity, and early and late Middle Ages. It was first created by the Thracians (5th century BC) and then consequently inhabited and built on by the Romans, the Byzantine, the Bulgarians and the Turks.

Together with Pliska and Preslav, Shoumen was an old Bulgarian fortification of 7th-10th centuries and it developed into a feudal town with a castle and an interior fortress, a number of churches, workshops (12th-14th centuries). This is the place where Tsar Ivan Shishman's inscription was found. The inscription announced the Tsar's visit to Shoumen.

The Arabian traveller Idrisi first mentioned it as *Simeonis (Shimeonit)* in 1153. Some consider that it comes from Tsar Simeon's name. In 14th century people called it *Shoumna* or *Shoumen*. Most probably it has the meaning of "shouma" (foliage) or "zashoumen" (covered up with branches) because it was situated in such an area. In 12th-14th centuries Shoumen was a significant military, administrative and economic centre surpassing even the old capital of Preslav, and growing outside the fortifications.

# NORTHEASTERN BULGARIA

The town fell under Turkish rule after a long siege. It was turned into a well-fortified military town with a big garrison within the fortress. It housed a lot of Turks, Jews, Tartars, and Armenians. The town was mentioned with different names like *Shoumena, Shoumna, Shoumoular, Soumounoum*, and of course in the last centuries of the domination as *Shoumen*. In 18$^{th}$ and particularly in 19$^{th}$ century it developed as an important crafts centre, which was one of the preconditions for an active cultural life. On 22$^{nd}$ May 1813 here was held the first in Bulgaria civil celebration of the day of the Saint brothers Cyril and Methodius, and the first theatre performance. In 1828 the first monastery school for young girls was founded. In 1846 the first amateur theatrical group in the schools were established. After the defeat of the Hungarian Revolution (1848) many Hungarian revolutionaries emigrated to Shoumen with Layosh Koshout at the head; these actively participated in the cultural life of the town. Due to them in 1851 the first symphonic orchestra conducted by Shafran was set up. Shoumen is the town of the first class school for young girls and the first communal cultural centre (1856). The first work of drama were written in Shoumen: "Mihal" (1853) by Sava Dobroplodni. The town hosted one of the first theatre performances (1856). The first Bulgarian short story "Miserable Family" (1860) by Vassil Droumev from Shoumen, founder of Bulgarian theatre, was written here, as well as "School Theatre - the Wealthy Man" (1864) by Dobri Voinikov from Shoumen, too. Born in Shoumen, Panayot Volov was one of the main apostles of the Fourth Revolutionary District at the time of the April Uprising (1876). He died on 25$^{th}$ May 1876 near Byala (Rousse district).

After the Liberation the town fell in decay because of the loss of markets for the crafts, the migration of Turks and the comparatively cheap and of high quality industrial goods from the West competing with the local production. The town gradually recovered and in 1882 the first Bulgarian brewery was established with Czech capital; Shoumensko Pivo beer" is still among those much sought after. In the period between 1950-1965 the town bore the name of *Kolarovgrad* but after that it regained its old name of Shoumen. Because of its proximity to the first capitals of Danubian Bulgaria (Pliska and Preslav), and the Madara Horseman, as well as because of its rich historical past, in 1981 Shoumen was chosen as centre of the celebrations of the 1300$^{th}$ anniversary of the foundation of the Bulgarian state by Khan Asparuh. The great Bulgarian composer Pancho Vladigerov was born in the town. The historical conditions and the natural environment make it a first-class tourist centre.

**Landmarks**: The **Founders of Modern Bulgaria Complex** (monument) (tel.: 054 52598, 52107)

*Vassil Droumev Theatre of Drama*

# NORTHEASTERN BULGARIA

is located on Ilchov Bair south of the town. With the means of architecture and sculpture the whole of the Bulgarian history from Khan Asparuh to Tsar Simeon is depicted. It was officially opened in 1981. There is an information centre and two restaurants. Working hours: 8.30 a.m.-5.00 p.m. all the week round.

The **Town Museum of History**. (15, Slavyanski Blvd., tel.: 054 57410) - founded in 1904 by Rafail Popov. Working hours: 8.30 a.m. - 5.00 p.m. Entrance fee: symbolic. The **Pancho Vladigerov Museum Complex** (136, Tsar Osvoboditel Str., tel.: 054 52123, working hours: 09.00 a.m.-12.00 a.m. and 2.00 p.m.-06.00 p.m.). The **Layosh Koshout House-Museum** (115, Tsar Osvoboditel, tel.: 054 57209, working hours: 9.00 a.m.-12.00 a.m. and 2.00 p.m.-6.00 p.m.). The **Panayot Volov** House-Museum (42, Tsar Osvoboditel Str., tel.: 054 63429, working hours: 9.00 a.m.-12.00 a.m. and 2.00 p.m.-6.00 p.m.). The **Dobri Voinikov House-Museum** (157, Tsar Osvoboditel Str., tel.: 054 56897, working hours: 9.00 a.m.-12.00 a.m. and 2.00 p.m.-6.00 p.m.).

There are four interesting cultural monuments in Shoumen traced back to the epoch of late Middle Ages. The first one is called **Bezistena**; it was built to serve the traders from Doubrovnik in 16$^{th}$ century. At present an original restaurant is housed there. The second one is **The Clock Tower** of 1741 being a stone prism with a built-in drinking-fountain (with rich ornamentation and an inscription). The interesting **Kourshoum Cheshma** (Bullet Drinking-Fountain) (1744) is located in the most lively in the past administrative and commercial part of the town. The drinking-fountain is covered with lead tiles where its name comes from.

The **Sveto Vuznesenie Church** (St. Ascension) of 1829 (48, Otets Paisii Str.) is of great interest, too. **Kazandgiiska Street** has been restored, a reminder of the 50 crafts in the past. One can see beautiful houses from the Revival Period in the **Cherkovna Quarter**.

There are a number of cultural institutes in Shoumen as well: Vassil Droumev Theatre of Drama (in the centre of the town, 72, Slavyanski Blvd., tel.: 054 52241). The Patilancho Puppet Theatre (in the central part of the town, 11, Todor Ikonomov Str., tel.: 054 55062, 57541). The Elena Karamihailova Art Gallery (81, Tsar Ivan Alexander, tel.: 054 42126,

*Madara Horseman*

# NORTHEASTERN BULGARIA

40171, working hours: 9.00 a.m. - 12.00 a.m. and 2.00 p.m. - 6.00 p.m. Shoumen is a university centre. There is the Konstantin Preslavski University.

**Accommodation**: The Shoumen Hotel Complex (four-star, in the central part of the town, Oborishte Square). It offers 430 beds, restaurants, bars, cafes, discos, halls, a swimming pool. The Madara Hotel (3-star, in the centre of the town, 1, Osvobozhdenie Square). It offers 200 beds, a restaurant, cafe-confectioneries. The Orbita Hotel (2-star, in the Kyoshkovete park). It offers 30 beds, a restaurant and a cafe. The Lyubomir Targovski Tourist House (Oborishte quarter, 8, Antim I Str.). It offers 14 beds in two-, and three-bed rooms.

**Tourist Information** - at the Committee on Tourism (in the central part of the town, zip code 9700, 17, Slavyanski Blvd., tel.: 054 59141, 55111). The Madara Horseman Tourist Association (15, Hristo Botev Str., tel.: 054 59456, 59528, 59167). At the hotels and the tourist house.

**Transport**. There are regular bus lines from Shoumen to Varna, Rousse, Turgovishte, Razgrad, Silistra, Karnobat, Pliska, Preslav and other smaller towns and villages in the district. The central bus station (tel.: 054 61618, 60193) and the railway station (tel.: 054 60155, 62537) are next to each other situated in the eastern part of the town, behind the town park. Shoumen is an important railway station on Sofia-Varna railway line. It is a starting point for the railway line to Karnobat. Near Shoumen is the town of Kaspichan where the railway forks to Rousse and Silistra. The nearest operating airport is that in Varna. There is public bus transport in Shoumen.

**Surrounding areas**. The **Kyoshkovete Park** is located in the west proximity of the town, on the territory of the **Shoumen Plateau National Park.** There are wonderful venerable beech-trees, numerous alleys, rest homes, tourist routes and Boukatsite Mountain Hut (5 km away from Shoumen, 1.5 km from the village of Troitsa, and 3 km from the village of Osmar; a bus line connects the three villages. It offers 20 beds; there are medieval monasteries cut in the rocks). In the Kyoshkovete are the remains of the **Shoumen Fortress** (2 km west of the town) - a real treasure for archaeologists (see the historical information). There is public bus transport.

Some 15 km east of Shoumen is the unique **Madara Historical-Archaeological Reserve** consisting of several sights of exceptional value. First of all, this is **the rock bas-relief of the Madara Horseman** representing a horseman with a sceptre in the right hand and a shepherd's crook in the left; a lion, a dog and a snake are depicted under the horse. It was considered a symbol of the victorious march of Bulgarian rulers at the dawn of Bulgarian state. The latest approach to the inscription is based on the Persian (East Indo-European) heritage. The horseman is the Earth correspondence of the Sun, the dog - of the Moon, the lion refers to the Lion constellation with the Regul main star. The computer analysis based on the latest software related to astronomy implies that the position of the Sun, the Moon and the Regul star as is on the bas-relief, has happened in 165AD (the year of the Snake). This year amazingly coincides with the year considered a beginning of Bulgarian statehood, as specified in the Name List of Bulgarian Khans, a written monument of the $8^{th}$ century. These lead to the conclusion that Bulgarians have Indo-European roots and

# NORTHEASTERN BULGARIA

culture and are a highly civilized state-founding people. This unique monument of worldwide importance is under the protection of **UNESCO**. At the bottom of the steep cliffs near the relief are the remains of buildings of various epochs - palaces, an ancient Bulgarian pagan sanctuary of 9$^{th}$ century, churches and monasteries of 11$^{th}$-14$^{th}$ centuries.

A flight of 386 steps in the rock lead to the **Madara Plateau** and the **Madara Fortress** - the remains of the Bulgarian fortress called Matora existed till 1386. At the south-west mouth of the Plateau is the **Roman Villa** - the remains of a Roman mansion (living and farm houses). The whole of Madara region is known as "the Bulgarian Troy". A tourist village sprang up in the immediate vicinity of the rocks; there is a rich archaeological museum, a hotel, a camping site and Madara Horseman Chalet (80 beds in two-, three-, four-, five-bed rooms, tel.: 261 through the operator of Madara village.)

One and a half kilometre away from Madara Rocks and the tourist village is the village of Madara with a railway station on the Sofia-Varna line and a regular bus line to Shou-men. Eight kilometres south-west of Shoumen is the village of Osmar famous for its renowned red wine called **Osmarski Pelin** (Osmar's Wormwood), which has as an ingredient the bitter herb of wormwood. There is regular bus transport.

The **Kabiyuk studfarm** is several kilometres north of the town. It is situated in a beautiful park with own race-course and ride hall (70 m long, 24 m wide). One can find here the unique horse museum, the summer residence of Prince Alexander Batenberg (a museum at present), a chapel with valuable icons. An excellent place for rest and horse riding practice. Regular bus transport available.

## VELIKI PRESLAV

The town of Veliki Preslav (population: 10 645; 120 m above sea-level) is situated on either banks of the Ticha River shortly before it flows into the Golyama Kamchia River. It is 365 km north-east of Sofia, 19 km south-west of Shoumen, 25 km south-east of Turgovishte, 23 km north-west of Smyadovo, and 37 km north-east of Vurbitsa. Successor of the second capital of Asparuh's state bearing the same name.

**The second capital of Danubian Bulgaria**. Its imposing ruins are to be found 2 km south of the present day town. Veliki Preslav was the capital of the Bulgarian kingdom from 893 till 969 in the epoch of its supreme might and in the boom of Old Bulgarian culture (the so called Golden Age). It sprang up in the first half of 9$^{th}$ century during the reign of Khan Omourtag (814-831) as a military camp with a fortified palace and garrison. Tsar Simeon (893-927) proclaimed it capital (thus moving it from Pliska). It established as an administrative, cult-religious, and cultural centre of medieval Bulgarian state, renowned for its remarkable monumental construction work, the achievements of applied arts, the stone plastic arts, the painted ceramics, the famous literary school.

Veliki Preslav grew systematically as a town. It has the same construction of gates, towers and walls as Pliska does. It had the same two fortification rings separating the Interior from the Exterior City, however the exterior zone is not the ditch typical for the ancient Bulgarians but a solid and high fortress wall. Following and improving their own tradition of construction work the Bulgarian masters first in Europe built a town with two concentric fortress walls - the exterior being 3.25 m thick, and the interior (the citadel) - 2.80 to 3 m thick.

**Preslav** is a pure Bulgarian name coming from "preslavun" (famous, most glorious),

# NORTHEASTERN BULGARIA

and the name **Veliki** (Great) was added when the capital turned into a really big and representative town for its time. The old Bulgarian capital occupied a territory of 3.5 sq. km. In the course of 28 years it was built on and improved by Tsar Simeon the Great, one of the most educated European rulers, an exceptional statesman, soldier and man of letters (a disciple of the Magnaur School in Constantinople). He made Preslav the most majestic town in the whole of south-eastern Europe second only to the capital of Byzantium. For comparison, the population of London in $10^{th}$ century was hardly fifteen thousand people, Paris had still not developed as a city, Madrid was a village, and Berlin and Moscow did not exist yet. The most talented Bulgarian men of letters of the time worked there - Yoan Ekzarh, Chernorizets Hrabur, Konstantin Preslavski, Prezviter Kozma, Tudor Doksov. Being followers of the mission of Cyril and Methodius, for several decades they turned the Old Bulgarian language from ecclesiastical into one of the richest literary languages of Europe at that time. In 969 Veliki Preslav was conquered by Prince Svetoslav of Kiev, and between 971 and 1186 it suffered the Byzantine rule and bore the name of *Johnanopolis*. In $13^{th}$-$14^{th}$ centuries it was a significant administrative centre, main bishop's residence. In 1388 the town was conquered and destroyed by the Turks. Some Turkish documents of 1573, 1585 and 1620 registered a village on the spot of the present day town with the name *Eski Stambolchouk* (Old Istanbul) bearing the memory of the old capital. The village had this name till 1878, and then it was called *Preslav*. In 1993 the town returned to the name signifying its biggest grandeur - *Veliki Preslav*.

There have been preserved remains of fortress walls, palaces, civil ensembles, workshops, public baths, water pipe systems. The most precious building in Veliki Preslav in the past (as well as a sight today) was the **Round (Golden) Church** built in 908. Its dome (gold-plated outside and inlaid on gold inside) covers the central building with 12 niches

*Remains of Veliki Preslav*

# NORTHEASTERN BULGARIA

(cut in the wall) and 12 white marble columns erected in between them. In respect of plan and rich mosaic and sculptural decoration, the Golden Church is a unique example of the Old Bulgarian architecture. It was a predecessor of the European Baroque with several centuries ahead of its time. It had good reputation during Middle Ages.

*Ceramic icon of St. Teodor Stratilat*

The whole region of the ruins was declared a **National Historical and Archaeological Reserve** (tel.: 0538 2630, 3243). A rich archaeological museum is functioning on its territory; it was founded 90 years ago. Of particular interest is the section about the painted ceramics of Preslav and especially the world-famous **ceramic icon of St. Teodor Stratilat**. The museum takes pride in Preslav's golden treasure and the unique collection of lead seals of Bulgarian and Byzantine rulers and dignitaries; these are exposed in the special hall. There is a bus line to the ruins and the museum.

**Landmarks** of the new town:

**The Ethnographic House** is a good example of Bulgarian customs in the past. Visitors are offered to hear authentic folklore, and taste the traditional "durpana banitsa" (specially made sheeted pasty) and the wonderful wines of Preslav. **The St. St. Peter and Pavel Church** was declared a monument of culture. **Tsar Simeon and the Bookmen Sculpture**

**Composition.** A monument in memory of the people of Preslav killed in 1912-1918 wars.

Veliki Preslav is a famous producer of wines and cognacs of high quality, which are sold in England, Belgium, the Netherlands, USA, Canada and Russia.

**Accommodation**: the Preslav Hotel (Simeon Veliki Str.)

**Tourist Information** - in the hotel and the Patleina Tourist Association (41, Boris Spirov Str., tel.: 0538 2628).

**Transport.** The town has bus and railway transport. There are regular bus lines to Shoumen, Turgovishte, Vurbitsa, Smyadovo, and other smaller villages in the region. The bus station is in the central part of the town (Boris Spirov Str.). The town is the final railway station on the Khan Kroum-Veliki Preslav railway line that connects it with the main line Sofia - Gorna Oryahovitsa - Varna and in this way with the national railway system. The railway station is located in the eastern industrial zone of the town of Veliki Preslav.

**Surrounding areas**. In the **Patleina area**, one and a half kilometres south-east of the town (there is a bus line) there is a **Bulgarian monastery dating back to 10th century (St. Pantheleimon)**. Except for being a centre of cultural life, Patleina is renowned for its unique medieval ceramics. This is the place where the ceramic icon of St. Teodor

# NORTHEASTERN BULGARIA

Stratilat made of 20 ceramic plates was found. It is one of the most eminent examples of our cultural heritage (it is kept in the museum at the ruins of Veliki Preslav). After withdrawing from the throne Prince (Tsar) Boris I spent the last years of his life in the monastery of Patleina. There is the Patleina Chalet in the region (tel.: 0538 2565) offering 36 beds in two-, three-, four-, five-, six-bed rooms.

**The Ticha Dam** - 14 km south of the town. A wonderful place for having a rest, taking sunbathes, fishing, practising water sports, water tourism. There are rest houses, private villas, as well as the Ticha Chalet (on the road between Veliki Preslav and Vurbitsa, regular bus line, tel. for reservations: 054 59456, 59528, 59167 - in the Tourist Association in Shoumen), offering 16 beds in two-, three-, and four-bed rooms.

**The town of Vurbitsa** - 37 km south-west of Veliki Preslav and south of Vurbitsa Pass in the Balkan Mountain Range. Another old Bulgarian town where in 17$^{th}$ century the Turks colonised Tartars from Krim because of the rebellious Bulgarian spirit. It was the Tartar wealthy man called Meadali Gerai who built the famous seraglio in the town (1830-1835, master Kolyo Dimov). There have been preserved **the St. Dimitur Solounski Church** of 1842, two-storey houses of interesting **Revival architecture**, like that of Hadzhi Vulchan (1868), old workshops, the school of 1873, the house of the Grouev brothers, etc. Four or five kilometres south-west of Vurbitsa is the **Vurbitsa resort**, at the north bottom of the Vurbitsa section of the Balkan Mountain Range. There is a mineral spring (for drinking only), rest homes, private villas, a forestry enterprise and the Vurbishki Prohod Chalet (76 beds in two suites and three-, four-, and five-bed rooms; reservations in the Tourist Association in Shoumen). There is regular bus transport to Vurbitsa, and from Vurbitsa to Veliki Preslav, Shoumen, Omourtag, etc.

## TURGOVISHTE

The town of Turgovishte (population: 40 775; 170 m above sea level) is situated at the southern foot of the low mountain of Preslav along either bank of the Vrana River. It is 339 km north-east of Sofia, 41 km west of Shoumen, 25 km north-west of Veliki Preslav, 24 km north-east of Omourtag, 100 km north-east of Veliko Turnovo, 36 km south of Razgrad, and 35 km south-east of Popovo. It was an ancient market settlement. A regional administrative centre.

**History**. The earliest vestiges of human life in the area date back to the Copper-Stone Era (Halcolite) of the 5$^{th}$-4$^{th}$ millennium before Christ (near the village of Ovcharovo). In the vicinity of the town remains of settlements and necropolises from the ancient times (the gold treasure from Kralevo) were found. The name of the present town was first mentioned in 16$^{th}$ century as *Eski Dzhoumaya* (*eski* - old, *dzhoumaya* - Friday; on that same day markets were organised in the Turkish settlements, so in this particular case it is rather a market place or if translated - "Old market"). It was first registered as such in a Turkish register of 1573, and in the following 17$^{th}$ century the traveller Hadzhi Kalfa gave it a short description. At first it was entirely an Oriental town. In the course of years a lot of Bulgarians settled to live there. The crafts underwent a brisk development together with

# NORTHEASTERN BULGARIA

the trade therewith. The well-known Eski Dzhoumaya Fair started at the end of 18th century and became the largest in the Danube district and one of the biggest and most representing in the Ottoman Empire. It used to commence on 14th May and lasted for 8 days. Traders came from the whole of the Ottoman Empire, from Russia and from the west European countries - Germany, Austria, and England - they offered industrial goods. Lots of cattle were sold at the fair, but most of all horses, so it was called "Haivan" or "Kamshik Panair" (Whip Fair). It always started with big horse races (koushii). At the beginning it was held in the central parts of the town but in 1865 - 1868 it moved to a special place outside the town with conveniences like inn, stables, cattle-sheds, eating-houses, bakery, wells, court place where problems and thefts were settled, etc. - prototype of nowadays market places. It was held till the end of 19th century. The material prosperity lead to cultural progress of the settlement. The small school was now transformed into a secular school in 1846 and in 1863 the construction of its new building of European style was completed (it was the most prominent building in Eski Dzhoumaya), this was where Pencho Slaveikov worked as a teacher for some time. In the winter of 1872 Angel Kunchev set up a revolutionary committee. The leaders of the Bulgarian National Revival, Sava Gerenov and Sava Katrafilov, spread the seeds of progress and national consciousness. The latter together with Nikola Simov-Kourouto (the colour-bearer) were members of Botev's detachment of armed volunteers. Both of them died a heroic death in the battles against the Ottomans.

During the Russian-Turkish War of Liberation (1877-1878) the inhabitants of the town showed great courage in defending the Bulgarian quarters from the Circassians and Bashibozouks. The town was liberated in January 1878.

In 1934 the town was renamed Turgovishte. It is more and more developing as a tourist centre. The traditional fair in Turgovishte known as the Spring Fair and Industrial Goods Expo was resumed.

**Landmarks**. There are more than 30 buildings of interesting architecture in the **old Revival quarter called Varosh**. Among them are the **St. St. Cyril and Methodius and Their Five Disciples school** (1863; 1, G.S.Rakovski Str.) where Spiridon Gramadov and Petko R. Slaveikov (who gave the plan for the construction) were teachers and where the latter started editing the "Gaida" (Bagpipe) newspaper. At present the building houses the **Museum of History** (tel.: 0601 25188, working hours: 9.00 a.m. - 12.00 a.m. and 2.00 p.m. - 5.00 p.m. except Mondays). **The Assumption Church** (1851; Ekzarh Yosiff Str., tel.: 0601 41236) is one of the most beautiful churches built in Bulgaria before the Liberation. **The house of Angel Hadzhi Droumev** (1863; 14, G.S.Rakovski Str.) is one of the most precious sights from the Revival Period in the town; it was built by the masters of Tryavna (the **Ethnographic Museum** at present). **The Nikola Simov-Kourouto Museum Exposition** (20, Karavelov Str.). **Sveshtarov's House** (1860). **The houses of priest Zahariev**, of **Ilia Katsarov** and others. **The Nikola Marinov Art Gallery** (Mourgash Str. tel.: 0601 27760) bears the name of the renowned Bulgarian artist born in the town and possesses a rich collection of his works.

**Monuments of Nikola Simov-Kourouto, of the Russian soldiers killed in the War of Liberation, of all those killed in the wars** and others. In Turgovishte there is a Theatre of Drama (Svoboda Square, tel.: 0601 23377) and a Puppet Theatre (Hristo Botev Str., tel.: 0601 25085). There is a branch of the Blagoevgrad University here.

**Accommodation**: the Mizia Hotel (in the centre of the town, 1 Svoboda Square, tel.: 0601 23753, fax: 0601 24693). Belia Lav Hotel (2, Skopie Str.). Chervenata Kushta Hotel (in the eastern part of the town, 40, Antim I Str.). Belia Kon Motel (on the way Sofia-Varna). Rai Hotel

# NORTHEASTERN BULGARIA

Complex (on the way Sofia-Varna). The Polyanitsa Motel (in the region of Polyanitsa). The Borovets House of Tourism (situated in the park of the same name at the south-eastern end of the town, 20 min. walk away from the centre). It offers 78 places, 1 suite and two-, four-, five-, and six-bed rooms. All above establishments have restaurants. There are many other places in the town offering original Bulgarian food. Here are two of them: Maikop (11, St. Karadzha Str.) and the Roden Kut Tavern (Tsar Osvoboditel Str.).

**Tourist Information** - available at the hotels, houses of tourism and the N. Simov Tourist Association (3, Benkovska Str., tel.: 0601 27651, 27744).

**Transport**. Bus and railway transport connects the town with the rest of the world. There are regular bus lines to Omourtag, Shoumen, Veliki Preslav, Razgrad, Popovo and other smaller villages in the district. The bus station is situated near the centre (N. Marinov Str., tel.: 0601 24316, 23101). The town is a railway station on Sofia - Gorna Oryahovitsa - Varna main railway line. The railway station is located in the northern part of the town (tel.: 0601 25236, 22959).

There is an airport adjacent to the town but at present there are no regular passengers flights. There is public bus transport functioning in the town of Turgovishte.

**Surrounding areas. The Turgovishte spring** is located 8 km south-west of the town. The temperature of the mineral water is 27°C, and the water debit is about 6 litres per second. It cures kidney and gastric-enteric diseases. A real resort has been set up in its vicinity - an open-air swimming pool, a prophylactic house, a hotel, and private villas. Part of the mineral water is bottled. There is a regular bus line to the town. In the immediate vicinity of the town is the interesting **Hunting Park, the Yukya Forest-Park, the Borovo Oko Lake,** and 7 km away is **the Park** in the Turgovishte gorge.

Twenty-four kilometres south-west of Turgovishte is the **town of Omourtag** where there are preserved the Menzilishkata drinking-fountain from 1779, the St. Dimitur Church from 1851 and six Revival houses among which is the one belonging to granny Ivanka Hadzhiiska (built in 1876) where she hid 200 women and children from the Turkish army during the War of Liberation. At present it houses the town museum. There is a regular bus line between Turgovishte and Omourtag.

**The Roman Bridge** is situated some 60 km south-west of Turgovishte between the villages of Vidanovo and Malko Dolyane, above the Stara River. In spite of its name it does not date back to Roman times, it was built in 16th-17th century. It is 60 m long, 4 m wide and the top-point height is 10 metres. It has the shape of a crescent with one central arc and 5 supplementary ones. It was built directly on the natural rock. This unique installation has been completely preserved; it fascinates with the exquisiteness of its architecture. In ancient times it was an important strategic road. The village of Stevrek is the point of departure (on the Omourtag-Elena way); there is bus transport from the village to Omourtag and Antonovo. The distance from the village to the bridge is 8 km (1.30-2 hours long walk) along the country road fit for vehicles. The road goes through the former village of Malko Dolyane.

**The Gurbatata drinking-fountain** is located 50 metres away from above mentioned Stara River, some 75 km south-west of Turgovishte and some 25 km west of Antonovo. It is a natural limestone rock, about 4 metres high and having the shape of an arc. On top there is an outfall where runs the water falling from the vertical cliff above the limestone ridge. So falling from the outfall the water forms a small cascade called the Gurbatata drinking-fountain (meaning a drinking-fountain crooked like a hunchback). The small village of Stara Rechka is the point of departure; a regular bus runs between the latter and Antonovo. One can get to the drinking-fountain from the village following a marked track for about an hour walk.

# NORTHEASTERN BULGARIA

## RAZGRAD

The town of Razgrad (population: 39 036 inhabitants, about 200 m above sea level) is situated on the Loudogorie Plateau (and is considered the capital of the Loudogorie), on either bank of the Beli Lom River. It is 375 km north-east of Sofia, 66 km south-east of Rousse, 49 km north-west of Shoumen, 36 km north of Turgovishte, 36 km north-east of Popovo and 108 km south-west of Silistra. A district centre.

**History**. Razgrad is the successor of the Roman settlement called *Abritus* (its ruins are situated near the town), the latter being established at the place of a Thracian settlement with an unknown name. The medieval Bulgarian settlement called *Hrazgrad* (Hrisgrad) sprang up upon the remains of the ruins of the Byzantine town already destroyed in the invasions.

In 1388 it fell under Turkish reign. Since 1573 on the town gradually grew into a craft centre. People reared silkworms. There was a trading colony from Dubrovnic dating back to 16th century.

It developed as a typical Oriental town. Bulgarians from the nearby villages gradually settled there and thus changed the ethnical pattern. In 1860 the first school opened its doors. The first Bulgarian poetess Stanka Nikolitsa Spaso-Elenina worked as a teacher in the Revival town of Razgrad.

On 1st March 1879 when the foundations were laid for the Mausoleum of the Russian liberators Prince Dondoukov-Korsakov was among the guests present. At that time Frank Grunanger was the town's architect.

For the last decades Razgrad has developed as a centre of pharmaceutical industry in Bulgaria.

**Landmarks**. The **St. Nikola Church** dates back to the end of 19th century. The **Clock Tower** is a slender stone body in the shape of parallelepiped with a wooden superstructure with a clockwork in it. It is 26.15 m high; master Todor Tonchev from Tryavna built it in 1864 replacing an old tower from 18th century. **The Museum of History** is situated both in the town and in the Abritus Archaeological Reserve (tel.: 084 24273, 27378, 42207). **The Ethnographic Complex** (Varosha Quarter, 20, Antim I Str., tel.: 084 36071, 36971). **The house-museum of Professor Dimitur Nenov** has the same address (tel.: 084 29777). **The Stanka and Nikola Ikonomovs Revival Museum Collection** (Varosha quarter, 7, St. Kliment Blvd, tel.: 084 29322). **The D. Danailov Art Gallery** (G.S.Rakovski Str.). **The Ilia Petrov Art Gallery** (Cyril and Methodius Str.). The bronze sculpture at the **Momina Cheshma**. Mausoleum of the Russian soldiers who died in the Russian-Turkish War of Liberation.

In Razgrad there is Anton Strashimirov Theatre of Drama (in the central part of the town) and a College for Chemical Technologies and Biotechnologies.

**Accommodation**: the Razgrad Hotel (in the southern part of the town, 15, Zheravna Str.). The Central Hotel (40, Beli Lom Str.). The Abritus Hotel (downtown). There are very interesting restaurants in Razgrad offering original Bulgarian specialities. Here are two of them: Bai Kiro and Sons Tavern (4, Maritsa Str., working hours: 9.00 a.m. - 12.00 p.m. all the week round) and The Academy Restaurant (11, Rakovski Str., working hours: 10.00 a.m - 3.00 a.m.).

**Tourist Information**: Diana Tours - an agency for complex tourists services (Bulgaria blvd., block Chaika, tel.: 084 22637). All hotels and the Buina Gora Tourist Agency (76, Knyaz Boris Str., tel.: 084 26761).

**Transport**. Bus and railway. There are regular bus lines to Rousse, Popovo, Turgovishte, Shoumen, Koubrat, Isperih and other smaller settlements in the district. The bus station is located in the eastern part of the town near the river (2, Bulgaria Blvd., tel.: 084 22356, 26979). The railway station in Razgrad (tel.: 084 22436, 6 km away from the town with a bus line) is situated on the oldest railway line in the country, i.e. Rousse - Varna. It makes

# NORTHEASTERN BULGARIA

it part of the national railway system. There is public bus transport in the town.

**Surrounding areas. The Abritus Archaeological Reserve** (2 km east of Razgrad). The Romans founded the ancient settlement in the middle of 1$^{st}$ century and during the reign of the Byzantine emperor Justinian (527-565) the fortress walls were fundamentally fortified. The walls surround an enclosure of 140 decares and parts of them are preserved; three towers as well as the southern and northern town gates have been partially restored. A large residential building occupying an area of 3300 sq. m. was restored. In 251 the Roman emperor Decius found his death in a battle between the Romans and the Goths near Abritus. In 1971 here was discovered a big ancient golden treasure consisting of 835 coins. A rich archaeological museum is open for guests (operating as a department of the Museum of History). There is a bus line round the town.

Some 10 km south of the town is **the Pchelina Forest-Park** (**Kovanluka**) offering excellent opportunities for rest, sports and tourism. Numerous holiday homes, restaurants, private villas as well as the Pchelina Chalet with 40 beds in two-, three-, and four-bed rooms. For reservations refer to the tourist agency in Razgrad. There is regular bus line.

One of the most charming places of the Loudogorie, i.e. the **Voden Nature Reserve** is situated 36 km north-east of Razgrad, along the Chairdere valley. The reserve is known for its venerable deciduous woods, the stockbreeding farm for aurochs, stags of fallow deer and others, and a lot of natural and historical sights. There are good accommodation facilities and a regular bus line to Razgrad.

**The Thracian Tomb near the village of Sveshtari** (40 km north-east of Razgrad and 6 km north-west of Isperih) has an exclusive decoration. It was declared a cultural monument of world significance and is under the protection of **UNESCO**. There is a regular bus line to the village from the town of Isperih.

# NORTHEASTERN BULGARIA

## TOUTRAKAN

The town of Toutrakan (population: 11 977, 100 m above sea-level) is situated on the high Bulgarian bank of the Danube River, 433 km away from the river mouth. It is 380 km north-east of Sofia, 60 km north-east of Rousse, 62 km west of Silistra and 70 km north of Razgrad.

**History**. It was built in Roman times as a fortress under the name of *Transmariska* by emperor Diocletian after a victory over the enemy's tribes. There was housed part of the 11$^{th}$ Legion of Claudius'. This information was drawn from a stone inscription dating back to 18 October 294. The name means "a settlement beyond the moors" signifying the opposite flat plane around todays Romanian town of Oltenitsa. During the reign of emperor Valent a raft-bridge was installed over the Danube River at the time of the war with the Goths (366). At the end of 10$^{th}$ century south Russian colonists settled here and called the town *Toutarakan*. Medieval Arabic geographers registered the town by the following names *Rekran, Zakatra, Trakan, Taraka*. Other mentioned it as *Tukvant, Torkan, Dourakam, and Tatkrakam*. In 15$^{th}$-16$^{th}$ centuries the town had a lot of water-mills (at the Danube Rriver) and wind-mills (on the hills by the bank), which existed till late and the last water-mill lasted till 1942.

The history of Toutrakan registers the names of two renowned Russian army leaders. On 10$^{th}$ May 1773 General Souvorov conquered the town. After the Russian armies retracted the Turks extended and fortified the fortress but this was no obstacle for General Koutouzov to conquer it on 11$^{th}$ October 1810.

In 19$^{th}$ century Toutrakan was a poor fishermen's, craftsmen's and vine-growing town; yet in its dockyards a lot of boats, small sailing vessels and water-mills were built. In 1862 a big church and a secular school were built, and in 1873 the communal cultural centre called Vuzrazhdane was founded. In 1867 near Toutrakan Panayot Hitov's detachment with Vassil Levski as a colour-bearer crossed the Danube from Romania into enslaved Bulgaria; in 1876 Tanyo Voivoda's detachment did the same.

At the beginning of 20$^{th}$ century Toutrakan's population was about 10 000 inhabitants and the town rivaled other towns like Vidin, Lom, Turnovo, Svishtov, Lovech and as far as trade was concerned it excelled them. At that time and in later days Toutrakan was the biggest fishing centre in the country on the Danube River. In 1913 the town was included in the territories of Romania under the name of Tourtoukai. However, the town fell into decay and its population reduced. In 1940 according the Krayova Agreement South Dobroudzha (including Toutrakan) was given back to Bulgaria. Because of its picturesque location on the hills by the Danube River, Toutrakan is known as the Danubian Turnovo.

**Landmarks**. The construction of the old buildings in the town was influenced by the Romanian architecture (one can at once notice the corrugated iron roofs). On top of the **town hills Sheremetitsa** and **Teketo** one can have a panoramic view of the Danube River and the plain around the Romanian town of Oltenitsa on the opposite side.

**The Danubian Fishing and Boat Construction Museum**, one in the county, is situated in Toutrakan (tel.: 0857 2152). It is housed in the solid building of the old town bath. Among the 500 exhibits depicting the history of fishing from ancient times till present day one can see nets, harpoons, anchors difans (fishing nets 150 m long), fishing boats typical of Toutrakan and the like. **The Town Museum of History** is arranged in an old house. **Remains of an ancient fortress and a medieval settlement**.

**Accommodation**: The Melin Hotel (11, Vassil Levski Str.).

**Tourist information**: in the hotel and in Aleko

# NORTHEASTERN BULGARIA

Tourist Agency (3, Docho Mihailov Str., tel.: 0857 3895).
**Transport**. Predominantly buses. There are regular bus lines to Rousse, Silistra, Razgrad, Koubrat and other towns and villages in the district. Toutrakan has a river station as well (tel.: 0857 2565), but since 1992 there have not been any passengers' trips along the Danube on behalf of Bulgaria.
**Surrounding areas. The Danube River** gives great opportunities for rest, sunbathing, fishing, water sports, and water tourism.
**Kandidiana-Negrianis** - remains of a Roman castle near the village of Malak Preslavets, some 30 km east of the town. It is supposed that this was the location of the Danubian palace of Khan Omourtag.
There are regular bus lines to Toutrakan.

## SILISTRA

The town of Silistra (population: 42 153; 20 m above sea level) is situated on the right (Bulgarian) bank of the river Danube, 375 kilometres from the river mouth, at the point where the river enters the territory of Romania and the terrestrial boundary between Bulgaria and Romania begins. It is 442 km and 122 km north-east of Sofia and Rousse respectively, 108 km north-east of Razgrad, 113 km north of Shoumen, and 92 km and 143 km north-west of Dobrich and Varna respectively. A regional administrative centre.
**History**. There are very few Bulgarian towns that can compete with Silistra in richness of historical past. The town is the successor of the Roman *Durostorum* (translated as "solid fortress", built by Emperor Trayan). It was first mentioned in 105. In 169 during the reign of emperor Marcus Aurelius Durostorum became a municipal - an independent town (in 1969 people celebrated 1800th anniversary of the town) that domineered as a centre of the Roman province of Dolna Mizia. The town was one of the early centres, which promoted Christianity. In 303 the soldier Dazius was beheaded, and the local inhabitant Emilian perished on the stake; both of them were partisans of the new Christian faith. They were declared saints and included in the catholic calendar.

The great commander Flavius Aecius was born here; he was the one who defeated Atila, the Huns' leader whom the inhabitants of Rome had considered a real horror. The successor of Rome, i.e. Byzantium, restored the ruins of the town during the reign of emperor Justinian in 6th century and gave it the name of *Dorostol*. Until 600 it had been an episcopal centre.

The Bulgarians called it *Drustur* and after the adoption of Christianity it became the main religious centre in the country. Under the Byzantine rule it was a main town in the

# NORTHEASTERN BULGARIA

region of Podounavie. In 1074 a rebellion against the Byzantine under the leadership of Nestor broke off. The town was an important fortress of the Bulgarian kingdom in 13$^{th}$-14$^{th}$ centuries. In 1388 the Romanian leader Mircha Stari conquered the town, and after 1413 it was within the territory of the Ottoman Empire.

The town received its present day name during the Turkish rule as a result of the preceding *Diristur* and *Dristra*. The poet Partenius Pavlovich was born in Silistra in 1695. During the Russian-Turkish wars at the end of 18$^{th}$ century and the first half of 19$^{th}$ century the great Russian generals Roumyantsev, Souvorov, Bagration, Koutouzov, Dibich Zabalkanski took part in battles near the fortress of Silistra (in fact there were two fortresses - Medgeditabia and Arabtabia on both hills above the town) which later on became part of the defensive rectangular of the Turkish empire (Rouschouk - Silistra - Varna - Shoumen).

In 1958 the inhabitants of Silistra received as a present the key to the fortress of Silistra which had been seized as a trophy on 12 June 1810 by generals Kamenski and Koutouzov, and kept in Sanct Petersburg. Between 1828 and 1835 Silistra was a free town as a result of its conquest by the Russian army with captain Georgi Mamarchev at the lead (a Bulgarian in Russian service). The great writer Lev Nikolaevich Tolstoy took part in the Russian siege in 1854. In 1812 a monastery school was established, and in 1891 - a pedagogical school, in Silistra. The Swiss Louie Aier spent some time teaching physical education (his name was associated with popularising a number of sports in Bulgaria) in the town (as well as in Rousse and Lom) and died as an officer in World War I near Doyran. From 1913 till 1940 the town was within the boundaries of Romania.

**Landmarks. The Town Museum of History** (in the central part of the town, Simeon Veliki Blvd., tel.: 086 27040, 23894). **The Ethnographic Museum.** In 1942 a **Roman tomb** was recovered (4$^{th}$ century, from the time of emperor Theodosius I). It is a tomb with arches, 3.20 m wide and 3.60 m long. The most interesting thing in it are the frescoes. It is situated in the south-eastern part of the town, at 7$^{th}$ September Str. **The Roman Necropolis** of an eminent magistrate from the time of emperor Prob (276-282). He had been buried together with his horses and chariot; very precious fragments of the chariot made of electron (gold and platinum) have been preserved. Parts of **the antique Roman fortress and the border fortification** were discovered at different places in the town and along the bank of the Danube River (in the town park). **The Art Gallery** is located in the centre, at 120, Simeon Veliki Blvd. (tel.: 086 26838).

There is a Drama Theatre named after Sava Dobroplodni (in the central part of the town, Simeon Veliki Blvd. tel.: 086 26937, 23201). Silistra is a university centre. There is a Higher Pedagogical School, branch of Rousse University.

**Accommodation**: The Zlatna Dobroudzha Hotel (in the central part of the town, 2, Dobroudzha Str.). The Silistra Hotel (in the central part of the town, 1, Ilia Bluskov Str.). The Orbita Hotel (in the southwestern part of the town, near the stadium, in the area of

*A pelican in Sreburna Reserve*

# NORTHEASTERN BULGARIA

Krepostta (the Fortress). 2-star, offers 20 double rooms and 6 three-bed rooms. Of great interest is the attractive restaurant at the TV tower with a wonderful panoramic view. Danube Tourist Hostel (on the bank of the Danube River, offers 33 beds in four-bed rooms). Among the numerous catering establishments there are several worth visiting: Beliyat Kalpak Restaurant (south-east of the centre, 51, Dobrich Str., 24-hour service, offers national specialities at reasonable prices), Beli Brezi Restaurant (in the southern part of the town, 92, 31$^{st}$ Regiment Str., working hours: 7.00 a.m. - 11.00 p.m., offers delicacies and national food in a cosy atmosphere), etc.

**Tourist Information** - at the hotels, at the tourist hostel and D. Mihailov Tourist Association (9, Dobroudzha Str., tel.: 086 27217)

**Transport**. Bus and railway transport connect the town with the rest of the world. There are regular bus lines to Rousse, Razgrad, Shoumen, Dobrich, Varna and other smaller towns and villages in the district. The bus station (tel.: 086 23418, 23997) and the railway station (tel.: 086 26813) are located next to each other in the Industrial zone (the west end of the town). The town is the final railway station on the local railway line Samouil-Silistra (an extension of the Rousse-Varna line) and thus is connected with the national railway system. Silistra has a river station, too, but for the time being the transportation of passengers along the Bulgarian coast of the Danube has been suspended. Cruises along the river are only carried out. There is regular public bus transport.

**Surrounding areas**. In the immediate proximity above the town is The Krepostta Park (The Fortress). There is a rich archaeological museum in it.

**The Sreburna Biosphere Reserve** is 16 km west of Silistra near a village having the same name. It comprises the Lake of Sreburna and the surrounding slopes of the Danubian bank occupying a territory of 600 hectares. In the periphery the lake is overgrown with cane and bulrush verdure, water lilies, marsh marigold, marsh fern, duckweed, etc. Various kinds of birds nest here - some 150 protected species of marsh birds like pelicans (the only colony in Bulgaria), black coots, water swallow, egrets, ibis, wild geese, 11 species of wild ducks, etc. Six species of fish, tortoises, snakes, etc. inhabit the area. There is a museum arranged. Felix Kanits who visited it in the second half of 19$^{th}$ century called the lake "the Eldorado of marsh birds". Being natural heritage of world significance the Sreburna Reserve is under the protection of **UNESCO**. There is regular bus transport from the town.

Eight kilometres west of Silistra is the biggest village in Bulgaria called **Aidemir** (9125 inhabitants). There is a regular public bus line to and from it.

The Alen Mak Chalet (5 km away from the town, in the rest area near the town, tel.: 086 20089) offers 30 beds in two-, three-, and seven-bed rooms. Nearby is a bus station of the town bus. It takes an hour or so to get there on foot.

**The Danube River** in the region of Silistra offers numerous opportunities for excursion tours, sunbathes, rest, water sports, water tourism. There are rest homes, private villas, two camping sites (Popina - on the bank of the river in the immediate vicinity of the port at the village of Popina, 35 km west of the town, 18 beds in two- and four-bed rooms, telephone for reservations: 318 through the operator of Popina village or at the Tourist Association in Silistra, there is regular bus transport; Vetren - on the bank of the river in the vicinity of Vetren village, 21 km west of the town and 2 km away from the Sreburna Reserve, 9 bungalows with 40 beds in two- and four-bed rooms, reservations at the Tourist Association in Silistra, regular bus transport to the town).

Half of all apricot orchards of Bulgaria grow in the region of Silistra.

# NORTHEASTERN BULGARIA

## DOBRICH

The town of Dobrich (population: 100 379; 220 m above sea-level) is situated on the Dobroudzha Plateau by the small Dobrich River. It is 512 km north-east of Sofia, 92 km south-east of Silistra, 51 km north-west of Varna, 34 km north-west of Balchik, and 37 km south-east of Yovkovo, the frontier post at the border with Romania. Known as the capital of Golden Dobroudzha. A regional administrative centre.

**History**. The first traces of life in the town date back to Antiquity. Remains of a Roman settlement ($3^{th}$-$4^{th}$ century) were discovered to the north of the centre and in the eastern part. An ancient Bulgarian settlement existed here in $8^{th}$ century. The modern town sprang up in $15^{th}$ century as a big market village. Unofficially the settlement was known as *Kourkouskelya* (dry port). According to the Turkish traveller Evlia Chelebi who visited the town in 1651 the latter numbered 2000 houses distributed in 7 quarters. It used to be a brisk trade and craft centre with 3 inns, 200 workshops, and a bazaar (market place) with 100 workshops. At the end of $18^{th}$ century and the beginning of $19^{th}$ century a lot of Bulgarians from the regions of Odrin, Kotel and Turgovishte settled here. In the course of $18^{th}$ century and part of $19^{th}$ century the town happened to be in the centre of the battle field of the Russian-Turkish Wars. The town was liberated three times in different periods of time before the War of Liberation of 1878. The first Bulgarian church in the town called St. Georgi was built in 1843. In the following year a monastery school in the church was opened. The town hospital was opened in 1866, and 3 years later started its urbanisation. In 1872 the first class school opened its doors.

During the Russian-Turkish War of Liberation the town gave a lot of translators, guides, and victuallers in help of the Russians. The army of general Zimmerman liberated the town on 27 January 1878 without leaving any damage. In 1882 at the insistence of the local inhabitants the town was called Dobrich (after the name of Dobrotitsa, Bulgarian leader in medieval times, ruler of the area). The town had four delegates at the Constituent National Assembly held in Turnovo. The opening of the railway line Razdelna - Dobrich - Kardam in 1911 and its extension to the Romanian town Medgidia in 1916 gave an impetus to its development.

This Bulgarian town continued to suffer from the vicissitudes of fate. The first Romanian occupation lasted till 1916, and after the Neuilly Treaty of 1919 was again included in the territory of Romania until 1940 when the Krayova Treaty was signed; and by means of peaceful mechanisms South Dobroudzha was once and forever given back to Mother Bulgaria. On 25 September 1940 the Bulgarian army entered Dobrich; since then this date has been the official holiday of the town. From 1949 till 1991 the town bore the name of *Tolbouhin* but after that it regained its old name. At present it is the centre of the largest grain-belt in the country called the Bulgarian granary. The town was closely associated with the life and works of Yordan Yovkov, a great Bulgarian writer. The actress Adriana Boudevska was born here.

**Landmarks**: **Yordan Yovkov Historical Museum** (in the town centre). **The Ethnographic House Museum** (in the centre of the town) is in one of the most interesting Revival houses (1861) and illustrates the living conditions, traditions, customs, crafts and culture of particular Bulgarian ethnographic groups emigrating from different parts of the country (the regions of Odrin, Kotel, Turgovishte, etc.). **The Ethnographic Complex Stariyat Dobrich** (Old Dobrich) (in the town centre, 37, $25^{th}$ September Str., tel.: 058 29307) has preserved the authenticity of the arts and crafts of the region. Sixteen workshops operate in the area of the museum.

# NORTHEASTERN BULGARIA

**The Archaeological Museum** (in the town centre, 2 General Gourko Str., tel.: 058 25491). **The House-Museum of Yordan Yovkov** (in the town centre, 4, General Gourko Str., tel.: 058 28159). **The House-Museum of Adriana Boudevska. The Art Gallery** (in the town centre, 14, Bulgaria Str., tel.: 058 28215, 29091) exibiting more than 3000 masterpieces of art - icons, paintings, sculptures, black and white drawings, works of applied arts. **Military Graveyard Memorial Complex-Museum. The remains of an ancient Roman settlement** ($3^{th}$-$4^{th}$ centuries) in the central and eastern parts of the town. **The historical St. Georgi Church** (in the centre of the town, $25^{th}$ September Blvd.). **The imposing monument to Khan Asparuh** - founder of the modern Bulgarian state, and many other **monuments.** All sights that are open to visitors and have the following working hours: 8.00 a.m. - 12.00 a.m. and 1.00 p.m. - 5.00 p.m. (Saturdays and Sundays are days off).

There is the Yordan Yovkov Theatre of Drama in Dobrich (in the town centre, 5 Bulgaria Str., tel.: 058 operator 863 extensions 25209, 25313) with big and chamber halls.

**Accommodation**: The Bulgaria Hotel Complex (four-star, in the town centre, 8, Svoboda Square). It offers 290 beds, two restaurants, bars, and a swimming pool. The Sport Palace Hotel (three-star, in the town centre, 1a, $25^{th}$ September Blvd.). It offers 100 beds, a restaurant, two bars, a fitness hall, etc. The Stariya Dobrich Inn (Old Dobrich) (two-star, situated in the ethnographic complex of the same name in the town centre). The Dobroudzha Hotel (three-star, 2, Nezavisimost Str.). The Rezidentsiyata Hotel and Restaurant (in Dobrotitsa quarter). The Dobrotitsa Tourist Hostel (a kilometre south of the centre, in the territory of the town park, near the stadium and the monument of Khan Asparuh). It offers 44 beds in two-, eight-, and more-bed rooms.

Catering establishments worth visiting: the Lebed Restaurant (three-star), the Bulgarsko Pivo Restaurant (four-star, 38, $25^{th}$ September Blvd.) as well as many others offering Bulgarian national food and pleasant entertainment.

**Tourist Information** - at the hotels and in Dobrotitsa Tourist Association (3, General Kisselov Str., tel.: 058 25382, 22219, 28551).

**Transport**. Dobrich has bus and railway transport. There are regular bus lines to Varna, Balchik, Silistra, Rousse, Kavarna, General Toshevo and other smaller town and villages in the district. The bus station is located in the eastern part of the town on the river bank (Russia Blvd., tel.: 058 22240). The railway station is on the line Razdelna-Kardam-Medgidia (Romania), which connects the town with the national and European railway systems. The former is situated in the opposite west end of Dobrich (Dobrichka Epopea Blvd. tel.: 058 39078, 23823). There is a transport agency in the town, too (tel.: 058 24432).

The town is 51 km away from the airport of Varna, 35 km away from the port of Balchik and 92 km away from the Danubian port of Silistra. There are public bus and trolley transport in Dobrich.

**Surrounding areas**. Six kilometres away from the town is **Kobaklaka area** situated in a thick oak forest. Here is to be found the three-star Dubovete Resort (the Oaks) with a restaurant

# NORTHEASTERN BULGARIA

offering 100 seats with exotic terrace (tel.: 058 42332, mobile phone: 048 953129). There is regular bus transport.

**The region called Botevska Gora** (Botev's Woods) is 16 km south-west of the town in the immediate proximity of the village of Botevo. Nearby is the Vedrinski Dam offering good conditions for rest, sunbathes, water sports, water tourism, and fishing. Here is a chalet named Botevo (reservations in the Dobrotitsa Tourist Association in Dobrich). It offers 24 beds in four-, and eight-bed rooms. The railway station Botevo (on the line Razdelna-Dobrich-Kardam) is a point of departure for the region; all passenger trains halt here. It takes 30 min. to get to the chalet on foot. If the railway station of Donchevo on the same line is a starting point then it will take 1 or 1.30 h on foot.

**The Batovo valley** is 26 km south-east of the town and it offers excellent opportunities for camping, outings, tourism and rest in the realm of the marvellous nature. The Prilep Tourist Hostel offers 25 beds in two rooms (telephone for reservations: 058 25440, 27602 in Dobrich). The villages of Batovo (45 min), Stozher (1.30 hours) and Debrene (1.30 hours) are the points of departure. There is regular bus transport from Dobrich to the three of them.

## PROVADIA

The town of Provadia (population: 15 000; 30 m above sea-level) is situated on the banks of Provadia River in the south end of the gorge of the same name. It is 435 km north-east of Sofia, 55 km south-east of Shoumen, 47 km west of Varna, and 17 km south-west of Devnya. The Bulgarian saltern.

**History**. The town is a successor of the Byzantine fortress *Provaton* (Provat) of $5^{th}$ century, which in Greek means "sheep". The Bulgarian medieval fortification town on the same place was called *Ovech*. The remains of these fortresses can be found right above the town in the region of Tashhisar. In different documents the town appeared with the names of *Bourfanto* and *Ovechgrad*.

In $13^{th}$-$14^{th}$ centuries the town was a prospering crafts and trading centre. Traders from Doubrovnik and Armenia came here to do business. Ovech was among the most important metropolitan centres in Bulgaria together with Turnovo, Preslav, Cherven, Drustur, and Sredets. It was also called *Purvada, Pravada* but after all the present day name of Provadia was kept which sounds similar to the first Greek name of the settlement. For decades on end this had been the place where the famous "singing carts" (over 3000 per year) were made; Yordan Yovkov glorified those in such a poetical manner. In 1844 the St. Nikola Church was erected, and in 1849 a secular school was opened with R. Bluskov as a first teacher there.

After the Liberation Provadia underwent a brisk development and now it is the west branch of the industrial axis Varna-Devnya-Provadia. Six kilometres south-east near the **railway station of Mirovo**

# NORTHEASTERN BULGARIA

is one of the biggest rock salt deposits in the country (about 3900 m deep), which serves for the production of cooking salt. All travellers that had once visited the town had been fascinated by its beauty - *"In my opinion there isn't a more wonderful place than this"*, *"A remarkable place"*, *"A town having too nice a view"*, *"An incomparable town"*!

**Landmarks**. **The Revival Architecture Museum Complex** in the ancient Varosha Quarter with the well known **Lambov's House**; **the Town Museum of History**; **the Svetoslav Obretenov's House-Museum**; **the St. Nikola Church** (1844); **the Clock Tower** (16th-17th century); **the Old Bazaar**.

**Accommodation**: Balneohotel. The Arkovna Chalet (in the Prolet Park in the rest zone near the town, 1.5 km away from the bus station and 2 km from the railway station). It offers 15 beds in two-, three-, four-, and six-bed rooms. Reservations in the Tourist Association in the town (see below).

**Tourist Information** - in the hotel and at the Ovech Tourist Association (13, Tsar Osvoboditel Str., tel.: 0518 2040).

**Transport**. Passengers travel to and from Provadia by bus and train. The railway station is on the main line Sofia-Gorna Oryahovitsa-Varna. There are regular bus lines to Varna, Shoumen, Devnya and other smaller towns and villages in the district. There is a bus station. Due to the short distance to Varna the town favours the use of air and sea transport.

**Surrounding areas**. The remains of the Medieval fortress (Byzantine, Bulgarian, Turkish) are situated immediately east above the town in the Tashhisar area (or Kaleto).

**The rampart** from Asparuh's state is also in the immediate proximity to the town.

**The baths** in Provadia are 7 km south-east, near the railway station of Mirovo (on the railway line Sofia - Gorna Oryahovitsa - Varna). The debit of the salty (14°C) and sulphurous (21°C) water altogether is about 5 litres per second. It is used in balneo-therapy and balneo-treatment. There is regular bus and railway transport to Provadia.

**The Petricha Chalet** is 30 km south-east of Provadia and 4 km away from the village of Avren. It offers 50 beds in two suites and two-, three-, and four-bed rooms. Reservations in the Tourist Association in the town of Beloslav. The village has a regular bus connection with Varna and Beloslav. It takes an hour to get to the chalet from Avren if you go on foot, and if you start at Razdelna railway station it will take 45 min. You can use your own car. **The historical fortress Petrich Kale** is 30 min walk away from the chalet. The Byzantine built it in $5^{th}$-$6^{th}$ centuries. In 1444 Vladislav Varnenchek destroyed it. There is a museum about the history of the fortress. The rocks around are excellent for climbing.

**The Lovkata Chalet** - a wonderful place for rest, sports and tourism; situated some 10 km east of Provadia and 3 km away from the village of Manastir. The buses of the line Provadia-Devnya stop here. It takes an hour to get from the village to the chalet, and about 2.30 h if you start in the town. The chalet offers 30 beds - one suite and two-, three-, and six-bed rooms. One can walk to the **Vulsheben Izvor** (Magic Spring) (4 km away) and to the Petricha chalet (1.30 - 2 hour walk). Reservations in the Tourist Association in Devnya (tel.: 0519 3411).

Seventeen kilometres north-east of Provadia is the **town of Devnya** - the biggest centre of industrial chemistry in Bulgaria; it sprang up as a settlement near the biggest karst springs.

The springs of Devnya are 30 in number and have a debit of 3670 litres per second with temp. 17°-20°C. It is where the Roman settlement called *Marcianopolis* (after the name of emperor Trayan's sister - Marciana) sprang up and was succeeded by the present day town.

There is an interesting **Museum of Mosaics** in Devnya. There is a regular bus line from Devnya to Provadia. Devnya is a railway station on the line Razdelna - Dobrich - Kardam.

# BULGARIAN BLACK SEA COAST

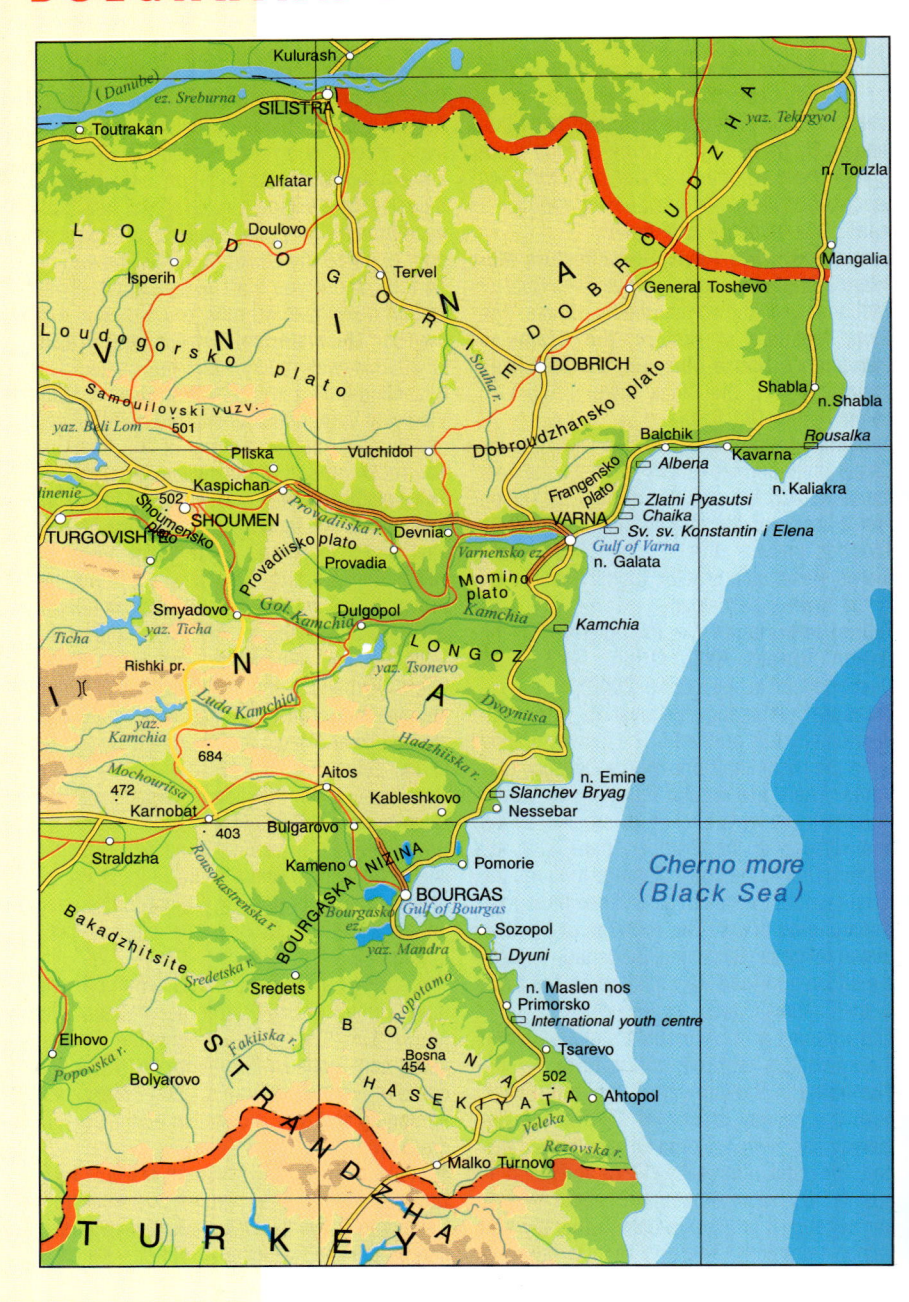

# BULGARIAN BLACK SEA COAST

## SHABLA

The town of Shabla (population: 4451) is situated some 24 km north of the Romanian boundary, 66 km north of Varna, and 536 km northwest of Sofia. In 1969 it was proclaimed a town.

**History**. An ancient Thracian settlement emerged at this place, then a Greek colony and later on the Roman town of *Karia* with a harbour was built in the vicinity of Cape Shabla. In early Byzantine time trade and crafts underwent brisk development. In later times the town fell into decay and only the fishermen's settlement was left. Except for fishing and the sea-related crafts the town is also known for its agricultural production. Not far from Shabla by the village of Tyulenovo there is an oil field where part of the population of the town earn their living nowadays.

**Landmarks**. There is an old community cultural centre, museum collection and an art gallery in the town. Every 24th May the town hosts a grand folklore festive of people's art and creativity noted for the songs, dances and applied art exhibitions. The beach here is clean and pleasant for recreation.

**Accommodation.** There is a small hotel in Shabla called Drouzhba Hotel offering 60 beds, as well as private lodgings and a camping site.

**Catering establishments**. Beside the restaurant at the hotel, in recent years Shabla offers sufficient catering opportunities at the small private restaurants and snack bars. There are grocer's stores, by-the-road caravans offering food and refreshment stalls. One can buy fruit and vegetables from the local producers.

**Transport**. Shabla is connected with Varna via Kavarna and with Dobrich by bus transport. The road to Varna is a first-class one and leads to the Romanian border northwards.

**Surrounding areas**. The archaeological excavations at Cape Shabla (about 5 km east of the town) are the most interesting site for the visitors. The foundations of an ancient Roman fortress may be seen and despite being a small one it had been an important centre of commercial contacts with the other settlements along the Black Sea coast. The Lake of Shabla is situated 3 km away of the town and it is a wonderful place for fishing and recreation. It is the nestling site for more than 100 000 wild geese. Nearby the town one can visit the **Ezerets Dam**. By the fishermen's settlement of Krapets (16 km north-east of the town) there is a camping site. **The Dourankoulak Moor** is further northwards and is famous for being a reserve for a number of marsh birds, some of them are registered in the Red Book of the fauna species in Bulgaria. On the big island in the Dourankoulak Moor the remains of the biggest Eneolithic settlement in Europe were excavated, as well as many other finds dating back to various periods of human civilization. There is a camping site, too. Nearby the town of Shabla is the yachting club where the annual yacht-regatta along the Black Sea coast starts.

*Kamen Bryag (Rocky Shore)*

# BULGARIAN BLACK SEA COAST

## ROUSSALKA

The resort of Roussalka was established in 1968 in the famous Taoukliman (Bay of the birds). This is a typical birds' colony in a pretty rocky area near the sea. It is 14 km east of the town of Kavarna, 59 km north-east of Varna, 529 km north-east of Sofia and 1 km away from the small village called St. Nikola. In the beginning Roussalka (Mermaid) predominantly received French holiday-makers while today a lot of Belgian, Dutch, Russian and Bulgarian tourists visit the resort.

**Accommodation and catering**. The resort offers 522 separate small houses (bungalows) facing the sea and enough sports and recreation equipment. It is situated on terraces according to the architectural decision. The resort offers opportunities and facilities for practicing of almost all kinds of water sports. There are many tennis-courts, biking alleys, fitness and balneology centres for water treatment and massage. There is a bar with entertainment programme, restaurants, discotheques and snack-bars.

Several small bays offer different beach conditions - sand, pebbles, bigger stones and rocks. The underwater world is interesting due to the peculiar relief of the rocks. Divers can find good opportunities for practising. There is a small firth with curative mud, yachting facilities, and an open-air theatre.

**The village of Kamen Bryag** (Rocky Shore) is in the vicinity of the resort and there are interesting rock formations, and wonderful rocky bays with many caves and reefs. This is the favourite site for students, trackers, hippies and tourists in search of privacy. The impressing **Yailata landslide** is situated 1 km south of the village.

# BULGARIAN BLACK SEA COAST

## KAVARNA

Kavarna (population: 12 225) is situated 48 km north of Varna, 518 km north-east of Sofia and 12 km away from Cape Kaliakra. It is a Black Sea port for passenger and cargo vessels of medium type.

**History**. Kavarna is the successor of the Thracian settlement called *Bizone*, the earliest finds dating back to the end of 6th century BC. Later on Greek settlers came here and turned it into one of the numerous Greek colonies along the Black Sea coast. In 1st century BC the town suffered severe earthquake that swallowed it almost completely. Then it was restored and included in the territory of the Roman Empire and consequently in that of Byzantium.

Nowadays traces of the old settlement are to be found on both the high and low parts of the area. After the foundation of the Bulgarian State on the Balkan Peninsula the town changed its name several times. It was called *Karvouna, Karbona, Karnava* and finally Kavarna. In the Middle Ages the invasion of the Tatars destroyed it. Later on the Boyar Balik restored it and it became independent principality named *Karvounska Hora*.

The Turks conquered it in 1393. The town moved slowly to its present day location. It suffered the Russian-Turkish Wars of 1828-1829 and of 1850, then it was restored but shortly before the liberation the inhabitants of Kavarna rebelled and as a result of the suppression of the rebellion, the town was put to fire and devastated by the bashibozouk (Turkish army of volunteers). 1200 people found their death.

The town of Kavarna was once again rebuilt and became an agricultural and fishing centre. Then it took part in the revolts of Dourankoulak

*Kaliakra*

# BULGARIAN BLACK SEA COAST

in 1900. Nowadays the town is an industrial centre; there is an agricultural technical school and a harbour.

**Landmarks.** On the high hill of Chirakman one can find the remains of Roman villas and walls, as well as of medieval buildings and churches. There is a museum hosting interesting exhibits of the town's history, the Thracian finds making special impression.

There is an excellent beach south of Kavarna. The interesting fishing harbour is much visited by tourists. Old buildings of the time of the Ottoman rule are preserved, today being used as warehouses. There is a small **Art Gallery** and local **Archaeological Museum** in the town.

**Accommodation**. The two well-known of the hotels in Kavarna are Siana Hotel and Dobrotitsa Hotel. One can find good conditions for the night in private lodgings at moderate prices. Close to the town is the camping resort of Morska Zvezda (Sea Star). It offers bungalows, camping area, caravans and tents at reasonable prices.

**Catering**. Near the harbour and in the centre of the town there are several big restaurants offering seafood and traditional Bulgarian cuisine. The small restaurants offer local dishes, pizzas, spaghetti, etc. The prices in the town are moderate and the products in the grocers' shops are cheap. The local producers sell fresh, fruits and vegetables. There are enough small snack-bars and pavilions in the town.

**Transport.** Kavarna is connected to Varna via Balchik and to Dobrich. There is regular bus transport as well as private transport - minibuses, taxis. One can use sea transport from the town to nearby Balchik, Kaliakra, some villages and small camping sites adjacent to the town, upon agreement with the fishermen.

**Surrounding areas**. **The climatic resort** in the village of Bulgarevo is situated 6 km east of Kavarna. The remains of the **ancient Timum Fortress** of Hellenes and Romans were found there. Six kilometres further eastwards is **Cape Kaliakra** where the ancient fortress called *Tirisis* was located. According to the legends it was a hiding place for the treasures of Lyzimah, successor of Alexander the Great. At the time of the Roman Empire the town bore the name of *Tetrasiada*, then during the Byzantine rule - *Akre*, and in the Middle Ages - *Kaliakra*. Today there are quite enough remains of those ancient settlements and part of them can be seen exhibited in a small museum sheltered under a limestone cave. There is a legend telling the story of several Bulgarian girls who chose to jump from the high cape with hair entangled with one another to avoid being converted to Islam by the Turks.

# BULGARIAN BLACK SEA COAST

## BALCHIK

The town of Balchik (population: 13 766) is 31 km north and north-east of Varna, 501 km away from Sofia, and is situated on the coast itself. There is a big harbour used for medium-size passenger and trade vessels.

**History**. The place was first inhabited by the Ionians in $5^{th}$ century BC. They founded a settlement and called it *Krouni* or *Krounoi* after the earlier Thracian settlements in the vicinity. The name of the town comes from the Greek word "izvori" (springs) as there are a lot of karst curative springs in the area. Later on it was renamed *Dionisopolis* after the name of Dionisius, God of wine and feasts. Some consider that the town was given this particular name because of the statue of Dionisius thrown out onshore.

The image of this god was on the coins minted here, and the town was also the most important centre, second only to Odessoss (Varna) on the northern Black Sea coast till the beginning of the new era. After a sequence of invasions at the time of the Roman Empire the town fell to decay. Later on it was included in the territory of Bulgaria. In $13^{th}$ - $14^{th}$ century it moved to Dzhina Bair, a natural fortification. It was ruled by the Boyar Balik, and so it was called Balchik. After the Crimean War (1853 - 1856) the town flourished and grew into a big corn-trading centre. After the Balkan War in 1913 it was included in the territories of Romania. Struck by the natural beauty of the place Queen Maria built a palace and a botanical garden, a chapel and a villa complex for the Romanian aristocrats. The town turned into a luxurious resort at the time. After 1940 Balchik was again included in Bulgarian territory.

**Landmarks**. Apart from the palace, the palace complex and the botanical garden - the biggest and most diverse in the Balkans, the town is attractive to tourists with its ancient atmosphere that has been preserved for centuries now. It is interesting to walk along and observe the Tatar Quarter with the pebbled streets and the houses made of stone and adobe.

**The Palace Complex** consists of the central palace with a high tower, numerous buildings in a modern style at the time, a many-terrace park, lanes and paths, stone summer-houses propped on marvellous columns facing the

*The Botanic Garden at the Palace*

# BULGARIAN BLACK SEA COAST

sea, a throne under an old tree where Queen Maria loved to sit and watch the sunset, a small chapel where her heart is preserved. There are more than 3000 rare and exotic species of plants in the botany garden. It is part of the teaching facilities of Sofia University. The whole complex was called *Tenha Yuva* (Quiet Nest).

**The Art Gallery** of the town is very interesting. The local museum is housed there as well. The coastal alley, 4 km long, is a nice place to stroll, so are the harbour and the small streets around. There is a small ethnographic museum and a beautiful old church called St. Nikola Church. The Revival complex with the old school in the town is quite well preserved.

**Accommodation.** The most popular hotels in the town are Dionisopolis Hotel, Balchik Hotel and Elite Hotel. One can reserve rooms at the palace as well. There are bungalows near the shore in the Tihiya Kut Resort (The Quiet Corner). The Tourist Information Centre is at 1, Ribarski Blvd., tel.: 05797 2034. There are many private lodgings offered in the town with their prices depending on the comfort and the distance to the beach or the centre. Not far from the town is the Bisser Camping offering bungalows and space for caravans to park and tents to put up.

**Catering.** Apart from the big restaurants in the palace, in the hotels and downtown, there are a number of small private restaurants, coastal stalls offering seafood, pizzas, spaghetti and other kinds of European cuisine. The grocer's shops are a good opportunity for practical tourists who cook for themselves.

**Transport.** There is regular transport to Dobrich, Varna and Albena. Apart from buses, there are numerous route-taxis and private minibuses, taxis and water transport to Varna and Albena.

**Surrounding areas**. **The area of Touzlata** is located 4 km east of the town and is well known for its curing mud. A balneo-centre was built here beside the two lakes, formed by old landslides. It receives patients suffering from joint disorders. A large recreational complex, a lot of villas, bungalows and a camping site are built here. There is a mineral spring with water temperature of 31°C. Near Balchik are the two big camping sites - Sandrino Camping and Beliyat Bryag Camping. They offer various opportunities for rest and water sports, clubs, bars, numerous bungalows for tourists having no camping equipment, small restaurants and stalls for sea and continental food.

Fifteen kilometres south-west of Balchik is **the village of Obrochishte** with a well-preserved fortress dating back to the early Ottoman rule. Travellers of that time used to compare it with the beauty of Baghdad.

*Balchik. In the park of the Palace*

# BULGARIAN BLACK SEA COAST

## ALBENA

The resort of Albena is situated 32 km north and north-east of Varna, 502 km north-east of Sofia and 12 km south-west of Balchik. It is located on a long sand stretch in the open northern part of Varna Bay. It was built in 1969 in an architectural style reminiscent of one of Walter Gropius' urban models and of the time of Bauhaus. Most of the hotels have a terrace-line structure with well-projected stories. The concept of this architecture is getting more sun in summer days.

The resort has three camping sites - Albena Camping, International Camping and Ekzotika Camping, which offer great opportunities for housing tourists and holiday-makers.

The **Batov River** is interesting with its location in a natural forest. Ovidius came here on his way to the country of his exile - Tomi (present Kyustendzha in Romania). To the north the shore is steep, formed of the yellow sandstone and limestone typical of the area. It is these stone slopes that gave the material for building the resort. It seems to match the landscape of the area in a most natural way. The resort was given its present name in honour of Albena, a female character of the great Bulgarian writer Yordan Yovkov, from the drama play of the same title "Albena". She is a symbol of purity and beauty in Bulgarian dramaturgy and literature. The area is rich of tennis courts, bars, casino, restaurants with entertainment performed by famous actors, children's playgrounds, swimming pools, golf playground. One can ride a bike or a horse, there are stunts with horses and cascade tricks, fans can rent automobiles, cutters, sail-boats, yachts, waterwheels and jets. The whole range of water sports facilities is available with the assistance of coaches.

There is an annual auto-rally called Albena held at the beginning of May, a folk festival for songs and dances from Dobroudzha, Zlatnata Antena (Gold Antennae) Festival for TV programs, bridge competition (in June), beach volleyball competition (in June or July), etc. Albena is a point in the route of the annual regatta. The resort hosts Vladimir Grashnov Annual Football Tournament, too.

**Accommodation.** At present the resort has 43 hotels functioning. From 4-star to 1-star categories the hotels offer different degree comfort and luxury to holiday-makers. Albena Resort is one the most expensive on the Black Sea coast, alongside with Dyuni and Roussalka. The most famous and representative is the 17-storey Dobroudzha Hotel, in Swiss style. The newly erected Maastricht Hotel is also notable. It was built with Bulgarian - Dutch funding and welcomes guests from all over Europe. Other famous hotels are

# BULGARIAN BLACK SEA COAST

Dobrotitsa, Drouzhba and Zdravets. There is an accommodation bureau and small private reservation agencies.

**Catering**. Apart from the numerous restaurants at the hotels, there are many restaurants and bistros offering various dishes - from continental European and traditionally Bulgarian to Indian and Chinese cuisine. The most popular and visited places offering entertainment and excellent specialties are: Picnic Orehite, Slavyanski Kut (Slavonic Corner), Starobulgarski Stan (Old Bulgarian Camp), Flambe Restaurant, Stariyat Dub (Old Oak), Ribarska Hizha (Fisherman's Hut) and especially Arabella ship-restaurant which serves incredibly delicious seafood.

**Transport.** There is regular transport to Albena from Balchik, Varna, Zlatni Pyasutsi (Golden Sands) and Dobrich. Apart from the regular town buses there are a lot of private minibuses, route and ordinary taxis, water transport from the small port in the resort.

**Surrounding areas.** Besides the village of Obrochishte mentioned in the section about Balchik, nearby is **the village of Kranevo** with remains of the ancient fortress *Kranea* and *Gerania*. There are many youth and school camps, as well as running mineral water in the village. The shore between Albena and Kranevo is high and extremely picturesque with sharply cut rocky formations. There are a lot of vine yards and small private gardens on the shore. The prices in Kranevo are far lower than those in Albena, besides there is a great capacity of private lodgings for foreign and Bulgarian tourists. The holidaymakers lodged in Kranevo often go to the beaches of Albena during the day.

Between Albena and Kranevo are the three big camping sites offering accommodation to tourists in bungalows and tents. There is a direct asphalt road through the area of Baltata connecting Kranevo and Albena. In the past the road was used by villains.

# BULGARIAN BLACK SEA COAST

## ZLATNI PYASSUTSI (GOLDEN SANDS)

The resort of Zlatni Pyassutsi is the largest one on the northern Black Sea coast (more than 1800 hectares). It is situated 18 km north-east of Varna, 488 km east of Sofia; it is bounded on the north by Kranevo and on the south by Chaika Villa Area, and merges with the St. St. Konstantin and Elena Resort. Above the resort is the Frengen Plateau of limestone structure, which is liable to landslide and erosion. The area is famous for the purest sand on the Black Sea coast. In Turkish times it was called *Ouzounkoum* - the long sands.

The resort is abundant in lush vegetation and with the numerous bushes and trees it resembles a real park. The mineral water running out of several big pipes onto the beach, as well as the marvellous deciduous wood bordering the Frengen Plateau turn Zlatni Pyassutsi into one of the pearls of the Bulgarian coast. The construction works commenced back around the year of 1950, and is still going on. Most of the alleys are asphalt-covered, the shore is paralleled by small streets, nice cosy hotels with picturesque parks around them, steps leading to small bays on both sides of the resort - favourite corners for tourists and holiday-makers in search for solitude.

The constant temperature of about 27°C and the microclimate of Zlatni Pyassutsi throughout the season make it a wonderful place for having a rest and fun. There is a casino, many bars, mini-golf playground, horse-carriages and attractive carts, water slides, good conditions and equipment for practising all kinds of water sports with the assistance of licensed coaches.

One can attend and participate in the following festive: the Strongest Man Competition, Miss and Mister "Zlatni Pyassutsi" Competition, competitions for all breeds of dogs, Satellite Tennis Tournament, Old-fashioned Auto Rally, International Festival for Standard and Sport Dances, etc.

**Accommodation.** The Zlatni Pyassutsi Resort offers at the disposal of its gueats 61 hotels and 10 luxury villas. The 4-star hotel category includes Yavor Hotel, Morsko Oko Hotel and Zlatna Kotva Hotel. The following hotels are of premium quality - Mars Hotel, Zora Hotel, Riviera Complex, Ambassador Hotel. Some of the hotels have swimming pools and fitness halls; most of them have exchange bureaus where the tourist companies leave up-to-date information as well.

# BULGARIAN BLACK SEA COAST

**Catering**. As is usual, each hotel has a snack-bar or a restaurant. There is a profusion of restaurants offering various kinds of specialties and entertainment in different styles. As a rule the best artists of the northern Black Sea coast dance and play here in Zlatni Pyassutsi. The following establishments are interesting for their architecture, entertainment programme and cuisine: Vodenitsata (The Water Mill), Tsiganski Tabor (Gypsy Tabor), Kosharite (Sheepfolds), Zlatna Ribka (Golden Fish), Kriva Lipa (Crooked Lime-tree) and Dionisus. The Indian restaurant has a chef from India and is of special interest to the visitors. There are a lot of snack-bars, fast food, grill- and toast-bars and various other ways to service the tourists.

**Transport**. The transport between Zlatni Pyassutsi and Varna is particularly well organised. Apart from the bus lines connecting the resort to the city and to the airport as well, there are a lot of minibuses, private route taxis and ordinary taxis. Because of the big competition the prices of the tickets are moderate.

**Surrounding areas**. In the immediate proximity of the resort is the interesting **Aladzha rock monastery**. It hosted Hesychasts in 12$^{th}$ century and has an interesting history. Nowadays only a small part of the frescoes are preserved but the experience of being in a monastery nestled on a high steep rock is unforgettable. The monastery is declared a cultural sight and houses a small museum.

## St. St. KONSTANTIN AND ELENA

The oldest resort on the Bulgarian Black Sea coast is only 9 km north-east of Varna and 479 km east of Sofia. Its construction began in 1908 in the vicinity of St. St. Konstantin and Elena Monastery and the purpose was to receive patients ill of tuberculosis. The church itself was built at the beginning of 18$^{th}$ century. Today the building of the monastery is a hotel and a restaurant of high category.

**Accommodation:** More than 50 hotels in the resort offer accommodation. First to mention is the 5-star Varna Grand Hotel equipped with swimming pools, lobby-bars and confectioneries, excellent restaurant, bar, fitness halls and many other additional facilities. Part of the Scientists' Rest Home is used as a hotel called Julio Curie. Other hotels offering excellent comfort are: Prostor Hotel, Roubin Hotel, Coral Hotel, Slunchev Den - a chain of four hotels, the Vakantsia Summer Resort with 25 villas and bungalows. For accommodation, information and reservations one may refer to the Tourist Bureau.

All hotels, bungalows and villas have been described in the article about St. St. Konstantin and Elena in Varna related chapter herein. Tourists should better make reservations on time as the resort is always packed throughout the high season.

**Catering**. The big restaurants at the hotels offer excellent food. Famous restaurants in the resort: Manastirska Izba (Monastery Cellar) - housed in the building of the monastery, Bulgarska Svatba (Bulgarian Wedding), Sedemte Odai (The Seven Old Bulgarian Rooms). Very interesting and much visited is the Sirius Fishing Ship restaurant, situated on a hill above the sea. It offers numerous fish specialties and seafood. As a rule the resort prices are high. Some tourists often prefer to eat in Varna.

# BULGARIAN BLACK SEA COAST

## VARNA

The city of Varna (population 314 539) is situated at the Bay of Varna, 470 km east of Sofia. Varna is the biggest city at the Bulgarian Black-sea coast. It is situated at the same latitude with Cannes, Nice, Monaco and Livorno. It is nestled in the deep valley between the Frengen Plareau and the Avren Plateau, where two lakes were formed during the polyotsen - the Beloslav Lake is to the west of the city and the other - Varna Lake is within the limits of the city itself.

Varna is a city over 110 km long, its width, including the new residential quarters is nearly 9 km. The city is like an amphitheatre and follows the curves of the Bay of Varna. It is surrounded by lots of gardens, vineyards and deciduous groves. Almost the whole territory is occupied with private country-houses and their small farms. The city is a regional administrative centre.

**History.** Varna has a history that could be traced back for thousand years. Due to its

*The Naval Museum*

**Transport.** Regular town buses run every ten minutes (from 6.00 a.m. till 11.00 p.m.) from the resort to the sea capital city. Many minibuses and route-taxis are a good opporture for quick transport to Varna.

**Surrounding areas.** Between St. Konstantin and Zlatni Pyassutsi is the small **Chaika Resort-Complex** offering sufficient accommodation and catering facilities. The **Evksinograd Residence** is located further southwards. It was built in a New Baroque style with exceedingly beautiful garden, park, fountains, and stairs leading down to the seashore. The residence can be visited with a special personal permit and tourists can have a look around in scheduled hours and days (usually on Fridays and Saturdays, reservations on tel.: 052 393140, 393150.

Almost next to Varna is the small resort of Pochivka (Rest) offering accommodation facilities. The new means for attracting tourists are interesting, i. e. barbecue and a programme performed by eminent actors who come here after their tours in the big resorts. Most of the hotels have parks and gardens, swimming pools for children.

The shore below Pochivka is interesting and picturesque with its typical rocky formations, slightly projected into the sea.

favourable location and visibility of almost 270 degrees the small cape, which now hosts the sea station, was inhabited by an ancient Thracian tribe - *Corbisy* in their small fishermen's settlement.

In 6th century BC a Greek polis (settlement) inhabited by colonists and settlers from Millet emerged here under the name of *Odessos*. The town became a fishing and farming colony and later on in the 5th century BC it turned into a real centre of commerce.

Up to the Roman domination the Thracian god Darzalas was worshipped rather than the common gods Apollo and Dionyssus. Old Greek and Roman sources evidence that in Darzalas' honour processions, mysteries, games and competitions were organised.

The town had been under the siege of the troops of Alexander of Macedonia in the middle of the 4th century BC but after the siege was put down the town was given autonomy within the limits of his Empire. After the uprising and its liberation during the rule of Lisimah the town re-established its supremacy at the north Black Sea coast. Up to the 1st century BC it was an independent polis and minted coins with the effigy of its patron god. Conquered by Mark Lukulus' legions, it became a Roman regional centre of great importance. There the great epic poet of Rome Ovidii stayed in his way to the town of Tommy (nowadays Kyustendzha, Romania) where he was sent on exile.

*The Dolphinarium*

Gradually Odessos lost its supremacy in the region, which was then gained by the town of *Martsianopolis* (nowadays Devnya) founded by the Emperor Trayan. Beeing conquered and devastated several times during the barbarian invasions it was for some time within the Byzantine Empire then out of its territories.

In 9th century it was already called Varna. It is supposed that the name originates from the horse people in Central Asia - toponymy (name of an area) and hydronymy (name of a water basin) in India (the river that runs into the Ganges at Varanassi) and from the concept of caste (colour). After the numerous wars between Bulgaria and Byzantine, the town was included in the territory of Bulgaria in the beginning of the 13th century during the reign of King Kaloyan. Its defence system consisted of three strongholds: one - at the Cape Galata; other - at Cape St. Dimitar and the third, called Petrich was near the lake of Beloslav.

Despite its reliable defence system, the town was conquered by the Turks in 1391 and it soon declined. In 1444, during the crusade of the Polish king Vladislav Yagello (Varnenchik) and the Hungarian leader Yanosh Huniady, the town was under the siege of the knights. Despite the fact that the troops of the Christian coalition fought bravely they suffered a complete defeat. The young king Vladislav was killed. The citizens of Varna built a mausoleum in his honour. In the course of time the town more and more acquired an Oriental outlook. Many Turks settled there. Mosques, konaks (town-halls) and Turkish baths were built. The construction of churches was strongly forbidden for a long time. Varna became a mighty stronghold, which guarded the north-east borders of the Ottoman Empire and a commercial and craftsmen' centre of great importance. During the Russian-Turkish War in 1828 the town was conquered by the Russian troops and hold under their rule for some time. An uplift of the national spirit began in the next decades. Schools, community centres and churches were built.

In 1878 Varna was finally liberated from Otto-

# BULGARIAN BLACK SEA COAST

man rule and became the most important Bulgarian seaport town. At the end of the 19th century it was connected with Sofia by railway. Many factories were opened, and industrial fishing was developing. Varna quickly established as a seaside resort as well, enhanced by the European fashion in architecture and water transport. Entertainment establishments and holiday houses were built. Varna won the fame of a favourite place for Bulgarian cultural elite. For a short time the city was renamed *Stalin*. After 1956 its previous name was reinstated. Varna became a centre of the North Black Sea coast and a starting point for the design and building of the numerous resorts around it. Marine business developed - from fishing to the transfer of goods between the East and the West. Nowadays Varna is an industrial city - the third biggest one in Bulgaria after Sofia and Plovdiv.

**Landmarks. The Roman Spa** are situated in the centre of the city. They were built in the $2^{nd}$ century during the reign of the emperor Antony Pii and were abandoned in the $5^{th}$ century during the barbarian invasion. After much research and restoration they are now preserved and are frequently visited by tourists and guests of the city. Pottery workshops were opened in the $14^{th}$ century, and later on a small residential quarter was built.

**The Roman Bath** dates back to the $3^{rd}$ century. It is built on layers of stones and bricks, bound by a mixture of plaster and crumbled tiles and bricks. The walls are grouted with water-resistant plaster, there are marble tiles on the floor and some of the premises were panelled in marble. In the $5^{th}$ century the building was considerably extended and reconstructed due to the development of that part of the city. Nowadays it is a sight of tourist and archaeological interest.

**The Holy Virgin Cathedral** is considered to be an emblem of the seaside capital of Bulgaria. It rises at the very city centre across from the theatre alley. Buses start from the square in front of it to all the vicinities and to the airport. A Revival master in the manner of Petersburg architecture built the church in 1866. Not until 1910 was it sanctified because its building and iconpainting took a lot of time. The woodcarving of the altar and the Episcopal stall are made by masters from the Debur school, Macedonia. The central wall paintings were completed in 1950. The **St. Nikola Church** is located near the Sea Garden Park and dates back to the 1866. It has very interesting wall paintings and ancient icons by masters, belonging to various iconpainting schools in Bulgaria.

**The Sea Garden Park** is another emblem of Varna. It dates from the end of the $19^{th}$ century, being finally completed in 1908. At that time the idea to place the busts of outstanding Revival figures in some of its valleys was accepted. Nowadays there is an amphitheatre; astronomic site, the first in the country, with an observatory, planetarium and a tower; many playgrounds for children, and a small channel, where they can practice rowing, as well as a pool for water wheels and a zoo.

**The open-air theatre** is a place, where various activities take place. These include the Varna Days of Music, the world famous International Ballet Competition and Varna Summer - a trienalle of arts. **The central sea baths and the beach** are located beneath the Sea Garden Park. They were built in the beginning of the century and are equipped with a polyclinic, water- and mud- cure complex, two quays, several restaurants and disco clubs.

**The Russian Monument** is in Primorski Park. It was erected in honour to the Russian soldiers who died in Varna in the War of Liberation.

**The Asparouh Bridge** connects the city centre with the residential quarterss Asparouhovo and Galata. It is the longest bridge in Bulgaria and works on it are still under way. Here the local club for extreme sports organises Bunji jumps. To the east of the bridge the Bay of Varna and the Cape Galata could be seen. To the west is the Varna Lake.

**The Clock Tower** was built in 1880 and it rises across the cathedral. Beneath the cathedral is

# BULGARIAN BLACK SEA COAST

one of the branches of the Theatre of Drama and the Club of the culture activists.

**The Festival Complex** is opposite the entrance of the Sea Garden Park. It is a modern building of aluminum, stone and glass. It has several stages, conference-halls, a big bazaar, and a sweet shop. Many exhibitions and festivals are held here as well as ballet and theatrical performances. **The Sports Palace** is located at the motorway to the resorts Zlatni Pyassutsi (Golden Sands), St. Constantin and Albena. Competitions in over 30 sports games take place there; exhibitions are held; concerts and performances take place, too. The design of the palace is actual copy of the Palace of Culture in Lagos, Nigeria, built by Bulgarian experts.

**The Dolphinarium** (Show-House) is one of the favourite attractions for children and guests of Varna. There are regular performances and demonstrations with the clever dolphins. Feeding the dolphins and taking pictures is allowed. Each year new stunts are performed here and the show gets more attractive, including performances by mime artists, clowns and actors. The **Theatre of Drama** is in the city-centre. It was built nearly a century ago after the fashion of Vienna. It houses a theatre, an opera - and philharmonic halls. Its foundations were laid by actors in the French Army during the Crimean War in 1856. The first Bulgarian theatre performance of Bulgarian drama was performed here. Not faraway is the **Puppet Theatre**, where the Golden Dolphin Festival of puppets takes place each year.

**Museums.** The **Archaeological Museum** is housed in a building that used to be a school during the Revival. Here visitors can see miniature models of pile dwellings from the Palaeolithic period; the hall to ancient arts and means of living; the hall to antique arts one of the biggest and most impressive collections in the country; some objects and church plate from the early ages of Christianity; objects of cult from the ancient Bulgarian ethnicity; the hall with exponents from the 13th-14th century, where the development of crafts at that time could be traced; the hall of Bulgarians applied arts and a lapidarium, where sarcophagi, tombstones, steles and tomb columns are displayed. The museum holds some rare objects from Egypt, Greece, Babylon and the Mediterranean countires, which were transported to ancient Odessos via the trade routes.

**The Museum of National Revival** is housed in a building from 1861, which was proclaimed a cultural monument. Patriotic citizens and scholars arranged the museum exhibition in 1959 and it has been enriched and extended many times. The original arrangement of St. Archangel Mihail Church can be seen on the ground floor. An impressive exhibition shows the struggle for religious enlightenment, national independence and the epic battles during the Russian-Turkish War of Liberation.

**The Naval Museum** is in the Sea Garden Park and possesses all the important documents and equipment of Bulgarian Navy from its foundation in 1878 up to the present. The great scientist Karel Shkorpil founded it in 1923. There are cannons, old anchors, and sea vessels and so on in the yard of the museum.

**The Vladislav Varnenchik Park-Museum** is to the north-east of the city, near the crossroads for Sofia and Dobrich. It was built in honour of the historical battle in 1444 when Czechs, Poles, Croatians, Hungarians and Bulgarians tried to resist the Turkish invasion in Europe. A mausoleum to Vladislav Varnenchik was built in 1934 on the foundations of an ancient Thracian tomb.

**The Ethnographic Museum** is housed in a Revival house from the 19th century. A typical arrangement of the house of Varna in that time is shown. Many kinds of jewellery are displayed, as well as clothing, formal national costumes, everyday life items and goods manufactured goods in the city and its vicinities.

**The Museum of Nature and Science** was founded in 1960 and it displays species typical of the Bulgarian flora and fauna. Geological and speleological miniature models show the

# BULGARIAN BLACK SEA COAST

## Varna

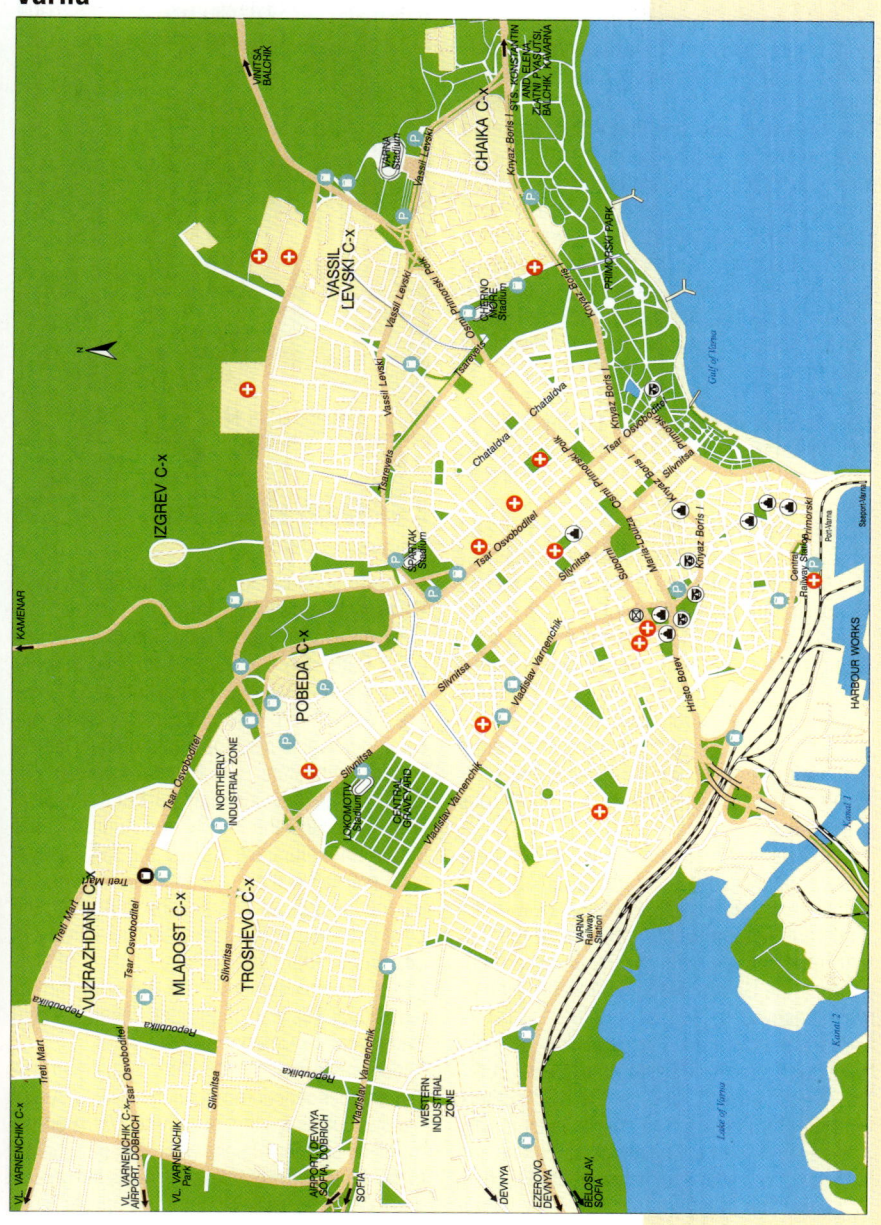

# BULGARIAN BLACK SEA COAST

stages of the formation of the lithosphere. There is a small board with the main kinds of stones and minerals. The exponents are displayed in three specialised halls - geology, flora and fauna.

**The Aquarium and the Black Sea Museum** were opened in 1932 - the first and the only marine biological station in the country. In 1954 the Scientific Research Institute on sea-related issues, fishing and industrial fishing was opened with the Aquarium. Hundreds of fish species are gathered here: molluscs, actinides, crabs, periwinkles as well as species of the fresh water rivers. A special place is occupied by the natural resources derived from the Black Sea, such as sea salt and oil.

**The Museum of Medicine** is the only one on the Balkan Peninsula. Medicinal plants and herbs are here on display, as well as surgical and other medical tools and clothing used in ancient times up till now. It was founded in 1869 as a private hospital with a small museum.

**The Museum of Art and History of Varna** has an exceptionally rich collection, one of its exhibits being the Gold Treasure of Varna - dating back 6000 years ago it is the oldest processed gold found in the world. 281 tombs were found in a necropolis dating back to the Halcolith Age. One of them contained more than 3000 golden articles (statehood attributes, jewellery, adorning, etc.), of the total 6 kg weight.

**The Art Gallery** was opened in 1950. It possesses paintings by the most outstanding Bulgarian artists as well as pieces of work by numerous foreign artists, donated to the gallery by private persons. A branch of the museum is the Georgi Veltchev Museum-House, where canvases by the prominent artist of Varna are displayed. An exhibition of icon-paintings from the Revival is arranged in the St. Atanas Church, built in the 13$^{th}$ century near the Roman spa. The church itself is very original with its mural paintings and icons and with its carved altar and bishop's throne. There is a collection of wood-cuts, etchings, liturgi-

*The theatre in Varna*

cal and canon books from Bulgarian Revival.

**Varna's festivals** are large in number, the most popular of them being: the International Choir Gathering - at the end of May, International Theatre Holidays - a part of Varna Summer Festival - in June; part of the aforementioned festival is also the International Gathering of Orchestras and Classical Music Ensambles - in July; again as part of the festival is the Jam Session in July and August. Other important cultural events are: the Folk Festival with international participants - in August; the International Ballet Competition in August; the Love is Folly Cinema International Festival - in September; the Golden Rose Festival of Bulgarian Cinematography; The Gold Dolphin International Festival of Puppet Theatres, held every year in October.

**Accommodation:** Varna offers virtually unlimited number of accommodation facilities. A well - known joke says that in summer Varna grows to the dimensions of Sofia whereas Sofia shrinks to the dimensions of Varna. As a rule the greater part of holiday-makers put up at private lodg-

# BULGARIAN BLACK SEA COAST

ings. There are several accommodation bureaus in the city which all exchange current information. The hotels at the disposal of the guests are a great number and continuously increase. Luxury hotels are the Black Sea Hotel, Odessa Hotel, Varnenski Bryag Hotel. The Moussala Hotel and the Orbita Hotel are cheaper ones. The latter is a hotel for international youth tourism. There are about 60 private hotels, most of them are 1- or 2-star hotels. The prices there are moderate. One of the best is the Breeze-II Hotel nearby Pochivka bus stop. Private lodgings can also be found directly not through the lodging offices.

**Catering**. Varna's most popular luxurious and offering special cuisine restaurants are: the Indian Maharany Restaurant, Maggy Restaurant and the Moussala Restaurant with a Viennese Cafe, the Paraklisa Restaurant, the FEB Restaurant, the Morska Sirena Restaurant, a chain of restaurants Mustang Food Bar, Happy Bar and Grill chain, Loza Restaurant, Morsko Konche Restaurant, and the Galateya Restaurant. Middle class restaurants, numerous private pubs and taverns are available even in the distant residential quarters of the city. Many of them are open 24 hours, others - as long as there are clients to be serviced. For those who prefer cooking for themselves there is a large chain of supermarkets with non-stop or regular working hours. There are a lot of market places as well. The most popular one is called Kolhoz.

A lot of small pizza shops and snack-bars that offer typically Bulgarian snacks such as sheeted pastries, cheese buns, dough nuts, boza (soft drink made of millet), and others. There are a great number of canteens, especially along the beach and in the Sea Garden Park where fish and seafood are offered. Every day one can buy freshly caught fish from the local fishermen at the sea station.

**Cinemas and theatres**. There are about ten cinemas functioning in Varna. Some of the best are in the city centre. The best is The Mustang Cinema. It is very comfortable and offers almost 24 hours of blockbusters. Stoyan Buchvarov Theatre of Drama is open during the whole holiday season with its three stages. Varna Opera and Philharmonic Orchestra also have their performances. The Puppet Theatre is also open throughout the season. As a rule, the theatres are on holiday during the summer, but in the beginning and at the end of the summer one can see many performances from all over the world at the Theatre and the Puppet Theatre Festivals, respectively. Good foreign theatrical companies are not an unusual event for the city. They perform attractive non-verbal shows, delivered for foreign guests, especially. In the open-air theatre pop and folk stars often have concerts, shows and ballet performances also take place there.

**Transport**. The fastest way to get to Varna is by airplane, it takes 50 min from Sofia to Varna. Varna Airport functions throughout the year. Planes in both directions fly 6 or 7 times a day during the summer. The airport phone number is 052 573323; the Balkan Ticket Office answers phone number 052 222248. The sea station provides sea buses to Balchik, Slunchev Bryag (Sunny Beach), Nessebur and Bourgas. The railway station phone number is 052 630414. The phone number of the booking office is 052 632347.

Varna is connected to all of the main railway lines in the country. There are express trains to Sofia and Plovdiv that reach for 7 and 4.30 hours

*The Sea Garden Park*

# BULGARIAN BLACK SEA COAST

respectively. Seats are limited so it is advisable to book sleeping car tickets a week before.

The bus station is 1.5 km away from the city centre. Its phone number is 052 448349. Buses for all the main destinations in the country start including Sofia from here. The Group Private Bus Company offers bus lines to all destinations (tel.: 052 256734). Buses travel to Athens and Istanbul as well as to some cities in Central and Eastern Europe. Their bus stop is in front of the cathedral. Varna's public transport offers over 60 bus lines that travel to various destinations. Some of the buses travel to the nearby resorts (20 km away from the city). There are trolley buses available in the city as well.

**Surrounding areas.** The famous **village of Vinitsa** is situated 10 km north-east of Varna, where the so-called Gagaouzi people live - they are Christians who speak Turkish and have very interesting customs and traditions. It is a favourite place where the citizens of Varna often go on picnics or for walks, it is also visited by a lot of tourists.

The **Cape Galata** is very attractive to a lot of tourists who seek solitude among nature. It is situated in the distant part of the Galata Quarter. There are wide meadows among deciduous groves and natural water springs with drinking water, and rocks convenient for fishing and cockle catching.

The **Romantika Resort** includes several hotels

*Pobitite Kamuni (The Rammed Stones)*

(tel.: 052 226317). It offers sports facilities for all kinds of water sports, cruises and voyages by the local water transport.

Around the Asparuh Bridge near the quarter of the same name the relics of the **rampart of Asparuh** can be seen. The great Bulgarian ruler built them 13 centuries ago in order to resist the raids of the Byzantine fleet.

To the south of the lake of Varna the **Dzhanavar Hill** can be visited. A basilica from the early Christian period is built here. In the 6$^{th}$ century there were fortifications to resist the raids of the Avari tribe.

The **Pobitite Kamuni** (Rammed Stones) are 18 km west of the city. They were formed by erosion about 50 million years ago. Dead cockles, sea species, and fossils are constituents of these stones, and of the sands around. Some of the stones have zoomorphic and anthropomorphic profiles. Many of them were place of worship or consecrated grounds during Thracian, Slavonic, and ancient Bulgarian times. Now they are an interesting tourist sight and a place where a lot of historic and adventure films have been made.

The **town of Devnya** is connected by the Varna Canal with the Varna Lake. It is famous for the industrial production of soda. There are remains of the ancient town of *Marcianopolis*, the second biggest town in ancient Bulgaria after Philipopolis. It was a stronghold against the numerous raids of the tribe of Dacians against the Emperor Trayan. In 3$^{rd}$ century it was so big that it was difficult to see it even from a bird's eye. The foundations of the defence walls, the rampart, the turrets, and the town's forum are in good condition. There are remains of other buildings as well.

The **Petrich Kale** rises opposite the railway station of Razdelna on Varna-Sofia railway line. The fortress was built in 5$^{th}$ century, later on it was destroyed down and rebuilt in 13$^{th}$-14$^{th}$ centuries. It was an important defence fortress in 1444 during the battles of Vladislav Varnenchik. The rocks near the fortress are perfect for mountaineering.

# BULGARIAN BLACK SEA COAST

## KAMCHIA

The mouth of the Kamchia River is one of the most beautiful sights along Bulgarian Black Sea coast. It is situated 34 km south of Varna and 504 km east of Sofia. The region is typical with its spacious beaches, starting from the area called Paletsa (The Thumb) in the north and ending to Cape Black near the village of Shkorpilovtsi in the south.

The recently built resort complex forks at the river mouth into Northern Kamchia and Southern Kamchia parts. The merging of two small rivulets springing from the Eastern Stara Planina Mountain - Louda Kamchia and Golyama Kamchia, forms the Kamchia River. Running down through the Balkan Mountain it meanders through a grove called **Longoza** (thick by-river grove). Over 40 species of beautiful trees, many species of bushes grow in the forest. Ferns, reed and yellow water lilies also grow here. Some tourists claim that the place is the earth's paradise; others call it a fairy tale place. The Ropotamo River, Dyavolska River (Devil's) and Veleka River have similar geological structure - sandstone, clay loam formations covered with wild vegetation in the quiet and large firth. Once Kamchia was called *Panisos* and the Slavs called it *Ticha*. Its contemporary name is of Kouman origin. The Romans built a stronghold called Erite on its left bank. The Lipovani tribe settled on its banks; actually they were offspring of Russian followers of the Gregorian Calendar who came here from the mouth of the Danube. Nowadays the frequently flooded area is a reserve under the protection of **UNESCO**. The reserve is 40 km in length (throughout Longoza to the river mouth) and 5 km in width in some of its parts. There are does, deer, sea hawks and eagles, wild boars, wild cats, etc.

**Accommodation**. There are several hotels in the two resorts. The preferred of them are the Kamchia Hotel and the Longoz Hotel. There are three large camping sites: Paradise, Pirin and Kamchia. Prices here are more than reasonable. Except for the hotels it is not necessary to make a reservation beforehand. Information about the hotels is available at the tourist agencies in Varna. Lodgings are offered in the villages in the vicinity.

*The mouth of the river Kamchia*

**Catering**. Apart from the large restaurants - Kamchia Restaurant, Lillie of Kamchia Restaurant, Kamchiiska Sreshta Restaurant, and the Hambarite Restaurant, which offer various dishes and show programs, there are a lot of small bistros, and pubs offering specialities from the sea and the river. There are a lot of stalls and a supermarket. In the villages in the vicinity one can buy fresh fruit and vegetables. There is a good restaurant in the area called Poda nearby the river mouth.

**Transport**. There is regular transport from Varna to Kamchia during the holiday seasons, and local transport from the villages in the vicinity. The water transport along the river is wonderful. Renting a boat is not only a way of transport but a tourist attraction as well.

**Surrounding areas**. The **Shkorpilovtsi Resort Complex** is near the village of the same name, and it spreads to White Cape in the south. There are two camping sites in it, the Izgev Camping, and the Horizon Camping. There is enough unoccupied space; there are restaurants and pubs in both the village and camping site.

One can go on foot to the Cape Black, hanging over the sea, with its old oak tree forest, and its spring of cold water. Further to the south there is a wide gulf with a drinking-fountain drawing its water from the Cape Black. Opposite it the Cape White can be seen with its lime rocks. To the north of the Cape Black is the village of Bliznatsi - 5 km away from the shore, to the south-west are the **villages of Old** and **New Oryahovo** with numerous rest houses around.

GUIDE BOOK

# BULGARIAN BLACK SEA COAST

## OBZOR

The town of Obzor (population: over 2000 inhabitants) is situated 65 km south of Varna, 73 km north of Bourgas and 530 km east of Sofia. It lies on the ridges of the Stara Planina Mountain that slope towards the sea and along the Dvoynitsa River. The ancient name of the town was *Navlohos* in Hellenic times, then it was given the name of *Heliopolis* (Town of the Sun) and in Roman times it was *Templum Jovis* (Jupiter's Temple).

During the Middle Ages the town was named *Kozyak* and was part of the Karvun principality and the fortress, successor of the ancient town. The Ottoman conquerors ruined the fortress to the last stone. Its present name Obzor was given in 1935.

The beach by the town is long and it extends from Cape St. Atanas on the north to the southern Cape Mona Petra. It is followed by a small nestling cove and a beach named Irakli. Once there was a village with the same name there, inhabited by Greek settlers who left it and settled to live with the Bulgarians in Obzor. Cape St. Nikola is several kilometres to the south where the Balkan Mountains touch the Black Sea. Then the central cape of the Stara Planina Mountain called **Emine** comes and it is considered to be the end of the Balkan Mountains. During the Middle Ages there was a fortress - Emona and the place around was called Paleokastro. Many monks and hermits lived in the rocks in those days and there were lots of small chapels and monasteries.

**Accommodation**. There are three camping sites with bungalows and enough space for tents between the village of Byala and the town of Obzor. Luna Camping and Prostor Camping work without advance reservation, as well as the Sluntse (Sun) Camping. The Ticha Hotel (medium category), Amore Tourist Hostel (low category) and plenty of private lodgings at moderate prices during the holiday season are located there. The Tourist Information Centre is located at 2, Ivan Vazov Street, tel.: 05504 3351.

**Catering**. In addition to the hotel restaurant, there is an emblematic establishment - Starata Kushta Restaurant (The Old House). There are small restaurants and refreshment stalls along the coast, as well as grocer's shops and fresh fruits and vegetables.

**Surrounding areas. The village of Byala** is situated not far to the north of Obzor. Once there was an ancient Greek fortress named *Aspro*. The camping site called Kristina is situated near the village. The wine of the extremely fine **Dimyat vintage** is produced in the village. There is a wonderful roadside establishment - Jackson Restaurant to the north on the road to Staro Oryahovo. **The village of Emona** near Cape Emine, to the south of Obzor is famous for being the birthplace of the Thracian king Rez. He participated in the Thracian War and was killed by Odysseus and Diomedus according to Homer's "Iliad".

# BULGARIAN BLACK SEA COAST

## ELENITE

Elenite is a resort situated east of Slunchev Bryag (Sunny Beach) at the beginning of an eight-kilometre long no through road. It is 50 km north of Bourgas and 442 km east of Sofia. The nearest village is Vlas. In the past it was given the name of a monastery destroyed by the Turks. The construction of the resort began in 1985. The resort complex consists of one-family bungalows and villas surrounded by lush green vegetation. The whole complex is designed as a park and offers deluxe holidays. This small separate settlement has its own private beach, several luxurious restaurants, sports facilities and equipment for water sports, tennis-court.

**The Vlas Camping** is situated not far away from Elenite. It offers accommodation in bungalows with toilet as well as enough space for tents. One can get to Elenite by minibus from Slunchev Bryag or by taxi, but most frequently holiday-makers come here in their own cars.

## SLUNCHEV BRYAG (SUNNY BEACH)

Slunchev Bryag Resort is situated 42 km north of Bourgas and 434 km east of Sofia. Its construction began in 1958. Practically, the resort is located on the whole territory between the land of the village of Vlas to the north and the town of Nessebur to the south. The construction began at the place where the two old wells providing water for Nessebur in the ancient times and the Middle Ages, had been. Nowadays there are more than 120 hotels and two camping sites, numerous places of entertainment. The Golden Orpheus International Festival of Popular Song, the Decade of Symphonic Music, part of the International Folklore Festival, fashion-shows, various beach competitions are held there. Hotels are also being built to the south of the Hadzhiiska River and an area of one-family luxury bungalows is being formed.

Lots of excursions in the country and abroad are organised for holiday-makers and tourists during the weekends or at the end of their holidays. The resort has tennis-courts, swimming pools, bowling, mini-golf playgrounds, yachts and sailboats, opportunities to develop and practice all water sports using the services of coaches, facilities and equipment, horse riding with coaches, water slides, a policlinic, and several big shopping centres for food, clothes and souvenirs. There is an amphitheatre with more than 1000 seats.

**Accommodation:** The most famous are Kuban Hotel, Bourgas Hotel and Diamond Hotel. The hotels Delta, Amphora, Zephyr, and Esperanto in the Black Sea Complex that is part of the resort. The two camping sites - Emona and Slunchev Bryag (Sunny Beach) cover a large area and therefore the sites there are practically unlimited. There are also bungalows in the camps, and these can only be reserved in advance.

# BULGARIAN BLACK SEA COAST

**Catering**. The hotel restaurants are three categories - deluxe, high and medium. Apart from them, there are plenty of other restaurants with different types of cuisine and entertainment. Some of the more famous restaurants are as follows: Chuchura (The Spout), Neptune, Hanska Shatra (Khan's Tent), Variety Show Bar, Strandzhanski Kolibi (Strandzha Huts), Magoura, Ribarska Hizha (Fisherman's Hut), etc. The Vyaturna Melnitsa Restaurant (Windmill) and Fregatata Restaurant (The Frigate) are attractive with their buildings made of wood and the marvelous cuisine and programs. There are lots of private restaurants, refreshment stalls, shops. The prices are high but the supply and the quality of the products are beyond any doubt.

**Transport.** There is a local transport in the resort - mini-train by which one can travel from the one end of the ten-kilometre beach to the other end. There is a regular bus transport from Nessebur and Bourgas to Slunchev Bryag, plenty of private minibuses, route and ordinary taxis, water transport to Nessebur and Bourgas. The ticket prices are moderate because of the competition and the flow of many tourists.

**Surrounding areas**. **Zora Holiday Complex** is situated here as well as the village of St. Vlas, and Elenite. The complex was built later than Elenite but of a similar style. The areas covered with trees along the Hadzhiiska River and the dunes between the road and the resort are very interesting. The town of Nessebur is so near with its new quarter extending to the north that it almost merges with the resort.

# BULGARIAN BLACK SEA COAST

## NESSEBUR

The town of Nessebur (9437 inhabitants) is situated on a small peninsula and on the land jutted out into the sea, 37 km north-east of Bourgas and 429 km east of Sofia.

Its beach is considered to be the best along the Black Sea coast. The big sandy strip of land between the town and the village of Ravda is covered with extremely fine and abundant clean golden sand. There are marvellous dunes next to the coast. The green copses by the sandy strips provide a cool breath of air during the hot days.

**History.** The town was founded on the place of a Thracian fisherman's settlement that was named *Menabryia*, which meant the town of Mena (the founder of the settlement). In the 6th century BC it was a colony of the Megarus tribe from ancient Greece, immigrants from Byzantium and Kalhedon. It remained the only Doric colony along the Black Sea coast, as the rest were typical Ionic colonies.

The Greeks named it *Messembria* and it grew into a big and well-fortified town-state with natural protection both from the land and the sea. It was equipped with water mains, a system of sewers, fortified walls, amphitheatre and numerous cult buildings the most impressive of which was the temple of Apollo. It became a commercial centre and plenty of goods from the Aegean and the Mediterranean regions were traded there. The excavated objects testify to a brisk trade with the ancient world.

The town maintained excellent relations with the neighbouring Thracian tribes and minted its own coins in 5th century BC. Two centuries later it grew so much that it founded its own colony called Navlohos near Obzor. The whole land between Nessebur and Obzor used to be a granary that supplied the two colonies with food as well as products of exchange and import. In 1st century BC the town fell under Roman rule and surrendered to Marcus Lukulus' legions so that it did not suffer any devastation. It was then that the constructions of the second colony of Messembria began, to the south of it - Anhialo (present day Pomorie).

In the early Middle Ages the town restored the fortress walls and until 812 it was part of Byzantium. In the same year it was conquered by Khan Kroum with no resistance put up, and was included in the territory of Bulgaria. Many a time the town was under the rule of the Bulgarians and then in the hands of the Byzantines.

During the reign of Ivan Alexander the town reached its cultural and economic boom, and it grew to the extent of occupying a huge territory of the land beyond the peninsula. It was approximately in this period of time when most of the churches of Nessebur were

# BULGARIAN BLACK SEA COAST

built and up to this day they are a unique decoration of the town. According to the world statistics Nessebur is the town having the biggest number of churches per capita. In 1366 the knights of Amadeus of Savoy conquered and devastated the town, and then sold it to Byzantium for 15 000 golden ducats. In 1453 shortly after Constantinople fell under Turkish domination the town was conquered by the Ottoman Empire and suffered decay. At the dawn of the Liberation it was a dilapidated fishermen's settlement, with well-developed viticulture on the soft hills above the town.

Today Nessebur is one of the resorts most preferred by tourists and it has been most attractive ever since the beginning of the century. The construction of the new town started at the time together with numerous rest homes, big and small hotels, and modern facilities for tourism and entertainment. The old buildings were restored and new houses in ancient style were built.

**Landmarks**. The churches in Nessebur are 41. Not all of them have preserved their full brilliance but even their present condition strongly impresses tourists. One of the oldest sights is the **Basilica** situated on the seashore, built most probably at the beginning of $5^{th}$ century. The building had three naves, however only the foundations have remained today. The **Old Bishop's Residence** located in the centre of the town is probably the most imposing one of all the churches in Nessebur. It is more than 25 m long and 22 m wide. The three naves were decorated with a colonnade and arches; stone and brick laid with a mosaic covered floor. **St. Ivan the Baptist Church** was built in $11^{th}$ century and is a typical cross domed church with three naves, and four brick-laid columns supporting the whole dome. There are some fragments of frescoes preserved dating back to $13^{th}$ century. There is a small archaeological museum arranged in the church.

**The St. Stefan Church** or the so-called New Bishop's Residence was built in $10^{th}$ century, too, and is situated in the vicinity of the harbour. It is three-nave. The exterior decoration is so picturesque that it marked the beginning of the future typical style of Nessebur expressed in the construction and decoration of churches of later times. The facade of the church is ornamented with built-in meanders of glazed ceramic figures of different colours, maiolicas and enamelled tiles that at the same time adorn and distinguish the architectural components. The main frescoes here were painted in $14^{th}$-$15^{th}$ centuries. The bishop's throne and the altar were made of wood later in $17^{th}$ century.

The subsequent picturesque style was best illustrated in the **St. Todor Church**; however only two facades have been preserved in their initial style. Today it has been restored, but the preserved decoration elements are unique in shape, colour, and variety of component combination. **The St. Paraskeva Church** was built in the same style. It is a small one-nave church. The ornaments match the architectonics of the building in a most natural way. Consoles with tiny arches slightly support the upper part of the dome and resemble children's sandcastle. **The St. St. Archangels Mihail and Gavrail Church** used to have a

# BULGARIAN BLACK SEA COAST

dome; its remains evidence of an interesting project and excellent performance. The restoration enables tourists see the architectural concept in the typical picturesque style.

In the ideal centre of the town itself is **the Pantocrator Church** with domes on a rectangular foundation. **The St. Yoan Aliturgetos Church** is considered to be the most beautiful one perched high above the harbour. It has three naves and the decoration of the facades is of unique beauty, particularly the eastern one facing the sea.

The remains of many parts of fortress walls have been found as well as the square turret, the round turret, a large part of the authentic medieval street pavement, and some of the Roman and Greek pavements, fortifications of different times and epochs, remains of administrative and other kinds of buildings. In spite of its small size the town is ever surprising tourists with the antiquities appearing all over the place.

During the Turkish rule only one church was built in 17th century - the St. Spas Church. The typical houses of Nessebur built in the unique style of 16th-19th centuries are interesting architectural monuments. So are the houses of Diamanti and that of Panayot Mouskoyani, which hosts an ethnographic exhibition, and that of Captain Pavel. The whole ensemble of the old quarters of Nessebur shows remarkable taste and mastership in the construction of houses, stone walls, and streets. The **Turkish bath** and the **windmill** at the beginning of the causeway are of particular interest.

**Accommodation.** The most famous hotels in the town are Messembria Hotel, Globus Hotel and Bourgas Hotel. In the town there is a tourist house and lots of small hotels. Private lodgings can be found without reservation in the old town; the inhabitants themselves offer their services to the tourists arriving to the town.

**Transport**. There is a regular transport connecting Bourgas and Pomorie to Nessebur and Slunchev Bryag (Sunny Beach). There are private taxis typical for the seaside towns due to the great number of tourists. The prices are moderate. There is water transport to Bourgas; one can often hire local boatmen to reach various places in the bay.

**Surrounding areas.** The **village of Ravda** is situated south of Nessebur and a sand strip connects both. There are melon fields, vines and gardens near the village where one can buy fresh agricultural products at low prices. There are numerous children's and youth camps, holiday houses and private lodgings. The **village of Aheloy** is situated on the motorway to Bourgas near the mouth of the Aheloy River. This is where the Bulgarian Tsar Simeon I destroyed the armies of the Byzantine emperor Lion Foka in the area called nowadays Kokalos because of the scattered bones of the killed soldiers. A vast firth with a sand strip parallels the distance from here to Pomorie and the long beach of excellent category is not yet built up. It borders the firth of Pomorie and the salt-mines by the town.

*Remains of Nessebur Fortress*

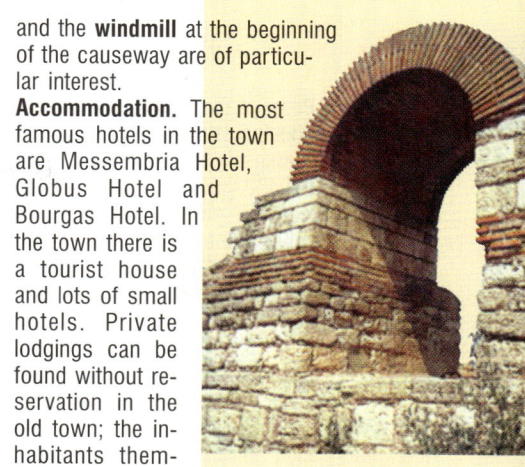

# BULGARIAN BLACK SEA COAST

## POMORIE

The town of Pomorie (population: 14 560) is situated on a peninsula projecting 5 km into the sea. The peninsula is 18 km north-east of Bourgas, and 408 km east of Sofia. Before entering the town one passes through a long and narrow causeway between the sea and the firth. The firth of Pomorie borders the peninsula and this gives the impression of jutting out into it.

**History**. There used to be a Thracian settlement here colonised by the Greeks in later times. A colony of the metropolis of Messembria was founded here in $5^{th}$ century BC. The town was called *Anhialo* being at the same time a colony of Apolonia as well (today's Sozopol). The town gradually worsened its relations with Messembria because the population of the latter was Doric in origin and the town was inhabited by the Ionic. The main occupation was fishing, mining and trading of sea salt. The shallow firth presented ideal conditions for that - it was where the first settlers discovered layers of salt in the sand. The ancient town was situated further inward onto the land in the area called Paleokastro where one can see its ruins scattered all over. During the Roman domination *Ulpia* was added to the name of the town and it surpassed even Apolonia in its glory for a long time. Anhialo regained its name in the Middle Ages. It suffered barbarian invasions and in $8^{th}$ century it was re-built by the Byzantine empress Irina. The town was intermittently under Bulgarian and then Byzantine domination, and vice versa, but more often in the Bulgarian territory. In 1366 it was conquered and resold to Byzantium by Amadeus of Savoy and his knights. It fell under Ottoman rule together with Nessebur in 1453.

At the time of the Kantakouzins family, successors of the last Byzantine emperors, the town became restive again; however Mihail - successor of the family had to escape to Romania. His plan did not succeed and he was hanged, but his sons managed to escape. After the Liberation the town regained its power and was of utmost importance in the Bourgas Bay. In 1906 the town burst in fire and nearly burnt down. It is known as a salt-mining centre; fruits and vegetables grow here; wine and tin productions are traditional for the place. Today the main occupation of its inhabitants is tourism; there is a mud-cure establishment. The mud-cure lake was discovered in $3^{rd}$-$4^{th}$ centuries BC and was later called the Holy Lake by Anna Komnina (a Byzantine female writer). The first mud-cure establishment was built here in 1902 after the curing properties of mud unique for Europe had been proved. The mud is good for bone and muscular disorders, radiculitis, rheumatism, sciatica, lumbago, discal hernia, etc.

**Landmarks**. The old churches - the **Transfiguration Church** (dating back to $18^{th}$-$19^{th}$ centuries has a valuable iconostasis and icons) and the **Assumption Church** ($19^{th}$ century). A stone bas-relief of St. Georgi is preserved in the **St. Georgi the Victorious Monastery of Pomorie**.

# BULGARIAN BLACK SEA COAST

A **museum collection** is arranged in the house of Peyo Yavorov, the reknown Bulgarian poet and there is a monument to his honour near the **Yavorov Rocks**. A domed **tomb-mausoleum** (3$^{rd}$-4$^{th}$ century) was found in the area of Kouhata Mogila near Europa Camping. It is interesting for the construction resembling a funnel and is open to visitors.

**Accommodation.** In Pomorie the majority of tourist use private lodgings. Most popular are the Anhialo Hotel, Pomorie Hotel and Byala Kushta Hotel (White House). Europa camping site offers accommodation in bungalows. Aheloy camping site is located 8 km north of the town and tourists having their own transport can use its services.

**Catering.** The most famous restaurants in the town are Tsarevets Restaurant and Peneka Restaurant. Apart from the restaurants at the hotels there are a number of small private establishments, refreshment stalls and shops. On can buy fresh fruits and vegetables at low prices from the local inhabitants directly or at the marketplace. Some rest homes (more than 30 in number) allow non-residential clients to dine at reduced vouchers.

**Transport.** Regular town transport connects Bourgas to Pomorie. Route taxis, minibuses and ordinary taxis run along the same route. Private water transport to Bourgas and Nessebur can be used upon agreement.

**Surrounding areas.** Despite Aheloy, the **village of Sarafovo** is 6 km south of Pomorie. Bourgas Airport is near the village and is open to international flights, too. The village is situated on the seashore and this in itself gives opportunities for recreation. Lodgings are offered. There are pleasant beaches.

**Atanassovo Lake** is located to the south of Sarafovo in a large lagoon. The waters of the lake are salty and used for salt-mining.

## BOURGAS

The city of Bourgas (population: 196 316) is the second largest city at the Black Sea coast and is a regional administrative centre. It is situated in the farthest western part of Bourgas Bay and is 390 km east of Sofia. It ranks fourth in size among the biggest cities in the country after Sofia, Plovdiv and Varna. Due to the low level of the coast three lagoon-lakes were formed: Atanassovo, Bourgas, and Mandren. The city is situated between the sea and the first two lakes, however it has grown so much that nowadays it almost touches the Mandra Lake.

**History.** Bourgas is a successor of the late Roman small town called *Deultum* founded by Emperor Vespasian as a military colony for veterans. Later it was called *Develt*, which served as a name for the present day village of Debelt. Three more villages were included in the present day territory of the city, i.e. Kastiacion, Skafida and Rossokastron. Later a curative settlement was built called *Aqua Kalidae*, arranged like Asclepionite around the mineral springs well known in the area. Thracian tribes lived here before the commencement of this construction work. The glory of the adjacent towns did not allow small fortresses to expand. In the Middle

# BULGARIAN BLACK SEA COAST

Ages a small fortress called *Pirgos* was erected, most probably used as a watch-tower in Bulgarian territories.

It was only in 17th century that Bourgas was given its present name and its location as it is now was determined. It was called *Ahelo-Bourgas*. After the Liberation it was called Bourgas, and was a small settlement with 2950 inhabitants. Ever since the town has grown and the population has increased almost 100 times. It became the centre of the Southern Black Sea coast, a city of well developed industry and trade, with a busy harbour. A number of plants, oil and chemical works producing more than 30 oil products for the country, were built; there was rapid agricultural development on the land by the city; salt and iron are mined in industrial quantities and traded far beyond the boundaries of the country. In 1903 the railway station in Bourgas started functioning.

**Landmarks. The District Museum of History** was founded in 1925 with the archaeological association. Today it houses an archaeological hall with a rich collection from the old colonies on the Black Sea coast. There are a number of ceramic vessels, objects from everyday life, coins and jewellery from antiquity, tombstones, plates of Thracian horse-riders, tools, and miniature models of ancient settlements. There are exhibits of modern history, photos of eminent Revival leaders, of Bulgarians born in the district having blazed a trail in the history of the native land.

**The Art Gallery** was established in 1945 with halls exhibiting foreign art, works of Bulgarian artists, and icons painted by Revival icon-painters.

**The Sea Garden Park** is situated on a high shore, all of it cut by flowerbeds, trees and sculptures. There is the bust of Adam Mizcewic, Polish writer and revolutionary, who stayed in the city in 1850. Within the park there is the casino, a small zoo and the open-air theatre, which houses the annual International Folklore Festival, and where part of the guests at the Golden Orpheus Pop-Festival perform.

**The central beach** is situated below the Sea Garden Park, a beautiful forked staircase in verdure leads to the beach. The sand is a mixture of various alloys of magnetite which are the reason for its dark colour. The city has a northern beach, too, close to the Izgrev Quarter, adjacent to the salt-mines.

**The St. St. Cyril and Methodius Cathedral** is situated near the marketplace, and is interesting for its marvelous frescos and wooden altar. **The Ethnographic Museum** has an interesting collection of traditional masks of koukeri, and costumes typical of the region, objects from everyday life, and ritual accessories. There is a video-hall where one can see ethnographic and historical films. A number of traditional Bulgarian fabrics and embroidery typical of the district are exhibited. The museum is arranged in a house from 1873, later declared a cultural monument.

**The Museum of Nature and Science** contains many exhibits describing the geological characteristics of the earth, the region, the flora and fauna. More than 1200 exhibits relating to insects and reptiles have been exposed. More than 140 species of fishes, plants growing in the district of Strandzha, protected and ende-

*Bulgaria Hotel*

# BULGARIAN BLACK SEA COAST

## Bourgas

mic species are on display.
**The Philharmonic, the Opera House, and the Theatre of Drama** are housed in three different buildings and function all through the season. Together with **the Puppet Theatre** they outline the cultural atmosphere in the city with their interesting concerts and performances. An interesting sight of Bourgas is the **Armenian Church** located close to Bulgaria Hotel. It was built in 1855 by the local Armenian minority supported by Bulgarians.

There are numerous festivals and holidays held in the city of Bourgas: Five days of the Classical German and Austrian music - at the end of April; International Festival of Children's Choirs - end of May; International Theatre Festival of Small Forms called "Theatre in a Suitcase" - May, June; Three-week Festival of Opera and Classical Music in Memory of the Conductor Emil Chakurov - July; International Folk Festival and A Week of the Arts for Children - August; International Pop- and Jazz-Session called "Bourgas and the Sea" - September; International Tournament in Standard and Latin-American Dances - December.

**Accommodation:** The city has many hotels of different categories, many private lodgings, there are two big camping sites in the proximity of Bourgas. The most famous hotels are Park Hotel, situated on the shore of Atanassovo Lake, deluxe category; Primorets Hotel; Bulgaria Hotel and Cosmos Hotel. Most expensive among them is the Bulgaria Hotel, the cheapest accommodation is found in the private hotels in the suburbs.

**Catering**. The city is full of restaurants, pubs, beer-houses, taverns, and refreshment stalls and grocer's shops. The most famous restaurants are National, Staryat Pristan (the Old Pier), Starata Gemiya (the Old Boat), Bourgaska Sreshta (Meeting in Bourgas), as well as the restaurants at the hotels. Most of the luxury restaurants have orchestras playing, some offer entertainment, too. As a rule the food in the city is cheap, especially if one shops in the suburbs or at the marketplaces. The practical tourists may use the services of the traditional bakeries, pizza houses, and self-service establishments.

**Transport**. Bourgas Airport is open for domestic and international flights throughout the year. One can receive information and book tickets on tel.: 056 684083; the booking agency in the city has the following tel.: 056 45605. There are flights to Sofia every day, and during the summer there are up to 7 flights daily in both directions. The flight to the capital city takes 40 min. The telephone of the railway station is 056 45022; booking office at tel.: 056 47023. The railway station in Bourgas has connections with all main directions round the country. The express train to Sofia travels less than 6.30 hours; it takes 3 hours to get to Plovdiv. Reservation in a sleeping car should be made at least a week earlier during the summer. The bus station is located next to the railway station, the telephone there is 056 24047. Buses in many directions including Sofia start from there. There are a lot of private carriers to the south and to the north of Bourgas to the towns and resorts situated some about 50 km away from the centre. The buses of the Group Company travel in various directions outside the country, too (tel.: 056 45360 for reservations). One can rent a bicycle at the corner of Mihailov Str. and Kirkov Str. There is regular city transport - buses, trolley-buses and route taxis.

**Surrounding areas**. **The lake of Pomorie** is located 20 km north

# BULGARIAN BLACK SEA COAST

of Bourgas and is surrounded by salt-mines and balneo-resorts. **Atanassovo Lake** is to the north, too, between the airport and the city. It is 10 km long and is a nestling site of many marsh and sea birds migrating from Gibraltar and the Bosphorus. Part of the lake is a biosphere reserve; bulrush and cane grow here, there are sites for fishing, swimming and having a rest. **Bourgas Lake** is a nestling site of numerous pelicans, ibis, and herons. It offers many opportunities for having a rest as well. **Mandren Lake** is 10 km south of the city and is also an important ornithological reserve with a large bird population in summer. Small lagoons are formed in it; it is appropriate for rowing tours and recreation. The lake is close to the road to Sozopol.

**The St. Anastassia Island** is 3 nautical miles east of the city. There is a well-preserved old church. The name of the island is associated with the exile of left-wing revolutionaries in 1923-1925, and of anti-Fascists in 1943-1944. That is why for some time after 1944 the island bore the name *Bolshevik*.

The **salt-mines** of Bourgas are a sight of interest. They border the Bourgas Lake, and some of them even stretch to the Atanassovo Lake. The **mineral public baths** are 13 km north-west of the city in the direction to Aitos. There are the remains of the old Roman town called *Aetos* built round the mineral springs. The settlement near the baths was called *Terma, Termopolis, Megaliterma*. In 16$^{th}$ century a Turkish hamam (bath) were erected; it is still existing and functioning. There is curing mud, a balneo-spa, a resort polyclinic, and a rest home.

**The village of Kraimorie** (old name *Kafka*) is to the south of Bourgas on the way to the old fortress of Pirgos. There is a nice beach near the village, as well as rest homes and private lodgings for the holiday-makers. **The Otmanli Park** is 15 km away from Bourgas near Cape Choukalya. It is situated in a thick forest on a territory of 6000 decares. There is a hunting reservation and bungalows for recreation.

## SOZOPOL

The town of Sozopol (population: 4 987) is situated 31 km south-east of Bourgas, and 421 km south-east of Sofia. The town lies on a small rocky peninsula in the farthest southern part of the Bourgas Bay. A one hundred-metre long strip of land connects it to the mainland. After 1925 the town started to grow in the direction of Harmanite Area and today it occupies considerably larger territory on the mainland.

**History**. The first settlements belonged to the Thracian tribes of Nipsei and Skirimian. In 7$^{th}$

*A typical Sozopol house*

# BULGARIAN BLACK SEA COAST

century BC Greek colonisers settled there and called the town after Apollo, the God of arts. *Apolonia* developed mainly as a trading centre for honey, wax, corn, wine, olive oil, olives, textiles, jewellery, and pottery. The numerous finds are evidence that this small town used to be the trading centre of the whole of the Black Sea coast. Much earlier in 13th century BC the argonauts led by Iazon, Heraklitis and Orpheus came ashore. The love for travelling and discovering made the inhabitants of Apolonia in those times travel, trade and found new colonies. So were founded the settlements of Anhialo and Pirgos, Termopolis and Aetos. The town was included in the union of sea town-states founded by Percales. Apolonia was frequently in economic and political dispute with the Doric inhabitants of Messembria; wars were even waged. At the time the island of Kirik was mainly inhabited. Apolonia sought help from Philip of Macedonia against the attacks of the Scythians. It was included in the territory of the Macedonian State at the time of Alexander the Great and was constantly subject to invasions but it struggled against the attacks of a number of Nomadic tribes flowing from north and west. The town fell under Roman domination in 1st century BC and was severely ruined by the armies of Marcus Lucul. It is an interesting fact that the Romans quickly restored the ruins, built new temples, and ordered a thirteen-metre high statue of Apollo by the sculpturer Kalamis. The statue was sent to Rome as an example of the arts of this particular Roman province. As early as 6th century Apolonia minted coins of its own. The Roman domination provided three centuries of peace until the invasion of the barbarian tribes. It was only in 5th century that the town was included in the territory of Byzantium.

During the reign of Khan Kroum it was within the borders of Bulgaria and like all other sea towns it frequently fell under the rule of Byzantium. In the Middle Ages it preserved its status of a district town. It was severely devastated in the middle of 14th century during an attack by the Genoa fleet. Later it was conquered and sold by the knights of Amadeus of Savoy. After a long siege the town fell under Turkish rule in 1453. Only wooden houses have been built there ever since; the oldest samples can be observed even today in the unique old streets. Sozopol welcomed the Liberation as small fishermen's settlement. Later the town became the biggest fishing centre of the Black Sea coast and developed recreation and tourism. The famous Tsar's Beach is located to the north of the town. Nestled between the rocks to the south of the town is the Raiski Beach (Paradise) and further southwards - the Kavatsite. The Harmanite Beach is immediately to the south of the so-called "new" town. An ancient necropolis was found here in 1993 and excavations are still going on.

**The landmarks** in Sozopol are many, but none of them can be separated from the rest since all of them impact the visitors as an attractive ensemble. **The ancient churches** from the Revival Period - St. Zosim Church and The Holy Virgin Church. The following **houses** are quite interesting: the house of Dimitur Laskaridis (17th century, now an art gallery), a fish trader, Ana Trendafilova's (the house

# BULGARIAN BLACK SEA COAST

with the sun), of Kourtidis, Lina Psarianova's (now arranged as Stenata Restaurant), of Grandmother Koukoulissa Hadzhinikolova (today housing the office of Sturshel Newspaper), Metropoliev's House (a medical centre at present), of Kreanoolu, etc. The **old cobbled streets** and high fences in front of which the old women sit and chat, knit laces and sell fig jam, are inseparable elements of a whole complex of three-centuries of history. Interesting places to visit are the **Archaeological Museum** and the **Art Gallery**.

At the beginning of September each year the town hosts the big Apolonia International Art Festival.

**Accommodation**. There are lodgings in the old part and in the new part of the town as well. The Radik Hotel and the Groudov Hotel are among the well-known ones. There are a lot of camping sites around Sozopol where many tourists spend their holidays: Kavatsite (The Willows), Smokinya (The Fig), Vesselie (Feast), Zlatna Ribka (Golden Fish) and Gradina (Garden). They offer bungalows of different categories, sites for caravans, tents and automobiles. The prices are quite moderate, the service and the hygiene are of good quality. The Tourist Information Centre is at Republikanska Str., tel.: 05514 3336.

**Catering**. The traditional establishments are the small coastal restaurants, small private places both in the old and new part of the town, the stalls for fish, the pizza-huts, the snack-bars scattered all over the camping sites. Interesting catering establishments are Vyaturnata Melnitsa (The Windmill), Sozopol Tavern, Athens Tavern, the restaurants Xantana, Neptun, Drouzhba Fishing Boat, Orpheus, Olymp and Lilia. Some of them are very interesting as they are built on ancient remains and houses after detailed archaeological research and restorations. Such an example is Stenata Restaurant (The Wall) whose basements were used as a warehouse for grain far back in time, and Kladenetsa Restaurant (The Well) which was built at the place of a spring, which

supplied the town with drinking water via water pipes. The prices at the restaurants are high, moderate prices one can enjoy at the camping sites and in the small restaurants along the beach. There are a lot of grocer's and marketplaces. One could buy fish directly from the fishermen at the quay.

**Surrounding areas**. To the north is the well-known resort at the **village of Chernomorets**, which borders the Gradina camping site. The Tourist Information Centre in the village is at 6, St. Nikola Str., tel.: 05510 2744. To the north there are marvelous rock juts, to the south - a river and canes of human size. There is an old church, a camping site called Chernomorets, rest homes and a lot of private lodgings.

To the south of Sozopol there are a number of fjords-like formations. The coast here is particularly high and cut in by the incoming waves. There are numerous secluded coves. **Mt. Bakurluka** (376 m high) is above the town, and some 20 km to the south is the mouth of **the Ropotamo River**. There is a biosphere reserve, camping sites, very near is the famous **Zmiiski Island** (of the Snakes).

# BULGARIAN BLACK SEA COAST

## DYUNI

The Dyuni Resort is situated some 12 km north of Primorsko and was completed in 1987 as a Bulgarian-Austrian project. It offers lots of hotels, villas and bungalows.
The Alepou Beach and Arkoutino Beach are visited by the tourists. They are wild and very beautiful places, which do not offer luxurious conditions for tourism and recreation. **Cape Maslen** is situated after the mouth of Roporamo River, in its last 20 kilometres after the biosphere reserve. Its rocky profile and high precipice down to the sea offer a great view to the tourists who have climbed it and beneath them there are small and quiet coves between the fiords covered with pebbles and seashells. Further southwards is the Perla Camping located in one of the most beautiful bays along the Black Sea coast. Here the beach gradually turns into a green grove; nearby is the marsh of Stomoplo. Two biosphere reserves cover this area - Vodna Lilia (water lily) and Velyov Vir. Via Pontica - the way of the migrating birds flying to the south passes from here. Every year at the end of the summer thousands of storks, pelicans, 33 species of birds of prey gather in the area and after having arranged themselves like a gigantic fan in the air (nobody knows why they follow this order) the birds with grandeur head southwards to spend the winter. The view is imposing and admirers visit this area to enjoy the unique scene.

## PRIMORSKO

The town of Primorsko (population: 2459) is a climate resort and a centre for youth tourism. It is situated 52 km south of Bourgas and 442 km south-east of Sofia. It lies on a cape jutting out between the Stamopolo Bay and the Dyavolski (Devil's) Bay. The old Turkish village bore the name of *Chenger*, and later on that of *Kyupria*.

Primorsko has a large beach zone and more than 80 rest homes, houses and summer camps for schoolchildren and students and an open-air theatre as well. The area is forested with deciduous trees and vegetation and is arranged as a park of numerous alleys in an old oak wood.

**Accommodation.** One can stay in Primorsko upon a booking in advance. During the summer season it would be a risk to rely on lodging without a reservation. The Tourist Information Centre is at 3$^{rd}$ March Street, tel.: 05561 3076.

**Catering.** The small restaurants and refreshment stalls are infinite in number. The local canteens at the rest houses and camps are much sought after. The prices are not high but the canteens require a preliminary reservation.

**Transport.** Several times in the day a bus runs to Bourgas and Sozopol. The telephone of the bus station is 05561 2613.

# BULGARIAN BLACK SEA COAST

## KITEN

The village of Kiten (population: 528) is situated at the south end of Primorsko Bay, 56 km south of Bourgas and 446 south-east of Sofia. The village is the successor of the *Urdoviza Fortress* situated on the cape itself. The Romans called the settlement *Oroudiza*. The town existed till the fall under Turkish domination and after that it was abandoned. One can still see ruins of the settlement lying on the cape. The river of Karaagach is very beautiful; it flows into the sea at the southern part of the Urdoviza Bay. The marsh mouth is full of fish. There are five camping sites in the vicinity: Atliman, Les, Koral, Koop and Yug.

There is a legend telling about a young woman called Stana who escaped from the harem of the Sultan. Amazed by her courage the Sultan promised to free the land she could reach on horseback. After a day's long ride the horse died on one of the beaches that up to this day bears the name of Atliman - the Bay of the Horse.

**Accommodation.** In Kiten there are enough private lodgings and camping sites on the beach. The local inhabitants are helpful, and the prices - comparatively low.

**Catering**. There are several small restaurants and plenty of snack bars. Local fishermen and producers offer fish, vegetables and fruits.

**Transport**. There are regular bus lines from Bourgas to Kiten, or one can take a taxi from Primorsko.

**Surrounding areas**. The **village of Lozenets** is situated 5 km away from Kiten in the direction of the Bulgarian-Turkish boundary. There are two camping sites near the village, Lozenets and Oasis.

# BULGARIAN BLACK SEA COAST

## TSAREVO

The town of Tsarevo (population: 6184) is 72 km south of Bourgas and 462 km south-east of Sofia. It is situated at the foot of Strandzha Mountain where it slopes to the sea. Mt. Papiya raises more than five hundred metres above the town. There are three spacious beaches in the vicinity.

In ancient times there was a colony named *Vassiliko*. It was only in 1912 that the town was included into the territory of Bulgaria. The name of Tsarevo dates back to 1930s, and it is a Bulgarian translation of its old name. After 1944 it was renamed into *Michurin*, but today it has regained its former name. It is an international port for medium passenger and cargo ships. The population earn their living with fishing, vine-growing, trade and tourism.

**Accommodation.** The camping sites of Arapya and Nestinarka offer great opportunities for accommodation at low prices for bungalows and camping. Chaika Hotel and the numerous private lodgings provide accommodation during the summer.

**Catering**. The most famous catering establishments in the town are Yalta Restaurant and the Passat Snack Bar. There are lots of small private restaurants, stalls, a marketplace and grocer's shops. Fish that can be bought at the port from local fishermen directly. Prices are low.

**Surrounding areas**. There are two villages to the south-west on the road to Malko Turnovo. They are famous for the nestinarski dances (barefoot dance on glowing embers), which are a tourist attraction nowadays. The actual ritual is held on 21st May when the old female fire-dancers perform.

The villages of **Kodolovo** and **Bulgari** are 22 and 17 km respectively away from Tsarevo. Another attraction is the village of **Gradishte** where Thracian mounds were found.

*The mouth of Veleka River*

# BULGARIAN BLACK SEA COAST

## AHTOPOL

The town of Ahtopol (population: 1364) is situated on a sharply jutted cape 87 km south-east of Bourgas and 477 km south-east of Sofia. The town is perched on the rocky peninsula at the place of a Thracian settlement. It was probably colonised in 6$^{th}$ century BC. Its name dates back to ancient times. The Romans called it *Peronticus*. The Byzantine leader Agaton restored the town after the barbarian invasions and gave it his own name *Agatopolis*. The Byzantine and the Bulgarians took it in turns. At the end of 14$^{th}$ century called was called *Ahtenbolu*. It was burnt down and devastated by sea pirates many a time. In 1918 it was completely burnt down again. The present day town was built anew. There are remains of a fortress wall. The Assumption Church and the St. Yani Monastery are interesting sights. High above the town is Mt. Malka Papia in the Strandzha Mountain.

**Accommodation**. The Elpida Hotel, the Dolphin Camping Site, the City Hotel, the Cherno More Hotel. Prices in Ahtopol are low, accommodation is no problem especially in the numerous private lodgings. The town is a much preferred resort by intellectuals and people in search of quietness and solitude. This particular place on Bulgarian Black Sea coast has the highest number of sunny and hot days during the season.

**Catering**. The most famous place is the small restaurant on the beach. There is a sufficient number of catering establishments offering various menues and products. Prices are low. Local producers and fishermen offer their products.

**Transport**. There is regular transport to Bourgas and Sozopol.

**Surrounding areas**. Five kilometres south of Ahtopol is the **mouth of Veleka River**, the most beautiful river all along the Black Sea coast in spite of the competitive characteristics of Kamchia and Ropotamo. The **village of Kosti** famous for the nestinarski dances (barefoot dances on glowing embers) is situated nearby the river mouth.

**The village of Varvara** is 3 km to the north, it is a favourite place for divers and skin-divers for it is full of stone cavities in the river banks and underwater "reefs" of shells. Usually people in search of nature and solitude come to spend their holidays here. The beaches of Varvara are rocky.

**The village of Sinemorets** is 10 km south of Ahtopol. There is a camping site and three beautiful beaches.

The last village on the coast is called **Rezovo**. It has a nice beach but is rarely used as a holiday place as it is too close to the national border and the border troops are stationed here.

# BULGARIAN MOUNTAINS

GUIDE BOOK

# BULGARIAN MOUNTAINS

It can safely be asserted that Bulgaria is a mountainous country. Approximately half of its territory is occupied by mountainous formations various in their area, height, nature and origin. All of them are a ring of the powerful range of the Alpine - Himalayan Massif comprising a multitude of mountainous systems on the two continents - Europe and Asia.

The mountains in Bulgaria are extremely diverse in kind. If they lack something, it is solely the "cosmic" altitudes and the everlasting snow and ice. Small and big, barren and forested, rounded and steep, low and high, rocky and openly Alpine all of them are accessible during the four seasons of the year and provide for limitless opportunities for recreation, sports and tourism.

Geographical science indicates the existence of 37 mountains on the territory of Bulgaria, 36 of them situated in the southern part of the country and the mountain range of Stara Planina is the border between Northern and Southern Bulgaria. It is namely the mountain range of **Stara Planina**, the longest and the biggest in area, known as the **Balkan Mountain,** too, which gave the name to our Balkan Peninsula. The second longest mountain range in our country is spread in parallel to it, to the south - **Sredna Gora**. These two mountains, except their magnificent natural endowments, are closely related to the history of our people as well. The most impressive mountainous system, however, is the Rila-Rhodope Massif, including **Rila, Pirin, the Rhodopes, Slavianka** and **Sturgach**.

**Rila** is the sixth highest mountain in Europe and the highest mountain on the Balkan Peninsula (Mt. Moussala 2925 m). **Pirin** is the most beautiful and Alpine-like Bulgarian mountain. **The Rhodope Mountains**, the greater part of which are on Bulgarian territory (a smaller part is in Greece), are the second in area and one of the most interesting of our mountains in relation to flora and fauna, the architecture of the settlements and the cultural traditions of the population. **Slavianka** and **Sturgach** are border Greek mountains. Slavianka is a very interesting tourist site famous for its fields of Pirin tea.

Two lower mountains are situated to the east of the Rila-Rhodope Massif - **Sakar** and **Strandzha**. Strandzha is closely related to the struggles of Bulgarian people for liberation from Ottoman Rule.

Another mountain system is the Plana-Zaval Group, including 5 mountains in it - **Zavalska, Viskiar, Lyulin, Vitosha** and **Plana**, situated in a line, to the south-east of the border with Serbia. The highest, biggest and most famous of them is the **Vitosha Mountain**. Located in the immediate proximity to the south of the capital city, it is the most visited mountain. The organised hiking movement in Bulgaria was commenced on the highest mount of this range - Mt. Cherni Vruh (2290 m). On 27$^{th}$ August 1895 at the appeal of the great Bulgarian writer and democrat Aleko Konstantinov, 300 citizens of Sofia climbed it on foot from Sofia-city - quite incredible for the time!

The Verila-Roui group comprises 7 comparatively low mountains, located between the border with Serbia and the Rila Mountain. These are **Roui** (bordering with Serbia and the highest in the group - 1706 m), **Ezdimir**, **Strazha, Lyubash, Cherna Gora, Golo Burdo** and **Verila**. In spite of their low altitude above sea level and their small area, each of these mountains is interesting in itself. The Ostritsa Reserve, for instance, is situated in **Golo Burdo** and it is extremely rich in endemic vegetation kinds.

The mountainous system of **Kraishte** has 11 individual mountain formations. Like in the Verila-Roui group, the mountains here are small in area and comparatively low. The highest of these mountains are those bordering with Serbia - **Milev** and **Kurvav Kamuk**, 1733 m and 1737 m respectively.

The Osogovo-Belassitsa mountainous group is situated in the south-west corner of Bulgaria. **Ossogovo** and **Belassitsa Mountains** are over 2000 metres high, and **Vlahina** and **Malashevska Mountain**, follow them closely in altitude. The fifth mountain within this group is **Ograzhden**. Four of the mountains are on the

# BULGARIAN MOUNTAINS

Bulgarian-Macedonian border, and Belassitsa is situated on the territories of 3 states - Bulgaria, Greece and Macedonia. Mt. Toumba (1881 m), is a knot between the three neighbouring Balkan countries.

Of all the 37 small and big mountains, 8 exceed the altitude of 2000 metres: Rila (Mt. Moussala - 2925 m), Pirin (Mt. Vihren - 2914 m), Stara Planina (Mt. Botev - 2376 m), Vitosha (Mt. Cherni Vruh - 2290 m), Ossogovo Mountain (Mt. Ruen - 2252 m), Slavianka (Mt. Gotsev Vruh - 2212 m), the Rhodopes (Mt. Golyam Perelik - 2191 m) and Belassitsa (Mt. Radomir - 2029 m). All of them are subject to tourist and sports related activities and the Rhodopes are quite densely populated as well.

The **high-mountain lakes** add to about 400 in number and they are scattered around cirques of the Rila and Pirin Mountains and one - in Stara Planina. There are a lot more natural lakes of different origin, mainly around the Rhodopes and fewer around Stara Planina. This is a priceless wealth of Bulgarian nature, which shall henceforward attract and charm thousands of fans.

The unique mountainous nature of Bulgaria is increasingly becoming a foremost concern for the state in view of its preservation for the present and the future generations. Dozens of biosphere reserves have been established and huge territories of Pirin, Rila and Stara Planina were declared National Parks. The **Pirin National Park** was included in the **UNESCO** list of protected territories and natural sites, representing supernational, universal values.

*Bachkovo Monastery*

The opportunities offered by Bulgarian mountains in relation to the pleasant and beneficial use of one's free time are great in number. For motor tourists there is branched road network providing access to the most interesting natural, historical and cultural places of interest, as well as to all the settlements and resorts. Hiking tourism opportunities are unlimited in number and hiking can be practised during all four seasons of the year. It is mainly for this purpose that over 300 chalets (for information and reservations contact tel.: 02 9801285) and high-mountain shelters were built in Bulgarian mountains, a sufficiently dense network, which allows for the longest mountain hikes to be concluded within one day.

Thousands of kilometres of marked trails provide a high degree of security when moving around in the mountains. The **four-colour marking** characteristic of most European countries with developed hiking is adopted in Bulgaria. The key colours in it are red, blue, green and yellow, and white colour is an auxiliary one. It should be known that the red marking, in principle, is for ridges. **Winter marking** consists of yellow-black metal stakes, at a height of between 3 and 4 metres and indicates the comparatively saf-

# BULGARIAN MOUNTAINS

est way along a certain route in the event of thick snow cover. The greater part of the routes, particularly in Rila, Pirin and along the ridges of Stara Planina, have azimuth table plates in addition to the numbering of the stakes.

There are very good ski-sports opportunities in four big ski-centres in the Bulgarian mountains - **Borovets** (Rila), **Pamporovo** (the Rhodopes), **Aleko** (Vitosha) and **Bansko** (Pirin). Of them Borovets has got the highest coefficient where the European Cup races are organised. Borovets was the host of a round of the World Cup as well. The smaller ski-centres of local importance include **Semkovo, Panichishte, Rilski Ezera (Rila Lakes), Malyovitsa** and **Govedartsi** in Rila, **Bezbog** in Pirin, **Petrohan, Kom, Strazhata, Beklemeto, Pleven, Uzana, Choumerna** in Stara Planina, **Zdravets, Byala Cherkva, Persenk, Yundola, Martsiganitsa** in the Rhodopes, **Vetrovala** and **Konyarnika** in Vitosha and others. Not only the slopes of the Alpine-like mountains of Rila and Pirin offer marvellous ski-tourism related conditions but so do Stara Planina, the Rhodopes, Vitosha, and Ossogovo as well.

Bulgarian mountains offer excellent conditions for one of the most attractive and emotional kinds of sports in the open air - **mountaineering**. Alpine sites in our country, which are of interest even to the most outstanding climbers in Europe add up to dozens. In the first place, without a rival, is the Malyovitsa mountain ridge of Rila - the cradle and centre of Bulgarian mountaineering - a vast Alpine "stadium", among which the most beautiful Bulgarian peak rises – **Mt. Malyovitsa** (2730 m). Other well-known Alpine sites are **Vihren** and **Stupalata** (the Stairs) in Pirin, **Vratsata, Lakatnik, Raiski Skali** (Paradise Rocks), **Severniya Dzhendem** (Northern Hell), **Muglizh** and **Karandila** in Stara Planina, **Kominite** (the Chimneys) and **Reznyovete** in Vitosha, **the gorge on Erma River**.

There are very good conditions for other modern mountainous sports, too - **mountain marathon**, **mountain biking, delta-** and **paragliding, rafting** and **kayaking**.

Their beauty, diversity and accessibility during all the seasons of the year make Bulgarian mountains an object of desire for home and international tourism.

The perfectly organised and equipped **Mountain Rescue Service (MRS)** and 15 well-trained dogs take care of the health, life and security of tourists and sportsmen in the mountains. About 50 permanent and 700 voluntary mountain rescuers provide for the security of the territory of all the Bulgarian mountains and through their dedicated labour and love for the people and the mountain they inspire calmness and more confidence in all nature admirers. T**he Central 24-hour Check Point** is located in the MRS Station in Lozenets quarter of the capital city, tel.: 02 9632000; 0481843; 088621286. A permanent radio connection is maintained with over 250 chalets and MRS check-points. Several central bases function with the Mountain Rescue Service - in Borovets, Malyovitsa, Bansko, Dobrinishte above Mt. Bezbog and Pamporovo, Mechi Chal above the town of Chepelare, as well as a great number of local bases - Aleko, Cherni Vruh and Opheliya in Vitosha Mountain, Vezhen, Buzov Dial, Uzana and Bulgarka in Stara Planina, Ossogovo in the mountains above the town of Kyustendil, Zdravets in the Rhodopes, above Plovdiv. There are a lot of temporary and permanent rescue check-points as well - Rezena and Konyarnika in Vitosha Mountain, Markudzhitsite and Tchatarluka in Rila, Chalin Valog, Yavorov Chalet and Shiligarnika in Pirin.

The Mountain Rescue Service structures have successfully participated in stamping out the consequences of earthquakes and other natural distasters in Turkey, Greece, Armenia, Egypt and in Bulgaria, as well. Since 2000 the Vitosha Life Insurance Company PLC offers mountain life insurance. The annual fee of 20 Leva covers first aid in the mountain, transport to a hospital and treatment.

# BULGARIAN MOUNTAINS

## RILA

**Rila is the highest mountain in Bulgaria and on the whole Balkan Peninsula**. It occupies the prestigious 6th place in the European "classification", preceded by: Caucasus (Mt. Elbrus - 5642 m), the Alps (Mt. Mont Blanc - 4807 m), Sierra Nevada (Mt. Mulasen - 3482 m), the Pyrenees (Mt. Aneto - 3404 m) and the Etna Volcano (3340 m). It is a central mountain for the peninsula and it is a main orographic and hydrographic junction. It is a composite part of the Rila - Rhodope Massif and occupies its north-western end.

The oldest name of the mountain is *Dounkas*, given to it by the Thracians. It means a place with a lot of water. Thracian is its other name *Roula*, which was altered by the Slav to Rila. It is also related to the water abundance of the mountain (it means "water mountain").

The key constructive element in the mountain is granite. There are also marble, crystalline schists and others here. The twofold glaciating

*Sedemte Rilski Ezera
(The Seven Rila Lakes)*

of Rila played an important part in the formation of its relief. The multitude of cirques, the well outlined trog (glacial) valleys, the Alpine peaks and the glacial lakes are evidence for this.

**The climate** of Rila is determined by its geographical situation, on the border between the continental and the transitional Mediterranean climate and the microclimate - by the altitude zones and by the soil and vegetation cover. The lowest average monthly temperature was recorded during the month of February on Mt. Moussala - 11.6°C below zero. The absolute minimal temperature so far in Bulgaria was measured in the same place - 31.2°C below zero (during February). During the month of August the average temperature of the mount is 5.4°C and the absolute maximal temperature measured on Mt. Moussala is 18.7°C.

The winds in Rila blow predominantly from the west and the south-west. There are rarely northwestern and north-eastern winds and they are more moderate, and the northern, southern and south-eastern winds do not play an essential role. The quantity of precipitation is significant, about 1200 mm fall on Mt. Moussala per year, about 80 per cent of them being snow. The snow cover on the parts of medium altitude and the Alpine parts of the mountain often exceeds 2 metres. All these enumerated climatic factors create prerequisites, mostly in the Alpine parts of the mountain, for avalanches.

Rila has the following boundaries (clockwise): on the north - the Dzhubrena River, the Klissoura Saddle and the Klissourchitsa River separate it from Verila Mountain. The Samokov Plain, the Bistritsa River, the Borovets Saddle, the Malka Slivnitsa, Slivnitsa and Maritsa Rivers (the Maritsa River up to Dolna Banya) separate it from Ihtiman Sredna Gora Mountain. Kostenets-Dolna Banya mountain valley, the Maritsa River up to its overfall with the Yadenitsa River separate Rila from the farthest south-eastern sprouts of Ihtiman Sredna Gora Mountain. To the east it borders on the Rhodopes through the Yadenitsa and Yundolska Rivers, the Yundola Saddle, Lyuta River, Avra-

# BULGARIAN MOUNTAINS

*Ivan Vazov Chalet in Rila*

mov's Saddle, the Dreshenets River and the Mesta River to Razlog mountain valley. On the south - Razlog mountain valley. It is separated from Pirin through the Rablevska River, Predela Saddle, and the rivers of Kulina, Elovitsa and Gradevska. On the west - the Valley of the Strouma River from the overfall with the Gradevska River to the overfall with the Dzherman River, the valley of the Dzherman River from the overfall with the Strouma River to the Doupnitsa Plain.

Within the so outlined borders Rila occupies the area of 2396 square kilometres.

On the basis of its orographic structures and characteristics and morphographic features the mountain is divided into 4 main parts - Eastern, Middle, North-Western and South-Western. The following rivers serve as their borders - Cherni (Black) Iskar, Levi (Left) Iskar, Beli (White) Iskar, Rilska, Iliina, Belishka and Stankova as well as the ridge saddles - Kobilino Branishte, Kadiin Grob and Gorni Kouki. Each of the main parts, on its part, is subdivided into several subparts bearing the names of the highest or central peak.

**Eastern Rila** is the highest (absolutely) and the most spacious of the 4 main parts and it comprises 37% of the total area of the mountain. Eastern Rila on its part is divided into 7 subparts. Three of them - the Moussala, Maritsa and Kovashki are situated on the Moussala edge and the remaining 4 - Slavov's, Belmeken, Ibur and Mustachal on the Ibur main edge. The two main edges cross at the junction Mt. Marishki Chal, situated at the main watershed on the Balkan Peninsula, between the water catchment areas of the Iskar, Maritsa and Mesta Rivers. The 11 highest peaks of the mountain raise in Eastern Rila headed by **Mt. Moussala** (2925.4 m). The second - **Mt. Malka (Little) Moussala** (2902 m) is situated to the east (they are linked by the narrow rocky edge Trionite (the Saws)). The third highest and unique between the altitude of 2800 and 2900 metres - **Mt. Irechek** (2852 m) is next to them, too. The lake groups of Moussalenski Ezera ("ezera" meaning lakes), Marichini Ezera, Ropalishki Ezera, Yakorouda Ezera and others are in this part as well. The highest lake in Rila is within the Moussala group - the **Ledenoto (Glacial) Lake** (2709 m), situated in the immediate proximity on the north under Mt. Moussala. There are 9 tourist chalets and 2 high-mountain shelters in Eastern Rila. The highest meteorological station in South-Eastern Europe, built in 1932 is situated on the Mount of Moussala.

**Middle Rila** is the smallest part of the mountain - it occupies only 9% of its area. Its relief, however, is the most Alpine with the average altitude above sea level - 2077.17 m. Middle Rila has two main ridges - Skakavishko and Riletsko separated by the valley of the Rilska River. They are linked by **Mt. Kanarata** (The Rock) (2691m), occupying a focal place in the orohydrographic characteristics of the whole mountain, known as the "navel" of Rila. Three subparts are outlined along the Skakavishki Main Ridge - Skakav, Marinkov and Shishkov. There are 3 subparts along the Rilets Ridge, too - Kanara, Rilets and Brichebor, i.e. Middle Rila has 6 subparts. The highest peak is **Mt. Karaalanitsa** (Black Meadow) - 2716 m (14th highest in Rila). The following peaks are remarkable, too: **Mt. Rilets** (2713 m), **Mt. Yosafitsa** (2697 m), **Mt. Aladzha Slap** (2684 m), **Mt. Vodniya Chal** (Water Peak) (2683 m). Middle Rila is rich in glacial lakes. Here are: the Fish Lakes, Prekorech Lakes, Mermer Lakes, Karaomerish Lakes, Dzhendem (Hell) Lakes, the Monastery Lakes. The biggest glacial lake on the Balkan Peninsula - Smradlivoto (Srinking) with the area of 212 decares is also in this part of the mountain. There are 3 chalets in Middle Rila and one high-mountain shelter.

**North-Western Rila**, which is divided into low and high (Alpine) parts, occupies 24% of the total area of the mountain and is the third biggest in relation to average altitude above sea level, too - 1555.73 m. Its low part comprises the oblong Govedartsi mountain valley and the so-called Lakatish Rila, which is a fore-mountain of the main massif of Rila. The high (Alpine) part is divided into Malyovitsa, Damga, Kalins, Otovish and Kabul subparts. The most prominent Alpine sites of Rila and Bulgaria are located in the Malyovitsa subpart. These are the **peaks**: **Mt. Malyovitsa** (2730 m, a symbol of Bulgarian alpinism and mountaineering), **Mt. Koupenite** (the highest of them - Mt. Goliam Koupen is the highest peak in North-Western Rila - 2731 м), **Mt. Elenin**, **Mt. Orlovets**, **Mt. Zliya Zub** (Evil Tooth), **Mt. Dvuglav** (Two-headed), **Mt. Lovnitsa, Mt. Petlite** (Roosters), **Mt. Orleto** (Little Eagle) and a number of others. Some of the biggest and significant lake groups are situated in this part of the mountain - Urdini Ezera, Malyovishki Ezera, Elenski Ezera, Gradinski Ezera, Popovokapski Ezera, as well as the biggest and most famous lake group on the Balkan Peninsula - Sedemte Rilski Ezera (The 7 Rila Lakes). There are 10 tourist chalets and 2 high-mountain shelters built up in North-Western Rila.

**South-Western Rila** comprises 30% of the mountain - the lowest part with the average altitude above sea level of 1306.63 m. It is divided into two main ridges - northern, consisting of Mechi Vruh and Tsarev Vruh subpart and southern, divided into Parangal, Kapatnik and Hurs. **Mt. Angel** is the highest in this subpart (2643 m). Some of the more remarkable peaks here are **Mt. Goliam Mechi Vruh** (Big Bear) (2618 m), **Mt. Uzunitsa** (2606 m), **Mt. Tsarev Vruh** (Tsar's Peak) (2378 m), **Mt. Kapatnik** (2170 m) and others. There are 2 tourist's chalets in South-Western Rila. One of the oldest biosphere reserves in Bulgaria is located on the territory of this part - **Parangalitsa**, known also for its centuries-old spruces.

Some of the most well-known **Bulgarian riv-**

*Mt. Moussala*

# BULGARIAN MOUNTAINS

ers flowing their waters in the direction of both the Black Sea and the Aegean Sea spring from Rila, i.e. the main watershed of the Balkans passes through it. Solely the **Iskar River** drains into the Black Sea, but its water catchment area in Rila is big enough including its initial tributaries Cherni (Black), Beli (White) and Levi (Left) Iskar as well as a lot of other smaller ones. The Chanakski Ezera (Chanak Lakes) in North-Western Rila are considered the spring of the Iskar River near the cirque of the 7 Rila Lakes. The longest Bulgarian river - the **Maritsa River** as well as the **Mesta River** empty in the Aegean Sea, beyond the territory of Bulgaria. The first flows out of Marichini Ezera (Maritsa Lakes), south of Mt. Moussala, and the second drains the southern slopes of Eastern Rila. The water catchment area of **Strouma River** (taking its rise from Vitosha Mountain) is spacious, too. It catches the waters of the western and south-western slopes of Rila and also empties into the Aegean Sea, on the territory of Greece. Among its Rila tributaries of greater importance are the Rila River, the Dzherman River, the Doupnitsa River and the Blagoevgrad Bistritsa River.

## RILA MONASTERY

Among the bosoms of Rila at the altitude of 1147 m above sea level, on the right bank of the Rila River is situated **the most outstanding monument** of Bulgarian culture and architecture of the Revival period - the Rila Monastery, known also as the Holy Rila Retreat. For centuries on end it played an extraordinary part in Bulgarian history, in the struggle of our nation for spiritual and political freedom.

It was founded during the 10$^{th}$ century by Sveti Ivan Rilski (St. John of Rila) - patron of Bulgaria. The Monastery was built as it stands now by Bulgarian master builders in 1816-1847. Whilst on the outside it reminds one of a powerful Medieval fortress, inside, the beauty of the Bulgarian Revival style emanates from the central **Birth of the Holy Virgin Church** and from the remaining monastery buildings, ornamented with colonnades, staircases and balconies.

The attention of the visitors is drawn to the first monastery kitchen (magernitsa) with its structure of octagons raising at the height of 22 metres crowned with a dome. In the middle of the monastery yard stands high the **Hrelyo Tower** - a powerful stone fortification, the sole preserved building of Medieval Times (1335). **The Preobrazhenie (Transfiguration) Chapel** housing mural paintings of the 14$^{th}$ century is on the top floor. The mural paintings in the remaining 3 chapels are remarkable, too, as well as the mural

*The Rila Monastery*

paintings on the arches of the yard facades, in the parlours, in the churches built in the areas surrounding the Monastery - all of them work of master builders from Samokov and Bansko Art School of the 19th century. Scenes from the Bible along with pieces of art of secular nature - the portraits of the founders of the Monastery are painted on the Cathedral. The enormous iconostasis in the Holy Virgin Monastery Church ornamented with open-worked wood-carving on walnut-tree wood, gilded later on, is a masterpiece of the art of wood-carving. The ceilings of the restored and furnished parlours, the interior of a monk's cell of the end of the 18th century and the beginning of the 19th century, the permanent ethnographic museum collection, the monastery library housing 16 000 volumes of valuable and unique books are of interest, too.

A **museum** has been arranged in the newly built eastern wing of the monastery building which houses the gate of the Hrelyo Church, ancient weapons of the monastery guards and certificates of merit of Bulgarian tsars. Ornaments, ancient coins and church plate are exhibited here. There is an entire hall dedicated to a collection of icons, brought as presents from all over the country. The wooden cross on which monk Rafail worked for 12 years (from 1790 to 1802), finally growing blind from this amazing work leaving for us behind a unique piece of art, is exceptional.

The Rila Monastery is under **UNESCO** patronage as a monument of an extraordinary value and significance for world culture.

One can get to the Monastery along a first-class asphalt road. There is regular bus transport connecting it to the town of: Rila (19 km), Blagoevgrad (40 km), Doupnitsa (44 km) and Sofia (110 km).

A tourist town has sprung round the Monastery, offering accomodation to the numerous visitors and admirers. If you have decided to **spend the night** here, you have a choice: it is the most romantic to do this in the Monastery itself and the cheapest way to do this, although with only basic conveniences, is in the tourist hostel (in seven-, nine- and twenty-bed rooms. The biggest hotel in the area - the Rilets Hotel is situated at a distance of 1 km in the direction of Kiril Meadow. The Tsarev Vruh

# BULGARIAN MOUNTAINS

## BOROVETZ

The oldest Bulgarian resort dating back to the year of 1896 when the mayor of the town of Samokov of that time built a wooden chalet there to alleviate the fate of his wife who was ill of tuberculosis. Today Borovets is the biggest, first-class mountain resort in Bulgaria. Spread out on the bordering Borovets Saddle as well as along the northern slopes of Moussala Ridge of Eastern Rila, amongst centuries-old coniferous forests, its altitude above sea level is from 1230 to 1390 m and its climate is one of the healthiest. It is pleasantly cool here in summer (the average July temperature is 15.2°C), and the winter is mild and snowy (the average January temperature being 4.8°C).

Borovets is connected to Samokov (12 km), Sofia (72 km), Kostenets Station (27 km), Doupnitsa (52 km) by a first-class road network. There is regular bus transport to them, the buses to Samokov running every 30 minutes.

The genuine charm of Borovets can be seen and felt in winter. Then harmony with nature is complete. The perfect opportunities for practising winter sports and skiing most of all attract thousands of fans of the mountains from Bulgaria and abroad. At their disposal are over 45 km of ski-runs varying in difficulty and grouped in 3 regions: Sitnyakovo - Martinov woodsheds - 8 ski-runs, Markoudzhik - 4 ski-runs and Yastrebets - 3 ski-runs. The Yastrebets ski-runs are first-class and all the ski races of

Hotel (two-star) has been completely renovated offering servicing of high quality and traditional Bulgarian cuisine in its several establishments. The asphalt road continues after the Monastery (into the mountain) for up to 7 to 8 km, to **Kirilova Polyana** (Kiril Meadow), where there is another tourist's settlement with accommodation and catering opportunities. After about 30-40 min walk eastwards along a marked route one can visit the retreat and the grave of Sveti Ivan Rilski, today with a small chapel nearby. There is a belief that the one who succeeds passing in the hole of the cave, where he had retreated as a hermit, without leaning on or touching the rocks is considered pious...

The Rila Monastery is a point from which one can set out on several marked **hiking routes around the Rila Mountain**:

To the Ribni Ezera (Fish Lakes) Chalet, through the above mentioned Kiril Meadow (4 to 5-hour walk), to Macedonia Chalet (a 5-hour walk), to the Ivan Vazov Chalet (a 5-hour walk), to the 7 Rila Lakes Chalet (6 to 7-hour walk), to the peak and the chalet of Malyovitsa (6 to 7-hour walk).

greater significance within the resort are held on them. Rounds of the World Cup on ski-Alpine disciplines are also held here. The Alpine skier Peter Popangelov, the Bulgarian legend in winter sports started from here, too. He contributed a lot to the international recognition of Borevets. There are dozens of ski-running and biathlon tracks, too. The resort is the regular host of races held in these sports.

A multitude of facilities (draglifts, baby tows, seat chain lifts) cross the mountain above Borovets, but the cabin cableway to Mt. Yastrebets is the most imposing one (2363 metres above sea level). The difference in altitude is 1046 m and the length of the route is 4827 m. Its capacity adds up to 1200 people per hour. The journey takes 23 min. Getting off of the cableway one faces the Paradise of Rila - the highest peaks of the mountain - Mt. Moussala, Mt. Malka (Little) Moussala, Mt. Irechek, Mt. Deno, Mt. Aleko.

**Hiking trails** may be undertaken from Borovets along marked routes to various sites in Rila: to Mt. Moussala (6 hours, and from the upper station of the cabin cableway - 3 hours), to Sitnyakovo Palace (1.30 hours), to Chakur Voyvoda Chalet (2.30 hours), to Saragyol Palace (3 hours), to the Maritsa Chalet (4.30 hours), to the Zavrachitsa Chalet (6 hours).

*A frozen fountain*

*An old villa in Borovets*

**Accommodation**: The Samokov Hotel is the most luxurious - 4 stars. The 3-star hotels are the most in number, the biggest of them being the Rila Hotel with 2000 beds. The Olymp Hotel is of medium size (308 beds); same goes for the Yastrebets Hotel (on the road to Beli Iskur, after the Bistritsa Palace and opposite Yastrebets-3 ski-run). The following hotels are smaller and very cosy as well: the Breza Hotel (55 beds in 7 single rooms, 21 double rooms and 2 suites), the Moura Hotel, the Flora Hotel (100 beds). The older but renovated hotels are as follows: the Bor (Pine) Hotel, The Edelweiss Hotel, the Sokolets Hotel, which also offer superb accommodation. The little houses of the following villa settlements are idyllic, too: Polyana (Meadow), Yagoda (Strawberry), Malina (Raspberry), the latter two belonging to Vilni Selishta PLC, Borovets. The little houses Yagoda and Malina host 4 people. Accommodation is on offer for tourists with more limited financial capacities, too: the Fournir Villa and the tourist chalet of Shoumnatitsa (at the distance of 3 km along the road to Dolna Banya and Kostenets. It goes without saying that there are a lot more hotels, private villas, holiday homes where one can get accommodation. In summer the prices for accommodation are reduced. There are a lot of public catering establishments, which offer various specialities from Bulgarian cuisine. The big, modern base of the Mountain Rescue Service is located at a 3 minutes-walk form the lower cabin cableway (tel.: 07128 292 and 312).

# BULGARIAN MOUNTAINS

## MALYOVITZA

Malyovitsa is a smaller resort than Borovets but there is no other resort in the Rila Mountain but also in the whole Bulgaria, which can compare with its beauty and grandeur. It is situated within the Malyovitsa sub-part of North-Western Rila, at about 1700 metres above sea level. An asphalt road connects it to the village of Govedartsi (13 km) and to the town of Samokov (27 km). There is a regular bus transport to the village of Govedartsi and once per day to the town of Samokov.

Malyovitsa is a **symbol of Bulgarian alpinism and mountaineering** and a natural base for alpine sports. Along with the sublime mount of Malyovitsa, a dozen more Alpine peaks rise within the region, which turn Malyovitsa sub-part into the most preferred site of high-mountain rock climbing in Bulgaria. It is namely here that the highest Alpine walls and the most difficult rock tours are located. One of the most beautiful high-mountains on the Balkan Peninsula - the **Strashnoto Ezero** (the Frightful Lake) is located in its proximity, too.

Unique in its kind on the Balkan Peninsula and one of the few in Eastern Europe, the **School for Training of Mountaineering Sports Qualified Staff** was established here during the 1950's. It is a centre for the training of mountaineers, instructors, hiking instructors, mountain guides, ski-tourism instructors, ski-lecturers etc., also known under the name of Central Mountain School of Malyovitsa (it was until recently called the **Hristo Prodanov Malyovitsa Training Centre** after the first Bulgarian who set his foot on Mount Everest).

Many marked **tourist hiking tracks** begin from the resort towards North-Western Rila: to the Ivan Vazov Chalet (7 hours), to the Ribni Ezera (Fish Lakes) Chalet (9 to 10 hours), to the Rila Monastery (6 hours), to the Strashno Ezero (Frightful Lake) Shelter (3 hours), to the BAC (Bulgarian Alpine Club) Shelter (2 hours), to the Vada Chalet (1.30 hours), to the Lovna (Hunter's) Chalet (2.30 to 3 hours), to the 7 Rila Lakes Chalet (8 hours along the ridge and 5 hours under it), to the Mechit Chalet (4 hours). The Malyovitsa Chalet (an old and a new building as well as wooden bungalows) is situated at an hour-walk from the resort, against the stream of the Malyovitsa River, at over 2000 metres above sea level, where one can find accommodation and buy some cooked warm food. The Mount of Malyovitsa can be climbed along a marked (summer and winter marking) trail for 2 to 3 hours leisurely walk. There are several ski-runs and ski-sports related facilities within the region.

**The accommodation facilities** are comparatively limited here. The Malyovitsa Hotel hosts the greatest number of beds (180) as well as a restaurant, a discotheque, a coffee bar, entertainment games hall, a souvenir shop, ski-equipment rental and

*Malyovitsa - chalet and mount*

# BULGARIAN MOUNTAINS

*On the way to Mayovitsa*

safekeeping services. The Training Centre hosts fewer beds and offers fewer conveniences - 4 beds and more per room. There is a restaurant here, too (self-service), a bar, a sports hall, a man-made Alpine wall, a museum of mountaineering. There are a lot of little cosy public catering establishments scattered round **Mecha Polyana** (Bear Meadow) where one can have a drink and a bite or just relax listening to nice music with a cup of coffee or a soft drink. There is a check-point of the Mountain Rescue Service in the building of the Training Centre (tel.: 07125 2382).

## MAJOR HIKING DEPARTURE POINTS

In addition to setting out from **Borovets, Malyovitsa and the Rila Monastery**, there are many tourist hiking departure points from many other settlements and resort related zones.

**The village of Govedartsi** - it is connected by regular bus transport links to Samokov (14 km) and Sofia (74 km). Marked tracks start from it to the Mechit Chalet (2 to 2.30 hours) and the Ovnarsko Tourist Base (2 hours), from which one can further explore the inner parts of Rila.

**The Dolna Banya Resort** is situated at the distance of 4 to 5 km south of the town of the same name, which is connected by a regularly running bus transport to Samokov (30 km), Borovets (20 km) and the nearby railway station of Kostenets (8 km). The **Gerginitsa Chalet** is located within the resort itself and there is a marked track leading to the **Venetitsa Chalet** (2 hours). Various trails round Eastern Rila set out from it.

**The resort of Kostenets** is situated at the distance of 9 km of the railway station of the same name, linked to it by regular bus transport. Two marked tracks set out from here - to the **Belmeken Chalet** (4.30 to 5 hours) and to the **Gourgoulitsa Chalet** (1.30 hours), which also branches into different directions further on.

**The resort of Yundola** - at the distance of 16 km from Velingrad, 26 km south from Septemvri and at the distance of 25 km from Yakorouda, connected by regular bus transport to them. A marked tracks for the **Kourtovo Chalet** (3 hours) and for the **sports town** beside the **Belmeken Dam Lake** (4.30 hours) sets out from it. The Yundola Pass and the resort respectively is the link between the Rila and the Rhodopes and the combined routes for the great Bulgarian mountains pass from here.

**The town of Yakorouda** - in the valley of the Mesta River, at the narrow-gauge railway line Septemvri - Dobrinishte. One can walk from here for 3 hours to the chalet and the resort of Treshtenik in Eastern Rila.

**The town of Belitsa** - is situated at the distance of 18 km south-west of Yakorouda. It is as departure point for the chalet and the resort of Semkovo (4 hours) in Central Rila, as well as for **Macedonia Chalet** (6 to 7 hours) in South-Western Rila.

**The Predela (Limit) Saddle**, where there is a small resort and tourist chalet. It is situated at the distance of 24 km from Simitli and at the distance of 14 km from Razlog. A lot of busses regularly running in both directions pass from here. The saddle is a border between Rila and Pirin and is often used as an interim point for combined hiking routes in

# BULGARIAN MOUNTAINS

our highest and most beautiful mountains. One can set out for the **Macedonia Chalet** in Rila from Predela (8 hours).

**Blagoevgrad** - the largest populated point at the foothill of Rila. It is connected to Sofia and the remaining parts of the country by bus and railway transport. One can get from this town to **Macedonia and Chakalitsa Chalets** in South-Western Rila for about one day.

**Doupnitsa** also a big town located at the north-western foothill of the mountain, linked by bus and railway transport to Sofia and the country. One can set out from the nearby villages of Bistritsa, Samoranovo and Resilovo to **Ivan Vazov, Otovitsa and Skakavitsa Chalets**.

**Sapareva Banya Resort**, situated at the distance of about 20 km east of the town of Doupnitsa, is linked by a regular bus transport to it. The hottest mineral spring in Bulgaria is here - 103.8°C. It is a starting point for the **resort of Panichishte** - 1.30 hours along the marked trail and 10 km along the road. A lot of marked tracks go further from Panichishte to the **Pionerska, Lovna, Skakavitsa, Rilski Ezera (Rila Lakes), the 7 Lakes, Ivan Vazov, Vada, Malyovitsa Chalets**, etc.

**The village of Klissoura** is located in the Klissoura Saddle, a border between Rila and Verila. It is situated at the distance of 25 km from Doupnitsa and at the distance of 15 km from Samokov and is linked to them by bus transport. The popular route through the 4 mountains: Vitosha, Verila, Rila and Pirin passes from here. From Klissoura one can get to the **Vada Chalet** for 5 hours and to the **Lovna Chalet** for 5.30 hours through the lowest part of Rila - Lakatishka Rila.

Although there is no trail setting out directly from **Samokov**, this little town situated at the northern foothill of the mountain is considered to be the entrance gate of Rila. One passes through Samokov for the most popular areas of the mountain - Borovets, Moussala, and Malyovitsa.

Almost all Rila chalets offer in summer something to eat, cooked warm food included.

# PIRIN

Pirin is the **most beautiful and most Alpine type of mountain** in Bulgaria. It is the second highest after the Rila Mountain (in Bulgaria) and third in the Balkan Peninsula (after Olympus of Greece - Mt. Mitika, 2917 metres). Pirin is situated in the south-western part of the country and covers the south-western corner of the Rila-Rhodope mountain massif. It is rather extended in shape to the north-west and south-east and is flanked by the rivers **Strouma** and **Mesta**.

The mountain has had different names through the centuries. From the Thracian *Orbelus* (Orbel), meaning "snowy mountain", through the old Slavic *Judenitsa* (meaning the fairies, which in the minds of the common people populated the mountains). Then came the later Slavic name *Perun*, connected with God Perun, who - according to the Slavic mythology - was supposed to have resided on Mt. Vihren and to have send fire in the form of lightning and thunder. The Turkish name it acquired later, *Beride,* means "spread out". According to the latest research, the name *Pirin* comes from the Haetic "perunash" - meaning "the rock" and the Thracian *Perintus* or *Pirintos*.

The mountain is formed predominantly from two types of rocks - granite and marble - which have so "interwoven" at some locations that the borders between them divide peaks, cirques and even lakes. Due to the prolonged freezing period of the Quarterner, Pirin has

*Edelweiss in Pirin*

GUIDE BOOK 343

# BULGARIAN MOUNTAINS

acquired an Alpine relief - rocky peaks and cliffs, deep cirques, well shaped glacier valleys and numerous lakes.

Pirin has the typical climate of a mountain but with a well-expressed Mediterranean influence, mainly through the valleys of the Strouma and Mesta rivers. This is why Pirin is the mountain with the greatest number of sunny days throughout the year in comparison to Rila, Stara Planina, Vitosha and Ossogovo. The average annual temperature in the area of the Vihren Chalet (at an altitude of about 2000 metres above sea level) is 3.7°C, the average temperature in January is 4.2°C below zero while in August it reaches 12.8°C. Precipitation (predominantly snowfalls) is higher in November and December and least in August. The average rain and snowfall at Mt. Vihren is within 1500 to 1600 millimetres per square meter annually. It is cloudy mostly in May and December. The dominating winds in winter are those from the north-west and during the summer - from south-western direction.

Pirin's borders (clock-wise) are: to the north - the Rila Mountain along the banks of the rivers Gradevska, Elovitsa and Kulina, the Predela Saddle (1142 metres above sea level) and the Rablevska River. To the east it is the Razlog Valley, the Momina Klissoura Pass and the Gotse Delchev Plain - the valley of Mesta River divides Pirin from the Rodopes. To the south, the border of the Pirin Mountain goes initially along the banks of the rivers Mutnitsa and

*Mt. Vihren*

Burovitsa, which separate it from the Stargach and Slavyanka mountains while the Paril Pass (1170 metres above sea level) separates the mountain from Slavyanka with the help of the rivers Goleshevska and Kalimanska. To the west, Pirin shares a border with the Petrich Plain, the Kresna Pass and the Simitli Plain - the bank of the Strouma River separates it from our western national border - the mountains Ograzhden, Malashevska and Vlahina.

The overall area of the Pirin Mountain is about 1210 square kilometres. In spite of this modesty of dimension and well formed upper ridge, it is divided into three parts - Northern Pirin, Mid-Pirin and Southern Pirin. Borders between them are the two saddles of the central ridge of the mountain - Todorova Polyana (1883 metres above sea level) and Popovi Livadi (Papaz Chair - 1430 metres above the sea).

**Northern Pirin** is the biggest in area (74% of the overall area of the mountain), the longest (42 km birds flight), the highest, the most spectacular and the most visited of the three. There are sixty peaks at an altitude of above 2500 metres. The highest of them is **Mt. Vihren** (2914 m) and **Mt. Kutelo** is the second above 2900 m (2908 m). There are aslo **Mt. Banski Suhodol** (2884 m), **Mt. Golyam Polezhan** (2851 m), **Mt. Maluk Polezhan** (2822 m), **Mt. Kamenitsa** (2822 m), **Mt. Bayuvi Doupki** (2820 m) and some others as

# BULGARIAN MOUNTAINS

well as the unique **Koncheto Karst Edge** (The Small Horse), which does not fall below 2810 metres. Along the Northern Pirin karst and granite ridges flow one after another but the three highest peaks and the Koncheto Edge are to be found on the main karst plateau edge, together with some other high and interesting side ridges - **Stupalata, Sredonos, Koteshki Chal, Tsurnomogilski Chal**. From the central ridge, Northern Pirin branches in four directions. From the north - Sinanitsa branch, which bears the name of the most spectacular and most often visited of all Pirin peaks, the **Mt. Sinanitsa** (2516 m). The higher peak along the Sinanitsa branch of the mountain is **Mt. Georgiitsa** (2589 m); Todorino mountain branch with the highest **Mt. Todorin** (2746 m) along the side-slopes of which are the best ski-runs in Pirin; the Polezhan branch with the highest **Mt. Golyam Polezhan** (2851 m) and with one of the most beautiful peaks - **Mt. Dzhengala** (2730 m); **Mt. Strazhite** (The Guards) (2810 m), **Mt. Gazei** (2761), **Mt. Disilitsa** (2700 m); the Kamenishko branch with the highest **Mt. Kamenitsa** (2822 m), which is spectacular and somehow full of a specific grandeur with its two peaks, **Mt. Malka Kamenitsa** (2679 m), **Mt. Yalovarnika** (2763 m), **Mt. Zubut** (2688 m) and **Mt. Kouklite** (2686 m).

This part of Pirin hosts all **glacial lakes** (140 - 150 in number) where among the most interesting lake groups are the Bunderishki Ezera, Vasilashki Ezera, Georgiiski Ezera, Vlahinski Ezera, Valyavishki Ezera, Kremenski Ezera, Samodivski Ezera and Gazeiski Ezera ('ezera' meaning lakes). The biggest lake in Pirin is the **Popovoto** (Papazgyol) - 124 decares - which is also the deepest - 29.5 metres. The glacial lake at the highest altitude in the Balkan Peninsula is the **Gorno Polezhansko Ezero** (at 2710 metres). **Tevnoto Ezero** is of particular interest not only with its position, dimensions and beauty but also with its historical significance - it is thus one of the symbols of the Pirin Mountain.

*A long the Koncheto Karst Edge*

Northern Pirin is the place where one can find almost all kinds of boarding facilities (except only two of the chalets). The area hosts 12 chalets and 4 shelters, which are at the disposal of mountaineers and tourists the year-round. Marking (winter and summer) is exceptionally clear and perfectly maintenained.

The smallest part of the Pirin Mountain is the **Mid-Pirin** sector, which amounts to 6.7% of the overall area. It is also the shortest and in its greater part is covered with broadleaf vegetation. Here is the kingdom of the Pirin tea, which grows along the highest and barren parts of the mountain. The highest peak in Mid-Pirin is **Mt. Orelyak** (Eagle) (2099 m) where at present a television transmission tower is in operation. Seen from the west, it looks like an eagle, with wings open and ready for flight. Other peaks of interest are **Mt. Baba, Mt. Chala, Mt. Senoto, Mt. Mourata** - all below 2000 metres. The southern part of this sector is marble-based while the northern part lies over granite. There are no lakes here. Only 2 chalets give shelter to visitors - Popovi Livadi Chalet (Papazchair) and Malina Chalet. The only marked track passes close by the ridge of the Mid-Pirin.

**Southern Pirin** lies over an area, amounting to 19.3% of the overall area. This is the lowest, most rounded and most rarely visited part of the mountain. Its highest parts are covered in coniferous trees (spruce, pine-trees), some-

# BULGARIAN MOUNTAINS

times accompanied by broadleaf (oak trees). The highest peak is **Mt. Sveshtnik** (Chandelier) (1975 m), followed by **Mt. Motorog** (1970 m), **Mt. Ushite** (The Ears), **Mt. Sarapelya**, etc. The mountain lies over granite in its central part and marble along the periphery. No lakes can be found here and no boarding facilities. There is only one marked mountain track between the Popovi Livadi Chalet and the village of Petrovo as part of the international E-4 highway.

**Pirin rivers** gather their waters from its snow-white peaks and blue lakes to pour them into the Strouma or Mesta rivers. The main ridge of the mountain is the division line between these two big Bulgarian rivers. Some bigger tributaries of the Strouma from north to south are the rivers: Vlahinska, Sandanska Bistritsa, Melnishka Reka and Pirinska Bistritsa (the longest river springing out of Pirin). The rivers that flow into the Mesta (north to south) are: Bela Reka, Iztok (collecting the greater part of the underground waters of the karst ridge), Glazne (flowing under this name after the spot where Banderishka and Demyanishka rivers merge their waters), Disilitsa, Retizhe (the beginning of which starts at the biggest Pirin lake - the Papazgyol), the Kameniza, Breznishka and Matnitsa rivers.

Because of the unique nature of the Pirin Mountain, in 1976 the **Pirin National Park** was found to cover - at present - nearly the whole of Northern Pirin to an area of some 40 000 hectares. Due to its extraordinary value and importance far outside of the country, in 1983 **UNESCO** decided to include the **Pirin National Park** as a biospere national park in the convention on the protection of the world's cultural and natural heritage. Three are three biospere reserves in Pirin, as well: **Bayuvi Dupki - Dzhindzhiritsa** (within the National Park), **Tissata** (in Northern Pirin, too) and **Orelek** (Mid-Pirin).

## MELNIK AND THE ROZHEN MONASTERY

Melnik is the smallest and one of the most fascinating town-museums in Bulgaria. Nestled amongst the lowest south-western fold of Pirin, it combines in it the memory of a prosperous past with the pastoral cosiness and the unique in its kind countryside. It dates back to Thracian times. The Romans after them and later on the Slavs finally developed the town and made it an important religious, cultural and administrative centre. It was at the end of the 6$^{th}$ century that the Slavs gave the town its today's melodious name.

The town was entered into the boundaries of Bulgaria after the 7$^{th}$ century. From the year of 1215 it was the capital of the independent despot Alexii Slav - boyar of the Melnik feudal principality and a son of Tsar Kaloyan's sister. After Bulgaria succumbed to Ottoman Rule, the town went into a decline but it reached its peak once again during the years of the Revival Period. Key occupation of the people in the region was the production of wines of high

*Melnik - town-museum*

quality, which matured in the sand wine cellars around and under the town itself. Its citizens enjoyed wealth and prosperity. They started to build big, rich and beautiful houses and to set aside funds for education. They maintained their national spirit vigilant. The prominent enlightener and patriot Emanuil Vaskidovich was born here and the Revival Period functionaries Neofit Rilski (Neofit of Rila) and Hristaki Pavlovich worked here.

After the Liberation Melnik remained under Ottoman Rule and was on decline. The new boundaries discontinued its traditional links of the Aegean Sea region and Vardar Macedonia. The phylloxera, which destroyed the renowned Melnik vineyards at the beginning of the 20th century, played a big part in the decline, too. Moreover, the town was almost completely destroyed by fire during the Balkan War. Yane Sandanski with his detachment of armed volunteers liberated the town in 1912 г. But no more than 1000 people were left from the old-time 12 000 inhabitants.

Nowadays the town has about 500 inhabitants but possesses great potential for the development of tourism. The remains of the old-time splendour are sufficient for one to be engulfed into the atmosphere of long past centuries. The old Melnik houses are impressive with their architecture in conformity with the laws of nature, with their wealth, with their wine-cellars, with Bulgarian sense of practicality and beauty.

The more popular of them are as follows: **Kordopoulovs' House** - the biggest residential building on the Balkan Peninsula from the Revival Period, housing extraordinary mural paintings and an enormous wine-cellar; **The Bolyar House** (the Byzantine one) - a valuable architectural monument of Medieval times, the oldest preserved residential building in our country; **Pashovs' House** - turned nowadays into a town museum of history; **Velevs'** and many others. The ruins of **St. Nikola Monastery** of the 12th century, the **Slavovs' Fortress** of the 13th - 14th centuries, **the Roman Bridge**, the ancient Turkish bath are of interest, too as well as the ruins of several churches, which in the old times added to 75 in number.

Melnik is situated among whimsical **sand pyramids** - some of the most fascinating natural phenomena not solely in Bulgaria, but on the Balkans as well. The Melnik and the Rozhen Rivers along with their tributaries deeply cut into the sandstones. Rains and weather did the rest, sculpting peculiar and bizarre shapes - Gothic temples, towers, columns, mushrooms, fish fins and what not else. A real paradise for human imagination and fantasy!

Melnik is situated at a distance of 20 km from the town of Sandanski and is linked through an asphalt road (12 km) to Sofia-Athens international road. There are regular bus connections with Petrich, Sandanski, Blagoevgrad and Sofia. The nearest railway station, Damyanitsa, on the Sofia - Koulata (Athens) railway line is at a distance of 12 km and there is a regular bus line to it.

There are different **accommodation** and catering capacities. The big Melnik Hotel-Restaurant in the centre of the town offers the greatest number of conveniences. The most preferred, however, are the **family hotels in the old houses**, which offer home cosiness and

# BULGARIAN MOUNTAINS

Bulgarian hospitality. Some of them are the Lumparovs' House, the Uzunovs' House, the Miloushevs' House, Rodina. Each of them offers original Bulgarian cuisine. The cheapest accommodation is in the tourist hostel, located in the ancient Paskalevs' house. There are about 20 private lodgings on offer, too.

The historical **Birth of the Holy Virgin Rozhen Monastery** is situated at the distance of 6 km north-east of Melnik. It was founded in 1217 and was repeatedly destroyed by fire and plundered. Today's church dates back to the year 1600, renovated in 1732, from which time period are most of its mural paintings. The Monastery Church has preserved mural paintings from 1597, 1611 and 1715, too. The mural paintings of the Rozhen Monastery as well as some iconostasis icons are exceptionally valuable monuments of our pictorial art. The church of the Monastery endows its visitors with its startlingly picturesque woodcarving of the altar iconostasis and the lectern. Unknown wood-carvers left their hearts in this extraordinary piece of art far before the commencement of the Revival Period - genuine evidence about the mastership of the Debur and Samokov Schools of Painting! There was a calligraphic school with the Monastery, too whose representatives - monks created the whimsical work of art "Interpretation of Jov", ornamented with 117 open-worked miniatures. Unfortunately it was taken to Jerusalem in 1647. The great Bulgarian revolutionary Yane Sandanski found shelter here during the last years of his life, too. His grave is nearby - beside the St. Cyril and Methodius Church, erected at his initiative.

There is regular bus line coming from Sandanski to the **village of Rozhen** (in the immediate proximity of the Monastery). Despite along the road, one can also reach Melnik in a 1 to 1.30-hour walk along a marked footpath through the Melnik Pyramids themselves - an incredible experience!

A marked tourist route sets out from the village of Rozhen to the Pirin Chalet (6 7 hours walk). One can get accommodation in the Monastery and there are several taverns in the village, offering traditional local cuisine and homemade Melnik wine.

## SHILIGARNIKA

The biggest ski-centre in Pirin is situated at the distance of 9 km south-west of the town of Bansko, to which there is an asphalt road. There is no regularly functioning transport to it. In 1985 a open-seat cableway was built with a difference between the two levels of 706 metres and the capacity of 800 people per hour. It services some of the best ski-runs in our country. Its upper station is at about 2450 metres above sea level in the locality of Echmishta, north under the rocky cairn of Mt. Todorka (2746 m). Here as well is the upper station of the draglift servicing the highest ski-run in Bulgaria - Platoto where one can go skiing even at the end of May. A little tourist settlement grew up around the lower station of the open-seat cableway with many public catering establishments - tea rooms, coffee bars, little restaurants and the Shiligarnika Hotel offering 15 beds, a cuisine with culinary specialities from the region, a 24-hour bar and own transport.

The road continues from the Shiligarnika to Bunderitsa Chalet (4 km) and Vihren Chalet (7 km), from which Mt. Vihren can be climbed or one can set out on some of the numerous marked hiking routes. One can find accommodation in the chalets.

## MAJOR DEPARTURE POINTS FOR HIKING TOURS

**The town of Bansko** is the entrance gate to Pirin (Bulgarian Shamoni). It is connected to the remaining parts of the country by bus and railway transport. It is 160 km south of Sofia. It offers a lot of accommodation and catering opportunities. There is a base of the Mountain Rescue Service, too (tel.: 07443 3075 and 3076). Marked tourist routes start from here for the **Bunderitsa Chalet** (3.30 hours), **Vihren Chalet** (4 hours) and **Damyanitsa Chalet** (4 hours), from where one can continue exploring Pirin in various directions and from the first two Mt. Vihren can be climbed for about 3 hours.

**The village of Dobrinishte** is situated at the distance of 6 km south of Bansko. It is connected by bus and railway transport, too. Last station of the narrow-gauge railway line Septemvri - Dobrinishte. There are good possibilities for accommodation in family hotels and private lodgings, offering traditional cuisine. A marked tourist track starts from the village to the Gotse Delchev Chalet (3 h, there is also a 11 km of asphalt road in same direction), from where on foot (2 h) or by an open-seat cableway one can get to the **Bezbog Chalet** beside the beautiful lake of the same name. The well maintained ski-run can be used in winter. One can continue in various directions from there along marked footpaths. The **Mocharata Tourist Base** is situated at about a 1.30 hours' walk west of the **Gotse Delchev Chalet**. One can get there directly from the village, too (3 to 3.30 h).

**The town of Gotse Delchev** - 212 km south of Sofia and 22 km north of the border with Greece. There is regular bus transport to it. One can depart from it along a marked hiking path to the **Popovi Livadi Chalet (Papazchair)** - 4.30 to 5 hours (there is a 16 km road too, but there is no regular transport). One can continue to Mid and Northern Pirin from there or set out in the opposite direction - to Southern Pirin. There are accommodation and catering opportunities in the town of Gotse Delchev.

**The town of Sandanski** - 165 km south of Sofia and 22 km north of Koulata (on the border with Greece), in the valley of the Strouma River. It is situated on the international road and the international railway line Sofia - Thessaloniki - Athens. There are accommodation and catering facilities. The **Popina Luka Resort** with the **Yane Sandanski Chalet** is located at the distance of 18 km north-east of it, in Pirin. There is no regular transport to it but one can hire a taxi. Marked tourist routes set out from there for: **Kamenitsa Chalet** (2 h), **Sinanitsa Chalet** (5 h), **Vihren Chalet** (7 h), **Tourichka Cherkva Resort** (1 h) and others.

**The town of Kresna** - also on the international railway and highway Sofia - Thessaloniki - Athens, 40 km south of Blagoevgrad. With modest accommodation possibilities but there is no problem as far as food is concerned. A marked tourist track starts out from there to **Sinanitsa Chalet** (8 to 9 h), from where various directions can be chosen.

**Predela Saddle** bordering between Rila and Pirin, at 1142 metres above sea level, on the road between Simitli and Razlog. A lot of regular bus lines pass from here. Besides the several holiday homes, there is the **Predela Chalet**, too, as well as a lot of public catering establishments. One can go from here for about 5 hours along a marked hiking path to the **Yavorov Chalet**, from where one can continue around the beautiful karst ridge of Northern Pirin.

**The town of Razlog** - 155 km south of Sofia and 6 km north of Bansko, with very good bus connections and a station at the narrow-gauge railway line Septemvri - Dobrinishte as well. There are perfect opportunities for accommodation and catering. A marked tourist track starts from it to the **Yavorov Chalet** (4.30 - 5 h). There is a truck road, too (16 km)

Food can be bought in almost all Pirin chalets in summer, cooked warm included.

# BULGARIAN MOUNTAINS

## STARA PLANINA

**Stara planina** is also known as "the Balkan". It is **the longest, the biggest and also the "most Bulgarian"** of all mountains. It extends throughout the entire length of the country - from the Bulgarian border with Serbia to the Black Sea coast. Being 550 kilometres long, like the back-bone of a fish it is such an inseparable part of the country and its history long become emblematic of Bulgaria, fortress of the national spirit. The highest peak - Mt. Botev - is at 2376 metres above sea level and ranks third in Bulgaria. Stara Planina divides Bulgaria in two - Northern and Southern Bulgaria.

The name Stara Planina is derived from the age of our lands (translated as "the old mountain"). Some of the older names, which have come to us are: *Haimon, Haimos, Hemus* (of Thracian origin) meaning "ridge", "division line", "border". In later time different parts of the mountain acquire individual names - *Sreburna Planina* (Silver Mountain), *Matornie Gori, Zigos, Imm.*

The name Stara Planina appears for the first time in 1533 in the notes of the Dalmacian traveller Antun Vranchich. The name *Balkan*, however, is older and there are several theories about its actual origin. In spite of the fact that this is not an official name, it has become the most popular since the last centuries. It is from the name Balkan that the name of the whole Balkan Peninsula is derived - often referred to with the collective "the Balkans".

In spite of the meaning of its name (old), as a geological formation this mountain is comparatively young. It is based on granite but there also are lime, gneiss and schist. In contrast to Rila and Pirin, only the highest parts of the mountain were covered with glaciers. The lack of completed cirques and the existence of a single lake of glacier origin is the most obvious proof of this theory. Part of the relief of Stara Planina, however, is decisively Alpine.

**Climate.** Stara Planina is situated on the **climatic border** between the mild-continental climate of Northern Bulgaria and the softer climate, resulting from the Mediterranean influences in the south. It is a natural barrier against the influx of northern winds to the south, which, especially during winter, are particularly unpleasant. Quite often, they are the cause of the so-called "falling winds" (bora, wild wind), which coming from the north find their way through the ridges of the mountain and literally "fall" on the Sub-Balkan Valley with great speed - sometimes up to 30 m/sec. Such winds are characteristic of the area round the town of Sliven. Stara Planina is the most windy and foggy of all Bulgarian Mountains. Average temperature values at Mt. Botev are - January

*Mazalat Chalet in Stara Planina Mountain*

# BULGARIAN MOUNTAINS

average temperature - 8.9°C below zero; July average temperature - 7.6°C and annual average temperature of 0.7°C below zero. Rainfalls are at their maximum in May and June and minimum (excluding the Mount Botev area) - in February. The snow cover is rather irregular not only in duration but also in territory. More snow and for a longer period of time falls and stays on the northern slopes of the mountain, while on the southern it will - in most areas - melt away quickly. Because of the powerful winds at the top of the mountain, and in particular the ridges, the formation of visors and avalanches is possible.

The western border of the mountain is the Vrushka Chouka Pass while on the north the natural border is the Danube Plain. In some cases, Stara Planina is accepted by geographers to include the so-called "Pre-Balkan" while in other cases only the mountain itself bears this name. However, such a division is difficult to make. To the south, the mountain is steep and its borders are clearly defined. From west to east Stara Planina touches upon the Sofia Valley, Sredna Gora with all its parts and the Gornotrakiiska (Upper Thracian) Lowland. Its connections with Sredna Gora are Gulubets, Koznitsa and Strazhata - natural orographic connections. To the east, the Balkan ends with Cape Emine, falling steeply down into the sea. Within these borders, Stara Planina covers an area of more than 25 000 square kilometres and the central chain alone amounts to 11 600 sq. km. The mountain has 29 peaks at an elevation of over 2000 metres, some of which are definitely Alpine and thus attractive for tourists and climbers.

This biggest Bulgarian mountain is divided into three parts - Western Stara Planina, Middle (Central) Stara Planina and Eastern Stara Planina. They are additionally divided into subparts, usually named after the settlements established there.

**Western Stara Planina** starts from the Vrushka Chouka Pass, which is located on the western border of the country with Serbia. It ends at the Zlatishki Pass (Kashana) which separates it from the Central part. This sector has the form of a bow opened to the east, which has a length of 215 kilometres as the bird flies. It is the longest section of the mountain and second in height with **Mt. Midzhur** (2168 m). Three other peaks are over the 2000-metres height - **Mt. Obov**, **Mt. Martinova Chouka** and the most popular and most often-climbed one - **Mt. Kom** (2016 m). The sub-divisions (west to east) along the main chain only (the Pre-Balkan part is excluded) are: Cape Babin with the peak of the same name - **Mt. Baba** (1108 m); Svetinikolska Planina with the highest point - **Mt. Haidoushki Kamuk** (1721 m); Chiprovska Planina with the highest in the whole division **Mt. Midzhour** (2168 m); Berkovska Planina with **Mt. Kom** (2016 m); Koznitsa with **Mt. Todorini Koukli** (1785 m); Golema Planina with **Mt. Choukava** (1588 m); Mourgash division with **Mt. Mourgash** (1687 m) with the meteorological station there; and Etropolska Planina with **Mt. Govedarnika** (1790 m).

In general, the relief of Stara Planina does not have a well-expressed Alpine character. The Vratsa mountain is an exception, which is within the Pre-Balkan. The karst of which it is formed, has given this particular mountain numerous Alpine formations. The natural **rock phenomenon Vratsata** is one supreme example and also the focal point of climbing activities in Bulgaria. The existence of many caves explains the speleological activities in this region. Here, too is the extremely picturesque Iskar Gorge, which is another true nature phenomenon. This part of the mountain has 23 tourist chalets and a great number of marked hiking tracks thus being an attraction for both Bulgarian and foreign tourists "on foot".

**Mid**, or **Central Stara Planina** starts from the Kashana Zlatishki Pass and ends at the pass Vratnik (Zhelezni vrata, in translation "metal gates") on the east. The length of this part of the mountain along a straight line is 185 kilometres. This is the highest and the most

# BULGARIAN MOUNTAINS

attractive part and it is most frequented by tourists from Bulgaria and abroad. Apart from the highest peak Mt. Botev, there are 24 other peaks at an altitude of above 2000 metres. This is the true Alpine part of the mountain along the central ridge between Mt. Ambaritsa and Mt. Botev. Mid Stara Planina is divided into the following sub-parts of the central mountain chain only (the Pre-Balkan part is excluded) (from the west eastwards) with the highest peak: Zlatishko-Tetevenska Planina with **Mt. Vezhen** (2198 m) - one of the most massive giants of Stara Planina; Troyanska Planina with **Mt. Golyam Koupen** (2169 m), which is the most Alpine in shape and the most picturesque peak in the whole mountain; this sub-part includes also **Mt. Ambaritsa** (2166 m), **Mt. Maluk Koupen** (2141 m), **Mt. Kostenurkata** (The Turtle), as well as the narrow Alpine ridge **Krusttsite** - one of the most emotional but also most dangerous places to cross if one wishes to discover the top ridge of the Balkan Mountain.

This sub-part houses also the **Steneto Gorge** (Gorge like a wall) in the valley of Cherni Osum River, which is a Nature Reserve; the Kalofer Mountain which is decorated by the highest peak in the whole of the mountain - **Mt. Botev** (2376 m). It is not in vain that its older name was **Mt. Iumruka** (The Fist) - it resembles a clenched fist, surrounded by stone cliffs and vertical walls attracting fog and tempest - as well as thousands of eager visitors. It is here that Nature has, indeed, created at will a mountain heaven - the Northern and the Southern Dzhendem, Raiski Skali (Heavenly Rocks) (a real challenge for the climber); Raiskoto Pruskalo (Heavenly Springer) (the highest water-fall in Bulgaria - 124 metres) close to the small but cosy mountain **Rai Chalet** (Paradise). At the very top of the mountain there is a television transmitter and a meteorological station.

The Kaloferska Planina division has another 12 peaks at an altitude of above 2000 metres. Starting from the second after Mt. Botev - **Mt. Golyam Kademliya** (2276 m) they are: **Mt. Mlechniya Chal** (2252 m), **Mt. Sarakaya** (Zhaltets - 2227 m), **Mt. Maluk Kademliya** (2228 m), **Mt. Paradzhika** (2211 m), **Mt. Mazalat** (2197 m), **Mt. Pirgos** (2195 m), **Mr. Yurushka Gramada** (2137 m), etc. The Stara Reka (Old River) Gorge (passing through Karlovo) has also been declared a Nature Reserve.

The Shipchenska Planina (Shipka Mountain) division of the Stara Planina is towered by the **Mt. Ispolin** (1524 m). The other peak - **Mt. Stoletov** (1328 m) is lower in the geographical sense, but unreachable in its historic importance. In August 1877 the Bulgarian volunteer army and the Russian regular forces held the most dramatic battle in the history of the Russian-Turkish War of Liberation in defence of the strategic Shipka Pass. Now, this sanctified peak hosts a 32 metre high memorial of granite - and the bones of the heroes - in memory of the days of glory. Another sacred place in the Shipchenska Planina is **Mt.**

# BULGARIAN MOUNTAINS

**Bouzloudzha** (1441 m) where in 1868 the volunteers in Hadzhi Dimitur's detachment held their last clash with the Turkish regiments and together with their leader, most of them met their death. On 20 July 1891 on the peak was held the congress for establishment of the Bulgarian Social Democratic Party (D. Blagoev). The highest point of the Trevnenska Planina (Tryavna Mountain) part of the Central Balkan is **Mt. Karadzhoolu Kula** (1511 m) and the last part of it is the Eleno-Tvurdishka Planina with **Mt. Choumerna** (1536 m).

There are 36 tourist chalets and about 10 high-mountain shelters in the Central Balkan. Hundreds of hiking tracks have been marked and most of them lead to important natural, historic and cultural places.

The Central Balkan National Park is established in this part of the mountain. Within its territory it hosts some 10 biosphere reserves, some of which have been included in **UNESCO** programme of preservation of nature.

**Eastern Stara Planina** starts from the Vratnik (Zhelezni Vrata) Pass and ends at the waters of the Black Sea. In spite of the considerable length of 155 kilometres (in a straight line) the mountain here loses its monolith shape, so typical of the other two parts. Its height drops rapidly (the highest peak is **Mt. Bulgarka** at 1181 metres) and there are no Alpine formations (with a few exceptions in the Sliven Mountain). Even the mountain ridges in this area are covered by broad-leaved trees.

As early as the Vratnik (Zhelezni Vrata) Pass, Eastern Stara Planina divides into two parallel chains - Udvoi Planina to the south and Mator Planina to the north, which is accepted to be the central ridge. Of Udvoi Planina the Sliven Mountain part deserves mentioning because of its height (here is the highest peak of the whole sector) and the Alpine character of the area around the Blue Rocks - the most beautiful and often visited sub-part of Eastern Stara Planina. Along the Mator Planina range one can count: Kotlenska Planina with the **Mt. Razboina** (1128 m) and the Vurbishka Planina with **Mt. Karaborun** (The Black Cape - 1053 m). From the gorge of the river Luda Kamchiya Mator Planina itself is divided in two parallel ridges, both of them reaching the sea. The northern is the Kamchiya Ridge with the highest peak **Mt. Kamenyak** (627 m) while the southern ridge is the Eminska Planina with the highest point being in the **Mandrabair Massif** (621 m). The latter is considered a continuation of the main ridge and finishes at Cape Emine with a lighthouse. Here, too ends the marked track, which follows the top ridge of the Stara Planina throughout its entire length starting from of Mt. Kom.

There are 10 tourist chalets built in this sector of the Balkan Mountain and several tourists hostels in the towns, offering boarding and food. In comparison with the other parts of the mountain range, it is less frequented. There are marked hiking tracks - especially in the Sliven Mountain, as well as some alpine mountaineering spots. Basic hiking route in this part of Stara Planina is the well-marked track along the Kom-Emine ridge. Over the greater part of the Central Stara Planina ridge runs the main Balkan water-separation line between the water-collecting systems of the White and Black seas.

The **Bulgarian rivers** of greater importance, which flow from the mountain to the north and into the sea via the Danube River are the rivers (west to east): Lom, Ogosta, Skat, Vit, Ossum, Yantra, Roussenski Lom and Kamchiya, the last flowing directly into the sea. To the south and into the White sea flow the rivers Stryama, Stara Reka, Toundzha and Mochouritsa. In its western and eastern end the ridge is no more a water-separation line and there are rivers flowing south but pouring into the Black Sea - Nishava (in the west) and Hadzhiiska (in the east), as well as some smaller rivers. The Iskar River and Louda Kamchiya River are the two that flow right across the main mountain ridge thus creating exceptionally picturesque gorges. Both flow to the north and drain into the Black Sea.

# BULGARIAN MOUNTAINS

## THE GORGE OF THE RIVER ISKAR

**The Iskar Gorge -** as it is commonly known - is a true pearl in the tourist necklace of Bulgaria. It is a natural miracle carved out of the stone breasts of the Stara Planina. For thousands of years the waters of the Iskar River have dug their way into the rock, carving out forms of incredible shape, which impress every visitor.

The gorge of the river Iskar starts from the Sofia Plain (550 metres above sea level), crosses the Pre-Balkan area and ends around the town of Cherven Bryag (95 m above sea level). The total length of the gorge is 156 km. The central - most beautiful and distinct - part of the gorge is actually located between the town of Novi Iskar and Lyutibrod village and is 67 kilometres long. It is this most impressive and picturesque part which is better known as the Iskar Gorge. From the very start of the gorge the valley narrows sharply to outline the well-visible meanders. The slopes of the valley are sometimes flatter, then steep and in the end - forbidding! Then come the fairytale sights of **Tserovo** and **Lakatnik railway stations**, where the beauty of the scenery is increased further by an amphitheatre of stone. At **Cherepish** the river struggles to find its way through a canyon-type valley between vertical walls of snow-white lime. After several kilometres one is struck by the awesome sight of the Ritlite, which serve to outline the border between the main Stara Planina chain and the rather modest forms of the Pre-Balkan.

For centuries, the heart of the Iskar Gorge has been difficult to access. The roads and tracks connecting both sides of the mountain were located high on the top of the mountain and ran parallel to its ridge. The railway line of today was built in 1889 (the double track line came some time later) and when this was completed, life along the river started to change. New settlements appeared, new people came in, new industries developed. Later came the road.

In most recent times, the best and most picturesque locations on both sides of the Iskar River, near the railway stations and bus stops, close to the villages and quarters host villa settlements (predominantly of citizens of the capital city), which only add additional colour to the gorge.

As early as the "gate to the Gorge" - the **town of Novi Iskar** - one can see the famous **Kutina Pyramids** (one-hour walk from Kurilo quarter but also accessible by car - about 15-20 minutes drive). The first 15 kilometres inside the gorge are hosting the houses and villas of Vlado Trichkov, Rebrovo, Lukovo, Thompson settlements. Among them the village of **Rebrovo** is well developed in economic sense. It is the initial point of several marked tourist tracks: the **Boukovets Chalet** (4 km from Batuliya village, accessible by regular bus plus a three-hour walk), **Leskova Chalet** (20 km., by regular bus to the Ogoya village and 2.5 hours of walking after that) as well as tracks leading into the Sofiiska mountain.

The only town in the gorge is **Svoge** (8351 citizens, 520 metres above sea level). Svoge is situated in the widest possible part of the gorge

# BULGARIAN MOUNTAINS

- it is where the Iskar River flows into its big left feeder, the Iskretska River. The town is 40 km to the north of Sofia and 60 km to the south-west of Mezdra. It is a resort with clean and fresh air, located among the most breathtaking of natural surroundings. Some 10 kilometres to the west, in the valley of the Iskretska River, one can visit the **village of Iskrets**, which hosts one of the biggest sanatoriums in the country for people suffering from lung diseases.

The past of the town of Svoge and the surrounding villages is reflected in the Archaeological Museum (Tsar Simeon Str., working hours 3 - 6 p.m.). The **St. Paraskeva Church** has preserved interesting frescoes from the 16th and 17th centuries. There is a monument in honour to the sacrifices in the war of 1912-1918. The town hosts the Kraft Jacob's Suchard Co. - a chocolate producing company. The town has a hotel - AIPI Hotel (12, Sofronii Vrachanski Str.).

**Tourist information** can be obtained in this hotel or from the Iskarski Prolom Tourist Association (15, Tsar Simeon Str., tel.: 0726 2593). Svoge is a railway station along the Sofia - Mezdra - Rousse (extending to Varna) line. Bus lines connect it to all neighbouring settlements. The central bus-station (tel.: 0726 3194) and the railway station (tel.: 0726 2310 and 2223) are close by in the centre of the town. Svoge is a starting point for hiking tours to the picturesque areas in all directions but there are no marked tracks.

After Svoge, along the gorge the train stops at **Tserovo**, **Bov**, and **Lakatnik**. These places are an entry to a miraculous, fantastic world. The rock walls and particularly those on the left bank of the river become more and more impressive, reaching a climax at the **Lakatnik Rocks** - a unique piece of nature's art! It is here that Bulgarian mountaineering made its first steps. These stone walls are the perfect challenge for any climber. The Alpine **shelter Orlovo Gnezdo** (Eagle's nest) has nestled among the rocks. It was built in 1938 by the members of Bulgarian Alpine Club and can host 4 mountaineers. Nearby is located the famous **Temnata Doupka Cave** and the **Zhitolub Karst Spring**, close to which there is a restaurant. A 1 hour-walk from Bov railway station takes the visitors (along a marked route) to one of the highest Bulgarian waterfalls, the **Skaklya Waterfall** (85 metres). From there along a marked track by the Zessele and Zimevitsa villages the **Proboinitsa Chalet** can be reached (3-3.30 hours).

Another marked track in the opposite, eastern direction, starts from Bov in the direction of the **Trastenaya Chalet** (4 hours). On the way to the chalet one can choose a marked hiking track to a small quarter where the national poet Ivan Vazov had stayed (the house is still preserved, 1.30 hours from the railway station). There are marked hiking tracks from the Lakatnik railway station to: **Trastenaya Chalet** (3.30-4 hours) from where one can reach the spectacular Stara Planina peaks **Mt. Izdrimets** (1493 m), **Mt. Yavorets** (1348 m), **Mt. Garvana**, etc. as well as **Proboinitsa Chalet** (4 h), **Parshevitsa Chalet** (4-5 hours) and **Byalata Voda Chalet** (7-8 hours) and others.

Further down the gorge are the Opletnya village and railway station and the stops Prolet and Eliseina. The slopes of the valley become somewhat smoother and calmer although the scenery is still spectacular. The **Purshevitsa Chalet** in the Vrachanski Balkan part of the mountain can be reached after a 4-hour walk starting from **Opletnya**. This is where the highest quality sheep-cheese and the well-known Balkan yellow cheese are produced. From the **Prolet** stop along the 15 km asphalt road from the direction of Eliseina, following the marks for about 3 hours one can reach the unique **Sedemte Prestola Monastery** nestled in the bosoms of the Balkan Mountain on the right bank of the most picturesque Gabrovnitsa River. The brother of Peter Delyan - King Georgi Gavril, built it in the 11th century. It was plundered and put to the torch in 1737 and in 1770 - was again restored. During the Turkish rule it was a place of refuge for the Bulgarian outlaws. In 1799 it was the hiding place of Sofronii Vrachanski, the notable Bulgarian revivalist. It was visited by Vassil Levski, the Apostle of Freedom and has hosted Ivan Vazov to write the "Klepaloto Bie" story (1899).

The church is of special interest its architecture being unique not only within the country but in Europe as well. It was built in 1815 and renewed in 1868. On both sides of the main nave there are three small chambers with separate entries, nave-thrones and iconostasis. It is from these 7 thrones ("sedemte prestola" meaning the seven thrones) that the name of the church is derived. Of particular interest is the big wooden chandelier Horoto (1815), made of 15 wooden parts well decorated with carvings. The monastery offers cheap lodging. It serves as a starting point for tourist tracks in many different directions throughout the mountain.

From **Eliseina** a regular bus (for Osenovlag village) reaches the Sedemte Prestola Monastery. Taken the opposite direction, to the west, the **Purshevitsa Chalet** can be reached along a marked hiking track (for about 5 hours). **Purshevitsa Chalet** can also be reached from the **village of Zverino** (where 40 members of Botev's detachment led by Boinovski crossed the Iskar River after they had lost the fight) along a marked track (5-5.30 hours walk). Some unmarked hiking tracks in the mountain lead also to the Sedemte Prestola Monastery (7-8 hours) and to **Leskova Chalet** (6.30-7 hours). After Zverino, the river is again "squeezed" between the white limestones and one is struck by the rock cliffs and the fairytale meanders. In most places the water washes the rocks and this is why the road and the railway line have been forced to find their way through numerous tunnels of different length. The historic **Cherepish Monastery** is located on the right bank of the river Iskar, between Zverino and Lyutibrod, not more than 1 kilometre from Cherepish railway station. The legend of this monastery, half hidden by the rocks and pressed against them by the river, is frightening. Ages ago it was here, that the army of Tsar Ivan Shishman (1323-1333) engaged into a fierce battle with the enemies of the kingdom. After the battle, they collected the skulls of the dead and made a heap of them on the spot, where the monastery is located today. Maybe it was in honour of our ancestors or maybe it was to help their souls rest in peace that a monastery was built on this spot and it was named the Cherepish Monastery (in Bulgarian "cherep" means "sculp"). The legend corresponds well with some local place-names: Shishmanovi Doupki, Shishmanets, etc.

Among the written documents, preserved and kept in the monastery, is the Cherepish Gospel, written on paper during the 15$^{th}$ century and kept in gold plating, made in the monastery itself. It comes to evidence the connections between the Cherepish Monastery and the monasteries in Aton. In a panegyric of 1623 three works of the Patriarch Evtimii have been found. Yonko Popvitanov painted some of the frescoes on the ceiling and the arcs. The wood-carved iconostasis and the bishop's throne are interesting pieces of art. The silver relics-holder of the 18$^{th}$ century and the knitted shroud of the 19$^{th}$ century add to the treasures of the monastery. It had also twice sheltered Sofronii Vrachanski.

One kilometer before the village of Lyutibrod - the practical end of the gorge - stand the **Ritlite** as the final, one of the most interesting nature phenomena of the whole Iskar Gorge. Four unique-shaped stone walls stand in parallel on both sides of the river and common people have correctly given them their name meaning the two sides of an ox car. Closer to the river they are 49 metres high while at the western end their height is up to 200 metres. The historic **Rashov Dol** is located to the south-west of the Ritlite, above the left river bank. In the early June 1876, 12 of the Botev volunteers led by Georgi Apostolov were killed here. A small memorial tomb and an engraved stone plate remind visitors of the death of these heroes. The adjacent area is now a park.

# BULGARIAN MOUNTAINS

**Mt. Okolchitsa** can be reached after a 3-hour walk along a marked track from the village of Lyutibrod. On the peak there is a **memorial** and a **chalet**. Okolchitsa is the place, where the poet and revolutionary Hristo Botev and his men met the Golgotha. There is also an asphalt road leading directly to the peak.

After Lyutibrod the gorge widens and enters its Pre-Balkan part. The impression is tempered but unexpectedly picturesque sites surprise visitors and tourists at the villages of Roman, Kunino, Karloukovo, Resselets.

It must be born in mind that the railway station in the town of Svoge is the only stop of express trains in the Iskar Gorge, otherwise only passenger trains have stops in the gorge. In addition, only Svoge offers accomodation facilities.

## TROYAN MONASTERY

In addition to its remarkable natural features, Stara Planina is also rich in valuable cultural and historical landmarks, which it has preserved during the centuries. One of its greatest wealth are the dozens monasteries nestled in its bosom. During the hard years of foreign rule the Bulgarian people looked for more concealed and secret places to create in them their Christian sanctuaries and keep the national spirit alive. There is no other mountain in Bulgaria, which has housed so many Christian temples and which has given so much to its people in its struggles for survival and spiritual rise!

A small part of this spiritual wealth are: the Chiprovtsi Monastery, the Klissoura Monastery, Sedemte Prestola Monastery (the Seven Thrones), the Cherepish Monastery, the Sopot Monastery, the Kalofer Monastery, the Glozhen Monastery, the Shipka Monastery, the Sokol Monastery, the Dryanovo Monastery, the Kilifarevo Monastery, the Kapinovo Monastery and dozens of others.

**The Holy Virgin Troyan Monastery** is situated in the northern folds of the Troyan Balkan (Central Stara Planina), on the left bank of the Cherni Ossum River. It is 10 km south-east of Troyan, between the villages of Oreshak and Cherni Ossum. There is a marked tourist route from the town of Troyan to the Monastery (about 4 hours).

The Troyan Monastery is the third biggest in Bulgaria and the third in significance as well. It was created at the end of the 15th century but the first written information about it was preserved from the 17th century. The monastery church is of main interest here as it was built by master Konstantin from Peshtera in 1835. Zahari Zograph (1849) painted the mural paintings in it. The carved wood iconostasis, work of a master from Tryavna (1839) is distinguished with genuine artistic qualities. The wood carving in the St. Nikola Monastery Chapel, created by Senior Monk Kipriyan in 1794 is amazing, too. The Monastery is famous for its miracle-working icon "Holy Virgin Troerouchitsa". It was a renowned literary centre, too and nowadays it is in possession of a rich and valuable library. During the time of the struggles for national freedom Troyan Monastery was a genuine revolutionary nest. All the monks took part in the revolutionary committee

# BULGARIAN MOUNTAINS

headed by the well-known Father Makarii. The Apostle of Freedom - Vassil Levski often came here, too. One of his trusted men was his courier Father David from the village of Vratsa (Stefanovo), senior monk and later on Father Superior of the Monastery. The room Levski hid in has been turned into a museum.

**The working hours** of the Monastery - from 7.30 a.m. to 7.30 p.m. (in winter to 6.00 p.m.) (no days off). All the regular buses running between the town of Troyan and the village of Cherni Ossum stop at the Monastery, around which a little tourist settlement of shops, restaurants, coffee bars developed.

There are **accommodation facilities** in the Monastery itself - 2 suites and 10 double rooms with their own sanitary facilities and shower. Low prices. Romantic atmosphere, silence and calm!

There are other accommodation facilities in the nearby (2 to 3 km) **village of Cherni Ossum**: Sherpa Family Boarding House - working in summer and offering 5 double rooms, a common bathroom and a lavatory. A yard with a trellis vine and a fireplace. The Spomen Family Hotel - 11 beds in 5 rooms with independent sanitary premises and a shower. There is central heating in winter. A 20-seat snack bar.

Accommodation can be found in the other neighbouring **village of Oreshak** (1 km from the Monastery) in the Zheravitsa Family Hotel with 12 beds in rooms with 2 and 3 beds with their own sanitary facilities. There is also a snack bar.

## MAJOR DEPARTURE POINTS FOR HIKING

### 1. In Western Stara Planina:

**The town of Chiprovtsi** - situated at the northern foothill of the Balkan Mountain, at the distance of 36 km from the town of Montana, with which there is a regular bus connection. A key set out point for Chiprovtsi Mountain. It is connected through roads to the **Velin Dyal Chalet** (5 km) and **Kopren Chalet** (20 km), and there are marked hiking routes to them, too.

**The town of Berkovitsa** - at the northern foothill of the Balkan Mountain, 89 km from Sofia, 24 km from Montana and 53 km from Vratsa, with which it maintains a regular bus connection. It is a station on the local railway line Boychinovtsi - Montana - Berkovitsa. It is the starting point for the **Kom Chalets** (new and old), to which there is a road, and one can get there along the marked tourist route for 3.30 to 4 hours. The pleasant Stara Planina **Mt. Kom** (2016 m), the champion of Berkovitsa Mountain, from which the marked tourist route along the whole ridge of the Balkan Mountain up to Cape Emine on the Black Sea coast, can be climbed in about 2.30 hours along a marked track (with winter and summer marking).

**Petrohan Pass (Petrohan)** - a bordering ridge between Berkovitsa Mountain and Koznitsa, through which the road from Sofia to Montana passes. It is at the distance of 71 km from Sofia and 42 km from Montana. All the regular buses going through the pass, stop there. There are several roadside catering establishments and the big **Petrohan Chalet** is located in the eastern direction at about a 30-minutes' walk (there is a road leading to it, too - 1.8 km). The tourist hiking route Kom - Emine passes through Petrohan, so it may be the starting point from which to set out either westward to the Kom Chalet and Mt. Kom and Berkovitsa, or eastward along the Stara Planina ridge.

**The town of Vratsa** - 116 km from Sofia. A starting point for a lot of marked hiking routes around the nearby Vratsa Balkan Mountain: **Ledenika Chalet** (to the illuminated cave of the same name - 2.30 hours, an open-seat cableway may be used too, saving about an hour and a half, **Purshevitsa Chalet** (3.30 hours), the **Chalet** and the **Memorial of Okolchitsa** (3-3.30 hours). **Vratsata** - the unique rocky paradise for mountaineers starts from the end of the town, too!

**The gorge of the Iskar River.** One can set out from almost any small station all along the whole gorge along a marked route west- or eastwards. The gorge itself is extremely beautiful and the view pleases one's eyes regardless of the fact whether you pass through it by train, by car, on a bike or on foot. One can set out in various directions from the village of Rebrovo, the town of Svoge, Bov railway station, the town of Lakatnik (with many interesting mountain climbing sites around), the village of Opletnya, Eliseina railway station, the village of Zverino and others (see the Iskur Gorge related section).

**The town of Etropole** - beside the Mali Iskar River at the northern foothill of Etropole Mountain. It is 25 km from Botevgrad and 87 km from Sofia and is connected to them through regular bus transport. Marked tourist hiking tracks set out from it for: **Roudinata Chalet** in the low massif Bilo (5 hours), from where one can reach Botevgrad in 2 to 2.30 hours, **Chavdar Chalet**, on the main Stara Planina ridge (4 hours), from where one can continue in various directions, **Strazhata Chalet** (already in the Central Stara Planina, 4 to 5 hours past the Etropole Monastery), from where one can get to the **Svishti Plaz Chalet** (about 3.30 hours) or the **Kashana Chalet** (2.30 hours).

**The city of Sofia.** Bulgaria's capital. From here, making use of the well arranged bus and railway transport, one can get to each smaller settlement or starting point (for instance Kremikovtsi, Buhovo, Yordankino, Chourek, Vitinya Pass - on the main ridge), from where marked hiking routes set out around the nearest sub-parts of Western Stara Planina.

## 2. In the Central Stara Planina

**The village of Ribaritsa** - one of the longest villages in Bulgaria, located along the two banks of the Beli Vit River, in the northern folds of the Zlatitsa - Tetevan Balkan Mountain, 12-13 km south-east of the town of Teteven, to which it is connected by means of a regular bus transport. Several marked hiking routes set out from here to: **Benkovski Chalet** (4 to 5 hours, depending on the selected option of the two), **Vezhen Chalet** (4 to 4.30 hours), **Eho Chalet** (3.30-4 hours). One can continue from them along the main Stara Planina Ridge, climb beautiful peaks, pass into Southern Bulgaria.

**The town of Zlatitsa** - it is situated immediately south in the lap of the Zlatitsa - Teteven Mountain, 75 km east of Sofia. The main highway Sofia - Karlovo - Bourgas as well as the main railway line Sofia - Karlovo - Bourgas pass through it. It is the starting point for the **Kashana Chalet** (15 km) along a road and the **Svishti Plaz Chalet** (3-3.30 hours) on foot along a marked route. Both chalets are on the Kom - Emine marking along the main ridge.

**The town of Pirdop** - 2 km east of Zlatitsa. A starting point for the **Paskal Chalet** (2 hours), from where a contact with the route Kom - Emine can be made.

**The village of Anton** - 10 km east of Pirdop. Also on the above mentioned highway and railway line, but solely passenger trains stop at this station. A starting point of marked hiking routes for **2 chalets**: **Momina Polyana**

*The geographic centre of Bulgaria*

# BULGARIAN MOUNTAINS

**Chalet** (north of the main Stara Planina Ridge - 5 hours) and **Planinski Izvori Chalet** (on the Stara Planina Ridge itself - 3.30 hours).

**The village of Hristo Danovo** - 24 km west of Karlovo at the southern foothill of the Troyan Balkan Mountain in the immediate proximity of the highway and the railway line Sofia - Karlovo - Bourgas (solely passenger trains stop there) and it is provided for as far as transport is concerned. Marked tourist routes start from it for the **Eho Chalet** (5 hours) and **Kozya Stena Chalet** (4 hours), on the very ridge of the Balkan Mountain.

**The town of Sopot** - the birthplace of the Patriarch of Bulgarian literature Ivan Vazov, 6 km west of Karlovo and it is connected to it through town buses. The main highway and the railway line Sofia - Karlovo - Bourgas pass through it, too. Marked tourist routes start from here for the **Nezabravka Chalet** (3 hours) and **Dobrila Chalet** (4 hours, on the ridge itself, under Mt. Ambaritsa). An open-seat cableway can be used, too which goes immediately above the **Nezabravka Chalet**.

**The town of Karlovo** - a big transport centre at the southern foothill of the Troyan Balkan Mountain, birthplace of the Apostle of Bulgarian Freedom Vassil Levski, as well as Hristo Prodanov, the first Bulgarian who stepped on the top of the world - Mount Everest. It is a starting point of marked routes for the three **chalets** in the Stara Reka Valley - **Houbavets Chalet** (2 hours), **Balkanski Rozi Chalet** (Balkan Roses) (3 hours) and **Vassil Levski Chalet** (4.30 h), for the **Ravnets Chalet** (in the massif of the same name - 2 hours), the **Ambaritsa Chalet** (about 6 hours), Mt. Botev - the highest peak of the Stara Planina (7 to 8 hours).

**The town of Kalofer** - spread out along the two banks of the Toundzha River, birthplace of the great Bulgarian poet - revolutionary Hristo Botev. It is situated on the main highway Sofia - Karlovo - Bourgas and has a station on the same railway line. It is linked to Karlovo by a bus line running every 30 minutes. It is the main starting point for climbing the Stara Planina highest peak - Mt. Botev along both summer and winter markings. The summer route passes through the **Rai Chalet** (5 hours) and another 2.30 to 3 hours to the peak and the winter route passes through 3 shelters and the aim is reached in about 7 hours.

**The village of Cherni Ossum** is situated beside the river of the same name at the northern foothill of the Troyan Balkan Mountain, 13 km from the town of Troyan and 2 to 3 km from the Troyan Monastery. It is connected to Troyan by regular bus transport. Beginning of a marked hiking route for one of the most well-known Stara Planina chalets - **Ambaritsa Chalet** (4 hours), providing for an access to the most beautiful and Alpine ridge of the Balkan Mountain. The village is the starting point for the Steneto Reserve, too; there is no marking, but one walks for some distance along a truck road.

**The town of Apriltsi** - it consists of 4 quarters (former villages) - Novo Selo, Zla Reka, Vidima and Ostrets, rather remote from each other. There is regular bus transport going to all of them from Toryan and Sevlievo, which are

# BULGARIAN MOUNTAINS

situated at the approximate distance of 25 and 35 km. Apriltsi is situated immediately north under the highest part of Stara Planina - the Kalofer Balkan Mountain and the marked tourist routes setting out from it, lead in this direction. There are 2 tourist chalets in the town itself - **Zora Chalet** and **Vidima Chalet**. One sets out from the quarter of Vidima for the big **Pleven Chalet** (2.30 to 3 hours), from where one can continue for the highest in the Stara Planina Mt. Botev - another 3 hours. One can set out from the quarter of Ostrets for the **Tuzha Chalet** (3 hours), from where one can continue to the highest peak of the mountain Mt. Botev - another 3 to 4 hours.

**The village of Tuzha** - in the south-eastern foothill of the Kalofer Balkan Mountain, 15 km east from Kalofer, a railway station of the railway line Sofia - Karlovo - Bourgas and near the main motorway of the same name. There is a regular bus line with Kazanluk and with the resort of Pavel Banya. It is the starting point for the **Roussalka Chalet** (13 km road and 2.30 hours along a marked footpath) and **Tuzha Chalet** (25 km road and 6 hours along a marked footpath route). Hiking tours may be initiated from the first chalet around the high Triglav (three-headed) Massif, and from the second one the highest peak of the mountain Mt. Botev can be reached or one can set out in another marked direction.

**The town of Gabrovo** - a key starting point from the north to the Shipka Mountain. A multitude of marked hiking tracks start from it: for the **Uzana Chalet** (4 hours, there is a 22 km road), in the proximity of which the geographical centre of Bulgaria is located, the **Bouzloudzha Chalet** (2.30 hours, but from the quarter of Yabulka, which is situated at the distance of centre of 17 km from the centre of the town), the **Sokolski Monastery** (1 hour from the Etura architectural ethnographic reserve, situated at the distance of 8 km from the centre of the town), **Shipka Pass** (2.30 hours from Etura), from where the legendary **Mt. Stoletov** - a symbol of Bulgarian Freedom can be climbed for 30 minutes.

**The town of Shipka** - it is located immediately to the south under the Shipka Pass and Mt. Stoletov, 12 km on a road from the town of Kazanluk, to which it is connected by a regular bus transport. A marked tourist footpath starts from the historic Shipka Monastery, which in 1.30 or 2 hours takes you up to the Monument on Mt. Stoletov, passing through the legendary Orlovo Gnezdo (Eagle's Nest).

**The town of Plachkovtsi** - in the northern approaches of the Tryavna Mountain, 23 km from Gabrovo and 7 km from Tryavna, to which it is connected by bus and a railway transport. A key starting point for this part of the Balkan Mountain. A marked route starts from there for **the chalets of Ivailo, Planinets and Armeets** (2.30 hours) and thence in another 30 minutes you can reach the **Bulgarian Woman Forest House** on the main Stara Planina Ridge. One can continue from there to the Krustets Station to the east, to the **Bouzloudzha Chalet** to the west, towards **the Izvora Tourist Base** and to the village of Muglizh to the south.

**The village of Muglizh** - opposite on the southern side to Plachkovtsi. It is situated at the distance of 13 km east of Kazanluk and it is connected to it through regular bus transport. It is connected through a truck road to the tourist base Izvora and the Bulgarian Women Forest House (28.5 km), and one can reach the ridge for 7-8 hours on foot along the marked footpath crossing the road.

**The town of Elena** - nestled in the northern

bosom of the Balkan Mountain, at the distance of 40 km south-east of Veliko Turnovo, to which it is linked by a regular bus transport. A starting point for hiking tours around the Elena - Tvurditsa Balkan Mountain. There are 26 km to the top point of the Tvarditsa Pass where the **Boukovets Chalet** is located and from where one can get to the **Chumerna Chalet** for 1.30 hours along a marked footpath. One can get directly to the **Choumerna Chalet** along a marked footpath route from the town of Elena in 6 to 7 hours.

## 3. In Eastern Stara Planina

Due to the fewer number of visitors to this part of the Balkan Mountain and the lack of sufficient boarding facilities and marked tourist routes here, we shall indicate only two departure points:

**The town of Sliven** - main starting point for the Sliven Balkan Mountain and for the whole Eastern Stara Planina. Open-seat cableway from the town to Sluncheva Polyana (Sunny Meadow), from where one can go to the **Karandila Tourist Complex** and **Karandila Chalet** in 20 to 30 minutes. One can get to it on foot from the town along a marked track in 3 to 3.30 hours. Hiking tours to the highest peak of the Eastern Stara Planina - Mt. Bulgarka (1181 m - 3 hours), to Mt. Malka Chatalka - 30 minutes, to Mt. Vratnik Pass (Zhelezni Vrata or Iron Gates) - 7.30 hours, to the shelters at Dragieva Cheshma (drinking-fountain) and Daula can be started from here. The climbing Alpine sites are in its proximity, too.

**The town of Kotel** - an old Bulgarian Revival Period town amidst the Balkan Mounatin, at the approximate distance of 50 km from Sliven. It is the only town through which the Kom - Emine ridge route passes. The highest peak of the Kotel Mountain - **Mt. Razboyna** (1128 m) can be climbed along this route in 1.30 to 2 hours. Again along it one can go to Vratnik Pass (Zhelezni Vrata or Iron Gates) for about 10 hours or to the Vurbitsa Pass in the opposite, east direction in 9 to 9.30 hours. One can reach the **architecture reserves of Zheravna and Medven** along other, not very well marked routes.

## KOM - EMINE ROUTE

The longest marked tourist route in Bulgaria passes along the central ridge of Stara Planina, named after the names of its two final points - **Mt. Kom** (2016 m), in the immediate proximity to the border with Serbia, and the Black Sea Cape **Emine** - the eastern end of the mountain and the country. It is approximately 650 km in length, measured with a mileage recorder of a bicycle along the terrain itself. The middle of the route is around the **Uzana Chalet** i.e. it coincides with the geographical centre of Bulgaria.

Dozens of Bulgarians pass along the unique mountain "highway" each year. The hiking tour takes normally between 20 and 25 days under summer conditions and approximately 1 month under winter conditions (with skis). Kom - Emine is an arena of marathon competitions as well, the official record for the time being 5 days and 17 hours! It is the completing part of the European Transitional Pedestrian Route E-3 and that is why this designation is indicated in the marking. All the normal daily hiking tracks finish at a chalet or another sheltering facility. Bathing in the Black Sea is mandatory, regardless of the season and the meteorological conditions.

# THE RHODOPE MOUNTAINS

The Rhodope Mountains are the most lyrical of Bulgarian mountains combining the relief of mild oval forms, the colourful "rugs" of nature animated by the architecture of picturesque villages, by the hospitality of the people and the legendary songs of Orpheus. Over 83 per cent of its area are on Bulgarian territory, the remaining are in Greece. It is located in the most southern part of the country and is the main mountain system in the Rila-Rhodope Massif. With its highest peak - **Mt. Golyam Perelik** (2191 m) it occupies the 7th place among Bulgarian Mountains.

The Rhodope Mountains do not have a clearly outlined orthographic skeleton. They are a huge maze of hills of different length, height and direction divided by deep river valleys. The mountain has left an imprint on the history of Bulgarian nation. Its present name has been preserved through the centuries since the legendary Orpheus. It has been also called *Slaveevi Gori (Nightingales' Woods)* and *Dospatdag* but these names haven't remained, and the Rhodope (Rodopa) has survived. The origin and the sense of this name still remains unclear. Some people relate it to the ancient pagan goddess Rhodopa but others argue that is composed of the Slavonic words "ruda" (ore) and "ropa" - pit and this hypothesis has some reason given the fact that the mountain has been known for its ore-mining since ancient times.

The Rhodope Mountains are some of the oldest mountains in Bulgaria, composed mainly of gneiss, amphibolits, karst and granite rocks. Very interesting are the karst areas with their deep river gorges, large caves and specific sculptured forms. The tuff in the Eastern Rhodopes has created strange natural sculptures - mushrooms, pyramids, etc. The mountain had not undergone a glacier period so typical glacier forms can not be found.

The location of the Rhodope Mountains in the south-eastern part of the Balkan Peninsula determines to a great extent the **climate** here. It is influenced both by the colder air coming from the north and by the warmer breeze from the Mediterranean (The White Sea coast). The average annual temperature in the Eastern Rhodopes is higher and steadier and is about 12°-13°C. The temperature in the Western Rhodopes under the influence of the higher altitude varies from 5°C to 9°C. The transitional character of the climate in the Rhodope Mountains is demonstrated in the annual record of precipitation. The maximum value of precipitation in the Eastern Rhodopes is in December, while the minimum is in August. On the contrary, in the Western Rhodopes summer rainfalls prevail. The mild climate combined with some other factors favours the development of recreation and tourist activities. The Pamporovo Resort is an excellent example, where the microclimate permits a thick snow cover to stand for a long time - a real paradise for skiing.

**The borders of the Mountain**. Clockwise, from the north it is the valley of the Maritsa river, that borders the Rhodope Mountains from the north and east; to the south - the White Sea Plain; to the west - the valley of Mesta River, the Dreshenets River, the Avramovi Kolibi Saddle, Lyuta Reka River, the Yundola Saddle, Yundola River and the river Yadenitsa till its pouring in Maritsa River. The western border of the Rhodope Mountains separates (or connects) it to Pirin and Rila. The mountain has an orthographic connection solely to the Rila Mountain - the saddles Avramovi Kolibi and Yundola.

The Rhodopes spread over 14 737 sq. km of which 12 233 sq. km are on Bulgarian territory, the remaining - in

*A distant house nestled in the Rhodopes*

# BULGARIAN MOUNTAINS

*Rhodopes landscape*

Greece. The mountain is about 220 km long and about 100-120 km wide with an average altitude of 785 m.

The Rhodopes have two main ranges - Western Rhodopes and Eastern Rhodopes. The border between them passes (from north to south) along the valley of Kayaliika River (right tributary to Maritsa River), Kitkata Saddle, Yailudere River, Borovitsa River, Kurdzhali Dam, Vurbitsa River to the Tri Kamuka Saddle on the Greek border. This division is made on Bulgarian territory only. The two ranges are subdivided into many subranges. What is typical for the Rhodope Mountains is that they are the most populated mountain in Bulgaria. Unlike the other high (over 2000 m) mountains in Bulgaria there are many towns and villages (14 of them are resorts) within the range. This fact provides essential advantages for development of tourism. The best conifer woods in Bulgaria are in the Rhodope Mountains as well as the best preserved natural environment in the country.

Fifteen reserves have been established, some of these are included in **UNESCO** list. There are many mineral water springs - a great natural wealth of the mountain. The European Pedestrian Route E-8 to Turkey passes through the Rhodope Mountains.

**The Western Rhodopes** is the bigger part (8061 sq. km, constituting 66% of the total area), the higher, more developed and visited part of the mountain. The highest and best known peaks are also here (more of 10 are over 2000 m) including the leader - **Mt. Golyam Perelik** (2191 m). Among the interesting peaks are **Mt. Shirokolushki Snezhnik** (Karlak - 2188 m), **Mt. Golyam Persenk** (2091 m) covered with the impenetrable spruce forest, the beautiful **Mt. Persenk** (2074 m), the blueberry paradise - **Mt. Batashki Snezhnik** (2082 m), the huge massif of **Mt. Syutkya - Golyama** (1286 m) and **Mt. Syutkya - Malka** (2078 m), the wonderful **Mt. Tourlata** (1800 m) with a sharp straight peak, overgrown with spruces, and many others. Some of the deepest and most picturesque river gorges are here, too - the Trigrad, Buinovsko, of the Gerzovitsa River, of the Mostova Sushitsa River and others. The rocky phenomenon Choudnite Mostove (Wonderful Bridges), the Chaira Lakes and the dams Dospat, Batak, Shiroka Polyana, Iglika, Toshkov Chark and others excellently fit into the environment. The unbelievable architecture reserves Shiroka Luka, Kovachevitsa, Momchilovtsi, Kosovo and many other interesting villages are in the Western Rhodopes, too. The town of Batak is also located here as well as the large tourist centres Smolyan and Velingrad, the winter resort of Pamporovo, the Christian sanctuary - Bachkovo Monastery, the ruins of Assenova Fortress and many others. There are approximately 40 tourist chalets and near 15 hostels and tourist dormitories in the Western Rhodopes. There are hundreds of kilometres marked tourist routes good not only for hiking and skiing but for mountain biking as well. The subranges of the Western Rhodopes with their highest peaks are: from the west to the east - Alabak with **Mt. Chernovets** (1834m), bordered by the Rila Mountain - there are 3 chalets and many marked hiking tracks; Velishko-Videnishki subrange with the **Mt. Golyama Syutkya** (2186 m) - the largest and the longest but with few chalets and relatively few marked tourist routes; Dubrash with **Mt. Beslet** (1938 m) bordered by the Pirin Mountain, where there are no tourist chalets but there is the village of Kovachevitsa (where there is a tourist hostel) - practically no marked tracks; Batashka Planina with **Mt. Batashki Snezhnik** (2082 m) - a lot of towns (Batak, Rakitovo, Peshtera, Bratsigovo) and Batak Dam. There are

# BULGARIAN MOUNTAINS

2 chalets and 3 toursit hostels as well as many marked routes; Perelik with **Mt. Golyam Perelik** (2191 m) - the leader of the whole mountain as well - this is one of the most visited areas. Here are the towns of Smolyan, Pamporovo Resort, the town of Shiroka Luka. There are 4 chalets, 1 tourist base and 3 tourist hostels, as well as tens of kilometres of marked tracks; Chernatitsa with **Mt. Golyam Persenk** (2091 m) - one of the most beautiful and definitely most visited subsection of the Western Rhodopes. Here are the rock phenomenon Choudnite Mostove (Wonderful Bridges) and the 7 Persenk Peaks. There are more than 10 chalets, some hostels and dormitories and this is the area with highest density of marked tracks; Dobrostan with **Mt. Staria Bunar** (1517 m) - a karst massif with many caves (some of them explored, others - not). There are 3 chalets and a tourist hostel as well as enough marked tracks.

One of the smallest subranges of the Western Rhodopes is the Prespan sector with **Mt. Prespa** (2000 m). The highest village in Bulgaria - Manastir (over 1500 m) is crouched in the northern foot of the peak. There are 6 chalets and 4 tourist dormitories and many kilometres of marked tracks. The range of Ardino is relatively less visited because of the border with Greece. The famous building Agoushevi Konatsi is here - in the village of Mogilitsa and in the hills of Kainadina, immediately to the south of Smolyan is **Mt. Srednogorets** (referred to as the Shipka Peak of the Rhodope Mountains). There are no chalets or hostels but nearby Smolyan offers lodging and food. Marked routes are available only in the Kainadina rocky area. The eastern sub-range of the Western Rhodopes is Zhulty Dyal (the Yellow range) with **Mt. Buchovitsa** (1319 m), but most impressive is **Mt. Alada** (1214 m) with the Alada Shelter next to it. Near the beautiful Belite Brezi area is the only **chalet** in the region with the same name. There are almost no marked tracks.

**The Eastern Rhodopes** are spread over a territory of 4127 sq. km, or about 34 per cent of the whole area of the mountain. This is a much lower part - the highest peaks are **Mt. Orlitsa** (1483 m) and **Mt. Veikata** (1463 m) on the Greek boundary. Here the large flat wood covered massifs of the Western Rhodopes are replaced by wide, low hills with almost no verdure, with rocks and cliffs. But this landscape is extremely interesting and one finds himself in an unbelievable world! Such an experience is offered to you in the valleys of the Borovitsa and Vurbitsa rivers and some smaller ones. Here are the large artificial dams Kurdzhali and Stouden Kladenets that together with the rivers mentioned above offer great opportunities for water tourism.

Due to their lower altitude the Eastern Rhodopes are much more populated than the Western part. Here are the major towns of Haskovo and Kurdzhali as well as the smaller Momchilgrad, Kroumovgrad, Kirkovo. There are about 10 tourist chalets and hostels here but the towns and villages provide additional lodging opportunities. There are marked hiking tracks, too. The opportunities for biking are very good given the road network spreading throughout the area.

The Rhodope Mountains are the greatest accumulator of water resources in the country although the Balkan watershed does not pass here. The rivers from the mountains flow into the Mediterranean Sea and the Aegean Sea. Three independent hydrographic systems have been formed - the Mesta River, the Maritsa River and the Arda River and only the latter takes its source from the Rhodope Mountains. The other larger rivers here are Dospat, Vucha, Chepelarska (Chaya), Borovitsa, Vurbitsa, Harmanliiska, Kroumovitsa and many others.

*Choudnite Mostove (Wonderful Bridges) nature phenomenon*

# BULGARIAN MOUNTAINS

## PAMPOROVO

Pamporovo is the second mountain winter resort in the country after Borovets. It is located 1650 m above sea level in the Perelik range (Boukova Planina) of the Western Rhodopes in one of the most beautiful places of the Orpheus mountain. It received its name from the convoys of mules of the Raicho Belev, a man from the town of Smolyan, which followed one another as the wagons of a train (from the Turkish word for "train" - pampor) carrying goods. A man from Chepelare - Chichovski - built the first tourist hostel here in 1933 thus establishing the present resort.

The specific combination of natural conditions makes the resort beautiful in summer and in winter alike - the large spruce forests, picturesque meadows, strange rocky forms (the Orpheus rocks and others), beautiful high peaks - **Mt. Snezhanka** (1925 m), **Mt. Mourgavets** (1858 m), **Mt. Orleto** and others. The mountain where Pamporovo is located is composed of marble that drains the water and dries the whole region. The hill has a hunchbacked form and is very airy so the air is always fresh.

Due to the influence of the Mediterranean climate the temperatures in the resort have small daily variations. The surrounding high peaks keep it from the winds and in winter preserve the snow cover on the northern slopes of the Snezhanka and Mourgavets peaks. The area is abundant in natural slopes where many ski-runs have been built with different category of difficulty, served by sophisticated technical equipment. The resort offers 5 chair lifts, 13 tow-lifts and 17 500 metres of alpine ski-runs. Pamporovo is 16 kilometres from Smolyan, 12 km from Chepelare, 35 kilometres from Devin, 83 km from Plovdiv and 240 km from Sofia. There is a regular bus line connecting it to these towns. The high transmission tower on Mt. Snezhanka helps the location of the resort to be esily indetified from far away (in a clear day). At the tower there ia a panorama coffee-bar and it is reached by a chair-lift. Pamporovo offers many **accomodation opportunities** for tourists. The only 5-star mountain hotel on the Balkans - Pamporovo Hotel is located in front of the Assumption Church. The 3-star hotels offer great comfort - Perelik Hotel, Arfa Hotel, Mourgavets Hotel and Prespa Hotel. The following are the 2-star hotels: Euridika, Rozhen, Orpheus, Panorama, Snezhanka. The one-star hotels are Belite Kushti, Bor, Duke's Place, Maistor Manol, Markoni, Gorski Rai. A pleasant atmosphere is also offered in the Malina cottage village. Visitors who can not afford above hotels can also find lodging in the **Stoudenets Chalet** and the **Smolyanski Ezera Chalet** (located near one of the beautiful lakes between Smolyan and Pamporovo that could be reached from Mt. Snezhanka by the chair-lift).

A number of cosy restaurants offer traditional Bulgarian (Rhodope) cuisine. An example is the Chevermeto folk restaurant (mehana) where the visitor should try the incredible Rhodope lamb shish-kebab.

Pamporovo is the starting point for many marked tourist tracks to: **Smolyanski Ezera Chalet** (2.15 hours or 0.40 hours with the two lifts), **Izgrev Chalet** (in Chernatitsa - 6 hours), **Momchil Yunak Chalet** (in Prespa - 4.30 hours), **Perelik Chalet** (under the mountain leader Mt. Golyam Perelik - 4.30 hours), the **village of Progled** (1.30 hours), the **town of Smolyan** (3 hours), the **Orpheus Rock** (20 min from Mt. Snezhanka), **Mt. Mourgavets** (1 hour). **Stoudenets Chalet** is a point of the European route E-8.

## BACHKOVO MONASTERY

Located on the right bank of the Chepelare Rriver (Chaya), above the Plovdiv-Smolyan road, 29 km away from Plovdiv, 89 km away from Sofia and 10 km away from Assenovgrad. This is **the second in size and importance** monastery in Bulgaria - a real Holy Cloister. A prominent Byzantine statesman, of Georgian origin, founded it in 1083. It does not look the same as it was when established because it was destroyed by fire more than once and then restored. The only part from its original structure that has survived is the charnel-house with an interesting architectural design. Another building, which has survived, is the **Saint Archangels Church** dating back to the 12th century, the ground floor of which was painted by Zahari Zograf and his students in the year 1841. Unique frescoes were discovered in the dining room of the monastery featuring ancient philosophers and writers. Sveta Bogoroditsa (The Holy Virgin) Cathedral Church (1604) is the place where a most valuable icon of the Holy Virgin Eleussa, dated from 1310 is kept (brought from Georgia). The museum of the Monastery has a rich exhibition of church plate, icons, books, the sword of Friedrich Barbarossa, the Crusader, the Sultan's firman from 1452, the wood-carved cross with miniatures. A fresco of the Doomsday, painted by Zahari Zograf in 1850 is retained in St. Nikolai Church and it is one of the most interesting pieces of Bulgarian Revival art. It is believed that Patriarch Evtimii was exiled by the Turks and died here. The broad branches of a Diasperus Lotus tree (dzhindzhifa), brought from Georgia more than two centuries ago stretch over the courtyard. Bachkovo Monastery is directly subordinated to the Holy Synod. **Accommodation** for more than 200 people is provided in its buildings, against a few Leva only. A real tourist settlement clusters around the monastery with lots of shops, restaurants and a big camping site. There is a tourist hostel in the near-by village of Bachkovo (1 km away) which has 54 beds in rooms of 4, 6 and more beds. Lodging can be found in the town of Assenovgrad as well.

Mountain hiking routes start from the Monastery: to **Martsiganitsa Chalet** (4 hours) in the Dobrostan Massif, to **Bezovo Chalet** (3.30 hours) again in the Dobrostan Massif, to **Momina Sulza Chalet** (via Bachkovo 2.30 hours).

## SHIROKA LUKA

This is a village - museum (an architecture and ethnographic reserve) well known not only throughout Bulgaria, but abroad as well, for its original Rhodope architectural style, musical traditions and history. It is located on the two banks of Shiroka Luka River and is 22 km away from the town of Devin, 12 km from Pamporovo Resort and 24 km from the town of Smolyan with which it is connected with a regular bus line. It is the centre of a region of 5 villages (Stoikite, Gela, Stickal and Solishta) populated by Christians and Muslems. It was

# BULGARIAN MOUNTAINS

founded after the most massive forceful conversion of the population of the Rodope mountain to the Islam during the Turkish domination (17th century).

A series of archaeological excavations in the area, near the village of Gela and Mt. Tourlata, resulted in the discovery of archaeological facts that show that the area was populated in most ancient times.

The residents of the village built the Holy Virgin Church in 1834 in 38 days only. The brothers Zahari and Dimitur Zograf painted the frescos and a school was opened in it only one year later. In those difficult years the village was a place where Bulgarian spirit and traditions were retained.

The natural conditions, the uncertainty prevailing in the centuries of the Ottoman rule, the national identity of the people and their economic prosperity were reflected in the **architectural style** of the houses that belong to the type of a "large Rhodope house". They are two-storied, with bay windows and high stone chimneys, thick walls, small windows, forged doors, internal wooden staircase and a small cellar with a hiding place. The rooms have cupboards hidden in the walls, closets, etc. The yards are small, stone paved, with an outdoor drinking-fountain. All this is built with exquisite taste in harmony with the environment. Most prominent among these houses are **Kalaidzhiiska, Uchikovs', Grigorovs', Bogdanov' houses**, **Zgourov Inn,** etc.

The arched bridges above Shiroka Luka River and some of its tributaries add romanticism to the village. The songs of the village are unique, melodious and very lyrical. They are sung to the accompaniment of kaba-bagpipe, flute and rebeck. The legendary Captain Petko Voivoda (The Commander) has visited the village many times. One of the two secondary music schools in Bulgaria is located here. Tourists would find especially fascinating the Pes Ponedelnik Koukerski Festival which takes place every first Sunday of March.

**Accommodation** is scarce: Chevermedzhiinitsata Hotel-Club. It is in a building, which is a monument of architecture and has 5 two-bed rooms. Vaska Hotel - is also in an old house with a beautiful panoramic view and it offers 3 rooms with 2, 3 and 4 beds. The most luxurious is the 3-star Margarita Family Hotel. Beds are also provided in private family houses. For information: Tourist Informational Centre, Shiroka Luka, tel.: 03030 573, e-mail: sh.luka@mbox.infotel.bg. Well marked hiking routes start from Shiroka Luka: to **Izgrev Chalet** in Chernatitsa (5 hours), **Perelik Chalet** (under Mt. Golyam Perelik - 3.30 hours), **Lednitsata Chalet** (4 hours) also in the Perelik range. It takes 1.30 hours walk on a truck road to reach the **village of Vurbovo** interesting for its location and architecture.

## MAJOR DEPARTURE POINTS FOR HIKING TOURS

### 1. In the Western Rhodopes

**Yundola Saddle and resort centre** - on the border between Rila Mountain and the Rhodopes, 16 km from Velingrad, 26 km from Belovo and 25 km from Yakorouda, are connected by regular bus lines. There are lots of rest homes, a tourist chalet, restaurants, shops. It is an intermediary point for combined routes in the two mountains and of the European route E-8. For 3.30 hours along a marked track one can reach the **Kladova Chalet** in the Alabak sub-range of the Rhodopes.

**Velingrad** - the biggest balneological resort in Bulgaria is also one of the most beautiful towns in the Rhodopes. It is the starting point for the Alabash Ridge. It is the main station of the narrow-gauge railway line Septemvri-Dobrinishte. It is also connected through regular bus lines with many towns and villages, including Pazardzhik (48 km) and Razlog (69 km). It is the beginning of a marked hiking track to the **Kladova Chalet** (3 hours), from where one can proceed to the **Milevi Skali Chalet** (5 hrs.) and **Ravno Bore Chalet** (another 2 hours).

**The town of Batak** - a town of rich history, 26 km to the south-east of Velingrad and very near Batak Dam. Regular bus lines connect it with Velingrad, Pazardzhik and Plovdiv. There is a tourist hostel. A hiking track starts to the **Teheran Chalet** (3.30-4 hours), from where in 3-3.30 hours one can reach the highest peak of the Batak range - Mt. Batakshki Snezhnik.

**The town of Devin** - is 82 km to the south of Pazardzhik and 46 km to the north-west of Smolyan, with which, along with many other towns (including Plovdiv) it is connected through regular bus lines. Hiking tracks start here to: **Orphei (Orpheus) Chalet** (5 hours) in the Devin mountain sub-range, from where one could proceed and reach in 3 hours the well known Kemerov Most (Kemer's Bridge), **Lednitsata Chalet** (from Nastan quarter - 6 hours) in the Perelik sub-range, from where there are different options - to the village of Shiroka Luka, **Perelik Chalet** and **Pamporovo**, **Trigradski Skali Chalet**. The bus from Devin to Trigrad passes through the Trigrad gorge and near the **Dyavolsko Gurlo Cave** (Devil's Throat).

**The town of Peroushtitsa** - 24 km to the south-west of Plovdiv, connected with a regular (every hour) bus line with it. Starting point for Chernatitsa. A hiking track starts here to the **Bryanovshtitsa Chalet** (3 hours), from where it proceeds to **Vurhovruh Chalet** (2.30 hours) or descends to the **Academic Chalet** (1 hour).

**The village of Hrabrino** - 12 km to the south of Plovdiv. Connected with it with a town bus line. Starting point for the **Academic Chalet** (1.30 hour), from where the track continues to the Vurhovruh Ridge of Chernatitsa to the **Bryanovshtitsa Chalet** (1.5 hrs.) and **Vurhovruh Chalet** (4 hours). The track is marked.

**Village of Gulubovo** - 17 km to the south of Plovdiv, connected with it with a regular town bus line. Starting point to the Byala Cherkva Ridge of Chernatitsa - along a marked track to **Zdravets Chalet** (1.30 hours), **Studenets Resort** (another 1 hour), **Byala Cherkva Resort** (another 1.30 hours), from where one can proceed to the **Ravnishta Chalet** (3.30 hours) and **Persenk Chalet** (6 hours).

**Village of Kouklen** - 14 km to the south of Plovdiv, connected with it through a town bus line. Near-by is the Kouklen Monastery (1 hour). From Kouklen there is a marked track to **Ruen Chalet** (2.30 hours), from where one can proceed to **Zdravets Chalet** (another 2 hours).

**Narechenski Bani** - one of the biggest balneological centres in Bulgaria, with many sanatoria, mineral water springs, hotels, restaurants, shops. Located 45 km to the south of Plovdiv and 54 km to the north of Smolyan. Regular bus lines connect it with these two towns and many other places. This is the beginning of marked tracks to **Byala Cherkva Resort** (3-4 hours passing Mt. Cherni Vruh - 1543 m altitude) in Chernatitsa, **Pashaliitsa Chalet** (3 hours) in Radyuva Mountain in the Prespa Range, **Mt. Zarenitsa** (1 hour) where one can see the remains of a medieval fortress. An asphalt road (6 km), with no marking, can take you to a very interesting village, known for its old architecture - **Kossovo**.

**Village of Orehovo** - 40 km to the south of Assenovgrad and 28 km to the north of Chepelare. A bus line connects it to Plovdiv (twice a day), Assenovgrad and Smolyan. 7 km away from it is the **village of Hvoina**, located on the main road Plovdiv-Smolyan, where many bus lines have a stop. It is the starting point to **Persenk Chalet** (2.30-3 hours) and **Kabata Chalet** (3 hours), from where in 3 hours and 1.30 hours respectively one can reach the phenomenal rocks **Choudnite Mostove**, near which, at 20 min walking distance from one another there are two chalets - **Choudnite Mostove Chalet** (immediately by the rocks) and above it - a bigger and better furnished **Skalnite Mostove Chalet**. All tracks are marked.

**Village of Zabardo** - 51 km to the south of Assenovgrad and 28 km to the north of Chepelare. Connected with Plovdiv by bus (once a day), with Assenovgrad and Smolyan as well. 13 km away from it is the Sinite Hancheta Inn, a bus stop on the main road Plovdiv-Smolyan. It is a starting point to the **natural phenomenon Choudnite Mostove** with the two chalets nearby (2.3-3 hours), from where one can proceed to **Persenk Chalet** (3 hours), **Izgrev Chalet** (5-6 hours), **Kabata Chalet** (1.30 hours) or climb Mt. Persenk (2074 m) in 2 hours. There is a direct route from Zaburdo to **Izgrev Chalet** as well. There is a hostel in the village. All tracks are marked.

**The town of Chepelare** - on the main road Plovdiv-Smolyan, located at respectively 73 km and 26 km from them, connected with regular bus lines. The biggest speleological centre in Bulgaria. The town hosts a **tourist house** and a **speleological museum**. This is the starting point for a marked track to **Izgrev Chalet** (2.30 3 hours) in Chernatitsa, from where one can proceed southwards along the watershed (to **Pamporovo** 6-7 hours, Shiroka Luka - 4 hours), or to the north (to **Persenk Chalet** - 6-7 hours, **Choudnite Mostove** - 5-6 hours. A main road (12 km) connects it to **Pamporovo Resort**.

**Rozhen Saddle** this the border between the Perelik and Prespa sub-ranges, located on the main road Plovdiv-Smolyan, it is 9 km away from Chepelare and 20 km to the north of Smolyan. All bus lines that cross the town stop there. There is a big motel with restaurant. The saddle is at an altitude of 1430 metres. A marked hiking track passes here, connecting the resort of Pamporovo (**Stoudenets Chalet** - 2 hours) and **Momchil Yunak Chalet** (3 hours) from where one can proceed in different directions.

**Smolyan** - the largest town in the Western Rhodopes, 100 km to the south of Plovdiv. Regular bus lines connect it to Sofia, Plovdiv and many other cities and villages. There are abounding accomodation facilities, many restaurants, entertainment opportunities. 16 km away from it is Pamporovo Resort. The town is the starting point for marked hiking tracks to the **Stoudenets Chalet** (Pamporovo - 3 hours), **Perelik Chalet** (5 hours) located near the highest peak in the mountain range - Mt. Golyam Perelik, Rodopska Shipka (with the monument below Mt. Srednogorets) - (3-4 hours), the village of Arda (7-8 hours). An 8 km road (town bus available, too) leads to the Smolyan lakes and the chalet thereby.

**The town of Assenovgrad** - 20 km to the south-west of Plovdiv, connected with it with bus and railway lines. This is the main starting point for the Dobrostan Massif. A marked hiking track leads to **Momina Sulza Chalet** (2 hours), **Bezovo Chalet** (another 1.30 hours) and **Martsiganitsa Chalet** (another 3 hours). 2.5 km to the south of the town is the historical Assenova Krepost. There is a tour-

# BULGARIAN MOUNTAINS

ist hostel in the town.

**The village of Manastir - the highest village in Bulgaria** (located at 1450 m above sea level). It is 20 km away from Luki, with a regular bus running between the two. An important starting point for the Prespa Sub-range. There is a tourist hostel. Marked hiking tracks lead to **Svoboda Chalet** (2.30-3 hours), **Prespa Chalet** (1.30-2 hours) and **Haidushki Polyani** (a small resort - 2 hours), located on the main watershed of the Prespa Range.

**The village of Novakovo** - located 24 km to the south-east of Assenovgrad, on the main road Plovdiv-Kurdzhali. Connected with the three towns by regular bus lines. Starting point for **Sini Vruh Chalet** (2 hours) in the Novakov Mountain (Prespa Sub-range), from where one can proceed to **Martsigaitsa Chalet** (7.30 hours), **Svoboda Chalet** (10-11 hours), passing by the forest guard house Aqua Tepe and Rodopsko Konche, **Aidaa Chalet** (9 hours) in the direction of the city of Haskovo.

## 2. In the Eastern Rhodopes:

**Kurdzhali** - the biggest town (together with Haskovo) in the Eastern Rhodopes. Kurdzhali is the main starting point to the most interesting places in the Eastern Rhodopes - the valleys of the rivers Borovitsa, Vurbitsa, Arda with the big dams built on them. There are almost no marked hiking tracks in the area and all tourist sites are accessible through regular bus lines and by car, of course.

**The town of Haskovo** - a starting point in the northern part of the Eastern Rhodopes. Located 78 km to the east of Plovdiv. Connected with other parts of the country by bus and railway lines.

9 km to the west of the town are **Haskovski Mineralni Bani**, which may be the starting point for hiking tours to the beautiful ridges Mechkovets and Dragoina. The route to **Aidaa Chalet**, (Aida) immediately below Mt. Mechkovets (760 m above sea level) takes 2 hours along a marked track, that passes by Sharapanite (remains from Thracian times). From the chalet one can proceed westward along a marked track leading to the **Sini Vruh Chalet** (9 hours), thus entering into the Western Rhodopes. A marked hiking track begins in the town to **the village of Dragoinovo,** crossing Dragoina Ridge (4-5 hours). There are no other marked tracks in the area, but all interesting sites are accessible via regular bus lines.

Every town and village in the Eastern Rhodopes can be the starting point for a route to natural sites, historical monuments or tourist chalets.

# BULGARIAN MOUNTAINS

## VITOSHA

Vitosha is the most visited Bulgarian mountain. It rises immediately above Sofia and is one of the symbols of our capital city. Few are the big cities in the world, and capitals are even fewer, that possess such a natural advantage. Vitosha Mountain is the most significant part of the Plana-Zavala Mountain System. With its highest peak - **Mt. Cherni Vruh** (The Black Peak) (2290 m) it occupies the fourth place among Bulgarian mountains.

Vitosha is **the cradle of hiking tourism in Bulgaria**. The date 27 August 1895 is considered the beginning of the organised tourist movement in the country. After the invitation of the renowned writer and democrat Aleko Konstantinov 300 men and women then climbed Mt. Cherni Vruh - something incredible and unbelievable in those times. Since then thousands of hikers climb the peak every year on this day.

In ancient times the mountain was named *Skomios, Skopios, Skombros,* meaning in Old Greek "the sharp, steep mountain". These names are preserved in the present name of Mt. Skoparnik. The name Vitosha appeared in the Middle Ages and for the first time it was used in a document from the 11th century. There are two versions about its origin: the first of them says that the name is of Thracian- Old Bulgarian origin and means a "binary", "dividing" mountain; the second (more likely to be true and acceptable) says that Vitosha comes from the personal name Vitosh. Vitosha is a typical dome-like mountain - one of the few in Bulgaria. It has a slightly prolonged profile from north-west to south-east. It consists primarily of granite rocks, but there are karst rocks as well especially in the southern part. A unique natural phenomenon are the so-called "stone rivers" (moreni) - piles of huge rounded granite stones along many of the river valleys, reaching up to 2 km in length and 50 m in width. Especially expressive and beautiful are the moreni in the Zlatni Mostove area (Golden Bridges). Similar phenomena can be seen in other Bulgarian mountains, too, the Vitosha moreni however being unique. They are the symbol of the mountain.

Since 1935 a meteorological station has been operating on Mt. Cherni Vruh, with many services, mostly in the chalets. Comparative data about Sofia and Mt. Cherni Vruh weather conditions: the average monthly and annual temperature - for the coldest month - January - in Sofia is 1.7°C below zero and on Mt. Cherni Vruh - 8.3°C below zero. For the warmest month - July in Sofia - 21.2°C and for Mt. Cherni Vruh - August - 9.0°C. The average annual temperature in Sofia is 10.5°C and at Mt. Cherni Vruh - 0.3°C. A characteristic feature of Vitosha climate is the inversion (mostly in December and January). When Sofia is covered by thick fog and cold, the Vitosha Mountain shines in sun and warmth. This happens in an average of 15 days per year. An average of 140 days per year are very cold on Mt. Cherni Vruh - the maximum values in these days are below zero and there are 222 frosty days (when only the minimum temperatures are below zero). The winter in the high parts of the mountain lasts between 5 and 7 months, and truly summer months are only July and August. The average precipitation rate on Mt. Cherni Vruh (mostly snowfalls) is 1178 litres per sq. m. and June is the most rainy month - 142 litres per sq. m., while September has the lowest figure - 71 litres per sq. m. Most thick snow coverage is formed in March. Mt. Cherni Vruh is quite inhospitable,

*Boyana Waterfall*

# BULGARIAN MOUNTAINS

having an average of 250 foggy days in the year and only 50 clear ones and it is one of most windy peaks in Bulgaria. With an average wind speed of 9.3 m/s it occupies the second place among the monitored peaks after Mt. Mourgash in Stara Planina (10.3 m/s) and before Mt. Botev (9.1 m/s) and Mt. Moussala (7.6 m/s). Only 7 per cent of the days on Mt. Cherni Vruh are windless.

Clockwise, the borders of the mountain are as follows: to the north and north-east - the Sofia Plain, to the west - the Egulo-Palakari Saddle (1195 m above sea level) separates the mountain from the Plana Mountain; to the south it reaches to the Samokov Plain, and the Buka Preslav Saddle (1090 m) separates it from Verila Mountain, the next to the west is the Pernik Plain, and to the north-west the border with the Lyulin Mountain passes through the Vladaya Saddle (860 m above sea level). Vitosha has an area of 278 sq. km - 18 and 20 km in length and width. In spite of its expressly compact nature, the mountain is conditionally divided into 4 main ranges - Northern, Eastern, South-Western and North-Western.

The slopes of the Northern Range descend steeply to the Sofia Plain above which dominates **Mt. Kamen Del** (1862 m above sea level) after which this range is also called the Kamendelski Range. On its turn it is divided into four sub-parts: Vladaya (without expressed peaks, but one of the most popular tourist sites - Zlatnite Mostove is located here); Knyazhevo (here the highest peak of the sector is **Mt. Luvcheto** (The Small Lion) (2052 m above sea level), as well as the peaks - **Mt. Sredets** (1969 m), **Mt. Chernata Skala** (The Black Rock) (1869 m), **Mt. Kopitoto** (1348 m with the TV-tower); Dragalevtsi - with the two-headed alpine peak - **Mt. Kominite** (1620 m), **Mt. Ushite** (1960), **Mt. Kamen Del** and others) and Simeonovo sub-part with no distinct peaks. There is a cabin cableway to the Aleko Challet.

**The Eastern Range,** also called Koupenski, borders the Plana Mountain. Some of the highest and well known peaks are here - **Mt. Golyam Rezen** (2277 m - the second after Mt. Cherni Vruh), **Mt. Maluk Rezen** (2191 m), the interesting **Mr. Golyam Koupen** (1930). The eastern edges of the Rezen peaks are particularly expressive - they offer a site for Alpine rock climbing. Under this crown of peaks spreads Bistrishko Branishte Reserve. The well-known Vitosha Resort and Aleko ski-centre are located in the eastern part as well.

**The South-Western Range** is the largest but least visited in the mountain. It borders the Verila Mountain. It is subdivided into three parts - the Vetren Part is the most eastward with the high peaks - **Mt. Skoparnik** (2226 m), **Mt. Koupena** (2195 m), **Mt. Siva Gramada** (2003 m); the middle part - Petrouska part which is the lowest with its **Mt. Petrous** (1454 m); and to the west end is the Bosneshka part with its flat and low ridge, where the highest peak is **Mt. Krasta** (1561 m); the longest cave in Bulgaria - Douhlata is located here as well as the interesting karst water spring - Zhivata voda.

**The North-Western Part** borders the Lyulin Mountain and is called Silimishki. It is dominated by the ridge beginning at **Mt. Samara** (2108 m) and then continuing with the peaks **Mt. Silimitsa** (2014 m), **Mt. Ostrets** (1836 m) and **Mt. Ostritsa** (1696 m). To the north of the ridge is the specific **Mt. Vladaiski Cherni Vruh** (1641 m).

The four main ranges of the mountain pile together to Mt. Cherni Vruh (2290 m) as a true centre of the mountain.

Part of the Balkan watershed, dividing the basins of the Black Sea and the White Sea (Aegian Sea and the Mediterranean Sea) passes along the mountain. The south-western rivers flow to river

# BULGARIAN MOUNTAINS

Strouma and thenon to the White Sea, while the eastern, northern and some of the western - through Iskar River and then the Danube flow to the Black Sea. The longest, the biggest and the most popular river taking its rise from the Vitosha Mountain is Strouma River. Its total length is 415 km, 290 of which - on Bulgarian territory. Mutnitsa, Kladnishka and Roudarshtitsa rivers are among its biggest tributaries from Vitosha. Among the bigger rivers flowing to Iskar are Palakaria (39 km long), Vulchi Dol River, Selskata (Zheleznishka) River, Bistrishka (Stara) River, Yanchevska River, Simeonovska River, Dragalevska River, Boyanska River, Perlovska River and Vladaiska River. There are no lakes in Vitosha. There were lakes in the past but they have been drained due to ore mining. A lot of artificial lakes have been built in the lower parts of the mountain near the resort villages, the most beautiful among which is the Boyana Lake (since 1906).

The year 1934 saw the establishment of the first **national park** in Bulgaria, enclosing the greater part of Vitosha and aimed at preserving for the next generations the beauties of the mountain. Vitosha, nevertheless, has been developed. There are more than 100 places for accomodation with almost 6000 beds (not counting beds provided in near-by villages), two cabin elevator lines, numerous open-seat lifts, catering facilities, mountain shelters, kilometres of asphalt roads. All these are concentrated mainly along the northern slopes of the mountain, facing Sofia. There are two main **tourist centres** - **Aleko** and **Zlatnite Mostove** (The Golden Bridges). The first is at about 1800 m above sea level in the eastern part of the mountain and is one of Bulgaria's biggest ski-centres. There are several hotels - the 3-star Prostor and Aglika Hotels, the 2-star Moreni Hotel. There is **Aleko Chalet** offering 88 beds in 3 suits and rooms of 2, 3, 4, 8 and more beds. The chalet is the starting point of the Bulgarian section of European hiking route E-4. Above it is the huge slope Stenata - the biggest natural ski-track in Bulgaria. Of course, there are lots of facilities to add to the comfort of skiers - open-seat lifts, snow-levelling trucks, special marking, etc. Near-by shops, booths, coffe-bars and restaurants offer wonderful opportunities for a pleasant stay. Behind Aleko Chalet is the office of the **Mountain Rescue Service** (phone: 02 9671155). Aleko is also the starting point for climbing the highest peak of Vitosha - **Mt. Cherni Vruh**. The steep climb, at a difference of altitude of approximately 500 m typically takes 1.30 hours, and for those who think it is difficult, there is an lift to **Mt. Maluk Rezen**, from where they can proceed along a flat route and reach the dreamed peak in 30 minutes only. All routes to the peak are marked by high metal pickets or pass by skiing facilities, thus reducing to the maximum the possibility of one getting lost. Still it is not recommended to climb the peak in bad weather!

On the peak itself, besides the meteorological station and the base of the Mountain Rescue Service (phone: 02 9671128), there is a tourist station where one can find shelter in bad weather (no beds, however). Tea and warm cooked food are also offered. Marked hiking tracks start from Aleko: to **Zlatnite Mostove** (2-3 hours, passing through the **Platoto**, **Bor Chalet**, **Tintyava Chalet**, **Momina Skala Chalet**), **Academic Youth Base** (1.30-2 hours), to the **village of Bistritsa** (1.30-2 hours), to **Simeonovo Quarter** (1.30-2 hours), to **Dragalevtsi Quarter** (1.30-2 hours), to **Prespa Chalet** (30 min). Besides on foot, from above villages and Sofia quarters, one can reach

*Mt. Cherni Vruh. The Meteorological Station*

# BULGARIAN MOUNTAINS

Aleko by car - 16 km on a road starting from Dragalevtsi Quarter, or by regular bus line No. 66 starting from Hladilnika Quarter; by Bai Krustyo-Goli Vruh chair-lift, whose first station is above Dragalevtsi and can be reached with bus line No. 93 starting from Hladilnika Quarter or with bus № 64 and then 20 minutes walk from the central square of Dragalevtsi; by the modern cabin-lift Simeonovo, starting in Simeonovo Quarter (to which one can take bus line No. 122 from Hladilnika or No. 123 from Durvenitsa).

**Zlatnite Mostove (Golden Bridges)** is the another popular **tourist centre**, located at an altitude of 1400 m above sea level in the Vladaya sub-part of the Northern Range of Vitosha. Most notorious here is the phenomenon we mentioned above - the moreni. In old times this was a place where gold was washed out of the sands, hence the name of the area and the tourist settlement. The Zlatnite Mostove Hotel-Restaurant is currently under reconstruction. Around it there are numerous booths, shops, coffee-bars, villas, rest houses, alcoves, a children playground. Zlatnite Mostove is also a starting point to **Mt. Cherni Vruh** (about 3 hours), which route passes by one of the oldest and most beautiful chalets in Vitosha - **Koumata Chalet** (1 hour) and **Konyarnika Ski-Centre**, which is at 15-20 min walk above the chalet. There are marked hiking routes in other directions as well: the **chalets Planinarska Pessen, Borova Gora and Boeritsa** (1 hour); the **chalets Edelweis and Zvezditsa** (about 1 hour), **Ostritsa Chalet** (a little bit more that 1 hour) and **Selimitsa Chalet** (yet another 1 hour), **Bor Chalet** (45 min), the **chalets Septemvri** (25 min), **Momina Skala** (30 min), **Rodina** (35 min) and **Tintyava** (45 min), the **chalets Sredets** (40 min.), **Esperanto** (45 min), **Kamen Del** (1 hour), **Planinets** (45 min), **Kikish Shelter** (1.15 hours), **Belite Brezi Chalet** (15 min) and Sofia **quarter Knyazhevo** (1.30 hours), **quarter Vladaya** (1 hour), the **Kopitoto Area** with the TV tower (1 hour). There are signs showing all tracks, and occasionally - information boards. Besides on foot from Sofia quarters Knyazhevo and Vladaya, to Zlatnite Mostove one

*A view to the highest peak in Vitosha Mountain*

can also drive along a 14 km road, starting from Boyana Quarter. A city bus line No. 261 is also available starting in Ovcha Koupel Quarter (by Slavia Stadium). There is a station of the Mountain Rescue Service in the **Ofeliite Area** - no phone line.

Another smaller tourist centre is established in the **area of Kopitoto** (1350 m above sea level - in the Knyazhevo part of the Northern Range) with a TV tower, newly built hotel-restaurant, shops, catering establishments, etc. The cabin-lift starting from Knyazhevo reaches this place, bus line No. 62 from Ovcha Koupel is also available. It takes 1.30-2 hours walk from Knyazhevo and about 1.30 hours from Boyana to reach the area. Marked tracks start here to **Zlatnite Mostove** (1 hour), **Planinets Chalet** (40 min), **Momina Skala Chalet** (45 min), **Esperanto Chalet** (40 min), etc.

A small tourist centre is formed around **Selimitsa Chalet** (1300 m above sea level, in the north-western range of the mountain). There are several rest houses and restaurants there. It takes a 15 minutes walk from there to reach the interesting **Saint Nikola Kladnitsa Monastery**. Marked tracks lead to **Ostritsa Chalet** (1 hour), **Edelweiss Chalet** (1.30 hours), **Mt. Selichitsa** (1.30 hours), **Mt. Cherni Vruh** (2.5-3 hours), the **village of Chuipetliovo** (2.5-3 hours). A starting point for this tourist centre is the **village of Kladnitsa** (3 km road, 1 hour walk along the road and then along a marked path). The village of Kladnitsa is 22 km away from Sofia and is connected to it by bus line No. 60, starting from Ovcha Koupel Quarter, and 16 km

# BULGARIAN MOUNTAINS

*Dragalevtsi Monastery*

away from Pernik, with which it is also connected with a regular bus line. 3 km before Kladnitsa is the **resort village of Roudartsi** with an open-air mineral water pool.

All chalets in Vitosha (about 15) offer tasty dishes from the Bulgarian cuisine. The marked tracks are typically broad alleys, very good for mountain biking. There are two special ski-tracks down the hill (Aleko - Dragalevski Monastery and Mt. Ushite - Knyazhevo).

Almost the whole mountain is surrounded by small resort villages and villa areas, who were picturesque mountin villages in the past and now some of them are Sofia suburbs. Chuipetlovo, Bosnek, Kladnitsa, Rudartsi, Marchaevo, Vladaya, Knyazhevo, Boyana, Dragalevtsi, Simeonovo, Bistritsa, Zheleznitsa, Yarlovo are starting points to the mountain, connected with Sofia and Pernik with regular bus lines, and offering lodging in family hotels and food in attractive restaurants. Sofia quarters of Knyazhevo, Dragalevtsi and Simeonovo are first stations of cable lifts (cabin- and open-chair).

There are a number of valuable historical monuments here, the most popular among them being the **Boyana Church** (1259), whose frescos in the traditions of the Turnovo Art School are the best of their kind in Europe retained from these early times. The church is included in the list of **UNESCO** of most valuable works of art. It is open from 9 to 12 a.m. and from 1 to 5 p.m. Tuesday through Saturday (phone: 02 685304). It is in the centre of Boyana Quarter (bus lines No. 64 and No. 107).

**The Dragalevtsi Monastery** was founded under the reign of Tsar Ivan Alexander in the middle of the 14$^{th}$ century. It had been one of the prominent monesteries of the so-called Mala Sveta Gora. During the Turkish yoke it was a centre of culture and dissent. Vassil Levski was often sheltered here and a secret revolutionary committee was established in the monastery in 1873. It is located 3 km above the village of Dragalevtsi on the road to Aleko. It takes 30-40 min walk from Dragalevtsi. The monastery is open to visitors all week round.

**The St. Georgi Church** in Bistritsa is located on the place where the main monastery of Mala Sveta Gora was in the past.

There are mineral water springs in some of the villages mentioned above - Roudartsi, Knyazhevo, Zheleznitsa.

Even though it is smaller in area than the other high mountains in Bulgaria, Vitosha has a lot of attractive advantages - high and beautiful peaks, thick woods, many tourist and two alpine sites, sufficient snow fall ensuring stable snow cover, pure air, hundreds of kilometres of well marked tracks, numerous lodging places and restaurants, comparatively well preserved nature, clean water, wonderful skiing facilities, rich history. Adding to all these its closeness to the biggest city, which is the capital of Bulgaria - this explains why the mountain is so often visited and so much loved.

*Boyana Church*

# NON-STANDARD TOURISM

## OPPORTUNITIES FOR NON-STANDARD TOURISM IN BULGARIA

### Sports tourism

As a country noted for its beauty and for the comparatively well preserved nature, Bulgaria offers various opportunities for practising non-standard tourism all the year round.

Hiking tourism (tracking) in Bulgarian mountains is most affordable and popular. Especially attractive in this respect are Pirin Mountain, Rila Mountain, Stara Planina (The Balkan Mountain), the Rhodopes, Vitosha and Sredna Gora Mountains. There are thousands of kilometres marked tourist routes throughout the mountains (summer and winter marking). Hundreds of chalets, tourist hostels, Alpine shelters, tourist homes and hotels are at the disposal of those willing to set out along the mountain tracks rucksacks on the back. The longest hiking track in Bulgaria follows the ridge of Stara Planina (The Balkan Mountain) starting from Mt. Kom close to the border with Serbia far away to Cape Emine at the Black Sea coast. These 650 kilometres take about 20-25 days but the tourists are inspired, full of energy and unforgetable experience. Fans of the mountain marathon also follow this rather long track the record being 5 days and 17 hours.

The most attractive tracking sites in Bulgaria include the highest peak in the Balkan Peninsula - Mt. Moussala (2925 m) located in Eatern Rila; the beautiful Alpine Malyovitsa sub-part of North-Western Rila; Pirin Mountain - one of the most attractive Alpine type of mountains not only in Bulgaria but in the whole of Europe as well; the Troyan and Kalofer Mountains in the Central Balkan; the highest peak in Vitosha Mountain - Mt. Cherni Vruh (2290 m). Summer and autumn (from June to October) are most favourable for hiking in the high mountains of Bulgaria.

Ski-tourism grows more and more popular and inspires many fans of the mountain and skiing. Most attractive opportunities in this respect are offered by the high Rila and Pirin Mountains. The long routes and the memorable coasting down the Alpine slopes covered with untrodden snow evoke deep emotions and make one feel a pioneer. The northern slopes of Stara Planina have a sufficient snow cover all the year round, too. Vitosha and Ossogovo Mountains are most suitable for one- and two-day hiking tours, as well as for training. The graduate changes of relief, smooth hill shapes, the lack of great variations in altitude, as well as the thick snow cover throughout the year make the Southern Rhodopes most attractive for skiing tours with narrow skis (for ski-running). Ski-mountaineering is an extreme of ski-tourism and is more and more widely practised. The Alpine relief of Rila and Pirin makes them real "stadiums" for its fans. The period from February to April is most favourable for ski-tourism and ski-mountaineering.

Mountain biking is still new to our country but grows increasingly an attractive and promising sports and tourist discipline. Far away enough from the smog, the noisy and hazardous streets and motorways, engulfed in the quietness of the mountain one can rest and recreate. The mountains of low and medium height meet this purpose - Sredna Gora, Verila, Golo Burdo, Plana, Lozenska, Konyavska, etc. Only the Rhodopes and some parts of Rila and Stara Planina among the high mountains (above 2000 m) offer good conditions for safe practising of above sport. The lots of truck ways and sufficient shelters make them preferred site for mountain biking. Only skilled bikers can practise it in the upper mountain parts. Summer and autumn (from June to September) are the best time for this sport. Our country offers very good mountaineering opportunities as well - the sport of the brave. The highest "grade" in this respect is given to Rila - the Malyovitsa sub-part being an Alpine Mecca to mountaineers. The highest rock walls

# NON-STANDARD TOURISM

are there with more than 400 metres variance in altitude. The climbing of Dyavolski Igli, Dvuglav, Zliyat Zub, Malyovitsa, Kamilata, Lovnitsa, Kouklata, Ushite and others is considered a professional certificate to every mountaineer. Pirin also offers sites of this type - the northern wall of Mt. Vihren, Stupalata, Momin Vruh, Sinanitsa, Atmegdan, Dzhengala, etc. Raiski Skali (Paradise Rocks) and the Northern Dzhendem (below Mt. Botev), Vratsata Massif, the gorge of the Iskar river do justice to Stara Planina as an Alpine mountain. Should we complete the list with some other sites at lower altitude (the gorge of the Roussenski Lom River, the gorge of Erma River above the town of Trun, Karandila above Sliven, Muglizhki Skali (the rocks above the village of Muglizh), Cape Kaliakra at the Black Sea and others) the picture becomes rather varied and attractive. Mountaineering in Bulgaria can be practised throughout the year depending on the skills and training of the fans and the altitude of the site.

There are relatively good conditions for water-tourism in Bulgaria. The Danube River and all other dams and big lakes offer opportunities all the year round. In some of the popular Bulgarian rivers - Iskar, Maritsa, Vit, Yantra, Strouma, Arda, etc. there are good conditions for water sports only from March to May during the spring high waters. Another variation of water-tourism becomes more popular recently - rafting (sailing down swift waters with a raft). The best opportunities offers Strouma River, but the fans keep trying along other rivers, as well.

Speleology is rahter popular in Bulgaria. The existence of vast karst areas (Karloukovo, the gorge of the Iskar River, the Dobrostan Mountain Massif and Trigrad Region in the Western Rhodopes, Ponor Mountain in the western part of the Balkan, the Pirin karst, some areas in the Vratsa sub-part of the Balkan Mountain) is an actual prerequisite. Some of the most interesting caves are electrified inside and open to visitors - Ledenika (in the Vratsa sub-part of the Balkan Mountain), Dyavolskoto Gurlo (Devil's Throat) and Yagodinska Cave (in the Western Rhodopes), Magourata (in Western Stara Planina).

Paragliding recently becomes quite popular in our country. This quick and non-standard way of moving along evokes unbelievable emotions and is one of the mass sports of the future nevertheless the expensive equipment and facilities for ensuring safety. The sites where one can dive in the air are numerous but the fans of paragliding prefer Mr. Goli Vruh (in Vitosha, above Sofia), the Malyovitsa area (in Rila), the Pochivaloto area (Central Stara Planina above the town of Sopot), Okolchitsa Chalet and memorial (Vratsa sub-part of the Balkan, above the towns of Vratsa and Mezdra), Albena Resort (at the Black Sea), the high ski-tracks in winter - Markudzhitsite and Yastrebets (in Rila), Shiligarnika (in Pirin) and Stenata (in Vitosha).

In Bulgaria there are certain conditions for non-standard relations with nature that shall not be overlooked, expressed in the form of horse-tourism, deltagliding, snowboarding, surfing, yachting, etc.

The pure natural environment and the variety of fauna ensure perfect opportunities for hunting and fishing tourism.

The more dynamic and stressful life between the concrete walls in the cities, lacking air and space makes contact with nature an actual need. Bulgarian nature, the available infrastructure, the traditions and the people living with them and observing them are ready to meet this need.

# NON-STANDARD TOURISM

## Esoteric tourism

Located in the heart of the Balkan Peninsula, Bulgaria has been a centre of esoteric doctrines since thousands of years. The most popular sites connected to these phenomena are the well preserved Thracian sanctuaries, Tangrist pagan sanctuaries, the sanctuaries of the Bogomils - being a base for future Katares and Albigenses to step on, the Hesychast Christian monasteries, the sacred sites of Dunov's White Brotherhood, the areas related to the energy phenomenon of Vanga the Prophet.

Thracian sanctuaries. The Sanctuary of Orpheus is located in the Rhodopes near the village of Gela, which is supposed to be his birthplace. The Rock of Orpheus (Orfeeva Skala) is in Pamporovo Resort. In this region are also the Trigrad Gorge, the Dyavolsko Gurlo Cave (The Devil's Throat), the sanctuary near the village of Mougla. Orpheus is one of the great Teachers of mankind, father of the first esoteric doctrine on the Balkans.

Tangrist sanctuaries. In the Loudogorie Mountain Region one can find the sanctuaries of the God Tangra (Tengri) close to the village of Madara, nearby the magic symbolic relief of the Madara Horseman. There are preserved sanctuaries in the Old Bulgarian capitals Pliska and Preslav. Tangrism is shamanism from Mid Asia brought by the Old Bulgarians during the Great Migration of Peoples from Pamir and Tyanshan Regions.

Sanctuaries of the Bogomils. In the Rila and Pirin Mountains as a rule, these are areas of high altitude (above 2000 m) and of high magnetic energy. Bulgarian doualists, whose followers are the Bogomils, being Tangrists and Christians at the same time, have built their own sanctuaries at these remote places because to the pursuit by the Orthodox Church. Later on the Bogomils were expelled from Bulgaria and they laid the foundations of the White Brotherhood, of the Katares and Albigenses in Western Europe.

Hesychast monasteries. These are the remarkable Ivanovski Skalni Manastiri (Ivan's Rock Monasteries/Churches) along the Roussenski Lom River, near the town of Rousse; the Aladzha Monasery in the rocks nearby the Zlatni Pyassutsi Resort (Golden Sands) at the Black Sea coast. The Krustova Gora (Wood of the Cross) area in the Western Rhodopes as well as the site near the Rila Monastery where St. Ivan Rilksi had retreated in 9$^{th}$ century are sites of great interest, too. The Hesychasts are an Orthodox sect teaching marginal asceticism and misteriousness of the rituals and life in solitude. The followers of this doctrine lived in caves and close to nature.

Sites of Dunov's White Brotherhood. In Sofia - the grave of Dunov the Teacher. In Rila - Sedemte Rilski Ezera (the 7 Rila Lakes) where the gatherings and the mysteries of Peter Dunov's followers are held. Peter Dunov the Teacher revived the White Borherhood in Bulgaria and enjoyed many followers in Europe and America.

The sites of Vanga the Prophet. The Roupite Area (between the towns of Sandanski and Petrich) where Vanga spent her last years are among the places in Bulgaria full of strong energy. Vanga went blind in her early childhood but acquired the endowment to reveal people's fate.

*The following two companies are among those specilized in non-standard tourism in Bulgaria:*

**ALEXANDER TOUR**
44, Pop Bogomil Str.
1202 Sofia, Bulgaria
**Tel.:** (359 2) 9832371
**Fax:** (359 2) 9833322
http://www.alexandertour.com

**MONDO**
Travel & Tourism Agency
2, Yanko Sakuzov Bul.,
Hotel Serdica, 1 fl., office 128
1504 Sofia, Bulgaria
**Tel./Fax:** (359 2) 9461767
(359 2) 91936/116
e-mail: mondo@interbgc.com

# INDEX

## INDEX OF TOWNS AND RESORTS

| | |
|---|---|
| Ahtopol | 329 |
| Aitos | 185 |
| Albena | 299 |
| Apriltsi | 222, 360 |
| Assenovgrad | 142, 370 |
| Balchik | 297 |
| Bansko | 90, 349 |
| Batak | 115, 369 |
| Belchinski Bani | 100 |
| Belogradchik | 194 |
| Berkovitsa | 189, 358 |
| Blagoevgrad | 94, 349 |
| Bodrost | 96 |
| Borovets | 100, 339 |
| Botevgrad | 208 |
| Bourgas | 319 |
| Bratsigovo | 117 |
| Byala | 262 |
| Byala Cherkva | 236 |
| Chepelare | 146 |
| Chernomorets | 325 |
| Cherven Bryag | 213 |
| Chiprovtsi | 191, 358 |
| Chirpan | 165 |
| Devin | 151, 369 |
| Devnya | 291, 310 |
| Dimitrovgrad | 166 |
| Dobrich | 288 |
| Dobrinishte | 92, 349 |
| Dolna Banya | 100, 342 |
| Dolni Dubnik | 231 |
| Dorkovo | 113 |
| Dryanovo | 245 |
| Doupnitsa | 97, 343 |
| Dyuni | 326 |
| Elena | 247, 361 |
| Elenite | 312 |
| Elhovo | 174 |
| Etropole | 210, 358 |
| Gabrovo | 239, 361 |
| Gorna Oryahovitsa | 259 |
| Gorna Stoudena | 236 |
| Gorni Dubnik | 231 |
| Gotse Delchev | 87, 349 |
| Govedartsi | 100, 342 |
| Grivitsa | 231 |
| Haskovo | 168, 371 |
| Haskovski Bani (Haskovo Mineral Baths) | 169, 371 |
| Hissarya | 132 |
| Kamen Bryag | 294 |
| Kalofer | 130, 360 |
| Karlovo | 125, 360 |
| Karlovski Bani (Karlovo Mineral Baths) | 130 |
| Karnobat | 184 |
| Kavarna | 295 |
| Kazanluk | 155 |
| Kiten | 327 |
| Kladnitsa | 104, 375 |
| Koprivshtitsa | 123 |
| Kostenets | 109, 342 |
| Kotel | 181, 362 |
| Kovachevitsa | 89 |
| Kozlodui | 199 |
| Kranevo | 300 |
| Kurdzhali | 170, 371 |
| Kyustendil | 101 |
| Lom | 198 |
| Loukovit | 214 |
| Lovech | 224 |
| Lyaskovets | 261 |
| Lyulyatsite | 242 |
| Malko Turnovo | 186 |
| Malyovitsa | 100, 341 |
| Marikostinovo | 84 |
| Medven | 183 |
| Melnik | 346 |
| Merichleri | 165 |
| Mezdra | 207 |
| Momchilovtsi | 150 |
| Momin Prohod | 110 |
| Montana | 202 |
| Narechenski Bani (Narechen Mineral Baths) | 369 |
| Nessebur | 315 |
| Nikopol | 232 |
| Obzor | 312 |
| Omourtag | 281 |
| Oryahovo | 201 |
| Pamporovo | 147, 150, 366, 370 |
| Panagyurishte | 107 |
| Panagyurski Kolonii | 106 |
| Panichishte | 98, 343 |
| Panitsite | 132 |
| Pavel Banya | 154 |
| Pavlikeni | 236 |
| Pazardzhik | 120 |
| Pchelinski Bani (Pchelina Mineral Baths) | 111 |
| Pernik | 103 |
| Peroushtitsa | 119, 369 |
| Petrich | 83 |
| Pirdop | 105, 359 |
| Plachkovtsi | 244 |
| Pleven | 227 |
| Pliska | 270 |
| Plovdiv | 135 |
| Pomorie | 318 |
| Popina Luka | 349 |

# INDEX

| | |
|---|---|
| Popovi Livadi | 89 |
| Pordim | 231 |
| Primorsko | 326 |
| Provadiya | 290 |
| Ravda | 317 |
| Razgrad | 282 |
| Razlog | 92, 349 |
| Ribaritsa | 218, 358 |
| Romanika | 310 |
| Roudartsi | 104, 376 |
| Roussalka | 294 |
| Rousse | 263 |
| Samokov | 99, 343 |
| Sandanski | 85, 349 |
| Sapareva Banya | 98, 343 |
| Sarafovo | 319 |
| Sevlievo | 237 |
| Shabla | 293 |
| Sheinovo | 159 |
| Shipkovo | 222 |
| Shiroka Luka | 367 |
| Shishkovtsi | 103 |
| Shkorpilovtsi | 311 |
| Shoumen | 272 |
| Silistra | 285 |
| Sliven | 177, 362 |
| Slivenski Bani (Sliven Mineral Baths) | 180 |
| Slunchev Bryag (Sunny Beach) | 313 |
| Smolyan | 148, 370 |
| Sofia | 62 |
| Sopot | 126 |
| Souhindol | 237 |
| Soungourlare | 185 |
| Sozopol | 323 |
| St. Konstantin & Elena | 302 |
| Stara Zagora | 160 |
| Starozagorski Bani (Stara Zagora Mineral Baths) | 164 |
| Svilengrad | 173 |
| Svishtov | 233 |
| Svoge | 354 |
| Teteven | 217 |
| Toutrakan | 284 |
| Troyan | 219 |
| Trun | 104 |
| Tryavna | 242 |
| Tsarevo | 328 |
| Tsigov Chark | 116 |
| Turgovishte | 279 |
| Varna | 303 |
| Vidin | 196 |
| Veliki Preslav | 276 |
| Veliko Turnovo | 250 |
| Velingrad | 111, 369 |
| Vinitsa | 310 |
| Vratsa | 204, 358 |
| Vurbitsa | 279 |
| Vurshets | 190 |
| Yablanitsa | 212 |
| Yambol | 175 |
| Yundola | 112, 342 |
| Zelin | 209 |
| Zlatitsa | 105, 359 |
| Zlatni Pyassutsi (Golden Sands) | 301 |

# INDEX OF LANDMARKS

- Abritus Archaeological Reserve (Razgrad) ... 283
- Aglikina Polyana (Sliven) ... 180
- Agoushevi Konatsi (Smolyan) ... 150
- Al. Stamboliiski Dam (Sevlievo) ... 238
- Aladzha Monastery (Zlatni Pyassutsi) ... 302
- Aleko Konstantinov's place of death (Pazardzhik) ... 122
- Aprilov's High School (Gabrovo) ... 240
- Arapovski Monastery (Assenovgrad) ... 145
- Arbanassi, the village of, Architecture Reserve (Veliko Turnovo) ... 256
- Asclepion of Paulatlia, remains of Roman spa (Kyustendil) ... 101
- Assenova Fortress (Assenovgrad) ... 144, 169

*The nearest point of departure is shown in brackets.

- Atanassovsko Lake (Bourgas) ... 319, 323
- Ayazmoto, Park M. Koussev (Stara Zagora) ... 162
- Baba Vida Fortress Museum (Vidin) ... 197
- Bachkovo Monastery ... 144, 367
- Bacho Kiro Cave (Dryanovo) ... 247
- Bakadzhitsite (Yambol) ... 177
- Balchik Palace (Balchik) ... 297
- Batak Dam ... 116
- Batoshevo Monastery (Apriltsi) ... 223
- Batovska Valley (Dobrich) ... 290
- Belassitsa Mountain ... 84
- Belenski Bridge (Byala) ... 262
- Belogradchik Rocks and Fortress ... 194
- Bessaparski Hills (Pazardzhik) ... 122
- Borovitsa, River (Kurdzhali) ... 171
- Botev Alley ... 200, 207
- Botev Park (Kozlodoui) ... 200, 205
- Bouynovsko Gorge (Devin, the Rhodopes) ... 153

# INDEX

- Boyana Church (Sofia) .................. 80, 376
- Bozhenishki Urvich (Botevgrad) ................ 209
- Bozhentsi, the village of, Architecture and Ethnographic Reserve ....................... 244
- Cape Emine (Obzor) ......................... 312, 362
- Cape Galata (Varna) ............................... 310
- Cape Kaliakra (Kavarna) ........................ 296
- Cape Maslen (Primorsko) ....................... 326
- Cherepish Monastery (Iskar Gorge) .......... 356
- Chertigrad, remains of a Thracian fortress (Etropole) ................... 211
- Cherven, remains of an ancient settlement (Rousse) ............................... 268
- Chervenata Cherkva Church (Peroushtitsa) ........................................... 120
- Chervenata Stena Biosphere Reserve (Assenovgrad) .......................................... 145
- Chiprovtsi Monastery, St. Yoan Rilski ....... 193
- Dolphinarium (Show-House) (Varna) ........ 306
- Domlyan Dam (Karlovo) .......................... 130
- Dourankoulak Plateau (Shabla) ................ 293
- Dragalevtsi Monastery (Sofia) ............ 80, 376
- Dryanovo Monastery (Dryanovo) ............... 246
- Dyavolsko Gurlo (the Rhodopes) .............. 153
- Elia's drinking-fountain (Nikopol) ............. 232
- Emenski Canyon (Pavlikeni) ..................... 237
- Erma River Gorge (Trun) ......................... 104
- Esperanto, the island of (Oryahovo) ......... 202
- Etropole Monastery, St. Trinity ................ 210
- Etura Architecture and Ethnographic Complex (Gabrovo) .................................. 240
- Evksinograd ............................................ 303
- Four Dams (Batak, the Rhodopes) ........... 116
- Geographic Centre of Bulgaria ................. 242
- Glozhene Monastery (Yablanitsa) ............. 212
- Golo Burdo Mountain ............................... 104
- Granitski oak-tree (Chirpan) .................... 166
- Hissarluka Park (Kyustendil, Ossogovo Mountain) ............ 102
- Hissarya Fortress ................................... 133
- Iovkovtsi Dam (Elena) ............................. 249
- Iskar Dam (Sofia) ..................................... 80
- Iskar Gorge .................................... 354, 358
- Ivanovski Rock Churches ........................ 269
- Izvorut na Belonogata (Haskovo) .............. 169
- Kabile Archaeological Reserve (Yambol) ................................................ 177
- Kabiyuk Horse Stud (Shoumen) ............... 276
- Kadin, Nevestin Bridge (Kyustendil) ......... 102
- Kailuka Park (Pleven) .............................. 230
- Kalofer Monstery .................................... 132
- Kamchiya, river mouth (Varna) ................ 311
- Kamuka (Klaeto) Fortress (Oryahovo) ...... 202
- Kapinovo Monastery (Elena) .................... 249
- Karlovo Waterfall (Souchouroum) ............. 130
- Kazanluk Thracian Tomb .......................... 156
- Kemerov's Bridge (Devin) ................ 153, 369
- Kenana Park (Haskovo) ........................... 169
- Kilifarevo Monastery (Veliko Turnovo) ...... 257
- Kladnitsa Monastery (Pernik) ............ 104, 375
- Klissoura Monstery (Berkovitsa) .............. 190
- Koprinka Dam (Kazanluk) ........................ 160
- Kozlodoui, the island of (Kozlodoui) ......... 200
- Kozyata Stena Biosphere Reserve (Troyan Balkan Mountain) ......................... 222
- Kukrinsko Hanche Museum (Lovch) ......... 227
- Kurdzhali Pyramids ................................. 171
- Kustova Gora (the Rhodopes) .................. 145
- Kutina Pyramids (Novi Iskar) .................... 354
- Lakatnik Rocks (Iskar Gorge) ................... 355
- Ledenika Cave (Vratsa) ............................ 206
- Lopoushanski Monastery (Chiprovtsi) ....... 193
- Lyaskovets (Petropavlovski) Monastery .... 257
- Lyulin Mountain ...................................... 104
- Madara, Hisotrical and Archaeological Reserve (Shoumen) .......... 275
- Madara Horseman (Shoumen) ................. 275
- Magourata, Rabisha Cave (Belogradchik) ....................................... 195
- Mausoleum - Charnel House (Pleven) ..... 230
- Memorial Complex, The Defenders of Stara Zagora ...................................... 162
- Memorial Complex, The Founders of Bulgarian State (Shoumen) .................. 273
- Mezek Thracian Tomb (Svilengrad) .......... 174
- Milin Kamuk (Vratsa) ............................... 207
- Montana Dam ......................................... 203
- Mr. Botev (Stara Planina) ........................ 132
- Mr. Moussala (Rila) ................................. 335
- Mr. Radomir (Belassitsa) .......................... 84
- Mr. Toumba (Belassitsa) ........................... 84
- Mt. Cherni Vrah (Vitosha) ................ 372, 374
- Mt. Gradishteto (Strandzha) .................... 187
- Mt. Kom (Stara Planina) .......................... 351
- Mt. Srednogorets (the Rhodopes) ............ 151
- Mt. Stoletov (Stara Planina) ............. 352, 361
- Mt. Vezhen (Stara Planina) ...................... 352
- Mt. Vihren (Pirin) .................................... 344
- Museum, Danubian Fishing and Boat Construction (Toutrakan) ................. 284
- Museum of Speleology and Bulgarian Karst (Chepelare) ...................... 147
- Museum of the Mosaics (Devnya) ............ 291
- Museum of the Rose (Kazanluk) .............. 157
- National Fair-Exhibition of People's Art Crafts (Oreshaka) .............................. 221
- National House of Speleologists, Peter Tranteev (Karloukovo) .................... 215

# INDEX

- Nicipolis ad Nestum, remains of a Roman town (Gotse Delchev) ............ 88
- Nikopolis ad Istrum, remains of a Roman town (Veliko Turnovo) .......... 258
- Nove, remains of an antique settlement (Svishtov) .................. 235
- Oborishte (Panagyurishte) ......................... 108
- Okolchitsa (Vratsa) ....................... 205, 357
- Old town of Plovdiv, Architecture Reserve .................................. 138
- Ossogovo Mountain ..................................... 102
- Pametnitzite Park (Svishtov) ...................... 235
- Panorama, Pleven Epic 1877 .................. 230
- Parangalitsa, Reserve (Blagoevgrad, Rilla) ................................ 336
- Patleina Monastery (Veliki Preslav) ........... 278
- Pchelina Forest Park (Razgrad) ................. 283
- Perperek, Medieval foretress (Kurdzhali, the Rhodopes) ......................... 171
- Petrova Niva, historical area (Malko Turnovo, Strandzha) ...................... 187
- Petrohan Pass (Berkovitsa) ................ 191, 358
- Plachkovo Monastery (Elena) ................... 249
- Pobitite Kamuni (Varna) .............................. 310
- Pokritiyat Most, bridge (Lovech) ................ 225
- Preobrazhenski Monastery ........................ 256
- Propadaloto (Cherven Bryag) .................... 213
- Raiskoto Pruskalo (Stara Planina) ............. 132
- Rashov Dol (Iskar Gorge) .......................... 356
- Ratsiaria, remains of a Roman town (Vidin) ............................... 198
- Rila Monastery ............................................ 337
- Ritlite, nature phenomenon (Lyutibrod) ..... 356
- Roman Bridge (Turgovishte) ...................... 281
- Ropotamo, river mouth .............................. 325
- Roupite (Petrich) ........................................... 84
- Roussenski Lom River Valley (Rousse) ...................................................... 268
- Rozhen Monastery (Melnik) ...................... 346
- Rozhen Observatory (Chepelare) .............. 147
- Samouil Fortress (Petrich) ........................... 83
- Sanctuary of the nymphs (Dimitrovgrad) ............................................ 169
- Sea Garden Park (Varna) .......................... 305
- Sedemte Prestola Monastery .................... 355
- Seven Rila Lakes ........................................ 336
- Sharapanite, Thracian wine cellars (Haskovo, the Rhodopes) ................. 169, 371
- Shegava, River (Kyustendil) ...................... 103
- Shipka - Bouzloudga, National Park-Museum ............................... 159
- Shirola Luka, the village of, Architecture and Ethnographic Reserve .... 367
- Shoumen Plateau Nature Park ................. 275
- Sinite Kamuni Nature Park (Sliven) .......... 179
- Skobelev Park (Pleven) ............................. 230
- Smolyan Lakes ........................................... 150
- Sokolski Monastery (Gabrovo) ......... 241, 361
- Sopot Dam (Troyan) .................................. 222
- Sopot Monastery, St. Spas ....................... 126
- Sreburna, Biosphere Reserve (Silistra) ...................................................... 287
- St. Anastassia, the island of (Bourgas) ..................................................... 323
- Steneto, Biospere Reserve (Troyan Balkan Mountain) ........................... 222
- Stob, the pyramids of (Rila) ........................ 96
- Stroupesh Monastery (Mezdra) ................ 208
- Sveti Vrach, Town Park (Sandanski) .......... 86
- Tevno Ezero, Lake (Pirin) ......................... 345
- The Holy Trinity Monastery (Veliko Turnovo) .......................................... 257
- Thracian rock sancturaies (Assenovgrad, the Rhodopes) .................. 145
- Thracian rock sanctury (Kurdzhali, the Rhodopes) ......................... 171
- Thracian tomb (temple), the village of Starossel (Hissarya) ............ 135
- Thracian tomb, the village of Alexandrovo (Haskovo) ......................... 169
- Thracian tomb, the village of Sveshtari (Isperih) ................................... 283
- Ticha Dam (Veliki Preslav) ....................... 279
- Touzlata (Balchik) ....................................... 298
- Trayanovi Vrata (Kostenets, Sredna Gora Mountain) ............................ 110
- Trigrad Gorge (Devin) ............................... 153
- Troyan Monastery ...................................... 357
- Tsarevets Archaeological Reserve (Veliko Turnovo) .......................................... 252
- Tsepina Fortress (Velingrad, the Rhodopes) ......................... 113
- Turgovishte Izvor, spring ........................... 281
- Uzana (Gabrovo) ....................................... 242
- Vardim, the island of (Svishtov) ............... 235
- Varosha Architecture and Historical Reserve (Lovech) ........................ 225
- Veleka, river mouth (Ahtopol) ................... 329
- Voden Nature Reserve (Razgrad) ............. 283
- Vratsata Gorge (Vratsa) ............................ 207
- Yagodinska Cave (Devin) .......................... 153
- Yailata Landslide ........................................ 294
- Zemen Gorge ............................................. 103
- Zemen Monastery ...................................... 103
- Zhaba Fortress (Bratsigovo) ..................... 118
- Zheravna, the village of, Architecture and Ethnographic Reserve (Kotel) ............. 182
- Zmiiski Island (Sozopol) ............................ 325

**TOUR GUIDE BULGARIA**
Second revised and expanded edition
© Evgheni Dinchev, Alexander Iliev, Roumen Naydenov, Dimiter M. Dimitrov,
  Petko Kolev, Lilyana Karagyozova, Sirma Nedeva, Georgi Vladimirov,
  Plamen Pavlov - authors
  Second Edition, Bulgaria

**Consultant:** Roumen Naydenov, Stoyan Minkovski, Plamen Pavlov
**Editor:** Adriana Momchilova
**Proof-reader:** Adriana Momchilova
**Photos rendered by** Vanya Stoikova Alexieva, Georgi Kitov, Doncho Donev, Ivailo Ivanov Ivanov, Maria G. Pencheva and Stoyan Minkovski are published in the edition.
**Format:** 16/60/84 quires 24

**ALEXANDER TOUR**
44, Pop Bogomil Str.
1202 Sofia, Bulgaria
Tel:/Fax: + 359/2/983 33 22;
983 23 71; 983 30 90; 983 55 68
http://www.AlexanderTour.com
e-mail: alextour@omega.bg

**TANGRA TanNakRa Publishing House Ltd.**
P.O.Box 1832, 1000 Sofia, Bulgaria
Tel: (02) 986 44 19
Fax: (359 2) 986 69 45
e-mail: Tangra@bitex.com
http://members.bitex.com/tangra
Wholesale and retail:
Book Exchange, Sofia, 11, Nikolai Rakitin Str., tel. (02) 43 53 05